D1436839

The Complete

BIRDWATCHER'S
Guide

The Complete

BIRDWATCHER'S
Guide

J O H N   G O O D E R S

Illustrated by
Alan Harris and Terence Lambert

KINGFISHER BOOKS

Acknowledgements

Page 10 Eric & David Hosking; 24 Courtesy, The Marconi Company; 25 Alan Harris top, Aquila Photographics bottom; 26 Stephen Dalton/NHPA top, Stephen Krasemann/NHPA bottom; 27 R. Tidman/NHPA top left, Melvin Grey/NHPA top right; 31 Brian Hawkes; 33 Brian Hawkes top left, Eric & David Hosking top right and bottom; 38 Heather Angel top and bottom left; 38/39 ZEFA; 39 Eric & David Hosking top right, Brian Hawkes bottom right; 42 from *Tetrad Atlas of the Breeding Birds of Devon* courtesy Devon Bird Watching and Preservation Society; 43 Tim Davies; 230 Mike Mockler/Swift Picture Library; 231 Martin King/Swift Picture Library; 232 Mike Read/Swift Picture Library; 233 Robert Iving/Swift Picture Library.

First published in 1988
by Kingfisher Books Limited
Elsley House, 24-30 Great Titchfield Street,
London W1P 7AD
A Grisewood and Dempsey Company
Some of the material in this book is taken from
*Kingfisher Field Guide to the Birds of Britain
and Europe* (1986).
Reprinted 1989
© Grisewood and Dempsey Limited 1986, 1988

BRITISH LIBRARY CATALOGUING IN PUBLICATION DATA
Gooders, John, *1937–*
    The complete birdwatcher's guide.
    1. Great Britain. Birds – Field guides
    I. Title   II. Harris, Alan, *1957–*
    III. Lambert, Terence
    598.2941

    ISBN 0-86272-369-8

Senior Editor: Janice Lacock
Editors: James Harrison, Jonathan Elphick
Design: Terry Woodley
Picture Research: Sarah Donald
Maps: Jeremy Gower, Malcolm Porter

Hand lettering by Jack Potter
Phototypeset by Roland Phototypesetting,
Bury St Edmunds, Suffolk
Colour separations by Newsele Litho, Milan
and Scantrans Pte Limited, Singapore
Printed in Italy by Vallardi Industrie Grafiche,
Milan.

Front cover: Green woodpecker
Back cover: Nuthatch
Spine: Top – Oystercatcher Bottom – Sanderling

CONTENTS

Preface

Not so long ago birdwatching was regarded as a slightly effete and definitely minority pursuit. In public places, like city parks, we were well advised to keep binoculars under our clothing for fear of being viewed at best as a crank, or at worst a peeping Tom. Today birdwatchers are a familiar sight and, in some favoured places, actually outnumber the locals and trippers combined. This is all very healthy, for the larger the birding army the more powerful the voice we have in the corridors of power for bird conservation. No one really knows how many birdwatchers there are in Britain and Ireland, but it is certainly tens of thousands and may actually be hundreds of thousands. What is certain is that the pursuit of birds has grown, is growing and will continue to grow in popularity.

From a conservation angle this is all very well. Today most of the best birding spots have been incorporated into bird reserves. There are hides sited at the prime vantage points, often with reception centres that put on educational displays and shops selling bird badges and stickers. Many have loos and some have audio guides to ensure that visitors see and understand what is going on around them. As a result birdwatching has changed radically over the past 25 years.

Today birds can be examined at really close range in some degree of comfort making it possible to pick out the individual feathers on, say, a moulting stint. This, in turn, has opened up new possibilities of finding rare birds. Once a rarity is sighted, there are queues of watchers waiting their turn to get into the hide, or risk a peep around the corner in their eagerness to see the bird. In the 1970s, this posed a problem when hordes of birdwatchers descended on an unsuspecting village. These have been largely solved in the 1980s by the adoption of a code of conduct and particularly by a more enlightened attitude on the part of reserve wardens. Today a major rarity is regarded more as a source of funds than as a source of problems.

There is, however, a certain sadness in the loss of loneliness that once characterized many of the formerly wild places. Estuarine walls that could be walked for miles without seeing a single person are a thing of the past. Sadly, the same is also true abroad. Not long ago I revisited northern Majorca and found it remarkably similar to Minsmere on a summer Sunday: hundreds of telescopes and tripods greeted every stop and every bird of note was shared by others rather than savoured alone.

On the plus side, birdwatching has never been easier to take up. There are bird clubs and reserves everywhere, and it is easy to meet birders and get involved in learning the business. It is the aim of this book to help by providing the information required to become a birder or improve one's skills.

In producing this book, I have enlisted the aid of several highly skilled helpers to further this task. Outstandingly, Alan Harris was persuaded to paint more of his skilful illustrations to add to the Kingfisher

Field Guide to the Birds of Britain and Ireland and extend the coverage of the identification section. As ever, they are masterful, showing a competence seldom seen among contemporary illustrators.

To complement Alan's critical studies I was fortunate to be able to call on Terence Lambert to produce some of his lovely paintings and drawings. Terence's work is quite different to Alan's, having a moody quality and fineness of finish that is less appropriate to identification illustrations. I have enjoyed Terence's friendship for ten years and it is always a pleasure to work with friends.

Frankly, the credits on the title page of a book like this should be as extensive as those that preceed a feature film. A new friend at Kingfisher Books was Jim Miles who acted as 'producer-director' of the whole business. Jim has been tenacious in ensuring that everyone did their bit and mainly did it on time. He has a remarkably persuasive way and was steadfastly helped by editors James Harrison and Jonathan Elphick whose paths have crossed with mine before.

Down in deepest Sussex I was fortunate enough to encounter Marion Waran and her amazing word machine. Not only does Marion produce fault-free copy, but she does it with such speed that it is quite impossible for a writer to keep up. Finally, as ever, my wife Robbie has taken the brunt of all of our other activities while I selfishly concentrated on the book. I think she understood.

JOHN GOODERS
EAST SUSSEX

Introduction

Anyone can watch and enjoy birds but it is more satisfying and rewarding if it is done well. This book is designed for those who would like to improve their birdwatching. It is, therefore, packed with easily accessible and readily digestible information that has been carefully chosen to concentrate on the main ingredients required to become a competent birdwatcher.

One of the most complimentary things that any birdwatcher can say of another is that he or she is 'competent'. The concept of competence picks out someone as knowledgeable and reliable; who knows their way around; who makes few mistakes, but is then able to correct them; and would rather correct an error and accept the embarrassment that follows, than stand out and defend an incorrect statement. The aim of being a 'competent' birdwatcher should be the goal of anyone interested in birds, no matter what the individual level of skill to which they aspire.

Unfortunately, there are many incompetent birdwatchers around and they are not all beginners. At the top of the pile, among experienced birders, such incompetence merits the description 'stringy' and the person becomes a 'stringer'. It is a description that should be avoided at all costs. Indeed, it is better to retire and take up croquet or crochet than to merit such a description! It is, of course, easy to avoid. Do not identify a bird, or make statements about birds unless you are absolutely sure of your ground.

Beginners do, of course, make plenty of mistakes and misidentifications along the road to competence. Slowly but surely all sensible people learn the art of caution, of not blurting out the first name that comes into one's head. As skill and knowledge improve one gains in confidence and can justifiably make larger claims. Nevertheless, caution should always remain the watchword.

The hoodwink phenomenon is well known among all competent birdwatchers. It consists of birdwatchers arriving to see a particular bird and promptly misidentifying something else as the bird they seek. Being told that such and such a bird is present makes it easier to find. Last autumn there was a small gathering of birders near my home to see a vagrant American Baird's Sandpiper. After a short time a fellow birder came up and told me where it was. Strangely it was in a completely different direction to where I was actually watching the bird. And only yesterday another birder told me 'I see the Garganey is still here', whereas, I could find nothing on the only Teal present that even hinted at such an identification. Both are simple examples of hoodwinking oneself into seeing features that are just not there. Caution is the essence and such caution comes only with experience and knowledge. It is the aim of this book to provide the knowledge on which caution is based.

Modesty forbids that I should describe this book as 'the first . . .', 'the greatest . . .', 'a break through . . .', etc, but I do think that it combines the main elements that make a competent birdwatcher. It is partly a field guide, partly a site guide, and partly a digest of useful background information. It thus answers the major queries of the novice birdwatchers: Which? Where? Why? Which bird is it? Where can I see it? Why does it do this or that? There are, of course, fine books available that attempt to deal with each of these major areas, but few try to cover them all, and none that I know of have attempted such detailed coverage.

Because of its size this is not a book to be carried around in the pocket, or the rucksack come to that. It does, however, deserve a place in the car for it aims to identify every bird that is at all likely to be seen in these islands, and guide you to the best places to watch birds, and provide background that may be consulted to find out when or why such birds are present and what they are doing.

To get the best from this book, the introductory section on birds and their lives should be read, re-read and digested. Parts of it should probably be learned, even by rote, so that full notes of the bird in the field, of its structure and feathering, can be made. The field and site guides (*see pages 44–229 and 230–333*) are equally important for they supply details of how and where birds can be found, their seasonal comings and goings, their nests and eggs, and all the various things that might help you get more from your watching. The checklist (*see pages 334–349*) provides the opportunity to keep a permanent record of the birds you spot, including rare visitors. Finally, there are lists of societies and useful addresses throughout Britain and Ireland who can provide further help and encouragement.

Birdwatching is not a science – it is a hobby, sport, pastime or passion. Although some watchers become scientists and may then be referred to as ornithologists, there is no need to feel at all guilty if you do not wish to join in the scientific study of birds. The important thing is to enjoy birds in your own way. It is our hope that this book may help you to fulfil that aim.

The Fascination of Birds

Not so long ago, birders were often frowned upon by a scientific establishment that regarded anything other than serious ornithological endeavour as frivolous. Regrettably, such attitudes still exist. Today, however, they have been challenged by an army of watchers who see no problem in simply enjoying birds in their own way. Birding has become a major part of the leisure industry, with a wealth of professional and semi-professional birders to service it. It is interesting to ask just why we find birds so fascinating.

Birders or birdwatchers (what they call themselves is largely irrelevant – though 'bird-spotters' or 'bird-lovers' are names that few would admit to) are essentially optimists. Day after day, they set out for some favoured bird haunt, perhaps hundreds of miles from their home. They walk for miles peering into bushes, scanning marshes, or straining their eyes to the horizon. Day after day, they return home, tired, hungry and often cold, with little to show for their efforts. Yet, as soon as possible, they are off to do it again. That is optimism. It also relates to the major reason why birds have such a strong fascination for us.

On the wing

Birds are the most mobile of all animals. Many, particularly in temperate and arctic lands, fly thousands of miles each year on migrations that take them from one hemisphere to the other. Because of this migrational drive, they may appear at places along the way only briefly. So when a birder sets off he has every hope of seeing birds that were not present a week, day, or even a few hours earlier. Some birds get lost along the way. They may drift hundreds or even thousands of miles off their regular course and become vagrants. For the birder the next bush may thus contain a real find, such as a Wryneck from northern Europe, a Barred Warbler from eastern Europe, an Icterine Warbler from eastern or northern Europe or a Pallas's Warbler from Central or eastern Asia, or even a Red-eyed Vireo or Black and White Warbler from North America.

It is the mobility of birds, their ability to cover hundreds of miles to make a distant landfall in only a few hours of non-stop flying, that stimulates our optimism. Put in its simplest terms, the birdwatcher does not know what he or she is going to see next – nor whether they will get good views, or only a fleeting glimpse. The skill of identifying a disappearing, fast-moving shape is as satisfying as any other skilful pursuit – and a lot more satisfying than most.

The standard equipment for birdwatchers used to be a pair of binoculars, but now telescopes and tripods are equally common.

Establishing patterns

Being so highly mobile, birds may breed in one area, winter in another, and regularly pass through others between the two. Ringing (*see page* 25) has shown that some of these birds return to the same breeding site year after year, like the Swallows that return each spring to nest in the same barn or garage. Less well known is the fact that these same birds also spend the winter on the same area of African veldt grassland, roosting in the same reed bed each winter. Perhaps even more remarkable is the fact that they will also follow the same route on each migrational journey and stop off at the same places along the way. Such an ordered, pre-determined existence is the normal mode of life of the vast majority of birds.

Resident species
Being a group of offshore islands at the edge of a large continental landmass, the British Isles has fewer breeding species than other nearby countries, since the water separating it has acted as a barrier. Yet our long coastline and our deep, food-rich estuaries offer a haven for birds from virtually every direction. We do have large numbers of resident birds that seldom move. The average Red Grouse, for example, will move no more than a mile from its birthplace throughout its life.

In general, these residents are omnivores, seed-eaters, or able to adapt to different foods at different times of the year. Thus they can cope with our differing seasons and the different foods that are then available. A few small birds get by without making such seasonal adjustments, however. The Goldcrest and Treecreeper both continue feeding on insects, spiders and their eggs throughout the hardest days of winter.

Winter visitors
Winter, the lean season for all birds, also sees thousands of birds arriving at our shores to avoid even harsher weather to the north and east. These hardy birds come to our marshes, fields and hedgerows because Britain enjoys relatively mild winters, thanks to the influence of the warming Gulf Stream. Continental Europe has no such current and is largely ice-bound in mid-winter.

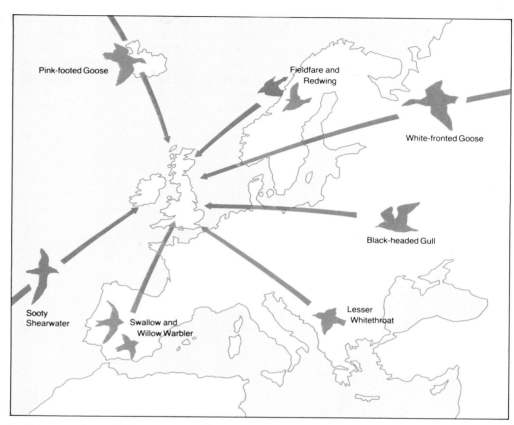

Other species, which are common here all the year round, include many individuals that leave our shores and are replaced by birds that have bred elsewhere. Starlings, Chaffinches, Blackbirds and even Robins fall into this category, along with millions of gulls.

Summer visitors
In summer, Britain, along with the rest of Europe, is invaded by birds that have spent the winter thousands of miles to the south. These summer visitors include millions of Willow Warblers and Swallows that cross the Sahara to reach us. Other summer visitors to Europe do not quite make it across the Channel, but may be quite common in France. Sometimes such birds may 'overshoot' in spring, bringing joy to the fortunate birdwatchers who manage to see them.

Birds fly to Britain from various directions. Winter visitors come from the north and east while summer visitors hail from the south-east and south-west.

How Birds Live

The main events in a bird's life are easily summarized. All birds are born as eggs that need the warmth of incubation to hatch. The chicks break their own way from the shell either naked and helpless, or well developed and able to feed themselves. They grow feathers and eventually develop powerful wings (except in a few flightless species). After adolescence, they become independent and seek their own territory. They mate, lay eggs and the cycle starts all over again.

Life cycles

All living British birds can fly and all incubate their own eggs, save for the Cuckoo which tricks other birds into performing this task for it. Some species build intricate nests, while others lay their eggs on bare rock. Some are highly colonial, while others are fiercely intolerant of their own kind. All birds do, however, establish their own territories.

The number of eggs laid, the number of clutches incubated in a season, the length of incubation, the role played by each sex in nest building, incubation and rearing of young, and the number of young safely reared varies enormously. The Manx Shearwater lays one egg, while the Grey Partridge may sometimes produce as many as 20. A Cuckoo's egg takes a mere 11 days to hatch, while that of the Fulmar takes almost two months. Young waders leave the nest soon after hatching, whereas young perching birds are blind, naked and helpless, and totally dependent on their parents. Blackbirds may rear four or five broods a year, whereas the larger birds of prey may abandon breeding altogether if they lose their eggs or chicks.

Lessons in survival

Having become independent, young birds require food, drink and shelter, and those that fail to find them die. In fact, most birds die within a few weeks of leaving the nest and few survive long enough to breed.

Taking the Goldfinch as an example, we find the young, newly independent birds forming flocks, often in company with adults that have finished breeding, or failed to do so. These flocks, or 'charms' as they are called, roam the countryside in their search for the seeds that have replaced the diet of caterpillars which they enjoyed as nestlings.

Even in the halcyon days of summer, when food is plentiful, there are still dangers. An inexperienced Goldfinch makes a relatively easy catch for a Sparrowhawk, cat, weasel or stoat.

It is, however, the short, cold days of winter that are the testing time for birds. Slowly the number of seeds available declines and food becomes harder to find. If snow covers the ground the Goldfinches must switch to another diet, move to milder climates, or starve.

Life-styles

Each species of bird has adapted to a particular life-style, a way of going about its life that is, in some way, different from every other bird that inhabits the same area. Were different species not separated in these ways, then they would compete directly one with another and the less well adapted would decline and disappear. The more opportunities, or niches, for birds to specialize, the more species will be able to inhabit a particular region. That is why Britain is relatively poorly endowed with species when compared to countries like Venezuela, Columbia or Thailand.

Almost all birds are aggressive in defence of their territory. Robins, however, are renowned for this and will fight with other males in both summer and winter.

Bird Calls

Birds produce a huge variety of songs and calls that serve a wide variety of purposes. Ornithologists have recorded and studied these calls in great detail, using the latest technology, and established whole batteries of meanings for them. The Great Tit, for example, utters no less than 57 distinct calls, each of which means something different. Despite their complexity, bird calls can be grouped into a few major categories: song, and alarm, threat, distress and contact calls.

The importance of bird song

Bird song serves a variety of purposes, the most important of which is to proclaim ownership of a territory and a readiness to breed. A song must, therefore, be clearly recognizable, far-carrying and regularly produced. Most of our better songsters are small, live among dense vegetation and are dull-coloured. They rely on their fine songs to find a mate and breed.

Woodland birds are among the loudest and most persistent of our songsters. Robin, Blackbird, Great Tit and Song Thrush all sing almost throughout the year. In spring each bird sings to inform others of its kind of its existence, and that it has established its domain over a small patch of the wood. Song also informs prospective mates of a potential partner's existence and makes location a relatively straightforward matter.

Some birds are remarkably similar in appearance and could, it is reasonable to assume, make mistakes in identification if their songs, too, were similar. Thus the Willow Warbler and Chiffchaff, which are closely related, small, greenish-yellow, summer visitors, have completely different songs. The Willow Warbler's little descending trill cannot be confused with the repetitive 'chiff-chaffing' of its relative. They thus do not waste time searching for or attacking the wrong species.

As well as including what may be – to humans – unmusical sounds, bird 'songs' may not even be vocal: examples are the curious bleating sounds made by a displaying Snipe as the wind rushes over its outer tail feathers, and the loud, far-carrying drumming that the woodpeckers make by striking their bills up to 15 times per second against carefully selected, resonant tree trunks or branches.

Sometimes called 'the watchdogs of the marshes', Redshanks are among the noisiest of birds, reacting to intruders with high-flying, yelping calls.

Alarm and contact calls

Though song is the most obvious and important of bird vocalizations, it is by no means the only way that birds communicate. The cackled alarm call of the disturbed Blackbird informs all other Blackbirds of the presence of danger. It is brief, far-carrying and easily understood.

If a predator, such as a roosting Tawny Owl, is discovered, many small birds will be attracted by the threat calls of the first to arrive on the scene. Soon, the innocent predator will be surrounded by a mass of screeching small birds and be driven to fly to another hiding place. Similarly, birds are attracted by the distress calls of an individual captured by a predator – or by a birdwatcher for ringing.

Finally, birds that habitually form flocks use contact calls to keep in touch with each other. Waders that feed regularly after dark have clear calls that keep them in contact with one another as they move from one part of an estuary to another. Geese maintain contact by a continual cackling during their long migrations. For the birdwatcher, a knowledge of bird songs and calls enables unseen birds to be located and identified. Its value cannot be overstressed.

Where Birds Live

Though many birds are common and widespread, inhabiting a variety of different life zones, the vast majority are creatures of habit. Knowing where they prefer to live is half the battle in finding them.

With some birds, there may be quite a choice of places to look for them. The Starling, for example, is a highly adapatable bird that has been able to exploit a wide range of different habitats. It is equally at home on a coastal marsh as it is in a city park. It nests as successfully in skyscrapers as it does in holes in trees. It feeds on bread in gardens and on leatherjackets and other insect grubs under the soil of ploughed fields. Such advantageous adaptability is unusual, however; many other birds are not nearly as flexible in their choice of habitat.

Man-made landscapes

Birds do then have preferred habitats and are, as a result, dependent on the continued existence of such life zones for their survival. Britain today consists almost entirely of man-made landscapes. Over the past thousand years we have cleared the forests to create fields separated by planted hedgerows. Today we are ripping out the hedgerows and filling in the dells.

Those who cry in protest at these changes should remember that the hedgerows themselves are artificial and just another stage in our manipulation of the lanscape. We have drained marshes, turned forests to moorland, enclosed and drained saltings and estuaries, ploughed heaths and downland and destroyed rivers by dredging and pollution. Along the way, many birds have lost their habitats and disappeared. Their place has been taken by other species better able to live in the new landscapes that we have created.

And where are we heading now? Will our highly mechanized farming techniques eventually finish off the Corncrake and Quail entirely as British breeding birds? Will the ploughing of heath and downland eventually eliminate the Stone-curlew? Will barrages across our estuaries wipe out huge numbers of waders that regularly stop-over and winter along there? Only time will tell. But it is clear that we must conserve the widest possible range of habitats if we wish to preserve the richness of our bird life.

It is understandable for conservationists to be often gloomy and despondent about habitat destruction, but while we change the landscape to the detriment of one species we may improve it to the benefit of another. Swallows, House Martins and Swifts have all increased their populations by being able to nest in our buildings instead of relying on natural caves. Sand Martins find more cliffs at our sand pits than ever existed naturally. Ducks and grebes find ideal resting or feeding sites at many of our reservoirs and gulls like them too, especially if they are located near our rubbish tips. Even the widely condemned, 'monoculture' tracts of planted conifers are, as they mature, much appreciated by the now widespread Crossbill.

Natural habitats

The habitats of the British Isles have been analysed and categorized in a variety of different schemes. For the sake of simplicity, we can divide Britain's bird habitats into uplands, woodlands, farmland, urban areas, freshwaters and coastlines. Each habitat has its characteristic birds, some of which cannot be found elsewhere.

Uplands

Britain has no spectacular mountain chains like the Alps or the Pyrennees and thus lacks many typically alpine species. We may have Choughs, but there are no Alpine Choughs or Wallcreepers, no Alpine Accentors or Snow Finches.

Most of our uplands consist of rough grassland for sheep-grazing and heather moorland, broken here and there by extensive plantations of conifers. There are also huge water-storage reservoirs, constructed to serve the lowland population with water and power, and some areas of bog. Sheep farming apart, the bare uplands are included mainly within sporting estates, totally geared to the rearing of our native Red Grouse.

Grouse moors are regularly burnt to provide fresh young heather shoots for grouse to feed upon. In general, this practice is beneficial, both to the moor and to the other species of birds that share the habitat. Here are Meadow Pipit and Twite, Wheatear and Ring Ousel together with their own special predator – the

Although Red Grouse are common on the hills of Britain they are found nowhere else.

The Crested Tit is confined to mature Scots pine plantations and is unknown in England.

Merlin. Never a common bird, this diminutive falcon is decidedly scarce and in need of help. Where buttresses and cliff faces break through they offer breeding sites to birds of prey like the Peregrine and Buzzard, as well as Golden Eagle and Raven.

Here too the damp, coarse-grass area hold the breeding waders that will later join immigrants from the Continent at our coastal marshes and estuaries. Dunlin, Golden Plover and Snipe are all widespread in the uplands, but in Scotland there are also breeding Greenshank and, more recently, Temminck's Stint, Wood Sandpiper and Purple Sandpiper. Colonization by arctic waders is doubtless due to our changing climate. They may be joined by other northern birds: today even Shore Lark and Lapland Bunting can be found in the far north of Britain.

Most uplands are situated in the north and west, where most of our rain falls. Here, the hills are broken by steep-sided gullies, where streams cascade between the rocks. In the valley bottoms they twist and turn over beds of pebbles and banks of shingle offering a home to Dipper, Grey Wagtail and Common Sandpiper.

Woodlands
The 'upland' woodlands that once covered vast tracts of our hills have been largely destroyed in the name of progress. Instead we have deer 'forests' and grouse moors that are identical and treeless to the eye, or rough grassland supporting a few sheep. Here and there remnants of a former glory can be found. At Rothiemurchus in the Spey valley, for example, there are still stands of the original Caledonian Forest of Scots pine. Here are Scottish Crossbill, Crested Tit, Black Grouse and Capercaillie, but alongside as well are huge new plantations of alien conifers that offer little to birds.

There are old woodlands in the Lake District and in Wales, too, but here they consist of oaks clinging tenaciously to the hillsides in areas where the land was simply not worth the effort of clearing. Among these woods Wood Warbler and Redstart, Pied Flycatcher and Tree Pipit abound. There are prospering populations of Buzzard and, in south-central Wales, a growing number of Red Kite. In lowland Britain clearance has been more complete and our landscape is one of the least forested in Europe.

In place of extensive natural woodlands we have a landscape broken up by hedgerows, wind breaks and copses of trees, with parks and gardens. These may offer refuge to a wide variety of forest birds, but most are too small to provide a home for the larger and shyer woodland birds. The Honey Buzzard, for example,

Estuaries are undoubtedly Britain's richest feeding grounds, providing food and shelter for a wide variety of species.

Where Birds Live

breeds in the New Forest, England's largest lowland woodland, and among the parks of Nottinghamshire's Dukeries. Elsewhere it is an erratic breeder. It needs large tracts of forest, but cannot find the right conditions this side of the English Channel. Yet another large woodland bird of prey has, in contrast, enjoyed spectacular success in recent years. Aided by escapes from falconry, the Goshawk is quickly building up a healthy population. Yet just a few years ago it was as scarce as the Honey Buzzard.

Woodlands are rich in birds and many of our most abundant species originated in this habitat. Blackbird, Song Thrush, Robin, Chaffinch, Wren, all are woodland birds that have found that our gardens meet their needs to perfection. Great and Blue Tits, Jays and Tawny Owls have all spread outward to occupy more open zones. Yet all retain a woodland base, for woods provide year-round food and shelter.

Farmland

Where the woods were cleared, they were replaced by farmland. At first, copses, hedgerows and wooded dells remained and the birds remained too. During the past 50 years farms and farming methods have changed out of all recognition and several once widespread birds have declined and may soon disappear.

Of course, farmland is good for some birds. Bullfinches benefit from fruit orchards, Woodpigeons descend in droves to feed on the cereal fields, and wild geese graze the winter wheat. Yet to farmers these are pests that they could well do without.

Few farmland birds are as well adapted to their habitat as the Barn Owl. These birds find their food almost entirely over agricultural land and are important in maintaining a check on the populations of small mammals. Yet, by felling old trees and converting or dismantling isolated barns, farmers are destroying the habitat of this splendid bird.

Farmers have a responsibility for the countryside, let us hope that they soon learn to act responsibly.

Urban areas

Large areas of Britain are covered with bricks, mortar and concrete and are home to the vast majority of the human population. Only birds that have learned to live alongside man have prospered here. Such birds are either tolerant of our presence, like the Blackbird and Robin in the city park and suburban garden, or like the Feral Pigeon and Black-headed Gull, actually benefit from our activities. Some birds find urban life particularly rewarding, and House Sparrows and Swifts have both prospered by taking over for nest-sites those portions of our homes that we do not use. Mallard, Coot and Moorhen find park ponds suit their needs perfectly, while Kestrels nest on ledges of chimneys and other tall buildings. All of these birds have been able to exploit man in one way or another, yet none have increased so dramatically as the gulls.

Virtually unknown inland a century ago, over a million gulls now winter inland every year. They feed on our rubbish tips and roost on our reservoirs – we have created the perfect gull environment. They are also becoming a pest. Worldwide, they pose a serious threat to aircraft, particularly modern jets, but they also threaten the existence of nature reserves where conservationists are now having to face up to the choice between gulls and other, scarcer, breeding species.

During the breeding season the auks – Guillemots and Razorbills – come to Britain's coastlines in enormous numbers.

Freshwaters

The British climate ensures that the country is well-supplied with large quantities of freshwater throughout the year. In the north and west there are lochs and loughs galore, supporting a wide range of breeding and wintering birds. The streams hold their typical birds, too, and most remain free of ice and available throughout the year. Only in the lowlands has man made a really determined effort to destroy some of our richest bird habitats. Marshes have been drained, lakes reclaimed and ponds filled. Streams and rivers have been straightened and canalized and seasonal floods controlled.

Yet such is our demand for water that having got rid of natural freshwaters, we immediately set about constructing artificial ones. The building of vast new lowland reservoirs has created some of the finest freshwater habitats in the country. Waters such as Abberton in Essex and Chew Valley in Avon are well established and noted haunts of birds. Newer waters such as Grafham and Rutland in the Midlands are maturing into top-class birding spots and there are many other smaller waters throughout the country.

The gravel extraction industry has played its part too. Flooded pits along river valleys, where gravel deposits occur, may be used by breeding birds even while they are still in active exploitation. Indeed, the Little Ringed Plover has used working pits throughout its twentieth-century colonization. Many used pits are filled with rubbish, but some are left to mature and offer living space to grebes, ducks and hosts of small birds. In many parts of the country exhausted pits have been converted to nature reserves.

Lowland waters are particularly important in winter. Many reserves, especially the larger ones, act as roosts for gulls, geese and ducks. Diving ducks and grebes feed in the water itself and may settle down happily for as long as the lake remains free of ice.

Coastlines

The British Isles enjoy some of the finest coastlines to be found in the world. There are spectacular cliffs, their ledges alive with nesting seabirds. There are offshore stacks and uninhabited islands where these and other birds may reach staggering numbers. And there are also sandy beaches, sometimes backed by protective marshes, where terns and Ringed Plovers may find a home. And there are estuaries, vast open areas of sand and mud upon which the Arctic-breeding waders descend on passage and for the winter – niches which land-locked European countries lack.

The Gannet finds its world headquarters around our coasts, with vast colonies, or 'gannetries', at St Kilda, the Bass Rock and Grassholm, but with new and growing colonies elsewhere. Guillemots crowd together so tightly on some cliff ledges that there seems no room for even a single extra bird. Razorbill, Puffin, Black Guillemot, Shag, Fulmar and Kittiwake all teem around our shores during the breeding season.

By August, however, these seabirds have moved out to the open ocean. It is then that the waders return to our estuaries. Hundreds of thousands of these birds flock to the Ribble and the Dee, to Morecambe Bay and Lindisfarne, to The Wash and the Humber, and to many other estuaries, too, each adapted to exploit the land between the tides. In the whole of Europe only the Dutch and German Waddensee compares with the estuaries of Britain. The dramatic spectacle of thousands of birds flighting in at high water can be compared only with the sight of a teeming cliff colony of seabirds. Britain and Ireland have them both.

Little Terns nest very close to the high tide line and have suffered a dramatic decline this century due to human disturbance. Conservation efforts have centred on denying people access to these areas.

Nests and Nesting

The vast majority of birds, and certainly all of those that breed in Britain today, share two features: they can fly and they lay eggs. Not surprisingly the two are closely linked. In order to fly efficiently, birds must have an appropriate power to weight ratio – and eggs add to the weight of a female bird.

Egg weight

Birds are descended from reptilian ancestors and have maintained the egg-laying facility of reptiles to the present day. The weight of an individual egg varies enormously according to species. In the case of the Kiwi of Australia the single egg amounts to some 17 per cent of the female's body weight, while the Willow Warbler's six or seven eggs each weigh only 5 per cent of its body weight. Yet the Ostrich egg, although it is the largest single cell on earth, forms only 1 per cent of the female's weight.

Egg weight depends on the life-style of the bird and on the size of clutch which it produces. Being flightless, the Kiwi and Ostrich can afford to lay large eggs. Although the Kiwi lays only a single egg, this is, at about 450g in weight, the largest relative to the size of the bird, of any living species. Although an Ostrich's egg is *relatively* smaller, it weighs up to 1.5kg, and up to 20 may be laid by a single female. The diminutive

Long-tailed Tits build delicate nests made of lichens and spiders' webs. As the young tits grow the nest expands to accommodate them.

Willow Warbler generally lays six or seven eggs which, combined, add up to a staggering 25 or 30 per cent of its body weight. If this species lacked the ability to lay eggs and, like a mammal, gave birth to six or seven living young which it would have to carry round as embryos in its body for many weeks or months, then its flying abilities would be, at best, seriously curtailed and, at worst, eliminated.

As a further refinement, female birds form the egg inside their bodies very quickly and are able to lay up to half their own weight in eggs within a few days. This has the advantage of exposing the eggs to predation in an unguarded nest for as short a time as possible.

The nesting ritual

All birds lay eggs, but the eggs vary considerably in size, colour and the time they take to hatch. Birds vary, too, in the location and construction of their nests, in the roles taken in incubation, in being monogamous or polygamous, even in tending or neglecting their young. The loving care and sharing of the parental role between their sexes shown by many common species is far from universal.

Typically the male establishes a territory and defends it. By singing, he attracts a mate and both then find a varying proportion of their food within this

exclusive zone. In the case of the Robin the vast majority of the food is found within the territory, while other species such as the Song Thrush or Chaffinch may forage more widely. The only element common to all our birds is that the territory will contain a nest site, but with most small birds there will be a choice of nest sites, plus a variety of song posts as well.

Most birds are in their finest plumage during the time that pairs are formed, usually in the early spring. At this time the Great Crested Grebe develops the colourful head adornments of crest and ear tufts that are so important in its courtship rituals. Before breeding the pair perform spectacular displays

designed to ensure that they reach the peak of readiness to breed at the same time and that the bond between them will remain strong throughout the season. They shake their heads, swim toward each other with necks low on the water, stand up and dance together, and make much of presenting weeds to each other. This elaborate behaviour ensures that nesting will be as successful as possible.

Different nests for different niches

Nests, too, vary from nothing to the most elaborate of structures. All are designed to protect the eggs from accident and predation. If birds did not lay eggs then the female would be able to carry her unborn young with her and use her experience to avoid predators. By leaving the (unhatched) young in a nest this ability is lost. Clearly, there must be an advantage in doing this. The Ringed Plover lays its eggs on the bare ground among shingle. As they resemble stones, they are easily overlooked and saved from predation by their superb camouflage. The disruptive camouflage of the sitting bird is also highly effective so, whether covered or uncovered, the eggs of the Ringed Plover are well protected without any nest at all.

Such a strategy can be compared with that of a cup-nesting species like the Reed Warbler or the Song Thrush. In this case the nest is an elaborate structure of vegetation carefully woven together to hold, not only the eggs, but also the growing brood of young. The eggs do not need to be highly camouflaged, but must be recognizable as belonging to the species concerned. In some cases even this necessity becomes redundant. The Kingfisher, for example, is a hole-nesting bird that, like most others, lays white eggs that are easier to see in the reduced light of a deep tunnel in an earth bank.

Body heat

Eggs need both warmth and protection in order to hatch, and this is provided by incubation. By coming into direct contact with the adult's body via an unfeathered area of its belly called the brood patch, body heat is passed through the shell to the developing chick. The details of incubation are as variable as egg size, colour and nest building. Some birds share the

incubation between the pair and both develop a brood patch. In others the female takes the larger share, while in others still she takes no part at all, leaving her mate to incubate and care for the chicks on his own.

Incubation may start with the first egg, as with the birds of prey and owls, or be delayed until the clutch is complete. There is an obvious advantage in having all the young hatch at the same time (delayed incubation) and leave the nest at more or less the same moment. In the case of the predators, with their feast-or-famine life-style, there is an advantage in having young at varying stages of development. If food is abundant, all the eggs will hatch and all the chicks fledge. If food is in short supply, there is an advantage in not spreading it evenly among the young, but in concentrating it on one or two of the oldest and strongest so that at least some young are successfully reared.

The incubation period varies too, from the 11 days for a Hawfinch to the 57 days of a Fulmar. When they hatch, some chicks dry out, stand up and leave the nest immediately. The waders and gamebirds are typical examples of birds that produce such precocious young. Others hatch blind, naked and helpless and spend several weeks being brooded and fed by their parents. Even after they leave the nest, the young of several species require regular feeding by the adults while they learn the skills they need to survive on their own.

The pebble-like eggs of the Ringed Plover are perfectly camouflaged on shingle. Unfortunately this does have a drawback – the nest is quite likely to be trampled on by large mammals, including humans!

Food and Feeding

Swallow: wide gape

Greenfinch: thick crushing bill

Redshank: neat probing bill

Robin: general purpose pick

Kestrel: hooked tearing bill

Curlew: slightly flexible bill

The size and shape of a bird's bill is totally adapted to its feeding routines and the type of food it eats.

By cutting down on all the inessentials in their adaption to flight, birds have had to dispense with hands and fingers. They have thus lost the main tools used by many other animals for feeding. To compensate, their bills have become adapted to perform a whole range of intricate manipulations.

A single glance at a bill can tell us much about how a bird lives and how it spends its life. The long downcurved bill of the Curlew is a perfectly adapted probe, ideally suited to finding food hidden deep in soft mud and sand. The strong, hooked bill of the Golden Eagle and other birds of prey is adapted for tearing up the flesh of its prey. But what if we were presented with the bill of the Crossbill and asked to explain its purpose? Would we come up with its perfect adaption to opening hard pine cones to extract the seeds? The variety of birds' bills is remarkable, but each one is geared to a particular mode of feeding or type of food. In most cases there are differences, albeit often subtle, that separate closely related birds.

Purpose-built bills
So a simple glance at a bird's bill will tell us much about the food it eats. The Swallow has a tiny bill that hides a huge gape that acts as a funnel in sweeping small flying insects from the skies. It is equipped with strong rictal bristles, hairs that grow outwards at the sides of the mouth, that increase this funnelling effect. Swallows, along with martins and swifts, can be regarded as the aerial equivalent of the great baleen whales. These huge mammals literally sieve their way through the seas, harvesting vast quantities of small crustaceans known as krill. Swallows, though more selective, find their food in a similar way. Nightjars are their nocturnal equivalents. They feed on night-flying moths and have an even larger gape with which to scoop up their prey.

In contrast, the Robin has a sharply pointed thin bill that is perfectly adapted to picking small prey from the leaves of trees and from among the debris of the woodland floor. They can often be seen tugging worms from the lawn, but this is derived from their woodland background where worms are often only hidden among fallen leaves. Their bills are not specifically designed

for digging, being instead a more versatile grasping and probing tool.

In fact, a great many insectivorous birds have bills very similar to that of the Robin. All of our warblers and chats have thin, picking bills, which is not surprising in view of their life-style. Being migrants, they can enjoy insect food throughout the year and travel long distances to ensure they find it. Chiffchaffs that return to Britain as early as March, long before insect life is abundant, often spend much of their time feeding on the ground. By late summer, when caterpillars are few and only adult insects are abundant, they often hover to catch them in the air. Their agility makes this a relatively successful strategy, but cannot be compared with the mastery of the flycatchers that specialize in this tactic.

Birds such as the Spotted Flycatcher show characters that combine the thin bills of the Robin with the wide gape of the Swallow. They hunt from a prominent perch and have long, broad wings similar to those of a Swallow to provide aerial mastery. With a brief dash they grab a passing insect in their scoop-like bills and close the mandibles shut with an audible snap.

In comparison, the bill of a Greenfinch appears a clumsy and unrefined sort of tool. As anyone who has handled one of these birds for ringing will tell you, they have powerful jaw muscles and sharp-edged bills that can give you a really nasty nip. These are seed-eaters that need considerable power to break into hard-coated seeds. The related Goldfinch has a conical bill too, though it is much thinner than that of the Greenfinch. It too feeds on seeds, but these are smaller and less hard-shelled than those favoured by the Greenfinch. Its problem is to pick them from thistle and teasel heads and thus the bill is more like that of a Robin than those of other finches.

One of the most formidable bills is that of the Hawfinch which is massive and capable of exerting a force of ten kilogrammes per square centimetre to crack open extra-hard cherry stones. If the Hawfinch has a nutcracker, then the Bullfinch has a pair of secateurs. In this bird the sides of the upper mandible are curved just like a pair of those favourite gardeners' tools. The Bullfinch's bill is perfectly adapted to snip off growing buds, a fact that fruit farmers know only too well. In winter they are equally adept at ripping off the wings of ash seeds.

Few groups of birds show such variation in bill shape as the waders; from the short picking bill of the Little Stint to the deep probe of the Curlew. Yet most waders have bills intermediate between these two extremes, like that of the Redshank, which is about one to one-and-a-half times the length of their heads. These less specialized birds can both pick for food and probe for it as well. The depth that a Curlew can reach into soft mud, however, gives it an advantage over shorter-billed birds by enabling it to reach the larger marine worms that live at greater depths. However, being a specialist worm-eater, it is also found on flooded fields in search of the terrestial equivalent of the marine worms, the earthworms.

Oystercatchers often feed on worms too, but these are mussel specialists that have adopted several distinct methods of dealing with these tough marine molluscs. Some individuals literally smash their way in. Others catch the mussels half open and carefully cut through the cartilage that attaches them to their protective covering. A similarly large, black and white wader, the Avocet has a delicate, upturned awl of a bill. When feeding it sweeps the upturned section from side to side through soft mud, grabbing whatever food is detected by the sensitive tip. The Turnstone, as its name implies, turns over stones to find the small creatures that hide there. Its short, stout and slightly upturned bill takes a lot of rough treatment as anyone who has watched these birds at close quarters will testify.

Among the ducks there are great variations in feeding techniques. Some dive to reach aquatic vegetation, while others do so to catch fish, or other animals. In general, vegetarian birds have to work harder for their food, and dabbling ducks spend long hours grazing or up-ending in shallow water. One of the most specialized members of the duck tribe is the Shoveler. One individual was watched feeding non-stop for over two hours without moving more than a yard.

Shovelers have huge spatulate bills armed with extensive lamellae along each edge that act as highly efficient filters. Huge quantities of water and soft mud

The diverse shapes of finch bills reflect the specific food each species eats.

Food and Feeding

The sharp talons of the Sparrowhawk perform two functions. As the bird catches smaller birds such as Chaffinches, they grasp and kill their prey at the same time.

are taken into the bill and ejected between the lamallae, leaving small particles of trapped food to be eaten. Just how many individual food items are consumed each day can only be guessed, but it must run into tens of thousands.

Other surface-feeding ducks may feed in the same way as the Shoveler but, lacking the huge bill and fine lamellae, feed on fewer and larger items of food. Teal, for example, have much smaller bills, but still feed mainly on the surface of muddy waters. Mallard are more adventurous, feeding opportunistically in a wide variety of ways. Although they are often seen up-ending in shallow water to obtain food from among bottom vegetation, they also feed on the surface. The elegance of the Pintail stems partly from its long thin neck, itself an adaptation to feeding by up-ending in deeper water than any of its near relatives. In this way it competes more with swans than with other ducks.

A great many ducks find their food by diving, though this group divides itself neatly into freshwater ducks and seaducks. Among the latter the powerfully billed Eider is a mussel and crab specialist. It thus frequents mainly rocky shores where such prey is most abundant. Similarly Scoter and Scaup are mainly seafarers that

feed on molluscs and crustaceans, sometimes forming huge flocks where their food abounds.

A highly specialized group of ducks is generally referred to as the 'sawbills'. Two, the Goosander and the Red-breasted Merganser, breed in northern Britain and are winter visitors further south. Both have laterally compressed, narrow bills armed with rows of sharp 'teeth' which are ideally suited to grasping the slippery fish that form their staple diet. But while mergansers are seaducks in winter, Goosanders are found mainly on freshwater.

Talons of death

Kestrels, along with other birds of prey, have departed from the norm by capturing their prey with their feet. As a result they have developed strong legs and toes equipped with long sharp claws, or talons. This in turn has allowed them to capture far larger prey than is taken by other birds and their bills have become powerful weapons capable of tearing small mammals and birds into edible-sized pieces. The hooked bill is a dismembering tool and not, as might be expected, a killing weapon. The larger the bill, the larger the prey that is taken.

Though Britain is not particularly well endowed with birds of prey, we do have representatives of most of the major groups of these birds. (Daytime birds of prey, but not owls are often known as 'raptors'.) Falcons, such as the Peregrine, are predominantly aerial killers of open country. Having selected a victim, they dive out of the sky at speed and deal their victim a killing blow with their powerful hind claw. Mostly they 'bind-to' and carry the prey away to a safe perch, but sometimes it falls to the ground and must be retrieved. These birds rely on speed and surprise for success.

The Sparrowhawk is a more opportunist hunter, though speed and surprise are essential elements in its attacks as well. While falcons have long pointed wings like a jet fighter's, hawks are round-winged birds with long tails capable of zig-zagging between trees and of rapid changes in direction. Their technique is to come in low, using all available cover, to appear from nowhere to grab small birds from the ground, or as they take off.

The harriers and the Golden Eagle are even more opportunistic hunters, quartering in a series of glides low over the ground in the hope of surprising prey at rest. Twisting and turning, they create as many chances as possible and work on a simple law of averages to provide their food. Not surprisingly, this hit-or-miss approach means spending much longer on the wing than birds such as falcons. Harriers, in particular, are always among the most obvious of birds in the areas they inhabit. Buzzards are opportunists too, but they adopt the shrike-like tactic of sitting and waiting for prey to come within range.

Feeding time

Birds feed in a variety of ways, on a variety of foods, and are adapted physically to achieve success in obtaining it. For most small birds, feeding occupies by far the largest part of their lives, though during the long days of summer there is time to establish a territory, to sing and to rear their young. Larger birds, especially the raptors, have more time to spare. For these birds, irregular meals are the rule – if they are hungry they hunt, if they are not, they sleep.

Just how much food a bird needs depends on its metabolism. The world's smallest birds, the hummingbirds, take in vast quantities of high-energy fuel in the form of nectar, but still have to semi-hibernate at night. Some of our smaller birds also consume vast quantities of food. In the case of Redshanks, studied on the Ythan Estuary north of Aberdeen, this amounted to a staggering 40,000 individual food items per day. Save for brief periods just before and after high tide, these birds feed continuously night and day.

Some of the best studied birds in Britain are the Great and Blue Tits of Oxford's Wytham Wood. Blue Tits here, doubtless no different from those in other parts of the country, fly up to six hundred insect-catching sorties a day when feeding their young. An adult, it was found, would bring five times its own body weight to feed its ever-hungry chicks during a single day. Such prodigious feats would seem to be the norm for the majority of our smaller birds, but may also be true for some of the larger ones as well.

Reed Warblers visit southern Britain, feeding on the superabundance of insects available during the long summer days.

Migration

Worldwide, the scale of bird migration is staggering, and even within the small area of the British Isles, millions of individual birds are involved. Some movements, like the passage of storks over Gibraltar and the Bosphorus, are dramatic while others are hidden by a cloak of darkness. To see and hear the flocks of wild geese make their autumn landfall at Loch Leven is a moving experience. To watch near-exhausted Starlings flight in from the sea along the east coast is equally dramatic. And, just occasionally, we get an impression of the vast unseen movements of warblers and chats that migrate by night when bad weather forces them to 'fall' from the sky and seek refuge where they can along some lonely promontory. Such sights represent merely the tip of the iceberg, for most birds manage their journeys without our ever being aware of their existence.

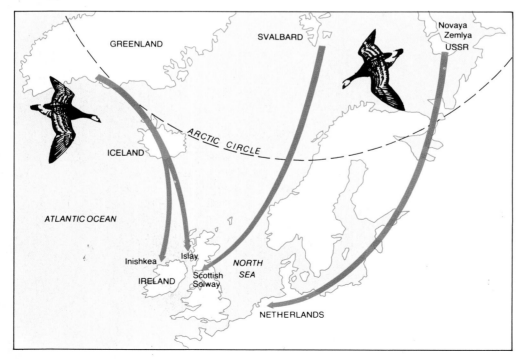

Radar image of chaffinches following the line of the French coast as they fly towards Kent.

Barnacle Geese belong to three distinct populations that nest in the Arctic and winter in temperate Europe. Their origins, destinations and routes are totally predictable.

Radar tracking

In the mid-1960s there was a vogue among dedicated birders for spending the first hour or so after dawn on October mornings on the roof of a tall building watching for daytime migrants. Soon after first light, flocks of finches and pipits would start to appear, all heading purposefully westward. One team of London observers counted no less than four million birds flying over the capital in a few brief weeks of autumn.

At about the same time other, more technically minded, ornithologists, were watching these same movements on specially adjusted radar screens. The scale of the avian traffic which they were privileged to observe was truly staggering. Perhaps the most dramatic radar picture of all, however, showed the whole coastline of southern England moving southward as thousands of nocturnal migrants rose into radar range and set off southward at dusk.

Changing food supplies

Migration is the method by which birds cope with seasonal variations in their food supply. The most obvious such variation is the superabundance of insect life in temperate and sub-arctic latitudes during summer. Lake Myvatn in northern Iceland is frozen solid and lifeless for much of the year, but in summer it is alive with the midges that account for its name – which, translated, means 'Lake of Flies'. Not surprisingly, there are plenty of birds to take advantage of this seasonal feast. Even in Britain sales of insect repellent rise dramatically when flies, mosquitoes and midges appear in May. It is this season of plenty that enables birds not only to feed themselves, but also to rear their young on high-protein insects. Migration is the means by which they are able to exploit this type of food.

At the end of the breeding season and before the onset of the cold days of winter, the birds must move southward to warmer climes, where insects are available throughout the year. Here, on the African plains, they share their food with other insect-eating birds that are resident there. Only by migrating back to the north at the end of winter do they avoid competing with these species during the breeding season.

The seasonal abundance of insect food in northern latitudes is, however, only one example of a trigger to migration. Waders, for example, can find plenty of insects and other small animals on the tundra when it suddenly blossoms into life during the brief arctic summer, but are unable to do so when the ground is frozen solid during the long, harsh winter. Geese may graze the rich meadow-like northern grasslands, but not when they are covered by several feet of snow. Skuas and birds of prey may feast on small mammals during the summer, but must leave before their prey hibernates for the winter. Insect specialists may make journeys of thousands of miles to find suitable wintering grounds, whereas waders and geese need move only a few hundred miles to warmer areas where snow is not a major barrier to feeding. Migration is thus not a simple phenomenon. There are enormous variations between species, but also between different populations of a single species and even between individual birds.

Patterns of migration

All Britain's Swallows leave to spend the winter in South Africa and all our Willow Warblers cross the Sahara, too. But a few Chiffchaffs manage to eke out a living in southern England throughout the winter, before being joined in spring by the bulk of the population that has passed the winter in the Mediterranean region. All three of these birds are classed as 'summer visitors'.

Another group of British birds is classed as 'winter visitors'; these include birds like the Pink-footed Goose which nests no further away than Iceland, but finds conditions in Britain much more favourable in winter. Redwings and Fieldfares swarm across the North Sea in autumn, only to return whence they came in March. Some stay on and breed, mainly in northern Britain. Yet other species breed to the north and east and winter to the south. Such birds, which normally neither breed nor winter in Britain, are classed as 'passage migrants'. Many waders, such as Little and Temminck's Stint, Wood and Curlew Sandpipers and Whimbrel, fall into this category. A few individuals of these do stay to breed or winter in this country.

The variations are infinite. Even birds that are classed as 'resident' are far from being so. True, the Red Grouse that breed on our moors seldom move more than a mile for the whole duration of their lives. Their close relative, the Ptarmigan, is similarly resident, but some individuals may make vertical migrations downward to avoid the harshest conditions on the high mountain plateaux. Distances may be minimal, but even this is a form of migration to take advantage of a seasonal food source.

Other so-called 'residents' are actually partial migrants, with some individuals making considerable journeys, while others remain more or less where they were born. Most of Britain's male Robins, for example, stay put and defend their territories throughout the year. A few females, however, make considerable journeys to spend winter in milder climes, though those of southern England are less likely to migrate than those farther north. The Robins of Scandinavia and Eastern Europe migrate south in winter, but Britain lies at the southern limit of this species' migratory zone. Presumably the advantages of migrating or not migrating are more or less in balance for the Robin in Britain. A similar balance exists for other partial migrants like the Blackbird and Song Thrush.

The ring being placed on this Greenfinch contains a serial number and a return address.

When set against a bushy background, mist nets become invisible to birds flying into them. They are thus the ideal way to capture birds for ringing.

Migration

Swallows are summer visitors to Britain and fly in excess of 6000 miles from South Africa every spring.

Each winter Smews fly from the Arctic to southern England, where they are largely confined to freshwater reservoirs and gravelpits. There are fewer males than females so spotting a male makes a birdwatcher's day.

Migration is a dangerous adventure for birds, and they will indulge in long and hazardous journeys only if there is an advantage in doing so. In other words, the advantages must outweigh the disadvantages of staying put. In the Arctic this balance is very apparent: it is a stark choice for most species between migrating and dying of starvation. In more temperate areas such as the British Isles, the balance is usually less clear cut for the birds.

Monitoring migration

Though man has been aware of bird migration for thousands of years, serious study of the phenomenon is comparatively new. Even as recently as the eighteenth century, the great parson-naturalist Gilbert White found it difficult to accept that Swallows did not hibernate at the bottom of ponds but made journeys of thousands of miles instead. By the nineteenth century, the concept of migration was widely accepted, though still little understood.

Only during the present century was the technique of ringing developed, enabling individual wild birds to be marked by lightweight rings bearing a serial number and a return address. At first birds were ringed while they were still nestlings, but gradually ever more ingenious methods of catching birds were developed. These enable fully adult, free-flying birds to be marked as well.

Today, the rings are made of lightweight, hard-wearing alloys that do not interfere in any way with the bird's normal life. Indeed, some individuals have worn the same ring without mishap for 30 years or more.

The results of ringing cannot be overstated. Swallows, for example, nest throughout Europe and winter throughout Africa. But British Swallows are found only in South Africa. Ornithologists had always suspected that the same Swallows returned to the same barn each year, and so (more or less) it has proved. What was surprising was that the same individuals return to the same piece of African veldt each winter and roost in the same reed bed each night. Our Swallows thus have two homes – one for summer for one for winter.

Bluethroats are scarce passage migrants as they fly from their breeding grounds in Scandinavia to their wintering grounds in the south. However, they have been known to nest in Britain on at least two occasions.

Although Whimbrel breed in north and west Scotland, the vast majority are passage migrants throughout Britain and Ireland.

Between their two residences lies one of the most daunting journeys in the world and many Swallows die of hunger or exhaustion along the way. Other small birds, too, make similar journeys and face the same life-threatening hazards.

Every autumn millions of small warblers such as the Willow Warbler and Whitethroat and chats such as the Redstart and Whinchat set out from our shores to fly to Africa. They can stop over to feed along the way, at least until they reach southern Europe. There they are faced with the Mediterranean, on the far side of which lies a narrow scorched strip of coastline with the great Sahara Desert beyond.

Among the olive groves of southern Europe these small waifs feed voraciously, sometimes doubling their weight in a few brief weeks. The extra weight is taken on in the form of fat that will be used as fuel during their long flight.

Finally they take off, climb to a few thousand feet and fly non-stop from Europe across the Mediterranean and Sahara to the African savannahs. The total flight takes about 40 hours and those that make it are those that do not stop off at an oasis, that are not killed by marauding falcons and do not run out of the reserves of fat that form their natural fuel. It is a remarkable journey and one that all birdwatchers should marvel at when the first Willow Warbler reappears to sing in British woodlands toward the end of April.

Sightings of Waxwings are usually infrequent in Britain. However, every five or six years they appear in large numbers owing to a combination of high populations and a failure of food crops in their Scandinavian breeding grounds.

The Structure of a Bird

The structure of birds is geared to the most important element in their lives – flight. Flight poses enormous problems in terms of weight and power, problems that even human intelligence has only managed to solve satisfactorily within the present century. The restrictions placed on flying animals are enormous and it is thus not surprising that the essential body plan of birds differs so little from species to species. Most birds are small and the only really large birds, such as the Ostrich, are flightless. The key to the success of birds as flying machines is the development of feathers.

Feathers

Birds evolved some 150 million years ago from reptilian ancestors which developed scales as a means of conserving body heat. The earliest birds developed scales on the forelimbs that, when spread, enabled them to glide from one tree to the next on rudimentary wings. Gradually proper feathers evolved, forming not only excellent body insulation, but also the functional feathers of wing and tail essential to propelled flight.

A feather is a remarkable structure. It consists of a central shaft lined with tightly packed barbs on either side. These in turn have rows of barbules that are locked together by small hook-like structures called barbicels. By running a feather through its bill a bird locks all of these elements together like a zip, forming a solid, but astonishingly lightweight, unit. Some feathers lack the locking structures and are designed purely for insulation – we call them 'down'. Others are particularly stiff or rigid and are used for flight like the wings and tail of an aircraft.

The main propulsion feathers are the primaries – the outer wing feathers, which vary in number from nine to twelve. These have stiff shafts and a tight structure of barbs and barbules that requires some effort to tear apart. The result is one of the highest strength-to-weight ratios imaginable, yet the feather remains flexible and perfectly adapted for flight. Primaries are asymmetrical, being narrow on the leading (forward) edge and wider on the trailing edge. They are attached to the bird's 'hand', overlapping outwards like slates on a roof, and, together with the muscles that move the 'hand', form the bird's

Most of the names given to parts of a bird's anatomy are easy to comprehend, but some are technical. All are worth learning as they aid understanding of how birds are built and can help in identifying them.

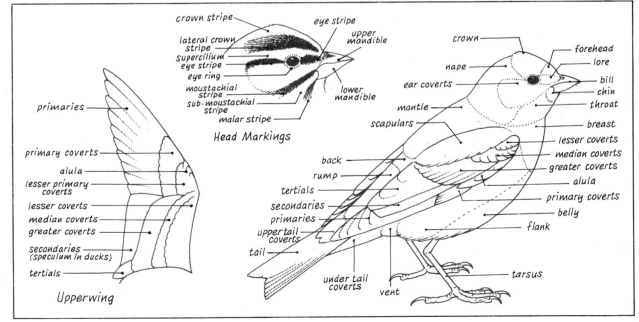

Head Markings

Upperwing

powerhouse. On the upward stroke of the wings the primaries open like a louvered window, letting air pass through easily. On the downward stroke the feathers overlap to form a solid paddle that pushes air downwards and backwards, creating a propulsive force to drive the bird though the air.

The secondary feathers of the wing vary in number according to the size of the bird. They grow from the forearm and are more symmetrical in shape than the primaries. Their main function is to provide lift, like the wings of an aircraft. Tail feathers too vary in number, as well as shape and size. They provide lift as well as steering and balance, but are also sometimes overdeveloped for other less functional uses such as recognition and courtship display.

Despite the lyrics of the nineteenth-century music-hall song, there are not 'forty thousand feathers on a thrush': a patient American researcher counted only just over three thousand on a similar-sized bird.

Feathers are, then, not only a bird's major characteristic, but the primary element in its adaptation to flight. Light, insulating and extremely strong, they are the most significant of all the adaptations to life evolved by birds.

Though feathers evolved from reptilian scales, birds did not entirely dispense with their ancestors' 'skin'. Birds' legs and feet are covered with scales, though here there is considerably more variation between species than there is in feather structure. A bird's legs and feet reflect its life-style. The long legs of herons are ideally suited to wading, the webbed feet of ducks are effective paddles, the sharp talons of eagles are splendidly designed to grab and kill prey, woodpeckers have sharp 'climbing-iron' feet that make tree climbing look simple. There are birds with tiny legs and feet that are no more than handy props on which to stand while they are not airborne. The legs of the highly aerial terns fall into this category, while the Swift has only the shortest of legs and four forward-pointing toes for clinging to its nest site, and is more or less helpless if grounded.

The normal arrangement of the toes is three pointing forward and one back, but in several groups the backward-pointing toe has become redundant and has disappeared. Waders such as the Oystercatcher are good examples of three-toed birds. Woodpeckers usually have only two toes that point forward, but two that point backward as an adaption to their climbing life-styles. Most swimming birds have webbed feet, but some like the grebes have semi-palmate feet with broad lobes along each toe that serve the same function.

Bills

If we can tell a great deal about a bird and the way it lives from its legs and feet, the design and shape of its bill can tell us much, much more. There are probes like the long, decurved bill of the Curlew and nutcrackers like the huge powerful bill of the Hawfinch. There are chisels like those of the Great Spotted Woodpecker and delicate tweezers like that of the Goldfinch. Even among a comparatively homogenous group like the ducks there are major differences in bill structure between the fish-eating Goosander and the filter-feeding Shoveler.

Muscles and skeleton

Perhaps the most obvious limitations on a bird's structure imposed by the demands of flight can be seen in its muscles and skeleton. Most of us have little understanding of bird anatomy, but if you carve a chicken or turkey, for example, it is easy to see where the meat is concentrated. In fact these are ground-dwelling walking birds with well developed 'drumsticks' and thighs. Most birds lack such development. Even with these birds, however, the bulk of the muscle is concentrated on the breast. This is the very heart of the bird's flight 'engines'. The breast actually consists of two muscles. The larger, outer one is the muscle that pulls the wing downward in the power stroke. An inner and much smaller muscle has the function of raising the wing at the completion of each downward stroke. The actual wing muscles are no more than tendons to carry the power to where it is required – a fact apparent to anyone who has eaten a chicken wing.

The large breast muscles are attached to the body on either side of a central keel on the sternum, or breastbone. The whole of the skeleton is shortened,

Broad like a Buzzard

Straight like a Fulmar

Rounded like a Partridge

Pointed like a Kestrel

Sharply angled like a Swallow

Long and thin like a Swift

Although the bone structure of the wing is similar in all birds, the shape of the feathered wing varies according to the bird's life-style.

The Structure of a Bird

Like an aircraft, birds alter their angle of approach when they come into land, lowering the 'undercarriage' only at the last minute.

Birds vary not only in size and plumage colours but also in shape. Many can be identified by silhouette alone.

finch-like

duck-like

wader-like

hawk-like

swallow-like

thrush-like

with little or no space between the foreparts and the hindquarters. Indeed, the backbone is virtually fused into the rear of the rib cage. Many of the bones, including those of the skull and the bill, are hollow and honeycombed internally, giving them lightness without sacrificing strength. The skeleton of birds is so designed for lightness that in some species it actually weighs less than the feathers.

Bird senses
Birds can hear and smell, but these senses are nowhere near as well developed as that of sight. Most birds have huge eyes and remarkable vision. Birds of prey certainly have better eyesight than humans, but all birds are able to absorb more information than we can by having a wider field of view than ours. The bird's eye is so important that it is protected by an extra eyelid, the nictitating membrane. In some aquatic species this has a transparent area that acts as a pair of underwater goggles and even compensates for the water's refraction, or bending of the light rays, which make objects seen from beneath the surface seem a short distance from their actual position.

Some birds have eyes at the sides of their heads. One of the most extreme examples is the Woodcock, a bird that can see just as well behind as in front. Other birds have forward-facing eyes with excellent binocular vision like ours. The owls are a prime example of birds with forward-facing eyes. To compensate for not being

able to see behind them, they have the remarkable ability to twist their necks through 180 degrees.

Saving weight
The internal digestive and reproductive systems of birds have been streamlined to save weight. Birds have no teeth (these would be too heavy for a flying animal) and have developed a powerful gizzard to grind down their food instead. They swallow grit regularly to aid the digestive process. They absorb energy very quickly and dispose of waste equally fast.

Even the strategy of laying eggs rather than giving birth to living young is another weight-saving device and females produce eggs remarkably quickly via a single ovary. An egg may form a significant percentage of a female's total body weight and a large clutch of eggs may amount to over half the parent's weight. Such a load would significantly affect the female's life-style and make her more vulnerable to predators, so placing the eggs somewhere safe (usually in a nest) and warming them by incubation through the latter stages of development makes sound evolutionary sense.

Birds are, then, structured in different ways according to their life-styles. Some have long legs, some short. Some have long bills, others short stubby ones. All birds have good eyesight, but some are particularly well endowed in this respect. All have made structural sacrifices to allow them the power of flight. It is this power that makes them so fascinating and so mobile, but it has not been achieved without loss.

Becoming a Birder

So far no one has marketed a do-it-yourself 'birder kit'. Though it would be easy enough to assemble the ingredients, the cost would be a little daunting to the average birdwatcher. Birding does not need to be an expensive hobby. It is certainly far cheaper than golf, and enthusiasts need a tiny fraction of the money spent by yachtsmen. Nevertheless, there are expenses that must be met.

Binoculars

Despite what some books say, it really is not possible to become a birder without a pair of binoculars. These may be obtained quite cheaply, but with glasses more than most consumer durables, you get what you pay for. Poor binoculars cut down on enjoyment and hold back the development of identification skills. A good pair might cost, at late 1980s prices, some £450, but there is a great deal of choice at around £70 to £150. If you spend less than that, you are likely to end up with optically poor binoculars that detract rather than add to your enjoyment of the birds.

When you decide to purchase a pair of binoculars, choose a reputable specialist supplier (ask an experienced birder's advice or scan the pages of a birdwatching magazine) and compare as many pairs as possible, preferably trying them out under field conditions.

Ideally, binoculars should give a magnification of between seven and ten times. Lower magnifications mean that you are unable to see the detail you require, while binoculars with higher magnifications are difficult to hold steady and have a narrow field of view. Never buy binoculars that are advertised as 'cross-Channel' or something similar; they are of no use to birders. The other feature of a binocular is the diameter of the object lens expressed in millimetres. This may vary enormously, but for birding something in the range of 30 to 50 (mm) is about right. Smaller object lenses let in little light and cut down the field of view. Larger object lenses give a bright image with a wide field of view, but are heavy to carry around your neck all day long. As with magnification, it is a matter of compromise to obtain the features that you need. My own choice is a pair of roof prism binoculars with no

Binoculars enable birdwatchers to sight Golden Eagles in the highlands of Scotland.

external moving parts to break or allow dust into the mechanism. The magnification is ten times, the object lens is 40mm. They are made in West Germany by one of the handful of top optical companies in the world and have served me well for nearly 20 years. A few years ago I had them adapted to focus closer so that I can enjoy detailed views of small birds.

Equipment and expertise

Binoculars are the only real essential, so anyone can start watching birds for £70 to £150 (1988 prices). However, you will soon realise that most other birders that you meet have considerably more equipment than a pair of binoculars. Walk along the East Bank at Cley and you will soon come across a khaki-clad figure weighed down with binoculars, telescope and tripod, and perhaps a single-lens reflex camera with a powerful telephoto lens and a motor drive hung over the shoulder, wearing a woolly hat festooned with badges of ornithological societies and naturalists' trusts, warm corduroy trousers, wellington boots, and an ancient thornproof jacket, its pockets bulging with a field guide or two, a notebook, and some obscure publications on bird identification or bird finding. In the car there may be a mobile tape recorder and collection of bird song cassettes, a shoulder pod for camera and telescope and a car-window-cum-hide telescope mount.

Just how much of this array of equipment one acquires is a matter of taste. All of it is useful and many birders have the lot. Its acquisition is, however, no indication of the level of expertise of the individual concerned. Today it is very difficult to separate the experts from the camp followers, for they all look the same. Once it was possible to pick out the experts by the amount of paint missing on their binoculars. Sadly, even this is no longer true. 'Distressing', the careful removal of paint from brand new binoculars to make them appear to have had daily use for the last twenty years or so, is easily achieved. Telescopes, jackets, jerseys and over-trousers, too, may all be 'distressed' prior to use.

The second item of basic equipment should be a good field guide. This will enable you to identify every bird you see, and most serious birders build up a library of such guides which they constantly update. They can be taken with you into the field (hence the name 'field guides') but they need not be lugged around all day when they can be left in a vehicle, and it is certainly a good habit to put them completely out of your mind until *after* making notes and drawings of a 'new' bird.

Contemporary field guides are remarkably good value and collecting them does not cost a great deal. Sensible clothing, waterproofs and wellingtons can all be obtained at reasonable prices.

Telescopes
The next big item which many birders acquire is the telescope. As with binoculars, there is a great range of instruments from which to choose. They range from about £100 to £1500 (late 1980s prices), but the instruments at the lower end of the market are perfectly adequate and an outlay of around £150 to £300 will produce a fine quality instrument. Not so long ago, birdwatchers could generally buy only brass telescopes about a metre long when extended. Today modern 'draw' telescopes have only a single draw-tube, while many are now prismatic, with no exterior moving parts. Once again my own preference is for the latter. 'Draw' telescopes tend to get wet inside and suffer from condensation on the lenses. If new, my own 'scope would cost £170 (late 1980s prices) and is a fine performer. The object lens is 60mm, but I think that 70mm would be better for gathering light and offer a wider field of view. As with most other modern 'scopes, it is easy to interchange the eyepiece, giving different magnifications, but I stick to a 25 times eyepiece and, if using another one, would go *down* in magnification rather than upwards. Zoom eyepieces have an initial appeal, but give a much narrower field of view at the same magnification and let in less light.

While it is difficult to borrow someone's binoculars, 'road testing' telescopes is simplicity itself. Find out about the latest rarity and head for the spot. There you will find a battery of 'scopes mounted on tripods, all focused on the same spot – the bird. Most birders will happily oblige you with a look and in a few minutes you can judge for yourself which is the best instrument and the most appropriate eyepiece. It is also easy to start a debate among any group of birders on the subject of telescopes . . . and that's another way to learn.

For what it's worth, my binoculars are West German Zeiss Dialyt 10 × 40B and my telescope a Kowa TS1 with a 25 times eyepiece . . . both of them are heavily distressed, of course.

Few can aspire to the quality of a field notebook like this but everyone can try to keep detailed records of everything they see and hear. Drawings are always a useful addition.

3 June 1985
Lower Twidlemarsh
Worcs:

Wind SW (5-6)
fresh → moderate
50%, sunny later

steep forehead

pale eyebrow

uniform underparts

pinkish legs

Teal 10
Redshank 2
Yellowhammer 10
Marsh Warbler
(1 singing)
Goldfinch
Greenfinch
Tree Sparrow
(several nesting)

Marsh Warbler

osier bed

Note association with meadowsweet & osiers

meadowsweet

Suitable equipment and sensible dull-coloured clothing are the major prerequisites for birdwatchers. Photographers will find few subjects as co-operative as Puffins near their cliff-top nests.

Lesser Spotted Woodpecker

The Field Guide Jungle

The first sensible field guides to British (and European) birds appeared in the early 1950s when books with colour plates were rare and colour printing was decidedly expensive. For technical reasons, this meant that the pictures of the birds had to be crammed on to pages quite separate from the text. It says much for the quality of both its illustrations and text that one of the first, *A Field Guide to the Birds of Britain and Europe*, by Peterson, Mountfort and Hollom, first published in 1954 by Collins, remains the best-selling field guide to the present day. Indeed, it has sold more copies than any other bird book, apart from its earlier American equivalent.

'Peterson', as it is affectionately known, was the major breakthrough in European birding and has shown three generations how to set about identifying birds. A major feature was its system of pointers, instantly and clearly drawing attention to the most important identification features for each bird – which soon became known as the 'Peterson' system after its inventor, the famous American bird artist Roger Tony Peterson.

Modern field guides

Inevitably, the publishing industry has moved on. Today high-quality four-colour lithography is widely used for a vast range of books. Colour printing has become much cheaper and it was quickly realized that the 'colour on every page' facility was ideally suited to the field guide. First, in 1970, came *The Hamlyn Guide to the Birds of Britain and Europe* (written by Bertel Bruun and illustrated by Arthur Singer) and soon after *The Birds of Britain and Europe, with North Africa and the Middle East*, published by Collins in 1972 (with text by Richard Fitter, illustrations by Hermann Heinzel and maps by John Parslow). Both were immediate successes for they allowed illustration, text and map on a single bird to be grouped together with obvious advantages to the consumer. The Collins guide, which has been updated several times, is the nearest rival to 'Peterson' in the best selling stakes, while the latest (1986) edition of the Hamlyn guide, renamed *The Country Life Guide to the Birds of Britain and Europe*, is also very popular.

By printing the text on a separate black plate the whole of Europe was opened up as a market. To produce a German edition all the publisher had to do was to drop the plate with the English text and substitute a German text. The same could be done for Sweden, France, Spain and Italy (to date, 'Peterson' has been translated into 12 different languages). Such guides seemed perfect. How could one improve on perfection?

'Designer' guides

There was, however, one drawback to the all-colour guides. Because European sales were essential to achieve the large print-run required to make the project economic, the guides had to include all the birds of Europe. To avoid making the book too huge and cumbersome, up to six species had to be crammed on to a spread (two pages). This allowed remarkably little room for text, which didn't matter for, say, a Robin, but which was unsatisfactory, to say the least, for some of the more difficult-to-identify species such as the gulls, terns, waders and warblers.

Sadly, few attempts have been made to overcome this problem, for publishers – and presumably the book-buying public – actually like the neatness of design of the all-colour guides. However, *The Shell Guide to the Birds of Britain and Ireland* by James Ferguson-Lees, with maps by Dr J. T. R. Sharrock, published in 1983 by Michael Joseph, made a fine attempt at a solution by ignoring design and going for what was seen as the guide to fit the birder, rather than the other way around. Texts run as long as is required and the illustrations by Ian Willis are excellent. It remains the best guide to every bird ever to have occurred in Britain up to the time of publication of this book. Somewhere, there is a middle road, with a well designed and attractive book that allows author and artist the space they need, while offering the observer all of the birds that he requires. One day someone will solve the problem.

The field guide jungle consists of the most amazing number of guides that attempt to identify our birds. At present several such guides appear each year, most soon disappear but those that are well produced have a remarkable shelf life and go on selling year after year.

Specialist guides

Because some birds are easy to identify and some difficult, that after all is the problem with 'designer field guides', several books have appeared in recent years that ignore the common, easily identified species. The first of these, brought out in 1974 by the admirable small publishers T. A. & D. Poyser, was *Flight Identification of European Raptors* by R. F. Porter, Ian Willis, Steen Christensen and Bent Pors Nielsen. This Anglo-Danish production runs to great detail on what is often a very difficult group of birds to identify and one for which the Peterson system is particularly inappropriate. This first-class book, in its revised and enlarged third (1981) edition, should be a compulsory item of luggage for any birder travelling in Europe who is likely to see birds of prey, especially in the eastern part of the continent. It is packed with information, and illustrated by a wealth of drawings and photographs, yet covers only 39 species. How can a 'normal' field guide cope with such difficult birds?

Also published by Poyser, in 1982, is P. J. Grant's *Gulls – a guide to identification*. Here again, this deals with an exceedingly confusing group of birds that, like the raptors, pass through a complex series of plumages before becoming adult. Packed with data, this book too should be owned by anyone who may expect to pick out one of the rarer gulls from the masses of common species. The second edition (1986) is considerably revised and enlarged, containing 280 new photographs of gulls.

'Group' guides

In the past few years this concept of 'group' guides to identfication has been picked up by the firm of Croom Helm, now Christopher Helm. Here, though, the books are illustrated in colour and cover all the species found in the World. *Seabirds – an identification guide* by Peter Harrison covers all of the world's seabirds in a major *tour de force*. But, while being an essential part of the serious birder's library, it is hardly a book for the field. Birding in Britain is unlikely to produce more than a tiny percentage of the species covered, though a trip through the southern oceans would be infinitely less rewarding without it.

Similarly *Shorebirds – an identification guide to the waders of the world* by Hayman, Marchant and Prater is a splendid work of rererence that, like *Seabirds* is an eye-opener to what could be expected in the way of rarities. The series continues with *Wildfowl – an identification guide to the ducks, geese and swans of the world*, and more are on the way.

One of the best sources of identification material is the monthly magazine *British Birds*, popularly known simply as 'BB'. Several issues each year feature major articles on the identification of 'difficult' birds. Wherever a major rarity occurs, many birders can be seen thumbing through the appropriate issue of 'BB' abstracted from their library. A paper by Grant and Jonsson on the small waders known as 'stints and peeps' has become a classic, taking the identification of these notoriously confusing birds into another phase of development. One friend of mine buys two copies of all these papers and books and creates a scrap-book by tearing them apart and using the material he needs. This is good news for publishers and authors, but it is something I have been unable to force myself to do.

Field guides are then compromises. They have to have a wide appeal to make economic sense and that means catering to both beginner and expert alike. Yet birdwatchers at these two extremes, as well as those between, demand different things from their guides. One day. . . .

Waders like this Greenshank, have always proved a problem for novice birdwatchers, though birders can pick them out at a glance.

35

Where to Go: What to See

Knowing where to go and what one is likely to see is half the battle in identifying birds. It is also essential if one is to develop as a birdwatcher. For the beginner a glance through the field guide section of a book like this can be both exciting and daunting: so many birds to see, so many problems in putting names to them.

'Hot spots'
One can, of course, enjoy watching birds anywhere, just as one can go climbing on the gentle sandstone outcrops of The Weald, or play golf on the local common. But just as there is something special for a climber about the peaks of Snowdonia and for the golfer to tread the hallowed turf of Gleneagles, so for the birder Cley, Elmley, Spurn, Fair Isle and Scilly are special places. Most of the best birding areas in Britain are coastal (*see map*) and it is to our shores that most birders travel at weekends and for their holidays. Wild marshes, isolated headlands, remote islands and lonely estuaries are the best places for birds, and birders throng to these 'hot spots' throughout the year.

There are however, a number of excellent inland hot spots, too. The Spey valley in the Cairngorms of Scotland (*see page* 251) sees an annual pilgrimage of birdwatchers keen to see its breeding specialities in late May and June. Where else could one reasonably expect to see Crested Tit or Capercaillie? The Ouse Washes in Cambridgeshire (*see page* 307) have their devotees too, with hordes of wild swans in winter and the summer spectacle of Black-tailed Godwits and Ruff in their splendid breeding plumage. Then there are those to whom an annual pilgrimage to the New Forest (*see page* 304) is essential. Where else could they readily expect to find breeding Honey Buzzard and Dartford Warbler? I could continue . . . Fetlar, Minsmere, Tregaron and Weeting Heath. All these places and many more can be found in the 'Where to Watch' section of this book, between pages 232 and 333.

Coastal sites are favoured by birdwatchers because they offer a variety of habitats and thus a variety of birds. You cannot reasonably expect to see seabirds such as Fulmar, Kittiwake and Puffin inland. Shorebirds such as Sanderling, Knot and Turnstone turn up only rarely away from the coast and most other waders are far more abundant along coastal marshes and estuaries than they ever are in inland. Yet a coastal wood or heath will also hold those species typically found in such habitats inland – so coastal sites have all the advantages with none of the disadvantages.

Rare birds
The coasts also have one other major advantage – they attract wanderers from afar, usually known as 'vagrants'. Before arriving safely in Britain, birds have to make a sea crossing and it is not surprising that at the end of what may have been a long and tiring journey, they are likely to alight at the first landfall. Thus exhausted vagrants tend to concentrate along our coasts. They do also find their way inland, even to the heart of our great conurbations, but most are found at the coast. Here birders, too, concentrate so the effect is reinforced. More birders frequent the coasts, so more birds are found there. Nevertheless, there does seem to be a genuine coastal bias to the occurrence of all migrants, including rare species.

A similar relationship between the habits of birdwatchers and numbers of birds seen exists with so-called 'weekend rarity' phenomenon. Most rare species are found at weekends. Of course, this does not mean that the birds can tell Saturdays and Sundays from weekdays and conveniently make their landfalls only on those days! It simply reflects the fact that most birders are out and about at weekends.

Personally, I am not convinced that one stretch of coastline is much better than another, for almost any area of cover will produce birds at one time or another. For long, Fair Isle was regarded as the ultimate birding spot in autumn, but now the Isles of Scilly have that reputation. The more adventurous birders had already shown that Shetland's Out Skerries were quite capable of producing Fair-Isle-standard rarities and those who like their rare birds without being surrounded by crowds of other birders, need not despair that Scilly has an October monopoly of such birds. Half of the rarities that occur on those islands are of eastern origins and they must pass through other areas on their way to their Scilly landfall.

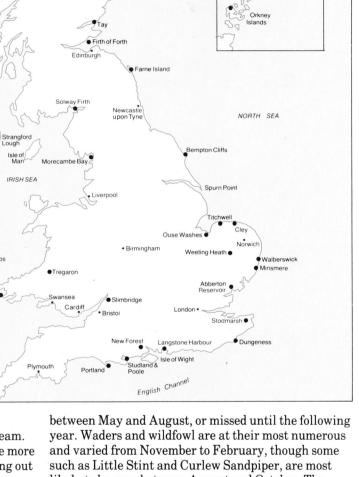

Outer
Hebrides

Inverness •
● Speyside
● Abernethy &
Loch Garten

ATLANTIC OCEAN

● Tay
● Firth of Forth
Edinburgh •

Islay

● Farne Island

Solway Firth ●

Belfast ●
Strangford
Lough
Isle of
Man
● Morecambe Bay

IRISH SEA

Galway ●

Dublin •

Akeragh Lough ●

● Wexford Slobs

● Tregaron

Skomer ●

Cape Clear ●

Swansea ●
● Cardiff
• Bristol

Plymouth •

Portland •

Isles of Scilly
•

Shetland Isles

● Unst
● Fetlar

● Fair Isle

Orkney
Islands

NORTH SEA

Newcastle
upon Tyne •

● Bempton Cliffs

Spurn Point

● Liverpool

• Birmingham

● Titchwell
● Cley
Ouse Washes ●
Norwich •
Weeting Heath ●
● Walberswick
● Minsmere
Abberton
Reservoir ●
London •
Stodmarsh ●

● Slimbridge

New Forest ●
Langstone Harbour ●
Studland &
Poole
Isle of Wight
● Dungeness

English Channel

*Any selection of favourite bird
spots must be personal, but sites
on this map would figure in most
people's lists. All can be
recommended for a good day's
birding.*

The importance of timing

For the novice birder, rarities should be only a dream.
It is essential to have a thorough grounding in the more
regular resident and visiting species before seeking out
exciting rarities. For beginners, visits to reservoirs,
gravel pits, estuaries, coastal marshes, heaths,
woodlands and the mountains are all part of a general
background. Timing such visits is important and trips
should be well planned to take place at the best time of
the year for the area concerned. The summering
warblers, chats and flycatchers must be looked for

between May and August, or missed until the following
year. Waders and wildfowl are at their most numerous
and varied from November to February, though some
such as Little Stint and Curlew Sandpiper, are most
likely to be seen between August and October. The
birder's year is a busy one, but a reasonably active
beginner should be able to see 200 species in a year.

The Field Guide section of this book gives wintering
and passage areas and breeding or resident
distribution, which will help considerably with your
forward planning of birdwatching trips.

Conservation

A hundred years ago our birds were in need of 'protection' and the concept of 'conservation' simply did not exist. Thus we had bird 'protectionists' and the embryonic Royal Society for the Protection of Birds (RSPB). At this time the major problem was to protect birds against deliberate acts of persecution and this impressive organization was founded in an effort to stop the mass destruction of birds for the feather trade. Great Crested Grebes were shot wholesale for their nuptial plumes and the species was reduced to the status of a threatened rarity. Egrets were similarly slaughtered in Europe for the fine 'aigrette' feathers. Sadly, most of our birds of prey were shot out of existence by gamekeepers or collectors and any bird that had the misfortune of becoming rare was ceaselessly persecuted both for its skin and its eggs. Today we have moved on, though the RSPB still has to guard our rarer birds against illegal trapping, egg collecting and falconry thieves.

Protection apart, the conservation movement is now more concerned with habitats than with individual birds. Recognizing the importance of places where birds can live, the RSPB has devoted a large proportion of its income to establishing a network of bird reserves throughout Britain. It might make sense to change the name to the 'Royal Society for the Conservation of Birds', but it would make no difference to the splendid work the RSPB does. The RSPB is already an extremely effective conservation organization. The basic thinking is that if the correct habitat is conserved or created then the birds will follow. At Minsmere in Suffolk (*see page* 303), the Society pioneered the idea of 'the Scrape' turning a relatively useless stretch of rough coastal grassland into a prime breeding and

Conservationists are highly concerned about acid rain. So far it has largely affected the continent, as here in Germany, where it is destroying the habitats of a number of birds.

Even National Nature Reserves like this one at Craigellachie are not immune to destruction when major roadworks are under construction.

feeding ground for a wide variety of birds. Almost overnight, this new habitat attracted breeding Avocets and terns and the original 'Scrape' has been copied throughout the country to the great benefit of these and many other species. The idea is to renew or recreate habitats that are in short supply, or under threat from various types of development, from tidal barrages and marinas to industrial complexes. But such active conservation is only one arm of the movement.

Seeking out a variety of bird-rich habitats and turning them into bird reserves may be essential, but such areas must then be prepared to receive visitors who wish to see how their money is being spent. For a long time, the leader in this field was The Wildfowl Trust, with its open-every-day turnstile approach to conservation. Most of the Trust's grounds are part zoo–part wildfowl refuge with both captive and wild birds on view. Here entertainment and education go hand in hand with great success. The RSPB approach has been somewhat different, but most reserves are now open most days of the year and can be visited without notice, often free. The educational role of reserves is regarded as highly important and the Society continues a quite phenomenal growth.

Similarly local naturalists' trusts (many of which are now called 'conservation' trusts) have become more aware of their public role. Many own or lease reserves where birds are of primary interest and most have arrangements for public visiting. The Norfolk Naturalists' Trust was first in the field in 1926 and it still leads the way with its excellent network of easily visited reserves. Slowly, but surely, even the Nature Conservancy Council, the government conservation organization, is following suit. Today more and more of our state-owned reserves are being opened up to visitors, though generally the NCC sees its role more as conservation than public relations.

A question of balance

The NCC is, however, highly active in other, perhaps more important, fields. In a tiny, over crowded island like the British Isles there are inevitably clashes of interest between conservationists on the one hand and developers on the other. Some developers are private individuals seeking no more than to build a housing estate on a small rural field. Others may be giant corporations and multi-nationals offering employment and prosperity to whole regions of the country. They may be government agencies seeking to construct new roads or nuclear power stations, or they may be factories or farmers polluting our watercourses.

All developments are carefully monitored by the NCC and the voluntary conservation bodies. It is easy to object to virtually any development that destroys even a small part of the countryside. Yet conservationists use electricity, oil, gas and the road system as much as anyone else. They need places to live, places to work and even new airports. Everything is a balance, so that the very things that we value are not destroyed in a headlong flight to material prosperity.

I must end this section with an earnest request: if you do not belong to the RSPB, join immediately.

Powerlines need to be carefully sited not only with regard to aesthetics but also to wildlife safety. Large numbers of Mute Swans are killed annually by cables.

Oil pollution at sea regularly kills thousands of birds each year. Many of the victims come ashore in a pitiable state like this unfortunate Guillemot.

Wider Horizons

It is perhaps inevitable that, having become an accomplished 'British' birder, one should begin to look farther afield in search of birds. At first, birding abroad was the preserve of a few intrepid pioneers who roamed as far afield as Spain's Coto Doñana, the Camargue of southern France and the Danube Delta in Romania. Accounts of such journeys into the 'wilderness' became the classics of ornithological literature at the end of the nineteenth century and the beginning of the present one. Books by R. B. Lodge, Abel Chapman, M. J. Nicholl and W. H. Hudson showed the way, though few were to follow.

Seeking new sites

After the Second World War, the Peterson guide covered the birds of Europe and soon there were car-loads of birders heading southwards across the Continent on stamina-testing birdwatching holidays to all manner of 'hot spots'. At first, they followed the well charted routes of their forebears, but later they branched out in search of pastures new. The Greek coast of Macedonia was an early favourite, with Lapland soon to follow. Then it was Turkey and Morocco, introducing birds that were not even to be found in 'Peterson'.

Britons, of course, had been watching birds throughout the world since the days of the Empire and there was a good chance that, if there was a bird book at all, it would be in English. The new band of birders were, however, new in almost every way. Mainly male, they were prepared to camp, sleep rough, bird from dawn to dusk and seldom bothered to pay their compliments to the ambassador. Eventually, they began to find their way right across Europe and the Middle East to India. It was then, at the end of the 1960s that the great travel revolution occurred. The intercontinental jet airliner arrived. The effect of the jetliner on our holiday and travel aspirations has been dramatic. The transformation of the airline industry into a highly competitive business (which some might describe as a 'cutthroat jungle') has been revolutionary. Today, long and exhausting car trips are out. The modern answer is to fly-and-drive. Yet even with the whole world at their doorstep, many British

birders regularly continue to head in the same direction – eastward.

Britain lies at the western edge of the great Palearctic zoogeographical region. To the west, across the Atlantic, lies the Nearctic region; to the south, the Ethiopian region. Both have 'foreign' birds, whereas to the east are birds that, while not exactly the same, show close affinities with our own. Besides, most recent bird colonists and rarities come from this direction and British birders, who have gradually grown to think of themselves as European birders, now increasingly see themselves as Western Palearctic or even Palearctic birders. (The Palearctic region is one of the great regions of animal distribution in the world: it comprises the whole of Europe, Africa north of the Sahara, and Asia north to the Himalayas.) It simply seems a natural extension of one's existing expertise.

Unlimited horizons

There are also those who venture farther afield. A trip to the Galapagos Islands off the coast of Ecuador is almost irresistible; a journey to Antarctica no longer merely a dream; a safari in Africa impossible to turn down, and so on. Some have even become global birders with life lists running into the thousands, though, in general, the world birder is an American phenomenon. I suppose, at the end of the day, most British birdwatchers get more pleasure out of seeing a new Palearctic bird than they do from a new penguin or earthcreeper; from seeing a bird that could conceivably find its way to these islands, than from seeing one that is destined never to budge from its home several thousand miles away.

On the opposite page the map shows a selection of some of the best spots to watch birds in the world. The choice is purely personal and includes many where I have enjoyed some of the best birding I have ever had the fortune to experience. In the tropics the number of species, though not necessarily the number of birds, rises dramatically. Venezuela and Ecuador both have well over a thousand species to search for. Kenya has produced more species in a single day than any other country. Yet my own favourites remain steadfastly Old World, and Palearctic in particular. Only Bharatpur, in

Bee-eaters, very rare visitors to southern England, are common on the continent and bring a touch of colour to any day's birding around the Mediterranean.

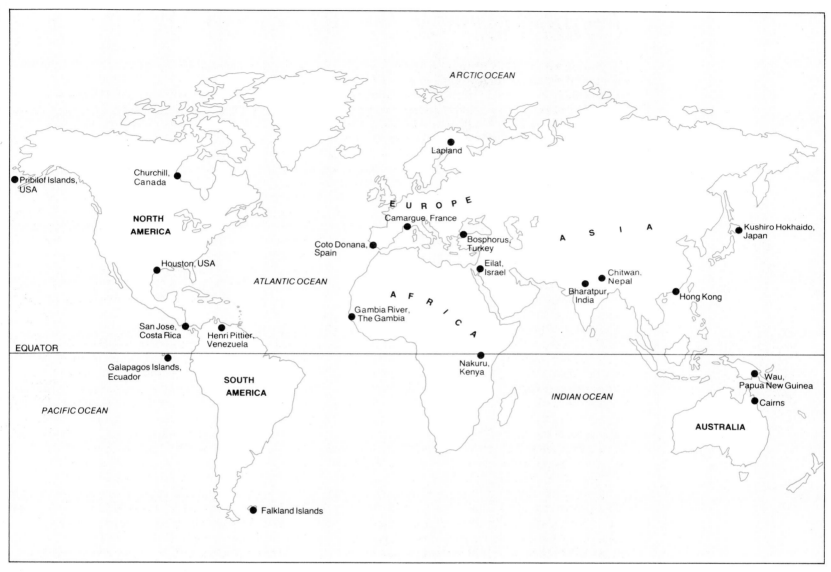

Pribilof Islands, USA

Churchill, Canada

NORTH AMERICA

Lapland

EUROPE

ASIA

Camargue, France

Kushiro Hokhaido, Japan

Coto Donana, Spain

Bosphorus, Turkey

Houston, USA

Eilat, Israel

ATLANTIC OCEAN

AFRICA

Chitwan, Nepal

Bharatpur, India

Hong Kong

Gambia River, The Gambia

San Jose, Costa Rica

Henri Pittier, Venezuela

EQUATOR

Galapagos Islands, Ecuador

SOUTH AMERICA

Nakuru, Kenya

INDIAN OCEAN

Wau, Papua New Guinea

Cairns

PACIFIC OCEAN

AUSTRALIA

Falkland Islands

ARCTIC OCEAN

northern India, would find its way into my top five sites; the rest are all in Europe.

There are, of course, places I have never been to but which are high on my list of possible future trips. The watery wildernesses of Arnhemland in northern Australia and the dense tropical rain-forests of Papua–New Guinea must be wonderful. The seabirds of South Georgia I would be sad to miss. The cranes of Zhalong in northern China (a cold winter–spring trip this) must be outstanding, not to mention the tundra wastes of Churchill in northern Canada. The marshes of northern Argentina and Uruguay, the wealth of birds unique to Madagascar and Hawaii, the Bald Eagles of Alaska, the magnificent Steller's Sea Eagles on the island of Kamchatka, in the USSR: I could go on and on . . . And if I was only allowed to choose just one wider horizon? Then, unhesitatingly, it would have to be Spain again!

The world's top birdwatching sites.

From Birder to Ornithologist

Birds are fascinating creatures and the birdwatcher finds great satisfaction in learning more about them. At first our primary aim is to recognize and put names to them and, with more than 8600 known species in the world, that may turn out to be a lot easier said than done. Many birders never get beyond identification, and there is nothing wrong with that. Others need to know more about birds and their lives. They ask themselves the questions 'Where?' 'When?' 'How?' and 'Why?' They seek understanding as well as skill. Such birders are likely to become ornithologists.

Ornithology is the scientific study of birds and, as such, it encompasses a wide variety of specializations. There is thus no one activity that picks out an ornithologist from a birder and, indeed, the two are often combined in a single individual. Someone examining the birds of a winter estuary may be searching for a rarity to add to their 'life list', or counting the number of individual birds present. Their appearance, equipment and techniques are the same. Only their aims differ. In fact, they may both actually keep the same records of their observations with species and numbers neatly tabulated in their notebooks.

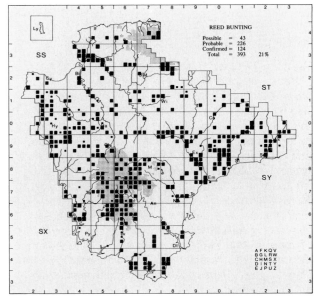

Intensive co-operative research such as that used to compile The Atlas of the Breeding Birds of Devon *is a feature of British ornithology largely instigated by the British Trust for Ornithology.*

Ornithologists do, however, carry out a wide variety of activities never undertaken by birders. They may preserve specimens, take measurements, dissect, count, sample, record, trap, weigh and so on. For most birders a little science can be both enjoyable and rewarding. Certainly, it is not necessary to spend one's time in a laboratory surrounded by specimens preserved in smelly formalin to be an ornithologist.

Amateur achievements

Britain has a long history of amateur field-work and some outstanding achievements as a result. The vast majority of ringers, for instance, are amateurs who pay for their own rings and equipment. The atlases of breeding and wintering birds, organized by the British Trust for Ornithology (BTO) and published by T. & A. D. Poyser, are the results of the efforts of over 10,000 amateur birdwatchers. The BTO's Common Bird Census that monitors the populations of our more abundant birds is the work of amateur enthusiasts. Most observatory work is carried out by enthusiasts who earn their living in totally unconnected ways. Indeed, almost everything we know about British birds has been discovered by non-professional ornithologists.

Becoming an ornithologist does not, therefore, involve a lengthy period of training at a university, or anywhere else come to that. It is simply a matter of being interested, observing and finding out. In its simplest terms it may involve no more than counting the birds at a garden feeder, in the garden itself, in a local park or wood, on a farm or some other area. It may involve watching and recording the behaviour of a common bird over a period of time, and understanding why it does what it does.

However, such individual research, while completely satisfying, may only duplicate work that has already been thoroughly researched. Much better is to join in a piece of co-operative research such as the variety of schemes organised by the BTO. By utilizing the efforts of a large number of individuals, the Trust has been able to considerably increase our knowledge and understanding of British birds. As well as organizing the Common Bird Census and research for the summer and winter atlases, it is responsible for the

administration of the national ringing scheme. By joining the Trust and participating in its work, one quickly finds out what is being done and what needs to be done. It is the prime base for individual field work and by far the best way of meeting others with the same interest.

If, however, individual research has a greater appeal, then still join the BTO and read the journal *Bird Study* avidly. Here you will find out what is being done and how your own ideas of research might fit into the general pattern. If you wish to specialize in a particular species, the BTO will soon put you in direct contact with anyone working on the same bird. If you want to become a ringer, the nearest ringing group may well take you under their wing. If migration fascinates you, then visit a bird observatory: again, the BTO has all the names and addresses to contact.

Becoming an ornithologist is not so much a matter of what you do, but more an attitude of mind: watch, listen, note and record. Watch carefully and inquisitively. Listen carefully and learn to tell the difference between a bird's calls in one circumstance and another. Keep careful notes of everything you see – even seemingly irrelevancies – and record your information in a way that makes it easy to retrieve. Most birdwatchers' notebooks are full of data arranged in chronological order. Most will disappear and never be seen in print. Modern computers make this a thing of the past, and their value for storing and retrieving data is obvious. In an increasingly computerized world, they may well come to be seen as an indispensable tool for the ornithologist.

The Field Guide

Identifying birds is largely a matter of knowing what to look for and where and when to expect what. A novice birdwatcher will see a bird, check through a book, find the illustration that most closely resembles the bird and put a name to it. This can lead to some terrible howlers. I have heard of young Robins being identified as White's Thrushes, of oiled Kittiwakes as Black Terns and so on. In each case a little knowledge would have shown the absurdity of the identification.

In this book all the background information on an individual bird is assembled on a single page. This total approach is in many ways similar to a recipe – miss one ingredient and the whole process can go wrong leading to misidentification, or an inedible dish. Thus illustrations alone are not sufficient evidence on which to base an accurate identification – the annotation, maps, seasonal and abundance charts and, of course, text must all be checked thoroughly.

Let us suppose that a dumpy, long-legged, grey bird with a long bill is seen on a marshy pool near the sea in September. A quick flick through the field guide section shows it is a wader. A more careful search eliminates the plovers because the bill is much larger than those birds and the head is smaller and less rounded. The godwits, curlews and snipe can be eliminated on bill length and shape, and Ruff and Woodcock because they are never grey. The leg colour of the bird is clearly not red or orange, so Ruff, the redshanks and Turnstone fall as well. Glancing through the feature notes we see that several of the

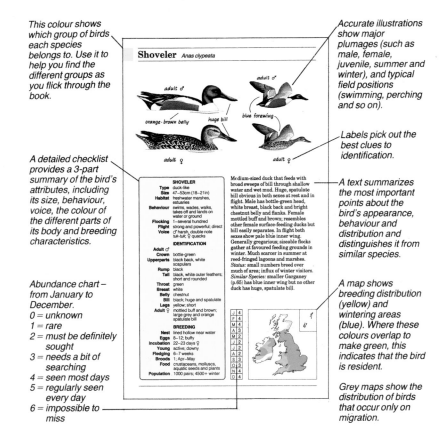

This colour shows which group of birds each species belongs to. Use it to help you find the different groups as you flick through the book.

Accurate illustrations show major plumages (such as male, female, juvenile, summer and winter), and typical field positions (swimming, perching and so on).

Labels pick out the best clues to identification.

A detailed checklist provides a 3-part summary of the bird's attributes, including its size, behaviour, voice, the colour of the different parts of its body and breeding characteristics.

A text summarizes the most important points about the bird's appearance, behaviour and distribution and distinguishes it from similar species.

Abundance chart – from January to December.
0 = unknown
1 = rare
2 = must be definitely sought
3 = needs a bit of searching
4 = seen most days
5 = regularly seen every day
6 = impossible to miss

A map shows breeding distribution (yellow) and wintering areas (blue). Where these colours overlap to make green, this indicates that the bird is resident.

Grey maps show the distribution of birds that occur only on migration.

remaining greyish waders have short bills and our bird has one that is certainly larger than its head and perhaps nearly twice as long. It is also straight rather than decurved and thus Knot, the stints, Dunlin, Sanderling and Curlew Sandpiper are eliminated. A check through the seasonal abundance chart shows that September is a top month for waders and does not help to narrow our choice. Likewise the maps show that most of these birds are widespread migrants. The text picks out the elegance of the Wood Sandpiper, a feature heightened by its long legs and speckled upperparts. Only the Greenshank seems similarly grey and elegant, but our bird does not have the very long bill of that species. So we end with possible identification of Wood Sandpiper.

Fortunately, not all identifications are so drawn out, but on each occasion the process is the same.

The illustrations
Each species is shown in its major plumages and in typical attitudes. These are intentionally somewhat diagramatical to show the salient points of each species. Similar birds are shown in similar poses to facilitate comparison.

The annotation
Labels pick out the main distinguishing features of each bird. Where a variety of plumages is shown a feature may be pointed out on one plumage only.

The Text
Written to compliment both the illustrations and annotations, the text describes each bird's appearance, how it moves, where it usually occurs and how it can be distinguished from similar species.

The Maps
These show the distribution of species using different colours to indicate breeding and wintering areas. Where these overlap, the two colours combine to produce a third. For the sake of simplicity we have not given information on passage, save only with a few species that neither breed nor winter with us.

The abundance charts
Seasonal abundance is shown month by month on a scale from 0–6. These numbers indicate not the number of birds, but the chances of actually seeing one – that is a combination of both number and visibility.

The order of birds
The birds in this book are arranged in systematic order. This arranges birds in their approximate order of evolution and to the beginner may seem confusing. Why not arrange the birds alphabetically, or by size, or by habitat, or by colour? The one great feature of the systematic order is that it groups similar birds together, thus making comparison so much easier. Use the coloured squares to help find the different groups.

Divers and grebes

Shearwaters, petrels, cormorants and gannets

Herons and spoonbills

Wildfowl

Birds of prey

Gamebirds, crakes and rails

Waders, skuas, gulls, terns and auks

Pigeons, cuckoos, owls, woodpeckers, nightjars and allies

Larks, swallows, wagtails, wrens, dippers, accentors and allies

Chats and thrushes

Warblers and flycatchers

Tits, nuthatches and treecreepers

Orioles, shrikes, crows and starlings

Sparrows, finches and buntings

DIVERS AND GREBES

Divers and grebes are perfectly adapted to an aquatic life-style. Indeed, they are seldom seen out of water and are extremely awkward on land. Sometimes they will haul themselves up on a lake shoreline, but many grebes spend their entire lives afloat and even construct a floating nest, while the divers seldom struggle more than a couple of metres to their waterside nest.

The feet are set well back on the body and are adapted to providing underwater propulsion. The toes of grebes are lobed, while those of divers are webbed like a duck's. They have long necks and long pointed bills ideally suited to catching fish. Their body feathers are dense, providing excellent insulation against the cold. Though both groups nest on inland waters, the divers become totally marine outside the breeding season. Although the Slavonian Grebe is generally found on tidal waters in winter, the other grebes mostly prefer freshwater.

These birds are expert divers that find their food – mainly fish – by pursuing it underwater. They can reach considerable depths and remain submerged up to a minute at a time, though most dives are shallow and brief. Several species are gregarious outside the breeding season, forming loose flocks at favoured feeding grounds. They take off after a laborious run over the water's surface, but fly quite strongly on long pointed wings.

Members of both families have distinctive summer and winter plumages, the latter being rather dull and uniform, creating some problems with their identification. Distinguishing the divers, in particular, needs great care in winter, but separating some of the grebes can be difficult, too.

Several of the grebes have developed elaborate breeding plumages and complex breeding rituals. Colourful plumes are a feature of some species and the Great Crested Grebe (*illustrated*), in particular, was brought to the verge of extinction by nineteenth-century plume hunters (the plumes were used mainly to adorn ladies' hats). Today all of these birds enjoy protection, but divers are often caught in fishing nets and, like so many other seabirds, are in constant danger from oil slicks.

Red-throated Diver *Gavia stellata*

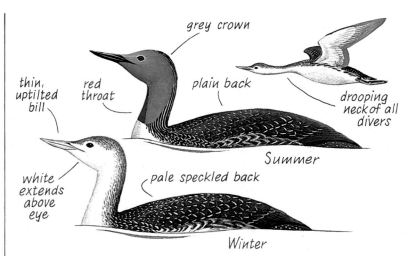

grey crown

thin, uptilted bill

red throat

plain back

drooping neck of all divers

white extends above eye

pale speckled back

Summer

Winter

Smallest of the divers and generally the most widespread and numerous throughout year. Breeds on small lakes, usually within flighting distance of sea. Winters in coastal waters, often in loose flocks. Thin, uptilted bill. Pale grey crown and rust-red throat in summer. In winter pale grey or brown back, spotted white. Like other divers, flies fast on long, pointed wings with head and neck drooping.
Status: scarce but widespread breeder in northern and western Scotland and north-western Ireland. Winters along all shores.
Similar Species: Black-throated Diver (p.48) and Great Northern Diver (p.49). All divers similar in winter, though Red-throated paler; smaller size distinguishes throughout year.

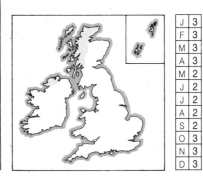

	RED-THROATED DIVER
Type	duck-like
Size	53–59cm (22in)
Habitat	freshwater, sea
Behaviour	swims, dives from surface, takes off and lands on water
Flocking	summer solitary; small flocks winter
Flight	strong and powerful; direct
Voice	harsh *kuk-kuk-kuk* in flight; wails and cackles in breeding season.

IDENTIFICATION

Ad.summer	
Crown	pale grey
Upperparts	brown
Rump	brown
Tail	brown; short and pointed
Throat	rust-red
Breast	white
Belly	white
Bill	black; short, thin, uptilted
Legs	black; short
Ad.winter	white head and throat; grey cap; pale grey back spotted white; grey bill
Juvenile	as Ad.winter, darker back

BREEDING

Nest	scrape at water's edge
Eggs	2; olive-buff, blotched black
Incubation	24–29 days, mainly ♀
Young	active; downy
Fledging	6 weeks
Broods	1; May–Sept
Food	fish, amphibians
Population	750+ pairs

J	3
F	3
M	3
A	3
M	2
J	2
J	2
A	2
S	2
O	3
N	3
D	3

Black-throated Diver *Gavia arctica*

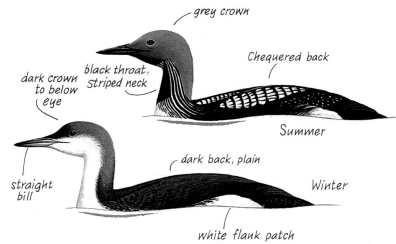

grey crown

Chequered back

dark crown to below eye

black throat, striped neck

Summer

straight bill

dark back, plain

Winter

white flank patch

Intermediate in size between Red-throated and Great Northern Divers. Breeds on larger lakes and winters offshore. In summer, largely black and white with two chequered ovals on back. Neck striped black and white with white foreneck. In winter, upperparts plain slate-brown in adult; slightly mottled in juvenile. White patch on rear flanks often obvious. Dark of crown extends below eye giving masked effect.
Status: scarce breeder in north and west Scotland. Winters along all shores, mostly in west.
Similar Species: Red-throated Diver (p.48) always paler and more slightly built. Great Northern Diver (p.49) has more massive head and bill and black, not grey, head in summer.

	BLACK-THROATED DIVER
Type	duck-like
Size	56–69cm (25in)
Habitat	freshwater, sea
Behaviour	swims, dives from surface, takes off and lands on water
Flocking	summer solitary; small flocks winter
Flight	strong and powerful; direct
Voice	grunts, croaks and loud wailing in breeding season

IDENTIFICATION

Ad.summer	
Crown	grey
Upperparts	black and white, with two chequered ovals
Rump	black
Tail	black; short and pointed
Throat	black
Breast	white
Belly	white
Bill	black; straight and pointed
Legs	black; short
Ad.winter	dark above, white below; white patch on rear flanks
Juvenile	as Ad.winter, speckly above

BREEDING

Nest	scrape at water's edge
Eggs	2; olive-brown, blotched black
Incubation	28–29 days ♂ ♀
Young	active; downy
Fledging	9 weeks
Broods	1; May–Sept
Food	fish, amphibians
Population	150–200 pairs

J	3
F	3
M	3
A	3
M	2
J	2
J	2
A	2
S	2
O	3
N	3
D	3

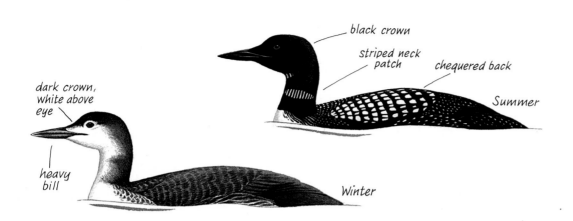

dark crown, white above eye

heavy bill

black crown

striped neck patch

chequered back

Summer

Winter

	GREAT NORTHERN DIVER
Type	duck-like, goose-like
Size	69–81cm (30in)
Habitat	freshwater, sea
Behaviour	swims, dives from surface, takes off and lands on water
Flocking	summer solitary; small flocks winter
Flight	strong and powerful; direct
Voice	summer – loud wails, cackling laugh; winter – occasional croaks, moans

IDENTIFICATION

Ad.summer	
Crown	black
Upperparts	black and white, two chequered ovals
Rump	black
Tail	black; short and pointed
Throat	black
Breast	white
Belly	white
Bill	black; straight and pointed
Legs	black; short
Ad.winter	brown above, white below
Juvenile	as Ad.winter, speckly back

BREEDING

Nest	scrape at water's edge
Eggs	2; olive-brown, blackish spots
Incubation	29–30 days ♂ ♀
Young	active; downy
Fledging	12 weeks
Broods	1; May–Sept
Food	fish, amphibians
Population	2000+ winter

This is the largest and generally least numerous of the three divers. The large, angular head and heavy bill distinguish it from the other common divers at all seasons. In summer, the head and neck are black, broken only by a narrow oval of white stripes on the neck. In flight, the wing beats are slower than those of the smaller divers.
Status: has bred and regularly summers in northern Scotland. It is a winter visitor to most coasts; more regular in north and west.

Similar Species:
White Billed Diver *Gavia adamsii* 75–90cm (29–35in)
Very similar to Great Northern, but with a larger, paler and distinctly shaped bill. Though much stouter, the bill is similar in shape to that of the smaller Red-throated with a straight upper mandible and a sharply angled gonys, giving an uptilted impression to the head. Its size and general coloration are otherwise similar to those of the Great Northern, with which it is most usually confused. In summer the plumage pattern is much the same as that of Great Northern, but with fewer white stripes on neck and fewer white 'squares' on back. The winter plumage is very similar to that of

Great Northern, but with a paler face and neck. Juveniles are more clearly barred on the upperparts than juvenile Great Northerns. A steeper forehead and more flattened crown are apparent in all plumages.
Range: breeds right round the North Pole, with a gap from Greenland to Scandinavia.
Migration: usually moves only as far as ice-free Arctic seas.
British Distribution: occasionally wanders in winter to shores of North Sea from Yorkshire to Shetland.
Other Similar Species: Black-throated Diver (p. 48).

White-billed Diver

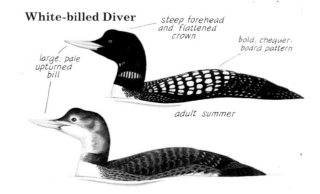

steep forehead and flattened crown

bold, chequer-board pattern

large, pale upturned bill

adult summer

J	F	M	A	M	J	J	A	S	O	N	D
3	3	3	2	1	1	1	1	1	2	3	3

Great Crested Grebe *Podiceps cristatus*

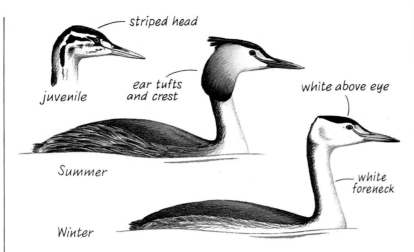

Largest grebe; widespread resident and winter visitor to lakes, reservoirs and coastlines. In summer, black cap and prominent russet and black head plumes (erected in display) preclude confusion. In winter, black cap extends *above* eye forming prominent white eyebrow; foreneck white. Juveniles heavily streaked on head. Dives expertly; flies laboriously after lengthy pattering over water's surface.
Status: widespread and quite numerous except in Scottish Highlands and Islands. In winter congregates at larger waters and sheltered coastlines. Some immigration from the Continent.
Similar Species: large size, long neck and sharply pointed bill separate from all grebes except winter Red-necked (p.50), which has no eyebrow and dusky, not white, foreneck.

J	5
F	5
M	5
A	5
M	5
J	5
J	5
A	5
S	5
O	5
N	5
D	5

GREAT CRESTED GREBE

Type	duck-like
Size	45–51cm (19in)
Habitat	freshwater, sea
Behaviour	swims, dives from surface, takes off and lands on water
Flocking	summer solitary; small flocks winter
Flight	laboured; direct
Voice	harsh barking *ra-ra* and variety croaking sounds

IDENTIFICATION

Ad.summer		
	Crown	black; crest
	Upperparts	brown
	Rump	brown
	Tail	brown; short and rounded
	Throat	white
	Breast	white
	Belly	white
	Bill	red; straight and sharply pointed
	Legs	green; short
Ad.winter		dark cap, white above eye, white neck
Juvenile		as Ad.winter, streaked head

BREEDING

Nest	floating mound in water
Eggs	4; white
Incubation	25–29 days ♂ ♀
Young	active; downy
Fledging	25–29 days
Broods	1 or 2; May–July
Food	fish
Population	6000–7000 pairs

Red-necked Grebe *Podiceps grisegena*

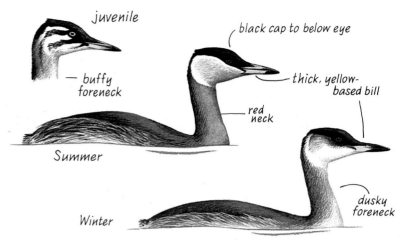

Mainly winter visitor and passage migrant to coastal waters. In summer, black cap extends to below eye; white cheeks and rust-red neck preclude confusion. In winter, overall pattern remains same but neck becomes dusky grey and cheeks less white. Yellow bill with dark tip. Often found in small groups in winter.
Status: scarce double passage migrant and winter visitor to east coast, extending westward along south coast to Dorset. Absent Ireland.
Similar Species: winter Great Crested Grebe (p.50). Red-necked slightly smaller with grey foreneck; shorter, thicker bill is yellow, not pink.

J	2
F	2
M	2
A	1
M	1
J	1
J	1
A	1
S	2
O	2
N	2
D	2

RED-NECKED GREBE

Type	duck-like
Size	40–46cm (17in)
Habitat	freshwater, sea
Behaviour	swims, dives from surface, takes off and lands on water
Flocking	1–10
Flight	laboured; direct
Voice	silent away from breeding grounds

IDENTIFICATION

Ad.summer		
	Crown	black
	Upperparts	brown
	Rump	brown
	Tail	brown; short and rounded
	Throat	rust-red
	Breast	rust-red
	Belly	white
	Bill	yellow, dark tip; straight and pointed
	Legs	black; short
Ad.winter		smudgy cap, grey foreneck
Juvenile		as Ad.winter; streaked head

BREEDING

Nest	floating mound in water
Eggs	4–5; white
Incubation	22–25 days ♂ ♀
Young	active; downy
Fledging	?
Broods	1; May–June
Food	small fish, crustaceans, molluscs, insects
Population	c100 winter

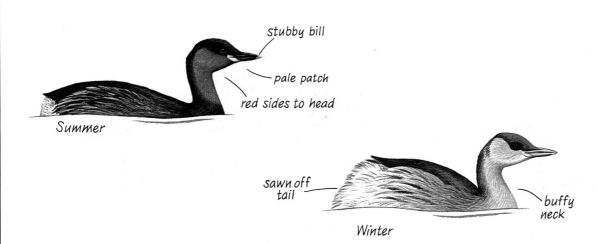

stubby bill

pale patch

red sides to head

Summer

sawn off tail

Winter

buffy neck

LITTLE GREBE

Type	duck-like
Size	25–29cm (10–11in)
Habitat	freshwater, estuaries
Behaviour	swims, dives from surface, takes off and lands on water
Flocking	colonial; small flocks winter
Flight	laborious; direct
Voice	brief *whit-whit*; loud, far-carrying whinnying song

IDENTIFICATION

Ad.summer	
Crown	black
Upperparts	black
Rump	brown
Tail	buff; short and rounded
Throat	rust-red
Breast	black
Belly	brown
Bill	black with yellow spot at base; short and stubby
Legs	green; short
Ad.winter and juvenile	brown above, buff below, dark cap

BREEDING

Nest	floating mound in water
Eggs	4–6; white
Incubation	19–25 days ♂ ♀
Young	active; downy
Fledging	44–48 days
Broods	2; Apr–July
Food	fish, insects, crustaceans, molluscs
Population	9000–18,000 pairs

The smallest, most widespread and numerous of the grebes. This bird is found on a variety of inland waters, mostly with plentiful submerged and emergent vegetation. In summer, it has rust-red cheeks, throat and neck and a bold yellow spot at the base of the bill. In winter the cap and upperparts are dark brown, with buffy throat, neck and flanks. In all plumages the 'sawn-off' tail is a good distinguishing feature, though the tails of other grebes, in particular the Black-necked and very rare Pied-billed, can look similar.
Status: a widespread breeding resident that is often quite numerous (with semi-colonial nesting) on favoured waters.

Similar Species:
Pied-billed Grebe *Podilymbus podiceps*
31–38cm (12–15in)
A chunky, heavily built grebe, shaped like a Little Grebe, but as large as a Slavonian. The bill is thick and conical and the head and neck are heavier and stronger than a Little Grebe's. The upperparts are grey, the flanks grey-buff, and the under tail coverts white, with a 'sawn-off' rear end like a Little Grebe. In summer, the ivory bill is marked by a vertical black band, an effect that is accentuated by the black forehead and chin. In winter, the bill is uniformly pale brown, and the face lacks dark markings. The juvenile has black and white streaks on its cheeks and the sides of its neck, and its foreneck is a dull orange.
Range: western United States, extending northwards into adjacent areas of Canada and south to the Mexican border.
Migration: whole population moves south to winter in Mexico and Central America.
British Distribution: a very rare vagrant, mostly to the south-west, since 1963.
Other Similar Species: Black-necked Grebe and Slavonian Grebe (p. 52).

Pied-billed Grebe

bill ring

uniform dark back

adult summer

adult winter

"sawn off" rear end

J	F	M	A	M	J	J	A	S	O	N	D
5	5	5	5	5	5	5	5	5	5	5	5

Slavonian Grebe *Podiceps auritus*

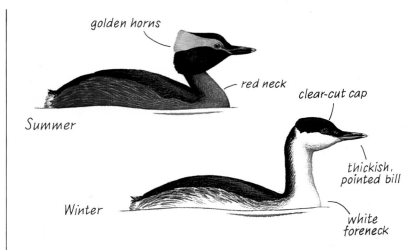

golden horns

red neck

clear-cut cap

Summer

thickish, pointed bill

Winter

white foreneck

Small grebe, only slightly larger than Little Grebe. In summer, black head marked by bold golden 'horns' extending through eye; neck and flanks rust-red. In winter, clear-cut black cap contrasts with white foreneck and flanks; back almost black. Generally gregarious at all seasons.
Status: rare breeder in northern Britain; scarce winter visitor, mainly to sheltered coasts and estuaries.
Similar Species: Black-necked (p.52) is separated by black, not red, neck in summer and grey foreneck and less clear-cut cap in winter. At all times, Slavonian has thicker, more symmetrical, bill.

SLAVONIAN GREBE	
Type	duck-like
Size	31–36cm (13in)
Habitat	freshwater, sea
Behaviour	swims, dives from surface, takes off and lands on water
Flocking	colonial; small flocks (up to 15) winter
Flight	laboured; direct
Voice	trills when breeding

IDENTIFICATION	
Ad.summer	
Crown	black, golden 'horns'
Upperparts	almost black
Rump	black
Tail	black; short and rounded
Throat	rust-red
Breast	rust-red
Belly	rust-red
Bill	black; short and pointed
Legs	black; short
Ad.winter	black cap, white throat
Juvenile	browner version of Ad.winter

BREEDING	
Nest	floating mound in water
Eggs	4–5; white
Incubation	22–25 days ♂ ♀
Young	active; downy
Fledging	?
Broods	1; May–July
Food	small fish, crustaceans, molluscs, insects
Population	50–60 pairs; 700 winter

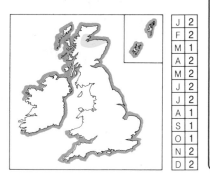

J	2
F	2
M	1
A	2
M	2
J	2
J	2
A	1
S	1
O	1
N	2
D	2

Black-necked Grebe *Podiceps nigricollis*

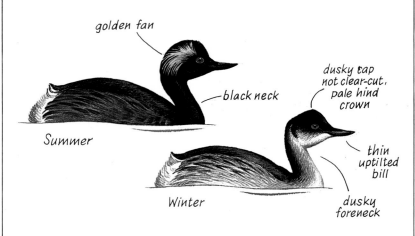

golden fan

black neck

dusky cap not clear-cut, pale hind crown

Summer

thin uptilted bill

Winter

dusky foreneck

Small grebe, similar in size to Slavonian but head rounder and bill thinner and uptilted. Decidedly less maritime than Slavonian in winter, frequenting large reservoirs and gravel pits, usually within easy reach of coast. Winter plumage is dark cap with pale area extending to hind crown; neck smudgy grey. In summer, head, neck and breast black broken only by golden fan of plumes extending from eye. Back black; flanks rust-red.
Status: breeds central Scotland, western Ireland and occasionally elsewhere. Winter visitor to southern Scottish and English waters.
Similar Species: Slavonian Grebe (p.52), especially in winter when Slavonian has more clear-cut cap, white (not grey) neck, and appears more black and white.

BLACK-NECKED GREBE	
Type	duck-like
Size	28–33cm (12in)
Habitat	freshwater
Behaviour	swims, dives from surface, takes off and lands on water
Flocking	colonial; small flocks winter
Flight	laboured; direct
Voice	quiet *poo-eep*; variety harsh notes

IDENTIFICATION	
Ad.summer	
Crown	black, golden 'fan'
Upperparts	black
Rump	black
Tail	black; short and rounded
Throat	black
Breast	black
Belly	rust-red
Bill	black; short and uptilted
Legs	black; short
Ad.winter	black above, greyish white below, smudgy cap, smudgy grey throat
Juvenile	as Ad.winter but browner

BREEDING	
Nest	floating mound in water
Eggs	3–4; white
Incubation	20–21 days ♂ ♀
Young	active; downy
Fledging	?
Broods	2; Apr–June
Food	insects, crustaceans, molluscs
Population	11–21 pairs; 120 winter

J	2
F	2
M	2
A	1
M	2
J	1
J	1
A	1
S	2
O	2
N	2
D	2

SHEARWATERS, PETRELS, CORMORANTS AND GANNETS

This is a rather mixed group of seabirds that, between them, occupy most of the marine habitats found around our shores. Some are widespread and familiar, others decidedly local and seldom seen from land. The shearwaters and petrels are among the most marine of all birds. Except when breeding, their lives are spent travelling the world's oceans and some make long migrations from one hemisphere to the other. They occur along our coasts only when storm-driven or when coming to land to breed.

The shearwaters are expert flyers, using the updraughts created by rolling waves to gain lift and gliding on stiffly held wings with the minimum output of energy. Storm-petrels (Storm Petrel, Leach's Petrel, Wilson's Petrel, Madeiran Petrel) have a more bat-like flight, though they are equally expert flyers.

Both groups have a peculiar tube-shaped nostril that helps them in finding their nests at night by smell. Apart from the Fulmar, which has increased dramatically and colonized most of the cliff-girt coasts of Britain and Ireland during the past hundred years, these birds remain little seen and little known by non-birders.

The cormorants, by contrast, are known to many people. Large, black seabirds with long necks and the distinctive habit of hanging out their wings to dry, they are a familiar sight along most of our shorelines. Though the non-expert may have difficulty in separating the Shag and Cormorant, the latter is much more likely to be seen inland and is larger, thicker necked and larger headed. They are gregarious birds that find their food by diving from the waters' surface usually close inshore, often at estuary mouths.

The Gannet (*illustrated*) is a huge black and white seabird and the only representative of a family of nine species that occupy all the oceans of the World.

Best called the North Atlantic Gannet, it finds its greatest stronghold around the coasts of Britain and Ireland and is increasing in numbers and spreading. Highly gregarious, North Atlantic Gannets pack together in dense breeding colonies, mostly on uninhabited islands, where the spectacle of thousands of these great birds provides one of the ultimate thrills of British birdwatching.

Fulmarus glacialis **Fulmar**

short, stubby bill

stiff wings

thick neck

Stocky, heavily-built seabird; glides and skims water with typical stiff-winged shearwater flight. Flaps wings more frequently than shearwaters. Head, neck and body white; wings, back and tail grey. Lacks any distinctive black and white pattern on wingtips. Short yellow bill; tube-nose visible at close quarters. Thick 'bull-neck' quite unlike any similar species; particularly noticeable in flight. Often gathers in large numbers round trawlers; decidedly gregarious at cliff breeding colonies.
Status: breeds along almost all coasts where suitable cliffs occur. In winter, widespread throughout Atlantic and North Sea.
Similar Species: easily confused with gulls, especially when perched on cliffs. Only grey, stiff-winged species at sea.

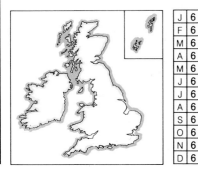

	FULMAR
Type	gull-like
Size	44–50cm (17–20in)
Habitat	sea and sea-cliffs
Behaviour	swims, perches on rocks, takes off and lands on water or cliffs
Flocking	colonial; sometimes huge flocks
Flight	strong and powerful; gliding
Voice	harsh crackle at breeding colonies
	IDENTIFICATION
Adult	
Crown	white
Upperparts	grey
Rump	grey
Tail	grey; short and square
Throat	white
Breast	white
Belly	white
Bill	yellow; short, tube-nosed
Legs	yellow; short
	BREEDING
Nest	bare ledge
Eggs	1; white
Incubation	55–57 days ♂ ♀
Young	helpless; downy
Fledging	46–51 days
Broods	1; May–Sept
Food	crustaceans, fish
Population	300,000 pairs

J	6
F	6
M	6
A	6
M	6
J	6
J	6
A	6
S	6
O	6
N	6
D	6

Puffinus griseus **Sooty Shearwater**

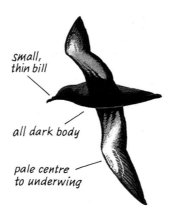

small, thin bill

wings set back on body

all dark body

pale centre to underwing

narrow stiff wings

Large, narrow-winged shearwater; scarce visitor from South Atlantic. Dark sooty coloration above and below; small head, thin bill; wings set well back on body. Pale underwing may be obvious at considerable range. Flies fast and direct on narrow swept-back wings, flapping frequently – more so than other shearwaters.
Status: regular, but scarce, visitor in summer and autumn to most coasts; more numerous in north and west and decidedly scarce on English coasts of Irish Sea.
Similar Species: with good views, coloration and purposeful flight preclude confusion with other shearwaters.

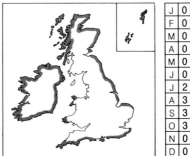

	SOOTY SHEARWATER
Type	gull-like
Size	39–44cm (15–17in)
Habitat	sea
Behaviour	swims, takes off and lands on water
Flocking	1–15
Flight	strong and powerful; gliding; direct
Voice	silent away from breeding grounds
	IDENTIFICATION
Adult	
Crown	black
Upperparts	black
Rump	black
Tail	black; short and rounded
Throat	black
Breast	black
Belly	black
Bill	black; short and thin
Legs	black; short
	BREEDING
Nest	crevice, burrow
Eggs	1; white
Incubation	?
Young	helpless; downy
Fledging	?
Broods	1
Food	squid, crustaceans, fish
Population	scarce migrant

J	0
F	0
M	0
A	0
M	0
J	0
J	2
A	3
S	3
O	3
N	0
D	0

Great Shearwater *Puffinus gravis*

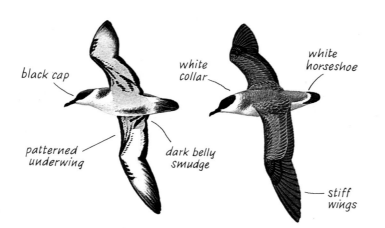

black cap

white collar

white horseshoe

patterned underwing

dark belly smudge

stiff wings

Large shearwater; flies with long, stiff-winged glides broken by short bouts of wing-flapping. Dark above and pale below. Dark cap, separated from mantle by narrow white collar, contrasts with white cheeks. Wings and rump brown with prominent white horseshoe at base of dark tail. Underparts white with dark ventral smudge. Dark tips to white axillaries (arm pits) and dark wing margins form distinctive underwing pattern.
Status: scarce annual visitor from South Atlantic late summer and autumn; mainly to south and west Ireland, Cornwall, and Durham and Yorkshire coasts. Occasionally gale-blown in large numbers.
Similar Species: similar to Cory's Shearwater (p.56), though flight more like Manx Shearwater (p.57).

	GREAT SHEARWATER
Type	gull-like
Size	42–49cm (16½–19in)
Habitat	sea
Behaviour	swims, takes off and lands on water
Flocking	1–15
Flight	strong and powerful; gliding
Voice	usually silent at sea; some raucous calls from feeding flocks
IDENTIFICATION	
Adult	
Crown	black
Upperparts	brown
Rump	white
Tail	black, white horseshoe at base; short and rounded
Throat	white
Breast	white
Belly	white, dark smudge
Bill	black; short and thin
Legs	pink; short
BREEDING	
Nest	crevice, burrow
Eggs	1; white
Incubation	?
Young	helpless; downy
Fledging	?
Broods	1
Food	fish, crustaceans, squid
Population	scarce migrant

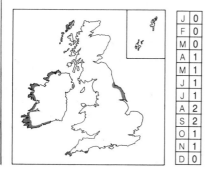

J	0
F	0
M	0
A	1
M	1
J	1
J	1
A	2
S	2
O	1
N	1
D	0

Cory's Shearwater *Calonectris diomedea*

grey crown

plain underwing

stiff wings

Large shearwater and uncommon visitor to Britain; seen mostly in autumn at sea. Typical long shearwater wings, held straight and stiff in flight, though slightly bowed when gliding. Flaps and soars more than Great Shearwater; flight more like Fulmar than Manx Shearwater. Dark above and pale below, with pale grey-brown head, brown wings and dark brown tail with narrow, pale rump.
Status: uncommon visitor in late summer and autumn, mainly to southern and western Ireland, Cornwall, and Durham and Yorkshire coasts. Breeds in Mediterranean.
Similar Species: Great Shearwater (p.56) has dark cap, prominent white rump and dusky ventral patch.

	CORY'S SHEARWATER
Type	gull-like
Size	43–48cm (17–19in)
Habitat	sea
Behaviour	swims, takes off and lands on water
Flocking	1–15
Flight	strong and powerful; gliding
Voice	silent away from breeding grounds
IDENTIFICATION	
Adult	
Crown	grey-brown
Upperparts	brown
Rump	brown
Tail	dark brown; short and rounded
Throat	white
Breast	white
Belly	white
Bill	yellow; short and thin
Legs	grey; short
BREEDING	
Nest	crevice, burrow
Eggs	1; white
Incubation	60 days? ♂ ♀
Young	helpless; downy
Fledging	?
Broods	1; May–Sept
Food	fish, crustaceans, squid
Population	scarce migrant

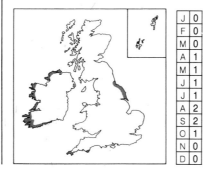

J	0
F	0
M	0
A	1
M	1
J	1
J	1
A	2
S	2
O	1
N	1
D	0

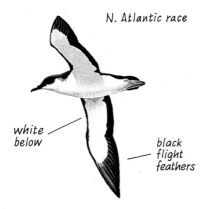

N. Atlantic race

white below

black flight feathers

black above

This is the most common and widespread of the British shearwaters and is usually seen in fast careering flight low over the sea, or resting on the water awaiting the cover of darkness to return to its breeding colonies. The British (or North Atlantic) sub-species *P. p. puffinus* is black above and white below, with broad black margins to the underwing. In typical shearwater flight it flashes alternately black and white as it turns low over the waves on straight, stiff wings. The Balearic sub-species *P. p. mauretanicus* is brown above and buff below.
Status: breeds on many islands in the north and west and elsewhere is a passage migrant. The Balearic sub-species is a scarce autumn visitor, mainly to south and west.

Similar Species:
Little Shearwater *Puffinus assimilis*
25–30cm (10–12in)
Like a small version of the Manx Shearwater. The size difference is often difficult to judge at sea, particularly in the absence of other birds. The black cap extends to the eye, not below it as in the Manx Shearwater, and the eye can often be seen as a black dot against a white

background. Shorter wings are suggestive of a Puffin, and the fluttering flight, like that of a Common Sandpiper, with fast wing beats and less gliding than Manx Shearwater, are the best way to pick it out.
Range: breeds on the Canary Islands, the Salvages, Desertas, Azores and Cape Verdes; on Tristan da Cunha and Gough Island; and around Australia.
Migration: spreads over oceans adjacent to breeding areas, generally reaching little further north than the coasts of Portugal.
British Distribution: a rare vagrant in spring and more frequently autumn to south-west Irish sea-watch stations.
Other Similar Species: Sooty Shearwater (p. 55), may be confused with Balearic.

Little Shearwater

tiny bill

eye shows as black spot

relatively rounded wings

	MANX SHEARWATER	
Type	gull-like	
Size	30–38cm (11½–15in)	
Habitat	sea and small islands	
Behaviour	swims, takes off and lands on water and ground	
Flocking	1–many thousands	
Flight	strong and powerful; gliding; undulating	
Voice	loud wails and screams at breeding colonies	

IDENTIFICATION

Ad.N.Atlan.		
Crown	black	
Upperparts	black	
Rump	black	
Tail	black; short and rounded	
Throat	white	
Breast	white	
Belly	white	
Bill	black; short and thin	
Legs	grey; short	
Ad.Medit.	brown above, buff below	

BREEDING

Nest	burrow, crevice
Eggs	1; white
Incubation	52–54 days ♂ ♀
Young	helpless; downy
Fledging	59–62 days
Broods	1; May–Sept
Food	fish, squid, crustaceans
Population	300,000 pairs+

J	F	M	A	M	J	J	A	S	O	N	D
0	1	2	2	3	4	3	3	2	2	1	1

Storm Petrel *Hydrobates pelagicus*

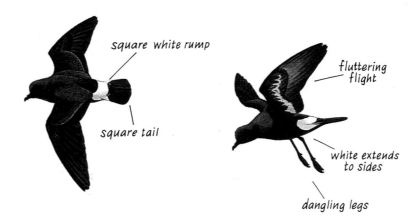

square white rump

square tail

fluttering flight

white extends to sides

dangling legs

This is a tiny, black, seabird marked by a prominent white rump. It is usually seen at sea in bat-like, fluttering flight with non-stop wing action, dipping to patter over the surface with wings raised and feet dangling to pick up food. The wings are straight, broad and rounded, and marked by a white underwing bar. The tail is square-cut with a broad white rump extending to the sides of the underparts. The feet do not project beyond the tail.
Status: a highly localized breeder on small islands off the coasts of Scotland, Wales and Ireland. Elsewhere it is seen only on passage or when blown off-course by gales.

Similar Species:
Wilson's Petrel *Oceanites oceanicus* 17–18cm (6½–7in)
Very like Storm Petrel, with a white rump and square tail, but marked by longer legs that extend beyond the tail tip in regular flight. When 'hopping over the water', the wings are held level or only slightly raised. Sometimes, the bird may 'stand' on the water, with wings rigid and webbed feet used as anchors. Other identifying features of Wilson's Petrel are its uniformly dark underwing (Storm Petrel has a variable

white line across its underwing coverts), rounder wings than Storm Petrel and a less bat-like flight with more gliding.
Range: breeds in huge colonies on small islands around the South Pole.
Migration: performs huge loop migrations into Indian and Atlantic Oceans, but extends less to the north in the Pacific. Reaches western North Atlantic by April to May and then eastern Atlantic coasts of Europe by August. May be relatively common off the coast of Iberia at this time.
British Distribution: an extremely rare vagrant to our south-western approaches, though seen regularly on ocean-going boat trips in the southern Irish Sea (in an area known as 'Wilson's Triangle').
Other Similar Species: Leach's Petrel (p. 59).

Wilson's Petrel

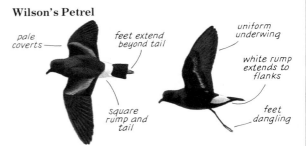

pale coverts

feet extend beyond tail

uniform underwing

white rump extends to flanks

square rump and tail

feet dangling

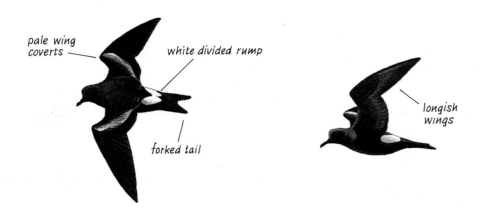

pale wing coverts

white divided rump

forked tail

longish wings

LEACH'S PETREL

Type	swallow-like
Size	19–22cm (7½–9in)
Habitat	sea and small offshore islets
Behaviour	swims, takes off and lands on water or ground
Flocking	1–20
Flight	hovers, glides; undulating
Voice	croons on nest; variety of screeches and repeated notes at colonies

IDENTIFICATION

Adult	
Crown	dark brown
Upperparts	dark brown
Rump	white, dark central stripe
Tail	dark brown; medium length and forked
Throat	dark brown
Breast	dark brown
Belly	dark brown
Bill	black; short and thin
Legs	black; medium length

BREEDING

Nest	burrow, crevice
Eggs	1; white
Incubation	41–42 days ♂ ♀
Young	helpless; downy
Fledging	63–70 days
Broods	1; May–June
Food	fish, plankton
Population	several thousand pairs

A black-brown bird whose long, pointed, angled wings have pale edges to the coverts, forming a pale inner wing bar. The tail is distinctly forked and the white rump bears a dark central stripe. The feet do not extend beyond the tail. The flight is shearwater-like, with short glides between bouts of leisurely wing-flapping. An experienced birder can tell this species from a Storm Petrel on the basis of flight alone. It is seldom seen following ships.
Status: confined as a breeding bird to a handful of remote islands off the coasts of Scotland and possibly also Ireland. Otherwise it is a scarce passage migrant and storm-driven waif.

Similar Species:
Madeiran Petrel *Oceanodroma castro*
18–20cm (7–8in)
Black-brown, like other storm-petrels (Storm Petrel, Leach's Petrel, Wilson's Petrel) and generally intermediate between closely related Leach's and Wilson's Petrels. It lacks the distinctly forked tail of Leach's and its shorter and broader wings give an impression of smaller size. Its rump is decidedly larger and whiter and its flight is even more shearwater-like, with long glides

on stiff wings. It is distinguished from the Storm Petrel by pale diagonal bars on upper wing (though less marked than on Leach's) and lack of white underwing bar. Though the tail is notched, this is often not apparent at sea.
Range: breeds in tropical areas of both the Atlantic and Pacific. In Atlantic found on Ascension, St Helena, Madeira, Cape Verde Islands and the Portuguese coast.
Migration: dispersal at sea, but with some indication of penetration along the eastern seaboard of the United States.
British Distribution: an exceptionally rare vagrant to the south and west.
Other Similar Species: Storm Petrel (p. 58).

Madeiran Petrel

forked tail

pale coverts

uniform underwing

square white rump

J	F	M	A	M	J	J	A	S	O	N	D
0	0	2	2	2	2	2	2	2	2	2	0

Cormorant *Phalacrocorax carbo*

adult summer

white face

pale belly first winter

thick bill

thick neck

adult winter

white face

white patch

Common, goose-like waterbird, occurring on coasts and less frequently on inland waters; often seen perched with wings outstretched. Adult glossy green-black with white face and round white flank patch in summer. Immature browner, with pale breast and belly. Swims low in water with uptilted head and heavy, yellow bill. Dives easily; often flies in 'V' formation like geese.
Status: found on all coasts, breeding mainly in north and west; also inland in lowland England and north and central Ireland.
Similar Species: Shag (p.60) is considerably smaller.

CORMORANT	
Type	goose-like
Size	84–89cm (33–38in)
Habitat	sea, estuaries, freshwater, islands, trees
Behaviour	swims, dives, perches on rocks and buoys, takes off and lands on water and ground
Flocking	colonial; small flocks
Flight	laboured; glides; direct
Voice	croaks and grunts on breeding grounds
IDENTIFICATION	
Adult	
Crown	black
Upperparts	black
Rump	black
Tail	black; medium length and rounded
Throat	white
Breast	black
Belly	black
Bill	yellow; straight and thick
Legs	black; short
Juvenile	brown above, buff below
BREEDING	
Nest	mound of seaweed on cliff or tree
Eggs	3–4; pale blue
Incubation	28–29 days ♂ ♀
Young	helpless; naked
Fledging	50–60 days
Broods	1; Apr–June
Food	fish
Population	8000 pairs

J	5
F	5
M	5
A	5
M	5
J	5
J	5
A	5
S	5
O	5
N	5
D	5

Shag *Phalacrocorax aristotelis*

crest

greenish-black

no white

buffy

first winter

thin bill

thin neck

dark face

adult summer

adult winter

Smaller version of Cormorant, though essentially marine along predominantly rocky coasts. Swims, dives and hangs out wings like Cormorant but seldom flies very high. Adult glossy green-black, with short tufted crest in summer. Bill black with yellow gape. Immatures brownish with black scaling to feathers; underparts buffy, chin paler.
Status: widespread in north and west, scarce where does not breed.
Similar Species: separated from Cormorant (p.60) at all times by smaller size, steeper forehead, smaller, thinner bill and thinner neck.

SHAG	
Type	goose-like
Size	72–80cm (28–31in)
Habitat	sea, sea-cliffs
Behaviour	swims, dives, perches on rocks and buoys, takes off and lands on water and ground
Flocking	colonial; 1–several thousand
Flight	laboured; glides; direct
Voice	grunts and hisses at breeding grounds
IDENTIFICATION	
Ad.summer	
Crown	green-black; crest
Upperparts	green-black
Rump	green-black
Tail	green-black; medium length and rounded
Throat	green-black
Breast	green-black
Belly	green-black
Bill	black with yellow gape; straight and thinnish
Legs	grey; short
Ad.winter	no crest, dark face
Juvenile	brown above, buff below
BREEDING	
Nest	mound of seaweed on cliff
Eggs	3; pale blue
Incubation	30 days ♂ ♀
Young	helpless; naked
Fledging	55 days
Broods	1; Mar–Apr
Food	fish
Population	52,000 pairs

J	3
F	3
M	3
A	4
M	4
J	4
J	4
A	4
S	3
O	3
N	3
D	3

dark, speckled

juvenile

first summer

white head and fore-wing

second summer

some black tips to wing feathers

third summer

white, black wingtips

thick neck and bill

adult

This is a large black and white seabird that nests at a few colonies, mainly on remote islets, often in enormous numbers. At sea it appears white and cigar-shaped with a pointed head and tail. The wings are long, straight and pointed with large black tips. It flies low over the water on stiff, shearwater-like wings, before rising with a series of flaps and starting another glide. It performs dramatic dives for fish, often from a great height. The adult has a yellow wash over the head. Immatures share the same basic shape, but are dark brown.
Status: often abundant around colonies and regularly seen passing offshore.

Similar Species:
Cape Gannet *Sula capensis*
85–100cm (33–39in)
Australasian Gannet *Sula serrator*
85–95cm (33–37in)
Until recently, any gannet seen off Britain could be safely assumed to be a North Atlantic Gannet *Sula bassana*; off South Africa, the Cape Gannet *S. capensis*; and off southern Australia and New Zealand, the Australasian Gannet *S. serrator*. The occurrence of a Cape Gannet in Spanish waters in 1980 has upset this arrangement.

Adults of the three species are distinguished by the presence and extent of black in the tail and on the secondary wing feathers. Adult North Atlantic Gannets have pure white tails, Cape Gannets have black tails and Australasian Gannets black central tail feathers. Beware, however, because North Atlantic Gannets in their fourth year also have black central tail feathers. They do, however, lack the completely black secondaries of the two other species.
Other Similar Species: all-dark juveniles separated from Cormorant (p. 60), by flight and behaviour.

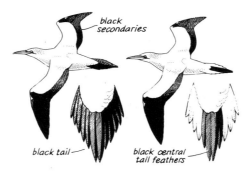

black secondaries

black tail

black central tail feathers

Cape Gannet　　**Australasian Gannet**

GANNET	
Type	goose-like
Size	86–96cm (34–37in)
Habitat	sea, sea-cliffs
Behaviour	swims, dives from air, takes off and lands on water and ground
Flocking	colonial; 1–several thousand
Flight	strong and powerful; glides, dives; direct
Voice	variety grunts and cackles at breeding colonies

IDENTIFICATION

Adult	
Crown	yellow
Upperparts	white, black wingtips
Rump	white
Tail	white; medium length and pointed
Throat	white
Breast	white
Belly	white
Bill	grey; straight and thickish
Legs	black; short
Juvenile	speckled dark brown, white rump
Second Year	dark brown, head and forewing becoming whiter

BREEDING

Nest	mound of seaweed
Eggs	1; white
Incubation	43–45 days ♂ ♀
Young	helpless; downy
Fledging	14 weeks
Broods	1; Apr–June
Food	fish
Population	150,000 pairs

J	F	M	A	M	J	J	A	S	O	N	D
4	4	6	6	6	6	6	6	6	6	4	4

HERONS AND SPOONBILLS

Easily identified, these large, long-legged wading birds are familiar to town and country dweller alike.

The Grey Heron (*illustrated*) is widespread and relatively numerous, but the three other regular British species are all rare and elusive, requiring either luck or a definite search to locate them.

The Grey Heron is most often seen waiting patiently beside a stream or lake for an unsuspecting fish to swim within range of its long, dagger-like bill. A master of stealth, it is an expert fisherman, able to extend its neck in an instant to grab its prey. Grey Herons are large birds that fly with slow beats of their arched wings and are frequently mobbed by smaller birds, especially Crows and Rooks.

Though generally solitary hunters, Grey Herons breed gregariously in heronries that may number up to a hundred pairs. These are situated in tree-top colonies, some of which have a history going back a hundred years or even more.

Because most heronries are used regularly year after year and as nests are large and easy to count, we know more about the population changes of this bird than any other. It is clear that the Grey Heron suffers great losses during hard winters, but that numbers quickly build up again to reach an upper limit, or population ceiling. During such winters Herons are often found along tidal waters and frequently along the shoreline itself.

Our only other breeding heron is the Bittern which is equally affected by bad weather when the reed beds it inhabits are frozen solid. At such times these secretive birds are forced to search for food along open ditches where their normally cryptic camouflage is completely ineffective. The Bittern population is, at present, slowly declining and, in any case, is limited by the number of suitable large reed beds available.

Two other members of this group, the Purple Heron and the Spoonbill, do not breed in Britain, but regularly pass through each spring. Sometimes a pair will stay late into summer, arousing expectation that they may nest. They are most frequent among the reed beds of East Anglia, a mere hundred miles from their nearest breeding grounds in Holland. Purple Herons, unlike Grey Herons, breed among reeds rather than in trees. They are thus easily overlooked. Spoonbills, on the other hand, feed in open waters, sifting food from the surface by sieving it out with their large spatulate bills. A sighting of either species is enough to make any birdwatcher's day.

Bittern _Botaurus stellaris_

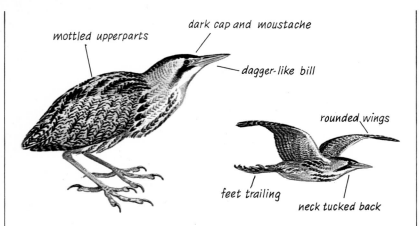

mottled upperparts

dark cap and moustache

dagger-like bill

rounded wings

feet trailing

neck tucked back

Large, secretive heron of dense reedbeds; more often heard than seen. Characteristic booming sounds more like distant foghorn than bird. Heavily camouflaged in shades of brown and buff; spends most of life hidden among reeds. Seen by chance during excursions across open areas, or in occasional flights with head tucked back and legs trailing behind. Close views reveal delicate plumage details as well as black crown and moustachial streak. Legs greenish yellow.
Status: decidedly scarce, breeding regularly only in East Anglia and Lancashire. Some winter wandering and immigration from the Continent.
Similar Species: rare Purple Heron (p.64) also appears brownish in flight.

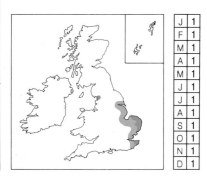

	BITTERN
Type	heron-like
Size	70–80cm (27–31in)
Habitat	freshwater marshes
Behaviour	wades, takes off and lands on ground
Flocking	solitary
Flight	laboured
Voice	deep, far-carrying _urrwoomp_, repeated

IDENTIFICATION

Adult	
Crown	black
Upperparts	brown and black, streaked
Rump	buff and brown, streaked
Tail	buff and brown, streaked; short and rounded
Throat	white
Breast	buff and brown, streaked
Belly	buff and brown, streaked
Bill	yellow; straight and thin
Legs	greenish yellow; medium length

BREEDING

Nest	platform of twigs, reeds on ground
Eggs	3–4; pale greenish blue
Incubation	21 days ♂ ♀
Young	helpless; downy
Fledging	6 weeks
Broods	1, sometimes 2; Apr–May
Food	fish, amphibians
Population	less than 35 pairs

J	1
F	1
M	1
A	1
M	1
J	1
J	1
A	1
S	1
O	1
N	
D	1

Purple Heron _Ardea purpurea_

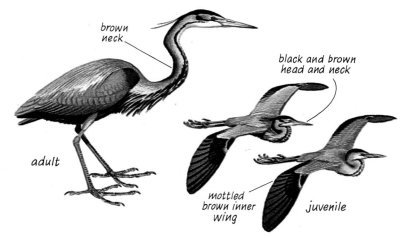

brown neck

black and brown head and neck

adult

mottled brown inner wing

juvenile

Slightly smaller than Grey Heron and considerably darker, both at rest and in flight. Head and neck warm brown with black crest and black streaking on neck. Back and wings grey with buffy tips to scapulars. Generally rather skulking.
Status: decidedly scarce, though annual, summer visitor to marshes and reedbeds; mostly southern and eastern England.
Similar Species: could be confused with Bittern (p.64) in flight, especially brown, mottled juvenile.

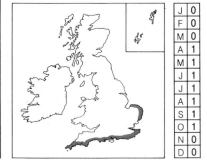

	PURPLE HERON
Type	heron-like
Size	75–85cm (29–33in)
Habitat	freshwater margins and marshes
Behaviour	wades, walks, takes off and lands on ground
Flocking	solitary
Flight	laboured; glides; direct
Voice	similar to Grey Heron but higher pitched

IDENTIFICATION

Adult	
Crown	black; crest
Upperparts	grey and buff
Rump	grey
Tail	grey; short and square
Throat	brown and black, streaked
Breast	brown and black, streaked
Belly	black
Bill	yellow; straight and thin
Legs	yellow; very long
Juvenile	brown above, buff below, mottled, lacks crest

BREEDING

Nest	platform of reeds in reedbed
Eggs	4–5; greenish blue
Incubation	24–28 days ♂ ♀
Young	helpless; downy
Fledging	42 days
Broods	1; Apr–May
Food	fish, insects, amphibians
Population	rare migrant

J	0
F	0
M	0
A	1
M	1
J	1
J	1
A	1
S	1
O	1
N	0
D	0

Ardea cinerea **Grey Heron**

Platalea leucorodia **Spoonbill**

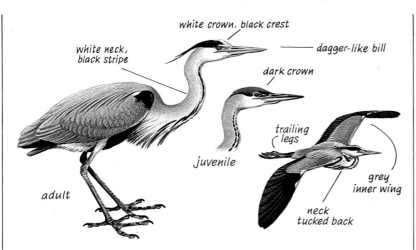

white neck, black stripe

white crown, black crest

dagger-like bill

dark crown

juvenile

trailing legs

grey inner wing

neck tucked back

adult

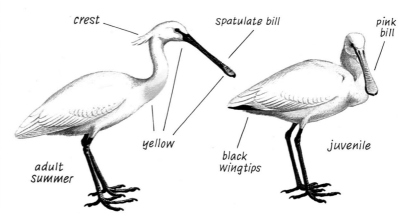

crest

spatulate bill

pink bill

yellow

black wingtips

juvenile

adult summer

Large, grey and white heron with long neck and dagger-like yellow bill. Flies with orange-yellow legs trailing behind and neck tucked into shoulders. Grey back; wings deeply bowed in flight. White head, neck and underparts; black crest and black streaking on neck. Frequents all wetlands. Nests colonially in heronries among tall trees; many have been used for more than a century.
Status: widespread resident throughout Britain and Ireland; population reduced by hard winters.
Similar Species: rare Purple Heron (p.64) could possibly be confused.

GREY HERON	
Type	heron-like
Size	90–100cm (35–39in)
Habitat	freshwater margins and marshes
Behaviour	wades, walks, takes off and lands on ground
Flocking	1–50
Flight	laboured; glides; direct
Voice	harsh *snark*
IDENTIFICATION	
Adult	
Crown	black; crest
Upperparts	grey
Rump	grey
Tail	grey; short and square
Throat	white
Breast	white, streaked black
Belly	white, streaked black
Bill	yellow; straight and thin
Legs	orange-yellow; very long
Juvenile	greyer, lacks crest
BREEDING	
Nest	platform of twigs high in trees
Eggs	3–5; pale greenish blue
Incubation	23–28 days ♂ ♀
Young	helpless; downy
Fledging	50–55 days
Broods	1; Feb–Apr
Food	fish, amphibians
Population	6500–11,500 pairs

Large, white, heron-like bird with large spatulate bill. Plumage all white with droopy crest and yellow wash at base of neck in breeding plumage; crest and neck wash lost in winter. Bill black with yellow tip; bare yellow patch on throat; long legs black. Flies with neck extended rather than tucked back like heron. Feeds with side-to-side scything action of bill in shallow water. Juveniles show black wingtips.
Status: scarce visitor, mostly spring and autumn, to south and east coasts. Breeds Holland.
Similar Species: rare Little and Great White Egrets are only other all-white, heron-like birds. Spoonbill can be picked-out at considerable distance by slightly creamy white (not pure white) plumage.

SPOONBILL	
Type	heron-like
Size	78–80cm (27–31in)
Habitat	freshwater marshes, estuaries
Behaviour	wades, walks, takes off and lands on water or ground
Flocking	1 or 2
Flight	glides, soars; strong, powerful and direct
Voice	silent
IDENTIFICATION	
Ad.summer	
Crown	white; crest
Upperparts	white
Rump	white
Tail	white; short and square
Throat	yellow
Breast	yellow
Belly	white
Bill	black, tipped yellow; large and spatulate
Legs	black; very long
Ad.winter	no crest or neck wash
Juvenile	as winter but black wingtips and pink bill
BREEDING	
Nest	platform of reeds and twigs in tree or bush
Eggs	4; spotted reddish
Incubation	21 days ♂ ♀
Young	helpless; downy
Fledging	7 weeks
Broods	1; Apr–May
Food	insects, crustaceans, molluscs, fish
Population	scarce passage migrant

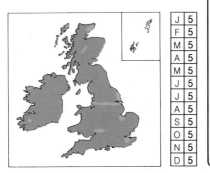

J	5
F	5
M	5
A	5
M	5
J	5
J	5
A	5
S	5
O	5
N	5
D	5

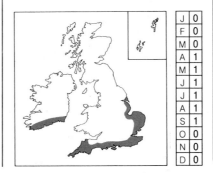

J	0
F	0
M	0
A	1
M	1
J	1
J	1
A	1
S	1
O	0
N	0
D	0

WILDFOWL

This large family is well represented in Britain and Ireland, with no less than 32 species occurring regularly. They can be neatly divided into three main tribes: swans, geese and ducks. Though numbers of all three breed in Britain and Ireland, our shores and generally mild winters offer a major wintering ground for birds that breed to the north and east of our islands. As a result, hundreds of thousands of wildfowl spend the months from November to March among our marshes, lakes and estuaries.

Wildfowl are excellent swimmers, with dense body plumage that they keep well oiled to provide insulation and buoyancy. The feet, which are webbed, are set well back on the body to provide propulsion while swimming, but are poorly suited to walking. They thus have a waddling gait that is somewhat comical on land. The neck is generally long and the bill usually spoon-shaped, or spatulate, for sieving food from the water. Wildfowl vary in size from the Teal, about 35cm long, to the Mute Swan, 160cm in length.

In winter Mute Swans are joined by two 'wild' swans from the north and east: Bewick's and Whooper. Sometimes all three may congregate together, but while Bewick's has a southerly distribution, the Whooper is more common in the north of Britain.

The geese that are mainly winter visitors may be divided into two groups: 'grey geese' and 'black geese'. Both groups are highly gregarious, often forming large flocks, particularly at their roosts.

Many ducks can be seen at their favoured roosts in daylight, sometimes packed together in their thousands. They can be easily divided on the basis of their method of feeding into surface-feeders and diving ducks. Shelduck (*illustrated*), Mallard and Pintail are typical examples of the former, Pochard and Tufted Duck of the latter.

There is a further sub-division of diving ducks into freshwater ducks (like Pochard and Tufted Duck) and seaducks. The latter include Eider, Long-tailed Duck and scoters. Many of these marine ducks remain well out of sight of land, but in some areas they feed close inshore.

Mute Swan *Cygnus olor*

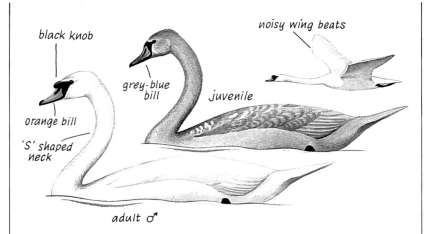

black knob
grey-blue bill
noisy wing beats
orange bill
'S' shaped neck
juvenile
adult ♂

Huge, familiar, white waterbird found on all types of freshwater; also occurs on estuaries and occasionally the sea. Adult completely white; legs black; bill orange with large black knob at base. Juvenile grey-buff with grey bill. Swims easily and walks with rolling gait. At all times holds neck in gentle 'S' shape. Flies with noisy wing beats after laborious pattering take-off over water.
Status: widespread and numerous resident throughout lowland Britain; gathers in substantial flocks outside breeding season. Sometimes nests in colonies.
Similar Species: Bewick's Swan (p.69) and Whooper Swan (p.68) are winter visitors that often join Mute Swan flocks. Both have black and yellow bills and noisy calls in flight.

	J	5
	F	5
	M	5
	A	5
	M	5
	J	5
	J	5
	A	5
	S	5
	O	5
	N	5
	D	5

MUTE SWAN

Type	goose-like
Size	145–160cm (57–63in)
Habitat	freshwater, estuaries, fields
Behaviour	swims, up-ends, walks, takes off and lands on water
Flocking	1–30, exceptionally several hundred
Flight	laboured; direct
Voice	various hisses and grunts of aggression during breeding season; silent in flight

IDENTIFICATION

Adult	
Crown	white
Upperparts	white
Rump	white
Tail	white; short and square
Throat	white
Breast	white
Belly	white
Bill	orange with black knob at base; duck-like
Legs	black; short
Juvenile	grey-buff with grey-blue bill

BREEDING

Nest	huge mound of vegetation, freshwater margins
Eggs	5–7; white, blue-grey wash
Incubation	34–38 days, mainly ♀
Young	active; downy
Fledging	4 months
Broods	1; Apr–May
Food	aquatic vegetation
Population	5000–6000 pairs

Whooper Swan *Cygnus cygnus*

straight profile
straight profile
pointed yellow area
straight neck
juvenile
adult

Winter visitor forming medium-sized flocks, often in association with other swans. Neck usually held straight. Yellow base to black bill, which extends forward to form clear point, accentuating flat crown-bill profile. Generally noisy, especially in flight, when wing beats produce whistling noise.
Status: regular winter visitor mainly from Iceland; largest numbers in Scotland and Ireland.
Similar Species: Mute Swan (p.68) is same size but has orange bill and holds neck in 'S'. Smaller Bewick's Swan (p.69) has concave (not flat) crown-bill profile.

	J	2
	F	2
	M	2
	A	1
	M	1
	J	1
	J	1
	A	1
	S	2
	O	2
	N	2
	D	2

WHOOPER SWAN

Type	goose-like
Size	145–160cm (57–63in)
Habitat	freshwater, estuaries, fields
Behaviour	swims, up-ends, walks, takes off and lands on water or ground
Flocking	1–100
Flight	laboured; direct
Voice	loud, trumpeting *whoop*

IDENTIFICATION

Adult	
Crown	white
Upperparts	white
Rump	white
Tail	white; short and square
Throat	white
Breast	white
Belly	white
Bill	black with yellow base; duck-like
Legs	black; short
Juvenile	brownish grey, pinkish bill

BREEDING

Nest	mound of vegetation at water's edge, usually island
Eggs	5–6; creamy white
Incubation	35–42 days ♀
Young	active; downy
Fledging	?
Broods	1; May–June
Food	grass, grain, roots
Population	1 or 2 feral pairs; 7000–9000 winter

concave profile

concave profile

noisy calls in flight

truncated yellow area

pinkish bill

juvenile

adult

BEWICK'S SWAN

Type	goose-like
Size	116–128cm (45–50in)
Habitat	freshwater, estuaries, fields
Behaviour	swims, up-ends, walks, takes off and lands on water or ground
Flocking	gregarious, 1–several hundred
Flight	laboured; direct
Voice	goose-like honking flight call

IDENTIFICATION

Adult	
Crown	white
Upperparts	white
Rump	white
Tail	white; short and square
Throat	white
Breast	white
Belly	white
Bill	black with yellow base; duck-like
Legs	black; short
Juvenile	brownish-grey, pinkish bill

BREEDING

Nest	huge mound of vegetation
Eggs	4; creamy white
Incubation	29–30 days
Young	active; downy
Fledging	40–45 days
Broods	1; June–July
Food	grass, grain, roots
Population	4000 winter

This is the smallest of the three British swans, though its size is most apparent in flight when its faster wing beats and noisy calls resemble those of a goose. The black bill has a truncated yellow area at the base, though this is difficult to see at a distance. A more useful field mark is the rounded crown, with a concave forehead and bill profile, and the shorter, often curved neck.
Status: a localized winter visitor from Siberia to traditional feeding grounds, such as the Ouse Washes (*see page* 307) and Slimbridge (*see page* 320).

Similar Species:
Trumpeter Swan *Cygnus buccinator*
122–140cm (48–55in)
Whistling Swan *Cygnus columbianus columbianus* 115–130cm (45–51in)
The two wild swans that are winter visitors to Britain have their New World equivalents in the Whistling and Trumpeter Swans of Canada and the United States. But while the large and highly endangered Trumpeter Swan is now regarded as a separate species from the similarly-sized Whooper Swan, the Whistling Swan is considered to be merely a sub-species of *C. columbianus*, like Bewick's *C. c. bewickii*.

The Whistling Swan makes a long south-easterly migration from the western shores of Hudson Bay to winter on the eastern seaboard from Virgina southwards and the odd individual may wander as far as Britain. The Trumpeter Swan breeds in Alaska, Alberta, Saskatchewan and parts of north-western USA. Northern populations migrate south to winter in south-eastern Alaska, British Columbia and areas within the US breeding range. Even though the Trumpeter Swan is unlikely to turn up in Britain, the heads of both birds are illustrated for the sake of completeness.
Other Similar Species: Whooper Swan (p. 68).

J	F	M	A	M	J	J	A	S	O	N	D
2	2	2	2	0	0	0	0	0	1	2	2

concave black bill

adult

Whistling Swan

adult

Trumpeter Swan

Bean Goose *Anser fabalis*

- dark head and neck
- orange bill
- uniform brown wing
- large head and bill
- orange legs

Large, 'grey' goose with dark neck and dark head. Favours damp grassland habitat. Upperparts brown, closely barred buff. Underparts buffy, narrowly barred brown on flanks. Orange legs; bill orange with variable black base. Gregarious.
Status: scarce winter visitor with only two small regular flocks in Solway and East Anglia. Elsewhere rare winter visitor after hard weather.
Similar Species: closely-related Pink-footed Goose (p.70) is smaller and prefers estuaries to damp grassland. Pink-footed and Greylag Goose both show obvious pale forewing in flight, commonly lacking in Bean Goose.

BEAN GOOSE

Type	goose-like
Size	71–89cm (28–35in)
Habitat	freshwater marshes, grassland
Behaviour	swims, walks, takes off and lands on water and ground
Flocking	1–100
Flight	strong and powerful; direct
Voice	low *ung-unk*, generally less vocal than other geese

IDENTIFICATION

Adult	
Crown	brown
Upperparts	brown, barred buff
Rump	white
Tail	white with grey terminal band; short and square
Throat	brown
Breast	buff
Belly	buff, barred brown
Bill	orange, black base; duck-like
Legs	orange; medium length

BREEDING

Nest	lined scrape near water
Eggs	4–6; white
Incubation	27–29 days ♀
Young	active; downy
Fledging	8 weeks
Broods	1; June–July
Food	grass, grain
Population	less than 150 winter

J	1
F	1
M	1
A	1
M	0
J	0
J	0
A	0
S	0
O	1
N	1
D	1

Pink-footed Goose *Anser brachyrhynchus*

- dark head and neck
- pink bill
- grey forewing
- small head and bill
- pink legs

Small 'grey' goose; highly localized winter visitor to Scotland and northern Britain. Small dark head and small pink bill with variable dark base; legs pink. Upperparts greyish brown, closely barred buffy white. Shows bold grey forewing in flight.
Status: numerous winter visitor from Iceland and Greenland forming enormous roosting flocks at traditional sites, mainly Scotland and Lancashire. Elsewhere rather scarce visitor after hard weather.
Similar Species: dark head and neck separate from all other 'grey' geese except Bean Goose (p.70), which lacks grey forewing and has larger head and thicker neck.

PINK-FOOTED GOOSE

Type	goose-like
Size	61–76cm (24–30in)
Habitat	freshwater, estuaries, grassland
Behaviour	swims, walks, takes off and lands on water and ground
Flocking	1–many thousands
Flight	strong and powerful; direct
Voice	highly vocal; high-pitched *unk-unk* and *wink-wink-wink*

IDENTIFICATION

Adult	
Crown	brown
Upperparts	grey-brown, barred buff
Rump	white
Tail	white with dark terminal band; short and square
Throat	brown
Breast	buff
Belly	buff, barred brown
Bill	pink, dark based; small and duck-like
Legs	pink; medium length

BREEDING

Nest	lined scrape, cliff-ledge
Eggs	4–5; white
Incubation	25–28 days ♀
Young	active; downy
Fledging	8 weeks
Broods	1; June–July
Food	grass, grain, potatoes
Population	81,000–104,000 winter

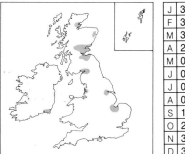

J	3
F	3
M	3
A	2
M	0
J	0
J	0
A	0
S	1
O	2
N	3
D	3

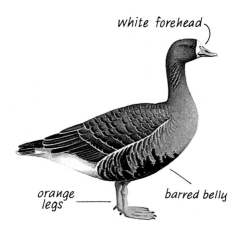

white forehead

orange legs

barred belly

uniform brown wing

barred belly

	WHITE-FRONTED GOOSE
Type	goose-like
Size	65–76cm (26–30in)
Habitat	freshwater marshes, grassland
Behaviour	swims, walks, takes off and lands on water and ground
Flocking	1–6000
Flight	strong and powerful; direct
Voice	high-pitched *kow-yow* and *ryo-ryok*; more musical than other geese

IDENTIFICATION

Ad.Russian	
Crown	brown
Upperparts	brown; barred
Rump	white
Tail	white with grey terminal band; short and square
Throat	brown
Breast	buff
Belly	brown, barred black
Bill	pink; duck-like
Legs	orange; medium length
Ad.Greenland	bill orange

BREEDING

Nest	lined scrape in bog or thicket
Eggs	5–6; white
Incubation	27–28 days ♀
Young	active; downy
Fledging	?
Broods	1; June–July
Food	grass, cereals, potatoes
Population	9000 Russian; 12,000 Greenland winter

This is the most widespread, though not the most numerous, of the 'grey' geese, found in a variety of habitats throughout Britain and Ireland. Its small size, broad white base to the bill and the bold, smudgy bars on the belly separate it from other similar regular geese. The bill is pink or orange (*see below*) and the legs orange. In flight, the lack of a grey forewing distinguishes it from the other 'grey' geese except the Bean Goose. *Status:* a widespread winter visitor. The pink-billed sub-species *A. a. albifrons* from Russia visits England and Wales, while the orange-billed sub-species *A. a. flavirostris* from Greenland occurs in Ireland, west Scotland and west Wales.

Similar Species:
Lesser White-fronted Goose
Anser erythropus 53–66cm (21–26in)
This is a smaller relation of the White-fronted Goose, though there is an overlap and size alone is no clear criterion of identification. A smaller, rounded head and shorter neck are useful identifying marks in all plumages. The adult has the white on the forehead extending over the crown to above the eye; fewer black bars on the belly; and a yellow eye-ring that is surprisingly obvious,

even at long range. Juveniles lack all of these features, though a faint eye-ring may be discernible at close range. The upper wing is, like the White-fronted's, uniform in flight, but when folded the wings extend well beyond the tail tip.
Range: from Arctic Scandinavia across Northern Siberia.
Migration: moves southward from Scandinavia to winter in the Balkans.
British Distribution: a more or less annual vagrant to Slimbridge in Gloucestershire (*see page* 320) in association with Whitefronts, or to the Yare Valley in Norfolk (*see page* 324) with Bean Geese.
Other Similar Species: Bean and Pink-footed Goose (p. 70); Greylag Goose (p. 72).

Lesser White-fronted Goose

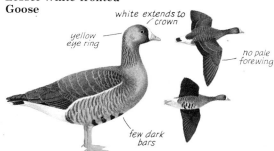

yellow eye ring

white extends to crown

few dark bars

no pale forewing

J	F	M	A	M	J	J	A	S	O	N	D
3	3	3	2	0	0	0	0	0	1	2	3

Greylag Goose *Anser anser*

large head and bill

orange bill

grey forewing

pink legs

Canada Goose *Branta canadensis*

large bill

white chin patch

brown back

black neck

brown wing

Largest and most frequently seen 'grey' goose; ancestor of most domestic geese. Upperparts dark brown, closely barred buff. Underparts, head and neck buff; some faint barring on flanks. Pink legs; orange bill (pink in eastern sub-species). In flight shows prominent pale grey forewing.
Status: native birds breed only in Outer Hebrides and nearby Scottish mainland, but many successful re-introductions in various parts of the country. Widespread visitor, mainly from Iceland.
Similar Species: overall size, large pale head and neck with large bill separate from all other 'grey' geese.

GREYLAG GOOSE	
Type	goose-like
Size	76–89cm (30–35in)
Habitat	freshwater, estuaries, grassland
Behaviour	swims, walks, takes off and lands on water or ground
Flocking	1–several hundred
Flight	strong and powerful; direct
Voice	deep *aahng-ung-ung*; highly vocal

IDENTIFICATION

Adult	
Crown	brown
Upperparts	brown, barred buff
Rump	white
Tail	white with grey terminal band; short and square
Throat	brown
Breast	buff
Belly	buff
Bill	orange; large and duck-like
Legs	pink; medium length

BREEDING

Nest	scrape near water
Eggs	4–6; white
Incubation	27–28 days ♀
Young	active; downy
Fledging	8 weeks
Broods	1; Apr–May
Food	grass, grain, roots
Population	700–800 pairs; 66,000 winter

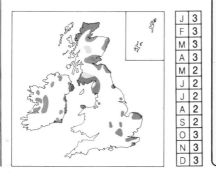

J	3
F	3
M	3
A	3
M	2
J	2
J	2
A	2
S	2
O	3
N	3
D	3

Largest of the 'black' geese; about same size as bulkier Greylag. Familiar inhabitant of ponds, lakes, reservoirs and other freshwater habitats; generally tame and often aggressive. Buffy brown above and buff below; long black head and neck broken only by white chin patch. Forms large flocks at end of breeding season (for moulting), otherwise in pairs and family parties.
Status: prospering after introduction from native North America, where is long distance migrant. Fresh birds continually flying free from wildfowl collections. Widespread in Britain but highly local in Ireland. Most birds resident, but some long distance migrations (for moulting) developing.
Similar Species: Barnacle Goose (p.73) has white face, grey (not brown) back and is much smaller.

CANADA GOOSE	
Type	goose-like
Size	90–100cm (36–40in)
Habitat	freshwater, marshes and margins, grassland
Behaviour	swims, walks, takes off and lands on water or ground
Flocking	1–1000
Flight	strong and powerful; direct
Voice	loud *wagh-onk* repeated

IDENTIFICATION

Adult	
Crown	black
Upperparts	brown, barred buff
Rump	white
Tail	white with black terminal band; short and square
Throat	black and white
Breast	buff
Belly	brown
Bill	black; large and duck-like
Legs	black; medium length

BREEDING

Nest	lined hollow beside water, often on island
Eggs	5–6; white
Incubation	28–30 days ♀
Young	active; downy
Fledging	9 weeks
Broods	1; Apr–May
Food	grass, aquatic vegetation, cereals, grain
Population	10,000 individuals

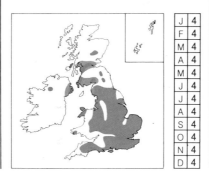

J	4
F	4
M	4
A	4
M	4
J	4
J	4
A	4
S	4
O	4
N	4
D	4

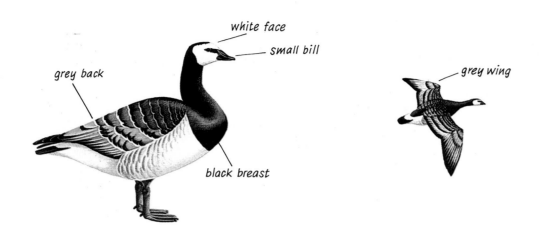

grey back

white face

small bill

grey wing

black breast

This is a strikingly attractive 'black' goose that is a highly localized winter visitor, forming large flocks in favoured areas. The back is grey, heavily barred with black and white. The neck and breast are black, while the face is white with a black crown. The underparts are white, with some pale barring on the flanks. In flight the wings appear grey with a black trailing edge. The small bill, as well as the feet, are black.
Status: largest numbers appear in western Scotland and western Ireland, but it has prospered with careful protection and now occurs irregularly in small numbers at other, mainly coastal, sites. There are, however, many escapes from wildfowl collections.

Similar Species:
Red-breasted Goose *Branta ruficollis* 51–58cm (20–23in)
This small 'black' goose has a striking harlequin face pattern and a bold white slash along the flank. Though colourful and easily identified in books and at close range, it may be more difficult to pick out from a flock of Barnacles or Brents at a distance. The adult has a tiny bill, large head and thick neck marked by a rust-red cheek spot,

neck and breast. A Redbreasted Goose is black above and below with a very prominent white flank. The combination of black and white on the body is the best means of picking it out at any distance. Juveniles have white, not rust-red, cheeks.
Range: breeds in the West Siberia tundra.
Migration: moves south-westward to winter around the Caspian and Black Seas.
British Distribution: a very rare winter visitor, most often to southern England, especially at Slimbridge (*see page* 320).
Other Similar Species: Canada Goose (p. 72); Brent Goose (p. 74).

Red-breasted Goose

bold white flank slash

black upper wings

very dark below

	BARNACLE GOOSE
Type	goose-like
Size	58–69cm (23–27in)
Habitat	grassland, estuaries
Behaviour	swims, walks, takes off and lands on water and ground
Flocking	1–several thousand
Flight	strong and powerful; direct
Voice	barking, puppy-like yaps with deeper growls

IDENTIFICATION

Adult	
Crown	black
Upperparts	grey, barred black and white
Rump	white
Tail	white with black terminal band; short and square
Throat	black and white
Breast	black
Belly	white
Bill	black; small and duck-like
Legs	black; medium length

BREEDING

Nest	lined depression, ledges of cliffs
Eggs	3–5; white
Incubation	24–25 days ♀
Young	active; downy
Fledging	7 weeks
Broods	1; June–July
Food	grass
Population	30,000 winter

J	F	M	A	M	J	J	A	S	O	N	D
3	3	3	2	1	0	0	0	1	3	3	3

Brent Goose *Branta bernicla*

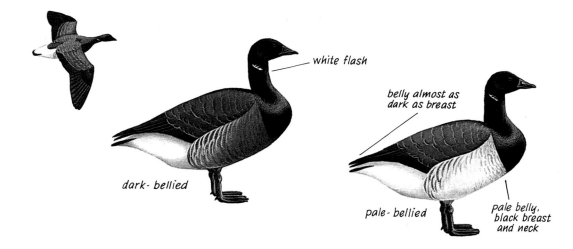

white flash

dark- bellied

belly almost as dark as breast

pale- bellied

pale belly, black breast and neck

This is the smallest and darkest of the 'black' geese and is predominantly an estuarine species that is regularly found feeding among coastal fields. Two distinct sub-species occur in Britain. The Pale-bellied sub-species *B. b. hrota* is dark brown above and buffy below, and the black of the head and neck ends abruptly to form a clear-cut breast band. Adults have a small white neck flash. The Dark-bellied race *B. b. bernicla* is similar, but lacks the contrast between the breast and belly. Juveniles of both sub-species have white bars across the folded wing and lack a neck flash.
Status: it has flourished with protection and is now an increasing and spreading winter visitor along most coastlines. The largest flocks tend to favour particular estuaries. The Dark-bellied Brent is found mostly in southern and eastern England, while the Pale-bellied Brent occurs in Ireland and north-east England.

Similar Species:
Black Brant *Branta bernicla nigricans* 56–61cm (22–24in)
Though not regarded as a separate species, the Black Brant is a sufficiently distinct sub-species to be recognized in the field. It is separated from our two regular sub-species of the Brent Goose by being considerably darker than either on the belly with a much bolder white neck flash. Unlike that of the Dark-bellied Brent, its dark belly contrasts with pale flanks.
Range: the Black Brant replaces the Brent in the Canadian Arctic westward to Alaska.
Migration: moves southward to winter along the Pacific coast of Canada and the United States south to California and Baja California (northern Mexico).
British Distribution: recognized more or less annually among Light-bellied Brent.
Other Similar Species: Barnacle Goose (p. 73); Canada Goose (p. 72).

Black Brant

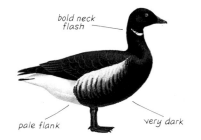

bold neck flash

pale flank

very dark

Alopochen aegyptiacus **Egyptian Goose**

Tadorna tadorna **Shelduck**

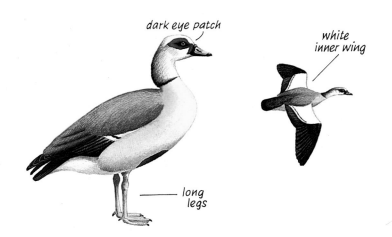

dark eye patch

white inner wing

long legs

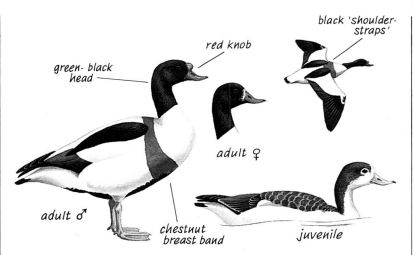

green-black head

red knob

black 'shoulder-straps'

adult ♀

adult ♂

chestnut breast band

juvenile

More like Shelduck than goose. Pinkish buff plumage, darker above and paler below. Shows black wingtips and tail and broad green speculum. Small pink bill with dark base and tip; dark patch around eye. Legs long and pink. Flies fast on broad wings; black on wings contrasts with white inner forewing, forming bold pattern. Spends much time on land and even perches in trees.
Status: scarce. Introduced from Africa in eighteenth century, now confined to parks and marshes in northern East Anglia.
Similar Species: none.

	EGYPTIAN GOOSE
Type	goose-like
Size	66–72cm (26–28in)
Habitat	freshwater, parks, fields
Behaviour	swims, wades, walks, takes off and lands on water or ground
Flocking	1–15
Flight	strong and powerful; direct
Voice	usually silent; some hissing and cackling
IDENTIFICATION	
Adult	
Crown	pinkish buff
Upperparts	rust or grey-brown
Rump	rust-brown or grey-brown
Tail	black and brown; short and square
Throat	pinkish buff
Breast	pinkish buff
Belly	pinkish buff
Bill	pink; small and duck-like
Legs	pink; long
Juvenile	as adult but lacks eye ring; bill and legs yellowish grey
BREEDING	
Nest	hole in tree or among rocks
Eggs	5–8; creamy-white
Incubation	28–30 days ♂ ♀
Young	active; downy
Fledging	?
Broods	1; Apr–May
Food	grass, other vegetation
Population	small feral, 400?

Large, goose-like duck showing bold black and white pattern. Head and neck dark bottle-green; rest of plumage white with broad, chestnut breast band and black stripe along folded wing. Bill bright red in a adult male with bulbous knob at base. Females and immatures have pinkish red bills (without knob) and less clear-cut breast and wing markings. In flight, main wing feathers are black and contrast with white forewing, forming large flocks in winter and for moulting. Generally gregarious, favours estuaries and muddy shores, though often breeds inland.
Status: resident along most coasts; most migrate late summer to N. Germany to moult; return in autumn.
Similar Species: none.

	SHELDUCK
Type	duck-like, goose-like
Size	58–64cm (22–25in)
Habitat	shorelines, estuaries, freshwater marshes
Behaviour	swims, wades, walks, takes off and lands on water or ground
Flocking	1–several hundred
Flight	strong and powerful; direct
Voice	whistling and growling
IDENTIFICATION	
Adult ♂	
Crown	bottle-green
Upperparts	white and black
Rump	white
Tail	white with black terminal band; short and square
Throat	bottle-green
Breast	chestnut
Belly	white
Bill	red with knob; duck-like
Legs	pink; medium length
Adult ♀	as ♂ but less clear-cut markings and pink-red, knobless bill
Juvenile	as ♀ but lacks breast band; grey-brown crown
BREEDING	
Nest	down-lined cup in burrow, hollow tree
Eggs	8–15; cream
Incubation	28–30 days ♀
Young	active; downy
Fledging	8 weeks
Broods	1; May–June
Food	crustaceans, molluscs
Population	12,000 pairs; 50,000 winter

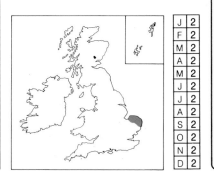

J	2
F	2
M	2
A	2
M	2
J	2
J	2
A	2
S	2
O	2
N	2
D	2

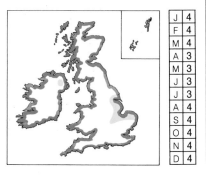

J	4
F	4
M	4
A	3
M	3
J	3
J	3
A	4
S	4
O	4
N	4
D	4

Mandarin *Aix galericulata*

MANDARIN

Type	duck-like
Size	41–47cm (16–18½in)
Habitat	freshwater, woodland
Behaviour	swims, walks, takes off and lands on water, vegetation or ground
Flocking	1–15
Flight	strong and powerful; direct
Voice	♂ whistle; ♀ kek

IDENTIFICATION

Adult ♂	
Crown	brown; crest
Upperparts	brown and black; orange 'sails'
Rump	black
Tail	black; short and rounded
Throat	brown and black
Breast	black and white
Belly	white
Bill	red; duck-like
Legs	yellow; short
Ad. ♀ and juv.	head grey, upperparts brown, underparts spotted

BREEDING

Nest	tree-hole
Eggs	9–12; buffy
Incubation	28–30 days ♀
Young	active; downy
Fledging	?
Broods	1; Apr–May
Food	nuts, seeds, insects
Population	300–400 pairs

J	F	M	A	M	J	J	A	S	O	N	D
2	2	2	2	2	2	2	2	2	2	2	2

orange 'sails'   bold white eyebrow   white eyebrow

adult ♂   adult ♂

adult ♀   green speculum   adult ♀

spotted flanks

One of our smallest ducks, most often found on small lakes in wooded countryside. The male has elaborate, multi-coloured plumage with a dark, droopy crest, white slash over the eye, green nape, chestnut 'whiskers' and orange flanks. Two orange 'sails' stand up on its back, though when flying these lie flat on the lower back. Though such a combination would seem unmistakable, at a distance the white slash over the eye is the best field mark. The female is dull in comparison. The head is grey marked by a narrow white eyebrow. The upperparts are brown, the underparts buff, heavily spotted with cream. There is a small crest at the nape.
Status: introduced from China and now well established, mainly in south-east England.

Similar Species:
Harlequin Duck *Histrionicus histrionicus* 41–45cm (16–18in)
A small sea duck that appears dark at any distance and which is easily overlooked, particularly the female. On a close approach the male is multi-coloured like a Mandarin, though the habitats of the two species are quite distinct. The flanks are dark orange-red, with head, neck and back blue-black, variously marked with patches

of white. The female resembles the considerably larger female Velvet Scoter, being dusky all over save for three pale patches on the sides of the head. It does, however, lack a white wingbar. Females also resemble female Long-tailed Ducks.
Range: the Harlequin breeds as near as Iceland and then in a great sweep across North America to eastern Siberia.
Migration: Icelandic birds seldom venture far, but American and Siberian birds make lengthy southward migrations.
British Distribution: a very rare vagrant to the far north of Scotland.
Other Similar Species: female American Wood Duck (an occasional escapee from waterfowl collections).

Harlequin Duck

bold head pattern   adult ♂

adult ♂   uniform dark wings

three pale face spots

adult ♀   adult ♀

Anas penelope **Wigeon**

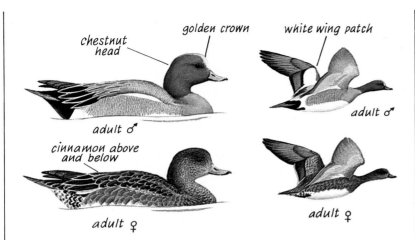

chestnut head · golden crown · white wing patch · adult ♂ · cinnamon above and below · adult ♂ · adult ♀

Anas acuta **Pintail**

long tail · chocolate head · pale forewing · adult ♂ · adult ♂ · heavily spotted · adult ♀ · base of neck low in water · pointed tail · adult ♀

Abundant winter visitor; often forming large flocks in favoured areas. Male has golden blase extending from forehead over crown. Rest of head and neck chestnut; body grey with white flash along flanks. Rear flanks white with black end to body. In flight, shows white patch on inner wing; lacking in female and first winter male. Small silver-grey bill. Female cinnamon-brown with delicate rounded head. Largest flocks feed on coastal grassland and most roost on estuaries. Often found alongside geese; also occurs at inland reservoirs and flooded ground. *Status:* widespread and numerous winter visitor; small numbers breed, mainly in north of Britain. *Similar Species:* male none; female more cinnamon than other surface-feeding ducks.

WIGEON	
Type	duck-like
Size	43–48cm (16–19in)
Habitat	estuaries, shores, marshes, grassland
Behaviour	swims, wades, walks, takes off and lands on water or ground
Flocking	1–several thousand
Flight	strong and powerful; direct
Voice	♂ high pitched whistle; ♀ growls

IDENTIFICATION

Adult ♂	
Crown	yellow and chestnut
Upperparts	grey
Rump	grey
Tail	black and white; short and pointed
Throat	chestnut
Breast	buff
Belly	white
Bill	silver-grey; small and duck-like
Legs	grey; short
Adult ♀	rufous; barred above and below

BREEDING

Nest	lined hollow near water
Eggs	7–8; creamy
Incubation	22–25 days ♀
Young	active; downy
Fledging	6 weeks
Broods	1; May–June
Food	grass, eelgrass, aquatic vegetation
Population	300–500 pairs; up to 200,000 winter

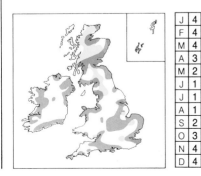

J	4
F	4
M	4
A	3
M	2
J	1
J	1
A	1
S	2
O	3
N	4
D	4

Slim, elegant duck; characteristic swimming attitude with foreparts lower in water than hindparts. Male has chocolate-brown head with vertical white stripe up back of long neck. Upperparts grey; long drooping black and white scapulars. Grey underparts; white rear flank patch and black rear end. Long tail has pointed central tail feathers. Bill silver-blue. Female grey-buff, boldly blotched brown above and below – the palest surface-feeding duck. In flight, male shows pale inner forewing; female virtually featureless. Pointed rear end more obvious in male than female. *Status:* scarce, very localized breeder. Winter visitor everywhere, but only common at favoured areas. *Similar Species:* Wigeon (p.77) also has pointed tail in flight.

PINTAIL	
Type	duck-like
Size	♂ 63–70cm (25–27in); ♀ 53–59cm (21–23in)
Habitat	marshes, estuaries
Behaviour	swims, up-ends, takes off and lands on water or ground
Flocking	1–several thousand
Flight	strong and powerful; direct
Voice	♂ growls and whistles; ♀ quacks

IDENTIFICATION

Adult ♂	
Crown	brown
Upperparts	grey; black and cream scapulars
Rump	grey
Tail	black; long and pointed
Throat	brown
Breast	white
Belly	white
Bill	silver-blue; duck-like
Legs	black; short
Adult ♀	buff and brown with distinctive spotting; pointed tail

BREEDING

Nest	lined hollow in vegetation
Eggs	7–9; yellowish white
Incubation	21–23 days ♀
Young	active; downy
Fledging	7 weeks
Broods	1; Apr–June
Food	aquatic vegetation, invertebrates
Population	less than 50 pairs; c 25,000 winter

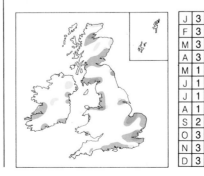

J	3
F	3
M	3
A	3
M	1
J	1
J	1
A	1
S	2
O	3
N	3
D	3

Teal *Anas crecca*

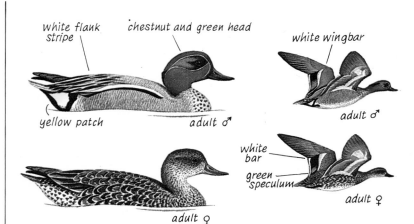

white flank stripe
chestnut and green head
white wingbar
yellow patch
adult ♂
adult ♂
white bar
green speculum
adult ♀
adult ♀

Small, fast-flying, highly gregarious duck. Often forms compact flocks that fly in twisting, turning formation, like waders. Male's chestnut head has bottle-green, yellow-edged area round eye. At any distance appears simply dark headed. Breast buff, spotted brown. Grey back and flanks separated by narrow black and white 'lateral line'. Black rear end encloses large yellow patch. In flight, shows inconspicuous bottle-green speculum and clearer white wingbar. Female brown and buff.
Status: uncommon but widespread breeder; huge winter influx.
Similar Species: similar to, but smaller than, all female surface-feeding ducks except Garganey (p.78), from which separated by green speculum and different face pattern.

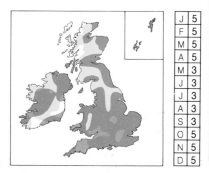

TEAL	
Type	duck-like
Size	34–38cm (13–15in)
Habitat	freshwater, estuaries
Behaviour	swims, wades, walks, takes off and lands on water or ground
Flocking	1–several hundred
Flight	strong and powerful
Voice	♂ whistles; ♀ quacks
IDENTIFICATION	
Adult ♂	
Crown	chestnut-brown
Upperparts	grey
Rump	black
Tail	grey; short and rounded
Throat	brown
Breast	buff, spotted brown
Belly	buff
Bill	grey; duck-like
Legs	black; short
Adult ♀	mottled brown and buff
BREEDING	
Nest	lined hollow in marsh
Eggs	8–12; creamy buff
Incubation	21–28 days ♀
Young	active; downy
Fledging	44 days
Broods	1; Apr–May
Food	aquatic vegetation, seeds
Population	3500–6000 pairs; 52,000 winter

J	5
F	5
M	5
A	5
M	3
J	3
J	3
A	3
S	3
O	5
N	5
D	5

Garganey *Anas querquedula*

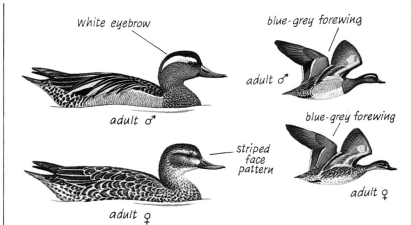

white eyebrow
blue-grey forewing
adult ♂
adult ♂
blue-grey forewing
striped face pattern
adult ♀
adult ♀

Dainty, Teal-sized duck easily overlooked in eclipse and female plumages. Male has maroon-brown head with bold white eyebrow, drooping black and white scapulars and grey underparts. Female has striped face pattern. In flight, shows pale blue inner wing like Shoveler.
Status: scarce summer visitor, mainly to south and east England; winters in Africa.
Similar Species: female and eclipse male like similar plumages of Teal (p.78) and much larger Mallard (p.79). Female similar to other female surface-feeding ducks but separated by pronounced face pattern. Some female and eclipse Teal, and many Mallard, show similar pattern but less pronounced.

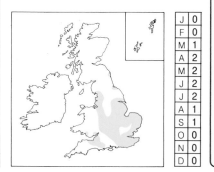

GARGANEY	
Type	duck-like
Size	37–41cm (14–16in)
Habitat	freshwater and marshes
Behaviour	swims, up-ends, takes off and lands on water or ground
Flocking	1–10
Flight	strong and powerful; direct
Voice	♂ crackling rattle; ♀ quacks
IDENTIFICATION	
Adult ♂	
Crown	maroon-brown
Upperparts	buff and brown
Rump	buff and brown
Tail	buff; short and square
Throat	brown
Breast	buff and brown
Belly	grey
Bill	grey; duck-like
Legs	grey; short
Adult ♀	spotted buff and brown with distinctive striped face pattern
BREEDING	
Nest	lined hollow, well-hidden near water
Eggs	8–11; buffy
Incubation	21–23 days ♀
Young	active; downy
Fledging	5–6 weeks
Broods	1; Apr–May
Food	aquatic invertebrates and plants
Population	less than 100 pairs

J	0
F	0
M	1
A	2
M	2
J	2
J	2
A	1
S	1
O	0
N	0
D	0

Anas strepera **Gadwall**

grey back and flanks

black rear end

adult ♂

white in wing

adult ♂

adult ♀

orange-yellow bill edges

adult ♀

Rather nondescript grey and brown duck, slightly smaller than Mallard. Resident at marshes and waters with growth of reeds. Male has mottled brown head and upperparts with dark eye stripe, similar to females of other surface-feeding ducks. Flanks finely barred grey. Best field mark is black rear end and white speculum, particularly in flight. Female has white speculum and yellow sides to bill. *Status:* nowhere numerous, mostly introduced and resident. Some Scottish birds migrate to Ireland; some winter visitors from northern Europe. *Similar Species:* only adult male Wigeon (p.77) show white in dark wing in flight. Female Pintail, Teal (pp.77–78), Mallard and Shoveler (pp.79–80) resemble both sexes adult Gadwall but all lack Gadwall's white in wing.

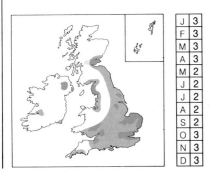

J	3	
F	3	
M	3	
A	3	
M	2	
J	2	
J	2	
A	2	
S	2	
O	3	
N	3	
D	3	

GADWALL

Type	duck-like
Size	48–54cm (18–21in)
Habitat	freshwater marshes, estuaries
Behaviour	swims, walks, takes off and lands on water or ground
Flocking	1–15
Flight	strong and powerful; direct
Voice	♂ whistles; ♀ quacks

IDENTIFICATION

Adult ♂	
Crown	brown
Upperparts	grey
Rump	black
Tail	black; short and square
Throat	brown
Breast	grey, spotted
Belly	grey, barred
Bill	black; duck-like
Legs	yellow; short
Adult ♀	mottled buff and brown with white speculum (as ♂) and yellow sides to bill

BREEDING

Nest	lined hollow by water
Eggs	8–12; creamy
Incubation	25–27 days ♀
Young	active; downy
Fledging	7 weeks
Broods	1; May–June
Food	aquatic vegetation
Population	250 pairs

Anas platyrhynchos **Mallard**

bottle-green crown

adult ♂

black rear end

adult ♂

blue and white speculum

brown breast band

adult ♀

orange-yellow bill

adult ♀

Common and widespread throughout year in wide variety of aquatic habitats, from wild marshes and floods to city-centre ponds. Male's bottle-green head separated from chocolate-brown breast by narrow white neck ring. Back and wings pale grey; underparts paler grey. Black rear end with two upward-curling feathers. In flight.head appears dark; dark blue speculum bordered fore and aft by white bars. Female resembles other female surface-feeding ducks; dark cap, dark eye stripe and orange-yellow bill aid separation. Generally gregarious. *Status:* mainly resident; breeds throughout area. Large winter influx from the Continent. *Similar Species:* female and eclipse male often show similar face pattern to much smaller Garganey (p.78).

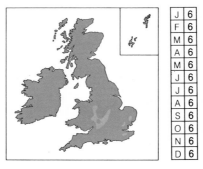

J	6	
F	6	
M	6	
A	6	
M	6	
J	6	
J	6	
A	6	
S	6	
O	6	
N	6	
D	6	

MALLARD

Type	duck-like
Size	55–62cm (22–24in)
Habitat	freshwater, marshes, estuaries
Behaviour	swims, up-ends, takes off and lands on water or ground
Flocking	1–several thousand
Flight	strong and powerful; direct
Voice	♂ whistles and grunts; ♀ familiar quack

IDENTIFICATION

Adult ♂	
Crown	bottle-green
Upperparts	pale grey
Rump	black
Tail	white; short and rounded
Throat	bottle-green
Breast	chocolate-brown
Belly	very pale grey
Bill	yellow; duck-like
Legs	orange; short
Adult ♀	mottled buffs and browns, orange-yellow bill, blue and white speculum

BREEDING

Nest	lined hollow on ground
Eggs	10–12; creamy
Incubation	28–29 days ♀
Young	active; downy
Fledging	7–8 weeks
Broods	1; Mar–July
Food	aquatic seeds, plants, invertebrates
Population	70,000–150,000 pairs; 300,000 winter

Shoveler *Anas clypeata*

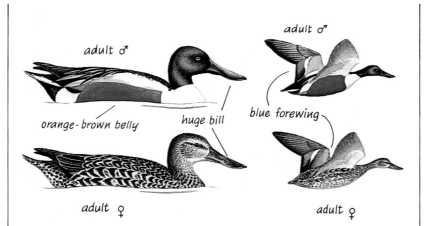

adult ♂

orange-brown belly   huge bill

adult ♀

adult ♂

blue forewing

adult ♀

Medium-sized duck that feeds with broad sweeps of bill through shallow water and wet mud. Huge, spatulate bill obvious in both sexes at rest and in flight. Male has bottle-green head, white breast, black back and bright chestnut belly and flanks. Female mottled buff and brown; resembles other female surface-feeding ducks but bill easily separates. In flight both sexes show pale blue inner wing. Generally gregarious; sizeable flocks gather at favoured feeding grounds in winter. Much scarcer in summer at reed-fringed lagoons and marshes. *Status:* small numbers breed over much of area; influx of winter visitors. *Similar Species:* smaller Garganey (p.78) has blue inner wing but no other duck has huge, spatulate bill.

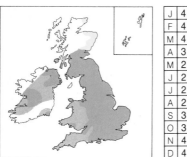

J	4
F	4
M	4
A	3
M	2
J	2
J	2
A	2
S	3
O	3
N	4
D	4

SHOVELER

Type	duck-like
Size	47–53cm (18–21in)
Habitat	freshwater marshes, estuaries
Behaviour	swims, wades, walks, takes off and lands on water or ground
Flocking	1–several hundred
Flight	strong and powerful; direct
Voice	♂ harsh, double note *tuk-tuk*; ♀ quacks

IDENTIFICATION

Adult ♂	
Crown	bottle-green
Upperparts	black back, white scapulars
Rump	black
Tail	black, white outer feathers; short and rounded
Throat	green
Breast	white
Belly	chestnut
Bill	black; huge and spatulate
Legs	yellow; short
Adult ♀	mottled buff and brown; large grey and orange spatulate bill

BREEDING

Nest	lined hollow near water
Eggs	8–12; buffy
Incubation	22–23 days ♀
Young	active; downy
Fledging	6–7 weeks
Broods	1; Apr–May
Food	crustaceans, molluscs, aquatic seeds and plants
Population	1000 pairs; 4500+ winter

Pochard *Aythya ferina*

grey back   rusty head

grey wings

adult ♂

adult ♂

pale eye ring and line

buff-grey wings

adult ♀

adult ♀

Compact diving duck with prominent sloping forehead and large bill. Male has grey body, chestnut head and black breast. At any distance whole of foreparts appear dark; body pale grey with dark rear end. Female greyish-brown, darker on head and neck. In flight shows inconspicuous pale grey wingbar. Highly gregarious, forming huge rafts at suitable waters. Flocks generally spend much time sleeping during the day. Dives mainly for aquatic vegetation. *Status:* widespread, but not a common breeder; often abundant winter visitor. *Similar Species:* none.

J	4
F	4
M	4
A	3
M	2
J	2
J	2
A	2
S	3
O	4
N	4
D	4

POCHARD

Type	duck-like
Size	44–48cm (17–19in)
Habitat	freshwater, sea, estuaries
Behaviour	swims, dives from surface, walks, takes off and lands on water
Flocking	1–2000
Flight	strong and powerful; direct
Voice	generally quiet; ♀ growls in flight

IDENTIFICATION

Adult ♂	
Crown	chestnut
Upperparts	grey
Rump	black
Tail	grey; short and rounded
Throat	chestnut
Breast	black
Belly	grey
Bill	grey; large and duck-like
Legs	black; short
Adult ♀	greyish brown with darker head and breast and dark rear end

BREEDING

Nest	mound of vegetation at or near water's edge
Eggs	6–11; greenish
Incubation	24–26 days ♀
Young	active; downy
Fledging	7–8 weeks
Broods	1; Apr–June
Food	aquatic plants, invertebrates
Population	400 pairs; many thousands winter

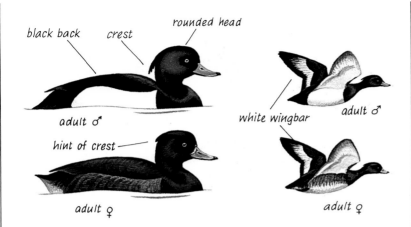

black back — crest — rounded head

adult ♂

hint of crest

adult ♀

white wingbar — adult ♂

adult ♀

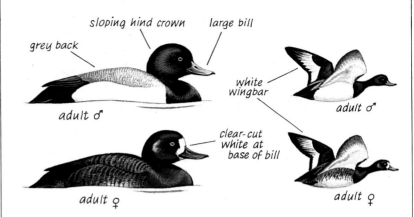

sloping hind crown — large bill

grey back

adult ♂

white wingbar

adult ♂

adult ♀

clear-cut white at base of bill

adult ♀

Dainty diving duck, with round head, drooping crest and short neck. Male has all-black breast, back and tail; black head has purple sheen; white flanks and underparts. Inconspicuous crest extends from hind crown. Female sooty brown, with paler barred flanks and less obvious crest. Grey bill often has white base in female. In flight both sexes show prominent, broad, white wingbar. Gregarious, often gathering in large winter flocks, frequently in company of Pochard. Dives easily, mainly for invertebrates.
Status: widespread breeding bird in small numbers; abundant winter visitor.
Similar Species: Goldeneye (p.82) is similarly black and white. White-faced females resemble female Scaup (p.81).

Marine equivalent of Tufted Duck and generally similar. Male has black, green-glossed head, black breast and rear end, grey back and white flanks and belly. Female has large, clear-cut white area at base of bill. In all plumages, steep forehead and backward-sloping crown create distinct head shape. Essentially coastal, gathering in large, sometimes huge, flocks at favoured feeding grounds; small numbers storm-driven inland.
Status: occasional rare breeder in extreme north; common winter visitor but large flocks highly localized, mainly in north.
Similar Species: female usually separated from female Tufted Duck (p.81) by white on face, but beware white-faced female Tufted inland. Male like male Tufted, but grey-backed.

TUFTED DUCK	
Type	duck-like
Size	41–45cm (16–17in)
Habitat	freshwater, estuaries
Behaviour	swims, dives from surface, takes off and lands on water or ground
Flocking	1–2000
Flight	strong and powerful; direct
Voice	generally silent; ♀ growls

IDENTIFICATION

Adult ♂	
Crown	black, glossed purple; crest
Upperparts	black
Rump	black
Tail	black; short and rounded
Throat	black
Breast	black
Belly	white
Bill	grey; duck-like
Legs	black; short
Adult ♀	brown above, buffy on flanks; reduced crest

BREEDING

Nest	lined hollow near water; well-hidden
Eggs	5–12; greenish
Incubation	23–25 days ♀
Young	active; downy
Fledging	6 weeks
Broods	1; Apr–June
Food	aquatic invertebrates, plants
Population	6000–8000 pairs; many thousands winter

SCAUP	
Type	duck-like
Size	46–51cm (18–20in)
Habitat	freshwater marshes, sea, estuaries
Behaviour	swims, dives from surface, takes off and lands on water or ground
Flocking	1–10,000
Flight	strong and powerful; direct
Voice	generally silent; ♀ growls

IDENTIFICATION

Adult ♂	
Crown	black, green-glossed
Upperparts	grey
Rump	black
Tail	black; short and rounded
Throat	black
Breast	black
Belly	white
Bill	grey; duck-like
Legs	black; short
Adult ♀	brown above, buffy on flanks, white face

BREEDING

Nest	lined hollow near water; open sites
Eggs	6–15; greenish
Incubation	24–28 days ♀
Young	active; downy
Fledging	5–6 weeks
Broods	1; May–June
Food	molluscs, aquatic vegetation
Population	c5 pairs; 16,000 winter

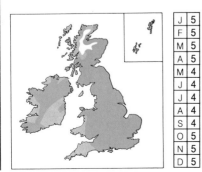

J	5
F	5
M	5
A	5
M	4
J	4
J	4
A	4
S	4
O	5
N	5
D	5

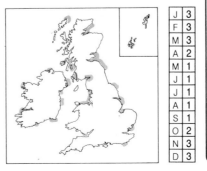

J	3
F	3
M	3
A	2
M	1
J	1
J	1
A	1
S	1
O	2
N	3
D	3

Long-tailed Duck *Clangula hyemalis*

pale face patch — black and white pattern

adult ♂ winter

long tail

adult ♂ summer

uniform wings

adult ♀ summer

appears 'neckless'

dark face patch

breast band

adult ♀ winter

Small, stocky seaduck. Large head, small bill and pointed tail; male has extended central tail feathers. Variable plumage always includes face patch. Summer male has dark brown head and neck; face silvery grey. Winter male has white head with grey patch on side of face. Female always has pale patch around eye; remaining upperparts broadly edged buff in summer, browner in winter. In flight, wings uniform brown in all plumages. Gregarious around coasts.
Status: winter visitor; most numerous on inshore waters in north and east where large flocks amount to at least half of British population.
Similar Species: none.

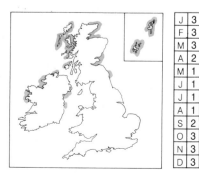

J	3
F	3
M	3
A	2
M	1
J	1
J	1
A	1
S	2
O	3
N	3
D	3

LONG-TAILED DUCK
Type	duck-like
Size	♂ 54–58cm (21–23in); ♀ 41–45cm (16–17in)
Habitat	sea, estuaries
Behaviour	swims, dives from surface, takes off and lands on water
Flocking	1–1000
Flight	strong and powerful; direct
Voice	♂ yodelling call; ♀ quacks

IDENTIFICATION
Ad.♂summer	
Crown	blackish brown
Upperparts	brown and black, edged buff
Rump	blackish brown
Tail	dark brown, white outer feathers; long and pointed
Throat	blackish brown
Breast	blackish brown
Belly	buff-grey
Bill	pink; small and duck-like
Legs	black; short
Ad.♂winter	paler on head with black and white back
Adult ♀	brown above with distinctive pale face patch

BREEDING
Nest	lined hollow hidden in vegetation
Eggs	5–9; yellow
Incubation	23–25 days ♀
Young	active; downy
Fledging	5 weeks
Broods	1; May–July
Food	molluscs, crustaceans
Population	10,000 winter

Smew *Mergus albellus*

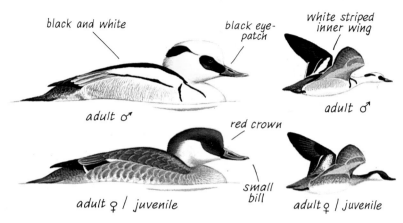

black and white

black eye-patch

white striped inner wing

adult ♂

adult ♂

red crown

small bill

adult ♀ / juvenile

adult ♀ / juvenile

Compact little duck and scarce winter visitor. Male white with narrow black lines on crown, back and flanks. Steep forehead and hint of crest create large-headed appearance; small bill, black facial mask. Female and first winter male – 'redheads' – have chestnut crown extending to below eye, white face, grey back and pale grey underparts. Mostly found in small flocks on inland waters, with 'redheads' predominating.
Status: scarce late winter visitor in variable numbers to south and east England; regular at a few favoured waters. Hard weather may bring larger numbers from the Continent.
Similar Species: male none; at distance, 'redheads' could be confused with Slavonian Grebe (p.52).

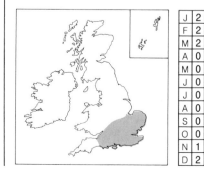

J	2
F	2
M	2
A	0
M	0
J	0
J	0
A	0
S	0
O	0
N	1
D	2

SMEW
Type	duck-like
Size	36–43cm (14–17in)
Habitat	freshwater, estuaries
Behaviour	swims, dives from surface, takes off and lands on water
Flocking	1–25
Flight	strong and powerful; direct
Voice	usually silent

IDENTIFICATION
Adult ♂	
Crown	white, black lines; slight crest
Upperparts	white, black lines
Rump	grey
Tail	grey; short and rounded
Throat	white
Breast	white
Belly	white
Bill	grey; small and duck-like
Legs	grey; short
Adult ♀	grey above, paler grey below; white cheeks, chestnut crown

BREEDING
Nest	unlined tree hole
Eggs	6–9; creamy
Incubation	30 days ♀
Young	active; downy
Fledging	10 weeks
Broods	1; May–June
Food	fish
Population	50–100 winter

Aythya fuligula **Tufted Duck**

Aythya marila **Scaup**

black back — crest — rounded head

adult ♂

hint of crest

adult ♀

white wingbar — adult ♂

adult ♀

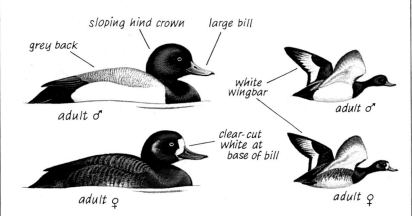

grey back — sloping hind crown — large bill

white wingbar

adult ♂

adult ♀

clear-cut white at base of bill

adult ♂

adult ♀

Dainty diving duck, with round head, drooping crest and short neck. Male has all-black breast, back and tail; black head has purple sheen; white flanks and underparts. Inconspicuous crest extends from hind crown. Female sooty brown, with paler barred flanks and less obvious crest. Grey bill often has white base in female. In flight both sexes show prominent, broad, white wingbar. Gregarious, often gathering in large winter flocks, frequently in company of Pochard. Dives easily, mainly for invertebrates.
Status: widespread breeding bird in small numbers; abundant winter visitor.
Similar Species: Goldeneye (p.82) is similarly black and white. White-faced females resemble female Scaup (p.81).

	TUFTED DUCK
Type	duck-like
Size	41–45cm (16–17in)
Habitat	freshwater, estuaries
Behaviour	swims, dives from surface, takes off and lands on water or ground
Flocking	1–2000
Flight	strong and powerful; direct
Voice	generally silent; ♀ growls

IDENTIFICATION

Adult ♂	
Crown	black, glossed purple; crest
Upperparts	black
Rump	black
Tail	black; short and rounded
Throat	black
Breast	black
Belly	white
Bill	grey; duck-like
Legs	black; short
Adult ♀	brown above, buffy on flanks; reduced crest

BREEDING

Nest	lined hollow near water; well-hidden
Eggs	5–12; greenish
Incubation	23–25 days ♀
Young	active; downy
Fledging	6 weeks
Broods	1; Apr–June
Food	aquatic invertebrates, plants
Population	6000–8000 pairs; many thousands winter

Marine equivalent of Tufted Duck and generally similar. Male has black, green-glossed head, black breast and rear end, grey back and white flanks and belly. Female has large, clear-cut white area at base of bill. In all plumages, steep forehead and backward-sloping crown create distinct head shape. Essentially coastal, gathering in large, sometimes huge, flocks at favoured feeding grounds; small numbers storm-driven inland.
Status: occasional rare breeder in extreme north; common winter visitor but large flocks highly localized, mainly in north.
Similar Species: female usually separated from female Tufted Duck (p.81) by white on face, but beware white-faced female Tufted inland. Male like male Tufted, but grey-backed.

	SCAUP
Type	duck-like
Size	46–51cm (18–20in)
Habitat	freshwater marshes, sea, estuaries
Behaviour	swims, dives from surface, takes off and lands on water or ground
Flocking	1–10,000
Flight	strong and powerful; direct
Voice	generally silent; ♀ growls

IDENTIFICATION

Adult ♂	
Crown	black, green-glossed
Upperparts	grey
Rump	black
Tail	black; short and rounded
Throat	black
Breast	black
Belly	white
Bill	grey; duck-like
Legs	black; short
Adult ♀	brown above, buffy on flanks, white face

BREEDING

Nest	lined hollow near water; open sites
Eggs	6–15; greenish
Incubation	24–28 days ♀
Young	active; downy
Fledging	5–6 weeks
Broods	1; May–June
Food	molluscs, aquatic vegetation
Population	c 5 pairs; 16,000 winter

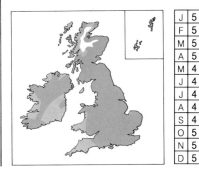

J	5
F	5
M	5
A	5
M	4
J	4
J	4
A	4
S	4
O	5
N	5
D	5

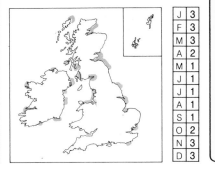

J	3
F	3
M	3
A	2
M	1
J	1
J	1
A	1
S	1
O	2
N	3
D	3

Eider *Somateria mollissima*

white back

flat forehead

white back and inner wings

adult ♂

adult ♂

flat forehead

adult ♀

adult ♀

Large, stocky seaduck. Male mainly white above and black below with pink tinge to white breast. Bold black mark extends over each side of crown. Pale green nape visible at close range. Female warm buff and brown, finely barred. Long, sloping forehead and longish bill form continuous line, creating wedge-shaped head with feathering reaching half way to bill tip. Immature male like female, but white developing from breast to back over first summer creates patchy effect. Forms small flocks in coastal waters; breeds colonially.
Status: resident along coasts of Scotland, northern Ireland and north-east England. Winter visitor elsewhere.
Similar Species: none.

EIDER

Type	duck-like
Size	55–61cm (21–24in)
Habitat	sea, estuaries
Behaviour	swims, dives from surface, takes off and lands on water
Flocking	1–several hundred
Flight	strong and powerful; direct
Voice	♂ dove-like cooing; ♀ repeated *gok-gok-gok*

IDENTIFICATION

Adult ♂	
Crown	white, black sides
Upperparts	white
Rump	black
Tail	black; short and rounded
Throat	white
Breast	white, pink-tinge
Belly	black
Bill	grey; duck-like
Legs	brown; short
Adult ♀	barred buff and brown above and below

BREEDING

Nest	lined hollow on island, coast or nearby river
Eggs	4–6; greenish
Incubation	27–28 days ♀
Young	active; downy
Fledging	60–75 days
Broods	1; May–June
Food	molluscs, crustaceans, other invertebrates
Population	15,000–25,000 pairs; 60,000 winter

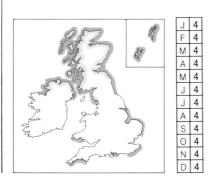

J	4
F	4
M	4
A	4
M	4
J	4
J	4
A	4
S	4
O	4
N	4
D	4

Goldeneye *Bucephala clangula*

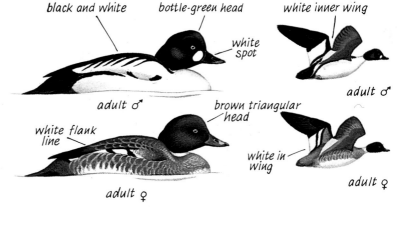

black and white

bottle-green head

white inner wing

white spot

adult ♂

adult ♂

white flank line

brown triangular head

adult ♀

white in wing

adult ♀

Medium-sized diving duck found on freshwater as often as on sea. Both sexes marked by steep forehead, peaked crown and sloping hind crown, giving head uniquely characteristic shape. Male has black, green-glossed head with white patch between bill and eye; upperparts black with transverse streaks across folded wing. Flanks and underparts white; rear end black. Female has chocolate-brown head, white neck band and grey body. In flight, both sexes have white inner wing with narrow, dark, central band(s). Generally gregarious, forming small, loose flocks.
Status: small numbers breed in Scotland; widespread winter visitor.
Similar Species: male Tufted Duck (p.81) also black and white, but should present no difficulties.

GOLDENEYE

Type	duck-like
Size	40–48cm (16–19in)
Habitat	freshwater, sea, estuaries
Behaviour	swims, dives from surface, takes off and lands on water
Flocking	1–15
Flight	strong and powerful; direct
Voice	silent except in courtship

IDENTIFICATION

Adult ♂	
Crown	black, glossed green
Upperparts	black; white wing streaked black
Rump	black
Tail	black; short and rounded
Throat	black
Breast	white
Belly	white
Bill	black; duck-like
Legs	yellow; short
Adult ♀	mottled grey with dark brown head and white neck-ring

BREEDING

Nest	unlined tree hole
Eggs	6–11; blue-green
Incubation	27–32 days ♀
Young	active; downy
Fledging	51–60 days
Broods	1; Apr–June
Food	molluscs, crustaceans
Population	27–57 pairs; 10,000–15,000 winter

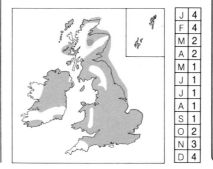

J	4
F	4
M	2
A	2
M	1
J	1
J	1
A	1
S	1
O	2
N	3
D	4

Melanitta nigra Common Scoter

uniform black

adult ♂

adult ♂

adult ♀

pale sides to face

adult ♀

All-black seaduck most often seen as small dark blobs bouncing among waves, or as all-dark birds flying fast and low over sea. Male black with yellow bill and black knob at base. Female brown with pale cheeks that may be picked out at considerable distances. Gregarious, usually forming flocks 10–100 strong.
Status: scarce breeder in extreme north and north-west; winter visitor to most coasts; non-breeders in summer.
Similar Species: Velvet Scoter (p.83).

	COMMON SCOTER	
Type	duck-like	
Size	46–51cm (18–20in)	
Habitat	sea	
Behaviour	swims, dives from surface, takes off and lands on water	
Flocking	1–several hundred	
Flight	strong and powerful; low; direct	
Voice	often silent; occasional harsh whistles	

IDENTIFICATION

Adult ♂		
Crown	black	
Upperparts	black	
Rump	black	
Tail	black; short and rounded	
Throat	black	
Breast	black	
Belly	black	
Bill	yellow, black knob at base; duck-like	
Legs	grey; short	
Adult ♀	brown with creamy cheeks; black bill with smaller knob	

BREEDING

Nest	lined hollow near water	
Eggs	6–9; creamy	
Incubation	27–31 days ♀	
Young	active; downy	
Fledging	6–7 weeks	
Broods	1; June–July	
Food	cockles, mussels, crustaceans	
Population	160–190 pairs; 35,000–50,000 winter	

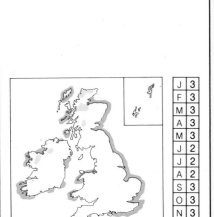

J	3
F	3
M	3
A	3
M	3
J	2
J	2
A	2
S	3
O	3
N	3
D	3

Melanitta fusca Velvet Scoter

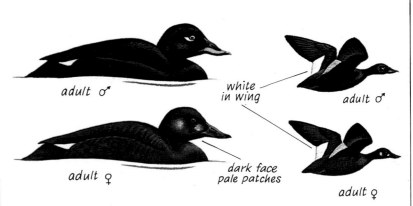

adult ♂

white in wing

adult ♂

adult ♀

dark face pale patches

adult ♀

Similar to Common Scoter, but generally scarcer; often forms mixed flocks. Male black with larger yellow bill. Female brown with two pale face patches. Both sexes show white in wing in flight; may also be visible at rest. When observing all-dark ducks on the sea at a distance, Velvet Scoter may betray their presence by flapping wings to reveal white patches.
Status: less numerous than Common Scoter. Winter visitor to inshore waters, except western Ireland.
Similar Species: Common Scoter (p.83) has no white in wing.

	VELVET SCOTER	
Type	duck-like	
Size	53–59cm (20–23in)	
Habitat	sea	
Behaviour	swims, dives from surface, takes off and lands on water	
Flocking	small flocks	
Flight	strong and powerful; low; direct	
Voice	mostly silent; some croaking	

IDENTIFICATION

Adult ♂		
Crown	black	
Upperparts	black	
Rump	black	
Tail	black; short and rounded	
Throat	black	
Breast	black	
Belly	black	
Bill	yellow; large and duck-like	
Legs	red; short	
Adult ♀	dark brown; pale face patches, grey bill	

BREEDING

Nest	lined hollow in open country, near water	
Eggs	7–10; creamy	
Incubation	27–28 days ♀	
Young	active; downy	
Fledging	6–7 weeks	
Broods	1; June–July	
Food	mussels, crabs, shrimps	
Population	2000+ winter	

J	2
F	2
M	2
A	1
M	1
J	0
J	0
A	0
S	1
O	2
N	2
D	2

Long-tailed Duck *Clangula hyemalis*

pale face patch

black and white pattern

adult ♂ winter

long tail

adult ♂ summer

uniform wings

appears 'neckless'

adult ♀ summer

dark face patch

breast band

adult ♀ winter

Small, stocky seaduck. Large head, small bill and pointed tail; male has extended central tail feathers. Variable plumage always includes face patch. Summer male has dark brown head and neck; face silvery grey. Winter male has white head with grey patch on side of face. Female always has pale patch around eye; remaining upperparts broadly edged buff in summer, browner in winter. In flight, wings uniform brown in all plumages. Gregarious around coasts.
Status: winter visitor; most numerous on inshore waters in north and east where large flocks amount to at least half of British population.
Similar Species: none.

	LONG-TAILED DUCK
Type	duck-like
Size	♂ 54–58cm (21–23in); ♀ 41–45cm (16–17in)
Habitat	sea, estuaries
Behaviour	swims, dives from surface, takes off and lands on water
Flocking	1–1000
Flight	strong and powerful; direct
Voice	♂ yodelling call; ♀ quacks
	IDENTIFICATION
Ad.♂summer	
Crown	blackish brown
Upperparts	brown and black, edged buff
Rump	blackish brown
Tail	dark brown, white outer feathers; long and pointed
Throat	blackish brown
Breast	blackish brown
Belly	buff-grey
Bill	pink; small and duck-like
Legs	black; short
Ad.♂winter	paler on head with black and white back
Adult ♀	brown above with distinctive pale face patch
	BREEDING
Nest	lined hollow hidden in vegetation
Eggs	5–9; yellow
Incubation	23–25 days ♀
Young	active; downy
Fledging	5 weeks
Broods	1; May–July
Food	molluscs, crustaceans
Population	10,000 winter

Month	
J	3
F	3
M	3
A	2
M	1
J	1
J	1
A	1
S	2
O	3
N	3
D	3

Smew *Mergus albellus*

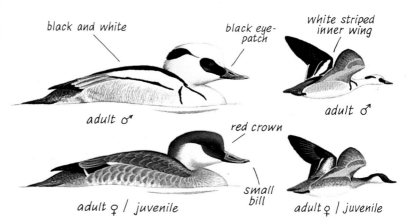

black and white

black eye-patch

white striped inner wing

adult ♂

adult ♂

red crown

small bill

adult ♀ / juvenile

adult ♀ / juvenile

Compact little duck and scarce winter visitor. Male white with narrow black lines on crown, back and flanks. Steep forehead and hint of crest create large-headed appearance; small bill, black facial mask. Female and first winter male – 'redheads' – have chestnut crown extending to below eye, white face, grey back and pale grey underparts. Mostly found in small flocks on inland waters, with 'redheads' predominating.
Status: scarce late winter visitor in variable numbers to south and east England; regular at a few favoured waters. Hard weather may bring larger numbers from the Continent.
Similar Species: male none; at distance, 'redheads' could be confused with Slavonian Grebe (p.52).

	SMEW
Type	duck-like
Size	36–43cm (14–17in)
Habitat	freshwater, estuaries
Behaviour	swims, dives from surface, takes off and lands on water
Flocking	1–25
Flight	strong and powerful; direct
Voice	usually silent
	IDENTIFICATION
Adult ♂	
Crown	white, black lines; slight crest
Upperparts	white, black lines
Rump	grey
Tail	grey; short and rounded
Throat	white
Breast	white
Belly	white
Bill	grey; small and duck-like
Legs	grey; short
Adult ♀	grey above, paler grey below; white cheeks, chestnut crown
	BREEDING
Nest	unlined tree hole
Eggs	6–9; creamy
Incubation	30 days ♀
Young	active; downy
Fledging	10 weeks
Broods	1; May–June
Food	fish
Population	50–100 winter

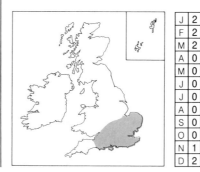

Month	
J	2
F	2
M	2
A	0
M	0
J	0
J	0
A	0
S	0
O	0
N	1
D	2

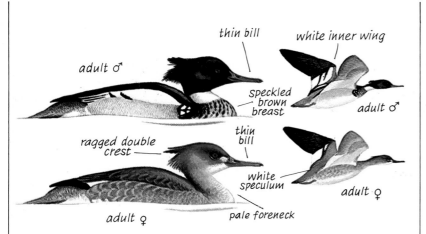

adult ♂ — thin bill — white inner wing — speckled brown breast — adult ♂

ragged double crest — thin bill — white speculum — adult ♀

adult ♀ — pale foreneck

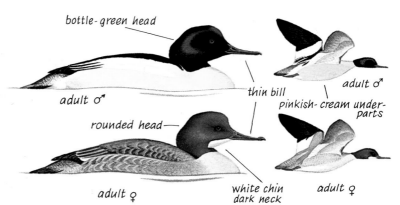

bottle-green head — thin bill — adult ♂ — pinkish-cream underparts

adult ♂ — rounded head — white chin dark neck — adult ♀

adult ♀

Long, slim duck with long, thin bill – a typical 'sawbill'. Male has dark bottle-green head with double crest extending from hind crown. Breast rufous brown, spotted black; forms breast band in flight. Head and breast separated by broad white collar. Upperparts black; flanks and underparts pale grey. Female has rusty head with similar double crest; foreneck and chin white. In flight, male shows black and white inner wing; female white speculum. Mergansers dive well to catch fish.
Status: breeds along rivers in north and west; large flocks in north-east in autumn, more widespread along most coasts in winter.
Similar Species: female Goosander (p.85); Red-breasted Merganser has thinner, horizontal-pointing crest and white foreneck.

RED-BREASTED MERGANSER	
Type	duck-like
Size	51–61cm (20–24in)
Habitat	freshwater, sea, estuaries
Behaviour	swims, dives from surface, takes off and lands on water
Flocking	1–several hundred
Flight	strong and powerful; direct
Voice	mostly silent; purrs and croaks in display

IDENTIFICATION	
Adult ♂	
Crown	green; double crest
Upperparts	black
Rump	grey
Tail	grey; short and rounded
Throat	white
Breast	brown, spotted black
Belly	pale grey
Bill	red; long, straight and thin
Legs	red; short
Adult ♀	grey with reddish head and similar double crest

BREEDING	
Nest	lined hollow, well hidden among rocks or tree roots
Eggs	7–12; buffy
Incubation	29–35 days ♀
Young	active; downy
Fledging	59 days
Broods	1; May–June
Food	fish
Population	2000–3000 pairs; 7500 winter

Typical 'sawbill' duck, found mainly on freshwater throughout year. Larger and bulkier than Red-breasted Merganser but with similar shape and similar long, thin, serrated bill. Male has green-glossed, black head with rounded crest, giving head unique shape. Back black; flanks and underparts white with warm, pinkish flush. White inner wing shows in flight. Female has white chin, rusty foreneck and hint of crest. Generally found on inland waters, occasionally larger flocks on sheltered estuaries.
Status: breeds on lakes, mostly in forested country in north.
Similar Species: Red-breasted Merganser (p.85); females most similar but Goosander has less ragged crest angled sharply downward towards back.

GOOSANDER	
Type	duck-like
Size	57–69cm (22–27in)
Habitat	freshwater
Behaviour	swims, dives from surface, takes off and lands on water
Flocking	1–50
Flight	strong and powerful; direct
Voice	generally silent; various courtship croaks and cackles

IDENTIFICATION	
Adult ♂	
Crown	black, green gloss; crest
Upperparts	black, white sides
Rump	grey
Tail	grey; short and rounded
Throat	green
Breast	white
Belly	pinkish white
Bill	red; long, straight and thin
Legs	red; short
Adult ♀	grey with reddish head and rounded crest

BREEDING	
Nest	lined tree hole or similar cavity
Eggs	7–14; creamy
Incubation	32–35 days ♀
Young	active; downy
Fledging	5 weeks
Broods	1; Mar–June
Food	fish
Population	900–1250 pairs; 4000 winter

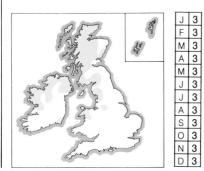

J	3
F	3
M	3
A	3
M	3
J	3
J	3
A	3
S	3
O	3
N	3
D	3

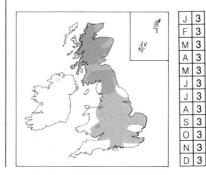

J	3
F	3
M	3
A	3
M	3
J	3
J	3
A	3
S	3
O	3
N	3
D	3

Ruddy Duck *Oxyura jamaicensis*

long tail

blue bill, white face

adult ♂

uniform upper wing

adult ♂

tail often hidden in water

adult ♀

bold face stripe

adult ♀

A dumpy little duck of oddly 'weight forward' appearance when its stiff tail is held invisible horizontally on the water. It looks decidedly more balanced when it holds its tail cocked upright. The male is russet, with a dark cap and nape enclosing a white face. The bill is a brilliant cobalt-blue. The female is brown above and brown and buff barred below. The prominent cap is dark brown and there is a distinctive dark line across the cheek below the eye. The bill is steel-grey and much less obvious than that of the male.
Status: introduced from North America to the West Midlands, where it is well established. Gradually spreading eastwards with movements southward in winter.

Similar Species:
White-headed Duck *Oxyura leucocephala* 43–48cm (17–19in)
Although there is no British record of this southern European duck, there are distinct possibilities of escapees and just a chance that, one day, one may wander northward or westward to our shores. The male is a similar chestnut colour to the Ruddy Duck, with white cheeks and a similar 'weight forward' stiff-tailed appearance. The white does, however, extend further over the head and a small black cap is confined to the top of the crown. Both the area around the eye and the nape are white. Also, the bright, cobalt-blue bill is larger and more bulbous. The female resembles the female Ruddy Duck, but the bulbous bill and dark cheek stripe are much more prominent.
Range: this is a slowly declining species, with a highly fragmented range from Spain, through the Mediterranean to Turkey and the southern Soviet Union.
Migration: winters in numbers only in central Turkey and the Caspian Sea area.
British Distribution: no wild birds recorded; beware escapees from wildfowl collections.

White-headed Duck

long tail

adult ♂

adult ♀

BIRDS OF
PREY

Among the most exciting and dramatic of all our birds are the diurnal (daytime) birds of prey, or raptors as they are often called. They are, sadly, a rather scarce group in Britain today. Though there are 16 regular British species, only two are at all numerous.

Continental Europe is far better endowed with raptors, both in terms of numbers and variety. An underlying reason is a general rule of biology that offshore islands such as ours have fewer animal species than adjacent continental landmasses; but added to this is the fact that British birds of prey were severely persecuted for a hundred years or more, and they are taking time to recover their former numbers. For example, Red Kites, all but exterminated last century, are still confined to mid-Wales, whereas they were once widespread throughout Britain. The news is not, however, all bad. Our islands now boast one of the strongest populations of the Peregrine in the world.

Birds of prey are generally a fairly similar-looking group of hook-billed birds that kill large prey with their razor-sharp curved talons. They are mostly sombrely coloured and pose identification problems for the beginner. Putting a name to a bird of prey is more a matter of checking shape, structure and behaviour than of picking out clear field marks.

What a bird does and how it behaves is not only the key to raptor identification, but is also a good indication of its life-style. Buzzards sit patiently on fence posts waiting, shrike-like, for prey to appear. Harriers glide low over the ground, hoping to surprise unsuspecting birds or rodents. Hawks pick out their victim and dash in, using the cover of trees or buildings to escape detection. Typical falcons rise high in the air before diving out of the sun like a fighter plane.

A Peregrine (*illustrated on previous page and below, chasing a Redshank and Lapwing*) actually looks like a fighter plane, though it existed for thousands of years before human flight.

British birds of prey have suffered from persecution, poisoning by pesticides, and most recently as a result of the large sums of money that can be made by illegally taking young birds from the wild and selling them to falconers, especially in the Middle East. Yet they have survived and in some cases increased. The Osprey has returned to Scotland unaided, the White-tailed Eagle only with a lot of help from conservationists. The Red Kites of Wales are as numerous as any time this century and Sparrowhawks are becoming widespread again twenty years after being decimated by pesticides. Even the summer-visiting Hobby is becoming more numerous and widespread after suffering a century of merciless egg stealing.

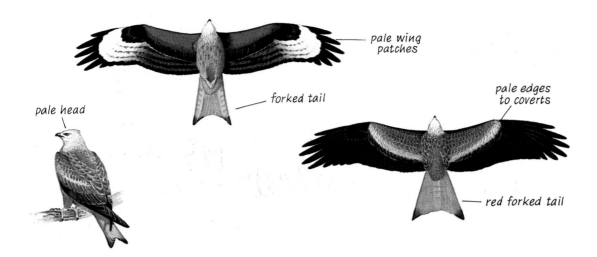

pale wing patches

pale head

forked tail

pale edges to coverts

red forked tail

RED KITE

Type	hawk-like
Size	58–64cm (22–25in)
Habitat	forests and woods
Behaviour	perches openly, takes off from vegetation and ground
Flocking	usually solitary
Flight	soars, glides; strong and powerful
Voice	repeated *he-he-heea*

IDENTIFICATION

Adult	
Crown	white
Upperparts	rufous
Rump	rufous
Tail	rufous; long and forked
Throat	white
Breast	rufous, streaked
Belly	rufous, streaked
Bill	yellow; hooked
Legs	yellow; medium length

BREEDING

Nest	twigs, plus rubbish in tree
Eggs	2–3; white, spotted red
Incubation	28–30 days ♀
Young	helpless; downy
Fledging	45–50 days
Broods	1; Mar–May
Food	mammals, birds, carrion
Population	variable, under 45 pairs

An uncommon, largely resident, bird of prey that is similar in size to the Buzzard, but which is far more angular and less bulky. In particular, the wings and tail are both longer and narrower. Both upperparts and underparts are rufous, though the head is pale, often almost white. In flight the upperwing is brown, with rufous coverts; the underwing brown, with prominent whitish patches on the outer wing. The rufous tail is deeply forked, almost translucent against the light, and is twisted from side to side as a rudder. Red Kites often hang on rising air over hillside updraughts.
Status: resident in central Wales and a scarce wanderer elsewhere in spring, autumn and winter, mainly in southern England.

Similar Species:
Black Kite *Milvus migrans*
53–59cm (21–23in)
A dark, brownish-grey raptor with the typical long wings and tail of a kite, but which is as likely to be confused with a young Marsh Harrier by inexperienced birders. The uniform dusky colouring is broken only by pale (not white) patches on the underwing and by similarly pale upper

wing coverts. Like those of the Red Kite, the wings are held bowed, but the tail is less forked and appears square-cut even when partially spread. Juveniles are more rufous and are more likely to be confused with Red Kites.
Range: breeds right across Europe to Eurasia, India and the Far East.
Migration: abandons most of its summer range to move southwards into Africa and tropical Asia, with huge concentrations at Gibraltar and the Bosphorus.
British Distribution: a rare visitor, mostly in spring, sometimes in autumn, mainly to south-eastern England and East Anglia.

Black Kite

obscure pale wing patches

palish wing coverts

slim "harrier" shape

shallow forked tail

J	F	M	A	M	J	J	A	S	O	N	D
2	2	2	2	2	2	2	2	2	2	2	2

White-tailed Eagle *Haliaeetus albicilla*

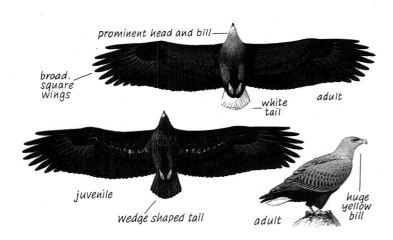

prominent head and bill

broad, square wings

white tail

adult

juvenile

wedge shaped tail

adult

huge yellow bill

Huge, bulky eagle with enormous broad wings and prominent head and bill. Adult mostly dark brown with pure white tail; large pale head with very large yellow bill. In flight, prominent head and bill and short white tail contrast with huge, square-cut dark wings. Juveniles share this shape, but have dark tails or only white centres to tail feathers, depending on age. Found by sea or near freshwater.
Status: exterminated as breeding bird in Scotland in 1916 but re-introduced to Rhum since 1975; first bred in 1985. Otherwise rare winter visitor.
Similar Species: immatures superficially similar to adult Golden Eagle (p.90); adult similar to immature Golden Eagle, which also has white tail but with black terminal band.

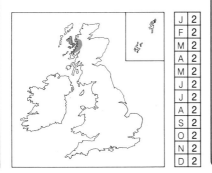

J	2
F	2
M	2
A	2
M	2
J	2
J	2
A	2
S	2
O	2
N	2
D	2

WHITE-TAILED EAGLE

Type	hawk-like
Size	69–91cm (27–36in)
Habitat	moors, sea
Behaviour	dives from air, perches openly, takes off from vegetation or ground
Flocking	usually solitary
Flight	soars, glides, aerial dive; strong and powerful
Voice	laughing *kok-kok-kok* while courting

IDENTIFICATION

Adult	
Crown	buff
Upperparts	dark brown
Rump	dark brown
Tail	white; short and rounded
Throat	dark brown
Breast	brown, streaked
Belly	brown
Bill	yellow; large and hooked
Legs	yellow; medium length
Juvenile	all brown but with white centres to tail feathers

BREEDING

Nest	huge mass of twigs on cliff or tree
Eggs	2; white
Incubation	34–45 days ♂ ♀
Young	helpless; downy
Fledging	70 days
Broods	1; Mar–May
Food	fish, carrion
Population	introduced Rhum, vagrant elsewhere

Golden Eagle *Aquila chrysaetos*

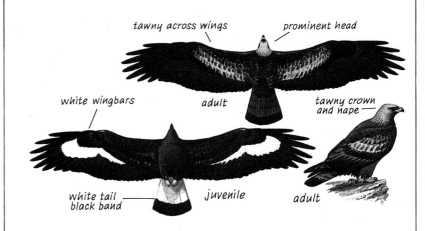

tawny across wings

prominent head

white wingbars

adult

tawny crown and nape

white tail black band

juvenile

adult

Large eagle of mountains and moorlands; virtually confined to Scotland. Adult dark brown with pale tawny crown and forewing. In flight, appears all dark from below. Juvenile has white tail with broad black terminal band and white base to outer primaries. From below, white tail less noticeable, but bold white line extends along all flight feathers. Flight powerful with deep wing beats; quarters hillsides like huge harrier. Long, broad wings held in shallow 'V' when soaring; dives on folded wings.
Status: sedentary in Scottish Highlands and Lake District.
Similar Species: White-tailed Eagle (p.90). Often confused with much smaller buzzards (p.94–95) but proportions of head, wings and tail quite different.

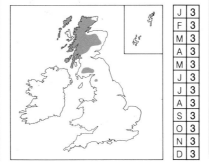

J	3
F	3
M	3
A	3
M	3
J	3
J	3
A	3
S	3
O	3
N	3
D	3

GOLDEN EAGLE

Type	hawk-like
Size	76–90cm (30–35in)
Habitat	moors and heaths, forests and woods
Behaviour	perches openly, takes off from vegetation or ground
Flocking	solitary
Flight	soars, glides; strong and powerful; laboured
Voice	yelping *kaa*; generally silent

IDENTIFICATION

Adult	
Crown	tawny-buff
Upperparts	brown
Rump	brown
Tail	brown; medium length, square
Throat	brown
Breast	brown
Belly	brown
Bill	yellow; hooked
Legs	yellow; medium length
Juvenile	brown with white wing flashes above and below; white tail with black band

BREEDING

Nest	massive structure of twigs on cliff or tree
Eggs	2; white, blotched brown
Incubation	43–45 days, usually ♀
Young	helpless; downy
Fledging	63–70 days
Broods	1; Feb–May
Food	small mammals, large birds
Population	250–300 pairs

Circus cyaneus **Hen Harrier**

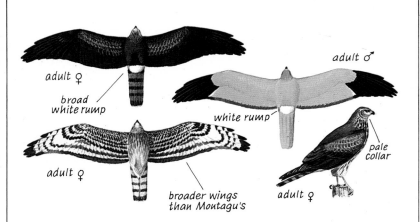

adult ♀

broad white rump

adult ♂

white rump

adult ♀

broader wings than Montagu's

adult ♀

pale collar

Circus aeruginosus **Marsh Harrier**

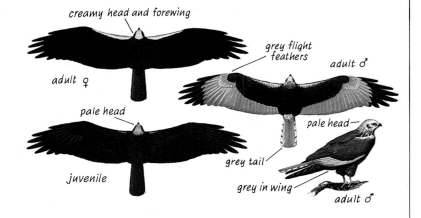

creamy head and forewing

adult ♀

grey flight feathers

adult ♂

pale head

juvenile

grey tail

grey in wing

pale head

adult ♂

Medium-sized harrier, between Montagu's and Marsh Harrier in size and bulk. Male pale grey above with white rump and black wingtips; breast grey, remaining underparts white. Female and juvenile brown above with bold white rump; streaked brown or buff below. Hunts low over moors and young conifer plantations in summer.
Status: scarce but increasing resident; breeds in hilly districts, more common in north than west. Regular passage migrant and winter visitor in small numbers, mainly to coasts (particularly east coast).
Similar Species: Montagu's Harrier (p.92). Females and juveniles especially similar – often jointly called 'ring-tail' harriers – though Hen Harrier bulkier, with larger white rump and paler head than breast.

HEN HARRIER	
Type	hawk-like
Size	43–51cm (17–20in)
Habitat	freshwater and marshes, moors and heaths, estuaries and shores
Behaviour	perches openly, takes off and lands on vegetation or ground
Flocking	1 or 2
Flight	hovers, soars, glides; laboured; undulating
Voice	mostly silent, cackles and squeals in courtship
IDENTIFICATION	
Adult ♂	
Crown	grey
Upperparts	grey
Rump	white
Tail	grey; long and square
Throat	grey
Breast	grey
Belly	white
Bill	black; hooked
Legs	yellow; medium length
Ad. ♀ and juv.	all brown with white rump, streaked below
BREEDING	
Nest	platform of sticks and twigs hidden in low vegetation
Eggs	4–6; pale blue
Incubation	29–39 days ♀
Young	helpless; downy
Fledging	37 days
Broods	1; Apr–June
Food	small birds and mammals
Population	500–600 pairs; ? winter

Largest of the harriers with typical slow, flap-and-glide flight creating lumbering appearance. Long wings, long tail and gliding flight near ground with wings held in 'V' identify as a harrier. Male brown with pale buff head and forewing edges. In flight, grey tail and large grey area on inner wing contrasts with dark wingtips and brown wing coverts. Female all brown with creamy head and forewing. Juveniles all brown with creamy head, similar to female. Found mostly over large reedbeds and marshes.
Status: rare breeder, mostly in East Anglia; scarce passage migrant and winter visitor, mostly east coasts.
Similar Species: Hen Harrier (p.91) and Montagu's Harrier (p.92). Marsh Harrier is bulkier and broader-winged than other harriers.

MARSH-HARRIER	
Type	hawk-like
Size	48–56cm (19–22in)
Habitat	freshwater marshes, moors, heaths, estuaries, shores
Behaviour	perches openly, takes off from vegetation or ground
Flocking	1 or 2
Flight	hovers, soars, glides; laboured; undulating
Voice	high-pitched *kee-a* in courtship
IDENTIFICATION	
Adult ♂	
Crown	buff
Upperparts	brown, dark wingtips
Rump	brown
Tail	grey; long and square
Throat	buff
Breast	brown, streaked
Belly	brown
Bill	black; hooked
Legs	yellow; medium length
Adult ♀	all brown with creamy head and forewing
Juvenile	all brown or similar to female
BREEDING	
Nest	platform of reeds in large reedbed
Eggs	4–5; blue-white
Incubation	33–38 days ♀
Young	helpless; downy
Fledging	35–40 days
Broods	1; Apr–May
Food	birds, eggs, small mammals, carrion
Population	32 pairs; ? winter

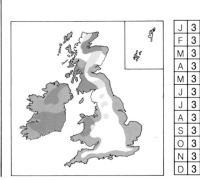

J	3
F	3
M	3
A	3
M	3
J	3
J	3
A	3
S	3
O	3
N	3
D	3

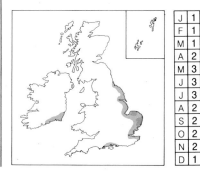

J	1
F	1
M	1
A	2
M	3
J	3
J	3
A	2
S	2
O	2
N	2
D	1

Montagu's Harrier *Circus pygargus*

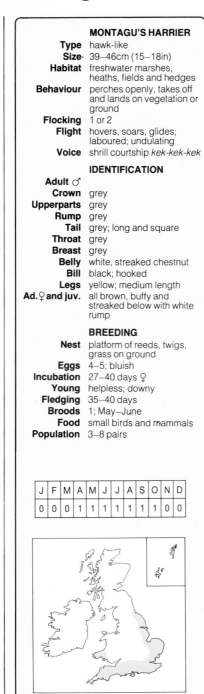

MONTAGU'S HARRIER	
Type	hawk-like
Size	39–46cm (15–18in)
Habitat	freshwater marshes, heaths, fields and hedges
Behaviour	perches openly, takes off and lands on vegetation or ground
Flocking	1 or 2
Flight	hovers, soars, glides; laboured; undulating
Voice	shrill courtship *kek-kek-kek*

IDENTIFICATION

Adult ♂	
Crown	grey
Upperparts	grey
Rump	grey
Tail	grey; long and square
Throat	grey
Breast	grey
Belly	white, streaked chestnut
Bill	black; hooked
Legs	yellow; medium length
Ad. ♀ and juv.	all brown, buffy and streaked below with white rump

BREEDING

Nest	platform of reeds, twigs, grass on ground
Eggs	4–5; bluish
Incubation	27–40 days ♀
Young	helpless; downy
Fledging	35–40 days
Broods	1; May–June
Food	small birds and mammals
Population	3–8 pairs

J	F	M	A	M	J	J	A	S	O	N	D
0	0	0	1	1	1	1	1	1	1	0	0

dark line across wings

adult ♂

dark cheek crescent

adult ♀

adult ♀

narrow white rump

no white rump

adult ♀

narrow wings

Generally smaller and slimmer than the otherwise similar Hen Harrier and much less common. The male is pale grey above, with black wingtips and a narrow black line across the upperwing. The underwing is marked by several lines of bars. The tail and rump are grey, with no more than a hint of white on the rump. The white underparts are streaked chestnut. The female, like the female Hen Harrier, is heavily streaked brown, buff and black, but is more lightly built with a narrower white rump. Juveniles are more uniformly rufous below.
Status: a scarce spring and autumn passage migrant and rare summer visitor to England, Wales and southern Ireland.

Similar Species:
Pallid Harrier *Circus macrourus*
41–48cm (16–19in)
Generally confusable more with the lightly structured Montagu's than the more bulky Hen Harrier. Male is even more lightly built than Montagu's and a much paler grey above; the flight is more buoyant and graceful. It lacks chestnut streaking on breast and the black wingtips form a pointed wedge rather than a square-cut tip. The female and juvenile are much more difficult

to separate from the female Montagu's, but both show a black eye stripe and a dark crescent on the ear coverts backed by a pale collar. These apparently obscure points create a distinctive head pattern, whether the bird is on the ground or in the air.
Range: breeds from north-eastern Romania across the southern Soviet Union.
Migration: occasionally erupts to western Europe, but usually moves southward through south-eastern Europe to Africa, and also to India and Burma.
British Distribution: an exceptionally rare straggler in spring and autumn.
Other Similar Species: Hen Harrier (p. 91).

Pallid Harrier

"diamond shaped" wingtips

very pale grey

narrow white rump

adult ♀

adult ♂

distinctive face pattern

adult ♀

adult ♀

Accipiter gentilis Goshawk

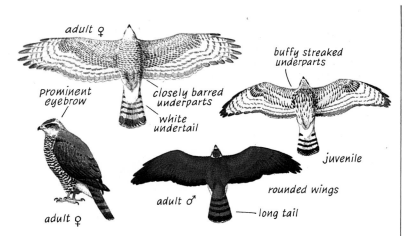

adult ♀

prominent eyebrow

closely barred underparts

white undertail

buffy streaked underparts

juvenile

adult ♂

rounded wings

long tail

adult ♀

Like large Sparrowhawk with rounded wings and long, banded tail. Adult brownish grey with darker cap and bold white eyebrow. Closely barred pale grey below, with particularly prominent white undertail coverts. Female about Buzzard-sized; much larger than male, which is only a little larger than female Sparrowhawk. Juvenile browner; streaked below. Dives and soars in spectacular display, often with white undertail coverts spread. Hunts like Sparrowhawk. *Status:* scarce but increasing resident in parts of England and Scotland following escape from falconry in 1960s. Rare passage migrant. *Similar Species:* Sparrowhawk (p.93); Goshawk is larger, bulkier and has slower wing beats.

GOSHAWK

Type	hawk-like
Size	48–58cm (19–23in)
Habitat	forests and woods, fields and hedgerows
Behaviour	perches openly, takes off from vegetation or ground
Flocking	solitary
Flight	soars, glides, aerial dive; strong and powerful; direct
Voice	chattering *gek-gek-gek*

IDENTIFICATION

Adult	
Crown	grey, dark cap
Upperparts	brownish grey
Rump	grey
Tail	grey; long and square
Throat	white
Breast	white, barred grey
Belly	white, barred grey
Bill	black; hooked
Legs	yellow; medium length
Juvenile	browner; streaked below where adult finely barred

BREEDING

Nest	twigs in tree
Eggs	2–3; pale blue
Incubation	36–41 days ♀
Young	helpless; downy
Fledging	45 days
Broods	1; Apr–June
Food	birds and mammals
Population	23–41 pairs

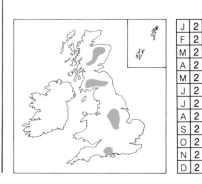

J	2
F	2
M	2
A	2
M	2
J	2
J	2
A	2
S	2
O	2
N	2
D	2

Accipiter nisus Sparrowhawk

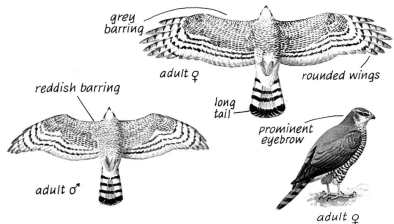

grey barring

adult ♀

rounded wings

reddish barring

long tail

prominent eyebrow

adult ♂

adult ♀

Fast-flying, agile hawk of woodlands and fields. Grey or grey-brown above, with clear, pale eyebrow in female. Male barred russet below; female barred grey. Both have long tails with at least four distinct bars showing. Dashing flight in pursuit of small birds makes confusion with Kestrel impossible. When soaring or travelling, shape is similar but Sparrowhawk flaps rounded wings quickly for a few beats before gliding. *Status:* widespread; increasing after 1960s pesticide disaster. *Similar Species:* Kestrel (p.96) has longer, more pointed wings and often hovers in flight. Goshawk (p.93) is larger and more bulky, although large female Sparrowhawk may be confused with small male Goshawk.

SPARROWHAWK

Type	hawk-like
Size	28–38cm (11–15in)
Habitat	forests and woods, fields and hedgerows, heaths
Behaviour	perches openly, takes off and lands on vegetation or ground
Flocking	solitary
Flight	soars, glides, aerial dive; strong and powerful; direct
Voice	loud *kek-kek-kek*

IDENTIFICATION

Adult ♂	
Crown	grey
Upperparts	grey or grey-brown
Rump	grey
Tail	grey and white, banded; long and square
Throat	white
Breast	whitish, reddish barring
Belly	whitish, reddish barring
Bill	black; hooked
Legs	yellow; medium length
Adult ♀	larger than ♂, brown above, pale eyebrow; heavily barred grey below

BREEDING

Nest	twigs in trees
Eggs	4–5; white, blotched dark brown
Incubation	42 days ♀
Young	helpless; downy
Fledging	32 days
Broods	1; Apr–June
Food	small birds
Population	15,000–20,000 pairs

J	4
F	4
M	4
A	4
M	4
J	4
J	4
A	4
S	4
O	4
N	4
D	4

Buzzard *Buteo buteo*

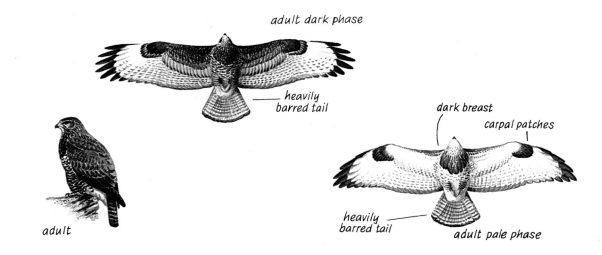

adult dark phase

heavily barred tail

dark breast

carpal patches

heavily barred tail

adult pale phase

BUZZARD

Type	hawk-like
Size	50–56cm (20–22in)
Habitat	moors and heaths, forests and woods, fields and hedgerows
Behaviour	perches openly, takes off and lands on vegetation or ground
Flocking	1; small soaring groups
Flight	soars, glides; laboured
Voice	mewing *pee-oo*

IDENTIFICATION

Ad.dark	
Crown	brown
Upperparts	brown
Rump	brown
Tail	brown, barred;short and square
Throat	brown
Breast	buff, dark patches on sides
Belly	brown
Bill	black; hooked
Legs	yellow; medium length
Ad.pale	variable, often almost white below, especially in flight

BREEDING

Nest	bulky sticks and twigs in tree, on cliff, rock outcrop, occasionally ground
Eggs	3–4; white, blotched reddish
Incubation	42 days, mainly ♀
Young	helpless; downy
Fledging	40–45 days
Broods	1; Mar–May
Food	small mammals
Population	8000–10,000 pairs

J	F	M	A	M	J	J	A	S	O	N	D
4	4	4	4	4	4	4	4	4	4	4	4

adult

This is the most common of our larger raptors. It prefers woods with open fields, but is also found on heathland and moors, especially in hilly districts. In France it is called *Buse Variable*, or 'Variable Buzzard', an apt name that draws attention to the extreme variations in plumage pattern exhibited by this bird. All birds of prey are best identified by structure rather than plumage characters, and none more so than the Buzzard. Pale-phase birds typically have white underwings marked by dark wingtips and dark carpal patches. The tail is usually heavily barred and the breast is dark, terminating in a more or less clear-cut band. Dark-phase birds additionally have the underwing coverts dark and are more or less completely dark on the body.

The Buzzard soars on broad wings held forward in a shallow 'V'. The head is small and the tail short. If a medium-sized raptor shows these characteristics and has dark carpals and a dark breast, it is a Buzzard.

Buzzards are so variable that uniformly dark birds may also be found, as well as birds that are almost pure white. White-breasted, white-tailed birds are startling in their appearance. In some plumages the Buzzard may even appear

white below with a smudgy brown breast and a white tail with a dark band – all features that are generally typical of the Rough-legged Buzzard. Remember the French name and be wary.

Status: a common resident of the hilly districts of the north of Ireland and the west of Britain. In the south it occurs as far east as Hampshire and is only a migrant or winter visitor elsewhere.

Other Similar Species: Rough-legged Buzzard and Honey Buzzard (p. 95).

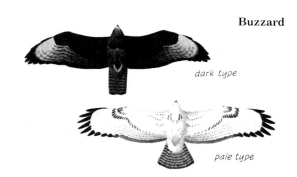

Buzzard

dark type

pale type

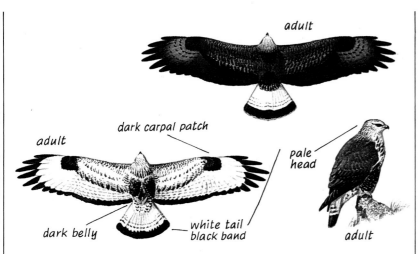

adult

adult

dark carpal patch

pale head

dark belly

white tail black band

adult

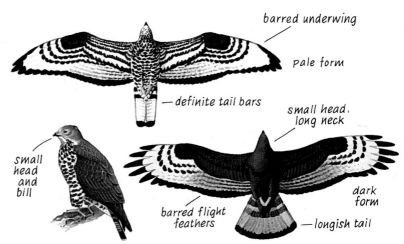

barred underwing

pale form

definite tail bars

small head, long neck

small head and bill

barred flight feathers

dark form

longish tail

Similar to Buzzard, but with less variable plumage pattern. Flight feathers always very pale, mostly white with a few indistinct bars. Underwing coverts vary from brown to white; carpal patch always black and prominent. Tail white with broad black sub-terminal band and up to four narrow, less distinct, bars towards tip. Dark belly or flank patches more obvious than Buzzard. Always pale headed. Soars on flat wings and frequently hangs on wind or hovers. *Status:* scarce winter visitor, mainly to east coasts; numbers vary from year to year.
Similar Species: Buzzard (p.94) and see above.

ROUGH-LEGGED BUZZARD

Type	hawk-like
Size	50–61cm (20–24in)
Habitat	freshwater marshes, moors, estuaries
Behaviour	perches openly, takes off and lands on vegetation or ground
Flocking	1–4
Flight	hovers, soars, glides; laboured
Voice	mostly silent

IDENTIFICATION

Adult	
Crown	white
Upperparts	brown
Rump	brown
Tail	white with black band and narrow bars near tip; medium length, square
Throat	buff
Breast	white, streaked brown
Belly	brown, blackish patches on sides
Bill	black; hooked
Legs	yellow; medium length

BREEDING

Nest	twigs on rock outcrop
Eggs	2–3; white, blotched
Incubation	28 days, mainly ♀
Young	helpless; downy
Fledging	40–42 days
Broods	1; May–June
Food	small mammals
Population	variable; ? winter

Rare summer visitor to large areas of woodland in southern England. Slimmer and more angular than similar Buzzard. Small head, thin neck and waisted, 'wasp-like' wings. Tail longer than Buzzard; wings droop when soaring. Plumage highly variable but carpals always dark and underwing has regularly spaced barring. Tail with terminal band and two other similar bands. Unique 'butterfly-like' display flight of male involves holding wings high above back and fluttering before diving. *Status:* very scarce summer visitor and passage migrant.
Similar Species: Buzzard (p.94).

HONEY BUZZARD

Type	hawk-like
Size	50–58cm (20–23in)
Habitat	forests and woods
Behaviour	takes off and lands on vegetation and ground
Flocking	usually solitary
Flight	soars, glides; strong and powerful
Voice	high-pitched *kee-a*

IDENTIFICATION

Adult	
Crown	brown
Upperparts	brown
Rump	brown
Tail	buff with brown bands; longish and square
Throat	white
Breast	brown, buff and brown barred or white
Belly	varies (as breast)
Bill	brown; hooked
Legs	yellow; medium length

BREEDING

Nest	sticks high in tree
Eggs	1–3; white, speckled reddish
Incubation	30–35 days, mainly ♀
Young	helpless; downy
Fledging	40–44 days
Broods	1; June
Food	larvae and adult wasps and bees; also amphibians, birds
Population	10–14 pairs

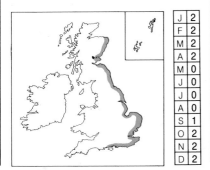

J	2
F	2
M	2
A	2
M	0
J	0
J	0
A	0
S	1
O	2
N	2
D	2

J	0
F	0
M	0
A	0
M	2
J	2
J	2
A	2
S	2
O	1
N	0
D	0

Kestrel *Falco tinnunculus*

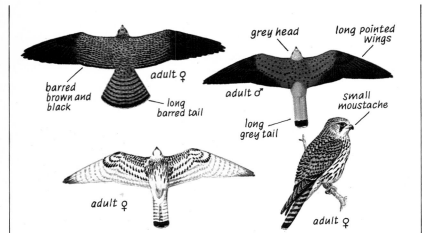

barred brown and black

adult ♀

long barred tail

grey head

long pointed wings

adult ♂

long grey tail

small moustache

adult ♀

adult ♀

Most common raptor frequenting farmland, moors, parks, heaths, coastlines, marshes and city-centres. Often seen hovering, especially over motorway verges. Male has grey head with thin black moustachial streak; grey tail with broad black sub-terminal band. Upperparts rufous brown spotted black with dark brown flight feathers. Underparts tawny with spotted streaks; underwing pale. Female all brown above with dark streaking on head, heavily barred back, and multiple dark tail bands. In flight, long tail and shallow beats of long, pointed wings distinctive.
Status: common and widespread resident.
Similar Species: Sparrowhawk (p.93) has rounded wings and distinctive flight.

J	5
F	5
M	5
A	5
M	5
J	5
J	5
A	5
S	5
O	5
N	5
D	5

KESTREL

Type	hawk-like
Size	33–36cm (13–14in)
Habitat	towns, marshes, moors, heaths, cliffs, forests, fields
Behaviour	perches openly, takes off and lands on vegetation or ground
Flocking	solitary
Flight	hovers, soars, aerial dive; strong and powerful; direct
Voice	high-pitched *kee-kee-kee*

IDENTIFICATION

Adult ♂	
Crown	grey
Upperparts	brown, spotted black
Rump	grey
Tail	grey, black terminal band; long and square
Throat	buff
Breast	buff, spotted black
Belly	buff, streaked on flanks
Bill	black; hooked
Legs	yellow; long
Ad.♀ and juv.	browner, heavily barred back; lacks grey on head and tail

BREEDING

Nest	bare ledge or hole
Eggs	4–5; white, heavily speckled brown
Incubation	27–29 days, mainly ♀
Young	helpless; downy
Fledging	27–39 days
Broods	1; Apr–June
Food	small mammals and birds
Population	c 100,000 pairs

Merlin *Falco columbarius*

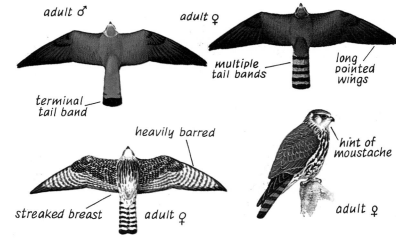

adult ♂

adult ♀

multiple tail bands

long pointed wings

terminal tail band

heavily barred

hint of moustache

streaked breast

adult ♀

adult ♀

Small, dark, fast-flying falcon of hills and moors; haunts coastlines and adjacent marshes in winter. Male smaller; blue-grey above with dark terminal band on tail. Female brown with multiple-barred buff and brown tail. Both sexes heavily streaked below and heavily barred across underwing. Flies low and fast in pursuit of smaller birds.
Status: resident in hilly districts of north and west, but nowhere common. Winter visitor elsewhere, mostly to coasts.
Similar Species: Hobby (p.97), a summer visitor, is also dark but with prominent white sides to neck and clear-cut, dark moustache; wings are longer, narrower and more angular.

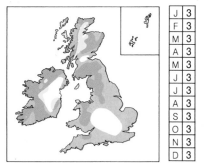

J	3
F	3
M	3
A	3
M	3
J	3
J	3
A	3
S	3
O	3
N	3
D	3

MERLIN

Type	hawk-like
Size	27–32cm (10–13in)
Habitat	moors, estuaries, freshwater marshes
Behaviour	perches openly, takes off and lands on vegetation or ground
Flocking	solitary
Flight	soars, glides, aerial dive; strong and powerful; direct
Voice	chattering *kee-kee-kee*

IDENTIFICATION

Adult ♂	
Crown	blue-grey
Upperparts	blue-grey
Rump	blue-grey
Tail	blue, dark terminal band
Throat	buff
Breast	buff, heavy blackish streaks
Belly	buff, heavy blackish streaks
Bill	yellow; hooked
Legs	yellow; short
Ad.♀ and juv.	brown above, heavily barred and streaked below

BREEDING

Nest	hollow on ground
Eggs	5–6; buff, heavily spotted reddish
Incubation	28–32 days, mainly ♀
Young	helpless; downy
Fledging	25–30 days
Broods	1; Apr–May
Food	small birds
Population	600–800 pairs

white half collar

'Swift-like' pointed wings

adult

juvenile

no red undertail

almost complete white collar

adult

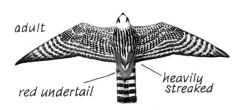

adult

red undertail

heavily streaked

Though it is similar to the more abundant Kestrel, its wings are longer and narrower, more Swift-like, and the tail slightly shorter. The upperparts are slate-grey, though there is an almost complete white 'neck ring' or 'collar' marked by prominent black 'moustaches'. The underparts are heavily streaked black on a white background, the underwing heavily barred. The undertail coverts are rust-red. Juveniles are dark brown above, streaked below, but lack the rufous undertail.
Status: a scarce, but increasing, summer visitor to south and central England; a scarce spring and autumn passage migrant elsewhere.

Similar Species:
Red-footed Falcon *Falco vespertinus*
28–31cm (11–12in)
Smaller than the Hobby, though of similar proportions, but with a longer tail. This is a gregarious little falcon that breeds in colonies and usually migrates in small to medium-sized groups. It perches openly like a shrike, often on telegraph wires, but also hovers like a Kestrel. The adult male is uniformly dark blue-grey marked by rufous undertail coverts and bright red eye rings,

legs and cere. The female is grey with darker barring on upperparts, tail and underwing. Her underparts and wing linings are a warm buff. Her head is paler and marked by dark eye-patches and 'moustaches'. There is a pale orange eye-ring. Juveniles are similar to females, but with considerably more streaking.
Range: breeds from east central Europe eastwards across Siberia to China.
Migration: the whole population moves westwards to winter in savannah Africa.
British Distribution: an annual, but rare, visitor to south and east England, mainly in late spring; sometimes in small parties.
Other Similar Species: Merlin, Kestrel (p. 96).

Red-footed Falcon

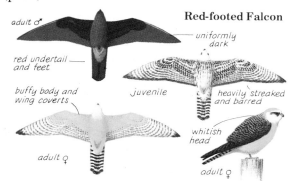

adult ♂

red undertail and feet

buffy body and wing coverts

uniformly dark

juvenile

heavily streaked and barred

whitish head

adult ♀

adult ♀

J	F	M	A	M	J	J	A	S	O	N	D
0	0	0	3	3	3	3	3	3	3	1	0	0

HOBBY	
Type	hawk-like
Size	30–36cm (12–14in)
Habitat	heaths, fields and hedges
Behaviour	perches openly, takes off and lands on vegetation
Flocking	1 or 2
Flight	soars, glides, aerial dive; strong and powerful; direct
Voice	*kew-kew* repeated; also high-pitched *ki-ki-ki*

IDENTIFICATION

Adult	
Crown	black
Upperparts	slate-grey, white 'neck ring' and black moustache
Rump	grey
Tail	grey, undertail coverts rust-red; medium length, square
Throat	white
Breast	buff, heavily streaked
Belly	buff, heavily streaked
Bill	yellow; hooked
Legs	yellow; short
Juvenile	dark brown above; lacks red undertail

BREEDING

Nest	old nest of other species in tree
Eggs	2–3; yellowish, speckled reddish
Incubation	28 days, mainly ♀
Young	helpless; downy
Fledging	28–32 days
Broods	1; May–June
Food	insects, small birds
Population	100–200 pairs

97

Peregrine *Falco peregrinus*

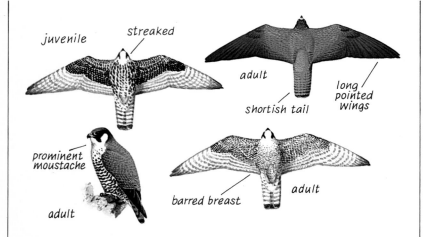

juvenile — streaked

adult

shortish tail — long pointed wings

prominent moustache

adult

barred breast — adult

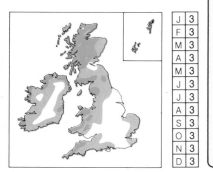

Large, robust falcon with shortish tail and long, angular wings. Flies with deep sweeps of long, pointed wings producing impression of immense speed and power. Upperparts slate-grey with paler rump and delicately barred tail. White face and sides of neck with bold black moustaches. Underparts and underwing finely barred. Juvenile brown above with heavily streaked body. Haunts cliffs, both coastal and inland; in winter also frequents estuaries where rests on ground or small hummock.
Status: scarce resident in hilly and coastal districts of north and west; elsewhere scarce winter visitor.
Similar Species: no other large falcons.

PEREGRINE

Type	hawk-like
Size	38–48cm (15–19in)
Habitat	moors, sea-cliffs, estuaries and shores
Behaviour	perches openly, takes off and lands on ground
Flocking	solitary
Flight	soars, glides, aerial stoop; strong and powerful; direct
Voice	loud *kek-kek-kek*; repeated *wee-chew*

IDENTIFICATION

Adult	
Crown	slate-grey
Upperparts	slate-grey, white face and sides of neck; prominent black moustache
Rump	grey
Tail	grey; shortish and square
Throat	white
Breast	white, barred black
Belly	white, barred black
Bill	yellow; hooked
Legs	yellow; short
Juvenile	brown above; heavily streaked

BREEDING

Nest	bare scrape on cliff
Eggs	3–4; buff, speckled red
Incubation	28–29 days, mainly ♀
Young	helpless; downy
Fledging	35–42 days
Broods	1; Apr–June
Food	birds
Population	less than 1000 pairs

J	3
F	3
M	3
A	3
M	3
J	3
J	3
A	3
S	3
O	3
N	3
D	3

Osprey *Pandion haliaetus*

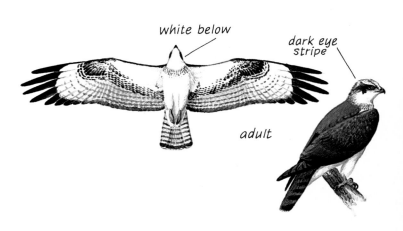

white below — dark eye stripe

adult

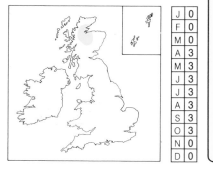

adult

Large, pale raptor, sometimes mistaken for large gull. Upperparts dark brown and grey; underparts white with black carpal patches, wingtips and wingbar. Flies gull-like on bowed wings. Head and nape white with prominent black eye stripe. Small head and long neck apparent at all times. Catches fish in spectacular feet-first dive; often after hovering high overhead. Found in lakes in forested areas in summer; reservoirs and other large waters at other times. Hunts in sea abroad.
Status: recolonised in 1955 after lengthy absence. Scarce (but spreading) summer visitor to Highlands of Scotland; elsewhere increasing passage migrant.
Similar Species: none.

OSPREY

Type	hawk-like
Size	51–59cm (20–23in)
Habitat	freshwater, sea, estuaries, forests and woods
Behaviour	perches openly; dives from air; takes off and lands on vegetation, ground, or water
Flocking	solitary
Flight	hovers, soars, glides, aerial dive; strong and powerful; direct
Voice	whistling *chew-chew*

IDENTIFICATION

Adult	
Crown	white
Upperparts	brown and grey
Rump	brown
Tail	brown; medium length, square
Throat	white
Breast	white, faint brown band
Belly	white
Bill	black; hooked
Legs	grey; medium length

BREEDING

Nest	mass of sticks in tree
Eggs	3; creamy, blotched reddish
Incubation	35–38 days ♂ ♀
Young	helpless, downy
Fledging	51–59 days
Broods	1; Mar–June
Food	fish
Population	27 pairs

J	0
F	0
M	0
A	3
M	3
J	3
J	3
A	3
S	3
O	0
N	0
D	0

This is a group of strong-legged, mostly walking birds that includes the partridges, pheasants, grouse and the more aquatic rails and crakes. Some of the latter, notably the Coot and Moorhen, have taken to a waterborne existence. They are generally poor flyers with rounded wings to give a short fast getaway, rather than prolonged economical flight. One of the gamebirds, the Quail, has, however, developed long pointed wings like a wader and is a long-distance migrant. Several of the rails, too, make long journeys and Coots migrate to winter with us.

As their name implies, gamebirds are a prime quarry of the sportsman, and the influence of shooting on their numbers is a major influence on the British landscape. Specially planted coverts are widespread throughout lowland Britain, offering perfect opportunities for introduced pheasants to breed. Even so, most of these 'wild' populations are augmented each season by hand-reared birds released a few weeks prior to the shooting season.

The place of the pheasants is occupied in Scotland and northern Britain by the Red Grouse, and huge areas of hillside are managed to produce the maximum amount of food for these birds. Shooting on 'The Glorious Twelfth' (of August) is one of the most expensive sports in the world. Other grouse are largely left in peace, but like the Black Grouse (*illustrated*) are confined to the hilly regions of the country.

Grey Partridges are highly prized too, but their numbers are dwindling, mainly due to changing agricultural techniques and a climate that has produced a series of wet springs.

Among the crakes and rails, only the Coot and Moorhen are widespread and numerous. Both are highly adaptable and very successful in exploiting man-made opportunities. In sharp contrast, the Water Rail is confined to the ever-decreasing reed and marsh areas and is badly hit when its wetland habitat freezes up in hard winters. It is the only European rail with a long bill and is generally well adapted to a life among dense vegetation.

Another inhabitant of dense aquatic vegetation, the Spotted Crake is only a rare summer visitor that is seldom seen. Its peculiar 'dripping tap' call, uttered late on summer evenings, is the only evidence many birders ever have of this most elusive of birds. It probably breeds every year, but seldom in the same place in consecutive seasons.

Closely related to the Spotted Crake, but adapted to dry land, the Corncrake has been a victim of changing agricultural practices. Harrowing, spraying and especially early harvesting have largely wiped out the lowland populations, leaving this once abundant bird to find a stronghold only in the north and west. Today, Ireland and the Outer Hebrides are almost the only areas where its call remains a summer sound.

Lagopus lagopus **Red Grouse**

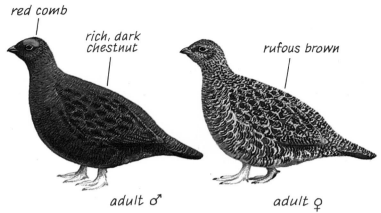

red comb

rich, dark chestnut

adult ♂

rufous brown

adult ♀

The grouse of grouse-moor fame; widespread resident of hilly, heather-clad regions. Sub-species of Willow Grouse, which is widespread in northern hemisphere. Most numerous in northern Britain where moorland is managed to suit its needs. Both sexes dark reddish brown, heavily spotted and barred black. Male considerably darker than female, with bolder red comb above eye. Generally seen when flushed from heather; flies away strongly before gliding back to cover on bowed wings. In early morning, often seen along moorland roads collecting grit. Colour and dumpy, rotund shape identify.
Status: largely confined to moorland of north and west Britain and Ireland.
Similar Species: Ptarmigan (p.101) is much scarcer and less widespread.

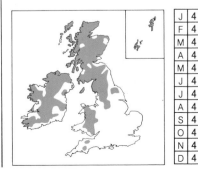

RED GROUSE	
Type	partridge-like
Size	33–39cm (13–19in)
Habitat	moors
Behaviour	walks, takes off and lands on ground
Flocking	1–15
Flight	glides; strong and powerful; direct
Voice	characteristic *go-back, go-back, go-back, back-back-back*
IDENTIFICATION	
Adult ♂	
Crown	red-brown, barred black
Upperparts	red-brown, barred black
Rump	red-brown, barred black
Tail	red-brown, barred black
Throat	red-brown, barred black
Breast	red-brown, barred black
Belly	red-brown, barred black
Bill	grey; short and stubby
Legs	white; short
Adult ♀	paler, reduced red comb
BREEDING	
Nest	hollow on ground
Eggs	6–11; yellowish, blotched dark brown
Incubation	20–26 days
Young	active; downy
Fledging	12–13 days
Broods	1; May–June
Food	heather
Population	less than 500,000 pairs

J	4
F	4
M	4
A	4
M	4
J	4
J	4
A	4
S	4
O	4
N	4
D	4

Lagopus mutus **Ptarmigan**

red comb

greyish-brown

dark lores

adult ♀ winter

adult ♂ summer

white belly

white wing

adult ♂ winter

Close relative of Red Grouse that lives at higher altitudes but is similarly resident and unknown away from breeding grounds. Mottled greys and browns camouflage against scant vegetation and broken rocks of high mountain tops. In winter, whole plumage white; in summer, only wingtips white. Even intermediate white and grey patchy birds difficult to see. Male has prominent red comb in summer; black mark between bill and eye in winter.
Status: scarce resident of mountain tops of Scottish Highlands.
Similar Species: in summer, Red Grouse (p.101) but Ptarmigan paler, in shades of grey-brown rather than russet. Slightly smaller than Red Grouse.

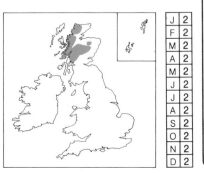

PTARMIGAN	
Type	partridge-like
Size	33–36cm (13–14in)
Habitat	moors
Behaviour	walks, perches openly, takes off and lands on ground
Flocking	1–15
Flight	glides; strong and powerful; direct
Voice	cackling *aar-aar-ka-ka-ka*
IDENTIFICATION	
Ad.♂summer	
Crown	grey-brown
Upperparts	grey-brown, barred black; white wingtips
Rump	grey-brown
Tail	black; short and rounded
Throat	grey-brown
Breast	grey-brown, barred black
Belly	white
Bill	black; short and stubby
Legs	white; short
Ad.♀summer	mottled brown and buff; underparts less white than ♂
Ad.winter	all white; ♂ dark area between bill and eye
BREEDING	
Nest	bare hollow on ground
Eggs	5–10; white, blotched dark brown
Incubation	24–26 days ♀
Young	active; downy
Fledging	10 days
Broods	1; May–June
Food	shoots, berries
Population	less than 10,000 pairs

J	2
F	2
M	2
A	2
M	2
J	2
J	2
A	2
S	2
O	2
N	2
D	2

Black Grouse *Tetrao tetrix*

red comb

dark, barred breast

white in wing

adult ♀

adult ♂

white undertail

lyre-shaped tail

notched tail

Large grouse of woodland margins and birch scrub, best seen at communal lekking grounds in early morning or evening. Generally gregarious, forming small flocks and family groups. Sexes quite distinct. Male (Blackcock) predominantly black, with longish lyre-shaped tail, erected in display to show bold white undertail. Large red comb above eye, bold white wingbar in flight. Female (Greyhen) heavily barred brown and black above, black and buff below. Longish tail shows distinct notch in flight.
Status: resident of moorlands in northern and western Britain; absent Ireland.
Similar Species: Capercaillie (p.102) is larger, has white bill and tail is a different shape.

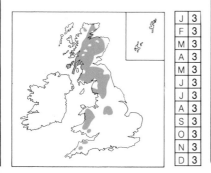

	BLACK GROUSE	
Type	partridge-like	
Size	♂ 51–56cm (20–22in); ♀ 40–44cm (15–17in)	
Habitat	moors, fields and hedgerows, forests	
Behaviour	walks, takes off and lands on ground	
Flocking	1–15	
Flight	glides; strong and powerful; direct	
Voice	roo-koo repeated at lek; a sneezed *chew-oosh*	
	IDENTIFICATION	
Adult ♂		
Crown	black	
Upperparts	black, white wingbar	
Rump	black	
Tail	black, undertail white; long and forked	
Throat	black	
Breast	black	
Belly	black and white	
Bill	black; short and stubby	
Legs	black; short	
Adult ♀	mottled brown and black above, black and buff below; notched tail	
Juvenile	like small, dull ♀	
	BREEDING	
Nest	hollow on ground	
Eggs	6–10; buffy, spotted brown	
Incubation	23–26 days ♀	
Young	active; downy	
Fledging	4 weeks	
Broods	1; May–June	
Food	shoots, berries	
Population	10,000–50,000 pairs	

J	3
F	3
M	3
A	3
M	3
J	3
J	3
A	3
S	3
O	3
N	3
D	3

Capercaillie *Tetrao urogallus*

white bill

red comb

orange breast

adult ♀

ragged beard

square tail

adult ♂

huge, wedge-shaped tail

Largest of the grouse; huge male reminiscent of Turkey. Native birds shot out of existence in eighteenth century but successfully re-introduced in nineteenth. Male black with brown back and wings; long tail spread and raised to form fan in display. Large head with ragged 'beard'; red wattle above eye; fearsome white bill. Highly aggressive, will even attack human intruders. Female smaller and camouflaged in barred shades of brown with distinctive orange breast. Confined to conifer forests.
Status: resident in Scottish Highland forests; unknown elsewhere.
Similar Species: smaller Black Grouse (p.102) has lyre-shaped tail in male; female lacks orange breast.

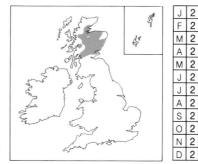

	CAPERCAILLIE	
Type	partridge-like	
Size	♂ 82–90cm (32–35in); ♀ 58–64cm (22–25in)	
Habitat	forests and woods	
Behaviour	walks, perches openly, takes off and lands on vegetation and ground	
Flocking	1–10	
Flight	glides; strong and powerful; direct	
Voice	crowing ko-ko-kok; series of clicks ending in pop	
	IDENTIFICATION	
Adult ♂		
Crown	black	
Upperparts	brown	
Rump	black	
Tail	black; long and rounded	
Throat	black	
Breast	black	
Belly	black; spotted white	
Bill	white; short and stubby	
Legs	grey; medium length	
Adult ♀	smaller; buff and brown with orange breast	
	BREEDING	
Nest	lined depression on ground	
Eggs	5–8; buff, blotched reddish	
Incubation	26–29 days ♀	
Young	active; downy	
Fledging	2–3 weeks	
Broods	1; Apr–June	
Food	shoots, berries, conifer needles	
Population	1000–10,000 pairs	

J	2
F	2
M	2
A	2
M	2
J	2
J	2
A	2
S	2
O	2
N	2
D	2

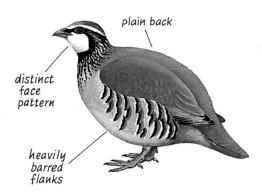

plain back

distinct
face
pattern

heavily
barred
flanks

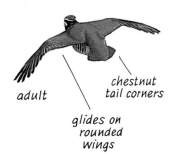

adult

chestnut
tail corners

glides on
rounded
wings

This stocky gamebird was introduced from the Continent from 200 years ago and has since spread over much of southern England and eastern Wales. Isolated populations further north into Scotland are the result of more recent introductions. The Red-legged Partridge is easily distinguished from our native Grey Partridge by its distinctive black and white face pattern, which consists of a black eye-stripe extending over the ear coverts and neck to join a broad, speckled breast band. This pattern encloses a creamy-white chin and throat. The flanks are pale blue, closely barred with chestnut, black and white. Like other partridges, it frequents open fields and prefers to run for cover rather than fly. When pursued, it flies low over the ground and glides on bowed wings, showing chestnut 'corners' to the tail. *Status:* resident in south, central and eastern England and on isolated sites to the north.

Similar Species:
Chukar *Alectoris chukar*
33–36cm (13–14in)
The Chukar has been introduced to several parts of Britain in recent years and now hybridizes with the Red-legged Partridge.

The two are very similar and closely related. The best distinguishing marks are the 'clean-cut' appearance of the Chukar, which lacks black spotting on the breast and has fewer, bolder, broader and more distinct flank stripes on a creamy background. *Range:* introduced from eastern Europe, where it extends in a broad band from Greece and Turkey across Asia to northern China.
Migration: resident.
British Distribution: patchy in southern and eastern England, including many hybrids with Red-legged Partridge.
Other Similar Species: Grey Partridge (p. 104).

Chukar

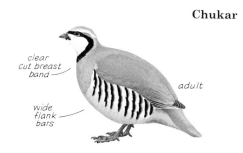

clear
cut breast
band

wide
flank
bars

adult

		RED-LEGGED PARTRIDGE
Type		partridge-like
Size		33–36cm (13–14in)
Habitat		heaths, fields
Behaviour		walks, runs, perches openly, takes off and lands on ground
Flocking		1–15
Flight		glides; strong and powerful; direct
Voice		loud *chuk-chuk-chukar-chukar*

IDENTIFICATION

Adult	
Crown	buff
Upperparts	buff
Rump	buff
Tail	buff; short and rounded
Throat	black and white
Breast	grey
Belly	orange
Bill	red; short and stubby
Legs	red; medium length

BREEDING

Nest	hollow on ground
Eggs	10–16; yellowish, spotted reddish
Incubation	23–25 days; often 2 nests, one incubated ♂, one incubated ♀
Young	active; downy
Fledging	10 + days
Broods	1 or 2; Apr–May
Food	seeds, leaves, insects
Population	100,000–200,000 pairs

J	F	M	A	M	J	J	A	S	O	N	D
5	5	5	5	5	5	5	5	5	5	5	5

Grey Partridge *Perdix perdix*

chestnut tail corners

grey breast

chestnut horseshoe

streaked back

♂

Stocky gamebird of open fields that prefers to run when threatened. When pressed, flies low over ground on bowed wings. Generally gregarious, occurring in small flocks (coveys). Pale, washed-out coloration makes it appear buffy at any distance. A closer approach reveals pale orange face, grey breast, brown bars on flanks and bold chestnut horseshoe on belly – reduced to chestnut smudge in female.
Status: declining resident of agricultural land throughout Britain and Ireland.
Similar Species: Red-legged Partridge (p.103).

GREY PARTRIDGE	
Type	partridge-like
Size	29–32cm (11–13in)
Habitat	heaths, fields
Behaviour	walks, runs, takes off and lands on ground
Flocking	1–15
Flight	glides; strong and powerful; direct
Voice	decelerating *krikrikri-kri-krikri*; also rusty hinge sound, *kirr-ik*

IDENTIFICATION

Adult	
Crown	buff
Upperparts	brown and black, streaked
Rump	buff
Tail	buff; short and rounded
Throat	orange
Breast	grey
Belly	buff; ♂ chestnut horseshoe, ♀ chestnut smudge
Bill	grey; short and stubby
Legs	grey; medium length

BREEDING

Nest	hollow on ground
Eggs	9–20; buff
Incubation	23–25 days ♀
Young	active; downy
Fledging	16 days
Broods	1; Apr–May
Food	seeds, leaves, insects
Population	c 500,000 pairs

J	5
F	5
M	5
A	5
M	5
J	5
J	5
A	5
S	5
O	5
N	5
D	5

Quail *Coturnix coturnix*

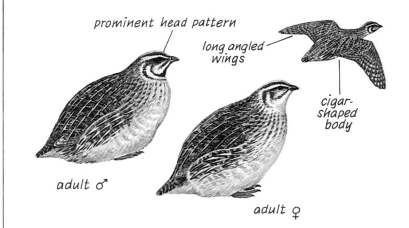

prominent head pattern

long angled wings

cigar-shaped body

adult ♂

adult ♀

Small, fast-flying, migratory gamebird; more often heard than seen. Ventriloquial call makes bird's location difficult to assess. Good views of bird on ground exceptional. Usually seen when flushed (deliberately or accidentally); flies when almost trodden on. Combination of stocky body and long, pointed wings is unique. Upperparts brown, streaked and barred; underparts warm buffy orange. Pattern of bold creamy eyebrow and dark facial streaks more pronounced in male than female.
Status: scarce and declining summer visitor.
Similar Species: none.

QUAIL	
Type	partridge-like
Size	17–18.5cm (6–7in)
Habitat	moors, heaths, fields, hedges
Behaviour	walks, runs, takes off and lands on ground
Flocking	solitary
Flight	glides; strong and powerful; direct
Voice	distinctive *whic-we-wic*, repeated; often rendered 'wet-me-lips'

IDENTIFICATION

Adult	
Crown	black and white
Upperparts	brown and black, pale streaks
Rump	brown
Tail	brown; short and rounded
Throat	white; ♂ black central stripe
Breast	buffy orange
Belly	white
Bill	black; short and stubby
Legs	grey; short

BREEDING

Nest	hollow on ground
Eggs	7–12; creamy, spotted brown
Incubation	16–21 days ♀
Young	active; downy
Fledging	19 days
Broods	1 sometimes 2; May–June
Food	seeds, insects
Population	?

J	0
F	0
M	0
A	2
M	2
J	2
J	1
A	1
S	1
O	0
N	0
D	0

Chrysolophus pictus **Golden Pheasant** Chrysolophus amherstiae **Lady Amherst's Pheasant**

yellow crown

red underparts

♀

brown legs

♂

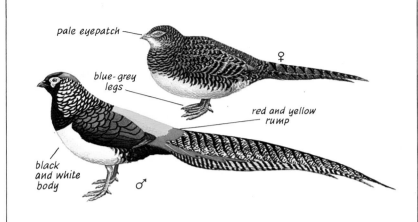

pale eyepatch

blue-grey legs

♀

black and white body

red and yellow rump

♂

Exotic pheasant introduced from South East Asia since end of nineteenth century; present breeding population from birds escaped from captivity. Male highly colourful and unmistakable with bright red underparts, golden crown and rump and long tail. Female much more subdued; mainly shades of rust and buff, heavily barred. Secretive and difficult to locate among dense stands of rhododendrons and conifers. Hybridizes with Lady Amherst's.
Status: still scarce; headquarters in Breckland and Galloway.
Similar Species: female similar to female Pheasant (p.106) but more rufous above. Female also easily confused with female Lady Amherst's Pheasant (p.105) but has brownish, rather than blue, legs.

Introduced in twentieth century from South East Asia. Male magnificent in black and white with orange rump, red uppertail coverts and extremely long black and white marbled tail. Female barred black and chestnut. Secretive; confined to conifer woods with dense undergrowth and rhododendron scrub.
Status: confined to area around Woburn where introduced.
Similar Species: female very similar to female Golden Pheasant (p.105) but has bluish legs and darker, more chestnut, breast.

	GOLDEN PHEASANT
Type	partridge-like
Size	♂ 89–109cm (35–43in); ♀ 61–71cm (24–28in)
Habitat	forests and woods
Behaviour	walks, runs, takes off and lands vegetation or ground
Flocking	1–15
Flight	laboured
Voice	harsh *chak*

IDENTIFICATION

Adult ♂	
Crown	yellow
Upperparts	yellow
Rump	red
Tail	brown and black; long and pointed
Throat	yellow
Breast	red
Belly	red
Bill	yellow; short and stubby
Legs	yellow; medium length
Adult ♀	rusty and black above; heavily barred buff below; long pointed tail

BREEDING

Nest	hollow on ground
Eggs	5–12; buffy
Incubation	22 days
Young	active; downy
Fledging	12–14 days
Broods	1; Apr–May
Food	shoots, berries, seeds
Population	500–1000 pairs

	LADY AMHERST'S PHEASANT
Type	partridge-like
Size	♂ 115–150cm (45–59in); ♀ 58–68cm (23–27in)
Habitat	forests and woods
Behaviour	walks, runs, takes off and lands on vegetation or ground
Flocking	1–15
Flight	laboured
Voice	*su-ik-ik-ik*

IDENTIFICATION

Adult ♂	
Crown	black, with black and white nape
Upperparts	green
Rump	red and yellow
Tail	black and white; very long and pointed
Throat	black
Breast	black
Belly	white
Bill	grey; short and stubby
Legs	bluish, medium length
Adult ♀	rusty and black above, heavily barred buff below; long pointed tail

BREEDING

Nest	hollow on ground
Eggs	6–12; buffy
Incubation	23 days ♀
Young	active; downy
Fledging	12–14 days
Broods	1; Apr–May
Food	shoots, berries, seeds
Population	100–200 pairs

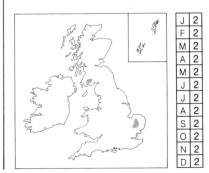

J	2
F	2
M	2
A	2
M	2
J	2
J	2
A	2
S	2
O	2
N	2
D	2

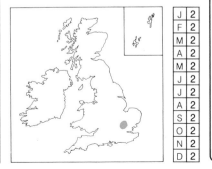

J	2
F	2
M	2
A	2
M	2
J	2
J	2
A	2
S	2
O	2
N	2
D	2

Pheasant *Phasianus colchicus*

PHEASANT	
Type	partridge-like
Size	♂ 75–90cm (30–35in); ♀ 52–64cm (20–25in)
Habitat	heaths, forests and woods, fields and hedges
Behaviour	walks, runs, takes off and lands on vegetation or ground
Flocking	1–15
Flight	glides; strong and powerful; direct
Voice	far carrying *kok . . . kok-kok*

IDENTIFICATION

Adult ♂	
Crown	green
Upperparts	brown, spotted black; lower back grey
Rump	russet
Tail	brown, barred black; long and pointed
Throat	green
Breast	brown, spotted black
Belly	brown, spotted black
Bill	buff; short and stubby
Legs	grey; medium length
Adult ♀	mottled buff and brown, speckled black; long, pointed, buff and black tail

BREEDING

Nest	hollow on ground
Eggs	7–15; plain olive-brown
Incubation	23–27 days ♀
Young	active; downy
Fledging	12–14 days
Broods	1; Apr–June
Food	shoots, seeds, berries
Population	100,000–500,000 pairs

J	F	M	A	M	J	J	A	S	O	N	D
6	6	6	6	6	6	6	6	6	6	6	6

red wattle

bottle-green head and neck

♂

♀

white neck ring

variants

The Pheasant is a widespread, ground-dwelling gamebird of woods, hedgerows and open fields, that has been introduced almost throughout these islands. It is absent only from the highest and bleakest areas, mainly in the north and west. The male is a stunning bird – though highly variable, it is typically a red-bronze, barred above and below with black. The head is an iridescent dark bottle-green with a bold red eye-wattle. The red-bronze tail is elongated and regularly barred black. The female is smaller, mottled and barred in shades of buff and brown with a shorter tail.
Status: a widespread resident, locally abundant where artificially reared.

Similar Species:
Green Pheasant *Phasianus versicolor*
♂ 75–90cm (30–35in) ♀ 52–64cm (20–25in)
This bird is a native of Japan, where it is resident. Like the Pheasant, it has been introduced to many parts of Europe and is remarkably similar to a melanistic form of that species. It is best identified in the male by the pale bluish or greyish rump and wing coverts. Females are not distinguishable. Common Pheasants introduced to Britain

and Ireland originate from many parts of their natural range, but include several isolated populations that differ quite strikingly.

In a nutshell, there is a western group which have no white collar; a western Asiatic group with white on the wings; a Mongolian group also with white on the wing, but more richly coloured; a white-rumped group in China; and a Far Eastern grey-rumped group.
Range: Japan.
Migration: resident.
British Distribution: unclear; see above.
Other Similar Species: Golden Pheasant and Lady Amherst's Pheasant (p. 105).

Green Pheasant

♂ *versicolor*

♂ *torquatus*

Rallus aquaticus **Water Rail**

long red bill

plain grey

white undertail

pinkish legs

barred flanks

trailing legs

Highly secretive, marsh-dwelling bird, similar to Moorhen but with long, red bill. More frequently heard than seen; calls sound more like a squealing pig than a bird. Laterally compressed for easy passage through dense vegetation, especially reeds. In winter, may emerge on open ground, though seldom far from water and cover. Upperparts dark brown, heavily streaked black; sides of head, throat and breast metallic grey. Flanks and belly barred black and white. Long legs and toes and short, rounded wings. Short, cocked tail frequently flicked showing white undertail coverts.
Status: widespread resident but not common; Continental birds are winter visitors.
Similar Species: only rail with long bill.

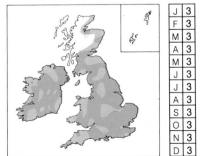

	J	3
	F	3
	M	3
	A	3
	M	3
	J	3
	J	3
	A	3
	S	3
	O	3
	N	3
	D	3

WATER RAIL

Type	rail-like
Size	27–29cm (10–11in)
Habitat	freshwater marshes
Behaviour	wades, takes off and lands on water or ground
Flocking	1–2
Flight	laboured; legs trailing
Voice	repeated *kip-kip-kip*; variety of shrill squeals and harsh grunts

IDENTIFICATION

Adult	
Crown	brown and black
Upperparts	brown, streaked black
Rump	brown and black
Tail	brown and black, undertail white; short and pointed
Throat	grey
Breast	grey
Belly	black and white, barred
Bill	red; very long and thin
Legs	pinkish or greenish; long

BREEDING

Nest	cup of reeds hidden above water
Eggs	6–10; creamy, spotted reddish
Incubation	19–20 days, mainly ♀
Young	active; downy
Fledging	7–8 weeks
Broods	2; Apr–June
Food	amphibians, vegetation, invertebrates
Population	2000–4000 pairs

Crex crex **Corncrake**

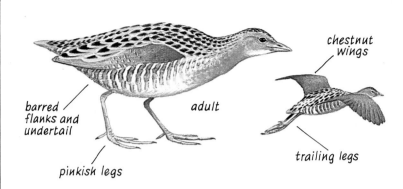

chestnut wings

barred flanks and undertail

adult

pinkish legs

trailing legs

Secretive summer visitor to hay and cereal fields. More often heard than seen, uttering harsh, rasping call; in some areas walks openly and even perches to call. When flushed, bold, chestnut wings and trailing legs diagnostic. Upperparts have black feather-centres edged with buffy brown, producing 'scalloped' effect. In summer, male has pale grey face and upper breast; less grey in winter. Underparts buff, barred chestnut, including undertail coverts; latter often obvious as bird walks away.
Status: summer visitor April–September. Once widespread, now decidedly scarce; still relatively numerous in Ireland and Hebrides.
Similar Species: short-billed rails, especially Spotted Crake (p.108) and rare Little and Baillon's Crake.

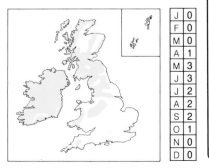

	J	0
	F	0
	M	0
	A	1
	M	3
	J	3
	J	2
	A	2
	S	2
	O	1
	N	0
	D	0

CORNCRAKE

Type	rail-like
Size	25–28cm (10–11in)
Habitat	fields and hedgerows
Behaviour	walks, takes off and lands on ground
Flocking	solitary
Flight	laboured; legs trailing
Voice	grating *crek-crek*, repeated

IDENTIFICATION

Ad.♂summer	
Crown	black and brown
Upperparts	black, brown feather margins; wings chestnut
Rump	buff and black
Tail	buff and black, undertail buff, barred chestnut; short and pointed
Throat	white
Breast	grey
Belly	buff, barred chestnut
Bill	yellow; short and pointed
Legs	pink; long
Ad.♂winter	less grey on breast (like ♀ and juvenile)

BREEDING

Nest	platform hidden on ground
Eggs	8–12; greenish, blotched brown
Incubation	15–18 days ♀
Young	active; downy
Fledging	5 weeks
Broods	1; May–June
Food	invertebrates, plants
Population	5000–6000 pairs

Spotted Crake *Porzana porzana*

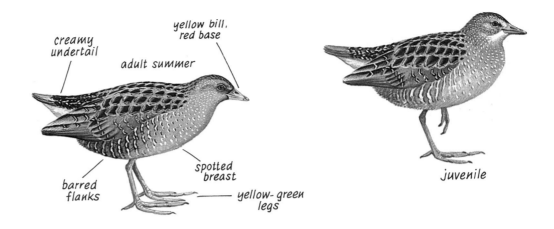

yellow bill, red base

creamy undertail

adult summer

barred flanks

spotted breast

yellow-green legs

juvenile

	SPOTTED CRAKE
Type	rail-like
Size	22–24cm (9–10in)
Habitat	freshwater marshes
Behaviour	wades, takes off from water or ground
Flocking	solitary
Flight	laboured
Voice	far-carrying *quip-quip-quip*, repeated for long periods

IDENTIFICATION

Adult	
Crown	brown
Upperparts	brown, streaked black
Rump	brown
Tail	brown, undertail creamy buff; short and pointed
Throat	grey
Breast	grey; white spots on sides
Belly	grey
Bill	yellow, red base; short and thin
Legs	yellow-green; long

BREEDING

Nest	cup of grasses over water
Eggs	8–12; buffy, blotched red
Incubation	18–21 days ♂ ♀
Young	active; downy
Fledging	25 + days
Broods	2; May–July
Food	invertebrates, vegetation
Population	0–4 pairs ?

J	F	M	A	M	J	J	A	S	O	N	D
0	0	1	1	2	1	1	1	1	1	1	0

This rare, skulking and highly elusive bird spends most of its time hidden deep among marshland vegetation. It is usually only heard late on warm, summer evenings when its repeated *quip-quip-quip* call echoes across the stillness. This call, which is instantly recognizable, has been likened to the slow drip-drip-drip of a tap into a half-empty barrel of water.

The upperparts are brown, heavily spotted with black centres to the feathers like those of a Water Rail. The face is grey with a dark mark through the lores. The underparts are grey, spotted with white on the sides of the breast, and a pattern of brown, black and white bars on the flanks. The undertail coverts are creamy, below a short, often cocked, tail. The bill is orange and yellow, the legs yellow-green.
Status: a summer visitor from April to October that probably breeds in small numbers. Otherwise only a scarce migrant.

Similar Species:
Little Crake *Porzana parva*
18–20cm (7–8in)
This is a smaller version of the Spotted Crake which is just as scarce and elusive. In summer the male is blue-grey below, with white bars beneath the tail. Females are similar, but creamy-white below. Like the juveniles, both sexes become creamy-buff in winter, with grey bars on the flanks and undertail. The Little Crake is thus always paler below than the Spotted Crake, with darker, bottle-green legs. The even rarer Baillon's Crake *P. pusilla* has flanks and undertail barred black on white.
Range: breeds in a highly fragmented range right across Europe to Central Asia.
Migration: leaves most of its range to winter mainly in Africa south of the Sahara.
British Distribution: irregular in south and south-west, mainly in spring or autumn.
Other Similar Species: Corncrake (p. 107).

Little Crake

red base to bill

under tail barring

grey flanks

adult ♂

adult ♀

unbarred flanks

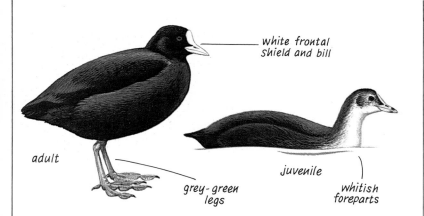

white frontal shield and bill

adult

grey-green legs

juvenile

whitish foreparts

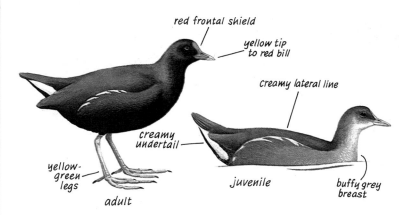

red frontal shield

yellow tip to red bill

creamy lateral line

creamy undertail

yellow-green legs

adult

juvenile

buffy grey breast

Bulky, sooty black waterbird distinguished by white bill and frontal shield. Juvenile brownish with whitish face and foreneck; lacks frontal shield. Swims buoyantly and frequently dives for food; also up-ends in shallow water. Walks well and often feeds on splashy grassland, though always adjacent to open water. Forms large winter flocks tightly packed together. Evades danger by running over water surface rather than flying. Once airborne, flies strongly on broad, rounded wings with long legs trailing behind.
Status: widespread resident; winter visitors arrive from the Continent October–April.
Similar Species: Moorhen (p.109) has red bill and white undertail.

COOT	
Type	duck-like
Size	36–40cm (14–16in)
Habitat	open freshwater, estuaries
Behaviour	swims, dives, wades, walks, takes off and lands on water
Flocking	1–1000
Flight	laboured; legs trailing
Voice	explosive *kook* or *teuk*

IDENTIFICATION

Adult	
Crown	black; white frontal shield
Upperparts	black
Rump	black
Tail	black; short and pointed
Throat	black
Breast	black
Belly	black
Bill	white; short and pointed
Legs	grey-green; medium length
Juvenile	brownish with whitish foreparts; lacks frontal shield

BREEDING

Nest	bulky cup among aquatic vegetation or adjacent bush
Eggs	6–9; buff, spotted black
Incubation	21–24 days ♂♀
Young	active; downy
Fledging	6–8 weeks
Broods	2; mid Mar–June
Food	mostly plants but omnivorous
Population	100,000 pairs

J	6
F	6
M	6
A	6
M	6
J	6
J	6
A	6
S	6
O	6
N	6
D	6

Common bird of ponds, rivers, canals and marshes; most often seen walking waterside banks with jerking, chicken-like movements of head. On land, long legs and toes obvious, as is white, cocked tail. In adult, white lateral line separates dark grey underparts from dark brown wings. Juvenile brown with whitish chin and foreneck; lateral line creamy; bill and legs dullish green. Swims well but flies laboriously with legs trailing after lengthy pattering take-off. Dives rarely. Seldom found in flocks.
Status: widespread resident except for higher hills; winter visitors arrive from September onwards.
Similar Species: Coot (p.109) is all black with white frontal shield and often forms large winter flocks.

MOORHEN	
Type	rail-like
Size	31–35cm (12–14in)
Habitat	freshwater, fields and hedges
Behaviour	swims, wades, walks, takes off and lands on water or ground
Flocking	1–15
Flight	laboured; legs trailing
Voice	loud *currick*; high-pitched *kik-kik-kik-kik*

IDENTIFICATION

Adult	
Crown	dark grey
Upperparts	dark brown, white lateral line
Rump	brown
Tail	brown, undertail black and white; short and pointed
Throat	dark grey
Breast	dark grey
Belly	dark grey
Bill	red, tip yellow; short and pointed
Legs	yellow-green; long
Juvenile	brown, whitish throat and foreneck; lateral line creamy; bill dull green

BREEDING

Nest	cup near ground
Eggs	5–11; buff, spotted
Incubation	19–22 days ♂♀
Young	active; downy
Fledging	6–7 weeks
Broods	2–3; Mar–Aug
Food	aquatic insects, molluscs, seeds, plants
Population	500,000–1,000,000 pairs

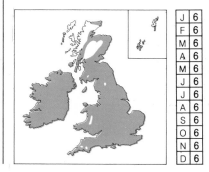

J	6
F	6
M	6
A	6
M	6
J	6
J	6
A	6
S	6
O	6
N	6
D	6

WADERS, SKUAS, GULLS, TERNS AND AUKS

This huge group of apparently diverse birds may belong to several families, but all are members of the order Charadriiformes and are relatively closely related.

Waders are long-legged birds that pick or probe for food in wetland areas. They vary from the elegant Greenshank and noisy Redshank (*illustrated opposite*) to the dainty Ringed Plover (*below*) with its delicate surface-picking bill. Thirty-five species of waders occur regularly in Britain. Some breed, some winter in flocks 50,000 strong, and others simply pass through on their way to and from their Arctic breeding grounds. In size, they range from the Curlew, which is as large as a Herring Gull, to the Little Stint, which is no larger than a House Sparrow. It is not overstating the case to say that without our estuaries huge numbers of these birds would simply cease to exist.

The gulls (seagulls to non-birders) are one of the most successful bird groups in the world. Highly adaptable, they have learned to live alongside man, benefiting from a huge range of human activities.

Terns, on the other hand, are sensitive to change and are easily disturbed while breeding. They are graceful, economical flyers that are among the longest distance migrants of all birds. Unfortunately, holidaymakers invade their nesting beaches in summer, accidentally trample their eggs and force them more and more into the confines of bird reserves. Although seen mainly at sea and along coasts, the terns include the 'marsh terns' that appear regularly at freshwater sites. These include the Black and White-winged Black Terns.

Skuas, though superficially similar to juvenile gulls, have all the power, menace and agility of a falcon. They are truly at home at sea, even though many of them rely on lemmings for food during the Arctic summer.

The auks are the northern equivalents of the penguins of the Southern Hemisphere, though they have (just) retained the power of flight. Breeding colonies pack themselves tightly together in an apparently disorganized mass on the steepest cliffs in northern and western Britain, but everywhere auks are in decline. Oil is a major cause and the cowboy tanker owners and skippers who wash their tanks at sea are the principal villains. Oil spills killing thousands of birds are reported by the media, but small spills and malpractice take an invisible toll month after month, year after year.

Oystercatcher *Haematopus ostralegus*

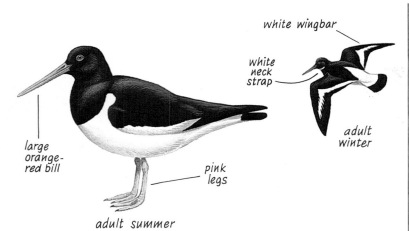

white wingbar

white neck strap

adult winter

large orange-red bill

pink legs

adult summer

Large, striking black and white bird with long, thick, orange-red bill and long, pink legs. Eyes red with bright orange-red eye ring. In winter, adult has brownish wash over black upperparts and white half collar. Juvenile as adult winter but browner above with only rudimentary half collar. Typically a bird of rocky and sandy shores; often gathers in large flocks on favoured estuaries. Highly vocal with loud piping calls; flies strongly, often low along shoreline. Frequently feeds on wet grasslands and freshwater marshes near sea; also along banks of shingle rivers.
Status: widespread coastal resident; winter visitors arrive August–April. Some British breeders migrate to France and Spain.
Similar Species: none.

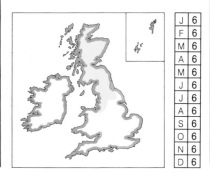

J	6
F	6
M	6
A	6
M	6
J	6
J	6
A	6
S	6
O	6
N	6
D	6

OYSTERCATCHER
Type	wader-like
Size	41–45cm (16–18in)
Habitat	marshes, estuaries and shores, fields
Behaviour	wades, walks, perches openly, takes off and lands on water or ground
Flocking	1–several thousand
Flight	strong and powerful; direct
Voice	loud, penetrating *kleep*; also *kleep-a-kleep*

IDENTIFICATION
Ad.summer	
Crown	black
Upperparts	black
Rump	white 'V'
Tail	white, black band; medium length, square
Throat	black
Breast	black, forming breast band
Belly	white
Bill	orange; long and thick
Legs	pink; long
Ad.winter	brownish black upperparts; white chin bar
Juvenile	browner upperparts than Ad.winter; legs grey

BREEDING
Nest	scrape
Eggs	3; buff, blotched black
Incubation	24–27 days ♂ ♀
Young	active; downy
Fledging	34–37 days
Broods	1; mid Apr–June
Food	molluscs, worms
Population	c 30,000 pairs; c 200,000 winter

Avocet *Recurvirostra avosetta*

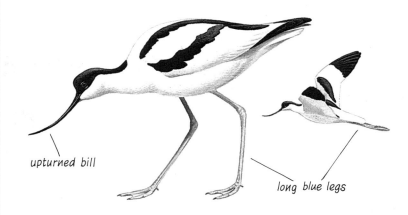

upturned bill

long blue legs

Large, elegant, black and white wader with long legs and distinctly upcurved bill. At rest, black areas form a white-filled oval pattern on wings. Scarce, seen mostly on coasts and marshes, mainly in south and east England. Feeds head-down with regular side-to-side scything movements of head and bill. Generally occurs in small groups; sometimes in much larger winter flocks. Often rather noisy.
Status: two regular breeding colonies in Suffolk, plus irregular breeding in other parts of East Anglia. Winters in Tamar Estuary, Devon. Elsewhere scarce passage migrant along south and east coasts in spring and autumn.
Similar Species: Oystercatcher (p.112) has more black plus straight orange-red bill.

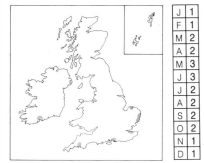

J	1
F	1
M	2
A	2
M	3
J	3
J	2
A	2
S	2
O	2
N	1
D	1

AVOCET
Type	wader-like
Size	41–45cm (16–18in)
Habitat	freshwater marshes, estuaries
Behaviour	wades, takes off and lands on water or ground
Flocking	1–100
Flight	strong and powerful; direct; legs trailing
Voice	loud *kloo-eet*

IDENTIFICATION
Adult	
Crown	black
Upperparts	black and white stripes
Rump	white
Tail	white; medium length, square
Throat	white
Breast	white
Belly	white
Bill	black; long, thin and upturned
Legs	blue-grey; very long
Juvenile	dark brown where adult black

BREEDING
Nest	bare scrape on ground, often on low island
Eggs	4; buff, spotted and blotched black
Incubation	22–24 days ♂ ♀
Young	active; downy
Fledging	6 weeks
Broods	1; Apr–May
Food	insects, crustaceans
Population	c 100 pairs

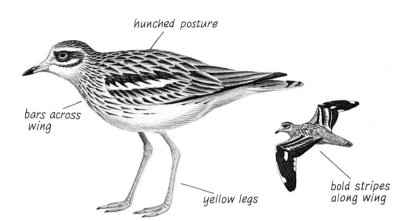

hunched posture

bars across wing

yellow legs

bold stripes along wing

STONE-CURLEW

Type	wader-like
Size	38–43cm (15–17in)
Habitat	heaths, fields
Behaviour	walks, runs, takes off and lands on ground
Flocking	1–2
Flight	strong and powerful; direct
Voice	rippling *coorree*, similar to tin whistle

IDENTIFICATION

Adult	
Crown	buff
Upperparts	buff, streaked black; black and white bars across wings
Rump	buff
Tail	buff, black tip; medium length, rounded
Throat	white
Breast	buff, streaked brown
Belly	white
Bill	yellow with black tip; short and pointed
Legs	yellow; long
Juvenile	paler with less marked wingbars

BREEDING

Nest	bare scrape
Eggs	2; creamy, speckled and blotched brown
Incubation	25–27 days ♂♀
Young	active; downy
Fledging	6 weeks
Broods	1 occasionally 2; Apr–May
Food	insects, worms
Population	c 300–500 pairs

This is a large plover-like summer visitor to stony or other sparsely vegetated ground, mainly in southern and eastern England. It is most active at dawn and dusk and, when disturbed, prefers to run rather than fly. It is buffy-brown, streaked with black above and on the breast. The wings have a bold horizontal white bar with a black border, that forms a conspicuous mark when the bird flies. The face pattern is a complex of black and white stripes marked by a large yellow eye. The legs are long and yellow. Though it is called 'curlew' because of its call, there is really very little similarity with the Curlew.
Status: a scarce and declining summer visitor to southern and eastern England, mainly to chalk downland, sandy heaths and shingle. It winters in southern Europe and Africa.

Similar Species:
Little Bustard *Tetrax tetrax*
41–45cm (16–18in)
This is the only similar-sized, ground dwelling bird that could reasonably be confused with the Stone-curlew. It is a bird of open plains with a more rounded, bulky body and a longer neck than that bird. Both

sexes are brown above, variously streaked and mottled with black, and white below. The male, in summer, shows a bold pattern of black and white on the neck that is particularly obvious in display. In both sexes the majority of the flight feathers are white. In flight it resembles a large duck, but with characteristically fast, shallow and fluttery wing beats.
Range: breeds right across Continental Europe though absent from large areas.
Migration: populations of northern France and Russia migrate.
British Distribution: a less-than-annual vagrant, mainly to the east coast of England, in winter.

Little Bustard

black and white neck pattern

much white in wing

♂ summer

adult ♀

♂ summer

J	F	M	A	M	J	J	A	S	O	N	D
0	0	1	2	2	2	2	2	2	1	1	0	0

Little Ringed Plover *Charadrius dubius*

yellow eye ring

white crown bar

no prominent wingbar

black bill

yellowish legs

adult

juvenile

Scarce summer visitor to inland freshwaters (especially gravel pits) of southern and central England. Smaller, slimmer version of Ringed Plover with similar round-headed appearance, short bill and typical 'run-stop' plover behaviour. Adult has white forehead with black band across crown bordered by narrow white line; yellow eye ring. In flight, lacks wingbar; shows white outer tail feathers. Juvenile similar but with darker brown (not black) head markings; breast band often incomplete.
Status: scarce summer visitor and passage migrant March–October.
Similar Species: Ringed Plover (p.114) has orange-yellow, not black, bill and shows wingbar in flight. Kentish Plover (p.115) is always paler sandy brown above.

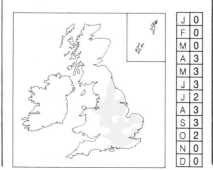

J	0	
F	0	
M	0	
A	3	
M	3	
J	3	
J	2	
A	3	
S	3	
O	2	
N	0	
D	0	

LITTLE RINGED PLOVER

Type	wader-like
Size	14–16cm (5–6in)
Habitat	freshwater
Behaviour	wades, runs, takes off and lands on ground
Flocking	1–2
Flight	strong and powerful; direct
Voice	short, down-slurred *piu*

IDENTIFICATION

Adult	
Crown	white, black and brown
Upperparts	brown
Rump	brown
Tail	black and white; short and square
Throat	white
Breast	white with black band
Belly	white
Bill	black; short and pointed
Legs	dull pink or yellow; medium length
Juvenile	brownish above; head and breast bands brownish, incomplete

BREEDING

Nest	bare scrape on ground
Eggs	4; buffish, spotted and streaked brown
Incubation	24–26 days ♂ ♀
Young	active; downy
Fledging	21–24 days
Broods	1 or 2; Mar–June
Food	insects, molluscs
Population	400–500 pairs

Ringed Plover *Charadrius hiaticula*

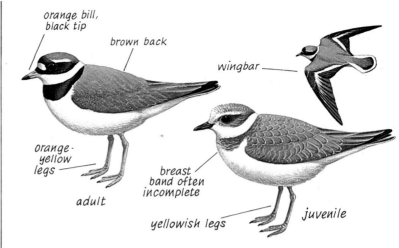

orange bill, black tip

brown back

wingbar

orange-yellow legs

breast band often incomplete

adult

yellowish legs

juvenile

Typical small 'banded' plover. Rotund shape with rounded head and short, stubby bill. Pattern of black and white on head and breast distinguish from all but two related species – see below. Orange bill and legs in adult; broad white wingbar in flight. Juvenile has brown head with creamy forehead and eyebrow (lacking in Little Ringed Plover) and smudgy, incomplete breast band. Bill black; legs yellowish. Runs fast and stands stock-still like other plovers. Often forms loose flocks and may gather in large numbers at suitable feeding grounds.
Status: resident breeder, passage migrant and winter visitor to coasts and estuaries. Also occurs and breeds inland but never commonly.
Similar Species: Little Ringed Plover (p.114) and Kentish Plover (p.115).

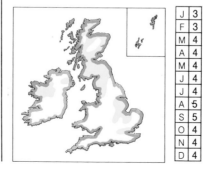

J	3	
F	3	
M	4	
A	4	
M	4	
J	4	
J	4	
A	5	
S	5	
O	4	
N	4	
D	4	

RINGED PLOVER

Type	wader-like
Size	18–20cm (7in)
Habitat	freshwater marshes, estuaries and shores
Behaviour	wades, runs, takes off and lands on water and ground
Flocking	1–100
Flight	strong and powerful; direct
Voice	melodic *tu-lee*

IDENTIFICATION

Adult	
Crown	black and brown
Upperparts	brown
Rump	brown
Tail	black and white; short and square
Throat	white
Breast	white with black band
Belly	white
Bill	orange; short and pointed
Legs	orange-yellow; medium length
Juvenile	brown head with creamy forehead and eyebrow; incomplete breast band; bill black; legs yellowish

BREEDING

Nest	bare scrape on ground
Eggs	4; buff, spotted brown
Incubation	23–26 days ♂ ♀
Young	active; downy
Fledging	25 days
Broods	2 sometimes 3; May–July
Food	invertebrates
Population	8000 pairs; 10,000–12,500 winter; more on passage

sandy cap

buffy back

wingbar

marks at side of breast

adult ♂

black legs

adult ♀

buffy

only a smudge at sides of breast

black legs

juvenile

KENTISH PLOVER

Type	wader-like
Size	15–17cm (6–6½in)
Habitat	freshwater marshes, estuaries and shores
Behaviour	wades, runs, takes off and lands on ground
Flocking	1–2
Flight	strong and powerful; direct
Voice	quiet *wit-wit-wit*; melodic *choo-wit*

IDENTIFICATION

Ad.♂summer	
Crown	sandy and black
Upperparts	buff
Rump	buff
Tail	white; short and square
Throat	white
Breast	white; incomplete black band
Belly	white
Bill	black, short and pointed
Legs	black; medium length
Ad.♀summer ♂ winter	crown, head markings and incomplete breast band buffy brown
Juvenile	paler; scaled upperparts; faint buff smudge at sides of breast

BREEDING

Nest	bare scrape on ground
Eggs	3; buff, spotted black
Incubation	24 days ♂ ♀
Young	active; downy
Fledging	25 days
Broods	2; Apr–June
Food	insects
Population	irregular passage migrant

Named after the English county where it formerly bred, this dainty little plover is now only a scarce migrant to the south and east coasts. It is smaller than the Ringed Plover, with an incomplete breast band that is actually no more than a dark smudge at either side of the breast. The bill and legs are black. In summer the male has black breast patches and black facial markings with a clear sandy-coloured crown. The winter male, female and juvenile have no more than buffy-brown breast patches. In all plumages the sandy colour of the upperparts is quite distinct from the two more common British 'ringed plovers'.
Status: a scarce migrant in spring, even scarcer in autumn, to south and east coasts; it has bred once in recent years.

Similar Species:
Greater Sand Plover
Charadrius leschenaultii
22–24cm (9–9½in)
Considerably larger than any similar plover that occurs in these islands. Generally a short-necked, large billed, long-legged version of the juvenile 'ringed plovers', though it is pale sandy-grey rather than brown. In summer the male is marked by

dark eye and crown markings and by a rufous band on the breast that extends to the nape. Females are duller. In winter the generally sandy-grey plumage is characteristic, but the long blue legs, heavy bill and complete lack of a white collar are also useful identification features.
Range: breeds from Turkey eastwards across the Asiatic steppes.
Migration: moves southward to winter along coasts of Africa, the Middle East and Asia.
British Distribution: an extremely rare vagrant to Britain.
Other Similar Species: Little Ringed Plover and Ringed Plover (p. 114).

Greater Sand Plover

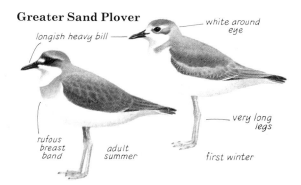

longish heavy bill

white around eye

rufous breast band

adult summer

very long legs

first winter

J	F	M	A	M	J	J	A	S	O	N	D
0	0	1	1	1	1	1	1	1	1	0	0	0

Dotterel *Charadrius morinellus*

eyebrows meet at nape

cleaner cut breast pattern

no wingbar

breast band

adult ♂

adult ♀

Small, rotund plover; easily overlooked on stony mountain-top habitat where well camouflaged among lichens and mosses. Summer adults have distinctive grey breast and chestnut underparts separated by white band. Prominent white eyebrows meet on nape. In winter and juvenile plumages, becomes greyish; marked only by white eyebrow and indistinct breast band. Plain wings and no distinctive tail pattern in flight. Runs and stops in typical plover manner.
Status: rare summer visitor; breeds on high stony ground on a few Scottish and Lakeland mountain-tops. Otherwise scarce passage migrant occurring most regularly in East Anglia in May.
Similar Species: none.

J	0
F	0
M	0
A	1
M	2
J	2
J	2
A	2
S	1
O	1
N	0
D	0

DOTTEREL

Type	wader-like
Size	20–23cm (8–9in)
Habitat	moors, fields
Behaviour	runs, takes off and lands on ground
Flocking	1–15
Flight	strong and powerful; direct
Voice	quiet *peep-peep* in flight; *titi-ri-titti-ri* repeated

IDENTIFICATION

Ad.summer	
Crown	black
Upperparts	grey; wings brown and black
Rump	buff and brown
Tail	buff and brown; short and rounded
Throat	white
Breast	grey, white band
Belly	chestnut
Bill	black; short and thin
Legs	yellow; medium length
Ad.winter and juvenile	grey above and below, good white eyebrow, indistinct breast band

BREEDING

Nest	hollow on ground
Eggs	3; buffy, spotted blackish brown
Incubation	21–26 days ♂
Young	active; downy
Fledging	4 weeks
Broods	1; May–June
Food	insects
Population	60–100 pairs; very scarce migrant

Lapwing *Vanellus vanellus*

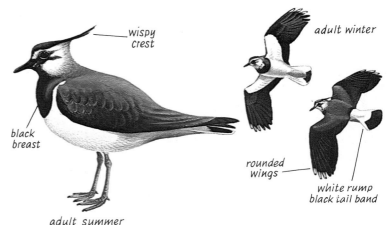

wispy crest

adult winter

black breast

rounded wings

white rump black tail band

adult summer

Common throughout Britain and Ireland. Looks black and white at any distance; distinctive crest. Close approach reveals upperparts have glossy green and purple sheen. Head white with intricate pattern of black markings; throat black, widening into black breast band. In winter, throat and upper breast become white. Gregarious outside breeding season.
Status: widespread and numerous breeding bird; huge winter influx from the Continent.
Similar Species: none.

J	6
F	6
M	6
A	6
M	6
J	6
J	6
A	6
S	6
O	6
N	6
D	6

LAPWING

Type	wader-like
Size	29–32cm (11–12in)
Habitat	freshwater marshes, moors, estuaries, fields
Behaviour	wades, walks, takes off and lands on ground
Flocking	1–1000
Flight	laboured; direct; aerial dive
Voice	plaintive *pee-wit*

IDENTIFICATION

Adult	
Crown	black and white; wispy crest
Upperparts	green-black
Rump	white
Tail	black and white, undertail pale brown; short and square
Throat	black and white
Breast	black
Belly	white
Bill	black; short and thin
Legs	dark red; long

BREEDING

Nest	hollow on ground
Eggs	4; buff, blotched black
Incubation	24–29 days, mainly ♀
Young	active; downy
Fledging	33 days
Broods	1; Mar–Apr
Food	invertebrates
Population	200,000 pairs; many hundreds of thousands winter

more black on face

adult northern summer

narrow wingbar

adult winter

black belly

adult southern summer

little streaking on buffy breast

adult winter

black and pale grey

black face and belly

adult summer

winter

black 'arm pits'

little streaking on white breast

winter

Medium-sized plover with typically rotund body, round head, short bill and long legs. Upperparts spangled black and gold. In winter, underparts whitish with buffy breast markings. In summer, southern sub-species has black belly extending to central breast stripe and grey face. Northern sub-species has more black on belly and breast with black face. In flight, shows faint wingbar and plain barred tail pattern. Found among hills in summer and in substantial flocks on marshes and grassland in winter.
Status: widespread and numerous winter visitor; breeds in most mountain districts.
Similar Species: similarly shaped Grey Plover (p.117) frequents estuaries and shores, and is spangled grey and black above; shows black 'arm pits' in flight.

GOLDEN PLOVER	
Type	wader-like
Size	27–29cm (10–11in)
Habitat	moors, heaths, fields, marshes
Behaviour	walks, runs, takes off and lands on ground
Flocking	1–1000
Flight	strong and powerful; direct
Voice	whistled *tlui*

IDENTIFICATION

Ad.summer	
Crown	black and gold
Upperparts	spangled black and gold
Rump	black and gold
Tail	black and gold; short and square
Throat	black
Breast	black, white margins
Belly	black, white margins
Bill	black; short and thin
Legs	grey; long
Ad.winter	lacks black face and underparts; buffy breast markings

BREEDING

Nest	scrape on ground
Eggs	4; buff, blotched brown
Incubation	27–28 days, mainly ♀
Young	active; downy
Fledging	4 weeks
Broods	1; Apr–June
Food	worms, insects
Population	30,000 pairs; 400,000 winter

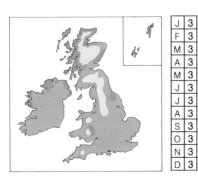

J	3
F	3
M	3
A	3
M	3
J	3
J	3
A	3
S	3
O	3
N	3
D	3

Similar to Golden Plover, but larger and confined to coasts, estuaries and adjacent marshes. Upperparts spangled grey and black. In winter, underparts white with grey speckling on breast. In summer, belly, breast and face black, with white margins on sides of breast and head. In flight, shows wingbar, white rump and black axillaries (arm pits). Legs longer than Golden Plover and extend just beyond tip of tail in flight. Found in large flocks on favoured estuaries and shorelines.
Status: common winter visitor and passage migrant to all coasts.
Similar Species: Golden Plover (p.117).

GREY PLOVER	
Type	wader-like
Size	28–31cm (11–12in)
Habitat	estuaries, shores
Behaviour	wades, walks, takes off and lands on water or ground
Flocking	1–1000
Flight	strong and powerful; direct
Voice	plaintive whistled *tlee-oo-ee*

IDENTIFICATION

Ad.summer	
Crown	grey and black
Upperparts	spangled grey and black
Rump	white
Tail	black and white; short and square
Throat	black
Breast	black, white margins
Belly	black
Bill	black; short and thin
Legs	black; long
Ad.winter	grey above, white below

BREEDING

Nest	hollow on ground
Eggs	4; buff, spotted
Incubation	23 days ♂ ♀
Young	active; downy
Fledging	?
Broods	1; June–July
Food	invertebrates, worms
Population	11,000 winter

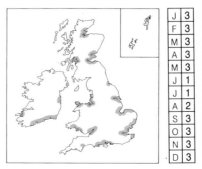

J	3
F	3
M	3
A	3
M	3
J	1
J	1
A	2
S	3
O	3
N	3
D	3

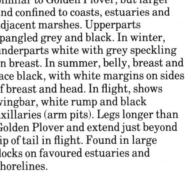

Knot *Calidris canutus*

short straight bill
eyebrow
chestnut underparts
wingbar
adult summer
grey rump
adult winter

Medium-sized, stocky shorebird similar to Dunlin, but considerably larger, with shorter bill and legs. Highly gregarious at all seasons with majority concentrated at relatively few favoured estuaries. In winter, grey above with pale feather margins; underparts white with faint speckling on breast and flanks; well marked eye stripe and eyebrow. In summer, mantle spangled black and chestnut; face and underparts chestnut; wings grey and black. In flight, shows faint wingbar and distinctive white rump; tail has grey terminal band.
Status: abundant, though localized, winter visitor and regular passage migrant.
Similar Species: winter Dunlin (p.122) but Knot much larger with proportionately shorter bill.

	KNOT	
Type	wader-like	
Size	24–27cm (9–10in)	
Habitat	estuaries and shores	
Behaviour	wades, takes off and lands on water or ground	
Flocking	1–20,000	
Flight	strong and powerful; direct	
Voice	low *knot*	

IDENTIFICATION

Ad.winter		
Crown	grey	
Upperparts	grey	
Rump	grey	
Tail	grey; short and square	
Throat	white	
Breast	grey	
Belly	white	
Bill	black; straight and thin	
Legs	dark green; medium length	
Ad.summer	face and underparts chestnut-red; mantle spangled black and chestnut; wings grey and black	

BREEDING

Nest	lined hollow	
Eggs	4; pale green, spotted brown	
Incubation	20–25 days ♂ ♀ ?	
Young	active; downy	
Fledging	20 days ?	
Broods	1; June	
Food	molluscs, crustaceans, worms	
Population	300,000 winter	

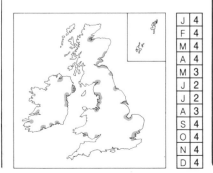

J	4
F	4
M	4
A	4
M	3
J	2
J	2
A	3
S	4
O	4
N	4
D	4

Sanderling *Calidris alba*

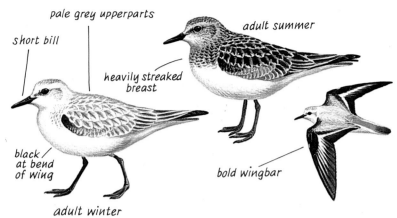

pale grey upperparts
short bill
adult summer
heavily streaked breast
black at bend of wing
bold wingbar
adult winter

Palest of the shorebirds with light grey upperparts and white below; prominent black mark at bend of wing. Gregarious, forms small flocks that characteristically feed in fast, running motion up and down beaches with movement of waves. In summer, head, breast and back spangled black and chestnut for brief period. Summer birds (especially juveniles) away from shoreline, may provoke thoughts of other, rarer, species or even juvenile Dunlin.
Status: widespread winter visitor and numerous passage migrant; confined to coasts and sometimes adjacent marshes.
Similar Species: no other wader runs up and down beach with the waves or is so pale in winter plumage.

	SANDERLING	
Type	wader-like	
Size	19–22cm (7–8½in)	
Habitat	shores	
Behaviour	wades, runs, takes off and lands on water or ground	
Flocking	1–100	
Flight	strong and powerful; direct	
Voice	*quit-quit*, repeated	

IDENTIFICATION

Ad.winter		
Crown	grey	
Upperparts	grey; black at bend of wing	
Rump	black and white	
Tail	black and white; short and square	
Throat	white	
Breast	white	
Belly	white	
Bill	black; short and straight	
Legs	black; medium length	
Ad.summer	head, back and breast spangled black and chestnut	

BREEDING

Nest	neat hollow on ground	
Eggs	4; greenish, spotted brownish	
Incubation	23–24 days ♂ ♀	
Young	active; downy	
Fledging	23–24 days	
Broods	1; June–July	
Food	molluscs, crustaceans	
Population	12,000 winter; 30,000 May	

J	3
F	3
M	3
A	3
M	3
J	1
J	0
A	2
S	2
O	3
N	3
D	3

short bill

rufous back

double white 'V' on back

black legs

adult summer

juvenile

narrow wingbar

a little breast streaking

adult winter

A small version of the Dunlin with a short straight bill and non-stop method of feeding. In winter, it is grey above, white below. In summer, the crown and upperparts are a warm brown with black feather centres and brown streaking at the sides of the breast. However, most visitors to Britain are autumn juveniles, with a prominent double white 'V' on the back.
Status: a scarce winter visitor and spring migrant that is more numerous in autumn.

Similar Species:
Semipalmated Sandpiper
Calidris pusilla 14–16cm (5½–6in)
This is the most abundant of the North American 'peeps' (as small sandpipers from that region are often called). It has been misidentified by more expert British birders than any other rare bird. Juvenile Little Stints, with their rufous colouring and bold white double 'V' on the back, present few problems. The Semi-palmated is a greyer bird with whitish or pale rufous tips to the feathers of the upperparts, creating a uniform scaly pattern. The rear scapulars are marked with a tiny anchor-like pattern. It has a solid, not split, eyebrow and a deep-based, blunt-tipped bill. The toes are

partially webbed, particularly between the outer two toes, but this feature is also shared with the Western Sandpiper *C. mauri,* a vagrant from eastern Siberia and Alaska.
Range: breeds across the Canadian and Alaskan Arctic.
Migration: the whole population moves southwards and eastwards to winter along the Atlantic seaboard, the Caribbean and South and Central America.
British Distribution: an extremely rare vagrant, mainly to the south-west, in autumn.
Other Similar Species: Temminck's Stint (p. 120), and several of the small North American sandpipers or 'peeps'.

Semipalmated Sandpiper

deep based blunt-tipped bill

no pale 'V'

solid, not split eyebrow

scaly pattern

winter

juvenile

LITTLE STINT

Type	wader-like
Size	14–15cm (5½in)
Habitat	marshes, estuaries
Behaviour	wades, walks, takes off from water or ground
Flocking	1–10
Flight	strong and powerful; direct
Voice	sharp *tyit*

IDENTIFICATION

Juvenile	
Crown	brown and black
Upperparts	brown and black; two white 'V's on back
Rump	black and white
Tail	black and white; short and square
Throat	white
Breast	buff; streaked on sides
Belly	white
Bill	black; short and straight
Legs	black; short
Ad.winter	grey above, white below, lacks 'V' on back
Ad.summer	spangled chestnut and black above, buffy breast

BREEDING

Nest	neat cup on ground
Eggs	4; pale olive, speckled brownish
Incubation	? mainly ♂
Young	active; downy
Fledging	?
Broods	1; June–July
Food	molluscs, crustaceans, worms
Population	10–12 winter; 200+ September

J	F	M	A	M	J	J	A	S	O	N	D
1	1	1	1	1	1	1	1	2	3	1	1

Temminck's Stint *Calidris temminckii*

short, thin bill

olive-grey back

grey streaked breast

greyish

juvenile

adult summer

yellow-green legs

white outer tail

Marginally smaller than Little Stint and much more grey and uniformly marked. Winter adult and juvenile grey above, with slightly paler feather margins. White below with grey breast. In summer, upperparts olive-grey with black streaks. Shortish legs and extended body shape, together with picking feeding action, recall Common Sandpiper rather than Dunlin or Little Stint. Prefers fresh marshes with emergent vegetation. *Status:* scarce, but regular, double passage migrant. Breeds regularly in small numbers in Scotland. *Similar Species:* Little Stint (p.119); Temminck's is more uniform and less 'contrasting' in all plumages.

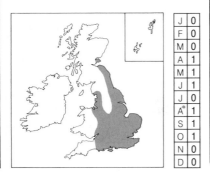

	TEMMINCK'S STINT
Type	wader-like
Size	13–15cm (5–5½in)
Habitat	freshwater marshes
Behaviour	wades, walks, takes off from water or ground
Flocking	1 or 2
Flight	strong and powerful; direct; flitting
Voice	high-pitched *trrrr-trrrr*
IDENTIFICATION	
Ad.winter and juvenile	
Crown	grey
Upperparts	grey
Rump	black and white
Tail	black and white; short and square
Throat	white
Breast	grey
Belly	white
Bill	black; short, straight and thin
Legs	yellow green; medium length
Ad.summer	upperparts olive-grey, speckled black; breast grey, streaked
BREEDING	
Nest	hollow on ground
Eggs	4; pale olive, speckled brownish
Incubation	21–22 days, mainly ♂
Young	active; downy
Fledging	15–18 days
Broods	1; June
Food	insects
Population	rare breeder; scarce passage migrant

J	0
F	0
M	0
A	1
M	1
J	1
J	0
A	1
S	1
O	1
N	0
D	0

Curlew Sandpiper *Calidris ferruginea*

decurved bill

long neck, rounded head

juvenile

square white rump

longish legs

adult winter

adult summer

buffy unstreaked breast

juvenile

Double passage migrant, mostly in autumn. Shape distinctive; long legs, long neck, decurved bill. White rump diagnostic. Adults constitute first wave of autumn birds (July–August); most show some chestnut feathers on breast. Later autumn wave (August–September) mainly juveniles; grey above with buffy feather margins giving scaled appearance. Buff wash over unstreaked breast. Some late adult migrants (September–October) are grey above and unstreaked white below. In spring, chestnut head and body contrast with grey wings. *Status:* regular in autumn, mostly August–September. Scarce in spring, mostly May–early June. *Similar Species:* Dunlin (p.120) is slightly smaller, shorter-necked and less elegant.

	CURLEW SANDPIPER
Type	wader-like
Size	18–20cm (7–8in)
Habitat	freshwater marshes, estuaries and shores
Behaviour	wades, walks, takes off and lands on ground
Flocking	1–15
Flight	strong and powerful; direct
Voice	*churrip*
IDENTIFICATION	
Juvenile	
Crown	grey
Upperparts	grey and buff
Rump	white
Tail	white, grey tip; short and square
Throat	white
Breast	buff-white
Belly	white
Bill	black, long and decurved
Legs	black; long
Ad.winter	grey above, white below; unmarked breast
Ad.summer	chestnut head and underparts; grey wings
BREEDING	
Nest	hollow on ground
Eggs	3–4; olive, blotched brown
Incubation	?; ♂ ♀
Young	active; downy
Fledging	?
Broods	1; June–July
Food	insects, molluscs, crustaceans
Population	variable; 100 to several thousand August–September; a few in spring

J	0
F	0
M	0
A	1
M	1
J	1
J	1
A	3
S	3
O	0
N	0
D	0

orange-red base to bill
uniform grey back
spotted breast
brown feather margins
adult summer
yellow legs
adult winter
narrow wingbar
winter

variants
adult ♂ winter
small head, long neck
white oval patches
broad buff margins to feathers create 'scaly' effect
orange-red legs
adult ♂ summer
buffy breast
adult ♀
juvenile

The most maritime of all shorebirds, seldom found away from rocky shorelines. Stockily-built, short-legged wader with bill about same length as head; base of bill orange-red. Few distinguishing features apart from shape and general dark coloration. In winter, head and breast dark grey with white eye ring and throat. Upperparts black with dark grey feather margins. Belly white with dark spots. In summer, back and wings dark with broad, brown edges to feathers. Head, neck, breast and belly heavily streaked. Feeds busily among rocks and seaweed, often in company with Turnstones (p.130).
Status: winter visitor to most suitable coastlines (October–April). Few in summer but has bred in Scotland.
Similar Species: no waders are as dark.

PURPLE SANDPIPER	
Type	wader-like
Size	20–22cm (7½–8½in)
Habitat	coasts
Behaviour	walks, wades, perches openly, takes off and lands on water or ground
Flocking	1–20
Flight	strong and powerful; direct
Voice	mostly silent; occasional *weet-weet*

IDENTIFICATION

Ad.winter	
Crown	dark grey
Upperparts	black and grey
Rump	black and white
Tail	black and white, short and rounded
Throat	white
Breast	dark grey
Belly	white, dark spots
Bill	black, orange base; straight and thin
Legs	yellow; short
Ad.summer	black and buff above; heavily streaked breast

BREEDING

Nest	leaf-lined hollow
Eggs	4; pale greenish, blotched brown
Incubation	21–22 days, mainly ♂
Young	active; downy
Fledging	3–4 weeks
Broods	1; June–July
Food	molluscs, crustaceans
Population	1 pair breeds; 15,000–25,000 winter

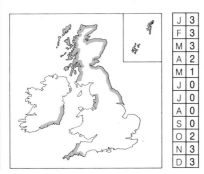

J	3
F	3
M	3
A	2
M	1
J	0
J	0
A	0
S	0
O	2
N	3
D	3

Rare breeder but relatively common double passage migrant and increasing winter visitor. Male (Ruff) much larger than female (Reeve). Male in summer, even on passage, boasts elaborate multi-coloured plumes on head and neck and has wattled, bare red face. Females, juveniles and males at other times have long necks, small heads, fine, medium-length, pointed bills and longish red, pink, yellow or green legs. Back always scalloped with buff margins to brown feathers.
Status: scarce breeder in East Anglia and north-west England; regular double passage migrant; scarce winter visitor.
Similar Species: Redshank (p.127) also has reddish legs but shape quite different. Juveniles may be confused with rare Buff-breasted Sandpiper.

RUFF	
Type	wader-like
Size	♂ 27–31cm (10–12in); ♀ 22–25cm (8–9in)
Habitat	freshwater marshes, flooded grassland
Behaviour	wades, walks, takes off from water or ground
Flocking	1–100
Flight	strong and powerful; direct
Voice	*chuck-uck*

IDENTIFICATION

Ad.♂winter and ♀	
Crown	buff
Upperparts	buff and brown, 'scalloped'
Rump	black and white
Tail	black and white; short and square
Throat	white
Breast	buff, speckled
Belly	white
Bill	black; straight and thin
Legs	pinkish red or yellowish; long
Ad.♂summer	elaborate head and neck plumes
Juvenile	uniformly buff below

BREEDING

Nest	hollow on ground
Eggs	4; olive, blotched brown
Incubation	20–21 days ♀
Young	active; downy
Fledging	?
Broods	1; Apr–May
Food	insects, invertebrates
Population	20+ Reeves; 1200 winter; several thousand passage

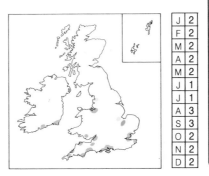

J	2
F	2
M	2
A	2
M	2
J	1
J	1
A	3
S	3
O	2
N	2
D	2

121

Dunlin *Calidris alpina*

DUNLIN	
Type	wader-like
Size	16–19cm (6–8in)
Habitat	marshes, estuaries and shores, moors
Behaviour	walks, wades, takes off from water and ground
Flocking	1–10,000
Flight	strong and powerful; direct
Voice	rasped *schreep*

IDENTIFICATION

Ad.winter	
Crown	grey
Upperparts	grey
Rump	black and white
Tail	black and white; short and square
Throat	white
Breast	white, streaked grey
Belly	white
Bill	black; long and thin, decurved at tip
Legs	black; medium length
Ad.summer	brown above; black belly patch
Juvenile	brown above, buff breast heavily streaked

BREEDING

Nest	hollow on ground
Eggs	4; greenish, blotched brown
Incubation	21–22 days ♂♀
Young	active; downy
Fledging	25 days
Broods	1; May–June
Food	molluscs, crustaceans
Population	4000–8000 pairs; 650,000 winter

J	F	M	A	M	J	J	A	S	O	N	D
5	5	4	4	4	3	3	4	4	5	5	5

longish bill
slight decurve

black belly

adult summer

buff feather margins

juvenile

streaked breast

adult winter

white wingbar

winter

white tail patches

This small wader breeds in small numbers on our inland moors, mainly in the north, but in winter it is the most abundant and widespread of our shore waders. Large numbers of visitors from the north and east form enormous flocks on our estuaries and shorelines. The Dunlin is a dumpy little bird that generally adopts a hunched-up attitude and also feeds very busily. In winter the upperparts are grey with paler feather margins, while the underparts are white, with grey streaking on the breast. In summer it is chestnut and black on the crown and back, while the breast is streaked and the belly boasts a bold black patch. The latter is quite distinctive. In autumn some birds retain remnants of their black bellies while on migration, though juveniles also have a scattering of black feathers from the lower breast to the belly. Otherwise the juvenile has buffy margins to the feathers of the upperparts and a buff, heavily streaked breast. There is often a pale 'V' on the back. *Status:* a widespread moorland breeder, spring and autumn passage migrant and abundant winter visitor to all coasts and muddy freshwater sites inland. This is the 'standard' small wader from which others have to be distinguished.

Similar Species: White-rumped Sandpiper
Calidris fuscicollis 16–18cm (6–7in)
Though easily overlooked among Dunlin, the White-rumped Sandpiper is more likely to be confused with other transatlantic rarities. It is short-legged and long-winged, like a Baird's Sandpiper, and has a similar horizontal stance. The white rump is a useful feature for identification.
Range: breeds in Arctic Canada as far west as the Alaskan border.
Migration: a huge loop migration to South America takes it out over the Atlantic.
British Distribution: a rare but annual visitor to the south and west and to East Anglia, mainly in autumn.

White-rumped Sandpiper

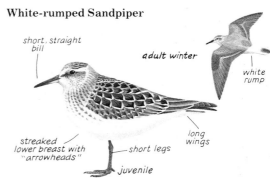

short, straight bill

adult winter

white rump

streaked lower breast with "arrowheads"

short legs

long wings

juvenile

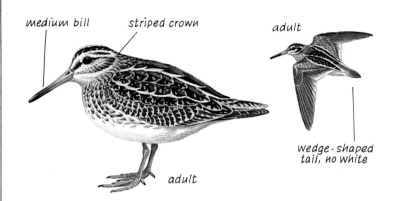

medium bill

striped crown

adult

wedge-shaped tail; no white

adult

very long bill

striped crown

rounded tail, white margins

Smaller, shorter-billed version of Snipe but much less common and more elusive, keeping itself well hidden in cover. Frequents freshwater marshes and flooded ground. Usually seen only when flushed; flies when in danger of being trodden on. Silent take-off and brief, low, straight flight with no towering or zig-zagging. No white on tail margins.
Status: passage migrant and winter visitor from September–April.
Similar Species: Snipe (p.123) is larger, with longer bill, zig-zag flight and harsh flight note.

JACK SNIPE

Type	wader-like
Size	18–20cm (7–8in)
Habitat	freshwater and marshes, fields and hedges
Behaviour	wades, walks, runs, takes off and lands on water or ground
Flocking	1–2
Flight	strong and powerful; direct
Voice	usually silent

IDENTIFICATION

Adult	
Crown	white with black stripe
Upperparts	brown and black, streaked
Rump	brown and black
Tail	brown and black; short and rounded
Throat	white
Breast	buff and brown, streaked
Belly	white
Bill	brown; straight and thin
Legs	green; medium length

BREEDING

Nest	lined cup on ground
Eggs	4; green, blotched brown
Incubation	17–24 days ♀
Young	active; downy
Fledging	?
Broods	1; June–July
Food	molluscs, worms, insects
Population	winter?

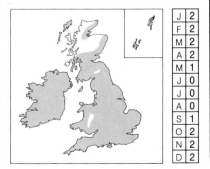

J	2
F	2
M	2
A	2
M	1
J	0
J	0
A	0
S	1
O	2
N	2
D	2

Heavily streaked, well camouflaged wader with long, straight bill. Mottled brown and black above with bold, buff stripes on back forming 'V'. Buff crown stripe and eyebrow plus dark eye stripe and dark margins to ear coverts produce distinctive striped pattern. Found mostly on freshwater marshes and flooded fields; generally gregarious. Tends to keep to cover but also feeds quite openly when not alarmed. If disturbed, flies off with pronounced zig-zagging, often towering into the air. Distinctive harsh flight note; also produces bleating sound in aerial diving display.
Status: widespread resident and abundant winter visitor.
Similar Species: Jack Snipe (p.123) smaller and usually silent with low, straight flight.

SNIPE

Type	wader-like
Size	25–27cm (9½–10½in)
Habitat	freshwater marshes, moors, fields
Behaviour	wades, walks, runs, takes off from water and ground
Flocking	1–100
Flight	strong and powerful, flitting, aerial dive
Voice	harsh *scarp*, repeated *chirper-chirper*; aerial 'drumming'

IDENTIFICATION

Adult	
Crown	dark brown with buff stripe
Upperparts	brown and black, streaked
Rump	brown and black
Tail	brown and black, edged white; short and rounded
Throat	white
Breast	buff and brown, streaked
Belly	white
Bill	brown; very long, thin and straight
Legs	green; long

BREEDING

Nest	lined hollow on ground
Eggs	4; pale green, blotched brown
Incubation	18–20 days ♀
Young	active; downy
Fledging	19–20 days
Broods	1, 2?; Apr–May
Food	worms, insects
Population	80,000–110,000 pairs; many thousands winter

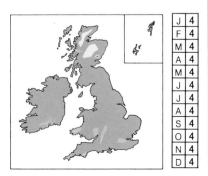

J	4
F	4
M	4
A	4
M	4
J	4
J	4
A	4
S	4
O	4
N	4
D	4

Woodcock *Scolopax rusticola*

WOODCOCK	
Type	wader-like
Size	32–36cm (12–14in)
Habitat	forest and woods
Behaviour	walks, takes off or lands on ground
Flocking	solitary
Flight	strong and powerful; direct
Voice	shrill *tssick* flight note when roding

IDENTIFICATION

Adult	
Crown	buff, transverse black bars
Upperparts	dark brown and buff, bars and stripes
Rump	brown and black
Tail	brown and black; short and rounded
Throat	buff
Breast	buff and brown, barred
Belly	buff and brown, barred
Bill	buff; very long and thin
Legs	pink; short and stout

BREEDING

Nest	leaf-lined hollow on ground
Eggs	4; buff, blotched brown
Incubation	20–23 days ♀
Young	active; downy
Fledging	5–6 weeks
Broods	2; Mar–May
Food	worms, insects
Population	10,000–50,000 pairs

J	F	M	A	M	J	J	A	S	O	N	D
2	2	2	2	3	3	3	2	2	2	2	2

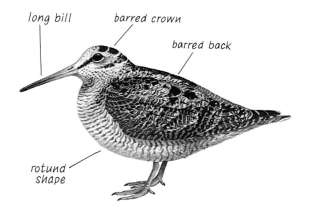

long bill — barred crown — barred back — rotund shape — rounded wings

A bulky, Snipe-like wader that is adapted to a life in moist open woodland. It is mottled and barred with rich chestnuts and browns above, and with buffs and browns below, the whole creating one of the most outstanding examples of cryptic camouflage in the entire world of birds. As well as this disguise, it has the habit of crouching immobile, even when closely approached, thus rendering itself virtually invisible on the ground. As a result, most Woodcock are seen in flight, especially during spring and summer evenings when they perform a courtship flight around their territory, known as 'roding'. This slow, rather owl-like flight over the tree-tops, indulged in at dawn as well as dusk, is accompanied by a low, croaking, frog-like sound followed by a thin *tssick* call.

In flight, Woodcock are distinctly bulky, round-winged birds with long, straight, downward-pointing bills. They breed among damp woodlands, flighting to feed in nearby marshy areas, mostly with a strong growth of emergent vegetation. Their nests and eggs are well camouflaged and just as difficult to locate as the sitting birds. Indeed, most nests are found by accident by flushing the bird at a range of a couple of metres. For generations there was great debate about the Woodcock's supposed habit of carrying its young in flight. It has now been established that Woodcock do have this remarkable ability, but that the method is to carry the chick between the legs and not in the bill as earlier naturalists had believed.

Status: resident virtually throughout Britain and Ireland; immigrants also arrive from the Continent.

Other Similar Species: Snipe (p. 123), has a similar, but longer, straight bill and is likewise cryptically coloured. It is, however, smaller, less bulky and is generally found in more open habitats.

Woodcock adult on nest

Limosa limosa **Black-tailed Godwit**

Limosa lapponica **Bar-tailed Godwit**

- long straight bill
- uniform greyish upperparts
- bold black and white wings
- adult winter
- black tail bar
- chestnut breast
- legs extend in flight
- chestnut ends at breast, white belly
- adult summer
- adult winter

- long bill, slightly uptilted
- streaking effect
- chestnut on whole of underparts
- no wingbar
- adult winter
- adult summer
- adult winter

Large, long-legged, long-billed wader of freshwater marshes, flooded fields and estuaries. In summer, adult has chestnut head, neck and breast with white chin and white eyebrow. Back spangled black and chestnut; wings grey. Belly white, barred black and brown. In winter, grey back and wings with no prominent streaking. Breast pale grey; belly white. Juvenile brown and buff; upperparts 'scalloped'. In flight, shows black band at tip of white tail and broad white wingbar.
Status: double passage migrant and winter visitor. Returned to breed in 1952 after lengthy absence; now breeds regularly in small numbers.
Similar Species: Bar-tailed Godwit (p.125) is smaller, has shorter legs and shorter, upturned bill; lacks wingbar.

Large, long-legged, long-billed wader of estuaries and shorelines; occasionally roosts in coastal freshwater marshes. In summer, males have chestnut underparts extending to undertail. Back spangled black and chestnut; wings grey. Summer females paler than males. In winter, upperparts buffy grey, heavily streaked black; underparts white. Juvenile streaked buff and black. In flight, appears uniformly greyish with white 'V' extending upwards from rump; feet barely extend beyond tail.
Status: double passage migrant and numerous winter visitor.
Similar Species: larger Black-tailed Godwit (p.125) shows bold pattern of black and white in flight (feet extend well beyond tail) and has barred white belly and white undertail in summer.

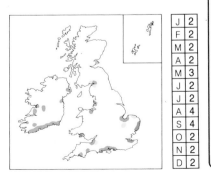

	BLACK-TAILED GODWIT
Type	wader-like
Size	38–43cm (14½–16½in)
Habitat	marshes, estuaries, fields
Behaviour	wades, walks, takes off and lands on water or ground
Flocking	1–200
Flight	strong and powerful; direct
Voice	loud *reeka-reeka-reeka*
IDENTIFICATION	
Ad.winter	
Crown	grey
Upperparts	grey
Rump	white
Tail	white with black band; short and square
Throat	white
Breast	pale grey
Belly	white
Bill	dark with pink base; very long, straight and thin
Legs	black; very long
Ad.summer	chestnut foreparts; barred white belly
Juvenile	upperparts dark brown and buff, scalloped; breast buff
BREEDING	
Nest	lined hollow on ground
Eggs	4; green, blotched brown
Incubation	22–24 days ♂ ♀
Young	active; downy
Fledging	4 weeks
Broods	1; Apr–June
Food	worms, molluscs, insects
Population	60–70 pairs; 10,000 winter; 16,500 autumn

J	2
F	2
M	2
A	2
M	3
J	2
J	2
A	4
S	4
O	2
N	2
D	2

	BAR-TAILED GODWIT
Type	wader-like
Size	36–40cm (14–16in)
Habitat	estuaries and shores, freshwater marshes
Behaviour	wades, walks, takes off from water and ground
Flocking	1–1000
Flight	strong and powerful; direct
Voice	*kirrick-kirrick*
IDENTIFICATION	
Ad.winter	
Crown	buff and brown
Upperparts	buffy grey, streaked black
Rump	white
Tail	barred black; short and square
Throat	white
Breast	buff
Belly	white
Bill	dark with pink base; very long and thin, upturned
Legs	black; long
Ad.summer	chestnut head and all underparts
Juvenile	heavily streaked and mottled black and buff above; breast buff with clear streaking
BREEDING	
Nest	lined hollow on ground
Eggs	4; olive, blotched brown
Incubation	20–21 days ♂ ♀
Young	active; downy
Fledging	?
Broods	1; May–June
Food	molluscs, worms
Population	58,000 winter

J	5
F	5
M	5
A	4
M	2
J	0
J	0
A	3
S	3
O	5
N	5
D	5

Whimbrel *Numenius phaeopus*

striped crown

bill decurved towards tip

white 'V' extends up back

Smaller version of Curlew that breeds in small numbers in northern Scotland but is otherwise double passage migrant. Central crown stripe, pale bordered black; pale eyebrow. Bill decurved towards tip. Upperparts greyish brown with dark centres and pale edges to feathers. Neck and breast buff with dark streaking. In flight, shows white 'V' up back; feet just protrude beyond tail. Distinctive call.
Status: scarce breeder in Scotland; regular double passage migrant April–June, July–October.
Similar Species: Curlew (p.126) lacks crown stripe and has longer, more decurved bill. (Beware young Curlews with short bills in autumn.) Also several other 'curlews' – all extremely rare.

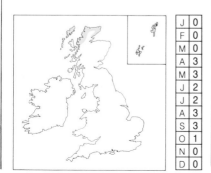

	WHIMBREL	
Type	wader-like	
Size	39–43cm (15–17in)	
Habitat	freshwater marshes, estuaries, moors	
Behaviour	wades, walks, takes off from water and ground	
Flocking	1–15	
Flight	strong and powerful; direct	
Voice	rapidly whistled *whi-whi-whi-whi-whi-whi-whi-whi*	

IDENTIFICATION		
Adult		
Crown	pale central stripe, bordered black	
Upperparts	greyish brown, dark feather centres	
Rump	white	
Tail	black and white; short and square	
Throat	buff and brown	
Breast	buff, brown streaks	
Belly	white	
Bill	black; long and decurved near tip	
Legs	grey; long	

BREEDING		
Nest	hollow on ground	
Eggs	4; olive-green, blotched brown	
Incubation	24–28 days ♂♀	
Young	active; downy	
Fledging	5–6 weeks	
Broods	1; May–June	
Food	molluscs, crabs	
Population	less than 200 pairs; over 2000 spring; less than 2000 autumn	

J	0
F	0
M	0
A	3
M	3
J	2
J	2
A	3
S	3
O	1
N	0
D	0

Curlew *Numenius arquata*

very long, curved bill

no crown stripes

white 'V' extends up back

Large shorebird with long legs and very long, decurved bill. Upperparts brown with buffy feather margins; underparts heavily streaked brown on neck and breast. In flight, shows uniform wings and white 'V' extending up rump. Generally gregarious, forming large flocks on estuaries, marshes and adjacent fields.
Status: widespread breeding bird, mainly in northern and western hill districts; also on lowland heaths and marshes. Numerous winter visitor and passage migrant.
Similar Species: Whimbrel (p.126) has striped crown, marked eyebrow and shorter bill with downward curve nearer the tip. Juvenile Curlew has shorter bill than adult and may be confused with Whimbrel.

	CURLEW	
Type	wader-like	
Size	51–61cm (20–24in)	
Habitat	freshwater marshes, estuaries and shores, moors and heaths, fields	
Behaviour	wades, walks, takes off and lands on water or ground	
Flocking	1–1000	
Flight	strong and powerful; direct	
Voice	drawn out *coor-lee*; bubbling call summer	

IDENTIFICATION		
Adult		
Crown	buff and brown	
Upperparts	buff and brown	
Rump	white	
Tail	buff and brown; short and square	
Throat	buff and brown, streaked	
Breast	buff and brown, streaked	
Belly	white	
Bill	black; very long and decurved	
Legs	grey; long	

BREEDING		
Nest	lined hollow on ground	
Eggs	4; olive, blotched brown	
Incubation	26–30 days, mainly ♀	
Young	active; downy	
Fledging	5–6 weeks	
Broods	1; Apr–June	
Food	worms, molluscs, crabs	
Population	40,000–70,000 pairs; 125,000 winter	

J	5
F	5
M	5
A	5
M	5
J	4
J	4
A	5
S	5
O	5
N	5
D	5

Tringa erythropus **Spotted Redshank**

- longer and thinner bill than Redshank
- clear eyebrow
- long, thin neck
- grey back
- buffy breast
- white 'V' extends up back
- all black with white spots above
- long red legs
- adult winter
- legs trail in flight
- no white trailing edge
- adult summer

Tringa totanus **Redshank** ▬

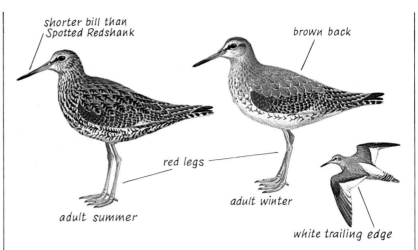

- shorter bill than Spotted Redshank
- brown back
- red legs
- adult summer
- adult winter
- white trailing edge

A more delicate and graceful version of Redshank with longer, darker bill and longer legs. In summer, adult is completely black above and below with white spangling on wings and back. In winter, upperparts grey; wing feathers spotted black with white margins. In late spring and early autumn, adults often show traces of black in plumage. Juveniles resemble Redshank more closely but brown upperparts finely spotted black and white. In flight white rump extends up back in a 'V'; no wingbar. Feet trail beyond tip of tail.
Status: regular double passage migrant and winter visitor in smaller numbers to south and east coasts.
Similar Species: Redshank (p.127) is less elegant.

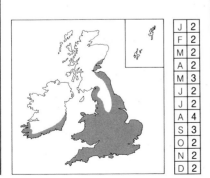

	SPOTTED REDSHANK
Type	wader-like
Size	29–32cm (11–12½in)
Habitat	freshwater marshes, estuaries
Behaviour	wades, walks, takes off from water or ground
Flocking	1–50
Flight	strong and powerful; direct
Voice	loud *choo-it*

IDENTIFICATION

Ad.winter	
Crown	grey
Upperparts	grey; wing feathers white margins, spotted black
Rump	white
Tail	black and white; short and square
Throat	white
Breast	grey
Belly	white
Bill	red; long and thin
Legs	red; long
Ad.summer	uniformly black with white speckling on upperparts
Juvenile	upperparts brown, spotted black and white; underparts white, barred brown

BREEDING

Nest	hollow on ground
Eggs	4; olive, blotched blackish
Incubation	?; ♂
Young	active; downy
Fledging	?
Broods	1; May–June
Food	molluscs, crustaceans
Population	100 winter; 700 September

J	2
F	2
M	2
A	2
M	3
J	2
J	2
A	4
S	3
O	2
N	2
D	2

Common and widespread wader of coasts, estuaries, inland marshes and wetlands. In winter, large flocks found on favoured estuaries; also occurs along rocky and muddy shores. Upperparts brown, paler and more uniform in winter. Underparts white with heavy streaking, particularly in summer. Legs and base of bill bright red. In flight shows broad white trailing edge to wing.
Status: breeds over large areas, particularly in north and west Britain and Ireland. Abundant passage migrant and winter visitor, mainly to coasts and estuaries.
Similar Species: Spotted Redshank (p.127) and beware red-legged Ruff (p.121).

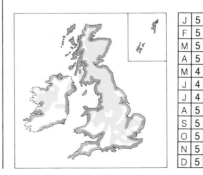

	REDSHANK
Type	wader-like
Size	26–30cm (10–11½in)
Habitat	freshwater marshes, estuaries and shores, fields
Behaviour	wades, walks, takes off from water and ground
Flocking	1–1000
Flight	strong and powerful; direct
Voice	melodic *tyew-yew-yew* ; and repeated *twek*

IDENTIFICATION

Adult	
Crown	brown
Upperparts	brown
Rump	white
Tail	black and white; short and square
Throat	white, heavy brown streaking
Breast	white, heavy brown streaking
Belly	white
Bill	dark brown, base red; long and thin
Legs	red; long

BREEDING

Nest	lined hollow on ground
Eggs	4; buff, blotched blackish
Incubation	23–24 days ♂ ♀
Young	active; downy
Fledging	30 days
Broods	1; Apr–June
Food	worms, molluscs, crustaceans
Population	40,000–50,000 pairs; 80,000 winter

J	5
F	5
M	5
A	5
M	4
J	4
J	4
A	5
S	5
O	5
N	5
D	5

127

Wood Sandpiper *Tringa glareola*

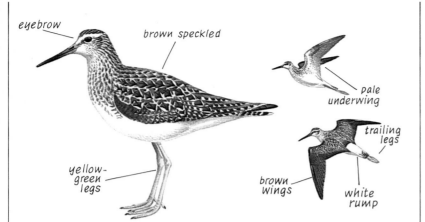

eyebrow
brown speckled
pale underwing
trailing legs
yellow-green legs
brown wings
white rump

Similar to Green Sandpiper but always browner above with heavily speckled plumage and more pronounced eyebrow. Slimmer build and longer, pale legs produce a more elegant impression. Generally occurs singly or in small groups on freshwater marshes, often where vegetation emerges above the water. In flight, shows white rump, barred tail and uniform wing, but never appears black and white like Green Sandpiper.
Status: regular double passage migrant, most numerous in autumn. Rare breeder in Scotland.
Similar Species: Green Sandpiper (p.128). Speckled upperparts may produce similar pattern to small female Ruff (p.121).

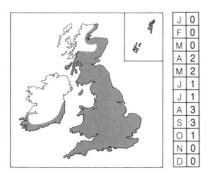

	WOOD SANDPIPER
Type	wader-like
Size	19–21cm (7–8in)
Habitat	freshwater marshes
Behaviour	wades, walks, takes off and lands on water or ground
Flocking	1–15
Flight	strong and powerful; direct
Voice	flat *chi-chi-chi*

	IDENTIFICATION
Adult	
Crown	brown
Upperparts	brown, speckled buff and white
Rump	white
Tail	black and white; short and square
Throat	white
Breast	buff, faint streaks
Belly	white
Bill	black; straight and thin
Legs	yellow-green; long

	BREEDING
Nest	hollow on ground
Eggs	4; pale green, blotched brown
Incubation	22–23 days, mainly ♀
Young	active; downy
Fledging	?
Broods	1; May–June
Food	molluscs, crustaceans, insects
Population	less than 5 pairs; passage 1000 or more?

J	0
F	0
M	0
A	2
M	2
J	1
J	1
A	3
S	3
O	1
N	0
D	0

Green Sandpiper *Tringa ochropus*

very dark, with small pale spots
dark underwing
uniform dark wings
shortish dark legs
white rump

Medium-sized wader; dark brown above and white below but always appears black and white at any distance. Speckled on breast; short white eyebrow. In flight, shows uniformly dark wings and back, white rump and barred tail. Generally solitary or in small groups on freshwater marshes, particularly along dykes and ditches. Bobs head and tail.
Status: double passage migrant but never numerous. Has bred in Scotland.
Similar Species: Wood Sandpiper (p.128) is paler brown above and has longer, paler legs and shorter, thicker bill

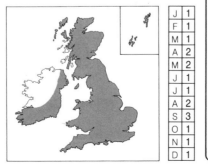

	GREEN SANDPIPER
Type	wader-like
Size	22–24cm (8½–9in)
Habitat	freshwater marshes
Behaviour	wades, walks, takes off from water and ground
Flocking	1–10
Flight	strong and powerful, direct
Voice	rising *tluit-weet-wit* of alarm

	IDENTIFICATION
Adult	
Crown	black and brown
Upperparts	dark brown
Rump	white
Tail	black and white, barred; short and square
Throat	white
Breast	white, brown streaks
Belly	white
Bill	black; straight and thin
Legs	dark green; medium length

	BREEDING
Nest	disused bird's nest in tree
Eggs	4; olive, spotted reddish brown
Incubation	20–23 days, mainly ♀
Young	active; downy
Fledging	4 weeks
Broods	1; Apr–June
Food	molluscs, crustaceans, insects
Population	very rare breeder; several hundred passage; 150–250 winter

J	1
F	1
M	1
A	2
M	2
J	1
J	1
A	2
S	3
O	1
N	1
D	1

Tringa nebularia Greenshank

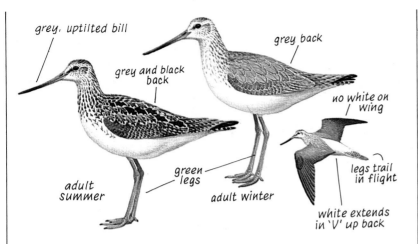

grey, uptilted bill

grey and black back

grey back

no white on wing

green legs

adult summer

adult winter

legs trail in flight

white extends in 'V' up back

Long-legged, long-billed, greyish wader of marshes and estuaries. Upperparts grey, marked with streaks of black in summer. Underparts mainly white, speckled grey in summer. Long green legs and long, grey, slightly upturned bill. Always appears graceful and elegant. In flight, wings uniformly dark grey with white rump extending in 'V' up back; feet extend beyond tip of tail.
Status: scarce breeder in Scottish Highlands and Islands and western Ireland. Double passage migrant, most numerous in autumn; scarce winter visitor to south-west England and Wales and coast of Ireland.
Similar Species: none.

GREENSHANK	
Type	wader-like
Size	29–32cm (11–12½in)
Habitat	freshwater marshes, moors, estuaries
Behaviour	wades, walks, takes off and lands on water or ground
Flocking	1–15
Flight	strong and powerful; direct
Voice	loud *tu-tu-tu*

IDENTIFICATION

Ad.winter	
Crown	grey
Upperparts	grey
Rump	white
Tail	grey; short and square
Throat	white
Breast	grey
Belly	white
Bill	grey; long and thin
Legs	green; long
Ad.summer	black streaks on upperparts; underparts speckled grey

BREEDING

Nest	hollow on ground
Eggs	4; buff, blotched brown
Incubation	24–25 days, mainly ♀
Young	active; downy
Fledging	4 weeks
Broods	1; May–June
Food	worms, molluscs, crustaceans
Population	800–900 pairs; 600 winter; 2000 September

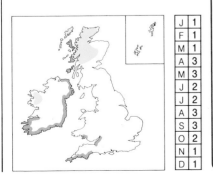

J	1
F	1
M	1
A	3
M	3
J	2
J	2
A	3
S	3
O	2
N	1
D	1

Actitis hypoleucos Common Sandpiper

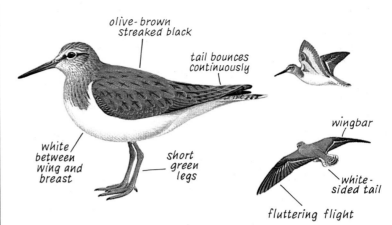

olive-brown streaked black

tail bounces continuously

white between wing and breast

short green legs

wingbar

white-sided tail

fluttering flight

Distinctive sandpiper with brown upperparts and white below. Brown streaking at sides of breast forms clear line above bend of wing; distinctive white wedge between the two. Clear-cut eye stripe and eyebrow. Short green legs accentuate long body; folded wings do not reach tip of tail. Continuous wagging motion when feeding and at rest. Flickering, shallow wing beats produce characteristic flight, usually low over water. Prefers margins of streams, dykes and ponds to open marshes; usually solitary.
Status: breeding summer visitor to hill districts of north and west. Common double passage migrant elsewhere.
Similar Species: Wood Sandpiper (p.128) and Green Sandpiper (p.128) also 'bob' but not continuously like Common Sandpiper.

COMMON SANDPIPER	
Type	wader-like
Size	18–21cm (7–8in)
Habitat	freshwater marshes, estuaries
Behaviour	wades, walks, takes off and lands on water or ground
Flocking	1–2
Flight	direct; flitting
Voice	whistled *sweeswee-swoo*

IDENTIFICATION

Adult	
Crown	brown
Upperparts	olive-brown
Rump	buff
Tail	buff; short and square
Throat	white
Breast	white, streaked buff on sides
Belly	white
Bill	black; straight and thin
Legs	green; short

BREEDING

Nest	hollow on ground
Eggs	4; buff, speckled brown
Incubation	20–23 days ♂ ♀
Young	active; downy
Fledging	13–21 days
Broods	1; May–June
Food	molluscs, crustaceans, insects
Population	50,000 pairs; 100 winter

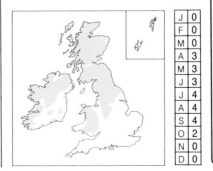

J	0
F	0
M	0
A	3
M	3
J	3
J	4
A	4
S	4
O	2
N	0
D	0

Grey Phalarope *Phalaropus fulicarius*

bill thicker and shorter than Red-necked

grey

adult winter

wingbar

red

adult ♀ summer

dark crown and eye patch

bold 'V's on back

juvenile

Similar to Red-necked Phalarope but slightly larger and decidedly more bulky, with stouter and proportionately shorter bill. In breeding plumage, rust-red on neck and underparts. Back is black with double buffy 'V' and broad buffy margins to wings. Crown, forehead and chin black, face white. Bill has yellow base. Winter and juvenile birds similar to Red-necked and best separated by stocky shape and thicker bill.
Status: autumn passage migrant in variable numbers, mostly storm-driven.
Similar Species: Red-necked Phalarope (p.131), see above.

GREY PHALAROPE	
Type	wader-like
Size	19–21cm (7–8in)
Habitat	freshwater, sea, estuaries
Behaviour	swims, wades, takes off from water and ground
Flocking	1–2
Flight	strong and powerful; direct
Voice	high-pitched *twit*
IDENTIFICATION	
Ad.winter	
Crown	grey
Upperparts	grey
Rump	black and white
Tail	black and white; short and square
Throat	white
Breast	white
Belly	white
Bill	black, yellow base; straight and thin
Legs	yellow; medium length
Ad.summer	chestnut red underparts; white face
Juvenile	dark brown on crown and back; dark eye mark
BREEDING	
Nest	hollow among vegetation in marsh
Eggs	4; pale green, blotched brown
Incubation	19 days ♂
Young	active; downy
Fledging	16–21 days
Broods	1; June–July
Food	insects, molluscs, crustaceans
Population	variable, autumn migrant

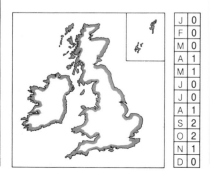

J	0
F	0
M	0
A	1
M	1
J	0
J	0
A	1
S	2
O	2
N	1
D	0

Turnstone *Arenaria interpres*

remnant face pattern

greyish

complex head and face pattern

rich chestnut

legs orange

adult winter

adult summer

complex pattern of bars and stripes

Stocky, short-legged, stubby-billed wader of coastal pools and beaches, especially rocky shores. Generally gregarious. Characteristic habit of turning stones in search of food; also picks and probes at surface. In summer, upperparts rich chestnut marked with black and buff. Head and neck white with intricate black markings extending to broad black breast band. Remaining underparts white. In winter, same overall pattern but in shades of grey. In flight, wingbar and wing patch combine with white rump and double tail bands to produce unmistakable pattern.
Status: common double passage migrant and winter visitor.
Similar Species: none.

TURNSTONE	
Type	wader-like
Size	22–24cm (8–9in)
Habitat	estuaries and shores
Behaviour	wades, walks, perches openly, takes off from water and ground
Flocking	1–300
Flight	strong and powerful; direct
Voice	distinctive rattling *tukatuk*
IDENTIFICATION	
Ad.winter and juvenile	
Crown	grey and black
Upperparts	grey and black
Rump	white
Tail	white, two black bands; short and square
Throat	white
Breast	grey
Belly	white
Bill	black; short and thin
Legs	orange; short
Ad.summer	rich chestnut above with bold black and white face pattern
BREEDING	
Nest	scrape on ground
Eggs	4; greenish, blotched brown
Incubation	22–23 days ♂ ♀
Young	active; downy
Fledging	?
Broods	1; May–July
Food	invertebrates
Population	25,000 winter

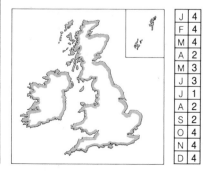

J	4
F	4
M	4
A	2
M	3
J	3
J	1
A	2
S	2
O	4
N	2
D	4

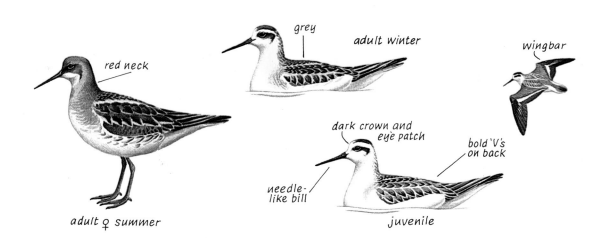

- red neck — adult ♀ summer
- grey — adult winter
- wingbar
- dark crown and eye patch
- bold 'V's on back
- needle-like bill
- juvenile

	RED-NECKED PHALAROPE
Type	wader-like
Size	17–19cm (6½–7in)
Habitat	freshwater marshes, sea
Behaviour	swims, wades, takes off from water and ground
Flocking	1–15
Flight	strong and powerful; direct
Voice	quiet *tyit*

IDENTIFICATION

Ad. ♀ summer	
Crown	grey
Upperparts	grey and buff; wings black and buff
Rump	black and white
Tail	black and white; short and square
Throat	white chin, red neck
Breast	orange-red
Belly	white
Bill	black; straight and fine
Legs	black; medium length
Ad. ♂ summer	as ♀ but paler
Ad. winter	grey above with eye mark
Juvenile	dark brown on crown and back; dark eye mark

BREEDING

Nest	neat cup in marsh
Eggs	4; pale green, blotched brown
Incubation	18–20 days ♂
Young	active; downy
Fledging	18–22 days
Broods	1; June–July
Food	insects, crustaceans
Population	40–50 pairs; variable autumn migration

J	F	M	A	M	J	J	A	S	O	N	D
0	0	0	0	2	2	2	1	2	2	0	0

This is a delicate little wader that spends most of its life swimming. It winters at sea, often well out of sight of land and usually in quite large flocks. In the breeding season the female has a slate-grey crown, nape, back and lower breast. The upperparts are marked by two bold, buff-coloured 'Vs'. The chin is white and the neck is orange-red, extending to the ear coverts and eye. The male is a duller version of his mate. In winter both sexes are grey above and white below, marked by a black 'comma' behind the eye. The bill is thin and pointed. The juvenile is dark brown above, with buffy feather margins and a double buff 'V' on the back. In all plumages a bold white wing bar is evident in flight.
Status: a rare breeder in Scotland and Ireland. Elsewhere, a scarce passage migrant in spring and autumn.

Similar Species:
Wilson's Phalarope *Phalaropus tricolor* 24–27cm (9½–10½in)
This transatlantic visitor is considerably larger than the other two phalaropes and generally swims less frequently. Instead, it feeds like a normal wader and may then be confused with species such as the Marsh Sandpiper. The bill is long and needle-like as in that species, but the shorter legs are yellow (in autumn). It is always much paler than any similar species.
Range: western Canada and adjacent United States.
Migration: southwards to South America.
British Distribution: though first recorded only in 1954 it is now a rare, but annual, visitor, mainly in the autumn, but also in spring and even summer. Most records have a westerly bias, but it also occurs elsewhere, except for northern Scotland.
Other Similar Species: Grey Phalarope (*opposite*).

Wilson's Phalarope

- face pattern
- ♀ summer
- needle like bill
- white rump
- adult winter
- pale grey
- first winter

Pomarine Skua *Stercorarius pomarinus*

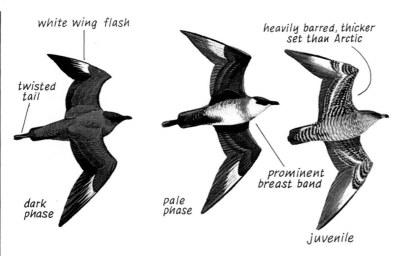

white wing flash

twisted tail

dark phase

heavily barred, thicker set than Arctic

prominent breast band

pale phase

juvenile

Like Arctic Skua, occurs in two phases – light and dark. Both phases show white wing flashes, but pale phase has smudgy breast band (more prominent than pale Arctic). Spring adults easily separated from Arctic by broad, twisted, central feathers extending well beyond rest of tail. In autumn and juveniles, structure more important than plumage details; Pomarine always heavier and more bulky than Arctic. Juvenile heavily barred above and below. Generally seen offshore during extended sea-watches in spring and autumn.
Status: regular but scarce passage migrant in first half of May and August–October off southern and western headlands.
Similar Species: Arctic Skua (p.132), see above.

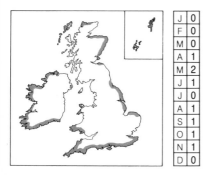

	POMARINE SKUA	
Type	gull-like	
Size	43–53cm (16–21in)	
Habitat	open sea; estuaries and shores	
Behaviour	swims, takes off and lands on water	
Flocking	1–10	
Flight	strong and powerful; direct; glides, aerial dive	
Voice	silent at sea	

IDENTIFICATION	
Ad.pale	
Crown	black
Upperparts	brown
Rump	brown
Tail	brown; rounded; central feathers long and twisted
Throat	yellow
Breast	buff; smudgy breast band
Belly	white
Bill	buff; short and thin
Legs	brown; medium length
Ad.dark	uniformly brown; white wing flashes
Juvenile	heavily barred; lacks long central tail feathers

BREEDING	
Nest	hollow on ground
Eggs	2; buff, spotted brown
Incubation	27–28 days ♂♀
Young	semi-helpless; downy
Fledging	5–6 weeks
Broods	1; June–July
Food	fish
Population	scarce passage migrant, mainly spring

J	0
F	0
M	0
A	1
M	2
J	1
J	0
A	1
S	1
O	1
N	1
D	0

Arctic Skua *Stercorarius parasiticus*

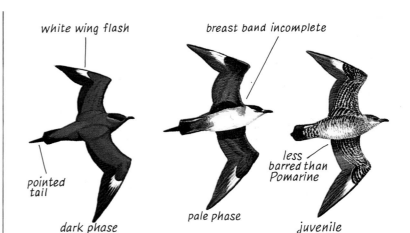

white wing flash

breast band incomplete

pointed tail

dark phase

pale phase

less barred than Pomarine

juvenile

Most commonly seen of the four skua species and the 'base' from which others must be differentiated. Fast, highly agile, dashing flight reminiscent of Peregrine. Pursues other seabirds. Occurs in two phases – light and dark – both of which show white wing flashes. Pale phase has dark cap and upperparts; underparts pale with indistinct dark breast band. Dark phase uniformly brown. Spring adults have two central tail feathers extended; absent in juveniles and (usually) autumn adults.
Status: summer visitor to far north; regular passage migrant to all coasts, especially in autumn.
Similar Species: lighter and more agile than Pomarine Skua (p.132) and heavier and less tern-like than Long-tailed Skua (p.133).

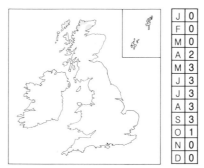

	ARCTIC SKUA	
Type	gull-like	
Size	38–48cm (14½–18½in)	
Habitat	sea, moors, estuaries	
Behaviour	swims, perches openly, takes off from water and ground	
Flocking	1–15	
Flight	strong and powerful; direct; glides, aerial dive	
Voice	high *kee-ow*; silent at sea	

IDENTIFICATION	
Ad.pale	
Crown	black
Upperparts	brown
Rump	brown
Tail	black; long central feathers
Throat	yellow
Breast	white; indistinct band
Belly	white
Bill	black; short and thin
Legs	brown; medium length
Ad.dark	uniformly brown; white wing flashes, as pale phase
Juvenile	heavily barred; lacks long central tail feathers

BREEDING	
Nest	unlined hollow on ground
Eggs	2; greenish, blotched brown
Incubation	24–28 days ♂♀
Young	semi-helpless; downy
Fledging	30 days
Broods	1; May–June
Food	fish
Population	1000 pairs; regular passage migrant, mostly autumn

J	0
F	0
M	0
A	2
M	3
J	3
J	3
A	3
S	3
O	1
N	0
D	0

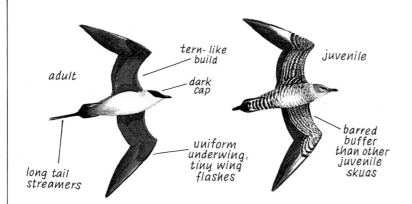

adult

tern-like build

dark cap

juvenile

long tail streamers

uniform underwing, tiny wing flashes

barred buffer than other juvenile skuas

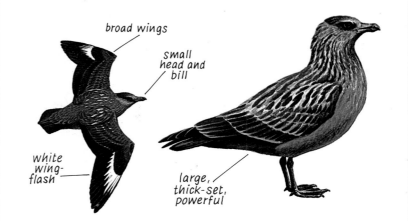

broad wings

small head and bill

white wing-flash

large, thick-set, powerful

Rarest of the skuas, occurring only in pale phase. Spring adults have very long central tail feathers, usually lacking in autumn and sub-adult birds. Upperparts greyish, not brown; underparts pure white. Dark cap more contrasting than in other pale phase skuas; wing flashes less pronounced. Juvenile barred as other skuas, but less rufous.
Status: scarce passage migrant to all coasts in spring and autumn.
Similar Species: pale phase Arctic Skua (p.132). Long-tailed lighter built than Arctic with more buoyant flight.

Largest of the skuas with uniformly dark brownish plumage and bold white wing flashes. Wings much broader than other skuas and flight less agile. Smaller head and bill than large gulls and easier, dashing flight, especially in pursuit of other seabirds.
Status: scarce breeder in far north of Britain; passage migrant to all other coasts.
Similar Species: often said to resemble large immature gull but not really confusable once seen.

LONG-TAILED SKUA

Type	gull-like
Size	38–56cm (14½–21in)
Habitat	sea, estuaries
Behaviour	swims, takes off and lands on water
Flocking	1–2
Flight	strong and powerful; direct; glides, aerial dive
Voice	silent at sea

IDENTIFICATION

Adult	
Crown	black
Upperparts	grey
Rump	grey
Tail	black; long central feathers
Throat	white
Breast	white
Belly	buff
Bill	black; short and thin
Legs	brown; medium length
Juvenile	heavily barred; lacks long central tail feathers and cap

BREEDING

Nest	unlined hollow on ground
Eggs	2; olive, blotched brown
Incubation	23 days ♂ ♀
Young	semi-helpless; downy
Fledging	3 weeks
Broods	1; June
Food	fish
Population	rare, passage migrant

GREAT SKUA

Type	gull-like
Size	56–61cm (22–24in)
Habitat	sea, estuaries, moors
Behaviour	swims, perches openly, takes off and lands on water or ground
Flocking	1–2
Flight	strong and powerful; direct; glides, aerial dive
Voice	harsh *uk-uk-uk*; nasal *skeerr*

IDENTIFICATION

Adult	
Crown	brown and black
Upperparts	dark brown, streaked buff
Rump	dark brown, streaked buff
Tail	dark brown and buff; medium length, rounded
Throat	buff and brown, streaked
Breast	buff and brown, streaked
Belly	buff and brown, streaked
Bill	black; stout
Legs	brown; medium length

BREEDING

Nest	unlined hollow on ground
Eggs	2; olive, spotted brown
Incubation	28–30 days ♂ ♀
Young	semi-helpless; downy
Fledging	6–7 weeks
Broods	1; May–June
Food	fish, eggs, birds
Population	3800 pairs; scarce passage migrant

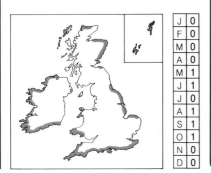

J	0
F	0
M	0
A	0
M	1
J	1
J	0
A	1
S	1
O	1
N	0
D	0

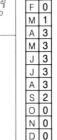

J	0
F	0
M	1
A	3
M	3
J	3
J	3
A	3
S	2
O	0
N	0
D	0

Mediterranean Gull _Larus melanocephalus_

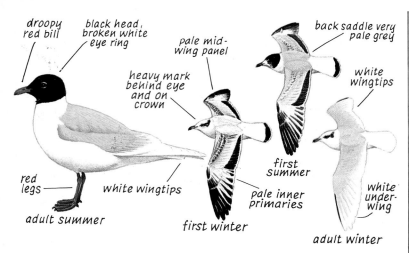

Very pale gull with heavy, droopy, red bill and red legs. Adult in summer has black, not brown, head with prominent broken white eye ring. Back and wings pale grey, with white primaries and white underwing. In winter, black head replaced by dark smudge behind eye and streaked hind crown. Uniform white primaries and underwing of adult facilitate identification at considerable range.
Status: rare breeder; scarce passage migrant and winter visitor.
Similar Species: adult Black-headed Gull (p.134). Juvenile more like Common Gull (p.137) than Black-headed, but with paler and more contrasting central wing panel. First winter Mediterranean and Common Gulls similar, but Common Gull has pale grey (not white) 'saddle' on back.

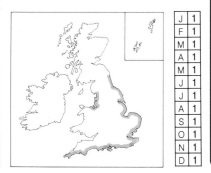

	MEDITERRANEAN GULL
Type	gull-like
Size	37–40cm (14–15in)
Habitat	freshwater marshes, sea, estuaries and shores
Behaviour	swims, wades, walks, perches openly, takes off from water and ground
Flocking	1–3
Flight	soars, glides; strong and powerful; direct
Voice	plaintive _kee-ow_

IDENTIFICATION

Ad.winter	
Crown	white, streaked hind crown
Upperparts	grey
Rump	white
Tail	white; medium length, square
Throat	white
Breast	white
Belly	white
Bill	red; short and thin
Legs	red; medium length
Ad.summer	black hood, white eye ring
Juvenile	brown across wings, pale central wing patch

BREEDING

Nest	lined hollow near water
Eggs	3; creamy, spotted black
Incubation	23–25 days ♂♀
Young	partly-active; downy
Fledging	35–40 days
Broods	1; May–June
Food	invertebrates, fish
Population	1–3 pairs; scarce passage migrant

J	1
F	1
M	1
A	1
M	1
J	1
J	1
A	1
S	1
O	1
N	1
D	1

Black-headed Gull _Larus ridibundus_

Most common and widespread gull, equally at home inland and along shorelines. In all plumages distinguished by white outer primaries creating a white forewing. Outer underwing dark. Adult in summer has chocolate hood, red bill and red legs. In winter, hood reduced to spot behind eye. First winter birds have pale grey backs with brown markings across wings. Gregarious, forming huge nocturnal roosts.
Status: widespread and numerous colonial breeder; abundant winter visitor.
Similar Species: Mediterranean Gull (p.134) and Little Gull (p.135).

	BLACK-HEADED GULL
Type	gull-like
Size	35–38cm (13–14½in)
Habitat	towns, marshes, moors, sea, shoreline, fields
Behaviour	swims, wades, walks, perches openly, takes off from water or ground
Flocking	1–40,000
Flight	soars, glides; strong and powerful; direct
Voice	repeated _kuk-kuk_; angry _kee-ar_

IDENTIFICATION

Ad.winter	
Crown	white
Upperparts	grey
Rump	white
Tail	white; medium length, square
Throat	white
Breast	white
Belly	white
Bill	red; short and thin
Legs	red; medium length
Ad.summer	chocolate hood
Juvenile	brown on head and back

BREEDING

Nest	scrape or cup of vegetation in marsh
Eggs	3; buffy, spotted black
Incubation	21–27 days ♂♀
Young	partly-active; downy
Fledging	5–6 weeks
Broods	1; Apr–May
Food	invertebrates, seeds
Population	150,000–300,000 pairs; huge numbers winter

J	6
F	6
M	6
A	6
M	6
J	6
J	6
A	6
S	6
O	6
N	6
D	6

red bill

black hood

dark underwing

adult winter

black 'W' across wings

dark crown

white wingtips

adult summer

first winter

A small, dainty, tern-like gull, that is most often seen feeding in flight, picking insects from the surface of water like a marsh tern. The adult has uniform, slightly rounded, pale grey wings that lack black tips. The underwing is a characteristic dark grey. In summer the head is black and the tiny bill red. In winter the dark hood is lost, being replaced by a dark hind crown and dark spot behind the eye; the bill is black. Juvenile and first winter birds have an inverted black 'W' across the upperwing in flight like the considerably larger and longer-winged Kittiwake.
Status: it has bred, but mainly a passage visitor, chiefly in late summer and autumn. It is also a scarce winter visitor.

Similar Species:
Bonaparte's Gull *Larus philadelphia*
30–33cm (12–13in)
Though nearer the size of a Little Gull, this American vagrant actually bears a strong resemblance to a small Black-headed Gull. Like that bird, it is pale grey above, marked by a white forewing, formed by the outer primaries, and a black trailing edge to the outer flight feathers. The bill is smaller and there is a single black spot behind the eye.

The major difference from the Black-headed Gull is the white underwing, compared with the dusky underwing, especially the primaries, of the larger bird. First winter birds are more like the equivalent Little Gull, though the inverted black 'W' is incomplete across the back and the outer primaries are still white, albeit edged black.
Range: breeds north-west Canada, Alaska.
Migration: migrates through the interior and to all coasts of the United States.
British Distribution: a very rare vagrant to coastal waters at almost any time of the year, mostly in the south-west.

Bonaparte's Gull

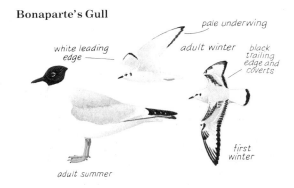

white leading edge

pale underwing

adult winter

black trailing edge and coverts

first winter

adult summer

	LITTLE GULL	
Type	gull-like	
Size	27–29cm (10–11in)	
Habitat	freshwater marshes, sea, estuaries and shores	
Behaviour	swims, wades, walks, perches openly, takes off from water or ground	
Flocking	1–100	
Flight	soars, glides, flitting; strong and powerful	
Voice	repeated *ka-ee* and low *ka-ka-ka*	

	IDENTIFICATION	
Ad.winter		
Crown	white, dark hind crown	
Upperparts	grey	
Rump	white	
Tail	white; medium length, square	
Throat	white	
Breast	white	
Belly	white	
Bill	black; short and thin	
Legs	black; short	
Ad.summer	black hood, red bill	
Juvenile	'W' across upperwing	

	BREEDING	
Nest	reeds and rushes	
Eggs	3; pale green, blotched black	
Incubation	20–21 days ♂ ♀	
Young	partly-active; downy	
Fledging	21–24 days	
Broods	1; May–June	
Food	invertebrates, fish, insects	
Population	double-passage migrant; scarce winter visitor	

J	F	M	A	M	J	J	A	S	O	N	D
2	2	2	2	2	2	2	3	3	3	2	2

Herring Gull *Larus argentatus*

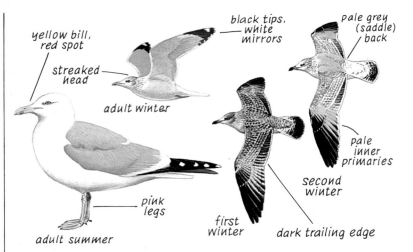

black tips, white mirrors

pale grey (saddle) back

yellow bill, red spot

streaked head

adult winter

pale inner primaries

pink legs

second winter

first winter

dark trailing edge

adult summer

Most common and familiar of the larger gulls. Grey back; grey wings with black tips and white 'mirrors'. Large yellow bill with red spot; flesh coloured legs. In winter, head variably streaked black. Immatures must be separated with care from Lesser Black-backed Gulls of same age. Juvenile Herring Gulls have wider pale margins to upperparts and pale inner primaries that break up hind wing pattern. First summer birds invariably have pale creamy upperparts, much paler than Lesser Black-backed. Second winter birds have pale grey 'saddles'.
Status: widespread resident and winter visitor; breeds along most coasts.
Similar Species: adult Common Gull (p.137) and immature Lesser Black-backed Gull (p.136) as above.

J	6	
F	6	
M	6	
A	6	
M	6	
J	6	
J	6	
A	6	
S	6	
O	6	
N	6	
D	6	

HERRING GULL

Type	gull-like
Size	53–59cm (20–23in)
Habitat	towns, freshwater marshes, moors, sea, sea-cliffs, estuaries, shores
Behaviour	swims, wades, walks, perches openly, takes off from water or ground
Flocking	1–10,000
Flight	soars, glides; strong and powerful; direct
Voice	loud ringing *kyow-kyow*

IDENTIFICATION

Adult	
Crown	white
Upperparts	grey; black wingtips with white 'mirrors'
Rump	white
Tail	white; medium length, square
Throat	white
Breast	white
Belly	white
Bill	yellow, red spot; straight and thick
Legs	pink; medium length
Juvenile	speckled brown above

BREEDING

Nest	cup of vegetation on cliff, dunes, marsh, building
Eggs	2–3; pale green, blotched brown
Incubation	25–33 days, mainly ♀
Young	partly-active; downy
Fledging	6 weeks
Broods	1; Apr–May
Food	virtually anything
Population	over 300,000 pairs

Lesser Black-backed Gull *Larus fuscus*

yellow bill, red spot

all dark back

adult winter

more marked trailing edge than Herring

second winter

yellow legs

narrow pale feather margins

first winter

lacks pale inner primaries

adult summer

Large, dark-backed gull with yellow legs and yellow bill with red spot. Scandinavian sub-species, *L.f. graellsii*, nearly as black on back as Great Black-backed, but considerably smaller. Like other large gulls, takes three years to acquire adult plumage but has slate-grey 'saddle' by second summer. Younger birds separated from Herring Gulls of similar age by narrower, paler margins to upperparts and bolder spots on underparts.
Status: widespread breeder mostly around coasts; passage migrant and increasing winter visitor.
Similar Species: adult Herring Gull (p.136) has lighter grey back and pink, not yellow, legs; immatures similar, see above. Adult Great Black-backed Gull (p.139) is much larger, almost black on back and has pale pink legs.

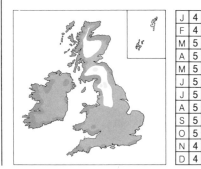

J	4	
F	4	
M	5	
A	5	
M	5	
J	5	
J	5	
A	5	
S	5	
O	5	
N	4	
D	4	

LESSER BLACK-BACKED GULL

Type	gull-like
Size	51–56cm (20–22in)
Habitat	marshes, moors, sea, estuaries, shores, fields
Behaviour	swims, wades, walks, perches openly, takes off from water and ground
Flocking	1–1000
Flight	soars, glides; strong and powerful; direct
Voice	variety of loud calls such as *kyow-kyow*, *kee-aa*

IDENTIFICATION

Adult	
Crown	white
Upperparts	slate-grey; black wingtips with white 'mirrors'
Rump	white
Tail	white; medium length, square
Throat	white
Breast	white
Belly	white
Bill	yellow with red spot; straight and thick
Legs	yellow; medium length
Juvenile	speckled brown above, buff below

BREEDING

Nest	lined hollow on flat ground
Eggs	3; olive, blotched blackish
Incubation	25–29 days ♂ ♀
Young	partly-active; downy
Fledging	35–40 days
Broods	1; Apr–June
Food	virtually anything
Population	c 50,000 pairs; fewer winter

small, rounded head and bill

yellow

adult

yellow

adult summer

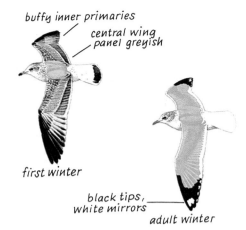

buffy inner primaries

central wing panel greyish

first winter

black tips, white mirrors

adult winter

This medium-sized gull's grey upperparts with black wingtips and white 'mirrors' create a similar pattern to that of the Herring Gull, but the head and bill are significantly smaller, giving the bird a more gentle look. The thin, yellow bill lacks a red spot. Juvenile and first winter birds show a dark trailing edge to the secondaries and a pale mid-wing panel. Second winter birds have a dark band (ring) on the bill.
Status: breeds inland in north and west Britain and Ireland, and is an abundant winter visitor elsewhere.

Similar Species:
Ring-billed Gull *Larus delawarensis*
46–51cm (18–20in)
First identified as recently as 1973, this American gull is very similar to the Common Gull. It is larger, with paler grey upperparts and a heavier bill with a dark band, or ring. The heavier bill and head, a darkish 'frown' over the eye and a pale iris (the latter in birds in their second summer and older) creates a fierce expression like a Herring Gull. Juveniles are spotted on tail, breast and flanks. First summer birds have yellow legs and bill, the latter with a broad dark band, and have a pale-grey saddle, not

a contrasting darker grey one. Adults have black wing tips, but their white mirrors are less extensive than the Common Gull's.
Range: replaces the Common Gull to the south, in North America.
Migration: many move southward to the Gulf of Mexico, though some winter in the northern United States.
British Distribution: regular, but scarce, in the south and west, mainly on the coast but also at inland reservoirs and other sites. It is most often seen in late February to April.
Other Similar Species: Kittiwake (p. 139), and first winter Mediterranean Gull (p. 134).

Ring-billed Gull

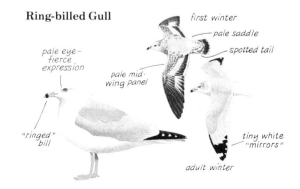

first winter

pale saddle

spotted tail

pale eye-fierce expression

pale mid-wing panel

tiny white "mirrors"

"ringed" bill

adult winter

COMMON GULL		
Type	gull-like	
Size	38–43cm (14–16½in)	
Habitat	towns, freshwater marshes, moors, sea, estuaries, shores, fields	
Behaviour	swims, wades, walks, perches openly, takes off from water or ground	
Flocking	1–1000	
Flight	soars, glides; strong and powerful; direct	
Voice	high *kee-aa*	
IDENTIFICATION		
Adult		
Crown	white	
Upperparts	grey; black wingtips with white 'mirrors'	
Rump	white	
Tail	white; medium length, square	
Throat	white	
Breast	white	
Belly	white	
Bill	yellow; short and thin	
Legs	yellow-green; medium length	
Juvenile	brown wings, grey 'saddle'	
BREEDING		
Nest	lined hollow on ground	
Eggs	3; pale green, blotched brown	
Incubation	22–27 days ♂♀	
Young	partly-active; downy	
Fledging	4 weeks	
Broods	1; May	
Food	worms, insects, molluscs	
Population	50,000 pairs; more winter	

J	F	M	A	M	J	J	A	S	O	N	D
5	5	5	5	5	5	5	5	5	5	5	5

Iceland Gull *Larus glaucoides*

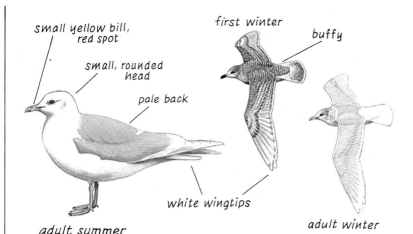

small yellow bill, red spot

small, rounded head

pale back

white wingtips

adult summer

first winter

buffy

white wingtips

adult winter

Decidedly scarce winter visitor; most common in the north but may occur along any shoreline. Adult has very pale grey back and wings with white primaries. First year birds are buffy; second year birds are pale creamy above and below – both have white primaries. Smaller, more rounded head, coupled with smaller bill and more benign expression are most reliable means of separating this bird from larger Glaucous Gull.
Status: scarcer than Glaucous Gull everywhere; winter visitor in variable numbers.
Similar Species: Glaucous Gull (p.138) is larger and has bigger head – see also above.

J	2
F	2
M	1
A	1
M	1
J	0
J	0
A	0
S	1
O	1
N	1
D	1

ICELAND GULL

Type	gull-like
Size	51–57cm (20–22in)
Habitat	sea, estuaries and shores
Behaviour	swims, wades, walks, perches openly, takes off and lands on water or ground
Flocking	solitary
Flight	soars, glides; strong and powerful; direct
Voice	shrill *kyow*

IDENTIFICATION

Adult	
Crown	buff
Upperparts	very pale grey
Rump	white
Tail	white; medium length, square
Throat	white
Breast	white
Belly	white
Bill	yellow with red spot; straight and thick
Legs	pink; medium length
Juvenile	buff with white primaries

BREEDING

Nest	vegetation on cliffs or islands
Eggs	2–3; ?
Incubation	?
Young	?
Fledging	?
Broods	1; June
Food	fish
Population	rare winter visitor

Glaucous Gull *Larus hyperboreus*

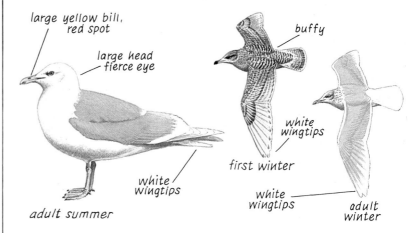

large yellow bill, red spot

large head fierce eye

buffy

white wingtips

first winter

adult summer

white wingtips

white wingtips

adult winter

Large, pale grey-backed gull – almost as large as Great Black-backed (p.158) Similar to Herring Gull (p.154) but lacks black tips in white primaries. Can be confused with much rarer Iceland Gull (p.156) but bill much longer and more powerful and head flatter with more fierce expression. Pink legs and yellow bill with red spot. Immatures pass through similar pattern of changes to Iceland Gull – all have white primaries.
Status: scarce; regular winter visitor to most coasts. More numerous in north.
Similar Species: Iceland Gull (p.138) as above.

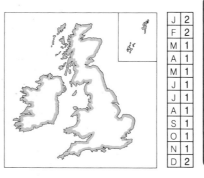

J	2
F	2
M	1
A	1
M	1
J	1
J	1
A	1
S	1
O	1
N	1
D	2

GLAUCOUS GULL

Type	gull-like
Size	58–69cm (22–27in)
Habitat	sea, estuaries
Behaviour	swims, wades, walks, perches openly, takes off and lands on water or ground
Flocking	1–2
Flight	soars, glides; strong and powerful; direct
Voice	harsh *kyow* like other large gulls

IDENTIFICATION

Adult	
Crown	white
Upperparts	grey
Rump	white
Tail	white; medium length, square
Throat	white
Breast	white
Belly	white
Bill	yellow with red spot; straight and thick
Legs	pink; medium length
Juvenile	buff with white primaries

BREEDING

Nest	bulky cup of vegetation on cliff or small island
Eggs	2–3; pale olive, blotched blackish
Incubation	27–30 days ♂ ♀
Young	partly-active; downy
Fledging	40–50 days ?
Broods	1; May–June
Food	fish, invertebrates, carrion
Population	scarce winter visitor

Larus marinus Great Black-backed Gull

Rissa tridactyla Kittiwake

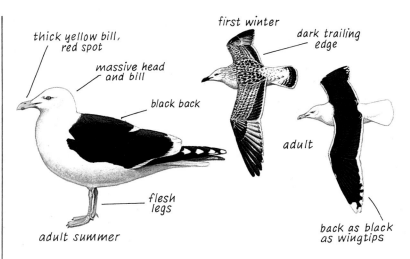

thick yellow bill, red spot

massive head and bill

black back

first winter

dark trailing edge

adult

flesh legs

adult summer

back as black as wingtips

'gentle head'

yellow bill

nape mark

juvenile

adult winter

adult summer

pale hind wing

black 'W'

black legs

black tips no mirrors

Massive gull that stands larger than Herring and Lesser Black-backed Gulls in all plumages. Sheer size of bird picks it out from any mixed gull flock. Adult has black back and wings, huge head and large, deep bill. Immatures have almost white margins to dark brown feathers of upperparts and are much more contrasted than Herring and Lesser Black-backed Gulls of similar age. Mainly marine, but penetrates inland in winter, mostly to rubbish tips and reservoirs.
Status: breeds along most western coasts; winter visitor elsewhere.
Similar Species: adult Lesser Black-backed Gull (p.136), especially Scandinavian sub-species *graellsii*, is as black above but smaller with less massive head and bill.

GREAT BLACK-BACKED GULL

Type	gull-like
Size	63–69cm (24½–27in)
Habitat	sea, estuaries, marshes
Behaviour	swims, wades, walks, perches openly, takes off from water or ground
Flocking	1–100s
Flight	soars, glides; strong and powerful; direct
Voice	harsh *owk*; also *uk-uk-uk*

IDENTIFICATION

Adult	
Crown	white
Upperparts	black; black wingtips with white 'mirrors'
Rump	white
Tail	white; medium length, square
Throat	white
Breast	white
Belly	white
Bill	yellow with red spot; large and thick
Legs	pink; medium length
Juvenile	buff brown with dark trailing edge to wing

BREEDING

Nest	large mass of sticks and seaweed on ground on island or rock
Eggs	2–3; olive, speckled brown
Incubation	26–30 days ♂ ♀
Young	partly-active; downy
Fledging	7–8 weeks
Broods	1; Apr–May
Food	seabirds, offal, rubbish
Population	22,000 pairs

Totally maritime gull about same size as Common Gull and superficially similar. Both species have small head, short yellow bill and benign expression. Kittiwake has shorter legs and longer, narrower wings; black wingtips lack white 'mirrors'. Immatures show black inverted 'W' across upperwings in flight (like much smaller Little Gull p.152) and black neck bar. Spends most of time at sea flying lightly and buoyantly; breeds on cliffs, forming large colonies.
Status: breeds on most cliff-bound shores, especially numerous in north and west.
Similar Species: Common Gull (p.137), as above.

KITTIWAKE

Type	gull-like
Size	38–43cm (15½–16½in)
Habitat	sea, cliffs
Behaviour	swims, perches openly, takes off and lands on water or ground
Flocking	1–1000s
Flight	soars, glides; strong and powerful; direct
Voice	repeated *kitti-week*

IDENTIFICATION

Adult	
Crown	white
Upperparts	grey; black wingtips
Rump	white
Tail	white; medium length, square
Throat	white
Breast	white
Belly	white
Bill	yellow; short and thin
Legs	black; short
Juvenile	black 'W' across wings, black tail band, black bill

BREEDING

Nest	neat cup of seaweed on tiny cliff ledge
Eggs	2; creamy, speckled brown
Incubation	25–30 days ♂ ♀
Young	partly-active; downy
Fledging	43 days
Broods	1; May–June
Food	fish
Population	*c* 500,000 pairs

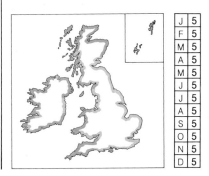

J	5
F	5
M	5
A	5
M	5
J	5
J	5
A	5
S	5
O	5
N	5
D	5

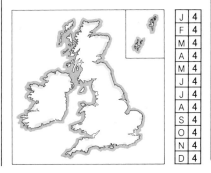

J	4
F	4
M	4
A	4
M	4
J	4
J	4
A	4
S	4
O	4
N	4
D	4

Sandwich Tern *Sterna sandvicensis*

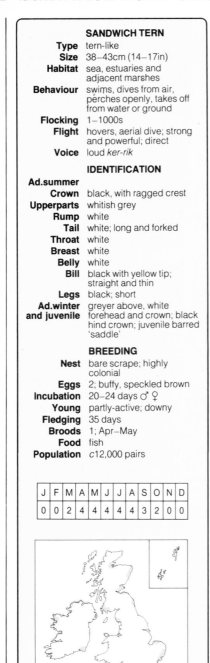

SANDWICH TERN	
Type	tern-like
Size	38–43cm (14–17in)
Habitat	sea, estuaries and adjacent marshes
Behaviour	swims, dives from air, perches openly, takes off from water or ground
Flocking	1–1000s
Flight	hovers, aerial dive; strong and powerful; direct
Voice	loud *ker-rik*

IDENTIFICATION

Ad.summer	
Crown	black, with ragged crest
Upperparts	whitish grey
Rump	white
Tail	white; long and forked
Throat	white
Breast	white
Belly	white
Bill	black with yellow tip; straight and thin
Legs	black; short
Ad.winter and juvenile	greyer above, white forehead and crown; black hind crown; juvenile barred 'saddle'

BREEDING

Nest	bare scrape; highly colonial
Eggs	2; buffy, speckled brown
Incubation	20–24 days ♂ ♀
Young	partly-active; downy
Fledging	35 days
Broods	1; Apr–May
Food	fish
Population	*c*12,000 pairs

J	F	M	A	M	J	J	A	S	O	N	D
0	0	2	4	4	4	4	4	3	2	0	0

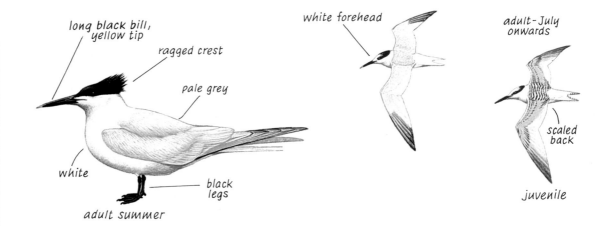

long black bill, yellow tip

ragged crest

pale grey

white

adult summer

black legs

white forehead

adult—July onwards

scaled back

juvenile

This is the largest of our regular terns, with typical buoyant flight on long narrow wings. The Sandwich is much paler above than either Common or Arctic Terns, especially in flight. Its legs and bill are black, the latter being long and tipped with yellow. The long black crown forms a ragged crest. In autumn the forehead is white, creating a capped appearance. Juveniles are patterned a scaly black and white on the upperparts. This is purely a coastal tern and is observed inland only when storm driven. It dives for food, usually close inshore.
Status: breeds in dense colonies at many suitable sites on all coasts. This is a summer visitor that moves southwards to the Mediterranean and the coasts of Africa.

Similar Species:
Lesser Crested Tern *Sterna bengalensis*
38–43cm (15–17in)
This is a recent arrival to our coastal waters that has begun to breed in Europe only over the past few years. It is becoming increasingly regular, especially along the east coast, and has been noted on a nest site among Sandwich Terns. Similar in size and appearance to that species, the Lesser Crested has a long orange-yellow bill and is generally darker grey above. The legs are black. Confusion is more likely with the larger and paler Royal Tern which has an orange-red bill and which is a very rare vagrant.
Range: widespread in tropical waters, though not in the Americas.
Migration: wanders at sea in the general area of its breeding colonies.
British Distribution: a very rare but annual visitor, chiefly to east coasts: visiting birds doubtless come from the Mediterranean, where it is an established breeder at sites along the North African coast.

Lesser Crested Tern

adult winter

ragged crest

first winter

adult summer

Sterna paradisaea Arctic Tern

juvenile

whole wing translucent

blood-red bill

adult summer

white trailing edge

white between crown and grey breast

grey

very short legs

less dark on forewing

first winter

Like Common Tern but with shorter, darker red bill (without black tip), longer tail and fully translucent wing when seen from below. Common Tern has translucent patch only on inner primaries. Generally greyer below with white cheeks standing out pure white. More confined to coast than Common Tern. Juveniles have less black on leading edge of wing than Common Tern and prominent white trailing edge to secondaries.
Status: summer visitor mainly to northern coasts; passage migrant in south.
Similar Species: Common Tern (p.141) as above.

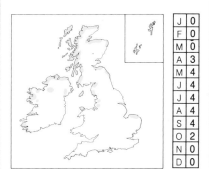

ARCTIC TERN	
Type	tern-like
Size	30–39cm (11–15in)
Habitat	sea, estuaries, freshwater marshes
Behaviour	swims, dives from air, perches openly, takes off and lands on water and ground
Flocking	1–1000
Flight	hovers, aerial dive; strong and powerful, direct
Voice	*key-rrr*, similar to Common Tern but briefer
IDENTIFICATION	
Ad.summer	
Crown	black
Upperparts	grey
Rump	white
Tail	white; long and forked
Throat	white
Breast	whitish grey
Belly	whitish grey
Bill	red; short and thin
Legs	red; short
Ad.winter and juvenile	white forehead
BREEDING	
Nest	bare scrape
Eggs	2; buffy, blotched brown
Incubation	20–22 days ♂ ♀
Young	partly-active; downy
Fledging	20–22 days
Broods	1; May–June
Food	fish
Population	c 40,000 pairs

J	0
F	0
M	0
A	3
M	4
J	4
J	4
A	4
S	4
O	2
N	0
D	0

Sterna hirundo Common Tern

orange-red bill, black tip

dark forewing

juvenile

dark trailing edge almost creates mid-wing panel

inner primaries translucent

grey back

adult summer

greyish

adult summer

first winter

Common and widespread summer visitor. Essentially pale grey above and white below but underparts have pale greyish wash. Black cap; red legs. Bill usually red with black tip but sometimes pure red or almost black. (Beware separating Common Terns from Arctic or Roseate Terns by bill colour alone.) Deeply forked tail; light and buoyant flight. Dives for food; also picks food from surface of water like Black Tern. Autumn adults and juveniles have black leading edge to wing that forms bar when wing is folded.
Status: summer visitor; breeds along most coasts in concentrated colonies, also inland in smaller numbers.
Similar Species: Arctic Tern (p.141) and Roseate Tern (p.142).

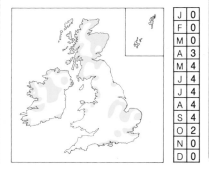

COMMON TERN	
Type	tern-like
Size	20–36cm (11–14in)
Habitat	sea, estuaries, inland freshwater
Behaviour	swims, dives from air, perches openly, takes off and lands on water or ground
Flocking	1–1000
Flight	hovers, aerial dive; strong and powerful; direct
Voice	harsh *key-arr*, *kirri-kirri*
IDENTIFICATION	
Ad.summer	
Crown	black
Upperparts	pale grey
Rump	white
Tail	white; long and forked
Throat	white
Breast	white
Belly	white
Bill	red with black tip; short and thin
Legs	red; short
Ad.winter and juvenile	white forehead; juvenile barred brownish on upperparts
BREEDING	
Nest	unlined hollow
Eggs	2–3; creamy, blotched black
Incubation	20–23 days, mainly ♀
Young	partly-active; downy
Fledging	28 days
Broods	1, 2?; May–June
Food	fish
Population	15,000–20,000 pairs

J	0
F	0
M	0
A	3
M	4
J	4
J	4
A	4
S	4
O	2
N	0
D	0

Roseate Tern *Sterna dougallii*

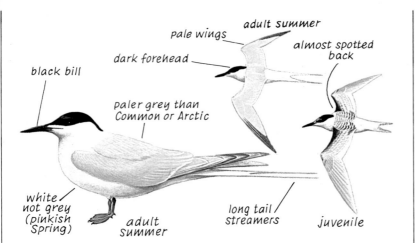

black bill

dark forehead

pale wings

adult summer

almost spotted back

paler grey than Common or Arctic

white not grey (pinkish Spring)

adult summer

long tail streamers

juvenile

Little Tern *Sterna albifrons*

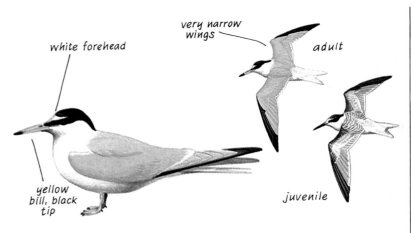

white forehead

very narrow wings

adult

yellow bill, black tip

juvenile

Rarest of the breeding terns with a few isolated colonies, mostly on islands, holding bulk of population. Elsewhere decidedly rare or overlooked. A small tern somewhere between Common and Little Tern in size but with long tail streamers boosting measured length. Best picked out from more abundant Common and Arctic Terns by paler colour – almost white above and below. Identification confirmed by black bill (some Common Terns have almost complete black bill) and tail streamers (may become broken). In spring has pink flush on breast.
Status: rare summer visitor and passage migrant; arrives later than other terns.
Similar Species: Common Tern (p.141) and Arctic Tern (p.141).

	ROSEATE TERN
Type	tern-like
Size	32–40cm (12–15in)
Habitat	sea, estuaries and adjacent marshes
Behaviour	swims, dives from air, perches openly, takes off and lands on water or ground
Flocking	1–100
Flight	hovers; strong and powerful; direct
Voice	kee-a, pee-pee-pee, similar to Common Tern

IDENTIFICATION

Ad.summer	
Crown	black
Upperparts	whitish grey
Rump	white
Tail	white; long and forked
Throat	white
Breast	white, pink flush in spring
Belly	white
Bill	black; short and thin
Legs	red; short
Ad.winter and juvenile	white forehead; juvenile scaled upperparts

BREEDING

Nest	unlined hollow
Eggs	1–2; creamy, speckled brown
Incubation	21–26 days ♂ ♀
Young	partly-active; downy
Fledging	27–30 days
Broods	1; June
Food	fish
Population	c 2500 pairs

Tiny, fast flying tern. Long, narrow wings, almost Swift-like in shape, flicker in fast wing beats. Essentially marine, feeding close inshore, diving for small fish; breeds along shingle beaches. Legs and bill yellow, the latter with black tip. Black cap always incomplete; forehead white.
Status: declining due to disturbance of breeding grounds; summer visitor to coasts.
Similar Species: small size separates from most other terns.

	LITTLE TERN
Type	tern-like
Size	23–26cm (9–10in)
Habitat	sea, estuaries and adjacent freshwater
Behaviour	swims, dives from air, perches openly, takes off from water and ground
Flocking	1–50
Flight	hovers, aerial dive; strong and powerful; direct
Voice	various chatterings; high-pitched, sharp *kitik*

IDENTIFICATION

Ad.summer	
Crown	black with white forehead
Upperparts	grey; black wingtips
Rump	white
Tail	white; medium length, forked
Throat	white
Breast	white
Belly	white
Bill	yellow, black tip; short and thin
Legs	yellow; short
Ad.winter and juvenile	more white on crown; juvenile sandy buff above, 'saddle' barred

BREEDING

Nest	bare scrape near sea
Eggs	2–3; olive, blotched brown
Incubation	19–22 days ♂ ♀
Young	partly-active; downy
Fledging	15–17 days
Broods	1; May–June
Food	fish
Population	c1800 pairs

J	0
F	0
M	0
A	1
M	2
J	2
J	2
A	2
S	1
O	0
N	0
D	0

J	0
F	0
M	0
A	3
M	3
J	3
J	3
A	3
S	2
O	1
N	0
D	0

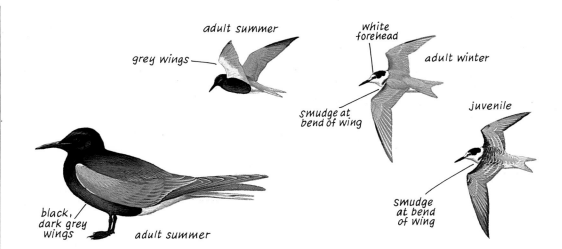

adult summer

grey wings

white forehead

adult winter

smudge at bend of wing

juvenile

black, dark grey wings

adult summer

smudge at bend of wing

In summer the adult Black Tern is all black with dark grey wings. The juvenile and winter adult are slate-grey above and white below with a black cap, white forehead and a black smudge at the sides of the breast. The tail is notched rather than forked. Black Terns feed by taking insects from the surface of water in flight. Their flight is easy and graceful, but erratic as they twist and swoop over the water.
Status: though it has bred on occasion, it is generally a regular passage migrant in variable numbers each spring and autumn. It is most numerous in south and east England.

Similar Species:
White-winged Black Tern
Chlidonias leucopterus 22–24cm (9–9½in). In summer plumage this is a stunning bird. The body, save for the rear end, is black, contrasting with the almost white wings and tail. The underwing coverts are black, as is the stubby bill. In this plumage it is unmistakable. In winter plumage, adults are similar to the Black Tern, but have a black patch behind the eye and only a hint of a greyish cap. They also lack a dark smudge at the sides of the breast. Juveniles are also

similar to juvenile Black Terns, but have a characteristic black 'saddle' and a pale rump. They also lack dark smudges at the side of the breast.
Range: from eastern Europe through Russia and Asia.
Migration: a summer visitor, wintering inland in Africa, India, China and other parts of Asia.
British Distribution: a rare spring and autumn passage migrant, with most occurring in August and September, mostly in the south and east. Now regular in small numbers every year at both inland and coastal sites.

White-winged Black Tern

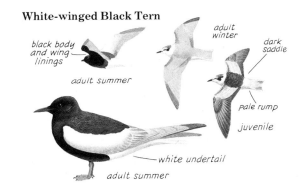

black body and wing linings

adult summer

adult winter

dark saddle

pale rump

juvenile

white undertail

adult summer

BLACK TERN	
Type	tern-like
Size	23–26cm (9–10in)
Habitat	freshwater marshes, sea, estuaries
Behaviour	swims, dives from air, perches openly, takes off from water and ground
Flocking	1–15
Flight	hovers, flitting; aerial dive; undulating
Voice	high-pitched *kik*

IDENTIFICATION	
Ad.summer	
Crown	black
Upperparts	black; dark grey wings
Rump	dark grey
Tail	grey; medium length, notched
Throat	black
Breast	black
Belly	black
Bill	black; short and thin
Legs	red-brown; short
Ad.winter and juvenile	grey above, white below, white forehead, dark smudge at sides of breast

BREEDING	
Nest	mound of vegetation in marshy lagoon
Eggs	3; buffy, spotted brown
Incubation	14–17 days, mainly ♀
Young	partly-active; downy
Fledging	4 weeks
Broods	1; May
Food	insects
Population	very rare breeder; several 100s spring and autumn

J	F	M	A	M	J	J	A	S	O	N	D
0	0	0	2	2	1	1	2	3	1	1	0

Guillemot *Uria aalge*

	GUILLEMOT
Type	auk-like
Size	40–44cm (15–17in)
Habitat	sea and cliffs
Behaviour	swims, dives from surface, perches openly, takes off and lands on water and ground
Flocking	1–1000s
Flight	laboured; direct
Voice	various growling and moaning notes

IDENTIFICATION

Ad.summer	
Crown	blackish brown
Upperparts	blackish brown
Rump	blackish brown
Tail	blackish brown; short and rounded
Throat	blackish brown
Breast	white
Belly	white
Bill	black; short and thin, pointed
Legs	black; short
Ad.winter	white throat and sides of face

BREEDING

Nest	bare cliff ledge
Eggs	1; highly variable, blotched black
Incubation	28–35 days ♂ ♀
Young	helpless; downy
Fledging	18–25 days
Broods	1; May–June
Food	fish, crustaceans, molluscs
Population	c 600,000 pairs

J	F	M	A	M	J	J	A	S	O	N	D
2	2	3	4	4	4	4	3	2	2	2	2

sharply pointed bill

adult summer

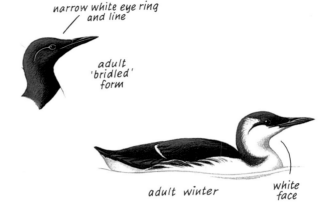

narrow white eye ring and line

adult 'bridled' form

adult winter

white face

Strictly marine, Guillemots swim and dive offshore, sometimes at considerable distances from land. These are gregarious birds, found mostly in flocks, that come to land only to breed, or when forced to do so by storms or if their feathers become oiled by pollution at sea. On land they stand upright, like penguins (to which they are not related), and breed in dense colonies on cliff ledges. The upperparts are blackish-brown, the underparts white. The head and neck are blackish-brown, and white tips to the secondaries form a white bar across the closed wing. In winter the neck and sides of the head become white, extending from the eye itself across the ear coverts. Some, 'bridled' Guillemots have a white eye ring and thin white line extending across the ear coverts.
Status: breeds mainly in the north and west, though found outside the breeding season along most coasts.

Similar Species:
Brünnich's Guillemot *Uria lomvia*
40–44cm (16–17in)
Though there is some degree of overlap, this species replaces the Guillemot in the high Arctic. It closely resembles the Guillemot,

but is virtually black above, with a thicker and shorter bill. At all seasons, a whitish line at the base of the bill is the best field mark, but in winter the black cap extends below the eye and there is no thin line across the ear coverts.
Range: breeds from Iceland and northern Norway eastwards through the high Arctic islands of Siberia, and in the North Pacific.
Migration: moves to ice-free seas in North Atlantic and North Pacific.
British Distribution: an extremely rare vagrant, almost always dead or dying.
Other Similar Species: Razorbill (p. 145); Puffin (p. 146).

Brünnich's Guillemot

thick bill, white mark

cap extends below eye

summer

winter

squarer bill than Guillemot

longish pointed tail

adult summer

adult winter

white face

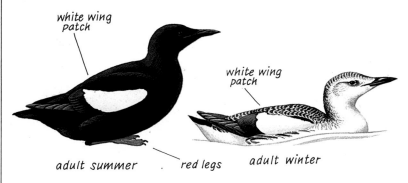

white wing patch

white wing patch

adult summer

red legs

adult winter

Similar to Guillemot; often forms mixed flocks. Generally blacker above. Bill shape much deeper than Guillemot, with distinctive vertical white line. In flight at sea, pointed tail particularly useful feature; gives bird elongated silhouette. Like Guillemot, black neck lost in winter. Nests in rock crevices rather than on open cliff ledges.
Status: breeds in north and west, often on same cliffs as Guillemot.
Similar Species: Guillemot (p.144) and Puffin (p.146).

Scarce seabird most often seen on water below nesting cliffs. In summer, plumage all black with bold white oval patch on wings. Feet and inside of mouth bright red. In winter, mottled greyish all over, with darker wings still marked by whitish ovals.
Status: scarce resident around northern and western cliffs; virtually unknown further south.
Similar Species: none.

RAZORBILL

Type	auk-like
Size	39–43cm (15–16½in)
Habitat	sea and cliffs
Behaviour	swims, dives from surface, perches openly, takes off and lands on water and ground
Flocking	1–100
Flight	laboured; direct
Voice	growls and grunts

IDENTIFICATION

Ad.summer	
Crown	black
Upperparts	black
Rump	black
Tail	black; short and pointed
Throat	black
Breast	white
Belly	white
Bill	black, vertical white line; short and thin
Legs	black; short
Ad.winter	throat and sides of face white

BREEDING

Nest	crevice or hole in cliff
Eggs	1; variable, blotched brown
Incubation	25–35 days ♂ ♀
Young	helpless; downy
Fledging	14–24 days
Broods	1; May–June
Food	fish, crustaceans, molluscs
Population	c 144,000 pairs

BLACK GUILLEMOT

Type	auk-like
Size	33–35cm (12½–13½in)
Habitat	sea and cliffs
Behaviour	swims, dives from surface, perches openly, takes off and lands on water or ground
Flocking	1–15
Flight	laboured; direct
Voice	whistling cries

IDENTIFICATION

Ad.summer	
Crown	black
Upperparts	black with white patches on wings
Rump	black
Tail	black; short and square
Throat	black
Breast	black
Belly	black
Bill	black; short and thin
Legs	red; short
Ad.winter	white below, grey above; black wings retain white oval patches

BREEDING

Nest	hole among boulders
Eggs	2; white, spotted blackish
Incubation	21–25 days ♂ ♀
Young	helpless; downy
Fledging	34–40 days
Broods	1; May–June
Food	fish, crustaceans, molluscs
Population	c 8500 pairs

J	2
F	2
M	2
A	3
M	3
J	3
J	3
A	2
S	2
O	2
N	2
D	2

J	1
F	1
M	2
A	2
M	2
J	2
J	2
A	2
S	2
O	2
N	1
D	1

Puffin *Fratercula arctica*

white face

multi-coloured bill

reduced bill

adult winter

less white face

adult summer

Small, comical seabird; forms colonies on offshore islands and sea stacks in north and west. Upperparts black; underparts white; face white. Outstanding feature is large parrot-like bill vertically striped in yellow and red. Size of bill reduced (horny plates at base shed) and colours paler in winter and juvenile plumages. At sea, short, rapidly whirring wings and white face are best features. Nests in burrows, but off-duty birds form groups that loaf around cliff-tops.
Status: locally abundant resident, especially in north and west; some winter wandering.
Similar Species: Guillemot (p.144) and Razorbill (p.145).

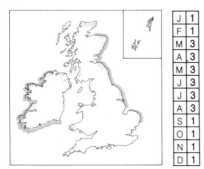

PUFFIN	
Type	auk-like
Size	29–31cm (11–12in)
Habitat	sea and cliffs
Behaviour	swims, dives from surface, walks, perches openly, takes off and lands on water or ground
Flocking	1–1000
Flight	laboured; direct
Voice	deep *arr-arr*
IDENTIFICATION	
Ad.summer	
Crown	black and white
Upperparts	black
Rump	black
Tail	black; short and square
Throat	black
Breast	white
Belly	white
Bill	blue-grey, red and yellow, striped; short and stubby
Legs	red; short
Ad.winter	bill smaller with paler colours
Juvenile	bill smaller and all dark
BREEDING	
Nest	burrow
Eggs	1; white
Incubation	40–43 days ♀ only
Young	helpless; downy
Fledging	47–51 days
Broods	1; May
Food	fish, crustaceans, molluscs
Population	*c* 500,000 pairs

J	1
F	1
M	3
A	3
M	3
J	3
J	3
A	3
S	1
O	1
N	1
D	1

Little Auk *Alle alle*

tiny, stubby bill

white face

summer

winter

Tiny, Starling-sized auk that is autumn and winter visitor in variable numbers, most often after severe storms. Upperparts black, underparts white. Throat and breast black in summer, white in winter. Bill short and stubby. Flies fast on whirring wings. Tiny size and rapid flight best features at sea.
Status: rare; storm-driven in late autumn and winter
Similar Species: none.

LITTLE AUK	
Type	auk-like
Size	20–22cm (7½–8½in)
Habitat	sea, estuaries
Behaviour	swims, dives from surface, takes off and lands on water or ground
Flocking	1–2
Flight	laboured; direct
Voice	silent at sea
IDENTIFICATION	
Ad.winter	
Crown	black
Upperparts	black
Rump	black
Tail	black; short and square
Throat	white
Breast	white
Belly	white
Bill	black; short and stubby
Legs	grey; short
BREEDING	
Nest	hole among rocks, often inland
Eggs	1; blue, spotted brown
Incubation	24 days ♂ ♀
Young	helpless; downy
Fledging	3–4 weeks
Broods	1; June–July
Food	crustaceans
Population	variable (less than 1000) autumn and winter

J	2
F	2
M	1
A	0
M	0
J	0
J	0
A	0
S	1
O	2
N	2
D	2

PIGEONS, CUCKOOS,
OWLS, WOODPECKERS,
NIGHTJARS
AND ALLIES

The species in this huge, amorphous group share few characteristics, save only that they follow each other in the normal systematic order in which zoologists the world over arrange birds, and that they are the only perching birds that do not belong to the order Passeriformes. In Britain and Ireland the total number of species amounts to only twenty, so it is also a simple matter of convenience to group such a rag-bag of species together in this way.

The largest groups are the pigeons, the owls and the woodpeckers, to which can be added a single (introduced) parrot, one kingfisher, one hoopoe, one cuckoo and one nightjar. Even the owls are divided among two distinct families.

Owls are nocturnal predators with large eyes, flat faces with excellent binocular vision and soft flight feathers to aid a silent approach. They are mostly camouflaged probably partly to escape predators and partly to avoid being 'mobbed' mercilessly by small birds during the hours of daylight. Most widespread and common, though absent from Ireland, is the Tawny Owl – the familiar hooting and 'tu-whitting' owl of wood and hedgerow. More widespread in global terms, but becoming progressively scarce in Britain, is the ghost-like Barn Owl (*illustrated*), most often seen at dusk. The decline of this splendid bird has been attributed to various causes, the most likely of which is the destruction and conversion of derelict and isolated farm buildings. They are also increasingly killed on roads. Short-eared Owls are daytime hunters that breed mainly in the north but are also winter visitors to our coasts from the Continent.

The pigeons and doves have largely benefited from the human transformation of our countryside. Woodpigeons are a major agricultural pest and the Collared Dove has spread from the Balkans during the present century largely by exploiting human cereal waste.

Like the Tawny Owl, woodpeckers are totally absent from Ireland, and even Britain's three species are only a fraction of the wealth of species to be found across the English Channel. They are expert tree climbers, are able to excavate their nesting chambers in living trees and find their food by hacking away the bark to reach insect pests below.

All in all, this highly variable group of birds consists of species that are easily identifiable and largely well known, even to non-birders. In the case of families consisting of only a single species, the British, in their usual insular way, have given them single-word names such as the Kingfisher and the Cuckoo. These are meaningless to foreign birdwatchers, who may encounter several species of kingfishers and cuckoos and, more sensibly, refer to the above two species as the Common Kingfisher and the European Cuckoo.

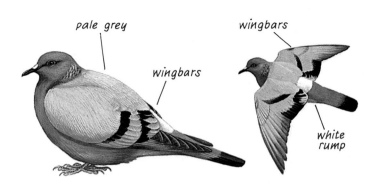

pale grey

wingbars

wingbars

white rump

mid-grey

tiny wingbars

no white rump

whole wing bordered black

Genuine Rock Doves are now confined to cliffs in extreme north and west. Elsewhere, they have interbred over the centuries with feral pigeons – domesticated Rock Doves escaped from captivity. Pigeons occur in wide variety of plumages, but genuine wild bird is pale grey with patch of irridescent purple and green at sides of neck. Folded wing shows two black bars. Rump white; tail broadly tipped black. Some feral pigeons show close resemblance to this plumage.
Status: highly localized resident in extreme north and west; feral birds widespread and numerous in cities and along cliffs.
Similar Species: Stock Dove (p.149) lacks white rump.

Grey above and paler grey below, with pale pink breast and less marked double wingbar than Rock Dove. In flight, shows grey wings with broad black borders – quite characteristic once seen. Tail broadly tipped black. Though found in similar areas to Woodpigeon, can be distinguished by lack of white on neck and wing.
Status: widespread resident.
Similar Species: Rock Dove (p.149) and Woodpigeon (p.150) as above.

ROCK DOVE

Type	pigeon-like
Size	31–35cm (12–13in)
Habitat	sea cliffs, towns
Behaviour	walks, perches openly, takes off and lands on ground
Flocking	1–100
Flight	glides; strong and powerful; direct
Voice	familiar *oo-roo-coo*, repeated

IDENTIFICATION

Adult	
Crown	grey
Upperparts	grey
Rump	white
Tail	grey, black tip; medium length, square
Throat	grey
Breast	grey
Belly	grey
Bill	black and white; short and thin
Legs	pink; short

BREEDING

Nest	crevices and ledges in cliffs and buildings
Eggs	2; white
Incubation	17–19 days ♂ ♀
Young	helpless; downy
Fledging	30–35 days
Broods	2 or 3; Mar–Sept
Food	seeds, grain
Population	*c*100,000 pairs

STOCK DOVE

Type	pigeon-like
Size	31–35cm (12–13in)
Habitat	forests and woods, fields and hedges, gardens, heaths
Behaviour	walks, perches openly, takes off and lands on vegetation and ground
Flocking	1–100
Flight	strong and powerful; direct
Voice	*coo-roo-oo*, repeated monotonously

IDENTIFICATION

Adult	
Crown	grey
Upperparts	grey
Rump	grey
Tail	grey, broad black tip; medium length, square
Throat	grey
Breast	pink
Belly	grey
Bill	red; short and thin
Legs	red; short

BREEDING

Nest	hole in tree or cliff
Eggs	2; white
Incubation	16–18 days ♂ ♀
Young	helpless; downy
Fledging	27–28 days
Broods	2–3; Mar–June
Food	crops, seeds, grain
Population	50,000–60,000 pairs

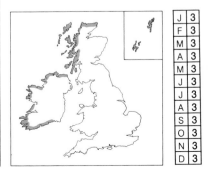

J	3
F	3
M	3
A	3
M	3
J	3
J	3
A	3
S	3
O	3
N	3
D	3

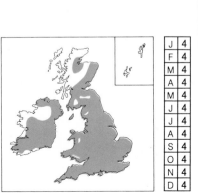

J	4
F	4
M	4
A	4
M	4
J	4
J	4
A	4
S	4
O	4
N	4
D	4

Woodpigeon *Columba palumbus*

white neck slash

white bars across wing

white wing edge

Largest of the pigeons; marked by white neck flash and broad white bar across open wings. Grey above, pinkish below. In flight, outer wing is black; tail grey with black terminal band. Familiar bird throughout the country, including city-centres.
Status: abundant and widespread resident; abundant winter visitor.
Similar Species: Stock Dove (p.149).

WOODPIGEON	
Type	pigeon-like
Size	39–43cm (15–16½in)
Habitat	forests and woods, fields and hedges, towns, gardens, heaths
Behaviour	walks, perches openly, takes off and lands on vegetation or ground
Flocking	1–1000
Flight	strong and powerful; direct
Voice	*coo-coo-coo-cu-coo*, repeated endlessly

IDENTIFICATION	
Adult	
Crown	grey
Upperparts	grey
Rump	grey
Tail	grey with black band; medium length, square
Throat	grey
Breast	pink
Belly	grey
Bill	red; short and thin
Legs	red; short
Juvenile	lacks white neck patch

BREEDING	
Nest	twig platform in tree
Eggs	2; white
Incubation	17 days ♂ ♀
Young	helpless; downy
Fledging	29–35 days
Broods	3; Apr–June
Food	crops, seeds, grain
Population	c 3,000,000

J	6
F	6
M	6
A	6
M	6
J	6
J	6
A	6
S	6
O	6
N	6
D	6

Collared Dove *Streptopelia decaocto*

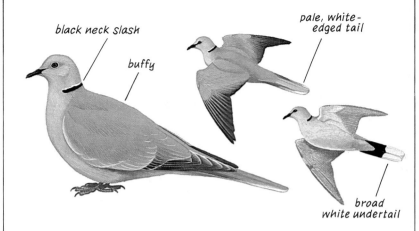

black neck slash

buffy

pale, white-edged tail

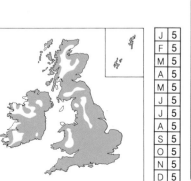

broad white undertail

First nested in Norfolk in 1955 and has since spread throughout the country. Pale buffy above, pinkish below; neat black line (collar) on sides of neck. In flight, undertail has black base and broad white tip. Haunts gardens with conifers as well as grain stores, where may form substantial flocks.
Status: widespread resident, reaches high densities in south-east; continued immigration probable.
Similar Species: Turtle Dove (p.151) is rust-brown on back.

COLLARED DOVE	
Type	pigeon-like
Size	29–32cm (11–12in)
Habitat	towns and gardens, fields and hedges
Behaviour	walks, perches openly, takes off and lands on vegetation or ground
Flocking	1–50
Flight	glides; strong and powerful; direct
Voice	*coo-cooo-coo* repeated at length; plaintive *weer*

IDENTIFICATION	
Adult	
Crown	buff
Upperparts	buff
Rump	buff
Tail	buff with white corners, undertail black with broad white tip; medium length, rounded
Throat	buff
Breast	buff
Belly	buff
Bill	brown; short and thin
Legs	red; short

BREEDING	
Nest	platform of twigs in tree
Eggs	2; white
Incubation	14 days ♂ ♀
Young	helpless; downy
Fledging	18 days
Broods	2–5; Mar–Sept
Food	seeds, grain
Population	30,000–40,000 pairs

J	5
F	5
M	5
A	5
M	5
J	5
J	5
A	5
S	5
O	5
N	5
D	5

bold black and white neck slash

black and brown

dark, white-edged tail

narrow white tail tip

TURTLE DOVE	
Type	pigeon-like
Size	26–29cm (10–11in)
Habitat	forests and woods, fields and hedges, gardens
Behaviour	walks, perches openly, takes off and lands on vegetation or ground
Flocking	1–50
Flight	strong and powerful; direct
Voice	purring *roor-rr*

IDENTIFICATION	
Adult	
Crown	grey
Upperparts	brown and black, 'scalloped'
Rump	brown
Tail	black edged white; medium length, rounded
Throat	pink
Breast	pink
Belly	white
Bill	black; short and thin
Legs	red; short

BREEDING	
Nest	platform of twigs in tree
Eggs	2; white
Incubation	13–14 days ♂ ♀
Young	helpless; downy
Fledging	19–21 days
Broods	2; May–June
Food	seeds
Population	c125,000 pairs

The Turtle Dove is a small, fast-flying dove whose call is a characteristic sound of summer. The head is greyish-brown extending to the back, and the body is a pinkish-grey below. Characteristic are the wing coverts, which are black broadly margined with rust-red, creating the 'turtle-shell' appearance from which the bird is named. In flight, at any distance, the upper parts appear rufous, thus effectively distinguishing it from any other regular pigeon. The longish tail is black beneath, with a clear white edge. A neck slash consists of several alternate stripes of black and white. Though generally found in pairs, it forms quite large autumn flocks at favoured feeding sites.
Status: a summer visitor to south, central and eastern England.

Similar Species:
Rufous Turtle Dove *Streptopelia orientalis* 32–34cm (12½–13in)
This bird, as its scientific name implies, is an eastern species that breeds no nearer Britain than the Ural Mountains in the USSR, and winters from India eastwards across the Orient. Although very similar to the Turtle Dove, it is larger and darker, with

less rufous and more black on the wing coverts. The pink breast is darker and the tail is fringed with grey, not white. These may seem subtle points, but they give the bird a heavier and darker appearance that is quite characteristic.
Range: replaces the Turtle Dove in Asia from central Siberia eastwards.
Migration: winters in India (where it is resident) southwards through the tropics.
British Status: an exceptionally rare vagrant.
Other Similar Species: Collared Dove (p. 150).

J	F	M	A	M	J	J	A	S	O	N	D
0	0	0	3	5	5	5	5	5	4	2	1	0

Rufous Turtle Dove

grey edges

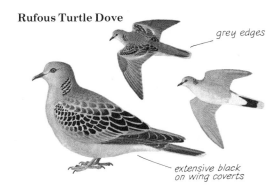

extensive black on wing coverts

Rose-ringed Parakeet *Psittacula krameri*

♀ ♂
red
neck ring
long green tail

Only parrot at large in Britain; introduced from India in 1960s. Plumage mainly green with blackish outer wings. Extremely long, pointed tail. Large, hooked, red bill. Male has narrow neck ring of pink and black. Often called Ring-necked Parakeet but several Asian parakeets have neck rings; Rose-ringed is the Indian name. *Status:* scarce but widespread resident in many areas; increasing and spreading. *Similar Species:* none.

	ROSE-RINGED PARAKEET
Type	parrot-like
Size	37–43cm (14–16½in)
Habitat	towns and gardens, fields and hedges
Behaviour	walks, perches openly, takes off and lands on vegetation or ground
Flocking	1–10
Flight	strong and powerful; direct
Voice	screamed *keeo-keeo*

IDENTIFICATION

Adult	
Crown	green
Upperparts	green
Rump	green
Tail	green; long and pointed
Throat	green
Breast	green
Belly	green
Bill	red; large and hooked
Legs	blue; short
Adult ♂	pink and black neck ring

BREEDING

Nest	tree hole
Eggs	3–4; white
Incubation	25–28 days ♀
Young	helpless; naked
Fledging	8 weeks
Broods	?
Food	seeds, fruit
Population	?

J	2
F	2
M	2
A	2
M	2
J	2
J	2
A	2
S	2
O	2
N	2
D	2

Cuckoo *Cuculus canorus*

small head and bill
juvenile
juvenile
adult ♀
long narrow wings
grey head and neck
adult
long tail
hepatic phase
adult
barred below

Harbinger of spring and Britain's most familiar bird call. Usually seen in flight when long pointed wings, long tail and small head are reminiscent of a hawk. When perched, often on overhead wire, appears ungainly and off-balance; seems to have difficulty folding wings. Upperparts and breast grey; underparts barred black and white. Juvenile darker; heavily barred above and below. Hepatic female is rare colour phase; chestnut above and white below. All females are heavily barred, like juvenile. *Status:* widespread summer visitor. *Similar Species:* beware female Sparrowhawk (p.93).

	CUCKOO
Type	pigeon-like/hawk-like
Size	32–34cm (12–13in)
Habitat	gardens, marshes, moors and heaths, woods, fields and hedges
Behaviour	hops, perches openly, takes off and lands on vegetation or ground
Flocking	1–2
Flight	direct
Voice	*cuc-coo* repeated

IDENTIFICATION

Adult	
Crown	grey
Upperparts	grey
Rump	grey
Tail	grey; long and rounded
Throat	grey
Breast	grey
Belly	black and white, barred
Bill	black; short and thin
Legs	yellow; short
Juvenile	mottled and barred brown, black, buff and white
Hepatic ♀	chestnut and white, heavily barred

BREEDING

Nest	parasitic
Eggs	8–12; highly variable, mimic host
Incubation	12½ days; by host
Young	helpless; naked
Fledging	20–23 days
Broods	not applicable
Food	insects
Population	17,000–35,000 pairs

J	0
F	0
M	1
A	3
M	4
J	4
J	4
A	3
S	3
O	2
N	0
D	0

bold facial disc

white breast

rare dark breasted form

pale rounded wings

flat white face

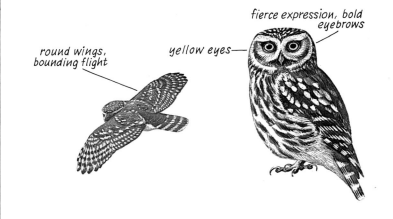

round wings, bounding flight

yellow eyes

fierce expression, bold eyebrows

The ghost-like, white owl of country folklore. Most often seen quartering fields at dusk when white underparts identify. Upperparts pale orange-buff with darkish spots. Flat-faced appearance with dark ring around facial disc. The dark-breasted form is a rare immigrant from central Europe.
Status: widespread resident but nowhere common; declining in numbers.
Similar Species: all other owls are brown and buff, except rare Snowy Owl, which is white, mottled black.

BARN OWL	
Type	owl-like
Size	33–36cm (12½–14in)
Habitat	heaths, woods, fields and hedges
Behaviour	perches openly, takes off and lands on vegetation or ground
Flocking	solitary
Flight	hovers, glides
Voice	variety shrill shrieks, hisses and snoring notes

IDENTIFICATION

Adult	
Crown	buffy orange
Upperparts	buffy orange, dark spots
Rump	buffy orange
Tail	buffy orange; short and square
Throat	white
Breast	white
Belly	white
Bill	grey; hooked
Legs	white; medium length

BREEDING

Nest	hole in tree or building
Eggs	4–7; white
Incubation	32–34 days ♀
Young	helpless; naked
Fledging	60 days
Broods	1–2; Mar–May
Food	small mammals, birds
Population	5000–10,000 pairs

Small brown and buff owl; most often seen perched openly during daylight. When disturbed, flies away with distinctive bouncing flight, like a woodpecker. Staring yellow eyes and prominent facial disc with bold 'eyebrows' create fierce expression.
Status: introduced resident England and Wales.
Similar Species: only tiny owl.

LITTLE OWL	
Type	owl-like
Size	21–23cm (8–9in)
Habitat	towns and gardens; heaths, woods, fields and hedges
Behaviour	perches openly, takes off and lands on vegetation or ground
Flocking	solitary
Flight	glides; undulating
Voice	plaintive *keeoo*

IDENTIFICATION

Adult	
Crown	brown and buff, spotted
Upperparts	brown and buff, spotted
Rump	brown and buff, spotted
Tail	brown and buff; short and square
Throat	brown and buff, streaked
Breast	brown and buff, streaked
Belly	white, streaked brown
Bill	grey; hooked
Legs	white; medium length

BREEDING

Nest	hole in tree or building
Eggs	3–5; white
Incubation	28–29 days ♀
Young	helpless; downy
Fledging	4–5 weeks
Broods	1, 2 ?; Apr–May
Food	insects, small mammals, small birds
Population	7000–14,000 pairs

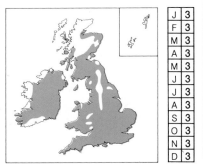

J	3
F	3
M	3
A	3
M	3
J	3
J	3
A	3
S	3
O	3
N	3
D	3

J	3
F	3
M	3
A	3
M	3
J	3
J	3
A	3
S	3
O	3
N	3
D	3

Short-eared Owl *Asio flammeus*

rounded head, yellow eyes

dark carpals

gliding, hovering harrier-like flight on long, rounded wings

Diurnal owl, associated with marshes and moorland; the owl most frequently seen hunting during daylight. Flat head and long, rounded wings with dark carpal patches above. Pale, almost white, below with dark wingtips and carpal patches. Quarters territory like a harrier – weaves, hovers and glides with wings held in shallow 'V'.
Status: resident mainly in north and along east coast of Britain; passage migrant and winter visitor elsewhere.
Similar Species: only regular diurnal owl of moors and marshes.

SHORT-EARED OWL	
Type	owl-like
Size	36–39cm (14–15in)
Habitat	freshwater marshes, moors, estuaries
Behaviour	perches openly, takes off and lands on ground
Flocking	1–2
Flight	hovers, glides; laboured
Voice	high-pitched *kee-aw*; deep *boo-boo-boo*

IDENTIFICATION	
Adult	
Crown	buff
Upperparts	brown and buff, barred
Rump	brown and buff, barred
Tail	brown and buff; short and square
Throat	brown and buff, streaked
Breast	brown and buff, streaked
Belly	pale buff
Bill	black; hooked
Legs	white; medium length

BREEDING	
Nest	hollow on ground
Eggs	4–8; white
Incubation	24–28 days ♀
Young	helpless; downy
Fledging	22–27 days
Broods	1 (sometimes 2); Apr–June
Food	small mammals
Population	1000+ pairs

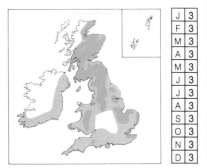

J	3
F	3
M	3
A	3
M	3
J	3
J	3
A	3
S	3
O	3
N	3
D	3

Long-eared Owl *Asio otus*

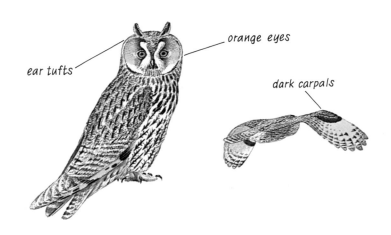

ear tufts

orange eyes

dark carpals

Medium-sized owl with striking orange eyes, prominent facial disc and conspicuous ear tufts. Upperparts mottled buff and brown; underparts buffy, streaked brown. Scarce and secretive owl, lacking obviously distinctive voice. Mainly found in old conifers; sometimes forms communal roosts in winter.
Status: widespread, but patchy, throughout Britain and Ireland. Continental immigrants in winter.
Similar Species: Tawny Owl (p.155) also occurs in woodlands.

LONG-EARED OWL	
Type	owl-like
Size	34–37cm (13–14in)
Habitat	forests and woods, heaths
Behaviour	takes off and lands on vegetation or ground
Flocking	solitary
Flight	glides; laboured; direct
Voice	low *oo-oo-oo*

IDENTIFICATION	
Adult	
Crown	buff and brown, mottled
Upperparts	buff and brown, mottled
Rump	buff and brown, mottled
Tail	buff and brown; short and square
Throat	buff, streaked brown
Breast	buff, streaked brown
Belly	buff, streaked brown
Bill	black; hooked
Legs	buff; medium length

BREEDING	
Nest	old nest of different species in tree
Eggs	4–5; white
Incubation	25–30 days ♀
Young	helpless; downy
Fledging	23–24 days
Broods	1 (rarely 2); Feb–May
Food	small mammals
Population	3000–10,000 pairs

J	2
F	2
M	2
A	2
M	2
J	2
J	2
A	2
S	2
O	2
N	2
D	2

large rounded head

dark eyes

flat head

broad rounded wings

This is the 'brown' or 'wood' owl of the countryman and the source of the most familiar hoots and shrieks. Though widespread and numerous, the Tawny Owl is surprisingly seldom seen. It hunts well after dark and hides away in a hole or among dense vegetation during the hours of daylight. The upperparts are brown, mottled and barred with buff and white, while the underparts are buff, becoming paler on the belly, and heavily streaked with brown and black. It has a well-marked facial disc with large dark eyes. In flight the wings are uniformly brown and well rounded.
Status: a widespread resident throughout Britain, but absent from Ireland.

particularly fierce expression. The densely barred breast and pale grey (spotted) scapulars help avoid confusion with any other European owl.
Range: resident in the great northern coniferous forests of Scandinavia, Siberia and North America that encircle the globe.
Migration: resident, but sometimes erupts southward during periods of food shortage.
British Distribution: an exceptional vagrant from both Europe and North America.
Other Similar Species: Long-eared Owl (p. 154).

Similar Species:
Hawk Owl *Surnia ulula*
34–41cm (13–16in)
This is an owl of the great northern conifer forests that just occasionally flies westwards to reach our shores. It is mainly active during the day and frequently perches quite openly. It is a predominantly grey owl with a long tail and large, well-marked rounded head. The facial disc is accentuated by broad black marks at either side and bold whitish eyebrows. The yellow eyes give this bird a

Hawk Owl

pale scapulars

dark sides to face

short, pointed wings

long tail

	TAWNY OWL	
Type	owl-like	
Size	36–40cm (14–15½in)	
Habitat	towns and gardens, heaths, forests and woods, fields and hedges	
Behaviour	perches openly, takes off and lands on vegetation	
Flocking	solitary	
Flight	glides; direct	
Voice	hooted *hoo-hoo-hoo-oo-oo-oo*; harsh *ke-wick*	

	IDENTIFICATION	
Adult		
Crown	brown, mottled buff	
Upperparts	brown, mottled buff	
Rump	brown, mottled buff	
Tail	buff and brown; short and square	
Throat	buff, streaked brown	
Breast	buff, streaked brown	
Belly	buff	
Bill	grey; hooked	
Legs	white; medium length	

	BREEDING	
Nest	hole in tree or building	
Eggs	2–4; white	
Incubation	28–30 days ♀	
Young	helpless; downy	
Fledging	32–37 days	
Broods	1; Mar–May	
Food	small mammals, small birds	
Population	50,000–100,000 pairs	

J	F	M	A	M	J	J	A	S	O	N	D
4	4	4	4	4	4	4	4	4	4	4	4

Nightjar *Caprimulgus europaeus*

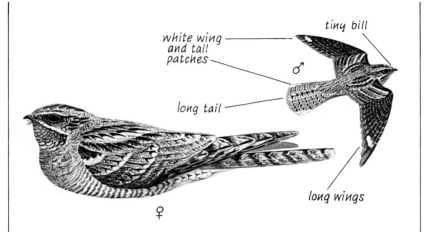

white wing and tail patches

tiny bill

♂

long tail

long wings

♀

Medium-sized nocturnal bird with long wings and tail. Heavily mottled and barred in browns, buffs and greys, creating excellent camouflage when bird nests on ground on open heaths. Male has conspicuous white patches on wings and tail, lacking in female. Best located by distinctive churring call (similar to that made by vibrating tongue in mouth), which continues for long periods. Claps wings in display. *Status:* widespread but scarce and declining summer visitor.
Similar Species: none.

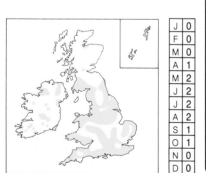

	NIGHTJAR	
Type	hawk-like/owl-like	
Size	25–28cm (9½–11in)	
Habitat	heaths, forests and woods	
Behaviour	takes off and lands on vegetation or ground	
Flocking	solitary	
Flight	glides; flitting	
Voice	distinctive churring	
	IDENTIFICATION	
Adult ♂		
Crown	grey	
Upperparts	brown, spotted	
Rump	brown	
Tail	brown, white patches; long and square	
Throat	buff and brown, barred	
Breast	buff and brown, barred	
Belly	buff and brown, barred	
Bill	black; short and thin	
Legs	buff; short	
Adult ♀	lacks white wing and tail patches	
	BREEDING	
Nest	bare hollow	
Eggs	2; white, spotted light brown	
Incubation	18 days ♂ ♀	
Young	partly-active; downy	
Fledging	16–18 days	
Broods	2; May–July	
Food	insects	
Population	3000–6000 pairs	

J	0
F	0
M	0
A	1
M	2
J	2
J	2
A	2
S	1
O	1
N	0
D	0

Swift *Apus apus*

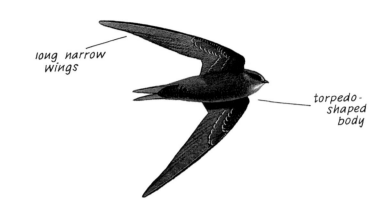

long narrow wings

torpedo-shaped body

Superficially similar to Swallow and martins but easily distinguished by longer and narrower sickle-shaped wings and all-black coloration. Most aerial of birds, coming to land (buildings and caves) only to lay and incubate eggs and feed young. Flickers wings and forms 'screaming' parties over colonies on summer evenings. *Status:* common summer visitor.
Similar Species: Swallow (p.165) and martins (p.164).

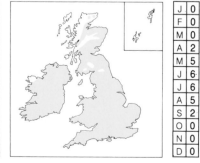

	SWIFT	
Type	swallow-like	
Size	16–17cm (6in)	
Habitat	towns, freshwater, moors, heaths, fields and hedges	
Behaviour	totally aerial, takes off and lands on buildings	
Flocking	1–1000	
Flight	glides; strong and powerful; flitting	
Voice	high-pitched scream	
	IDENTIFICATION	
Adult		
Crown	black	
Upperparts	black	
Rump	black	
Tail	black; short and forked	
Throat	grey	
Breast	black	
Belly	black	
Bill	black; short and thin	
Legs	black; short	
	BREEDING	
Nest	leaves and debris inside building	
Eggs	3; white	
Incubation	14–20 days ♂ ♀	
Young	helpless; naked	
Fledging	5–8 weeks	
Broods	1; May–June	
Food	insects	
Population	*c*100,000 pairs	

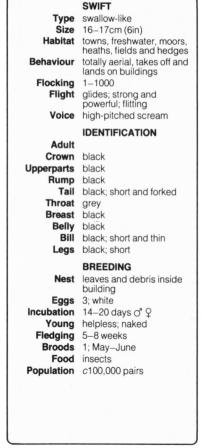

J	0
F	0
M	0
A	2
M	5
J	6
J	6
A	5
S	2
O	0
N	0
D	0

Alcedo atthis **Kingfisher**

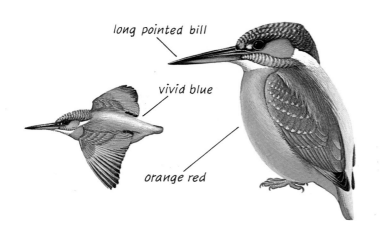

long pointed bill

vivid blue

orange red

Exotic, jewel-like bird, most often seen as a flash of bright blue as it dashes upstream. Confined to small streams, though may move to larger rivers and even coastal marshes during hard weather. Upperparts blue-green with vividly blue rump; underparts bright orange-red. Catches fishes by diving head-first into water.
Status: declining resident, becoming decidedly scarce.
Similar Species: none.

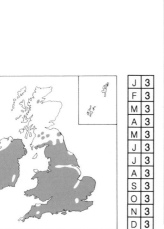

KINGFISHER	
Type	unique
Size	15–16cm (5½–6in)
Habitat	inland freshwater
Behaviour	dives from air, perches openly, takes off and lands in vegetation
Flocking	solitary
Flight	direct; aerial dive
Voice	metallic *chee*, or *chee-kee*, often rapidly repeated

IDENTIFICATION	
Adult	
Crown	blue-green, barred black
Upperparts	blue-green; wings barred black
Rump	bright blue
Tail	blue-green; short and square
Throat	white
Breast	orange-red
Belly	orange-red
Bill	black; straight and thin
Legs	red; short

BREEDING	
Nest	hole in bank
Eggs	6–7; white
Incubation	19–21 days ♂ ♀
Young	helpless; naked
Fledging	23–27 days
Broods	2; Apr–June
Food	fish
Population	5000–9000 pairs

J	3
F	3
M	3
A	3
M	3
J	3
J	3
A	3
S	3
O	3
N	3
D	3

Upupa epops **Hoopoe**

crest

black and white wings

decurved bill

Distinctive at rest and in flight. Sandy fawn above and below, marked by long erectile crest with black margin. Wings and tail black with broad white bars. Short legs and long, black, decurved bill. Spends much time on ground where may be surprisingly inconspicuous; also perches freely in trees.
Status: summer visitor to Mediterranean; overshoots in spring to reach southern England and Ireland. Occasionally stays to breed.
Similar Species: none.

HOOPOE	
Type	unique
Size	27–29cm (10–11in)
Habitat	gardens, heaths, woods, fields
Behaviour	perches openly, walks, takes off from vegetation or ground
Flocking	solitary
Flight	laboured; undulating; flitting
Voice	distinctive *poo-poo-poo*, repeated

IDENTIFICATION	
Adult	
Crown	sandy fawn; crest tipped black
Upperparts	black with white bars
Rump	black with white bars
Tail	black with white bars; medium length, square
Throat	sandy fawn
Breast	sandy fawn
Belly	white
Bill	black; long and decurved
Legs	grey; short

BREEDING	
Nest	hole in tree, building or rocks
Eggs	5–8; greyish
Incubation	16–19 days ♀
Young	helpless; downy
Fledging	20–27 days
Broods	1 (2?); Apr–June
Food	insects
Population	rarely breeds; variable passage migrant

J	0
F	0
M	1
A	1
M	1
J	1
J	1
A	1
S	1
O	0
N	0
D	0

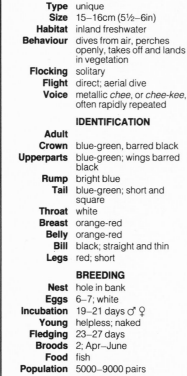

Wryneck *Jynx torquilla*

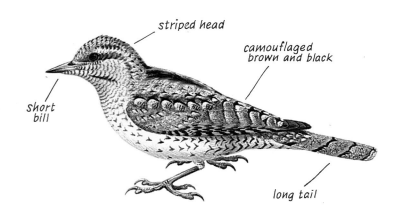

striped head

camouflaged brown and black

short bill

long tail

Highly elusive, well-camouflaged relative of the woodpeckers; spends most of its time on the ground or perched inconspicuously in bushes. Does not behave like a woodpecker, although voice similar to Lesser Spotted. Upperparts brown, variously mottled, streaked and barred with black, buff and grey. Short bill, striped head pattern and long tail produce unusual appearance. Name comes from habit of twisting neck right round when startled or handled.
Status: formerly bred southern England; now in process of colonizing Scotland. Regular but scarce passage migrant – especially in autumn on south and east coasts.
Similar Species: none.

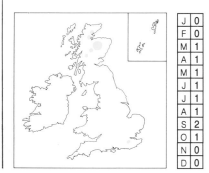

WRYNECK	
Type	woodpecker-like
Size	15–16cm (5½–6in)
Habitat	gardens, heaths, woods, fields
Behaviour	perches openly, hops, takes off from vegetation or ground
Flocking	solitary
Flight	direct
Voice	far-carrying *kyee-kyee-kyee*, repeated

IDENTIFICATION	
Adult	
Crown	buff and brown
Upperparts	brown with black, buff and grey markings
Rump	buff and brown
Tail	grey, barred black; long, square
Throat	buff
Breast	barred buff and brown
Belly	barred buff and brown
Bill	black; short and thin
Legs	brown; short

BREEDING	
Nest	hole in tree or wall
Eggs	7–10; white
Incubation	12–14 days, mainly ♀
Young	helpless; naked
Fledging	19–21 days
Broods	1, occasionally 2; May–June
Food	insects
Population	0–10 pairs; passage migrant, small numbers autumn

J	0
F	0
M	1
A	1
M	1
J	1
J	1
A	1
S	2
O	1
N	0
D	0

Green Woodpecker *Picus viridis*

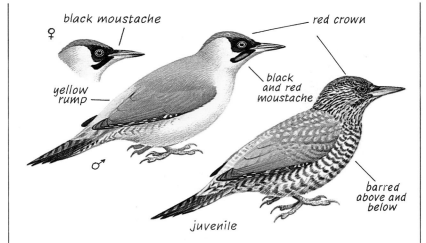

black moustache

♀

yellow rump

♂

red crown

black and red moustache

juvenile

barred above and below

Large green and yellow woodpecker which spends much time on ground, feeding. Bright red crown; moustachial stripe red, bordered black in male, pure black in female. Upperparts green, rump yellow, tail dark brown and pointed. Underparts white with faint greenish wash; undertail barred brown. Dagger-like silver-grey bill; grey legs. Typical undulating flight. Unlike other woodpeckers, rarely drums.
Status: widespread resident of woods and heaths in most of Britain except northern Scotland; absent Ireland.
Similar Species: only large green woodpecker to occur in Britain.

GREEN WOODPECKER	
Type	woodpecker-like
Size	30–33cm (11½–13in)
Habitat	gardens, woods, heaths, fields
Behaviour	climbs, hops, takes off from vegetation or ground
Flocking	1–2
Flight	laboured; undulating
Voice	loud, laughing *keu-keu-keu*

IDENTIFICATION	
Adult	
Crown	red
Upperparts	green
Rump	yellow
Tail	dark brown, barred below; short and pointed
Throat	grey
Breast	grey
Belly	white with greenish wash
Bill	silver-grey; short and thin
Legs	grey; short
Juvenile	face and underparts heavily barred black; less conspicuous moustaches

BREEDING	
Nest	bare tree hole
Eggs	5–7; white
Incubation	18–19 days ♂ ♀
Young	helpless; naked
Fledging	18–21 days
Broods	1; Apr–May
Food	insects
Population	15,000–30,000 pairs

J	3
F	3
M	3
A	3
M	3
J	3
J	3
A	3
S	3
O	3
N	3
D	3

Dendrocopos major Great Spotted Woodpecker   *Dendrocopos minor* Lesser Spotted Woodpecker

black crown — red nape
white ovals
♂
no red on crown
♀
red crown
juvenile

buffy crown
♀
red crown
ladder back
♂

Most common and widespread of the three British woodpeckers. Upperparts black broken by white cheeks, neck patch, and two bold white ovals on back. Underparts buffy white; red undertail coverts. Adult male has red patch on hind crown (lacking in female). Juvenile has red crown. Largely confined to woodland; climbs trees easily. Both sexes frequently drum on dead wood producing loud, far-carrying hollow sound. Deeply undulating flight.
Status: widespread resident; absent Ireland.
Similar Species: much smaller and more elusive Lesser Spotted Woodpecker (p.159) lacks red undertail and white ovals on back.

GREAT SPOTTED WOODPECKER

Type	woodpecker-like
Size	22–24cm (8–9in)
Habitat	woods, gardens, hedges
Behaviour	climbs, takes off and lands on vegetation
Flocking	1–2
Flight	laboured; undulating
Voice	loud *tchack*; also far-carrying, hollow drumming

IDENTIFICATION

Adult ♂	
Crown	black; red patch on nape
Upperparts	black and white; bold white ovals on back
Rump	black
Tail	black, undertail red; short and rounded
Throat	white
Breast	buffy white
Belly	buffy white; red on lower belly
Bill	grey; short and thin
Legs	grey; short
Adult ♀	lacks red on nape
Juvenile	red crown

BREEDING

Nest	tree hole
Eggs	4–7; white
Incubation	16 days, mainly ♀
Young	helpless; naked
Fledging	18–21 days
Broods	1; May–June
Food	insects
Population	30,000–40,000 pairs

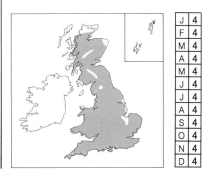

J	4
F	4
M	4
A	4
M	4
J	4
J	4
A	4
S	4
O	4
N	4
D	4

Tiny, sparrow-sized, black and white woodpecker; spends most of its time among the woodland canopy where easily overlooked. Agile climber, often on thin twigs near tops of trees. Male has red crown, female buffy white. Upperparts black, boldly barred white across back; white cheeks. Underparts buffy white. Both sexes drum on dead branches producing faster, higher-pitched sound than Great Spotted. Frequently calls early in breeding season. Needs dead and decaying trees for nesting.
Status: resident breeder in England and Wales.
Similar Species: Great Spotted Woodpecker (p.159) is larger and has white shoulder patches and red undertail.

LESSER SPOTTED WOODPECKER

Type	woodpecker-like
Size	14–15cm (5½–6in)
Habitat	heaths, woods, hedgerows, parks
Behaviour	climbs, takes off and lands on vegetation
Flocking	solitary
Flight	undulating
Voice	high-pitched *kee-kee-kee-kee*, repeated; similar to Wryneck

IDENTIFICATION

Adult ♂	
Crown	red
Upperparts	black, barred white
Rump	black
Tail	black; short and rounded
Throat	white
Breast	buffy white
Belly	buffy white
Bill	grey; short and thin
Legs	grey; short
Adult ♀	lacks red crown

BREEDING

Nest	tree hole
Eggs	4–6; white
Incubation	14 days ♂ ♀
Young	helpless, naked
Fledging	21 days
Broods	1; May–June
Food	insects
Population	5000–10,000 pairs

J	2
F	2
M	2
A	2
M	2
J	2
J	2
A	2
S	2
O	2
N	2
D	2

LARKS, SWALLOWS, WAGTAILS, WRENS, DIPPERS, ACCENTORS AND ALLIES

This group contains several quite different families, most of which have one or only a handful of representatives in Britain and Ireland. It is thus more a grouping of convenience than one of shared characteristics. Nevertheless, these are mainly small birds, most of which (the larks and wagtails) are ground-dwelling, though they also include the most aerial of British birds, the Swallow (*illustrated*) and closely related martins and, most aerial of all, the unrelated Swift. Most are insect eaters, though some take seeds, while the Dipper, looking like an overgrown version of the Wren, lives mainly on aquatic invertebrates, which it can catch by walking underwater – dippers are the only perching birds to do so.

By far the largest group is that comprising the pipits and wagtails, slim elegant birds often found alongside water. But while the three wagtails are straightforward to identify, the pipits are easily confused by the unwary, and may pose problems even for the experienced birder, especially as two or more very similar sub-species, or races, may be present together. Fortunately these birds have distinctive voices and the calls are the easiest way of separating them.

Three species of larks occur in these islands, though only the Skylark is at all numerous. In fact, it is the most widespread of all our birds, occurring in a wide range of habitats, from coastal marshes to inland moors. The once widespread Woodlark is declining so fast that it seems only a matter of time before it disappears altogether.

This grouping also includes two quite remarkable colonists – the Wren is a New World bird, called the Winter Wren in the United States, that has spread right across Asia to the Atlantic coasts of Europe. It is the only member of its large family that has colonized from America. The Dunnock belongs to a family that is otherwise restricted to the highest mountains of the Old World.

Woodlark *Lulluala arborea*

eyebrows meet at nape

black and white mark at bend of wing

short tail

white corners to tail

Small, stockily-built lark; scarce inhabitant of heaths and open woodlands. Favours areas of short grass with scattered trees and shrubs, on which it frequently lands. Similar to Skylark but tail obviously shorter and only hint of crest; prominent pale eyebrows meet at nape. Small black and white patch at bend of wing. Upperparts streaked brown and buff; underparts white with brown and buff streaks on breast. Distinctive song uttered from tree-top or in flight; melodic and liquid series of repeated phrases.
Status: fast-declining resident of southern England.
Similar Species: Skylark (p.162).

WOODLARK	
Type	lark-like
Size	14.5–16cm (5½–6in)
Habitat	heaths, woods
Behaviour	walks, takes off and lands on vegetation or ground
Flocking	1–2
Flight	hovers; undulating
Voice	fluty *too-loo-eet*
IDENTIFICATION	
Adult	
Crown	buff and brown
Upperparts	buff and brown, streaked
Rump	buff and brown
Tail	buff and brown, tipped white; short and notched
Throat	white
Breast	white, streaked buff
Belly	white
Bill	brown; short and thin
Legs	pink; medium length
BREEDING	
Nest	cup on ground
Eggs	3–4; buffy, spotted brown
Incubation	12–16 days ♀
Young	helpless; downy
Fledging	15–17 days?
Broods	2; Mar–May
Food	seeds, insects
Population	200–400 pairs

J	1
F	1
M	1
A	2
M	2
J	2
J	2
A	1
S	1
O	1
N	1
D	1

Skylark *Alauda arvensis*

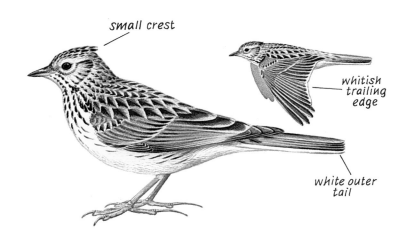

small crest

whitish trailing edge

white outer tail

Heavily-streaked, ground-dwelling bird of wide variety of habitats; common and widespread at all seasons. Most often seen in towering song flight during spring and early summer. Thickish bill and bulky shape distinguish from pipits; noticeable crest and long, white-edged tail separate from Woodlark. Gregarious outside breeding season.
Status: breeds throughout Britain and Ireland; also double passage migrant and winter visitor in large numbers.
Similar Species: Woodlark (p.162).

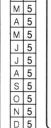

SKYLARK	
Type	lark-like
Size	17–18cm (6½–7in)
Habitat	moors, heaths, fields, marshes
Behaviour	walks, takes off and lands on ground
Flocking	1–100
Flight	hovers; undulating
Voice	liquid *chirrup*, also fine warbling song in towering flight
IDENTIFICATION	
Adult	
Crown	buff and brown; small crest
Upperparts	buff and brown; heavily-streaked
Rump	buff and brown
Tail	buff and brown, white-edged; long and notched
Throat	white
Breast	buff; streaked brown
Belly	white
Bill	brown; short and thickish
Legs	pinkish; medium length
BREEDING	
Nest	cup on ground
Eggs	3–4; greyish, blotched brown
Incubation	11 days ♀
Young	helpless; downy
Fledging	20 days
Broods	2–3; Apr–June
Food	seeds, insects
Population	2,000,000–3,000,000 pairs

J	5
F	5
M	5
A	5
M	5
J	5
J	5
A	5
S	5
O	5
N	5
D	5

bold face pattern

white outer tail

winter

♂ summer

	SHORE LARK
Type	lark-like
Size	16–17cm (6–6½in)
Habitat	estuaries and shores
Behaviour	walks, takes off and lands on ground
Flocking	1–15
Flight	undulating
Voice	shrill *tseep* or *tseep-seep*, similar to wagtail or pipit

IDENTIFICATION

Adult	
Crown	buff; black 'horns'
Upperparts	buff and brown
Rump	buff
Tail	buff and brown, white outer feathers; medium length, notched
Throat	yellow
Breast	black crescent
Belly	white
Bill	black; short and thin
Legs	black; short
Juvenile	darker above, spotted buff-white; lacks black and yellow face pattern

BREEDING

Nest	cup on ground
Eggs	4; greenish, speckled brown
Incubation	10–14 days ♀
Young	helpless; downy
Fledging	?
Broods	2; May–June
Food	seeds, insects
Population	less than 100 autumn; has bred

The Shore Lark is a scarce autumn and winter visitor to the east coast of Britain and is usually confined to shorelines, saltmarshes and coastal shingle with a growth of sparse vegetation. It is well camouflaged and often difficult to locate until it flies. The upperparts are buffy-brown and the underparts white. It shows white outer tail feathers and has a distinctive black and yellow face pattern. The crown has two tiny black 'horns' that can be seen only at very close range, which are responsible for its American name of Horned Lark. The face pattern is subdued in winter but still quite unmistakable. It usually occurs in small flocks, often in the same areas occupied by Snow Buntings. *Status:* a scarce and highly localized passage migrant in autumn and an even scarcer winter visitor. A few pairs have bred in Scotland in recent years.

Similar Species:
Short-toed Lark *Calandrella brachydactyla* 13–15cm (5–6in)
A darkish patch at the sides of the neck is often difficult to see and frequently obscured as the bird turns its head. A combination of pale, stubby bill, sandy or greyish upper

parts and a darkish bar across the closed wing are the best field marks, but once seen, the thickset shape, size and white underparts are characteristic.
Range: right across the Mediterranean basin, through southern Russia and Iran to north-western China.
Migration: winters in Africa and southern Asia.
British Distribution: increasingly identified, especially in autumn when most birds are of the grey eastern sub-species, at Fair Isle (*see page* 264) and the Isles of Scilly (*see page* 284).

Short-toed Lark

conical bill

smudge at breast sides

white

note: colour variation

J	F	M	A	M	J	J	A	S	O	N	D
2	2	1	0	0	0	0	0	0	0	2	2	2

Sand Martin *Riparia riparia*

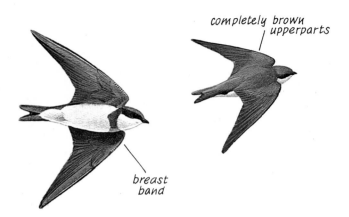

completely brown upperparts

breast band

Smallest of the Swallow-like birds, with shallow, forked tail and sharply angled wings. Erratic flight with less frequent glides than similar species. Upperparts sandy brown; underparts white. Distinctive brown breast band. Always gregarious, forming highly vocal, twittering flocks; frequently gathers to feed over water. Nests in colonies in sand-banks and cliffs. In winter and on passage roosts among dense reeds, often in company with Swallows.

Status: widespread summer visitor, except to northern and western isles. Sharp decline in mid-1980s associated with drought in Africa.

Similar Species: Swallow (p.165) and House Martin (p.164) have blackish upperparts.

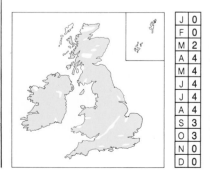

	SAND MARTIN
Type	swallow-like
Size	11–12cm (4½–5in)
Habitat	inland freshwater, sea cliffs
Behaviour	aerial, takes off and lands on ground
Flocking	1–100s
Flight	flitting
Voice	continuous twittering, harsh *chirrup*
	IDENTIFICATION
Adult	
Crown	sandy brown
Upperparts	sandy brown
Rump	sandy brown
Tail	sandy brown; short and notched
Throat	white
Breast	sandy brown band
Belly	white
Bill	black; short and thin
Legs	black; short
	BREEDING
Nest	hole in sand-bank; colonial
Eggs	4–5; white
Incubation	1–12 days ♂ ♀
Young	helpless; downy
Fledging	19 days
Broods	2; May–June
Food	insects
Population	less than 250,000 pairs

J	0
F	0
M	2
A	4
M	4
J	4
J	4
A	4
S	3
O	3
N	0
D	0

House Martin *Delichon urbica*

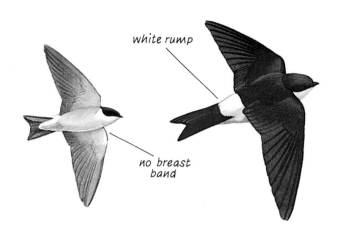

white rump

no breast band

Compact, black and white, Swallow-like bird. Common summer visitor, nesting mostly under eaves of buildings; usually forms colonies. Requires nearby source of soft mud to construct nearly spherical nest, which is well known in many small towns and villages. Blue-black on crown and back; black wings and tail; prominent white rump and pure white underparts. Usually gregarious but does not join communal roosts of Swallows and Sand Martins in reed beds. Often seen feeding over freshwater.

Status: common and widespread summer visitor.

Similar Species: Swallow (p.165) and Sand Martin (p.164).

	HOUSE MARTIN
Type	swallow-like
Size	12–13cm (4½–5in)
Habitat	towns, inland freshwater
Behaviour	aerial, takes off and lands on buildings
Flocking	1–100
Flight	glides; flitting
Voice	harsh *chirrup*, quite unlike other 'swallows'
	IDENTIFICATION
Adult	
Crown	blue-black
Upperparts	blue-black, wings black
Rump	white
Tail	black; short and forked
Throat	white
Breast	white
Belly	white
Bill	black; short and thin
Legs	white; short
	BREEDING
Nest	mud dome under eaves; colonial
Eggs	4–5; white
Incubation	13–19 days ♂ ♀
Young	helpless; downy
Fledging	19–25 days
Broods	2–3; May–June
Food	insects
Population	300,000–600,000 pairs

J	0
F	0
M	3
A	3
M	5
J	5
J	5
A	5
S	4
O	4
N	3
D	0

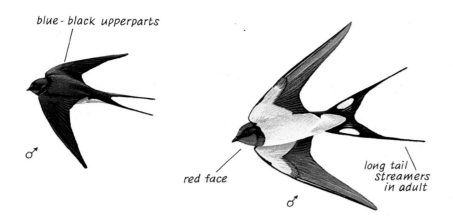

blue-black upperparts

♂

red face

long tail
streamers
in adult

♂

SWALLOW	
Type	swallow-like
Size	16–22cm (6½–8½in)
Habitat	gardens, freshwater, marshes, moors, fields
Behaviour	aerial, takes off and lands on buildings
Flocking	1–100s
Flight	glides; flitting
Voice	high-pitched *vit-vit-vit*; song, a twittering trill

IDENTIFICATION	
Adult	
Crown	dark metallic blue
Upperparts	dark metallic blue
Rump	dark metallic blue
Tail	blue-black; long and forked
Throat	red
Breast	dark metallic blue; narrow band
Belly	pale cream to rich pink
Bill	black; short and thin
Legs	black; short
Juvenile	lacks tail streamers

BREEDING	
Nest	mud cup inside outbuilding
Eggs	4–5; white with reddish spots
Incubation	14–16 days, ♀ alone?
Young	helpless; downy
Fledging	17–24 days
Broods	2–3; May–June
Food	insects
Population	500,000+ pairs

This is a summer visitor to our farms and gardens that most frequently nests inside barns, sheds, garages and outbuildings. Its flight is fast and highly acrobatic as it searches for and catches insects on the wing. The wings are long and angled, the tail deeply forked, with streamers in the adults that are longer in the male than the female. When spread, the tail shows a row of white spots. The upperparts are a metallic blue-black. The face and throat are dark red, bordered below by a narrow, dark breast band. The underparts vary from pale cream to rich pink.
Status: a common and widespread summer visitor.

Similar Species:
Red-rumped Swallow *Hirundo daurica*
17–18cm (6½–7in)
Formerly confined to the south-west and south-east of Europe, the Red-rumped Swallow has successfully expanded its range northwards in recent years. It is thus increasingly wandering northwards to our shores, especially in spring. The body is more robust and torpedo-like than a Swallow's, a shape accentuated by the tail streamers that turn distinctly inwards. The

upperparts are black, with a less metallic blue sheen, and the entire underparts, a narrow collar and a broad rump are rusty-pink.
Range: from the Mediterranean eastwards through the Middle East to India, China and Korea and also across the savannah grasslands of Africa in the Sahel zone.
Migration: northern birds winter in Africa and southern Asia.
British Distribution: an increasingly seen vagrant northwards from Spain and France, overshooting especially in late April and early May, mainly to eastern England.
Other Similar Species: House Martin and Sand Martin (p. 164).

Red-rumped Swallow

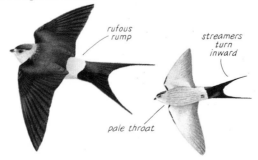

rufous
rump

streamers
turn
inward

pale throat

J	F	M	A	M	J	J	A	S	O	N	D
0	0	2	4	5	5	5	5	5	4	2	0

Tree Pipit *Anthus trivialis*

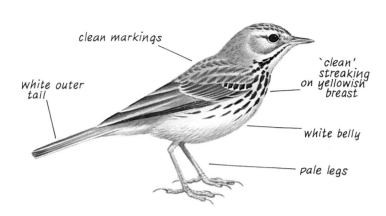

clean markings

white outer tail

'clean' streaking on yellowish breast

white belly

pale legs

Similar to more widespread and abundant Meadow Pipit but summer visitor only, preferring open woodlands and overgrown heaths with plentiful perches. Brown streaks on buff upperparts, buffy yellow breast and white flanks; conspicuous buffy eyebrow. Voice distinct, frequently uttered in song flight starting and terminating on perch.
Status: summer visitor to Britain; absent from Ireland except on passage.
Similar Species: Meadow Pipit (p.167) has (mostly) different habitat and call; streaking less clear and clean. See also Rock Pipit (p.166).

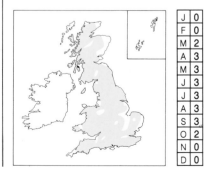

TREE PIPIT	
Type	wagtail-like
Size	14–16cm (5½–6½in)
Habitat	heaths, woods
Behaviour	walks, perches openly, takes off from vegetation or ground
Flocking	solitary
Flight	direct; hovers
Voice	harsh *tees*; also a loud descending trill with drawn-out *see-see-see* ending
IDENTIFICATION	
Adult	
Crown	buff, streaked brown
Upperparts	buff, streaked brown
Rump	buff, streaked brown
Tail	buff, streaked brown, white outer feathers; medium length, notched
Throat	buff
Breast	buffy yellow, streaked brown
Belly	white
Bill	brown; short and thin
Legs	pinkish; medium length
BREEDING	
Nest	cup on ground
Eggs	4–6; variable, speckled brown
Incubation	12–14 days ♀
Young	helpless; downy
Fledging	12–13 days
Broods	1–2; May–June
Food	insects
Population	50,000–100,000 pairs

J	0
F	0
M	2
A	3
M	3
J	3
J	3
A	3
S	3
O	2
N	0
D	0

Rock Pipit *Anthus spinoletta*

pale eyebrow more prominent

'petrosus'

darker than Meadow Pipit

dark legs

brown back

'spinoletta' summer

rufous breast

prominent eyebrow

grey outer tail

fewer streaks on whiter belly

brown back

dark legs

'littoralis' spring

dark legs

white streaked breast

'spinoletta' winter

Three distinct sub-species occur. The British Rock Pipit *A.s.petrosus* breeds on rocky shores. Streaked black on olive above; streaked black on buff below; short eyebrow; grey outer tail. Scandinavian Rock Pipit *A.s.littoralis* winters along coasts. In spring, streaked brownish above with prominent eyebrow. White belly; fine streaking on pinkish breast; grey outer tail. Continental sub-species *A.s.spinoletta* (Water Pipit) is winter visitor to inland marshes. Unstreaked back; bold eyebrow; white outer tail. Finely-streaked white breast in winter; unstreaked pinkish in spring. All three darker than Meadow Pipit (p.167) with more diffuse streaking, longer bill and darker legs.
Status: resident and winter visitor.
Similar Species: see above.

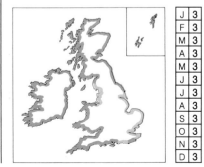

ROCK PIPIT	
Type	wagtail-like
Size	15–16.5cm (6–6½in)
Habitat	coasts, estuaries, freshwater marshes
Behaviour	walks, perches openly, takes off from ground
Flocking	1–15
Flight	direct; hovers
Voice	clear but harsh *weest*
IDENTIFICATION	
A.s.petrosus	
Crown	grey
Upperparts	grey, diffuse brown streaks
Rump	grey
Tail	black with grey outer feathers; medium, notched
Throat	buff
Breast	buff, diffuse brown streaks
Belly	buff
Bill	black; short and thin
Legs	dark; medium length
A.s.spinoletta	unstreaked browner upperparts, whiter below; white outer tail feathers
A.s.littoralis	in spring, cleaner streaking above and below; prominent eyebrow
BREEDING	
Nest	cup hidden on ground
Eggs	4–6; grey, spotted brown
Incubation	14 days ♀
Young	helpless; downy
Fledging	16 days
Broods	2; Apr–May
Food	insects
Population	50,000 pairs; variable numbers in winter

J	3
F	3
M	3
A	3
M	3
J	3
J	3
A	3
S	3
O	3
N	3
D	3

white outer tail

pale legs

streaked breast

streaking less contrasting

darker/greyer type

MEADOW PIPIT	
Type	wagtail-like
Size	14–15cm (5½–6in)
Habitat	marshes, heaths, coasts, estuaries, fields
Behaviour	walks, perches openly, takes off and lands on ground
Flocking	1–50
Flight	direct; hovers
Voice	thin, high-pitched *tissip* or *eest*; also an accelerating trill in parachuting display flight

IDENTIFICATION	
Adult	
Crown	buff, streaked dark brown
Upperparts	olive-brown or greyish, streaked dark brown
Rump	buff, streaked dark brown
Tail	buff, streaked dark brown, white outer feathers; medium length, notched
Throat	white
Breast	buff, streaked dark brown
Belly	white
Bill	brown; short and thin
Legs	pinkish; medium length

BREEDING	
Nest	cup on ground
Eggs	3–5; variable, spotted brown
Incubation	11–15 days ♀
Young	helpless; downy
Fledging	10–14 days
Broods	2; Apr–June
Food	insects
Population	3,000,000+

J	F	M	A	M	J	J	A	S	O	N	D
5	5	5	5	5	5	5	5	5	5	5	5

The Meadow Pipit is widespread and numerous at all seasons and is often abundant among coastal marshes and on beaches in winter. The upperparts are variably olive-brown or olive-grey, variably streaked with black or dark grey. The breast is buffy and the belly white, with clear streaks of black on breast and flanks. The outer tail feathers are white and the legs pinkish-brown. Though all pipits share this basic pattern, they may be separated by leg colour and by the degree of cleanness of their streaking. Meadow Pipits are gregarious, forming flocks in winter and on migration. *Status:* a widespread resident and abundant spring and autumn passage migrant and winter visitor.

Similar Species:
Tawny Pipit *Anthus campestris*
16–17cm (6–6½in)
The Tawny Pipit is substantially larger than our common pipits and is generally paler with less streaking, particularly on the underparts. Adults are pale sandy above, with any streaked effect confined to the pale margins of the flight feathers. The underparts are very pale buff. A line of dark spots forms a bar across the closed wing.

Juveniles are darker and more streaked on the back and upper breast, but are always paler and greyer than any of the common pipits. In all plumages the shape is reminiscent of a wagtail, as are the calls. *Range:* it breeds right across Eurasia from Spain to northern China. *Migration:* a summer visitor, wintering in Africa and southern Asia. *British Distribution:* a regular, if rare, autumn visitor to south and east England, mainly in September. Very rare in spring. *Other Similar Species:* Tree Pipit in summer and Rock Pipit in winter (p. 166).

Tawny Pipit

dark spots form line

unstreaked

adult

finely streaked

juvenile moulting to first winter

Pied Wagtail *Motacilla alba*

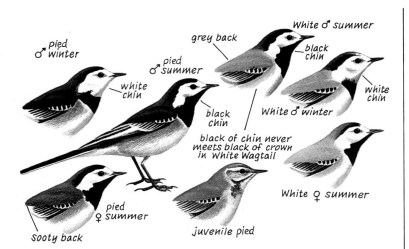

- ♂ pied winter
- white chin
- pied ♂ summer
- black chin
- grey back
- White ♂ summer
- black chin
- White ♂ winter
- white chin
- black of chin never meets black of crown in White Wagtail
- White ♀ summer
- pied ♀ summer
- sooty back
- juvenile pied

Grey Wagtail *Motacilla cinerea*

- black bib
- very long tail white outer feathers
- ♂ summer
- yellow undertail
- ♀ summer ♂ winter
- yellow undertail

Familiar black and white wagtail; widespread resident of open habitats with and without water. Common sub-species in British Isles is *M.a.yarrellii*. Male mainly black above with white face, white margins to flight feathers and white outer tail. Black bib terminates in broad black breast band; remaining underparts white. Female similar but with slate-grey back. Juveniles and first winter birds have grey backs and are similar to Continental sub-species *M.a.alba*, known as the White Wagtail. White Wagtails regularly occur on migration and have uniform grey backs.
Status: widespread resident.
Similar Species: Grey Wagtail (p.168) often lacks almost all yellow on underparts in winter – particularly in first winter plumage.

Largest of the three British wagtails and the one most closely associated with water, especially fast-running streams. In winter also found near waterfalls, weirs and sometimes lakes, reservoirs, watercress beds and even farmyards. Upperparts grey with white eyebrow, black wings, yellow-green rump, and long, white-edged, black tail. Underparts white with yellow undertail coverts and variable amount of yellow on breast. In summer, male has prominent black bib.
Status: widespread and common resident, but winter visitor only to large areas of eastern England; summer visitor to northern Scotland.
Similar Species: Yellow Wagtail (p.169) and Pied Wagtail (p.168).

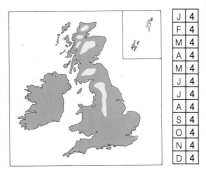

J	4
F	4
M	4
A	4
M	4
J	4
J	4
A	4
S	4
O	4
N	4
D	4

PIED WAGTAIL

Type	wagtail-like
Size	17–18cm (6½–7in)
Habitat	inland freshwater, fields, gardens
Behaviour	walks, perches openly, takes off from vegetation or ground
Flocking	1–10
Flight	undulating
Voice	harsh *chis-ick*; also a disjointed twitter

IDENTIFICATION

M.a.yarrellii

Crown	black, white face
Upperparts	black, white-tipped flight feathers
Rump	black
Tail	black, white outer feathers; long and notched
Throat	black bib in summer; white in winter
Breast	black band
Belly	white
Bill	black; short and thin
Legs	black; medium length
M.a.alba	back pale grey at all times

BREEDING

Nest	cup on ground
Eggs	5–6; grey, speckled brown
Incubation	12–14 days, ♀ only ?
Young	helpless; downy
Fledging	13–16 days
Broods	2; Apr–June
Food	insects
Population	c 500,000 pairs

J	3
F	3
M	3
A	3
M	3
J	3
J	3
A	3
S	3
O	3
N	3
D	3

GREY WAGTAIL

Type	wagtail-like
Size	18–20cm (7–8in)
Habitat	inland freshwater, marshes
Behaviour	walks, perches openly, takes off from vegetation or ground
Flocking	1–2
Flight	undulating
Voice	metallic *tzitzi*; also a warble reminiscent of Blue Tit

IDENTIFICATION

Ad.♂ summer

Crown	grey, white eyebrow
Upperparts	grey, wings black
Rump	yellow-green
Tail	black, white-edged; long and notched
Throat	white; black bib
Breast	yellow
Belly	white
Bill	black; short and thin
Legs	pink; medium length
Ad.♀, winter♂	less yellow below; lacks black bib

BREEDING

Nest	neat cup in crevice beside stream
Eggs	4–6; buffy, mottled greyish
Incubation	11–14 days, mainly ♀
Young	helpless; downy
Fledging	17 days
Broods	1, occasionally 2; Apr–May
Food	insects
Population	25,000–50,000 pairs

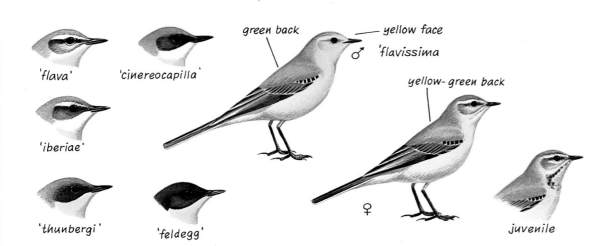

'flava'　　'cinereocapilla'

'iberiae'

'thunbergi'　　'feldegg'

green back — yellow face

♂ 'flavissima'

yellow-green back

♀

juvenile

	YELLOW WAGTAIL
Type	wagtail-like
Size	16–17cm (6½–7in)
Habitat	inland freshwater, marshes, estuaries, fields
Behaviour	walks, perches openly, takes off and lands on ground
Flocking	1–15
Flight	undulating
Voice	loud *see-ip*; also a disjointed warble

IDENTIFICATION

Ad. *flavissima*	
Crown	green
Upperparts	green, wings black and white
Rump	green
Tail	black, white-edged; long and notched
Throat	yellow
Breast	yellow
Belly	yellow
Bill	brown; short and thin
Legs	black; medium length
Other sub-sp.	adults vary in head colour

BREEDING

Nest	cup on ground
Eggs	5–6; greyish, speckled brown
Incubation	12–14 days, mainly ♀
Young	helpless; downy
Fledging	17 days
Broods	1–2; May–June
Food	insects
Population	c 25,000 pairs

J	F	M	A	M	J	J	A	S	O	N	D
0	0	2	3	4	4	4	4	3	2	0	0

This is a slim, elegant summer visitor to damp meadows and marshes that is distinguished by its yellow underparts, green back and typical bobbing of the long, white-edged tail. The several distinct sub-species differ mostly in the colour and pattern of the head markings. Such differences are more obvious in spring males. Birds that breed in Britain, which belong to the sub-species *M. f. flavissima*, usually have yellow heads; others have blue, black, grey and even white heads. These occur in Britain only as rare vagrants, but one sub-species, the Blue-headed Wagtail *M. f. flava*, is a regular passage migrant and, just occasionally, breeds. Yellow Wagtails are gregarious birds outside the breeding season.
Status: a widespread summer visitor to England, Wales and central Scotland.

Similar Species:
Citrine Wagtail *Motacilla citreola*
16–17cm (6–6½in)
Though superficially like a Yellow Wagtail, this rare visitor is actually larger in the body and shorter in the tail than that species. The head and underparts are yellow; the back is pale grey. The summer

male has a black half-collar at the base of the nape. Juveniles are white below and pale grey above, with black and white wings. In all plumages the grey back and bold white double wing bar help pick out this species.
Range: this species is a summer visitor that breeds in Central Asia.
Migration: migrates southwards to winter throughout Southern Africa.
British Distribution: a rare vagrant that occurs almost annually at Fair Isle (*see page 264*) and occasionally elsewhere in eastern Britain.
Other Similar Species: Grey Wagtail (p. 168).

Citrine Wagtail

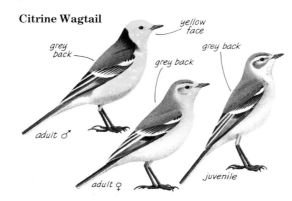

yellow face

grey back

grey back

grey back

adult ♂

adult ♀

juvenile

Waxwing *Bombycilla garrulus*

crest

black bib

yellow on wings and tail

Dipper *Cinclus cinclus*

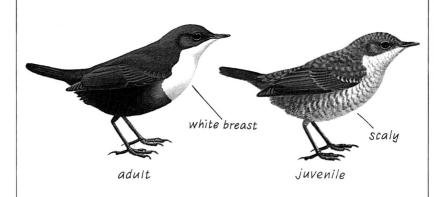

white breast

scaly

adult

juvenile

Decidedly Starling-like in shape and size, but pinkish brown in colour. Swept-back crest, black lores and chin patch broken by white moustachial streak produce 'cross' expression. Black wings marked by tiny wax-like spots of red and yellow; black banded tail tipped yellow. Irrupts in numbers every five or six years; roams hedgerows and gardens in flocks, sometimes a hundred or more strong; otherwise no more than a rarity.
Status: irregular autumn and winter visitor from Scandinavia and northern Russia, mainly to east coast; numbers variable.
Similar Species: in flight can be mistaken for Starling (p.213).

	WAXWING
Type	unique/starling-like
Size	17–18.5cm (7in)
Habitat	gardens, heaths, hedgerows
Behaviour	perches openly, hops, takes off from vegetation or ground
Flocking	1–100
Flight	direct
Voice	tinkling trill

IDENTIFICATION

Adult	
Crown	pinkish brown; swept-back crest
Upperparts	pinkish brown; black wings spotted red and yellow
Rump	grey
Tail	grey, black banded, tipped yellow; short and square
Throat	pinkish brown, black bib
Breast	pinkish brown
Belly	pinkish brown
Bill	black; short and thin
Legs	black; medium length

BREEDING

Nest	cup in conifer
Eggs	5; pale blue, spotted black
Incubation	13–14 days ♀
Young	helpless; naked
Fledging	15–17 days
Broods	1; May–June
Food	berries
Population	variable, up to several hundred in autumn and winter

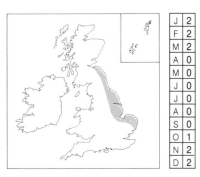

J	2
F	2
M	2
A	0
M	0
J	0
J	0
A	0
S	0
O	1
N	2
D	2

Portly, short-tailed, blackish bird marked by bold white gorget; reminiscent of large, white-breasted Wren. Confined to fast-running streams; most often seen from bridges or riverside paths. Spends much time searching for food among tumbling, rock-strewn waters where wades, swims and dives with complete mastery. Usually solitary, often perching openly on rocks; may be quite tame. Territory can be 2 km or more long but only as wide as a river or stream across.
Status: resident in northern and western hilly areas; some immigration of Continental birds in winter.
Similar Species: none.

	DIPPER
Type	wren-like
Size	17–18.5cm (7in)
Habitat	inland freshwater
Behaviour	swims, dives from surface, wades, walks, perches openly, takes off from water or ground
Flocking	solitary
Flight	direct
Voice	*zit-zit*

IDENTIFICATION

Adult	
Crown	chocolate-brown
Upperparts	black
Rump	black
Tail	black; short and notched
Throat	white
Breast	white
Belly	chestnut-brown
Bill	brown; short and thin
Legs	pinkish; medium length
Juvenile	slate-grey above, scaly patterning on whitish breast

BREEDING

Nest	dome in hole beside stream
Eggs	5; white
Incubation	15–18 days ♀
Young	helpless; downy
Fledging	19–25 days
Broods	2–3; Mar–June
Food	aquatic insects
Population	*c* 30,000 pairs

J	3
F	3
M	3
A	3
M	3
J	3
J	3
A	3
S	3
O	3
N	3
D	3

barred back

tail often cocked

barred flanks

thin bill

grey face

streaked flanks

adult

One of most widespread and numerous birds of Britain and Ireland, easily recognized by small size and cocked tail. Chestnut above, with clear pale eyebrow and barred back and wings. Underparts buffy; some barring on flanks. Spends much time hunting through dense ground cover, where presence betrayed only by characteristic calls and loud, wheezing song. Quite tame in gardens.
Status: widespread and numerous.
Similar Species: none; wrens are New World birds and this is the only species to have colonized the Old World.

WREN	
Type	wren-like
Size	9–10cm (3½–4in)
Habitat	gardens, marshes, heaths, sea cliffs, woods, hedges
Behaviour	flits, hops, perches openly, takes off from vegetation or ground
Flocking	1–2
Flight	laboured; direct
Voice	repeated *tic-tic* and *clink*; also a loud ripping warble ending in wheezing *chur*

IDENTIFICATION	
Adult	
Crown	chestnut brown
Upperparts	chestnut brown, darkly barred
Rump	chestnut brown
Tail	chestnut brown; short and square
Throat	buffy
Breast	buffy
Belly	buffy, flanks barred
Bill	brown; short and thin
Legs	brown; medium length

BREEDING	
Nest	dome in hole in bank
Eggs	5–8; white, speckled red
Incubation	14–17 days ♀
Young	helpless; downy
Fledging	15–20 days
Broods	1; Apr–May
Food	insects
Population	10,000,000 pairs

Tame garden and woodland bird; spends most of its time crouched low on ground searching for food. Seldom moves far from cover; usually perches openly only when singing. Flicks wings more or less continuously. Flies low and briefly in undulating flight. Easily overlooked among House Sparrows but grey foreparts and thin bill separate easily. Back and wings brown, liberally streaked with black; brown streaking on flanks. Juvenile has less grey on head and entire underparts are streaked.
Status: common and widespread resident; some autumn migrants from the Continent stay to winter here.
Similar Species: extremely rare Alpine Accentor.

DUNNOCK	
Type	sparrow-like
Size	14–15cm (5½–6in)
Habitat	gardens, heaths, woods, fields and hedges
Behaviour	flits, perches openly, hops, takes off from vegetation and ground
Flocking	1–2
Flight	undulating
Voice	jingling, staccato warble

IDENTIFICATION	
Adult	
Crown	grey-brown
Upperparts	brown, streaked black
Rump	dark grey
Tail	brown and black; medium length, notched
Throat	grey
Breast	grey
Belly	whitish grey; brown streaks on flanks
Bill	black; short and thin
Legs	flesh; medium length

BREEDING	
Nest	cup in tree or bush
Eggs	4–5; bright blue
Incubation	12–13 days ♀
Young	helpless; downy
Fledging	12 days
Broods	2–3 ?; Apr–May
Food	insects, berries
Population	*c* 5,000,000 pairs

J	5
F	5
M	5
A	5
M	5
J	5
J	5
A	5
S	5
O	5
N	5
D	5

J	5
F	5
M	5
A	5
M	5
J	5
J	5
A	5
S	5
O	5
N	5
D	5

CHATS AND THRUSHES

The Turdidae (chats and thrushes) are well represented in Britain and Ireland and include some of our most familiar and abundant birds. Indeed the Robin, Blackbird, Song Thrush and Mistle Thrush breed throughout these islands and have strong, healthy populations.

These are mostly ground-dwelling birds and even those most frequently seen perched, such as the Stonechat and Redstart, find the majority of their food on the ground.

Most chats and thrushes are of woodland origin and have evolved a dash-and-stop method of feeding, similar to that of the plovers. Outstandingly, both Robin and Blackbird have adapted to suburban gardens and here reach high population densities. They frequently become quite tame and often construct their nests in the most unnatural of sites.

All chats and thrushes fly strongly and many are migrants, or at least partial migrants. Wheatear, Nightingale, Redstart, Bluethroat and Whinchat (*illustrated*) are long-distance migrants and early summer visitors to these latitudes. Even Robins and Song Thrushes migrate, though many of them remain in our gardens throughout the year. Two species are winter visitors from further north and east – the Redwing and Fieldfare. Both now breed in small numbers in the north, but tens of thousands pour in to spend the winter among our damp fields and hedgerows.

Black Redstarts have colonized Britain during the past fifty years. On the Continent, these are birds of rocky outcrops among forests that take readily to burned-out woodland and suburban gardens. In Britain, they first occupied sea cliffs along the south coast, but quickly moved into the bomb-sites of central London during the Second World War. As these sites were redeveloped, the birds simply transferred their allegiances to nearby power stations and railway marshalling yards. Today power stations are the Black Redstarts' major stronghold, though during passage periods they may turn up on allotments, around farm buildings and so on.

By and large, chats and thrushes are easily observed birds that pose few problems of identification. There are, however, a host of southern and eastern species that occur irregularly in these islands and which may tax the skill of even the most experienced birder.

Robin *Erithacus rubecula*

red face and breast

scaled above and below

juvenile

adult

The most familiar and popular of garden and woodland birds; generally confiding with people. Upright, plump little bird; perches openly and hops on the ground. Adult warm olive-brown with red face, chin and breast. Sides of breast pale grey; belly white. Juvenile has brown head, wings and tail with brown barring on buffy back and breast; indistinguishable from adults after moult (June–August).
Status: widespread and numerous resident throughout year. Often large influx of Continental birds in autumn; some northern females also migrate southwards and to the Continent in autumn.
Similar Species: Redstart (p.176), Stonechat (p.177), Crossbill (p.222) and Bullfinch (p.224) all have 'red' breasts but none are orange-red.

J	6
F	6
M	6
A	6
M	6
J	6
J	6
A	6
S	6
O	6
N	6
D	6

ROBIN

Type	chat-like
Size	13–15cm (5–6in)
Habitat	towns and gardens, heaths, woods, hedges
Behaviour	flits, perches openly, hops, takes off from vegetation and ground
Flocking	solitary
Flight	undulating
Voice	thin *tic-tic-tic*, repeated; leisurely warble

IDENTIFICATION

Adult	
Crown	brown
Upperparts	brown
Rump	brown
Tail	brown; medium length, notched
Throat	orange-red
Breast	orange-red, sides pale grey
Belly	white
Bill	brown; short and pointed
Legs	brown; medium length
Juvenile	lacks red breast, scaly above and below

BREEDING

Nest	cup on ground, in tree stump or on bank
Eggs	5–6; white, speckled reddish
Incubation	12–15 days ♀
Young	helpless; downy
Fledging	12–15 days
Broods	2–3; Apr–June
Food	insects
Population	5,000,000 pairs

Bluethroat *Luscinia svecica*

bold eyebrow

♂ summer white spotted 'cyanecula'

first winter

moustache

blue breast

♂ summer red spotted 'svecica'

♀

rusty tail patches

Scarce passage migrant seen mostly at coastal observatories. Adult male has distinctive cobalt-blue throat and breast with dark blue and red breast bands. Spot in centre of breast is red in *L.s.svecica* and white in *L.s.cyanecula*. Adult female has white throat and breast marked by dark brown breast band extending as moustache to base of bill. Small smudge of red at centre of breast. Most birds passing through Britain are first winter; males have just a hint of blue and red above breast band; females lack both colours on breast. Seldom venture far from dense cover; flit back if disturbed, showing rusty tail patches – best field mark.
Status: rare migrant; has bred once.
Similar Species: none.

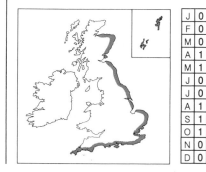

J	0
F	0
M	0
A	1
M	1
J	0
J	0
A	1
S	1
O	1
N	0
D	0

BLUETHROAT

Type	chat-like
Size	13–15cm (5–6in)
Habitat	heaths, shores
Behaviour	flits, hops, takes off from vegetation and ground
Flocking	solitary
Flight	undulating
Voice	penetrating *tic-tic*; also thin *hweet*

IDENTIFICATION

Ad.♂ svecica summer	
Crown	brown
Upperparts	brown
Rump	brown
Tail	brown, sides rusty; medium length, notched
Throat	blue
Breast	blue, red spot in centre
Belly	white
Bill	brown; short and thin
Legs	brown; medium length
Ad.♂cyanecula summer	as above but white spot on breast
Ad.♀ and juv.	as ♂ with less pronounced breast marks

BREEDING

Nest	cup on ground
Eggs	5–7; greenish, speckled reddish
Incubation	14–15 days ♀
Young	helpless; downy
Fledging	14 days
Broods	1–2; May–June
Food	insects
Population	bred once; scarce migrant spring and autumn

warm brown

rufous tail

adult

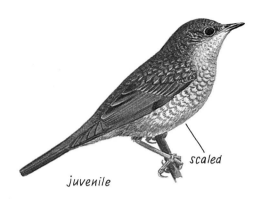

scaled

juvenile

NIGHTINGALE	
Type	chat-like
Size	16–17cm (6–6½in)
Habitat	heaths, woods
Behaviour	flits, takes off or lands on vegetation
Flocking	solitary
Flight	direct
Voice	long song of liquid trills with *peeoo* notes at beginning; also harsh *tchak* and *whooeet* contact notes

IDENTIFICATION	
Adult	
Crown	rufous brown
Upperparts	rufous brown
Rump	rust-red
Tail	rust-red; longish and rounded
Throat	white
Breast	creamy white
Belly	white
Bill	brown; short and pointed
Legs	grey; medium length
Juvenile	paler above and below with scaly markings; rust-red tail

BREEDING	
Nest	cup well hidden close to ground
Eggs	4–5; mottled reddish
Incubation	13–14 days ♀
Young	helpless; downy
Fledging	11–12 days
Broods	1; May–June
Food	insects
Population	10,000 pairs

J	F	M	A	M	J	J	A	S	O	N	D
0	0	0	2	3	3	3	2	2	1	0	0	0

The Nightingale is a fabulous songster that is more often heard than seen. The song is a virtuoso performance of liquid trills that ends in a crescendo. It is most commonly heard well after dark when most other species have ceased singing, but may also be picked out during the day, especially soon after the birds' arrival, when competing males are establishing their territories. At most times the bird remains hidden deep among tangled vegetation, but it does occasionally perch quite openly. When disturbed it dives into cover, showing the characteristic rust-red, conspicuously rounded, tail. The adult is a warm, rufous-brown above, merging with the creamy underparts. Juveniles are marked with scale-like crescents like a juvenile Robin, but have a rust-red tail.
Status: a summer visitor to south-east England from late April onwards.

Similar Species:
Thrush Nightingale *Luscinia luscinia* 16–17cm (6–6½in)
Though the two species of nightingale overlap in range, this species replaces the more common species to the east and north. It prefers marshy and flooded forests, rather than the dry woodland and bush country favoured by the Nightingale. The Thrush Nightingale is a darker, less rufous, brown and there is a mottling of brown on the breast. The tail too is less rusty. These are, however, fine points on a bird that is every bit as skulking as its close relative. The song is, however, both louder and lacks the crescendo of the Nightingale.
Range: from Denmark and south-eastern Europe eastwards across the southern Soviet Union to central Siberia.
Migration: migrates south-westwards through the Middle East to winter in Africa.
British Distribution: a rare spring vagrant (very rare in autumn), mainly to Fair Isle (*see page* 264).

Thrush Nightingale

less rufous

mottled breast

adult

Black Redstart *Phoenicurus ochruros*

white wing flash

red tail

♂ summer

♂ winter

red tail

♀

dusky breast

Colonizing summer visitor but still scarce. Favours demolition sites, industrial complexes, power stations and railway sidings; also sea cliffs. Attention often drawn by brief warbling song. Perches openly with rusty tail shimmering. Flies strongly; often feeds on ground. Summer male has black head, back, breast and belly; bold white flash on wings. In winter, black areas become dark grey; black remains on throat; underparts dirty white. Female is brown, darker above, paler below; juvenile as female but lightly barred; both have rust-red tails. *Status:* scarce summer visitor to southern and central England. Passage migrant; most numerous late autumn, some stay through winter.
Similar Species: female and juvenile Redstart (p.176) are lighter brown.

J	1
F	1
M	3
A	3
M	3
J	2
J	2
A	2
S	3
O	3
N	1
D	1

BLACK REDSTART

Type	chat-like
Size	14–15cm (5½–6in)
Habitat	cliffs, towns and cities
Behaviour	perches openly, takes off from vegetation or ground
Flocking	solitary
Flight	undulating; flitting
Voice	brief *sip* or *tissic*; short warble

IDENTIFICATION

Ad.♂summer	
Crown	black
Upperparts	black; white flash on wings
Rump	rust-red
Tail	rust-red, medium, notched
Throat	black
Breast	black
Belly	grey-black
Bill	black; short and pointed
Legs	black; medium length
Ad.♂winter	greyer above, throat remains black; underparts dirty white
Ad.♀	brown, darker above, paler below; rust-red tail
Juvenile	as ♀, lightly barred

BREEDING

Nest	cup hidden in hole or crevice
Eggs	4–6; white
Incubation	12–16 days ♀
Young	helpless; downy
Fledging	12–19 days
Broods	2–3; Apr–June
Food	insects
Population	*c* 30–100 pairs

Redstart *Phoenicurus phoenicurus*

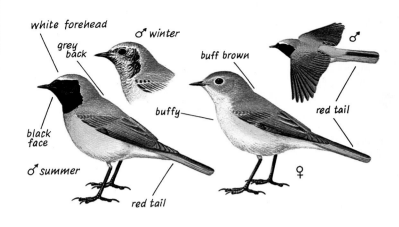

white forehead

grey back

♂ winter

buff brown

♂

black face

♂ summer

buffy

red tail

red tail

♀

Summer visitor to old woodlands and heaths with scattered trees. Perches on lower branches of trees and bushes and makes pouncing sallies to ground; also flits among vegetation. Orange-red tail frequently shimmered. Summer male has dove-grey crown and back; wings brown. White eyebrows meet on forehead; rest of face black. Underparts orange-red; tail orange-red with darker centre. Female also has orange-red tail but is buffy brown above (darker on wings) and buffy below. Juvenile similar to female but speckled.
Status: widespread summer visitor to Britain, April–October; more common in north and west. Decidedly local in Ireland. Also passage migrant; often numerous in autumn.
Similar Species: Black Redstart (p.176) is darker and has different habitat.

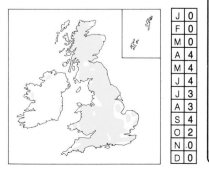

J	0
F	0
M	0
A	4
M	4
J	4
J	3
A	3
S	4
O	2
N	0
D	0

REDSTART

Type	chat-like
Size	13.5–14.5cm (5¼–5¾in)
Habitat	woods, heaths, parks
Behaviour	flits, perches openly, hops, takes off from vegetation or ground
Flocking	solitary
Flight	direct; flitting
Voice	*hooeet*, brief warble

IDENTIFICATION

Ad.♂summer	
Crown	grey
Upperparts	grey; wings brown
Rump	rust-red
Tail	rust-red; medium length, notched
Throat	black
Breast	orange-red
Belly	creamy white
Bill	black; medium length, short and pointed
Legs	black; medium length
Ad.♂winter	face more greyish; underparts duller orange-red
Ad.♀summer	buff-brown above, buffy below; rust-red tail

BREEDING

Nest	cup hidden in bank, tree roots or tree hole
Eggs	6–7; pale blue
Incubation	11–14 days ♀
Young	helpless; downy
Fledging	14–20 days
Broods	2; May–June
Food	insects
Population	*c* 50,000–100,000 pairs

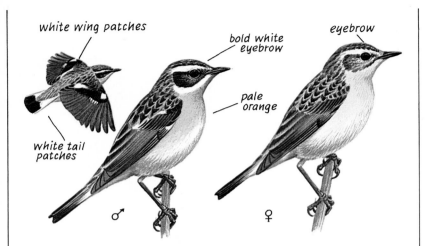

white wing patches

bold white eyebrow

eyebrow

pale orange

white tail patches

♂

♀

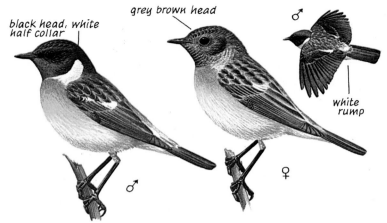

black head, white half collar

grey brown head

♂

white rump

♂

♀

Widespread summer visitor and passage migrant to open heaths and downland; most often seen perched atop a small bush. Pounces to ground to feed; often returns to same perch. In summer, adult has brown upperparts, heavily streaked black; white flash in closed wing. Prominent, creamy white eyebrow; dark ear coverts. Underparts pale creamy orange. In flight, shows white patch on inner wing and white patches either side of tail. Female a more subdued version of male. In winter, male more like female.
Status: summer visitor April–September. Double passage migrant in good numbers, particularly in autumn.
Similar Species: closely related Stonechat (p.177) lacks prominent eyebrow in all plumages.

WHINCHAT	
Type	chat-like
Size	12–13cm (4¾–5in)
Habitat	heaths, downland
Behaviour	perches openly, takes off and lands on vegetation or ground
Flocking	solitary
Flight	direct; flitting
Voice	metallic *tic-tic*; brief warble

IDENTIFICATION

Adult	
Crown	brown, streaked black
Upperparts	brown, streaked black; white wing patches
Rump	brown, streaked black
Tail	brown centre, white patches on sides, black band at tip; short and square
Throat	creamy orange
Breast	creamy orange
Belly	creamy orange
Bill	black; short and pointed
Legs	black; medium length

BREEDING

Nest	cup on ground at base of bush
Eggs	5–7; pale blue, finely speckled brown
Incubation	13–14 days ♀
Young	helpless; downy
Fledging	17 days
Broods	1–2; May–June
Food	insects
Population	20,000–40,000 pairs

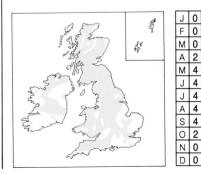

J	0
F	0
M	0
A	2
M	4
J	4
J	4
A	4
S	4
O	2
N	0
D	0

Widespread chat, present throughout year; prefers gorse habitats. Perches prominently on tops of bushes and pounces to ground. Flies low, showing greyish white rump and white patches on wings. In summer, male has black head bordered by prominent white half collar. Back and wings dark brown, streaked black; tail dark brown. Breast orange-red. In winter, male paler with more obviously streaked upperparts and less reddish breast. Female much paler than male with dark, not black, head. Eastern sub-species paler and greyer with little colour on breast.
Status: resident and winter visitor.
Similar Species: Whinchat (p.177) is summer visitor, has prominent eyebrow and creamy, not reddish, breast.

STONECHAT	
Type	chat-like
Size	12–13cm (4¾–5in)
Habitat	heaths, grassland
Behaviour	perches openly, hops, takes off and lands on vegetation or ground
Flocking	solitary
Flight	direct; flitting
Voice	metallic *chak-chak* also jingling warble

IDENTIFICATION

Adult ♂	
Crown	black
Upperparts	dark brown, streaked black; white wing patches
Rump	greyish white
Tail	dark brown; medium length, square
Throat	black, white half collar
Breast	orange-red
Belly	white
Bill	black; short and pointed
Legs	black; medium length
Adult ♀	paler, orange-buff breast; lacks black head

BREEDING

Nest	cup on ground at base of bush
Eggs	5–6; pale blue, lightly-speckled brown
Incubation	14–15 days ♀
Young	helpless; downy
Fledging	12–13 days
Broods	2–3; Apr–June
Food	insects, worms
Population	30,000–60,000 pairs

J	2
F	2
M	3
A	4
M	4
J	4
J	4
A	4
S	4
O	3
N	3
D	2

Wheatear   *Oenanthe oenanthe*

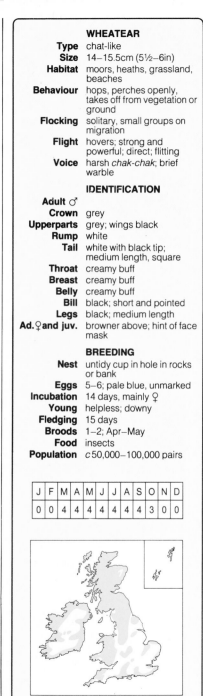

The Wheatear is a widespread summer visitor to open country that seldom perches higher than a rock or fence post. Typically, it adopts an upright posture, with sudden darting movements and equally sudden 'bobbing' actions of its body and flicking of its tail and wings. It feeds on insects by pouncing to the ground or making short, fluttering dashes in the air. In flight, it shows a distinctive white rump and black and white tail pattern. The Greenland sub-species *O. o. leucorrhoa* is larger, with longer wings.

Status: a common summer visitor from March to October, as well as a numerous spring and autumn passage migrant.

Similar Species:
Black-eared Wheatear
Oenanthe hispanica 14–15cm (5½–6in)
The adult male is easily separated from the common Wheatear but in other plumages separation is far from simple. Adult males of the western sub-species *O. h. hispanica* have black wings contrasting with a sandy back and crown, and a white belly. Two distinct forms show either a black mask (white-throated), or black mask, chin and throat (black-throated). The tail pattern is similar to the common Wheatear's. Adult males of the eastern sub-species *O. h. melanoleuca* show a similar pattern, but are paler, often white rather than sandy, and in the black-throated form the black extends further down the throat. Females and juveniles are similar to the common Wheatear, but with a darker mask and larger dark areas on the wings.

Range: a summer visitor through Mediterranean Europe to Turkey and Iran.
Migration: migrates to winter along the Sahel zone of Africa.
British Distribution: a rare spring and autumn vagrant, mostly to the south-west.

Black-eared Wheatear

Turdus torquatus **Ring Ousel**

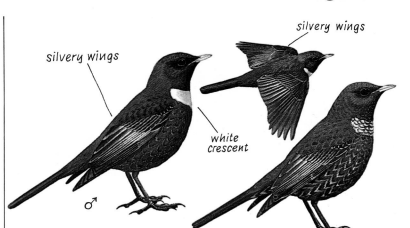

silvery wings

silvery wings

white crescent

♂

♀

Turdus merula **Blackbird**

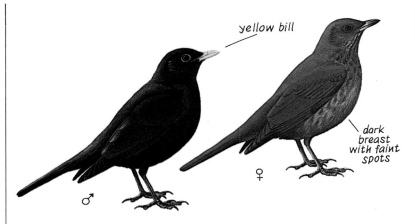

yellow bill

dark breast with faint spots

♂

♀

Summer visitor to mountains and moorlands with screes and rocky outcrops. Behaviour much as Blackbird but much less confiding. Flies swift and low showing silvery wings. On passage, often skulks in dense cover. In summer, male black with brownish wash; distinctive white crescent across breast. Silvery wing linings form obvious pale panel on folded wing. In winter, male browner with scaly markings; white feathers on breast band have buff, scaly tips. Adult female like winter male. Juvenile brown above with narrow, pale edges to wing feathers; heavily barred below.
Status: widespread summer visitor to north and west. Scarce passage migrant March–November.
Similar Species: Blackbird (p.179) lacks white crescent and silver wings.

	RING OUSEL
Type	thrush-like
Size	23–25cm (9–10in)
Habitat	mountains and moorlands
Behaviour	hops, runs, perches openly, takes off and lands on vegetation or ground
Flocking	solitary, small flocks
Flight	strong and powerful; direct
Voice	harsh *chak-chak*; also a loud *peu-u peu-u*

	IDENTIFICATION
Adult ♂	
Crown	black-brown
Upperparts	black-brown; wings have silvery edges
Rump	black-brown
Tail	black-brown; medium length, square
Throat	black-brown
Breast	white crescent
Belly	black-brown
Bill	pale yellow; medium length, pointed
Legs	black, medium length
Adult ♀	subdued colours
Juvenile	scaled; lacks white crescent on breast

	BREEDING
Nest	cup on ground
Eggs	4–5; pale blue, blotched brown
Incubation	13–14 days ♂ ♀
Young	helpless, downy
Fledging	13–14 days
Broods	1–2; Apr–May
Food	worms, insects, berries
Population	8,000–16,000 pairs

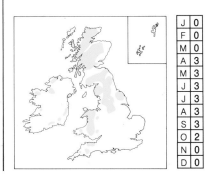

J	0
F	0
M	0
A	3
M	3
J	3
J	3
A	3
S	3
O	2
N	0
D	0

One of the most familiar of British birds, common to woodlands, fields and gardens; as much at home in towns as countryside. All-black male has yellow bill and eye ring. Female browner, with subdued speckling on breast varying considerably from rufous brown to greyish brown. First winter males retain dark brown wing feathers; distinguishes from older, black-winged birds. Generally highly territorial, though Continental immigrants often arrive in large autumn flocks.
Status: widespread and numerous resident; common passage migrant and winter visitor throughout Britain and Ireland.
Similar Species: Ring Ousel (p.179).

	BLACKBIRD
Type	thrush-like
Size	24–27cm (9½–11in)
Habitat	gardens, heaths, woods, hedges
Behaviour	perches openly, walks, hops, takes off from vegetation or ground
Flocking	1–15
Flight	strong and powerful; direct
Voice	loud harsh chatter of alarm; also a fluty warble

	IDENTIFICATION
Adult ♂	
Crown	black
Upperparts	black
Rump	black
Tail	black; medium length, square
Throat	black
Breast	black
Belly	black
Bill	yellow; short and thin
Legs	black; medium length
Adult ♀	underparts mottled grey-brown or rufous brown; brownish bill

	BREEDING
Nest	cup in tree or bush
Eggs	4–5; light blue, spotted red
Incubation	11–17 days ♀
Young	helpless; downy
Fledging	12–19 days
Broods	2–3; Mar–May
Food	insects, worms, berries
Population	7,000,000 pairs

J	6
F	6
M	6
A	6
M	6
J	6
J	6
A	6
S	6
O	6
N	6
D	6

Fieldfare *Turdus pilaris*

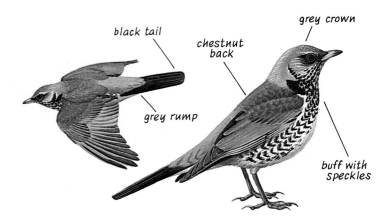

black tail

grey rump

chestnut back

grey crown

buff with speckles

Large, typical thrush with densely speckled breast washed buffy yellow. Head, nape and rump dove-grey – latter particularly useful field mark in flight. Wings and back chestnut-brown; tail black. Pattern of head and face markings produces 'cross' expression. Generally gregarious, forming quite substantial flocks along hedgerows and in fields.
Status: scarce breeder in northern England and Scotland; abundant winter visitor throughout Britain and Ireland.
Similar Species: related Mistle and Song Thrush (pp.181, 180) and Redwing (p.181) have less densely speckled breasts, less chestnut backs, and lack grey crown and rump.

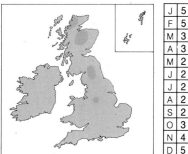

J	5
F	5
M	3
A	3
M	2
J	2
J	2
A	2
S	2
O	3
N	4
D	5

FIELDFARE

Type	thrush-like
Size	24–27cm (9½–11in)
Habitat	heaths, woods, fields and hedges, gardens
Behaviour	perches openly, hops, walks, takes off from vegetation or ground
Flocking	1–100s
Flight	strong and powerful; direct
Voice	harsh *chak-chak*, normally in flight

IDENTIFICATION

Adult	
Crown	dove-grey
Upperparts	chestnut-brown
Rump	dove-grey
Tail	black; medium length, notched
Throat	buffy yellow
Breast	buffy yellow, speckled black
Belly	white, speckled black
Bill	yellow; short and thin
Legs	black; medium length

BREEDING

Nest	cup in fork of tree
Eggs	5–6; pale blue, reddish markings
Incubation	11–14 days ♀
Young	helpless; downy
Fledging	12–16 days
Broods	1–2; Apr–June
Food	worms, insects, berries, fruit
Population	very rare breeder; abundant winter visitor

Song Thrush *Turdus philomelos*

brown back

buff with speckles

Neat, medium-sized thrush found in woods, fields and gardens. Brown above; white neatly spotted with black below; creamy yellow wash on breast. Head has clear eyebrow and moustachial streak. Characteristic habit of repeating song phrase three or four times.
Status: widespread resident throughout Britain and Ireland; passage migrant and winter visitor.
Similar Species: can be confused with Redwing (p.181) in winter and Mistle Thrush (p.181) throughout year.

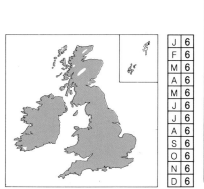

J	6
F	6
M	6
A	6
M	6
J	6
J	6
A	6
S	6
O	6
N	6
D	6

SONG THRUSH

Type	thrush-like
Size	22–24cm (8½–9½in)
Habitat	gardens, heaths, woods, fields
Behaviour	perches openly, hops, walks, takes off from vegetation or ground
Flocking	1–15
Flight	strong and powerful; direct
Voice	variety of repeated phrases; *chuk* alarm call

IDENTIFICATION

Adult	
Crown	brown
Upperparts	brown
Rump	brown
Tail	brown; medium length, square
Throat	buff
Breast	creamy yellow, spotted black
Belly	white, spotted black
Bill	black; short and thin
Legs	pink; medium length

BREEDING

Nest	neat cup in tree or bush
Eggs	4–6; pale blue, speckled black
Incubation	11–15 days ♀
Young	helpless; downy
Fledging	12–16 days
Broods	2–3; Mar–June
Food	worms, snails, insects, berries
Population	1,000,000–3,500,000 pairs

Turdus iliacus Redwing

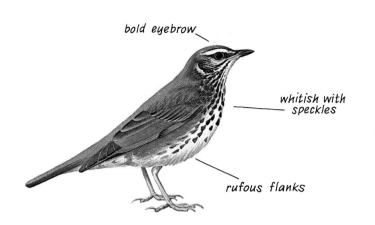

bold eyebrow

whitish with speckles

rufous flanks

Common winter visitor, forming flocks that roam through fields and hedgerows. Brown above, with brown ear coverts separating and accentuating bold eyebrow and double moustachial streak; face markings give distinctly 'cross' look. Whitish underparts spotted in clear streaks, with bold rust-red patch along flanks. Flight fast and direct like Song Thrush; unlike undulating flight of Mistle Thrush.
Status: widespread and abundant winter visitor; recent breeder in northern Scotland.
Similar Species: smaller than Song and Mistle Thrushes (pp.180, 181), which lack rust-red on flanks and prominent face patterns.

	REDWING
Type	thrush-like
Size	20–22cm (8–9in)
Habitat	gardens, heaths, woods, fields and hedges
Behaviour	perches openly, hops, walks, takes off from vegetation or ground
Flocking	1–100
Flight	strong and powerful; direct
Voice	soft *seeip* in flight

IDENTIFICATION

Adult	
Crown	brown
Upperparts	brown
Rump	brown
Tail	brown; medium length, square
Throat	whitish
Breast	whitish, streaked brown
Belly	whitish, streaked brown; rust-red flanks
Bill	black; short and thin
Legs	yellow; medium length

BREEDING

Nest	cup against tree trunk
Eggs	4–5; pale blue, speckled brownish
Incubation	11–15 days ♀
Young	helpless; downy
Fledging	10–15 days
Broods	2; Apr–June
Food	berries, worms, insects
Population	30–60 pairs; abundant winter visitor

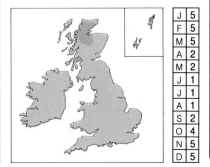

J	5
F	5
M	5
A	2
M	2
J	1
J	1
A	1
S	2
O	4
N	5
D	5

Turdus viscivorus Mistle Thrush

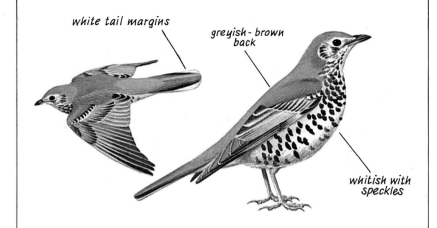

white tail margins

greyish-brown back

whitish with speckles

Largest of the thrushes with distinctly greyer and paler appearance than Song Thrush. Upperparts buffy grey-brown with pale margins to flight feathers. Underparts white, heavily spotted black. In undulating flight, shows grey-brown rump and white corners to tail. Generally less gregarious than other thrushes; forms small, loose groups but seldom large flocks. Song similar to Blackbird but generally with faster delivery.
Status: widespread resident.
Similar Species: Song Thrush (p.180) is smaller and darker, has warm yellowish wash on breast and prominent eyebrow. See also Fieldfare (p.180).

	MISTLE THRUSH
Type	thrush-like
Size	26–28cm (10–11in)
Habitat	gardens, heaths, woods, fields and hedges
Behaviour	perches openly, hops, walks, takes off from vegetation or ground
Flocking	1–15
Flight	strong and powerful; undulating
Voice	loud *tuk-tuk*

IDENTIFICATION

Adult	
Crown	grey-brown
Upperparts	grey-brown
Rump	grey-brown
Tail	grey-brown, white corners; medium length, square
Throat	whitish
Breast	whitish, spotted black
Belly	whitish, spotted black
Bill	black; short and thin
Legs	yellow; medium length

BREEDING

Nest	cup in fork of tree
Eggs	4–5; blue, spotted reddish
Incubation	12–15 days ♀
Young	helpless; downy
Fledging	20 days
Broods	2; Mar–May
Food	berries, worms, insects
Population	300,000–600,000 pairs

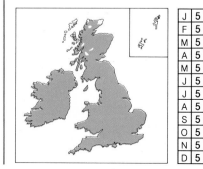

J	5
F	5
M	5
A	5
M	5
J	5
J	5
A	5
S	5
O	5
N	5
D	5

WARBLERS AND FLYCATCHERS

Although our two regular flycatchers, the Spotted and the Pied, are familiar and easily picked out, the warblers have always posed problems for the beginner. These are small, active birds that frequent a variety of well vegetated habitats. They are often difficult to observe, but are easily identified by their songs and calls.

They are chiefly insect-eaters and long-distance migrants, though many species fill up on autumn fruits and berries before making their long southward journeys. Two warblers, the Dartford Warbler and Cetti's Warbler, are resident and suffer huge drops in numbers, or 'population crashes', during hard winters. The Dartford Warbler is a resident on the heathlands of the southern counties of England and has

been to the verge of extinction and back more times than anyone can remember. Cetti's Warbler is a more recent colonist that seemed to be well established until the harsh winters of the mid-1980s decimated its British population. In most years a few Blackcaps and Chiffchaffs overwinter, especially in the south-west.

They are expert flyers that frequently fly directly into a bush rather than alight on the outside and then hop in. They will feed aerially like flycatchers and hover like Goldcrests. They also frequently lack clear identification features. Only in the eighteenth century did the great British

naturalist Gilbert White satisfactorily separate the three 'leaf' warblers – Willow Warbler, Wood Warbler (*illustrated*) and Chiffchaff. The Willow Warbler is our most numerous summer visitor.

Two 'crests' now breed with us, though both are more abundant at other times of the year. The Goldcrest is more widespread, while the Firecrest is confined to southern England.

Cetti's Warbler *Cettia cetti*

chestnut-brown

prominent rounded tail often spread

Grasshopper Warbler *Locustella naevia*

streaked back

rounded tail

Resident of dense bushy undergrowth, often at edge of reed beds and invariably alongside water. Always secretive and elusive, but presence revealed by uniquely explosive call. Usually sighted as dark brown bird flitting from one bush to another. Clearer views reveal rich chestnut-brown upperparts with clear, pale eyebrow and strongly rounded tail. Underparts whitish. Sometimes cocks tail to reveal barred undertail coverts.
Status: recent colonizer; scarce resident in southern and eastern England. Numbers seriously decline after hard winters.
Similar Species: in summer can be confused with Reed, Marsh, and Savi's warblers (pp.186–187); with reasonable views easily distinguished by dark coloration of upperparts.

	CETTI'S WARBLER
Type	warbler-like
Size	13.5–14.5cm (5–5½in)
Habitat	inland freshwater and marshes
Behaviour	flits, takes off and lands on vegetation
Flocking	solitary
Flight	flitting
Voice	explosive *chetti-chetti-chetti*

IDENTIFICATION	
Adult	
Crown	chestnut-brown
Upperparts	chestnut-brown
Rump	chestnut-brown
Tail	chestnut-brown; medium length, rounded
Throat	whitish
Breast	whitish
Belly	whitish
Bill	black; short and thin
Legs	buff; medium length

BREEDING	
Nest	cup in thick vegetation on or near ground
Eggs	4; chestnut
Incubation	♀?
Young	helpless; downy
Fledging	?
Broods	1; Apr–May
Food	insects, seeds
Population	100–200 pairs

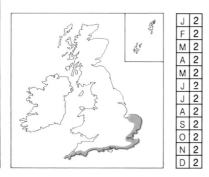

J	2
F	2
M	2
A	2
M	2
J	2
J	2
A	2
S	2
O	2
N	2
D	2

Summer visitor to heaths, young conifer plantations, scrub and edges of reed beds. One of 'streaked-back' marshy warblers; upperparts buffy streaked with dark brown; short and inconspicuous pale eyebrow. Underparts buff with faint breast streaking. Most frequently observed at dawn or dusk when produces continuous reeling call – like rewinding of fishing reel.
Status: widespread summer visitor throughout Britain and Ireland.
Similar Species: Sedge Warbler (p.223) has more pronounced streaking above and bold creamy eyebrow. Savi's Warbler (p.186) has similar call, but lower pitched and briefer; lacks streaked back.

	GRASSHOPPER WARBLER
Type	warbler-like
Size	12–13cm (4½–5in)
Habitat	marshes, heaths, plantations
Behaviour	flits, takes off and lands on vegetation
Flocking	solitary
Flight	flitting
Voice	ventriloquial reeling

IDENTIFICATION	
Adult	
Crown	buffy brown, dark streaked
Upperparts	buffy brown, dark streaked
Rump	buffy brown, dark streaked
Tail	buffy brown; medium length, rounded
Throat	buff
Breast	buff, faint streaking
Belly	buff
Bill	black; short and thin
Legs	buff; medium length

BREEDING	
Nest	cup on or near ground
Eggs	6; white, speckled brownish
Incubation	13–15 days ♂ ♀
Young	helpless; downy
Fledging	10–12 days
Broods	2; May–June
Food	insects
Population	25,000 pairs

J	0
F	0
M	0
A	2
M	3
J	3
J	3
A	3
S	3
O	2
N	0
D	0

dark crown

bold eyebrow

streaked back

adult

streaking more contrasting

yellow brown rump more marked than adult

juvenile

rounded tail

This is a summer visitor to a wide variety of wetland habitats, including reed beds, bushy margins, ditches and dykes. The upperparts are heavily streaked black on brown, with the streaking of the crown often quite heavy, giving the bird a capped appearance. A broad, creamy eyebrow extends almost to the nape and contrasts with a narrow, black eyestripe. The underparts are buffy, especially on the flanks. Though Sedge Warblers often keep well hidden, they also perch quite openly and, in spring, make short vertical song flights in which they may hover in mid-air.
Status: a common and widespread summer visitor throughout Britain and Ireland.

Similar Species:
Aquatic Warbler *Acrocephalus paludicola*
12–13cm (4½–5in)
Though a streaked *Acrocephalus* similar to the Sedge Warbler, this is a decidedly more elusive bird that spends most of its time deep inside aquatic cover. The upperparts are sandy coloured with clear black streaks, forming a more contrasting pattern than that of the Sedge or any other similar warbler. A creamy central crown stripe contrasts with dark lateral crown stripes

and long creamy eyebrows to produce a striped effect unlike any plumage of any other regular European warbler.
Range: a summer visitor from Holland eastward across northern Europe to the Black Sea and west central Siberia. Also occurs in Italy, Yugoslavia, Hungary and eastern Austria.
Migration: moves southward to winter in tropical Africa.
British Distribution: a regular autumn visitor in August and September to the south coast of England, mainly to Dorset.
Other Similar Species: Grasshopper Warbler (p. 184) and Marsh Warbler (p. 186).

Aquatic Warbler

bold striped pattern

first winter

SEDGE WARBLER	
Type	warbler-like
Size	12–13cm (4½–5in)
Habitat	inland freshwater and marshes
Behaviour	flits, takes off and lands on vegetation
Flocking	solitary
Flight	flitting
Voice	harsh grating notes mixed with melodic phrases and mimicry

IDENTIFICATION	
Adult	
Crown	brown, streaked black
Upperparts	brown, streaked black
Rump	yellow-brown
Tail	brown, streaked black; medium length, rounded
Throat	buffy white
Breast	buffy white
Belly	white
Bill	black; short and thin
Legs	grey; medium length
Juvenile	yellower rump

BREEDING	
Nest	cup in vegetation, on or near ground
Eggs	5–6; pale green, speckled buff
Incubation	13–14 days mainly ♀
Young	helpless; naked
Fledging	10–12 days
Broods	1; May–June
Food	insects
Population	c 300,000 pairs

J	F	M	A	M	J	J	A	S	O	N	D
0	0	0	4	5	5	5	5	5	4	0	0

Marsh Warbler *Acrocephalus palustris*

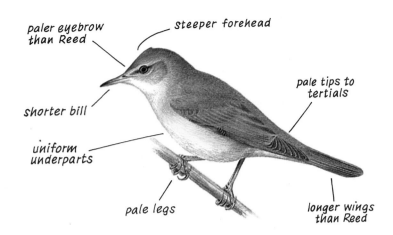

paler eyebrow than Reed

steeper forehead

shorter bill

uniform underparts

pale legs

pale tips to tertials

longer wings than Reed

Uncommon and extremely elusive summer visitor to southern England. Uniform olive-brown upperparts and buff and white underparts. Very similar to more widespread Reed Warbler, but generally more olive above and whiter below, with flatter crown and slightly longer wings. Prefers areas of willows and rushes near water to stands of pure reed. Best identified by song – a remarkable mimic; harsher notes reminiscent of Greenfinch.
Status: breeds regularly only in West Midlands; elsewhere rare passage migrant.
Similar Species: Reed Warbler (p.187) as above.

	MARSH WARBLER
Type	warbler-like
Size	12–13cm (4½–5in)
Habitat	inland freshwaer, marshes, fields
Behaviour	flits, takes off and lands on vegetation
Flocking	solitary
Flight	flitting
Voice	rich phrases, loud trills, harsh notes; mimic

IDENTIFICATION

Adult	
Crown	olive-brown
Upperparts	olive-brown
Rump	olive-brown
Tail	olive-brown; medium length, rounded
Throat	white
Breast	buffy white
Belly	white, flanks creamy
Bill	brown; short and thin
Legs	pinkish; medium length

BREEDING

Nest	cup in dense vegetation, near ground
Eggs	4–5; pale blue
Incubation	12 days ♂ ♀
Young	helpless; naked
Fledging	10–14 days
Broods	1; May–June
Food	insects
Population	50–75 pairs

J	0
F	0
M	0
A	0
M	2
J	2
J	2
A	2
S	2
O	2
N	0
D	0

Savi's Warbler *Locustella luscinioides*

lacks dagger-like bill of Reed Warbler

warm buffy flanks

unstreaked back

rounded tail

Summer visitor to southern reed beds, where often perches on reed-tops. Reeling song similar to Grasshopper Warbler, but lower pitched and usually with briefer phrases. Upperparts uniform buff-brown; underparts buff. Barely hint of an eyebrow; distinctly rounded tail. Very similar to Reed Warbler, though lacking its sloping forehead and long bill; song best means of separating.
Status: re-colonized East Anglia and south-east England from 1960s, but declined in 1980s; today decidedly scarce.
Similar Species: plumage similar to Reed and Marsh warblers (pp.186–187); call resembles that of Grasshopper Warbler (p.184).

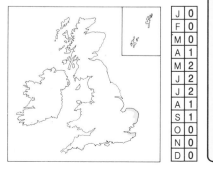

	SAVI'S WARBLER
Type	warbler-like
Size	13–14cm (5–5½in)
Habitat	reed beds
Behaviour	perches openly, takes off and lands on vegetation
Flocking	solitary
Flight	flitting
Voice	reeling, lower and briefer than Grasshopper Warbler

IDENTIFICATION

Adult	
Crown	buff-brown
Upperparts	buff-brown
Rump	buff-brown
Tail	buff-brown; medium length, rounded
Throat	buff
Breast	buff
Belly	white
Bill	brown; short and thin
Legs	brown; medium length

BREEDING

Nest	cup in reeds
Eggs	4–5; white, speckled brown
Incubation	12 days ♀
Young	helpless; downy
Fledging	12–14 days
Broods	2; Apr–May
Food	insects
Population	less than 20 pairs

J	0
F	0
M	0
A	1
M	2
J	2
J	2
A	1
S	1
O	0
N	0
D	0

sloping forehead

rusty rump

dagger like bill

buffy flanks

brown legs

The Reed Warbler is a summer visitor to various types of wetland habitats, though with a definite preference for reeds. It tends to skulk in deep cover, but perches openly on reed tops, especially while singing. The upperparts are a warm brown with a distinct rufous wash on the rump. The underparts are whitish with buffy flanks. Such a plumage pattern is shared by several closely related species, and distinguishing the Reed Warbler from them is difficult. The sloping forehead reaches a peak at the top of the crown, thus accentuating the length of the dagger-like bill. The legs are brown, rather than pale like a Marsh Warbler's, and the tail rounded.
Status: a common summer visitor to the southern half of England and South Wales.

Similar Species:
Great Reed Warbler *Acrocephalus arundinaceus* 18–20cm (7–8in)
Though similar to the Reed Warbler, this is a much larger and bulkier bird, with a very loud, harsh song that is quite unmistakable. The upperparts are brown, marked by a reasonably prominent eyebrow and a brown eyestripe that extends from the bill to behind the eye. The underparts are

creamy-buff. The large bill and head, the large rounded tail and the short, rounded wings are all distinguishing features. In flight the Great Reed Warbler resembles a thrush rather than a warbler, though it frequents waterside vegetation.
Range: a summer visitor to temperate Continental Europe.
Migration: the whole population winters in Africa south of the Sahara.
British Distribution: though it breeds just across the Channel, it is only a rare vagrant northwards to Britain, mainly in spring.
Other Similar Species: Sedge Warbler (p. 185) and Marsh Warbler (p. 186).

Great Reed Warbler

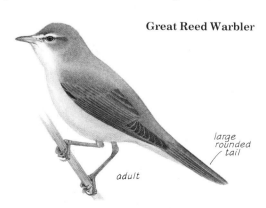

large rounded tail

adult

	REED WARBLER	
Type	warbler-like	
Size	12–13cm (4½–5in)	
Habitat	inland freshwater and marshes	
Behaviour	flits, takes off and lands on vegetation	
Flocking	solitary	
Flight	flitting	
Voice	series of harsh, grating notes – *jag-jag*, *chirrug-chirrug*	

IDENTIFICATION

Adult		
Crown	brown	
Upperparts	brown	
Rump	rufous brown	
Tail	brown; medium length, rounded	
Throat	white	
Breast	whitish	
Belly	whitish, flanks buff	
Bill	brown; short and thin	
Legs	grey-brown, medium length	

BREEDING

Nest	deep cup in reeds
Eggs	4; pale green, spotted olive
Incubation	11–12 days ♂ ♀
Young	helpless; naked
Fledging	11–13 days
Broods	1; Apr–June
Food	insects
Population	40,000–80,000 pairs

J	F	M	A	M	J	J	A	S	O	N	D
0	0	0	3	5	5	5	5	4	2	0	0

Icterine Warbler *Hippolais icterina*

large bill

pale wing panel

long wings

blue legs

square tail

The Icterine Warbler is a largish, rather nondescript warbler marked by a long, dagger-like bill and a sloping forehead. It is thus similar in shape to a Reed Warbler and in some plumages may be confused with that species. In spring it is olive above and yellowish-white below, with a short generally indistinct eyebrow. The legs are blue, the tail square. Summer adults have a pale panel in the wing formed by the margins of the inner flight feathers. The wings are long, with the exposed primaries forming about a third of the overall folded length. It frequents bushy areas and moves about vegetation rather awkwardly, crashing through foliage rather than flitting gracefully. Juveniles are paler, but still have a pale wing panel.
Status: a scarce, but regular, mainly autumn visitor to the east and south coasts.

Similar Species:
Melodious Warbler *Hippolais polyglotta*
12–13cm (4½–5in)
Rather nondescript, being brownish-green above and creamy-yellow below, but the bill is shorter, the head more rounded and the tail shorter, giving the species a distinctly plumper appearance. Also, the wings are short and rounded, the exposed primaries forming only a quarter of the length of the folded wing. The legs are usually grey, though occasionally bluish.
Range: a summer visitor from Portugal to northern France and southwards through Italy and North Africa.
Migration: moves southward to winter in Africa.
British Distribution: a regular, but scarce, autumn visitor to the south and south-west coasts of England, to Wales and to southern Ireland.
Other Similar Species: Reed Warbler (p. 187).

rounded head

Melodious Warbler

no mid-wing panel

short, rounded wings

adult

Sylvia undata **Dartford Warbler**

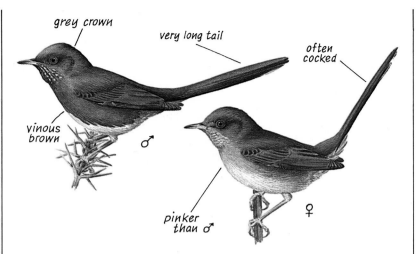

grey crown

very long tail

often cocked

vinous brown

♂

pinker than ♂

♀

Tiny, elusive warbler generally well hidden in thick cover of dense stands of gorse and heather; most easily seen while singing in early spring. Upperparts grey-brown, greyer on head; underparts dark vinous brown with sparse white flecking on throat. Outstanding feature is long tail; often cocked when perching. Juveniles browner above and buffy below. Flies on rounded, whirring wings with long tail trailing.
Status: scarce resident, confined to few heathland areas in southern England; suffers population crashes during severe winters.
Similar Species: no other warbler has long tail and dark underparts.

DARTFORD WARBLER

Type	warbler-like
Size	12–13cm (4½–5in)
Habitat	heaths
Behaviour	flits, takes off and lands on vegetation
Flocking	solitary
Flight	flitting; undulating
Voice	harsh *chur* or *tic*; also a scratchy warble

IDENTIFICATION

Adult ♂	
Crown	grey
Upperparts	grey-brown
Rump	grey-brown
Tail	black; long and rounded
Throat	vinous brown, white flecked
Breast	vinous brown
Belly	white
Bill	black; short and thin
Legs	yellow; medium length
Adult ♀	underparts pinker
Juvenile	browner above, buffy below

BREEDING

Nest	cup near ground in thick vegetation
Eggs	3–4; white, spotted reddish
Incubation	12–13 days, mainly ♀
Young	helpless; naked
Fledging	11–13 days
Broods	2–3; Apr–June
Food	insects
Population	200–300 pairs

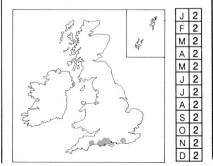

J	2
F	2
M	2
A	2
M	2
J	2
J	2
A	2
S	2
O	2
N	2
D	2

Sylvia borin **Garden Warbler**

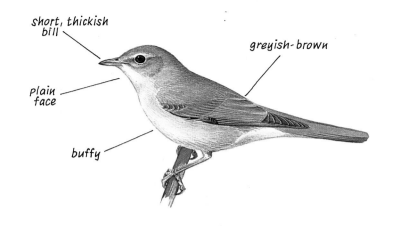

short, thickish bill

greyish-brown

plain face

buffy

Compact summer visitor, virtually devoid of field marks. Upperparts greyish brown, underparts buffy white. Short, stubby bill is best identification feature. Frequents open deciduous and mixed woodland with plenty of undergrowth, as well as scrub, overgrown hedgerows and young plantations. Mostly skulks, even when singing.
Status: summer visitor to England, Wales, southern Scotland and central Ireland; double passage migrant.
Similar Species: nondescript appearance could confuse with variety of warblers, including Icterine Warbler (p.188); song similar to Blackcap (p.190), but more subdued and usually longer lasting.

GARDEN WARBLER

Type	warbler-like
Size	13–15cm (5–6in)
Habitat	gardens, heaths, woods, hedges
Behaviour	flits, takes off and lands on vegetation
Flocking	solitary
Flight	flitting
Voice	fine but quiet warbling

IDENTIFICATION

Adult	
Crown	grey-brown
Upperparts	grey-brown
Rump	grey-brown
Tail	brown; medium length, notched
Throat	buffy white
Breast	buffy white
Belly	buffy white
Bill	black; short and stubby
Legs	grey; medium length

BREEDING

Nest	cup in bush
Eggs	4–5; white, blotched brown
Incubation	11–12 days ♂ ♀
Young	helpless; naked
Fledging	9–10 days
Broods	2; May–June
Food	insects, berries
Population	60,000–100,000 pairs

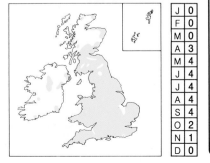

J	0
F	0
M	0
A	3
M	4
J	4
J	4
A	4
S	4
O	2
N	1
D	0

Blackcap *Sylvia atricapilla*

black cap · grey back

rust cap

♂

♀

Best known for its delightful song, which some compare to Nightingale; has greater variety of notes and phrases than Garden Warbler. Male has sooty black cap and grey back; greyish white below. Female has rusty cap; browner above and buffy below. Frequents open deciduous or mixed woodland with well-developed undergrowth; generally keeps well hidden among vegetation. Some birds overwinter and visit bird tables.
Status: widespread summer visitor, except to extreme north and west; passage migrant; scarce winter visitor to southern England and south-eastern Ireland.
Similar Species: male could be confused with Marsh Tit (p.200) and Willow Tit (p.201) but is larger and slimmer.

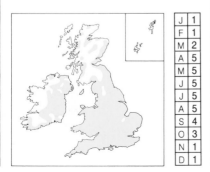

	BLACKCAP
Type	warbler-like
Size	13–15cm (5–6in)
Habitat	gardens, heaths, woods, hedges
Behaviour	flits, takes off and lands on vegetation
Flocking	solitary
Flight	flitting
Voice	a varied warble

IDENTIFICATION

Adult ♂	
Crown	sooty black cap
Upperparts	grey
Rump	grey
Tail	grey; medium length, notched
Throat	greyish white
Breast	greyish white
Belly	white
Bill	black; short and thin
Legs	black; medium length
Adult ♀	rusty cap; browner above, buffy below

BREEDING

Nest	cup in bush or tree
Eggs	5; white, blotched reddish
Incubation	12–13 days ♂ ♀
Young	helpless; naked
Fledging	10–14 days
Broods	2; May–June
Food	insects, berries
Population	*c* 200,000 pairs

J	1
F	1
M	2
A	5
M	5
J	5
J	5
A	5
S	4
O	3
N	1
D	1

Lesser Whitethroat *Sylvia curruca*

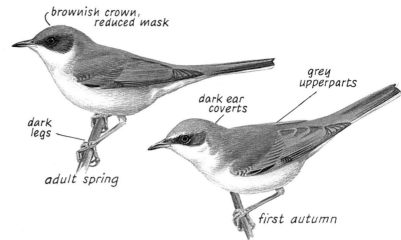

brownish crown, reduced mask

grey upperparts

dark ear coverts

dark legs

adult spring

first autumn

Generally a skulking bird of bushy scrub, tall hedgerows and young conifers. Attractive warbler, basically grey above, white below. Male has prominent, dark ear coverts, giving masked appearance. Legs dark; tail has white outer feathers. Song similar to rattle of Yellowhammer but lacking final flourish.
Status: summer visitor mostly to southern England; passage migrant especially to south and east coasts.
Similar Species: Whitethroat (p.191) is slightly larger, rusty brown above and pinkish below.

	LESSER WHITETHROAT
Type	warbler-like
Size	13–14cm (5–5½in)
Habitat	heaths, woods, hedges
Behaviour	flits, takes off and lands on vegetation
Flocking	solitary
Flight	flitting
Voice	hard *tac-tac*; also a single-note rattle

IDENTIFICATION

Adult	
Crown	grey
Upperparts	grey
Rump	grey
Tail	black, white outer feathers; medium length, square
Throat	white
Breast	white
Belly	white
Bill	black; short and thin
Legs	grey; medium length

BREEDING

Nest	neat cup in low bush
Eggs	4–6; white, blotched olive
Incubation	10–11 days ♂ ♀
Young	helpless; naked
Fledging	10–11 days
Broods	1–2 ?; May–June
Food	insects
Population	25,000–50,000 pairs

J	0
F	0
M	0
A	3
M	4
J	4
J	4
A	4
S	4
O	3
N	1
D	0

grey crown

prominent rusty wings

white throat

♂

buffy legs

brownish crown

♀

A summer visitor to our heaths, commons, hedgerows and scrub-covered areas that has declined rapidly since 1968 due to drought in its winter quarters in the Sahel region, on the southern fringe of the Sahara. The bird is marked by a white throat that is particularly obvious in the singing male, but by far the best field mark is that the wing feathers have rusty reddish margins, which are apparent in all plumages. The head is grey in the male, brownish in the female and juvenile. The white throat is set off by a pinkish breast and a white belly. The tail is boldly edged with white and the legs are a pale horn colour. Though Whitethroats often skulk in dense cover, males in spring frequently perch atop a bush to sing. They also have a short, dancing song flight.
Status: a widespread summer visitor to all areas except the Scottish hills.

Similar Species:
Subalpine Warbler *Sylvia cantillans*
11.5–12.5cm (4½–5in)
This is a tiny relative of the Whitethroat found in Mediterranean scrub. It is grey above and orange-pink below, marked by a white throat in all plumages save that of the adult male, which is a deeper orange-red

below with a bold white moustachial streak. The tail, like that of a Dartford Warbler, is long, the wings relatively short and rounded. In some plumages the wings are rather rufous, but never rusty reddish like the Whitethroat's. It has bold white outer tail feathers.
Range: it is a summer visitor to the Mediterranean.
Migration: winters on the southern edge of the Sahara.
British Distribution: a very rare vagrant, mostly in spring to Fair Isle (*see page* 264) and Shetland.
Other Similar Species: Lesser Whitethroat (p. 190).

Subalpine Warbler

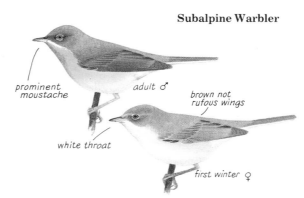

prominent moustache

adult ♂

brown not rufous wings

white throat

first winter ♀

	WHITETHROAT
Type	warbler-like
Size	13–15cm (5–6in)
Habitat	gardens, heaths, woods, hedges
Behaviour	flits, takes off and lands on vegetation
Flocking	solitary
Flight	undulating; flitting
Voice	hard *tac-tac*; song, a brief scratchy warble

IDENTIFICATION

Adult ♂	
Crown	grey
Upperparts	greyish brown, wings brown with rusty margins
Rump	greyish brown
Tail	greyish brown; medium length, square
Throat	white
Breast	pinkish
Belly	white
Bill	buff; short and thin
Legs	buff; medium length
Ad.♀and juv.	buffy brown head

BREEDING

Nest	cup near ground
Eggs	4–5; pale blue, speckled olive
Incubation	11–13 days ♂ ♀
Young	helpless; naked
Fledging	10–12 days
Broods	2; May–June
Food	insects, berries
Population	500,000–700,000 pairs

J	F	M	A	M	J	J	A	S	O	N	D
0	0	0	4	5	5	5	5	5	1	0	0

Wood Warbler *Phylloscopus sibilatrix*

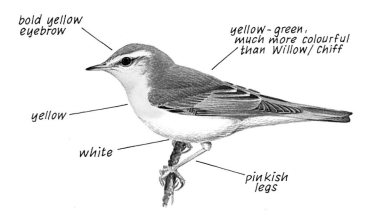

bold yellow eyebrow

yellow-green, much more colourful than Willow/Chiff

yellow

white

pinkish legs

The Wood Warbler is a summer visitor to dense deciduous woodland with scant undergrowth. It is a little larger than both the Willow Warbler and Chiffchaff, and is much more brightly coloured than either. It is greener above with bright yellow on the face and breast, and pure white below. The bold yellow eyebrow contrasts with a darker eyestripe. The legs are pale pinkish.
Status: a summer visitor that is decidedly more numerous in the west than the east, though it is virtually absent from Ireland.

Similar Species:

Arctic Warbler *Phylloscopus borealis*
11.5–12.5cm (4½–5in)
This rare vagrant is less colourful than the Wood Warbler, being olive above and whitish below, more like a Willow Warbler. It is distinguished by having a single narrow, white bar across the folded wing, formed by the tips of the greater coverts. In some plumages there is also a second bar formed by the tips of the median coverts; in winter both bars may be faint, though seldom totally lacking. The best field marks are the head shape and pattern. The bill is larger than that of some other *Phylloscopus* warblers and this is accentuated by the

sloping forehead which gives the appearance of a Reed Warbler or other *Acrocephalus*. The eyebrow is long and extends well beyond the eye, with an upturn towards the nape. It is accentuated by a clear olive eyestripe from bill to ear coverts.
Range: a summer visitor from northern Sweden right across northern Asia to the Bering Straits and Alaska. Also southwards to China.
Migration: winters in South-east Asia.
British Distribution: an annual vagrant in small numbers to Fair Isle (*see page* 264) and elsewhere, mainly in September.
Other Similar Species: Chiffchaff (p. 194) and Willow Warbler (p. 193).

Arctic Warbler

eyebrow extends to nape

single narrow wingbar

prominent eyestripe

pale legs

first winter

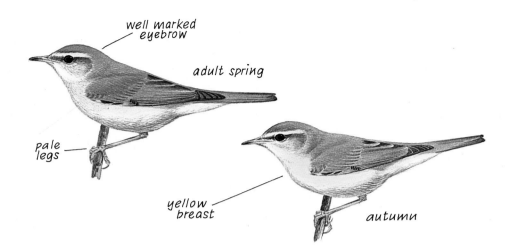

well marked
eyebrow

adult spring

pale
legs

yellow
breast

autumn

WILLOW WARBLER

Type	warbler-like
Size	10.5–11.5cm (4–4½in)
Habitat	heaths, woods, hedges
Behaviour	flits, takes off and lands on vegetation
Flocking	solitary
Flight	flitting
Voice	weak *hoo-eet*; also a descending warbled trill, repeated

IDENTIFICATION

Adult	
Crown	olive-brown
Upperparts	olive-brown
Rump	olive-brown
Tail	olive-brown; medium length, notched
Throat	buffy yellow
Breast	buffy yellow
Belly	buffy white
Bill	black; short and thin
Legs	pale brown; medium length
Juvenile	yellower below

BREEDING

Nest	dome on ground
Eggs	6–7; white, speckled reddish
Incubation	13 days ♀
Young	helpless; downy
Fledging	13–16 days
Broods	1–2; Apr–June
Food	insects
Population	3,000,000 pairs

Though easily distinguished by song, it is very similar to the Chiffchaff in appearance and the two are often lumped together as 'Willow-chiffs' during migration when birds may be seen briefly and not heard singing. The upperparts are olive-brown to buffy-olive, depending on season and age; the underparts are buffy-yellow to pale greyish. A clean-cut eyebrow extends well beyond the eye. It is always a more cleanly-cut bird overall than the Chiffchaff, with pale (not dark) legs.
Status: a widespread and abundant summer visitor to all parts of Britain.

Similar Species:
Greenish Warbler *Phylloscopus trochiloides* 10–11cm (4–4½in)
Though the Greenish Warbler is similar to both the Willow Warbler and Chiffchaff, the presence of a pale wing bar formed on the closed wing by the tips of the greater coverts is sufficient to distinguish it in summer adult and first winter plumages. At other times the wing bar may be faint, or even absent altogether, making the Greenish Warbler easily confusable with a Chiffchaff, which has similar dark legs. The upperparts are pale olive and the underparts dull white,

with no hint of yellow. The eyebrow is creamy and bold, more so than in the Chiffchaff. Some eastern sub-species of the latter also show a wing bar.
Range: a summer visitor to the eastern Baltic, extending right across Asia.
Migration: winters south in India and south-east Asia.
British Distribution: a rare, but annual, autumn vagrant to the east, south and south-west coasts in September and October. Also occasionally seen in spring on the east coast.
Other Similar Species: Chiffchaff (p. 194) and Wood Warbler (p. 192).

J	F	M	A	M	J	J	A	S	O	N	D
0	0	1	4	6	6	6	5	4	1	0	0

Greenish Warbler

well marked
eyestripe

prominent extended eyebrow

single narrow
wingbar

whitish

dark
legs

first winter

Goldcrest *Regulus regulus*

golden crest

♀

plain head

juvenile

plain face, no eyebrow, no eye stripe

olive-green

moustache

♂

Smallest British bird; tiny but decidedly rotund, with shortish tail. Crown has distinctive golden-orange blaze bordered by black. Face remarkably plain with large, dark eye and fine moustachial streak. Back olive-green; wings black with broad white margins and clear, single (sometimes double) wingbar. Underparts buffy white. Ever-active; flicks wings continuously during non-stop search for food among trees. Shows marked preference for conifers. In winter often associates with tit flocks. *Status:* common and widespread resident.
Similar Species: closely related Firecrest (p.195) also has orange crown stripe bordered by black, but has distinctive face pattern.

GOLDCREST	
Type	warbler-like
Size	8.5–9cm (3½in)
Habitat	gardens, heaths, woods, hedges
Behaviour	flits, takes off and lands on vegetation
Flocking	1–10
Flight	hovers; undulating; flitting
Voice	high-pitched *zi-zi-zi-zi*, repeated; song similar but ending in flourish
IDENTIFICATION	
Adult	
Crown	golden blaze, bordered black; lacks eye stripe and eyebrow
Upperparts	olive-green; wings black with white margins, wingbar
Rump	olive-green
Tail	black; medium length, notched
Throat	white
Breast	buffy white
Belly	buffy white
Bill	black; short and thin
Legs	black; medium length
BREEDING	
Nest	cup high in tree
Eggs	7–10; white, speckled brown
Incubation	14–17 days ♀
Young	helpless; downy
Fledging	16–21 days
Broods	2; Apr–May
Food	insects, spiders
Population	1,000,000–1,500,000 pairs

J	5
F	5
M	5
A	5
M	5
J	5
J	5
A	5
S	5
O	5
N	5
D	5

Chiffchaff *Phylloscopus collybita*

short, less marked eyebrow than Willow Warbler

adult spring

buffy white

dark legs

autumn

yellowish

Widespread summer visitor; named after its characteristic call. Inhabits open woodland but occurs in gardens and scrub on passage. Olive-brown above, dull buffy white below. Eyebrow and eye stripe less distinct than very similar Willow Warbler. Always appears as less well marked and less clean-cut version of Willow Warbler, with shorter eyebrow and (usually) dark legs. Active little bird; flits about foliage in non-stop feeding. Sometimes feeds on ground; continuously flicks wings.
Status: common summer visitor everywhere but highest hills of north; passage migrant; winter visitor to south-west England.
Similar Species: Willow Warbler (p.193) and Wood Warbler (p.192).

CHIFFCHAFF	
Type	warbler-like
Size	10.5–11.5cm (4–4½in)
Habitat	heaths, woods, hedges
Behaviour	flits, takes off and lands on vegetation
Flocking	solitary
Flight	flitting
Voice	distinct *chiff-chaff-chiff-chaff*, repeated; also *hueet*, especially on passage
IDENTIFICATION	
Adult	
Crown	olive-brown
Upperparts	olive-brown
Rump	olive-brown
Tail	olive-brown; medium length, notched
Throat	buffy white
Breast	buffy white
Belly	buffy white
Bill	black; short and thin
Legs	black; medium length
Juvenile	yellower below
BREEDING	
Nest	dome on ground
Eggs	4–9; white, speckled purple
Incubation	13–14 days ♀
Young	helpless; downy
Fledging	12–15 days
Broods	1–2; Apr–May
Food	insects
Population	300,000 pairs

J	1
F	1
M	2
A	5
M	6
J	6
J	5
A	4
S	4
O	3
N	1
D	1

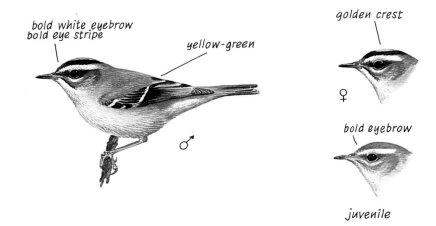

bold white eyebrow
bold eye stripe

yellow-green

♂

golden crest

♀

bold eyebrow

juvenile

FIRECREST	
Type	warbler-like
Size	8.5–9cm (3½in)
Habitat	gardens, heaths, woods, hedges
Behaviour	flits, takes off and lands on vegetation
Flocking	1–2
Flight	hovers; undulating; flitting
Voice	*zit-zit-zit*; song similar, often ending abruptly

IDENTIFICATION	
Adult	
Crown	golden blaze, bordered black; prominent eye stripe and eyebrow
Upperparts	yellow-green; wings black with white margins, wingbar
Rump	yellow-green
Tail	black; medium length, notched
Throat	white
Breast	white
Belly	white
Bill	black; short and thin
Legs	black; medium length

BREEDING	
Nest	cup high in tree
Eggs	7–11; pale buffy, speckled brown
Incubation	14–15 days ♀
Young	helpless; downy
Fledging	19–20 days
Broods	2; May–June
Food	insects, spiders
Population	*c* 40 pairs

J	F	M	A	M	J	J	A	S	O	N	D
1	1	2	2	2	2	2	2	2	3	3	1

The Firecrest is very similar to the more widespread Goldcrest, with a similar high-pitched call and active, non-stop search for food among conifers. It is, however, quite distinctive if seen well. The upperparts are greener, with an even more contrasting pattern of black and white on the wings. Though it has a golden crest, like the Goldcrest, its facial pattern of black and white stripes is quite different. The eyebrow is broad and white, contrasting with a lateral black crown stripe. There is also a dark stripe through the eye and a narrow dark moustachial streak. This pattern compares with the blank, almost unmarked 'face' of the Goldcrest. Though similar, the calls and song of the two 'crests' are distinctive once learned.
Status: a rare breeding bird in south-eastern England. It is also a regular autumn migrant and scarce winter visitor in most years to southern England.

Similar Species:
Pallas's Warbler *Phylloscopus proregulus*
8.5–9.5cm (3¼–3½in)
This tiny relative of the Chiffchaff and Willow Warbler is like the Firecrest in both size and behaviour. It often hovers,

'crest'-like, to reach the underside of leaves. The upperparts are olive-green, the underparts white. It has a pale crown stripe, dark lateral crown stripes, a bold white eyebrow and a narrow dark eye stripe, all of which combine to give its head a distinct 'zebra' appearance. The wings have two bold bars, the legs are dark and it shows a pale yellowish rump.
Range: a summer visitor to the far eastern Soviet Union, China and the Himalayas.
Migration: moves southward to winter in northern India, south-east Asia and China.
British Distribution: increasingly identified, mainly on the east coast of England in late October and early November.
Other Similar Species: Goldcrest (p. 194).

Pallas's Warbler

pale crown stripe plus
dark lateral crown stripes

bold double wingbar

dark eye
stripe

first winter

Spotted Flycatcher *Muscicapa striata*

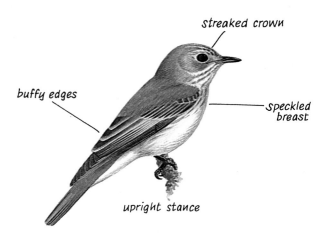

streaked crown

buffy edges

speckled breast

upright stance

Most frequently seen perched upright on fence or twig, flying out to catch passing insects and returning to original or nearby perch. Agile flight on large wings; snap of bill audible at close range. Solitary or in pairs. Upperparts greyish brown; narrow, pale edges to inner flight feathers and wing coverts. Crown streaked brown and buff. Underparts white; buff-brown streaking on breast. Short, broad black bill. First winter birds differ only in having broader buff margins to wing feathers.
Status: widespread summer visitor.
Similar Species: female and first winter Pied Flycatcher (p.196) also brownish, but with extensive white in wing; lack streaked breast.

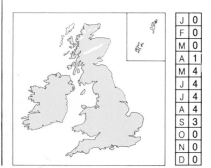

	SPOTTED FLYCATCHER
Type	chat-like
Size	13.5–14.5cm (5½–6in)
Habitat	gardens, heaths, woods, hedges
Behaviour	perches openly, takes off and lands on vegetation
Flocking	1 or 2
Flight	strong and powerful; flitting
Voice	weak *tzee*

IDENTIFICATION

Adult	
Crown	brown and buff
Upperparts	greyish brown; wings pale-edged
Rump	greyish brown
Tail	greyish brown; medium length, notched
Throat	buffy
Breast	white, streaked buff-brown
Belly	white
Bill	black; short and broad
Legs	black; short

BREEDING

Nest	cup against wall or tree trunk, often near ground
Eggs	4–5; pale blue, blotched reddish
Incubation	11–15 days ♀
Young	helpless; downy
Fledging	12–14 days
Broods	1–2; May–June
Food	insects
Population	100,000–200,000 pairs

J	0
F	0
M	0
A	1
M	4
J	4
J	4
A	4
S	3
O	0
N	0
D	0

Pied Flycatcher *Ficedula hypoleuca*

white forehead

white in wing

white in wing

cocked tail

♂

♀

Stout little bird with tiny bill. Like Spotted Flycatcher perches openly watching for passing insects, but returns to same perch less frequently. Summer male black above with white forehead and bold area of white in wing; underparts white. Female, winter male and first winter birds similar, but brown above with smaller white area in wing. Takes readily to nest boxes in open oak and birch woods.
Status: summer visitor to north and west Britain; passage migrant elsewhere, including eastern Ireland; sometimes numerous; usually regarded as important element of Scandinavian migration.
Similar Species: Spotted Flycatcher (p.196) has streaked breast.

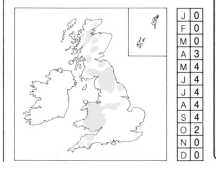

	PIED FLYCATCHER
Type	chat-like
Size	12–13cm (4½–5in)
Habitat	woods
Behaviour	perches openly, takes off and lands on vegetation
Flocking	solitary
Flight	strong and powerful; flitting
Voice	*whit* or *tic*; also a repeated *zee-chi* ending in flourish

IDENTIFICATION

Ad.♂ summer	
Crown	black and white
Upperparts	black, with white in wing
Rump	black
Tail	black, white outer feathers; medium length, square
Throat	white
Breast	white
Belly	white
Bill	black; tiny
Legs	black; short
Ad.♀, winter♂	brown above; less white in wing

BREEDING

Nest	cup in tree hole or nest box
Eggs	4–7; pale blue
Incubation	12–13 days ♀
Young	helpless; downy
Fledging	13–16 days
Broods	1; May–June
Food	insects
Population	20,000 pairs

J	0
F	0
M	0
A	3
M	4
J	4
J	4
A	4
S	4
O	2
N	0
D	0

TITS, NUTHATCHES AND TREECREEPERS

These are essentially woodland birds, several of which have made a highly successful transition to gardens. Indeed, they are the bread-and-butter birds of the bird-gardener. Blue and Great Tits, in particular, come readily to bird tables, to hanging food and to nest boxes, though other species, including the Nuthatch (*illustrated*), lag only a little behind in exploiting our generosity. Though they occupy distinct territories during the breeding season, they are essentially gregarious throughout the rest of the year and form the basis of most mixed flocks of birds that scour our countryside for food during the winter. Typically Blue and Great Tits dominate, but among conifers Coal Tits are often numerous and a flock of Long-tailed Tits may also join in. Marsh and Willow Tits are usually in a minority, but Nuthatches, Treecreepers and, in autumn, both Willow Warblers and Chiffchaffs, may be seen in these mixed flocks.

Bearded Tits belong to a quite distinct family – the parrotbills – that have their centre of distribution in China. There,

they are predominantly inhabitants of bamboo forests and it is, therefore, not surprising that our Bearded Tits are confined to the similar reed beds. Indeed, there are few birds that show such a total preference for a particular vegetation type. Though they could probably spread throughout much of the country, the lack of suitable stands of reeds sadly restricts these attractive little birds to south and east England.

In contrast, Crested Tits are confined to the old forests of the Scottish Highlands, where Scots Pine is the dominant tree. Though they are slowly spreading into new plantations as these mature, the birds show no inclination to wander. They are thus completely unknown elsewhere in the country. It is strange but true that the English birdwatcher is more likely to

see an Asiatic Pallas's Warbler or an American Blackpoll Warbler than a Crested Tit.

Though tits are largely resident, there is some evidence of migration and occasional large eruptions of Continental tits do arrive on our shores. This is particularly true of Bearded Tits, whose populations quickly outgrow their restricted breeding grounds, but both Great and Blue Tits, too, have occasionally arrived in large numbers from the Continent.

grey crown

black moustache

tawny, black and white streaking

♂

very long tail

♀

BEARDED TIT	
Type	tit-like
Size	16–17cm (6–6½in)
Habitat	reed beds
Behaviour	flits, takes off and lands on vegetation
Flocking	1–15
Flight	laboured; direct
Voice	loud *pting*, repeated in flight

IDENTIFICATION	
Adult ♂	
Crown	blue-grey
Upperparts	orange-brown; black and white wing margins
Rump	orange-brown
Tail	orange-brown; long and rounded
Throat	white
Breast	orange-buff
Belly	orange-buff
Bill	yellow; short and thin
Legs	black; medium length
Adult ♀	head orange-brown

BREEDING	
Nest	cup near ground, over water
Eggs	5–7; white, speckled brown
Incubation	12–13 days ♂ ♀
Young	helpless; naked
Fledging	9–12 days
Broods	2–3; Apr–May
Food	insects, seeds
Population	*c* 400 pairs

This is a small, buff-brown bird distinguished by an inordinately long tail. As its alternative name of Bearded Reedling implies, it is confined to extensive stands of reeds, where it is most often seen flying low over the reed tops on short whirring wings with the long tail streaming out behind. It also perches on the reed tops. The male is a rich orange-brown above, with bold black and white margins to the wings. The head is blue-grey, marked by droopy black moustaches; both these features are lacking in the female. The distinctive, twanging *pting* call is repeated as a contact note in flying flocks and often before flight.
Status: the absence of large reed beds from many parts of the country restricts the distribution of this largely resident little bird. It is confined to southern and eastern England, with its major strongholds in East Anglia. It does, however, frequently erupt elsewhere in autumn.

Similar Species:
Penduline Tit *Remiz pendulinus*
10.5–11cm (4–4½in)
Like the Bearded Tit, this bird lives among wetland vegetation, though it prefers overgrown ditches to reed beds. The male is

boldly marked, with a chestnut back and a bold black mask through the eye. The female is paler above and has a greyish head with only a rudimentary mask. It is best located by its plaintive *tsee* call.
Range: has a patchy breeding range extending from southern Spain to eastern Europe and from the Baltic to Greece, Turkey and the southern Soviet Union. Has extended westwards to reach Holland in recent years.
Migration: mainly resident, though eastern birds may move southwards.
British Distribution: an exceptionally rare vagrant that first occurred in 1966, but which may become more regular in future by virtue of its westerly expansion of range.

Penduline Tit

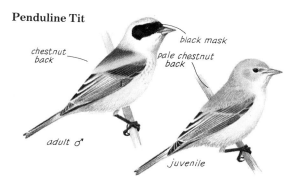

chestnut back

black mask

pale chestnut back

adult ♂

juvenile

J	F	M	A	M	J	J	A	S	O	N	D
2	2	2	2	2	2	2	2	2	2	2	2

Long-tailed Tit *Aegithalos caudatus*

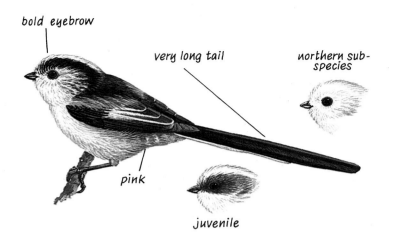

bold eyebrow

very long tail

northern sub-species

pink

juvenile

Small, active bird with tail longer than body – no other woodland bird has such a long tail. Crown white with bold black stripe over eye extending to black back; tiny black bill. Wings black and white with broad pink band across upper edge; tail black with white outer feathers. Underparts white with pink undertail coverts. Juveniles lack pink and have sooty black heads. Rare northern sub-species has all-white head. Usually found throughout year in small flocks up to twenty strong. Prefers hedgerows and woods with plentiful secondary growth, as well as bushy heaths and commons.
Status: widespread resident.
Similar Species: none.

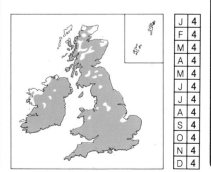

	LONG-TAILED TIT	
Type	tit-like	
Size	13.5–14.5cm (5½–6in)	
Habitat	heaths, woods, gardens, hedges	
Behaviour	flits, takes off and lands on vegetation	
Flocking	1–15	
Flight	laboured; flitting	
Voice	continuous *zee-zee-zee* contact call among flock	

IDENTIFICATION

Adult	
Crown	white, black eye stripe
Upperparts	black and white, wings pink-banded
Rump	black and white
Tail	black, white outer feathers; long and rounded
Throat	white
Breast	white
Belly	white, pink undertail
Bill	black; tiny
Legs	black; medium length
Juvenile	lacks pink; head sooty black

BREEDING

Nest	dome in bush
Eggs	8–12; white
Incubation	12–14 days, mainly ♀
Young	helpless; naked
Fledging	14–18 days
Broods	1–2; Mar–Apr
Food	insects, seeds
Population	150,000 pairs

J	4
F	4
M	4
A	4
M	4
J	4
J	4
A	4
S	4
O	4
N	4
D	4

Marsh Tit *Parus palustris*

glossy cap

small bib

Name misleading as haunts deciduous woods and hedgerows. Typical tit with round head, short bill, black cap and uniform buff-brown upperparts. Behaviour also typical – ever-active forager through tree canopy, often in company of related species. Great care needed to distinguish from very similar Willow Tit; Marsh Tit cap shiny (not dull), bib small (not large and diffuse); lacks pale panel in wing. Marsh Tit is neat and elegant little bird; Willow Tit decidedly scruffy. Calls quite different.
Status: widespread resident in England, Wales and southern Scotland.
Similar Species: Willow Tit (p.201) as above.

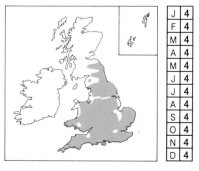

	MARSH TIT	
Type	tit-like	
Size	11–12cm (4½–5in)	
Habitat	heaths, woods, hedges, gardens	
Behaviour	flits, takes off and lands on vegetation	
Flocking	1–5	
Flight	undulating; flitting	
Voice	distinctive repeated *pitchoo-pitchoo-pitchoo*, also repeated *chip-chip*	

IDENTIFICATION

Adult	
Crown	shiny black cap
Upperparts	buff-brown
Rump	buff-brown
Tail	buff-brown; medium length, notched
Throat	black bib
Breast	white
Belly	white
Bill	black; short and stubby
Legs	black; medium length

BREEDING

Nest	cup in hole in rotten wood
Eggs	6–9; white, spotted reddish
Incubation	13–17 days ♀
Young	helpless; downy
Fledging	16–21 days
Broods	1–2; Apr–May
Food	insects, seeds
Population	70,000–140,000 pairs

J	4
F	4
M	4
A	4
M	4
J	4
J	4
A	4
S	4
O	4
N	4
D	4

pale wing edges

dull, sooty cap

large bib

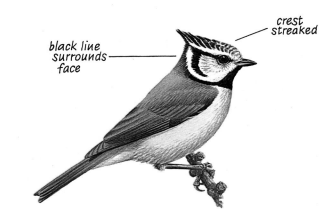

crest streaked

black line surrounds face

Very like closely related Marsh Tit and found in similar habitats, especially damp alder and birch woods. Somewhat ill-kempt appearance. Distinguished from Marsh Tit by dull black cap, larger white cheeks, larger and more diffuse black bib and (especially in winter) pale wing panel. In summer, must have dead rotting trees in which to excavate nest hole. *Status:* widespread resident in England, Wales and southern Scotland. *Similar Species:* Marsh Tit (p.200).

WILLOW TIT	
Type	tit-like
Size	11–12cm (4½–5in)
Habitat	heaths, woods, hedges, gardens
Behaviour	flits, takes off and lands on vegetation
Flocking	1–2
Flight	undulating; flitting
Voice	buzzing *erz-erz-erz*; also high-pitched *zi-zi-zi*

IDENTIFICATION

Adult	
Crown	dull black cap
Upperparts	buff-brown, pale wing edges
Rump	buff-brown
Tail	buff-brown; medium length, notched
Throat	black bib
Breast	white
Belly	white
Bill	black; short and stubby
Legs	black; medium length

BREEDING

Nest	self-excavated cavity, thinly lined
Eggs	6–9; white, speckled reddish
Incubation	13–15 days ♀
Young	helpless; downy
Fledging	17–19 days
Broods	1; Apr–May
Food	insects, seeds
Population	50,000–100,000 pairs

Typically active, often associating with other tits but confined to areas of old Scot's Pine with broken tree stumps and scattered birches. Grey-brown upperparts with prominent black and white streaked crest. Face white with clearly marked black eye stripe, black bib and black line extending to enclose ear coverts. Underparts whitish. *Status:* scarce, confined to central Scottish Highlands. *Similar Species:* only 'crested' tit.

CRESTED TIT	
Type	tit-like
Size	11–12cm (4½–5in)
Habitat	forests and woods
Behaviour	flits, takes off and lands on vegetation
Flocking	1–15
Flight	undulating; flitting
Voice	trilled *chirr-chirr-rr*

IDENTIFICATION

Adult	
Crown	black and white, crest
Upperparts	grey-brown
Rump	grey-brown
Tail	grey-brown; medium length, notched
Throat	black bib
Breast	whitish
Belly	whitish
Bill	black; short and stubby
Legs	black; medium length

BREEDING

Nest	cup in excavated hole in old stump
Eggs	4–8; white, speckled purple
Incubation	13–18 days ♀
Young	helpless; downy
Fledging	17–21 days
Broods	1; Apr–May
Food	insects, seeds
Population	*c*1000 pairs

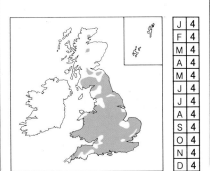

J	4
F	4
M	4
A	4
M	4
J	4
J	4
A	4
S	4
O	4
N	4
D	4

J	3
F	3
M	3
A	3
M	3
J	3
J	3
A	3
S	3
O	3
N	3
D	3

Coal Tit *Parus ater*

white nape patch

grey back

bold double wingbar

Smallest tit, most often found among conifers, but also visits mature deciduous and mixed woodland, gardens and bird tables. Grey-blue above, with double white wingbar; underparts greyish white. Crown and substantial bib glossy black; white patch on nape distinguishes from other woodland tits. Gregarious, often associating with other tits, particularly outside breeding season.
Status: widespread and common resident except in extreme northern and north-western isles.
Similar Species: white nape patch unique. Call similar to Goldcrest (p.194); song to a similar phrase of Great Tit (p.203).

COAL TIT	
Type	tit-like
Size	10.5–11.5cm (4½in)
Habitat	woods, hedges, heaths, gardens
Behaviour	flits, takes off and lands on vegetation
Flocking	1–15
Flight	undulating; flitting
Voice	high-pitched *zee-zee-zee*; also a repeated *weecho-weecho-weecho*
IDENTIFICATION	
Adult	
Crown	black, white nape
Upperparts	grey-blue, white wingbars
Rump	grey-blue
Tail	grey-blue; medium length, notched
Throat	black bib
Breast	greyish white
Belly	greyish white
Bill	black; short and stubby
Legs	black; medium length
BREEDING	
Nest	cup in tree hole
Eggs	7–9; white, speckled reddish
Incubation	14–18 days ♀
Young	helpless; downy
Fledging	16–19 days
Broods	2; Apr–May
Food	insects, seeds
Population	1,000,000 pairs

J	5
F	5
M	5
A	5
M	5
J	5
J	5
A	5
S	5
O	5
N	5
D	5

Blue Tit *Parus caeruleus*

greenish crown

blue crown

blue wings

eyebrow and eye stripe

juvenile

adult

Most common and familiar of tits; comes readily to bird tables and other feeders; will also occupy nest boxes and use bird baths. Wings pale blue with single white wingbar; back greenish. Underparts yellow with neat dividing line on centre of breast. White cheeks enclosed by dark line from eye to chin.
Status: abundant and widespread resident of Britain and Ireland.
Similar Species: Great Tit (p.203) larger with black cap and face pattern, and bold black line down breast.

BLUE TIT	
Type	tit-like
Size	11–12cm (4½–5in)
Habitat	gardens, marshes, heaths, woods, hedges
Behaviour	flits, takes off and lands on vegetation
Flocking	1–30
Flight	undulating; flitting
Voice	*tsee-tsee-tsee*; also harsh *churr*
IDENTIFICATION	
Adult	
Crown	pale blue
Upperparts	greenish, wings pale blue
Rump	greenish
Tail	pale blue; medium length, notched
Throat	blue bib
Breast	yellow
Belly	yellow, dark dividing line
Bill	black; short and stubby
Legs	black; medium length
Juvenile	crown greyish
BREEDING	
Nest	cup in tree hole or nest box
Eggs	7–12; white, speckled reddish
Incubation	12–16 days ♀
Young	helpless; downy
Fledging	15–23 days
Broods	1; Apr–May
Food	insects, seeds, nuts
Population	5,000,000 pairs

J	6
F	6
M	6
A	6
M	6
J	6
J	6
A	6
S	6
O	6
N	6
D	6

Parus major **Great Tit**　　　　　*Sitta europaea* **Nuthatch**

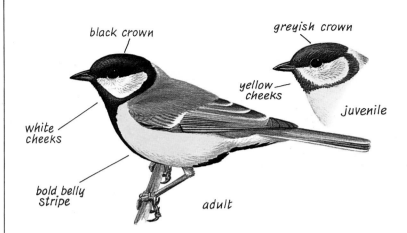

black crown

greyish crown

yellow cheeks

white cheeks

juvenile

bold belly stripe

adult

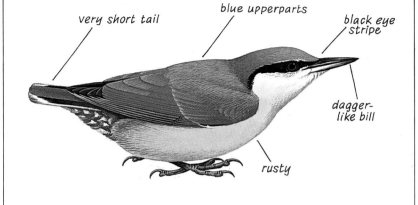

very short tail

blue upperparts

black eye stripe

dagger-like bill

rusty

Largest and most clearly marked of all the tits, with shiny black cap and bib joined by bold black line enclosing white cheeks; black stripe down yellow bib and belly (wider in male than female). Back green, wings and tail pale blue; latter with white outer feathers. Common in all types of woods, including pure conifer stands where often most abundant bird. Comes readily to gardens where aggressive at feeders. Joins mixed tit flocks outside breeding season. Has wide variety of calls and songs – fifty-seven distinct forms described.
Status: common and widespread resident of Britain and Ireland.
Similar Species: Blue Tit (p.202) is much smaller and has fainter belly line and paler cap and head pattern.

GREAT TIT	
Type	tit-like
Size	13.5–14.5cm (5½in)
Habitat	gardens, marshes, heaths, woods, hedges
Behaviour	flits, takes off and lands on vegetation
Flocking	1–30
Flight	undulating; flitting
Voice	*see-saw* and *teecha-teecha-teecha* most common

IDENTIFICATION

Adult	
Crown	black
Upperparts	green; wings pale blue, white outer feathers
Rump	pale blue
Tail	pale blue; medium length, notched
Throat	black bib
Breast	yellow, black centre stripe
Belly	yellow, black centre stripe
Bill	black; short and stubby
Legs	black; medium length
Juvenile	crown greyish black

BREEDING

Nest	cup in tree hole or nest box
Eggs	8–13; white, spotted reddish
Incubation	13–14 days ♀
Young	helpless; downy
Fledging	16–22 days
Broods	1; Mar–May
Food	insects, seeds
Population	3,000,000 pairs

J	6
F	6
M	6
A	6
M	6
J	6
J	6
A	6
S	6
O	6
N	6
D	6

Agile tree-climber, similar to woodpeckers but with ability to climb up and down trees. Does not undulate in flight like woodpecker. Upperparts pale blue with bold black eye stripe and black wingtips. Throat white; remaining underparts warm buff, with chestnut on flanks. Tail short and square. Produces sounds by hacking at nuts wedged in tree crevice with sharply pointed bill.
Status: widespread resident of England and Wales.
Similar Species: none.

NUTHATCH	
Type	woodpecker-like
Size	13.5–14.5cm (5½in)
Habitat	woods, hedges, heaths, gardens
Behaviour	climbs, takes off and lands on vegetation
Flocking	1–2
Flight	strong and powerful; direct
Voice	high-pitched *chwit-chwit*; also a repeated *kee-kee-kee*

IDENTIFICATION

Adult	
Crown	pale blue
Upperparts	pale blue, black wingtips
Rump	pale blue
Tail	pale blue; short and square
Throat	white
Breast	warm buff
Belly	warm buff
Bill	black; short and thin
Legs	buff; medium length

BREEDING

Nest	tree hole, plastered mud
Eggs	6–9; white, spotted reddish
Incubation	14–18 days ♀
Young	helpless; downy
Fledging	23–25 days
Broods	1; Apr–May
Food	seeds, nuts, insects
Population	20,000 pairs

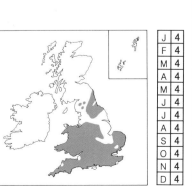

J	4
F	4
M	4
A	4
M	4
J	4
J	4
A	4
S	4
O	4
N	4
D	4

Treecreeper *Certhia familiaris*

TREECREEPER

Type	woodpecker-like
Size	12–13cm (4½–5in)
Habitat	woods, heaths, hedges, gardens
Behaviour	climbs, takes off and lands on vegetation
Flocking	solitary
Flight	undulating
Voice	Goldcrest-like *tsee-tsee*

IDENTIFICATION

Adult	
Crown	buff and brown, streaked
Upperparts	buff and brown, streaked
Rump	rusty brown
Tail	brown; medium length, pointed
Throat	white
Breast	white
Belly	white
Bill	black; long and thin, decurved
Legs	grey; medium length

BREEDING

Nest	cup behind bark
Eggs	6; white, speckled reddish
Incubation	14–15 days ♀
Young	helpless; downy
Fledging	14–16 days
Broods	1–2; Apr–June
Food	insects
Population	150,000–300,000 pairs

J	F	M	A	M	J	J	A	S	O	N	D
4	4	4	4	4	4	4	4	4	4	4	4

long decurved bill

streaked upperparts

white

pointed tail

This is a familiar woodland bird that climbs the trunks and limbs of trees using its long, decurved bill to search the bark for insect food. It is well camouflaged and easily overlooked and shows a remarkable ability to put a tree between itself and the would-be observer. The upperparts are mottled and streaked brown, buff and black with a rusty rump and plain brown, pointed tail feathers with protruding shafts. There is a bold double wingbar. The underparts are pure white. Its high-pitched *tsee-tsee* call is often the first indication of its presence and it frequently associates with mixed tit flocks outside the breeding season.
Status: a widespread resident in woodland throughout the country.

Similar Species:
Short-toed Treecreeper
Certhia brachydactyla 12–13cm (4½–5in)
This continental species is very similar to the Treecreeper and should be identified only with the greatest of care. In general the plumage pattern of the two species is the same, but the Short-toed is less rufous and more greyish-brown, with a finer, less distinct eyebrow. Below, its flanks are washed with buff-brown. Most of the calls are similar to those of the Treecreeper, but a Chaffinch-like *chink* is confined to the Short-toed.
Range: continental western Europe as far as the Russian border and into North Africa where it is resident; range includes the Channel Islands, where it is the only breeding treecreeper.
Migration: none.
British Distribution: an exceptional vagrant to south and south-east Britain from across the English Channel.

Short-toed Treecreeper

indistinct eyebrows

tawny flanks

ORIOLES, SHRIKES,
CROWS AND
STARLINGS

These are generally medium to large species that include some of the most abundant and familiar of our birds. Crow, Rook, Jackdaw and Starling are familiar almost everyday sights, and the spectacular urban roosts of the latter are a feature of the lives of many city dwellers and commuters. But this group also contains some of the most elusive and rare of our breeding birds.

Once widespread enough to merit the country name of 'Butcher-bird' (from its habit of impaling its prey on thorns), the Red-backed Shrike is in imminent danger of extinction as a British breeding bird.

While the shrike suffers a decline, the Golden Oriole is on the increase. Today it breeds in several south-eastern counties, with a thriving colony in East Anglia.

Rook, Jackdaw, Crow and Jay (*illustrated*) are all widespread and successful species. Several have learned to live happily alongside humans, with the colonial Rook and Jackdaw and the more solitary Crow being prime examples. A rare member of the crow family, the red-billed Chough, is confined to a few windswept cliffs and quarries of the west. Ravens, too, are resident and unknown away from their upland

strongholds. It was not always so. Largely carrion eaters, having a strong association with sheep pastures, they were once widespread in Britain and Ireland. Persecution may well have been the main cause.

Save perhaps for the House Sparrow, no bird in the world has been more successful than the Starling. Though the Starling is an abundant breeder throughout these islands, our birds are joined by a huge influx of winter visitors every autumn. At this time roosts of over a million birds have been located in several country areas.

Oriolus oriolus Golden Oriole

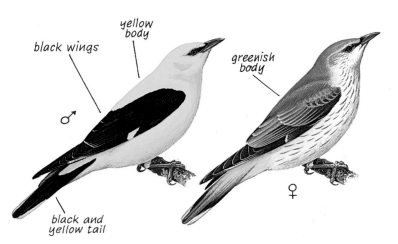

black wings

yellow body

greenish body

♂

black and yellow tail

♀

Boldly coloured but self-effacing woodland bird; more often heard than seen. Male bright yellow with black wings and black base to tail. Females and younger males greenish and black, with varying amounts of white and some streaking on breast. Bill red. Except when flies, easily overlooked among canopy of large deciduous trees. *Status:* rare summer visitor, mostly to East Anglia.
Similar Species: none.

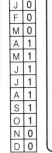

J	0
F	0
M	0
A	1
M	1
J	1
J	1
A	1
S	1
O	1
N	0
D	0

GOLDEN ORIOLE

Type	pigeon-like
Size	23–25cm (9–10in)
Habitat	heaths, woods, hedges
Behaviour	flits, perches openly, takes off and lands on vegetation
Flocking	1–2
Flight	strong and powerful; undulating
Voice	flute-like whistle *weela-weeo*

IDENTIFICATION

Adult ♂	
Crown	yellow
Upperparts	yellow, black wings
Rump	yellow
Tail	black and yellow; medium length, square
Throat	yellow
Breast	yellow
Belly	yellow
Bill	red; short and thin
Legs	black; medium length
Ad.♀, Sub-ad.♂	greenish above, white with streaking below

BREEDING

Nest	cup suspended in tree
Eggs	3–4; white, spotted brown
Incubation	14–15 days, mainly ♀
Young	helpless; downy
Fledging	14–15 days
Broods	1–2 ?; May–June
Food	insects, berries, fruit
Population	c 20 pairs

Pica pica Magpie

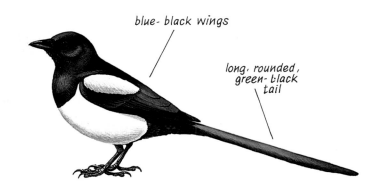

blue-black wings

long, rounded, green-black tail

Large black and white crow, with distinctive long, wedge-shaped, green-glossed tail. Black head, breast and back; wings black with glossy blue wash and bold, white oval patches. Belly white. Mainly scavenger and robber, often seen in early morning picking at corpses along roads. Usually solitary or in small groups.
Status: widespread resident; has moved into city-centres in present century.
Similar Species: only large black and white bird of the countryside.

J	6
F	6
M	6
A	6
M	6
J	6
J	6
A	6
S	6
O	6
N	6
D	6

MAGPIE

Type	crow-like
Size	42–50cm (16½–20in)
Habitat	heaths, woods, hedges, gardens
Behaviour	perches openly, hops, takes off from vegetation or ground
Flocking	1–15
Flight	laboured; direct
Voice	harsh *chak-chak-chak*

IDENTIFICATION

Adult	
Crown	black
Upperparts	black, blue-black wings with white patches
Rump	black
Tail	green-black, long and wedge-shaped
Throat	black
Breast	black
Belly	white
Bill	black; short and thin
Legs	black; medium length

BREEDING

Nest	dome of twigs in bush or tree
Eggs	5–8; pale blue, blotched olive
Incubation	17–18 days ♀
Young	helpless, naked
Fledging	22–28 days
Broods	1; Apr–May
Food	nestlings, eggs, carrion, seeds, insects
Population	250,000 pairs

Red-backed Shrike *Lanius collurio*

It spends much of its time sitting on the top or side of a bush or low tree or on a telegraph wire or post, waiting to pounce on a large insect or small bird. Like other shrikes, it has the somewhat unendearing habit of impaling its prey on thorns or barbed wire to serve as a larder. The male is a lovely bird with a pale grey crown and nape, and a black mask through the eye. The back and wings are rust-red, the rump grey and the tail black with white edges. The underparts are white. The female, dull in comparison, is sandy brown above with a dark smudge through the eye and heavily barred underparts. Juveniles and first winter birds are similar to the female, but with heavier barring below as well as barring on the upperparts, creating a scaly impression. *Status:* although an increasingly scarce summer visitor to southern England, it may be colonizing Scotland.

Similar Species:
Woodchat Shrike *Lanius senator*
16–18cm (6–7in)
Male and female are similar, with a rich chestnut cap, black facial mask and upperparts, and white underparts. The white scapulars form two distinct ovals on the back and, in flight, the white outer tail feathers and white rump show well. The female is slightly duller than the male. Juvenile and first winter birds are buff-brown and scaled above and below like juvenile Red-backed Shrikes. They do, however, have two pale ovals on the back. *Range:* summer visitor to most of western Europe and around the Mediterranean, extending south-eastwards.
Migration: winters in Africa.
British Distribution: a regular, though rare, double passage migrant, with an eastern bias in spring and a western bias in autumn.
Other Similar Species: Great Grey Shrike (p. 209).

Woodchat Shrike

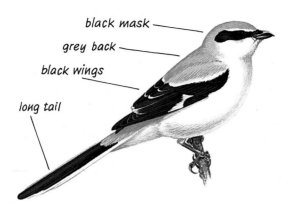

black mask

grey back

black wings

long tail

This is a medium-sized, grey and white winter visitor that occurs regularly in small numbers. The crown, back and rump are pale grey, while the wings and the long tail are black; both are marked with white. A black mask extends from the bill through the eye. The underparts are white, though there is sometimes a pinkish flush on the breast. It often sits openly on the top of a bush or telegraph post, where its glistening white breast is noticeable at considerable distances. Like other shrikes it feeds by pouncing on its prey. It is generally solitary.
Status: a scarce, perhaps declining, winter visitor to eastern Scotland and England, often returning to favoured sites every year.

Similar Species:
Lesser Grey Shrike *Lanius minor*
19–21cm (7½–8in)
Smaller than the Great Grey Shrike, though the difference in size is seldom of much use in the field. Like the Great Grey, this is a grey and white shrike marked by black wings and tail. It is, however, shorter in the tail and tends to sit more upright than the Great Grey. The major distinction however, is the black mask that in the Lesser Grey is larger and extends from the forehead rather

than the lores. It also lacks a white eyebrow. Males in summer have a pinkish wash over the breast. The juvenile is greyish-buff above, marked with fine crescents and a fading black mask behind the eye.
Range: breeds from France in a broadening band to central Siberia.
Migration: moves to the savannah grasslands of Africa in winter.
British Distribution: a very rare spring and autumn vagrant, mainly to the east coast; most records in the first week of June.
Other Similar Species: Red-backed Shrike (p. 208).

Lesser Grey Shrike

black mask extends over forehead

dark mask

adult

juvenile

	GREAT GREY SHRIKE	
Type	chat-like	
Size	23–25cm (9–10in)	
Habitat	heaths, hedges	
Behaviour	perches openly, takes off and lands on vegetation	
Flocking	solitary	
Flight	direct	
Voice	harsh *chek-chek*	

	IDENTIFICATION	
Adult		
Crown	grey	
Upperparts	grey, black wings with white patches	
Rump	grey	
Tail	black with white patches; long and rounded	
Throat	white	
Breast	white	
Belly	white	
Bill	black; short and stubby	
Legs	black; medium length	

	BREEDING	
Nest	cup in bush	
Eggs	5–7; white, spotted reddish	
Incubation	15 days ♂, mainly ♀	
Young	helpless; naked	
Fledging	19–20 days	
Broods	1; Apr–May	
Food	birds, voles	
Population	scarce winter visitor	

J	F	M	A	M	J	J	A	S	O	N	D
2	2	2	1	0	0	0	0	1	2	2	2

Chough *Pyrrhocorax pyrrhocorax*

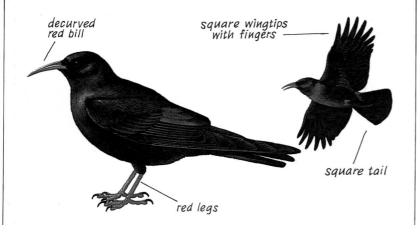

decurved red bill

square wingtips with fingers

square tail

red legs

Black, crow-like bird with thin, decurved, red bill and red legs. Wings broad and square, with deep fingering at tips. Found only along cliff-lined shores and in mountain gorges and quarries, where masterful flight involves diving, soaring and aerobatics. Gregarious, forming flocks where numbers sufficient.
Status: scarce and highly localized resident in Islay, Scotland and west Wales and Ireland.
Similar Species: Jackdaw (p.210) is similar size and colour and shares habitat and behaviour, but wings more rounded and lacks red bill and legs.

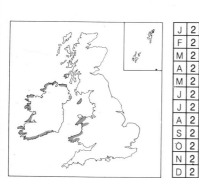

J	2
F	2
M	2
A	2
M	2
J	2
J	2
A	2
S	2
O	2
N	2
D	2

CHOUGH
Type	crow-like
Size	36–41cm (14–16in)
Habitat	moors, sea cliffs
Behaviour	walks, perches openly, takes off and lands on ground
Flocking	1–15
Flight	soars, glides, aerial dive; strong and powerful
Voice	ringing *keear*, repeated

IDENTIFICATION
Adult	
Crown	black
Upperparts	black; wingtips deep-fingered
Rump	black
Tail	black; medium length, square
Throat	black
Breast	black
Belly	black
Bill	red; decurved, long and thin
Legs	red; medium length

BREEDING
Nest	cup on ledge in cave or crevice
Eggs	3–4; pale green, blotched brown
Incubation	17–23 days ♀
Young	helpless; downy
Fledging	38 days
Broods	1; Apr–May
Food	insects, worms, seeds
Population	less than 1000 pairs

Jackdaw *Corvus monedula*

short bill

grey nape

more rounded wings

white eye

longer tail than Chough

Smallest crow; typical black plumage broken by grey nape, not often visible at distance. Short, stubby bill distinguishes from Crow and Rook. Gregarious, forming flocks in wide variety of habitats. Performs aerobatics (like much rarer and more localized Chough) along cliff-lined shores, gorges and, in towns, cathedrals, and so on. Feeds mostly on farmland, often in company with Rooks.
Status: widespread and common resident of Britain and Ireland.
Similar Species: Rook (p.211) and Carrion Crow (p.211) are bigger with larger bills; Chough (p.210) is rare, with red bill and legs.

J	6
F	6
M	6
A	6
M	6
J	6
J	6
A	6
S	6
O	6
N	6
D	6

JACKDAW
Type	crow-like
Size	32–34cm (12½–13½in)
Habitat	towns, heaths, sea cliffs, woods, hedges
Behaviour	walks, perches openly, takes off from vegetation or ground
Flocking	1–200
Flight	soars, glides, aerial dive; laboured; direct
Voice	high-pitched *kya*; distinctive *chak*

IDENTIFICATION
Adult	
Crown	black, grey nape
Upperparts	black
Rump	black
Tail	black; medium length, square
Throat	black
Breast	black
Belly	black
Bill	black; short and stubby
Legs	black; medium length

BREEDING
Nest	variable; twigs in tree or cliff hole; also holes in buildings, chimneys
Eggs	4–6; pale blue, spotted brown
Incubation	17–18 days ♀
Young	helpless; downy
Fledging	28–32 days
Broods	1; Apr–May
Food	worms, nestlings, eggs, small mammals, grain
Population	c 500,000 pairs

Corvus frugilegus **Rook**

bare face

lacks bare face

juvenile

thinnish bill

slimmer, less bulky than Crow

adult

Highly gregarious crow, forming large flocks, roosts, and colonial nesting groups, called rookeries, in tall clumps of trees. Crown has distinct peak above eye. Bare skin around base of bill main distinguishing feature; absent in juvenile. Similar to Carrion Crow, but slimmer and more angular, especially in flight. Feeds mostly on arable land, taking more pests than crops.
Status: widespread and common resident, but more numerous in east than west.
Similar Species: Carrion Crow (p.211) as above.

ROOK	
Type	crow-like
Size	44–47cm (17–18½in)
Habitat	hedges, fields, woods, heaths
Behaviour	perches openly, hops, walks, takes off from vegetation or ground
Flocking	1–200
Flight	laboured; direct
Voice	cawing *kaah*

IDENTIFICATION

Adult	
Crown	black
Upperparts	black
Rump	black
Tail	black; medium length, square
Throat	black
Breast	black
Belly	black
Bill	grey; short and thin
Legs	black; medium length
Juvenile	lacks bare face patch

BREEDING

Nest	cup of twigs high in tree; colonial
Eggs	3–5; pale blue-green, blotched brown
Incubation	16–20 days ♀
Young	helpless; downy
Fledging	29–30 days
Broods	1; Mar–Apr
Food	worms, insects, seeds
Population	1,500,000 pairs

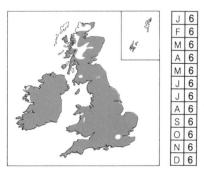

J	6
F	6
M	6
A	6
M	6
J	6
J	6
A	6
S	6
O	6
N	6
D	6

Corvus corone **Carrion Crow**

grey body, black wings

heavy bill

Hooded Crow

Carrion Crow

Large, familiar, all-black bird with heavy bill and aggressive habits. More strongly built than Rook and usually found in pairs, though larger numbers may roost together in winter and gather at rich food sources, such as rubbish tips. Generally a scavenger. In northern and western Scotland and in Ireland, replaced by sub-species *C.c.cornix* (Hooded Crow), which has grey back, belly and rump.
Status: widespread in Britain and Ireland.
Similar Species: Rook (p.211) and Raven (p.212).

CARRION CROW	
Type	crow-like
Size	45–49cm (18–19in)
Habitat	towns, heaths, estuaries, woods, hedges
Behaviour	perches openly, hops, walks, takes off from vegetation or ground
Flocking	1–10
Flight	laboured; direct
Voice	loud *kraa-kraa*

IDENTIFICATION

Ad.*C.c.corone*	
Crown	black
Upperparts	black
Rump	black
Tail	black; medium length, square
Throat	black
Breast	black
Belly	black
Bill	black; short and heavy
Legs	black; medium length
Ad.*C.c.cornix*	grey back, belly and rump

BREEDING

Nest	cup near top of tree
Eggs	4–6; greenish blue, speckled brown
Incubation	18–20 days ♀
Young	helpless; downy
Fledging	4–5 weeks
Broods	1; Mar–May
Food	carrion, birds, eggs, insects, worms, grain
Population	1,000,000 pairs

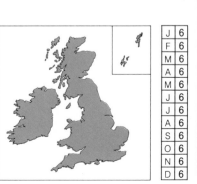

J	6
F	6
M	6
A	6
M	6
J	6
J	6
A	6
S	6
O	6
N	6
D	6

Raven _Corvus corax_

thick, heavy bill

beard

wedge-shaped tail

Largest crow, similar to Carrion Crow, but considerably bigger with more powerful head and bill, shaggy beard and large wedge-shaped tail. Found in mountainous and hilly areas, and along cliff-lined coasts; frequently soars like bird of prey. Mainly a scavenger, but also kills small birds and mammals.
Status: widespread in hilly districts of north and west.
Similar Species: Carrion Crow (p.211) smaller with less massive head and bill.

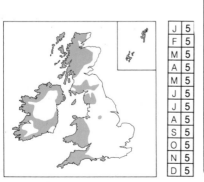

	RAVEN
Type	crow-like
Size	60–67cm (23½–26½in)
Habitat	moors, heaths, sea cliffs
Behaviour	hops, walks, perches openly, takes off from vegetation or ground
Flocking	1–15
Flight	soars, glides; laboured; direct
Voice	hollow _pruk-pruk_

IDENTIFICATION

Adult	
Crown	black
Upperparts	black
Rump	black
Tail	black; long and wedge-shaped
Throat	black, shaggy beard
Breast	black
Belly	black
Bill	black; short and heavy
Legs	black; medium length

BREEDING

Nest	large cup on ledge or fork in tree
Eggs	4–6; pale greenish blue, spotted brown
Incubation	20–21 days ♀
Young	helpless; downy
Fledging	5–6 weeks
Broods	1; Feb–Mar
Food	carrion, birds, mammals, eggs, snails, grain
Population	5000 pairs

J	5
F	5
M	5
A	5
M	5
J	5
J	5
A	5
S	5
O	5
N	5
D	5

Jay _Garrulus glandarius_

streaked crown

brownish-pink

black moustache

Large woodland bird with distinctive plumage, rounded wings and long tail. Crown streaked black and white; black moustachial streak. Back buff-brown; underparts pinkish buff. Wings and tail black; in flight shows bold white rump and white patches on inner wing. Small but distinctive blue and white barred patch on primary coverts. Generally secretive; presence often detected by harsh cries. Gregarious only in early spring.
Status: widespread resident of wooded areas, except northern Scotland.
Similar Species: none.

	JAY
Type	crow-like
Size	33–36cm (13–14in)
Habitat	forests, hedges, heaths, gardens
Behaviour	perches openly, hops, flits, takes off from vegetation or ground
Flocking	1–10
Flight	laboured; direct
Voice	harsh _kaaa_

IDENTIFICATION

Adult	
Crown	black and white, streaked
Upperparts	buff-brown, black wings
Rump	white
Tail	black; medium length, square
Throat	white
Breast	pinkish buff
Belly	pinkish buff
Bill	black; short and thin
Legs	buff; medium length

BREEDING

Nest	cup in tree fork
Eggs	5–7; pale green, speckled buff
Incubation	16–17 days ♂ ♀
Young	helpless; naked
Fledging	19–20 days
Broods	1; Apr–May
Food	nuts, nestlings, worms, insects
Population	100,000 pairs

J	5
F	5
M	5
A	5
M	5
J	5
J	5
A	5
S	5
O	5
N	5
D	5

yellow

glossy black

summer

heavily speckled breast

winter

grey brown

juvenile

STARLING	
Type	unique
Size	20.5–22.5cm (8–9in)
Habitat	gardens, marshes, moors, sea cliffs, estuaries, woods, hedges
Behaviour	flits, perches openly, walks, takes off from vegetation or ground
Flocking	1–100,000
Flight	glides; strong and powerful; direct
Voice	variety of wheezing calls; much mimicry

IDENTIFICATION	
Ad.summer	
Crown	black
Upperparts	black, wings tipped brown
Rump	black
Tail	black; short and square
Throat	black
Breast	black
Belly	black
Bill	yellow; short and thin
Legs	red; medium length
Ad.winter	head and underparts spotted white
Juvenile	grey-buff with white chin

BREEDING	
Nest	untidy; in hole in tree, cliff, building, nest box
Eggs	5–7; pale blue
Incubation	12–15 days ♂ ♀
Young	helpless; downy
Fledging	20–22 days
Broods	1–2; Apr–May
Food	insects, seeds, fruit
Population	4,000,000–7,000,000 pairs

This is a noisy and aggressive bird that walks with a waddling swagger. It is a highly successful and abundant species that is gregarious outside the breeding season, forming huge flocks, particularly at favoured roosts. The upperparts are glossy black with brown margins to the wing feathers. The head, back and underparts are glossy black in summer, and spotted with white in winter. The bill is yellow and the legs reddish-brown. Juveniles are grey-buff with a whitish chin patch and black bill and legs. The angled, pointed wings and the short tail create a characteristic flight silhouette.
Status: an abundant and widespread resident, as well as a winter visitor.

Similar Species:
Rose-coloured Starling *Sturnus roseus* 20.5–22.5cm (8–9in)
The Rosy Starling breeds in the southern Soviet Union and migrates westwards in huge numbers from time to time. The adult is pale pink with black head, wings and tail. The legs are pinkish, the bill shorter and more thrush-like than a common Starling's and a yellowish-horn colour. There is little chance of anyone mistaking the identity of

this bird in adult plumage. The juvenile is sandy-buff above and paler below, with some fine streaking on the breast. A pale eyebrow extends around the darker ear coverts and the wings and tail are brown with paler edges to the feathers.
Range: breeds from Russia to central Siberia and southwards to Iran.
Migration: winters in India, but occasionally erupts westward and may then breed in the countries of eastern Europe.
British Distribution: a rare vagrant, mainly from June to September, that may occur almost anywhere and usually does so in Shetland.

Rose-coloured Starling

pale eyebrow

short bill

juvenile

J	F	M	A	M	J	J	A	S	O	N	D
6	6	6	6	6	6	6	6	6	6	6	6

SPARROWS, FINCHES AND BUNTINGS

This is a relatively similar group of small seed-eating birds that have adapted in their different ways to exploit all of the major seed-producing plants in Britain and Ireland. They are generally gregarious, forming single-species or mixed flocks that roam the countryside, feeding in their different ways. They differ mainly in the shape of the bill, for while all are specialized for seed-eating, the seeds themselves differ enormously. Goldfinches (*illustrated*), for example, have tweezer-like bills for picking the delicate seeds from thistles, while the Hawfinches have powerful 'nutcrackers', able to deal with hard cherry stones. Siskins can extract the seeds of alder trees with their quite delicate bills, whereas Crossbills have a 'prising' bill that is exquisitely geared to opening strong pine cones and removing the seeds.

Being a specialist, each species depends on the availability of its particular food plant; eliminate the food and you eliminate the species. Yet intensive studies of individual species, largely at the request of the farming community, have shown that depredations such as those of the Bullfinch on the buds of fruit trees are more complex than at first appears. Bullfinches normally feed on the seeds of ash trees, and it is only when these fail or run out in the late winter that they turn their attention to fruit buds. Thus the better the ash crop, the less the damage to fruit trees. Orchard owners should plant more ash.

Chaffinches and Bramblings are both largely dependent on the crop of beechmast (beech fruit) in our woods and spend the winter turning over the leaf litter to get at their food. Competition between the two is eliminated by the Bramblings leaving each spring to breed further north. Similarly, Twites and Linnets often form huge mixed flocks around our estuaries and on our coastal marshes, but here too the Twites avoid competition by moving to higher altitudes and latitudes.

Perhaps the most successful member of the group is the House Sparrow, which is not a finch at all, but a member of the same family as the African weaver birds.

Its ability to live alongside humans and to take advantage of almost every change in the environment is quite remarkable. Yet it seems quite likely that its numbers have actually declined in our cities during the present century. The change from horse-drawn transport, with its attendant grain spills, to the motor-car must have reduced the urban food supply of Sparrows quite dramatically. Yet they remain the chirpy inhabitants of every part of the country occupied by man.

House Sparrow *Passer domesticus*

grey crown

pale eyebrow

large bib

♂

♀

Tree Sparrow *Passer montanus*

brown crown

white half collar

small neat bib

Most familiar of British birds, found everywhere permanently inhabited by people. Male streaked brown and black above, with chocolate nape and grey crown; black bib widens out across breast. Female buffy and brown with streaked back, prominent pale eyebrow and double wingbar; lacks bib. Usually gregarious; forms huge post-harvest flocks in late summer. Nests in holes in houses, but also in bushes when these not available.
Status: widespread resident.
Similar Species: Tree Sparrow (p.216).

HOUSE SPARROW	
Type	sparrow-like
Size	14–15.5cm (5½–6in)
Habitat	gardens, marshes, heaths, sea cliffs, estuaries, woods, hedges
Behaviour	flits, perches openly, hops, takes off from vegetation or ground
Flocking	1–500
Flight	direct
Voice	*chirrup*; various twitters

IDENTIFICATION

Adult ♂	
Crown	grey
Upperparts	brown and black, streaked
Rump	grey
Tail	brown and black; medium length, notched
Throat	black bib
Breast	black and white
Belly	white
Bill	brown; short and stubby
Legs	pinkish; medium length
Ad.♀ and juv.	buff and brown above; lack bib

BREEDING

Nest	dome in hole in building, sometimes tree; colonial
Eggs	3–5; grey, blotched dark grey
Incubation	11–14 days, mainly ♀
Young	helpless; naked
Fledging	15 days
Broods	3; Apr–June
Food	seeds, insects, bread
Population	3,500,000–7,000,000 pairs

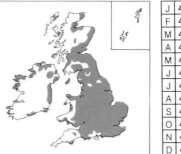

J	6
F	6
M	6
A	6
M	6
J	6
J	6
A	6
S	6
O	6
N	6
D	6

Both sexes resemble male House Sparrow, but slightly smaller with upperparts more clearly streaked black and brown. Crown chocolate-brown; tiny black bib; black comma on white cheeks. White half-collar visible at considerable distance – best field mark. Underparts white. Prefers parkland and gardens, but often associates with flocks of House Sparrows. Colonial nester, often in boxes erected for tits.
Status: widespread resident, but curiously absent from some western areas.
Similar Species: House Sparrow (p.216).

TREE SPARROW	
Type	sparrow-like
Size	13.5–14.5cm (5½–6in)
Habitat	gardens, heaths, woods, fields and hedges
Behaviour	flits, perches openly, hops, takes off from vegetation or ground
Flocking	1–15
Flight	direct
Voice	distinct *chup-chup*; also *tek-tek*

IDENTIFICATION

Adult	
Crown	chocolate-brown
Upperparts	brown and black, streaked
Rump	buff
Tail	brown; medium length, notched
Throat	black bib
Breast	white
Belly	white
Bill	black; short and stubby
Legs	red; medium length

BREEDING

Nest	dome in tree hole, among rocks or against walls
Eggs	4–6; pale grey, spotted brown
Incubation	11–14 days ♂ ♀
Young	helpless; naked
Fledging	12–14 days
Broods	2–3; Apr–June
Food	seeds, insects
Population	250,000 pairs

J	4
F	4
M	4
A	4
M	4
J	4
J	4
A	4
S	4
O	4
N	4
D	4

Fringilla coelebs **Chaffinch**

blue-grey crown

buffy crown

creamy breast

pinkish breast

broad wingbar

♂

♀

Most common finch, found in wide variety of habitats. Often seen beside roads, where may fly up showing white outer tail feathers and bold, white, double wingbar (in both sexes). Male has blue-grey crown and pinkish breast. Female duller, in shades of buff. Forms large winter flocks.
Status: numerous and widespread resident; winter visitor.
Similar Species: female similar to female House Sparrow (p.216) but Chaffinch distinguished by bold, white, double wingbar.

CHAFFINCH

Type	finch-like
Size	14.5–16cm (5½–6½in)
Habitat	gardens, heaths, woods, fields and hedges
Behaviour	flits, hops, perches openly, takes off from vegetation or ground
Flocking	1–200
Flight	undulating
Voice	loud *pink-pink*; delicate song ending in flourish

IDENTIFICATION

Adult ♂	
Crown	blue-grey
Upperparts	brown, wings black and white
Rump	buff
Tail	black and white; medium length, notched
Throat	pinkish
Breast	pinkish
Belly	pinkish
Bill	blue-grey; short and stubby
Legs	brown; medium length
Adult ♀	buff-brown above; buffy cream below

BREEDING

Nest	neat cup in low vegetation
Eggs	4–5; pale blue, scrawled red
Incubation	11–13 days ♀
Young	helpless; downy
Fledging	12–15 days
Broods	1–2; Apr–May
Food	seeds, fruit
Population	7,000,000 pairs

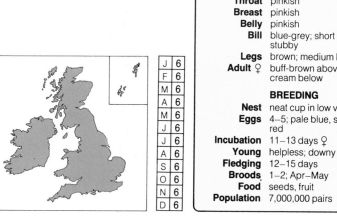

J	6
F	6
M	6
A	6
M	6
J	6
J	6
A	6
S	6
O	6
N	6
D	6

Fringilla montifringilla **Brambling**

black head and back with scaling

black crown and back

scaled black on buff

♂ summer

bright orange breast

♂ winter

♀

Similar and closely related to Chaffinch, often associating in winter flocks, where may be overlooked. Winter male has blackish upperparts, liberally edged buff on crown and back. Tail black; shows square white rump in flight. Breast bright orange; belly white. Buff margins lost in summer; head and back become pure black with broad orange band below. Female more heavily edged buff at all seasons.
Status: regular and numerous winter visitor, although more abundant in east; 2–10 pairs breed in north.
Similar Species: Chaffinch (p.217).

BRAMBLING

Type	finch-like
Size	14–15cm (5½–6in)
Habitat	heaths, woods, fields and hedges
Behaviour	flits, hops, takes off and lands on vegetation or ground
Flocking	1–100
Flight	undulating
Voice	hard *tswick* and *chik*

IDENTIFICATION

Ad. ♂ winter	
Crown	black and buff
Upperparts	black and buff
Rump	white
Tail	black; medium length, notched
Throat	orange
Breast	orange
Belly	white
Bill	yellow; short and stubby
Legs	red; medium length
Ad. ♂ summer	cap black; back bordered orange
Adult ♀	paler than winter ♂

BREEDING

Nest	cup in pine tree, near trunk
Eggs	5–7; pale blue, blotched red
Incubation	11–12 days ♀
Young	helpless; downy
Fledging	11–13 days
Broods	1; May–June
Food	seeds, berries
Population	2–10 pairs breed; common winter visitor

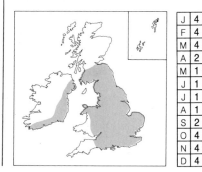

J	4
F	4
M	4
A	2
M	1
J	1
J	1
A	1
S	2
O	4
N	4
D	4

Serin *Serinus serinus*

streaked, often little yellow

yellow rump

bright yellow breast

♂   ♀

Tiny yellow finch with bright tinkling song; pure yellow rump a bold field mark. Male has yellow head, back and breast, marked with variable amount of brown streaking. Wings dark with yellowish edges. Less yellow on female, but heavier streaking, particularly on breast. Short stubby bill creates large, round-headed appearance.
Status: rare vagrant, gradually becoming more regular; beginning to breed (1–7 pairs).
Similar Species: Siskin (p.219).

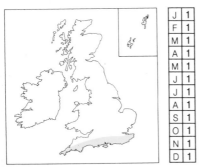

	SERIN
Type	finch-like
Size	11–12cm (4½–5in)
Habitat	gardens, heaths, woods, hedges
Behaviour	flits, perches openly, takes off and lands on vegetation
Flocking	1–2
Flight	undulating
Voice	twittering jangle of notes

IDENTIFICATION

Adult ♂	
Crown	yellow
Upperparts	yellow, streaked brown, wings black
Rump	yellow
Tail	black; medium length, notched
Throat	yellow
Breast	yellow, streaked brown
Belly	white
Bill	buff; short and stubby
Legs	brown; medium length
Adult ♀	less yellow; heavier streaking

BREEDING

Nest	neat cup in bush or tree
Eggs	4; pale blue, spotted brown
Incubation	13 days ♀
Young	helpless; downy
Fledging	14 days
Broods	1–2; Apr–May
Food	seeds
Population	1–7 pairs

J	1
F	1
M	1
A	1
M	1
J	1
J	1
A	1
S	1
O	1
N	1
D	1

Greenfinch *Carduelis chloris*

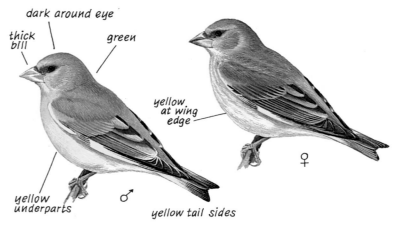

dark around eye

thick bill

green

yellow at wing edge

yellow underparts   ♂   yellow tail sides   ♀

Chunky, thick-set finch with substantial white bill. Male green above, with bold yellow margin to folded grey wing; yellowish below. Female paler and browner. In flight, shows yellow at base of primaries and incomplete yellow edges to tail. Largest and most common of green-yellow finches; found in range of habitats, but most at home in parkland and gardens.
Status: widespread and numerous resident of Britain and Ireland.
Similar Species: female similar to female House Sparrow (p.216) but Greenfinch has narrow yellow edge to folded wing.

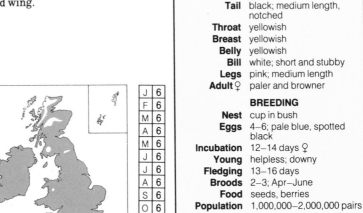

	GREENFINCH
Type	finch-like
Size	14–15cm (5½–6in)
Habitat	gardens, marshes, heaths, woods, hedges
Behaviour	flits, perches openly, hops, takes off from vegetation or ground
Flocking	1–100
Flight	undulating
Voice	nasal *skeer*, *chup-chup* flight call

IDENTIFICATION

Adult ♂	
Crown	green
Upperparts	green; grey wings yellow-edged
Rump	green
Tail	black; medium length, notched
Throat	yellowish
Breast	yellowish
Belly	yellowish
Bill	white; short and stubby
Legs	pink; medium length
Adult ♀	paler and browner

BREEDING

Nest	cup in bush
Eggs	4–6; pale blue, spotted black
Incubation	12–14 days ♀
Young	helpless; downy
Fledging	13–16 days
Broods	2–3; Apr–June
Food	seeds, berries
Population	1,000,000–2,000,000 pairs

J	6
F	6
M	6
A	6
M	6
J	6
J	6
A	6
S	6
O	6
N	6
D	6

Carduelis carduelis Goldfinch

crimson face

lacks face pattern

juvenile

yellow wingbar

white rump

bright yellow in black wing

adult

Attractive, easily identified finch with distinctive face pattern of crimson, white and black. Back warm brown; wings black with broad yellow band apparent both at rest and in flight. Shows bold white rump in flight. Feeds on teazles; prefers gardens and overgrown areas. Mostly gregarious. *Status:* widespread resident except in north.
Similar Species: none.

GOLDFINCH

Type	finch-like
Size	11.5–12.5cm (4¾in)
Habitat	gardens, heaths, woods, fields and hedges
Behaviour	flits, perches openly, hops, takes off from vegetation or ground
Flocking	1–100
Flight	undulating
Voice	sweet tinkling

IDENTIFICATION

Adult	
Crown	crimson, black and white
Upperparts	brown; wings black, yellow bars
Rump	white
Tail	black; medium length, notched
Throat	crimson
Breast	buff
Belly	white
Bill	white; short and stubby
Legs	buff; medium length
Juvenile	lacks head pattern; more buffy

BREEDING

Nest	cup in bush
Eggs	4–7; blue, spotted blackish
Incubation	12–14 days ♀
Young	helpless; downy
Fledging	13–16 days
Broods	2; Apr–May
Food	seeds
Population	300,000 pairs

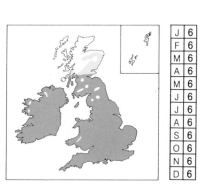

J	6
F	6
M	6
A	6
M	6
J	6
J	6
A	6
S	6
O	6
N	6
D	6

Carduelis spinus Siskin

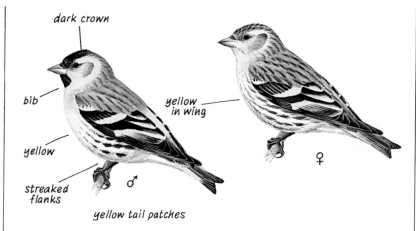

dark crown

bib

yellow

streaked flanks

♂

yellow in wing

♀

yellow tail patches

Small woodland finch found mostly near damp areas; has particular liking for alder. Male greenish above, yellowish below with streaked flanks. Crown black, forming distinct cap; small black bib. Wings black with bold yellow wingbars; yellow rump. Female much duller with yellow only in wings and tail; upperparts grey-green, underparts buffy with streaking above and below. Agile feeder, hanging upside down, tit-like, to extract seeds; comes to red-peanut feeding nets in late winter. Gregarious in winter.
Status: winter visitor; breeds in many parts of Britain and Ireland, especially north and west.
Similar Species: Serin, Greenfinch and Redpoll (pp.218, 218, 221).

SISKIN

Type	finch-like
Size	11.5–12.5cm (4¾in)
Habitat	woods, hedges, heaths, gardens
Behaviour	flits, perches openly, takes off and lands on vegetation
Flocking	1–50
Flight	undulating
Voice	*tsu*, *tsu-weet*; various twitterings

IDENTIFICATION

Adult ♂	
Crown	black cap
Upperparts	green; black wings, yellow wingbars
Rump	yellow
Tail	black and yellow; medium length, notched
Throat	black bib
Breast	yellow
Belly	white
Bill	white; short and stubby
Legs	brown; medium length
Adult ♀	greyish green above; buffy and streaked below

BREEDING

Nest	cup high in conifer
Eggs	3–5; pale blue, speckled reddish
Incubation	11–14 days ♀
Young	helpless; downy
Fledging	13–15 days
Broods	2; Apr–May
Food	seeds
Population	20,000–40,000 pairs

J	3
F	3
M	3
A	3
M	2
J	2
J	2
A	2
S	3
O	3
N	3
D	3

Linnet *Carduelis cannabina*

red forehead

white wing flashes

white in tail

brown back

red breast

♂ summer

♀

Small finch abundant in open areas, especially coastal marshes and shingle in winter. Summer male distinguished by red forehead and breast; grey head, brown back. Female lacks red; streaked above and below. Male loses red in winter. Both sexes show white in tail and wings in flight. Gregarious, often forming huge flocks, sometimes with smaller numbers of Twite.
Status: widespread and numerous resident.
Similar Species: Twite (p.220) very similar to female Linnet but much more heavily streaked.

LINNET	
Type	finch-like
Size	13–14cm (5–5½in)
Habitat	heaths, estuaries, woods, hedges, gardens
Behaviour	flits, perches openly, hops, takes off from vegetation or ground
Flocking	1–500
Flight	undulating
Voice	high-pitched twittering in flight

IDENTIFICATION

Ad.♂summer	
Crown	red
Upperparts	brown
Rump	buff
Tail	black and white; medium length, notched
Throat	buff
Breast	red
Belly	buff
Bill	grey; short and stubby
Legs	grey; medium length
Ad.♂winter	lacks red
Adult ♀	lacks red; streaked above and below

BREEDING

Nest	cup in bush
Eggs	4–6; pale blue, speckled reddish
Incubation	10–14 days ♀
Young	helpless; downy
Fledging	14–17 days
Broods	2–3; Apr–June
Food	seeds
Population	800,000–1,600,000 pairs

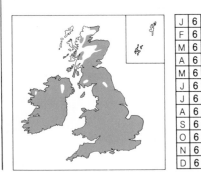

J	6
F	6
M	6
A	6
M	6
J	6
J	6
A	6
S	6
O	6
N	6
D	6

Twite *Carduelis flavirostris*

yellow bill

distinctly streaked

buffy throat

pink rump

streaked black on buff

♂ summer

♂ winter

Northern, upland equivalent of Linnet. Regularly winters along coasts, often in association with large flocks of Linnets; shows similar markings in flight. In all seasons and plumages, Twite warm, buffy brown bird, heavily streaked black above and below. Linnet never as heavily streaked, even in juvenile plumage. Twite has pink rump but difficult to see. Juvenile and winter birds have yellow, not grey, bills.
Status: resident in northern and hilly areas; winter visitor to coast, except in south-west.
Similar Species: Linnet (p.220) as above.

TWITE	
Type	finch-like
Size	13–14cm (5–5½in)
Habitat	moors, estuaries, woods, fields, gardens
Behaviour	hops, perches openly, takes off and lands on ground
Flocking	1–500
Flight	undulating
Voice	similar to Linnet, but harder

IDENTIFICATION

Ad.summer	
Crown	brown, streaked black
Upperparts	brown, streaked black
Rump	pink
Tail	black; medium length, notched
Throat	buff
Breast	buff, streaked black
Belly	white
Bill	grey; short and stubby
Legs	black; medium length
Ad.winter and juvenile	bill yellow

BREEDING

Nest	cup on ground
Eggs	5–6; pale blue, speckled reddish
Incubation	12–13 days ♀
Young	helpless; downy
Fledging	15 days
Broods	1–2; Apr–May
Food	seeds
Population	20,000–40,000 pairs

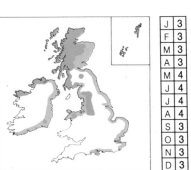

J	3
F	3
M	3
A	3
M	4
J	4
J	4
A	4
S	3
O	3
N	3
D	3

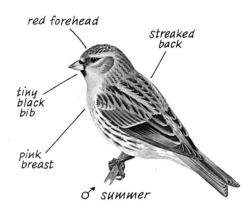

red forehead

streaked back

tiny black bib

pink breast

♂ summer

♀

	REDPOLL	
Type	finch-like	
Size	11.5–13cm (4½–5in)	
Habitat	heaths, woods, hedges, gardens	
Behaviour	flits, perches openly, takes off and lands on vegetation	
Flocking	1–50	
Flight	undulating	
Voice	buzzing nasal trill in flight	

IDENTIFICATION

Adult	
Crown	red
Upperparts	buff, streaked brown
Rump	buff, streaked brown
Tail	black; medium length, notched
Throat	black bib
Breast	pink, streaked buff
Belly	white
Bill	buff; short and stubby
Legs	black; medium length
Ad.♂summer	loses streaking below, apart from on flanks

BREEDING

Nest	cup in tree
Eggs	4–5; pale blue, speckled reddish
Incubation	10–13 days ♀
Young	helpless; downy
Fledging	11–14 days
Broods	1–2; Apr–June
Food	seeds
Population	300,000+ pairs

J	F	M	A	M	J	J	A	S	O	N	D
4	4	4	4	4	4	4	4	4	4	4	4

The Redpoll is a small, streaked finch that is almost totally restricted to trees and which hangs acrobatically, like a tit, from twigs when feeding. As its name suggests, it had a red forehead, as well as a neat black bib. The upperparts are heavily streaked black on brown; the underparts are white, streaked with blackish-brown on the flanks. In summer, the male has a pale pink wash over the breast. Like the other *Carduelis* finches, Redpolls have distinctly notched tails. They are similar to Linnets in size and shape. The northern sub-species, *C. f. flammea*, known as the Mealy Redpoll, is larger, greyer and paler above, with whiter wing bars and rump. It is a winter visitor from northern Europe. Redpolls are found mainly among birches, alders and conifers and are easily identified by their buzzing calls.
Status: a widespread resident and winter visitor.

Similar Species:
Arctic Redpoll *Carduelis hornemanni*
12–13.5cm (4½–5½in)
This bird replaces the Redpoll in the high Arctic and is generally similar in appearance. Some ornithologists consider the two as belonging to the same species,

especially as the Mealy race of the Redpoll shows characters intermediate between the two. The Arctic Redpoll is much paler than the Redpoll, but with a similar red forehead and black bib. The head and nape are almost greyish-white, the underparts are virtually devoid of streaking, there are two white bars on the wing, and the rump is white.
Range: breeds in high Arctic Scandinavia, Siberia, Greenland and Canada.
Migration: moves southward only to avoid the harshest conditions.
British Distribution: an autumn and winter vagrant to the east coast, indicating a Eurasian rather than New World origin.
Other Similar Species: Siskin (p. 219).

Arctic Redpoll

pale head

white rump

adult ♂

Crossbill *Loxia curvirostra*

	CROSSBILL
Type	finch-like
Size	16–17cm (6–6½in)
Habitat	forests
Behaviour	flits, perches openly, takes off and lands on vegetation
Flocking	1–15
Flight	undulating
Voice	distinctive *jip-jip*

	IDENTIFICATION
Adult ♂	
Crown	reddish
Upperparts	brown
Rump	reddish
Tail	black; medium length, notched
Throat	reddish
Breast	reddish
Belly	reddish
Bill	grey; short and stubby
Legs	black; medium length
Adult ♀	grey-green, lightly streaked

	BREEDING
Nest	twiggy cup high in conifer
Eggs	3–4; pale blue, spotted purple
Incubation	13–16 days ♀
Young	helpless; downy
Fledging	17–22 days
Broods	1; Jan–Apr
Food	pine seeds
Population	1000–4000 pairs

J	F	M	A	M	J	J	A	S	O	N	D
2	2	2	2	2	2	2	2	2	3	3	2

chunky crossed bill

♂

♀

This is a chunky, thick-set finch with a large head and a substantial bill. Its name derives from the bill's distinctively crossed mandibles, which are visible at close range. The male is a dirty reddish on the crown, back, rump and underparts, with dark brown wings and tail. The female is grey-green, with light streaking above and below. When seen in flight, its chunky shape, with a large head and short tail, is a useful identification feature. Crossbills are generally gregarious birds that regularly erupt from the Continent and which, as a result, now breed in many parts of the country where new plantations mature to provide food. They are confined to mature conifers, where they feed by extracting pine seeds from the cones with their bills.
Status: a widespread but localized resident, irregular autumn and winter visitor.

Similar Species:
Two-barred Crossbill *Loxia leucoptera*
14–15cm (5½–6in)
Of all the crossbills, this is by far the most distinctive, the others differing almost entirely in the size and shape of the bill and head. The Two-barred Crossbill is, as its name implies, marked by a bold, double white wingbar and white tips to the inner secondaries. The male is a paler, pinker bird than the Crossbill, with a thinner, less bulky bill. The female is more yellowish-green than the Crossbill, particularly on the rump; the streaking of the upperparts produces a more contrasting effect.
Range: breeds right across Eurasia and North America in the conifer zone.
Migration: largely resident, but does erupt, usually in the company of Crossbills.
British Distribution: a rare autumn and winter visitor during Crossbill irruption years.
Other Similar Species: Scottish Crossbill.

Two-barred Crossbill

pinkish red
♂
double white wing-bar
streaked flanks
streaked
♀

larger crossed bill than
Crossbill

♂

♀

This is the only bird species to breed solely in Britain, having been separated from the common Crossbill in the 1970s on the basis of its larger bill. Otherwise, it is identical to the more widespread bird. Scottish Crossbills live in the old Caledonian forests of Scots Pine in the Highlands and are similarly coloured reddish in the male and yellowish-green in the female. They are gregarious birds that breed in the late winter. There is no evidence of movement from their range, and any birder would be hard put to justify a claimed identification away from the Highlands. Conversely, it is difficult to prove a sighting of common Crossbills in northern Scotland, although they do occur in this area.
Status: resident in Scots Pine forests of Scottish Highlands.

Similar Species:
Parrot Crossbill *Loxia pytyopsittacus*
16.5–17.5cm (6½–6¾in)
Though slightly larger than both common and Scottish Crossbills, this bird differs mainly in the size of its bill and head. These are disproportionately large, giving the bird a decidedly top-heavy appearance. The lower mandible of the bill, in particular, is

very bulbous and the head is flattened and elongated. In other respects the plumage is very similar to that of the other crossbills. It prefers pines to other conifers.
Range: confined to Scandinavia and adjacent areas of Russia.
Migration: mainly resident, but erupts with common Crossbills.
British Distribution: a rare autumn and winter vagrant to the east coast that has bred in East Anglia in recent years.
Other Similar Species: Crossbill (p. 222).

Parrot Crossbill

very stout bill
large head

♂   ♀

	SCOTTISH CROSSBILL
Type	finch-like
Size	16–17cm (6–6½in)
Habitat	forests
Behaviour	flits, perches openly, takes off and lands on vegetation
Flocking	1–15
Flight	undulating
Voice	distinctive *jip-jip*, as Crossbill

	IDENTIFICATION
Adult ♂	
Crown	reddish
Upperparts	brown
Rump	reddish
Tail	black; medium length, notched
Throat	reddish
Breast	reddish
Belly	reddish
Bill	grey; short and stubby
Legs	black; medium length
Adult ♀	grey-green, lightly streaked

	BREEDING
Nest	twiggy cup high in conifer
Eggs	3–4; pale blue, spotted purple
Incubation	13–16 days ♀
Young	helpless; downy
Fledging	17–22 days
Broods	1; Jan–Apr
Food	pine seeds
Population	c1000 pairs

J	F	M	A	M	J	J	A	S	O	N	D
2	2	2	2	2	2	2	2	2	2	2	2

Bullfinch *Pyrrhula pyrrhula*

short stubby bill / black cap / white rump / bright pink / ♂ / ♀ / juvenile

The Bullfinch is a portly, bull-necked finch of gardens and hedgerows that is mostly seen singly or in pairs. The male has a black crown, a thick, black conical bill and a bright pink breast. The upperparts are a pale dove-grey. The female is similar, but with a pale pinkish-buff breast and pinkish-grey back. Both sexes have black wings marked by a bold white wingbar, and a black tail with a white rump patch. The latter, which is square-cut, is a sure means of identification as the birds flit along a hedgerow.

Status: a widespread resident that is absent only from the extreme west and north-west.

Similar Species:
Scarlet Rosefinch *Carpodacus erythrinus*
14–15cm (5½–6in)
Though about the same size as a Bullfinch and, in many parts of its range, also an inhabitant of hedgerows and even gardens, the Scarlet Rosefinch bears more of a similarity to a crossbill than a Bullfinch. The male is pinkish on the head, back, breast and rump. The belly is white, the wings and tail brown. There is a pinkish wingbar. Females and first year birds are dull grey-brown above and whitish below,

streaked with brown on the breast. The pale conical bill and the black eye are the best field marks on what is otherwise a rather sparrow-like bird.
Range: breeds right across Eurasia, from the Baltic to China and the Bering Straits.
Migration: moves southwards to winter in India and South-east Asia.
British Distribution: a rare vagrant, mainly in autumn, predominantly to Fair Isle (*see page* 264) and the east coast. It is, however, annual in both spring (late May–early June) and autumn (late August–early October).
Other Similar Species: crossbills (pp. 222–3).

Scarlet Rosefinch

silver bill / pink / silver bill / featureless face / ♀ / spring ♂

Coccothraustes coccothraustes **Hawfinch**

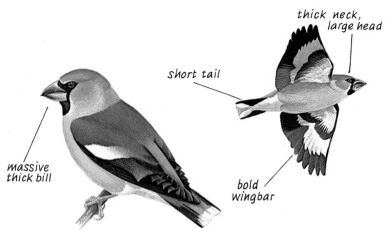

short tail

thick neck, large head

massive thick bill

bold wingbar

Stout finch with huge, thick, grey bill. Large head and bill, thick-set body and short tail obvious in flight; broad wingbars above and below diagnostic. Crown rufous, back brown, wings black, rump and underparts buff. Generally elusive and difficult to find; inhabits old woods and parks, often perching immobile for long periods. Forms communal roosts in winter. *Status:* widespread resident; absent northern Scotland and Ireland. *Similar Species:* none.

	HAWFINCH
Type	finch-like
Size	16–17cm (6–6½in)
Habitat	woods, gardens, parks
Behaviour	flits, perches openly, takes off and lands on vegetation
Flocking	1–15
Flight	strong and powerful; direct
Voice	Robin-like *zik* or *tic*

	IDENTIFICATION
Adult	
Crown	rufous
Upperparts	brown, wings black and white
Rump	buff
Tail	buff with white tip; short and notched
Throat	black bib
Breast	buff
Belly	buff
Bill	grey; short and stubby
Legs	red; medium length

	BREEDING
Nest	twiggy cup in tree
Eggs	5; pale blue, spotted blackish
Incubation	9–14 days ♀, occasionally ♂
Young	helpless; downy
Fledging	10–14 days
Broods	1; Apr–May
Food	seeds, nuts
Population	5000–10,000 pairs

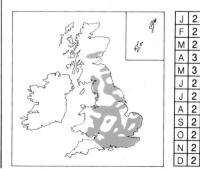

J	2
F	2
M	2
A	3
M	3
J	2
J	2
A	2
S	2
O	2
N	2
D	2

Plectrophenax nivalis **Snow Bunting**

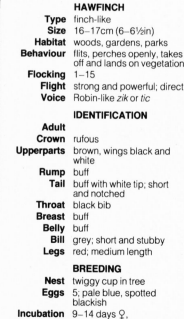

white in wing

buffy marks on head

white head

white in tail

♂ winter

♀ winter

♂ summer

Breeds on high mountain tops; winters along shorelines where forms large flocks. Flies like pieces of white paper blowing in wind. At all times shows much white in wing and tail. Summer male mainly white with black back; wings black and white. Female, juvenile and winter male have mottled upperparts and variable amounts of streaking or buff on head. Feeds on shingle and among dunes, keeping low on ground. *Status:* scarce breeder in Scottish mountains; regular but local visitor to east coast. *Similar Species:* none.

	SNOW BUNTING
Type	bunting-like
Size	16–17cm (6–6½in)
Habitat	moors, shorelines
Behaviour	hops, perches openly, takes off and lands on ground
Flocking	1–500
Flight	strong and powerful; direct; flitting
Voice	loud *tsweep*

	IDENTIFICATION
Ad.♂ summer	
Crown	white
Upperparts	black and white
Rump	white
Tail	black and white; medium length, notched
Throat	white
Breast	white
Belly	white
Bill	black; short and stubby
Legs	black; medium length
Ad.♂ winter, Ad.♀ and juv.	white below, mottled above; buffy head markings

	BREEDING
Nest	cup on ground in rocks
Eggs	4–6; pale blue, spotted reddish
Incubation	10–15 days ♀
Young	helpless; downy
Fledging	15–20 days
Broods	2; May–July
Food	seeds
Population	6–17 pairs; local winter visitor in some numbers

J	3
F	3
M	2
A	1
M	1
J	1
J	1
A	1
S	1
O	3
N	3
D	3

Lapland Bunting *Calcarius lapponicus*

	LAPLAND BUNTING
Type	bunting-like
Size	14–16cm (5½–6½in)
Habitat	marshes, estuaries, moors
Behaviour	hops, perches openly, takes off and lands on ground
Flocking	1–15
Flight	strong and powerful; direct
Voice	rolling *rrrrp*

	IDENTIFICATION
Ad.♀,♂ winter	
Crown	black and white with stripe
Upperparts	rusty and black, streaked
Rump	rusty and black, streaked
Tail	black and white; medium length, notched
Throat	white
Breast	streaked buff
Belly	white
Bill	yellow; short and stubby
Legs	black; medium length
Ad.♂ summer	black head with bold, creamy eyebrow

	BREEDING
Nest	cup on ground
Eggs	5–6; greenish, mottled reddish
Incubation	10–14 days mainly ♀
Young	helpless; downy
Fledging	11–15 days
Broods	1; May–June
Food	seeds
Population	has bred; scarce winter visitor

J	F	M	A	M	J	J	A	S	O	N	D
2	2	2	1	1	1	1	1	1	1	2	2

This is a scarce, ground-dwelling bunting that usually perches no higher than a large rock or similar object. It is virtually confined to the east coast. In summer plumage the male has a black head with a rich chestnut nape and a prominent creamy eyebrow extending behind the eye. The upperparts are brown, streaked with black and white, while the wings are more chestnut and the underparts pure white. The female, juvenile and winter male bear a strong resemblance to a female Reed Bunting. They differ in having a pale central stripe on the crown, more rusty on the wings and, in the case of the male, a chestnut nape.
Status: a scarce autumn and winter visitor to the east coast; a rare breeder in Scotland.

Similar Species:
Rustic Bunting *Emberiza rustica*
14–15cm (5½–6in)
The Rustic Bunting is marked in all plumages by raised crown feathers that form a characteristic crest. The male in summer has a black head with a bold white eyebrow behind the eye and a white chin. It also has a broad chestnut breast band that extends along the flanks to form a series of chestnut blotches. The upperparts are streaked brown and black. The female, first winter and winter male resemble other female buntings more closely, but have a whitish eyebrow behind the eye, dark brown or even black cheeks, a dark moustachial streak and often more than a hint of a chestnut breast band.
Range: breeds from Scandinavia right across Eurasia to the Bering Straits.
Migration: winters southwards in China.
British Distribution: a less-than-annual vagrant in May and in September and October, mainly to the east coast, but particularly to Fair Isle (*see page 264*) and Scilly (*see page 284*).
Other Similar Species: Reed Bunting, female (p. 229).

Rustic Bunting

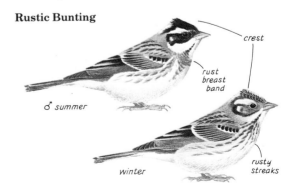

rusty back

rusty rump

very yellow head

♂

more yellow on head than Cirl ♀

♀

The Yellowhammer is a yellow bunting most often seen perched on a wire or the top of a bush, uttering its well known little song about a 'little bit of bread and no cheese'. The male has a bright yellow head and underparts and rusty-brown streaked wings. The female is similar, but with less yellow and generally darker head markings. Both sexes have a prominent rusty rump that is an excellent field mark as the bird flies. Though generally found singly or in pairs, Yellowhammers frequently form winter flocks at favoured feeding grounds.
Status: a widespread resident almost throughout the country.

Similar Species:
Ortolan Bunting *Emberiza hortulana*
15.5–16.5cm (6–6½in)
The summer male is grey-green on the head and breast with a yellowish throat and moustachial streak. The remaining upperparts are brown, streaked with black, save for a dull yellowish rump. The underparts are orange-buff. The female and winter male are similar, but duller coloured, with spotting on the breast. First winter birds are paler, less rufous above, with considerable streaking on the sides of the

head and breast. The pale chin and moustache are creamy-coloured. In all plumages the reddish bill and legs and a pale eye ring are useful field marks.
Range: breeds right across mainland Europe as far east as central Siberia.
Migration: moves southward to winter in Africa and the Middle East.
British Distribution: a regular, but scarce, double passage migrant with peaks in early May and from late August to the end of September. Fair Isle (*see page* 264) has a near monopoly of spring records.
Other Similar Species: Female Yellowhammer may be confused with rarer female Cirl Bunting (p. 228).

Ortolan Bunting

grey-green
pale yellow
pale eye ring
summer ♂
pinkish bill
juvenile
pink legs

YELLOWHAMMER

Type	bunting-like
Size	16–17cm (6–6½in)
Habitat	heaths, fields and hedges, gardens
Behaviour	hops, perches openly, takes off and lands on vegetation or ground
Flocking	1–50
Flight	direct
Voice	familiar 'little-bit-of-bread-and-no-cheese'

IDENTIFICATION

Adult ♂	
Crown	yellow
Upperparts	rust-brown and black
Rump	rusty
Tail	black and white; medium length, notched
Throat	yellow
Breast	yellow
Belly	yellow
Bill	grey; short and stubby
Legs	buff; medium length
Adult ♀	less yellow, darker head markings

BREEDING

Nest	cup in low bush
Eggs	3–5; white, blotched purplish
Incubation	11–14 days ♀
Young	helpless; downy
Fledging	16 days
Broods	2–3; Apr–June
Food	seeds, berries
Population	1,000,000 pairs

J	F	M	A	M	J	J	A	S	O	N	D
5	5	5	5	5	5	5	5	5	5	5	5

Cirl Bunting *Emberiza cirlus*

rusty back

black and pale yellow head

black chin

♂

♀

buffy rather than yellow

Male distinguished by bold head pattern of black and pale yellow; greenish breast band, pale yellow underparts and rusty, streaked back. Female rufous buff above, creamy buff below – heavily streaked. Decidedly local and declining resident; inhabits bushy slopes, old hedgerows, parks and gardens – often near sea.
Status: scarce resident in south-west England.
Similar Species: female confusable with female Yellowhammer (p.227), but Cirl never yellow and lacks rusty rump.

	CIRL BUNTING	
Type	bunting-like	
Size	15.5–16.5cm (6–6½in)	
Habitat	fields and hedges, heaths, parks, gardens	
Behaviour	perches openly, hops, takes off and lands on vegetation or ground	
Flocking	1–2	
Flight	direct	
Voice	*sip*, also a quick rattle	

IDENTIFICATION

Adult ♂		
Crown	black	
Upperparts	rust and black	
Rump	olive	
Tail	rust and black; medium length, notched	
Throat	black	
Breast	pale yellow; greenish band	
Belly	pale yellow	
Bill	buff; short and stubby	
Legs	buff; medium length	
Adult ♀	streaked rufous buff above, creamy buff below	

BREEDING

Nest	cup low among bushes	
Eggs	3–4; white, speckled black	
Incubation	11–13 days ♀	
Young	helpless; downy	
Fledging	11–13 days	
Broods	2–3; May–June	
Food	seeds, berries	
Population	40–167 pairs	

Month	Value
J	2
F	2
M	2
A	2
M	2
J	2
J	2
A	2
S	2
O	2
N	2
D	2

Corn Bunting *Miliaria calandra*

short, thick neck

stubby bill

both sexes streaked

pink legs

Chunky, thick-set bunting that appears almost neckless. Streaked buff and brown above and below; both sexes similar to other female buntings. No white in tail. Perches openly, usually near ground in fields and open bushy areas. Sings with head thrown back; legs trail in fluttering flight. Gregarious in winter.
Status: locally abundant resident; absent from many areas, especially in north and west.
Similar Species: all female buntings (pp.225–229), but Corn Bunting larger and plumper.

	CORN BUNTING	
Type	bunting-like	
Size	17–18.5cm (6½–7½in)	
Habitat	heaths, fields and hedges, gardens	
Behaviour	perches openly, hops, takes off and lands on vegetation or ground	
Flocking	1–2	
Flight	direct	
Voice	jingling rattle	

IDENTIFICATION

Adult		
Crown	streaked buff and brown	
Upperparts	streaked buff and brown	
Rump	buff	
Tail	brown; medium length, notched	
Throat	white	
Breast	streaked buff and brown	
Belly	streaked buff and brown	
Bill	buff; short and stubby	
Legs	pink; medium length	

BREEDING

Nest	cup on ground or in bush	
Eggs	4–6; white, spotted grey	
Incubation	12–14 days ♀	
Young	helpless; downy	
Fledging	12+ days	
Broods	1–2; Apr–May	
Food	seeds, berries	
Population	30,000 pairs	

Month	Value
J	4
F	4
M	4
A	4
M	4
J	4
J	4
A	4
S	4
O	4
N	4
D	4

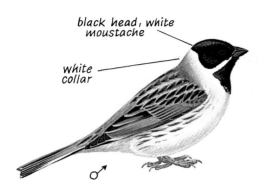

black head, white moustache

white collar

♂

streaked crown

♂ winter

♀

black moustache

REED BUNTING

Type	bunting-like
Size	14–16cm (5½–6½in)
Habitat	marshes, heaths, fields, gardens
Behaviour	flits, perches openly, takes off from vegetation or ground
Flocking	1–10
Flight	direct
Voice	several deliberate notes ending in a hurry

IDENTIFICATION

Adult ♂	
Crown	black
Upperparts	streaked brown and black; white collar
Rump	grey
Tail	black and white; medium length, notched
Throat	black
Breast	white
Belly	white
Bill	black; short and stubby
Legs	black; medium length
Adult ♀	heavily streaked brown and buff above, buffy below; eyebrow and moustache

BREEDING

Nest	cup on or near ground
Eggs	4–5; pale grey and black
Incubation	12–14 days, mainly ♀
Young	helpless; downy
Fledging	10–13 days
Broods	2–3; Apr–June
Food	seeds
Population	c 600,000 pairs

Though originally a typical marshland bird, the Reed Bunting has shown a remarkable spread to drier habitats, even including gardens, in recent years. The male has a black head marked by a white moustache and collar. The remaining upperparts are rufous, heavily streaked with black. The underparts are white with brown streaking along the flanks. The female is similar to other female buntings: heavily streaked buff and brown above and buffy below. A bold creamy eyebrow and a smudgy black moustache are useful distinguishing features. The winter male is similar to the female, but with a subdued version of the black head of summer. Both sexes show white outer tail feathers.
Status: a widespread and numerous resident.

Similar Species:
Little Bunting *Emberiza pusilla*
13–14cm (5–5½in)
This species looks like a small version of the female Reed Bunting. It is no larger than a Meadow Pipit, with a shorter tail than most buntings. The upperparts are brown rather than rufous, with bold clear-cut black streaking. The underparts are white, with

fine black streaks on the breast and flanks. It is, however, the head pattern that clinches identification, with a black lateral crown stripe and chestnut cheeks outlined with black. The bill is thinner and more pointed than that of most buntings and the legs are pink.
Range: breeds in Eurasia from Finland eastwards to the Bering Straits.
Migration: moves southwards to winter in China and South-east Asia.
British Distribution: a very rare autumn vagrant to Fair Isle (*see page 264*) and sometimes elsewhere. Exceptional in spring.
Other Similar Species: other female buntings (pp. 225–229).

Little Bunting

striped crown

chestnut cheeks with black outline

thin bill

♂ summer

♀ winter

white, streaked black

J	F	M	A	M	J	J	A	S	O	N	D
5	5	5	5	5	5	5	5	5	5	5	5

The Site Guide

Any guide to birdwatching localities inevitably involves making choices and is therefore personal. Birds can, of course, be seen anywhere, but some places are better than others and are generally acknowledged as such. These sites may or may not be bird reserves. They may have particularly scarce habitats. They may, by virtue of their geographical position, have the ability to attract birds. Or they may be simply the best available area in an otherwise rather dull region. Many birders have their own small patch that they watch regularly and that by dint of hard work may produce all manner of species. It may be a local park, garden or open space – a sort of urban Fair Isle – but such places are seldom rewarding for the casual visitor. Thus this guide concentrates on the top birding spots in the British Isles, rather than on places where an individual or small group has managed to see a few interesting birds.

By and large the best birding spots are coastal, simply because coastlines have most of the habitats that are found inland as well as those that are not. Thus a good coastal site will have farmland, woodland, heath and hedgerow as well as shoreline, cliffs, marsh and estuary. Additionally, shorelines offer a haven to land-birds making lengthy sea crossings and duck migrants may, on occasion, appear in huge numbers. It is then not surprising that coastlines attract birdwatchers in large number.

Some areas have, over the years, built up a remarkable reputation for producing scarce or interesting birds. Fair Isle, Scilly and Cley fall into this category and the number of skilled observers that they attract tends to maintain their reputation. Other areas may be equally as good but, because they are not subject to such continual observation, fail to produce interesting birds. This phenomenon can be regarded as the geographical equivalent of the 'weekend rarity bias' that has been mentioned elsewhere. There are, however, quite genuine reasons why these places maintain their reputation and any beginner could do a lot worse than make his first major outing to a place such as Cley.

There are, however, many other places that are worthy of attention and it should be a major aim to get to know them well and learn about the normal bird populations and their regular comings and goings. This may involve frequent visits to a particular area of woodland, marsh, reservoir or even heath or moorland. The most rewarding sites are usually at water because that is where the birds themselves are found in their greatest number and variety. In seeking such local 'hot spots' the Ordinance Survey Maps are invaluable.

When I lived in London I regularly visited the London hot spots, and evening visits to Barn Elms Reservoir and weekends trips to Staines were, for a while, part of my routine. I did, however, hanker after a spot of my own and by scouring the appropriate OS map discovered a miniscule, old-fashioned sewage farm along the River Wandle. Having cycled over to seek permission I was delighted to find a tiny settling lagoon, an overgrown dump area and a wet grassy field forming an oasis right in the middle of Merton's urban sprawl. Within weeks I was seeing Greenshank, Little Stint and Common Sandpiper right in my own backyard, so to speak. There were no other birdwatchers and it was a joy to watch what were otherwise 'coastal' birds in such an environment. Less

The elusive Dartford Warbler is only found on a few heathland areas in southern England. Of the sites mentioned in this guide, the most likely are Arne, Brownsea Island and Studland Heath in Dorset (see pages 237, 247 and 324), the New Forest in Hampshire (see page 304) and Thursley Common in Surrey (see page 327).

anyone tries to find this little gem, I must inform you that the area is now the industrial estate right next to Wimbledon football ground.

About the same time I also started scouring my local common every day. It, too, was surrounded by suburban London, but the comings and goings of small migrants were fascinating, even if the numbers were small. The best birds were far from outstanding – Wood Warbler, Pied Flycatcher, Redstart, Wheatear – but by urban London standards they were really very exciting. Quite recently a friend who still lives in the area managed to find a Pallas's Warbler, so even national scale rarities are not out of the question. Such local-patch birding may be immensely rewarding, but daily visits are really essential if the scale of migration is to be appreciated.

Inevitably, every birder will also develop his or her own favourite coastal location, too, that has the variety of habitats necessary to attract and hold a good variety of birds. For many years all of my weekends and holidays were spent on a particular stretch of the East Anglian coast. Eventually, however, the journey became somewhat tedious and I turned my attention to the Kent–Sussex border country where I now live. It is nowhere near as beautiful or as lonely as my East Anglian stomping ground, but it does produce some fabulous birds.

Some watchers never settle for a favourite spot at all. These gipsy-like birders flit from one spot to the next, partly on impulse and partly in search of reported rarities. Mostly they will be visiting places covered in this book but birds can and do appear at all manner of strange places and the gipsys will follow. Residents of a small Hampshire village once reported a strange nocturnal sound and were worried enough to call in the Electricity Board to investigate. Eventually, someone thought it might be a bird and contacted an experienced local. The sound turned out to be an off-course Scops Owl and the village was inundated by birders for several weeks. It is, of course, not listed here.

With so many birders now travelling the length and breadth of the country, it is easy for records to go unreported. Nevertheless, virtually the whole country is covered by a network of local recorders who are responsible for assembling the records of birds for the local bird report. In the society section at the end of this guide you will find the addresses of most local bird clubs – remember they would like your records. If in doubt the British Trust for Ornithology will be happy to put you in touch with the relevant recorder. Most importantly, if you spot a rare bird report it instantly to the warden (if there is one) or to the local society.

How to use the site guide

The sites detailed in this guide are arranged alphabetically rather than geographically. This makes it easy to find a site known by name. To find sites near a particular town or route, refer to the key map (*see page* 233) which shows their exact location within Britain and Ireland. They can then be found by turning to the page indicated. Each site is treated uniformly under standard headings.

Name

Each site is named and placed in its appropriate county or region. This is followed by the relevant map

The Black-tailed Godwit can be seen at many freshwater marshes and estuaries around Britain and Ireland both during spring and autumn passage and when wintering. Large flocks winter at Gayton Sands, Langstone Harbour, Chichester Harbour, Studland Bay, the Exe Estuary and the Ribble Estuary (see pages 270, 287, 253, 324, 263 and 313) while many Icelandic birds regularly spend the winter on the Shannon Estuary, Co. Limerick (see page 317). The only place where large numbers of birds breed regularly is the Ouse Washes (see page 307).

The Site Guide

The Glen More Forest which surrounds Loch Morlich in Scotland (see page 251) contains many ancient Scots pine trees and is the home of the Scottish Crossbill, Crested Tit and Capercaillie. There is also a fair chance of seeing Osprey around the Loch.

reference with OS for Ordinance Survey; OSNI for Ordinance Survey Northern Ireland; and IOS for the Ordinance Survey of the Irish Republic. The maps referred to are the modern 1:50,000 series except for Ireland where they are the $\frac{1}{2}$ inch series. Each grid square represents one square kilometre.

Location
Under this heading a general indication of where the area lies is given, usually with the distance from the nearest large town or city. A good road atlas will then help you look in the right direction.

Habitats
In general the wider the range of habitats the greater the variety of birds that will use a particular area. The habitats found in each area are summarized, giving an idea of the sort of landform to be expected.

Birds
It is impossible to list every bird found in each area so this section is inevitably selective. The most

interesting regular species are picked out along with the possibilities of seeing other scarcer birds, and particular attention is drawn to seasonal differences. Planning visits, for example, to watch waders is generally best in spring when all the summer visitors have arrived and when all the birds are singing.

Access
This section gives precise directions about how to get to the area, usually from the nearest large town, and certainly from the nearest main road. Details about footpaths, trails and hides are also incorporated.

Permits
Where necessary these are detailed, giving places and times where they may be obtained. Bear in mind that such information does tend to change quite rapidly, especially where small, largely voluntary organizations are involved.

I would be pleased to hear of major changes and developments to any of the featured sites c/o the publishers.

Key map to the birdwatching sites and their page references.

The Isles of Scilly (see page 284) have long been a popular birdwatching site. Of the 375 species that have been recorded there, many have been rarities, including numerous American species that have lost their way over the Atlantic. October is the best time for spotting these birds.

Unst/328 Fetlar/266
SHETLANDS Out Skerries/306
Lerwick/290
Foula/269 Noss/305
Loch of Spiggie/295

Fair Isle/264

Papa Westray/309
Marwick Head/301 **ORKNEYS**
The Loons/297 Birsay Moors + Cottasgarth/243
Hobbister/277 Copinsay/257
Hoy/281

Clo Mor/255 Faraid Head/265 John O'Groats/284
Handa/274 Dunnet Head/261
Kyle of Tongue/285

Inverpolly/282 Loch Fleet/292
Dornoch Firth/259

Balranald/239 Culbin Bar
Beinn Eighe/241 Findhorn Bay/258 Loch of Strathbeg/295
Loch Druidibeg/292 **INVERNESS** GlenMuick + East Grampian/272 Bullers of Buchan/249
Ythan Estuary/333
Loch Garten/293 **ABERDEEN**
Rhum/313 Abernethy Forest/235 Cairngorms/251
Insh Marshes/282 Fowlsheugh/269

Loch of Lowes/294

Eden Estuary/262
Largo Bay + Kilconquhar Loch/288 Fife Ness/267
Loch Leven/294 Isle of May/283
EDINBURGH Bass Rock/240
Islay/283 **GLASGOW** Aberlady Bay/234
Lochwinnoch/296 Leith + Musselburgh/290 St Abb's Head/315

Lindisfarne/291
Rathlin Island/312 Ayr/238 Farne Islands/266
Lough Foyle/299 Coquet Island/257
Loch Ryan/296 Hauxley/274 Washington/330
Larne Lough/288 Caerlaverock/250
Lough Neagh/299 **BELFAST** Loch Ken/293 Geltsdale/271
Strangford Lough/323 Teesside + Cowpen Marsh/325
St Bees Head/316 **MIDDLESBOROUGH**

Allen Pools/236 Leighton Moss/289 Bempton Cliffs + Flamborough Head/242
Carlingford Lough/252 Hest Bank/276 Hornsea Mere/280
Walney Island/330 Morecambe/302
Fleetwood/268 Pilling/310 Blacktoft Sands/245 Spurn Head/322
Ribble Estuary/313 **LEEDS**
Ainsdale Sands/235 Fairburn Ings/265 Tetney/326
Martin Mere/301 Theddlethorpe + Saltfleetby/326
North Bull, Dublin/305 Hilbre/277 **LIVERPOOL** Rostherne Mere/314 **MANCHESTER**
South Stack/321 Mersey Estuary/302 Goyt Valley/272 Clumber/255 + The Dukeries Gibraltar Point/271
DUBLIN Gayton Sands/270 Holme/279 Blakeney Point + Harbour/244
Lavan Sands/289 Shotton Pools/318 Frampton Marsh/270 Titchwell/327 Cley/254
Newborough Warren/304 Connah's Quay/256 Hunstanton/281 Holkham + Wells/278 Hickling Broad/276
Coombes Valley/256 Holbeach/279 Horsey Mere/280
Bardsey Island/239 Lake Vyrnwy/286 Rutland Water/314 Snettisham/321 Breydon Water/248
Shannon Estuary/317 Blithfield Reservoir/246 Ouse Washes/307 **NORWICH** Benacre/243
Akeragh Lough/236 Wyre Forest/332 Wicken Fen/332 Strumpshaw Fen/324 Walberswick/329
BIRMINGHAM East Wretham Heath/262 Weeting Heath/331 Blyth Estuary/246
Dyfi Estuary/261 Eyebrook Reservoir/264 Grafham Water/273 Minsmere/303
Ynys-hir/333 Draycote Water/259 The Lodge/297 Alton Water/237 Havergate Island/275
Wexford Slobs/331 Pitsford Reservoir/311 Landguard Point/287
Tacumshin Lake/325 Tregaron/328 Abberton Reservoir/234 Fingringhoe Wick/267
Gwenffrwd + Dinas/273 Old Hall Marshes/306 Walton-on-the-Naze/329
Skelligs/319 Bradwell/247
CORK Forest of Dean/268 Cliffe + Halstow/253
Cape Clear/250 Blackpill/244 Slimbridge/320 Staines Reservoir/322 Shellness/318
Skomer/319 **SWANSEA** **BRISTOL** Barn Elms Reservoir/240 Elmley Sandwich Bay/317
Cork Harbour/258 Burry Inlet/249 **CARDIFF** **LONDON/298** Marshes/263 Stodmarsh/323
Oxwich Bay/308 Kenfig/285 Thursley Common/327
Lundy/300 Chew Valley Lake/252 Chichester Harbour/253 Rye Harbour/315
Langstone Harbour/287 Arundel/238 Dungeness/260
New Forest/304 Pett Level/310
EXETER Brownsea Island/247 Pennington Marshes/309 Beachy Head/241
Exe Estuary/263 Arne/237 Pagham Harbour/308
Radipole + Lodmoor/312 Studland Heath/324
St Ives/316 Hayle Estuary/275 Portland/311
Land's End/286 Marazion Marsh/300 **PLYMOUTH**
Isles of Scilly/284 Slapton Ley/320

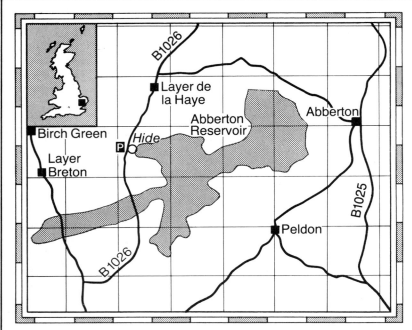

ABBERTON RESERVOIR, ESSEX OS 168

Location: 4 miles south of Colchester.

Habitats: this is one of lowland Britain's largest man-made waters; it has banks at the western end, large shallow bays and, in autumn, considerable areas of open mud.

Birds: one of the very best reservoirs in the country for divers, grebes, wildfowl, gulls and terns. Great Crested and Little Grebes are present throughout the year, and winter brings the scarcer grebes plus divers and ducks, especially Wigeon, Gadwall, Shoveler, Pochard and Tufted, with good numbers of Goldeneye. Smew, Goosander and Bewick's Swan are frequently present.

During spring and autumn passage periods waders are present, with Little Stint and Curlew Sandpiper turning up regularly, especially in autumn. Black Tern and Little Gull are also regular and it is a poor migration season that does not produce Garganey and Red-crested Pochard.

Access: much of the reservoir is visible from the B1026. After 5½ miles there is a parking area on the right. A turnstile (small charge) leads to a hide. The main causeway lies ½ mile south. Follow the B1026 and signs to Layer Breton for a secondary causeway.

Permits: not required.

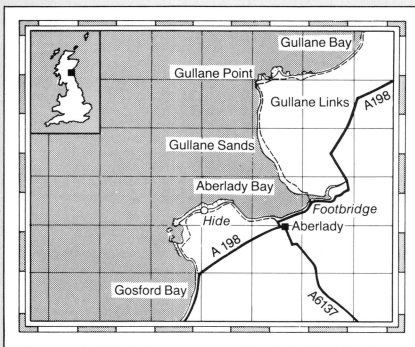

ABERLADY BAY, EAST LOTHIAN OS 66

Location: about 12 miles east of Edinburgh, on the south shore of the Firth of Forth.

Habitats: intertidal mud, backed by low-lying dunes.

Birds: winter is probably the best season, when there are flocks of Pinkfeet, Whooper Swans, and many seaducks, including Eider, Scoter, Velvet Scoter and Long-tailed. The sea also holds impressive concentrations of divers, as well as of Slavonian and Red-necked Grebes. Waders are abundant, with all the usual species plus Purple Sandpiper and, sometimes, Ruff. During passage periods, visitors regularly include Black-tailed Godwit, Curlew Sandpiper and Little Stint. Aberlady boasts one of the most important wader roosts in Scotland. In summer, terns are often present and Eider breed locally. Gannets breed nearby at Bass Rock (*see page* 240).

Access: leave Edinburgh on the A1 eastwards and turn left on the A198 to Aberlady. About ½ mile beyond the village is a car park where a footbridge crosses a stream and a footpath leads out along the eastern shore. This is best visited on a rising tide.

Permits: write for a car park permit to Department of Leisure, Recreation and Tourism, Brunton Hall, Musselburgh, Edinburgh EH21 6AF.

ABERNETHY FOREST, HIGHLAND OS 36

Location: this area lies to the east of the River Spey and north of Aviemore a few miles from Boat of Garten.

Habitats: a huge area of old Scots Pine forest, together with new plantations at various stages of maturity.

Birds: this area is best visited in summer. Although you will have to mingle with hordes of visitors to see the Ospreys at Loch Garten (*see page* 293), the forest specialities – Capercaillie, Black Grouse, Crested Tit and Scottish Crossbill – are best seen early in the morning, when few tourists are about. Additionally, there are Goshawk, Hen Harrier and Merlin. Redstart, Siskin, Dipper and Common Sandpiper should all be seen. Long-eared Owl is as elusive as elsewhere.

Access: access to this National Nature Reserve is freely available over many tracks and roads. The best areas lie to the south of Loch Garten and can be approached via the minor road to Tulloch just north of Auchgourish. Find Mhor Cottage for a Blackcock lek (communal display ground of male Black Grouse), but do not disturb the birds. Continue to Forest Lodge.

Permits: not required.

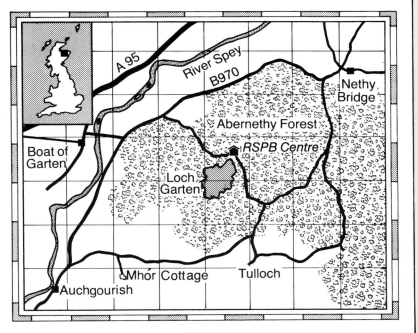

AINSDALE SANDS, LANCASHIRE OS 108

Location: this shoreline lies between Southport and Formby.

Habitats: the tide exposes considerable areas of intertidal sand, backed by an extensive area of dunes and dune slacks. There are also extensive plantations of pines.

Birds: this area is often overshadowed by other, more famous, locations nearby, but has always had its own band of dedicated devotees. It is best during spring and autumn passage periods, when the dune thickets hold many small migrants and the shoreline may be full of waders. The latter are more numerous in winter, when large numbers of both Black-tailed and Bar-tailed Godwits, Sanderlings, Turnstones and the more widespread species may be seen. Skuas and terns are usually present in autumn, often with a few auks. Even in summer exciting birds are possible at this site.

Access: from Freshfield Station in Formby walk northwards up the road along the landward side of the railway and cross to Fisherman's Path. This leads to Massam's Slack and the shore. To the north a road leads to Ainsdale-on-Sea for seabirds. Other areas are of restricted access forming part of a National Nature Reserve.

Permits: not necessary for casual birding.

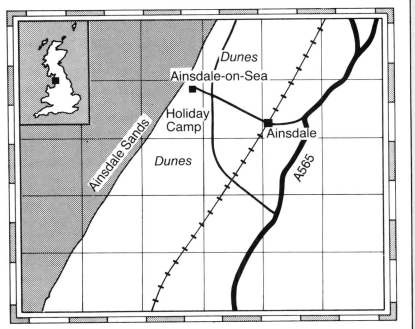

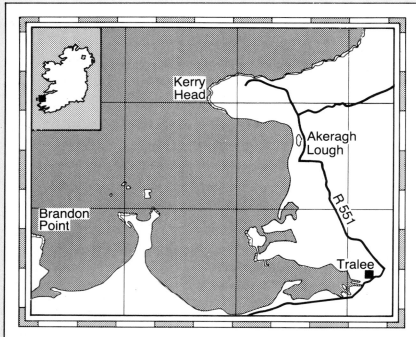

AKERAGH LOUGH, CO. KERRY, IRISH REPUBLIC IOS½ 20

Location: this small area of freshwater lies in northern Kerry just a few miles north of Tralee. The quickest route for visitors across the Irish Sea is by air to Shannon, then by roads N18 and N21 to Limerick and Tralee; or by air to Cork then by road N22 to Tralee.

Habitats: there are three fresh-to-brackish water pools here that, in winter, are joined to form a larger flooded area. This is the only stretch of permanent freshwater in northern Kerry.

Birds: the nearest stretch of freshwater to America, Akeragh's international fame rests on the extraordinary array of transatlantic vagrants that it attracts every year. It is difficult to predict what might turn up here in autumn, but Pectoral Sandpipers, Lesser Golden Plovers, one of the dowitchers and White-rumped and Baird's Sandpipers must be regarded as distinct possibilities. The Lough also holds the occasional American duck as well as the more usual European species.

Access: leave Tralee northwards on the R551 and view Akeragh on the left before Ballyheige village. Do not ignore the intertidal areas of Tralee Bay. Brandon Point, about 20 miles to the west, is a major autumn sea-watch station.

Permits: the area is private and permits are not available.

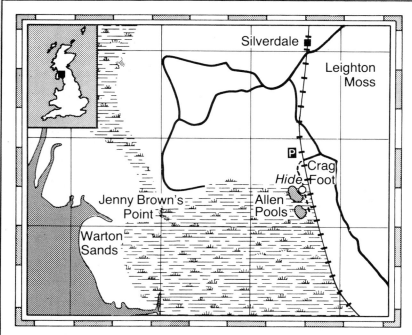

ALLEN POOLS, LANCASHIRE

OS 97

Location: a few miles west of Carnforth in the northeast of Morecambe Bay; part of the RSPB Morecambe Bay reserve.

Habitats: a huge area of intertidal sand and saltmarsh, where the RSPB has created two pools on the Carnforth Saltings, one of which is dedicated to the memory of Eric Morecambe – not only a very funny man, but also a bird-lover and dedicated conservationist.

Birds: Greylag Geese, Pintail and Shoveler are particularly fond of this area. The winter landscape is dominated by the huge flocks of waders, with Knot the most abundant. There are also many Dunlin, Oystercatcher and Bartailed Godwit, along with lesser numbers of Turnstone, Redshank and Sanderling. During spring and autumn passage periods other species occur, including large flocks of Ringed Plover, particularly in spring, together with Spotted Redshank, Black-tailed Godwit and Little Stint. Terns are often present in spring and autumn, and there is usually a good collection of the more common gulls.

Access: leave the M6 at exit 35 to Carnforth and take the road toward Silverdale. At Crag Foot take a left under a railway bridge to the car park and hides.

Permits: free access to the pools at all times.

236

ALTON WATER, SUFFOLK OS 169

Location: this relatively recent reservoir lies 5 miles south of Ipswich, between the estuaries of the Stour and Orwell.

Habitats: flooding a shallow valley has created a lowland reservoir with a highly indented and shallow shoreline that is particularly attractive to passage and wintering wetland birds. Its position, near many well-established bird resorts, makes it one of the best reservoirs in the country.

Birds: Alton Water has become one of Britain's major strongholds of breeding Great Crested Grebes. Greylag Geese, too, find it attractive and, in winter, they are joined by large numbers of ducks that regularly include marine species, such as Long-tailed Duck, Scaup, Goosander and Smew. Passage waders are often interesting, but the lengthy shoreline does make locating them something of a lottery. Snipe, as well as regular Jack Snipe, are present in winter.

Access: leave Ipswich southwards on the A137 toward Colchester and turn left towards Tattingstone. Before the village a causeway crosses the higher part of the reservoir. Beyond the village lies another viewpoint. Continue via Stutton to the dam, where there is a car park.

Permits: not required for access as detailed above.

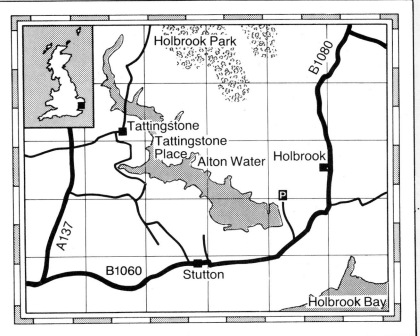

ARNE, DORSET OS 195

Location: the Arne peninsula lies on the south side of Poole Harbour, a few kilometres east of Wareham off the road to Swanage.

Habitats: sandy heath, covered with heather, ling, gorse and stands of pines with birch scrub. Also large areas of intertidal mud with reed beds and saltmarshes.

Birds: Arne's most famous bird inhabitant is the Dartford Warbler. More birdwatchers have 'ticked' this species here than at any other site. Other typical heathland birds include Nightjar and Stonechat. A good variety of waders may be seen on the mudflats and saltings, both in winter and on passage (*see also Brownsea Island, page* 247). Black-tailed Godwit, Spotted Redshank and Avocet winter here, and in autumn may be present in quite large numbers. They are joined by Curlew Sandpiper, Little Stint, Greenshank and often a few terns. Both Buzzard and Sparrowhawk breed in the area.

Access: leave Wareham on the A351 towards Swanage and turn left after ½ mile in Stoborough. Continue to Arne village and the car park and RSPB reception. There is free access to the Shipstal area. A nature trail starts opposite the church.

Permits: not required. Groups may arrange for escorted visits by writing to: The Warden, Syldata, Arne, Wareham BH20 5BJ.

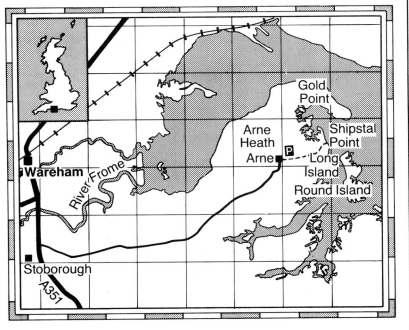

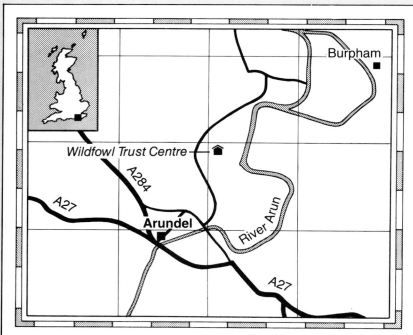

ARUNDEL, WEST SUSSEX OS 197

Location: this Wildfowl Trust Refuge lies just a ½ mile north of Arundel between Chichester and Worthing and is well signposted from the A27 roundabouts.

Habitats: a series of pools has been created alongside the River Arun to house a fine collection of captive wildfowl. There is also a more natural lagoon surrounded by an extensive growth of reeds.

Birds: the wildfowl collection here includes a fine and representative array of the world's ducks, geese and swans, including feral Canada and Greylag Geese and several species of seaducks not usually on view at such refuges. During passage periods scarcer waders, including Green Sandpiper, are often seen. In winter the 'natural' lagoon is frequently visited by other waders, as well as good numbers of Water Rails, Snipe and the occasional Bittern or flock of Bearded Tits. Only a short distance to the north lie the flooded fields at Greatham Bridge, where early autumn waders are often worth more than a brief look.

Access: leave the A27 at Arundel and follow signs to the Wildfowl Trust Refuge. Park on the right after one mile.

Permits: there is an entrance charge, though Wildfowl Trust members are allowed in free.

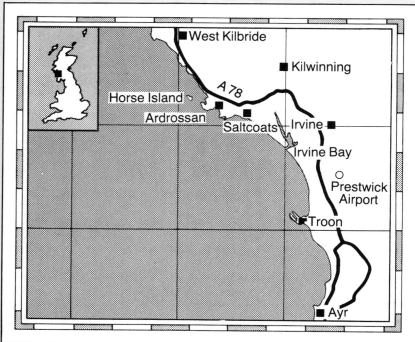

AYR, STRATHCLYDE OS 70

Location: 30 miles south-west of Glasgow at the mouth of the Firth of Clyde. The major bird areas lie between Troon and West Kilbride.

Habitats: the intertidal area is not huge, but still offers excellent opportunities to see a great variety of seabirds.

Birds: in summer there are good tern colonies on the RSPB's Horse Island to the north of Ardrossan. The birds can be seen easily from the town itself. Eider, Gannet and Guillemot are also present at this time. Spring and autumn passage brings a wider variety of species, but it is in winter that this coast really comes into its own. Divers are then plentiful and there is a sizeable herd of Whooper Swans at Irvine-Garnock estuary. Seaducks include regular Red-breasted Merganser, Scoter and Eider. Waders may be abundant and Purple Sandpipers are always present. The South Bay at Troon is a likely spot for this bird, as well as for Glaucous and Iceland Gulls among the roosting flocks. Another good spot is Doonfoot Bay, south of Ayr.

Access: leave Glasgow southwestwards on the A737 and turn right to Dalry on the A780 and again on the A781 to West Kilbride. The A78 coast road is excellent, with easy access to the seafront at Ardrossan, Troon, Ayr and Doonfoot Bay.

Permits: landing on Horse Island may be arranged with the RSPB, 17 Regent Terrace, Edinburgh EH7 5NB.

BALRANALD, NORTH UIST, WESTERN ISLES OS 18

Location: this RSPB reserve lies on the west coast of North Uist between the villages of Tigharry and Paiblesgarry.

Habitats: this is a harsh, crofting landscape surrounded by a rocky shoreline with huge dune beaches. There are areas of marsh and loch and flower-strewn coastal grasslands. Typical of the Outer Hebrides, these rich grazing lands have been built up on lime-rich shell-sand. They are called by their Gaelic name *machair* (pronounced 'mackar') and have a rich birdlife.

Birds: a typical range of Outer Hebridean birds that includes Corncrake and sometimes Red-necked Phalarope. The former is more often heard than seen, though Balranald is one of the best places for this declining species in Britain. Red-necked Phalaropes are often present in the second half of May. Other breeding wetland birds include several duck species (notably Wigeon, as well as Gadwall, Teal, Shoveler and Eider), while Arctic Terns are often abundant. Black Guillemot, Dunlin and Ringed Plover all breed.

Access: by air to Benbecula, then northwards across the causeways to North Uist. Follow the A865 westward and turn left to Hougharry. There is a visitor reception cottage at Goular.

Permits: access is free at all times, but keep to the marked paths.

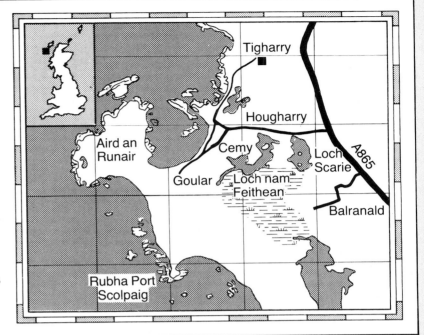

BARDSEY ISLAND, GWYNEDD

OS 123

Location: this island lies off the tip of the Llŷn Peninsula, which forms the northern arm of Cardigan Bay.

Habitats: Bardsey is a small island with areas of farmland, a conifer plantation, a few cliffs and a hill that rises to 170m.

Birds: though Manx Shearwater breed on the east side of the hill and Shag, Razorbill, Kittiwake and Chough nest on the cliffs, Bardsey is essentially a migration watch point. A bird observatory was established in 1953 and a succession of rare and scarce birds has been recorded since, especially in autumn. The lighthouse at the southern end of the island was for long a major killer of small migrants and, though the death roll has now been reduced, birds are still attracted during overcast conditions.

Access: there is a regular boat service (at present early on Saturday mornings) from Pwllheli. Accommodation at the Observatory, from March to November, is in dormitories. Inquiries (enclose s.a.e.) to The Secretary, Mrs H. Bond, 21a Gestridge Road, Kingsteignton, Newton Abbot, Devon. Contact Bardsey Trust, Tyddyn Du Farm, Criccieth, Gwynedd, for cottages to rent.

Permits: see above.

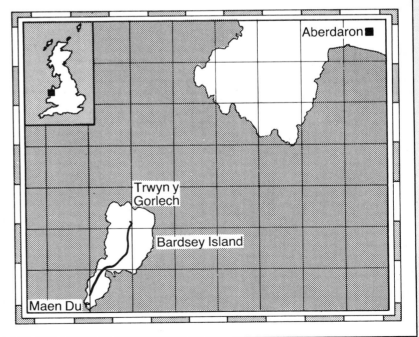

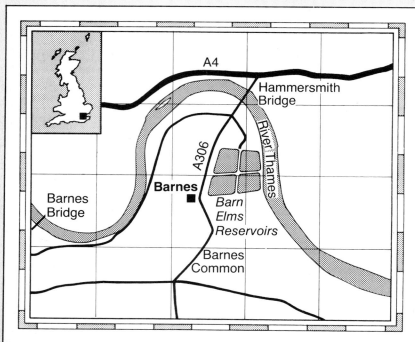

BARN ELMS RESERVOIR, LONDON OS 176

Location: West London, south of Hammersmith Bridge.

Habitats: four concrete-banked reservoirs in a suburban landscape only a few yards from the Thames. The banks offer little in the way of food, but still manage to attract a few waders on spring and autumn passage. In winter the waters offer a safe refuge and feeding opportunities to a remarkable collection of ducks.

Birds: in winter Barn Elms holds great rafts of Tufted Duck and Pochard, together with Gadwall, Goosander and Wigeon. The latter graze the grassy banks and nearby playing fields. Hard weather may bring in the occasional Scaup or even Long-tailed Duck. Great Crested Grebes are regular and occasionally one of the scarcer grebes or even a diver may also be present. Black and Common Terns are regular in spring and autumn and, although Common Sandpipers are the most regular passage waders, there is often a Dunlin, Little Stint or Ringed Plover present.

Access: from Hammersmith, cross the bridge and turn left at the traffic lights on the south bank into Merthyr Terrace. The reservoir entrance is 180m away, at the end of this road.

Permits: must be obtained in advance from Thames Water, New River Head, Rosebery Avenue, London EC1R 4TP.

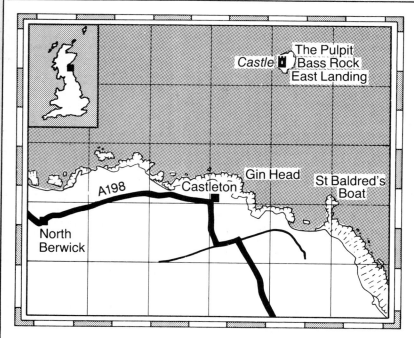

BASS ROCK, EAST LOTHIAN OS 67

Location: off the southern shore at the mouth of the Firth of Forth, about 3 miles north-east of North Berwick and some 20 miles east of Edinburgh.

Habitats: this is a monolithic lump of rock rising precipitously from the sea that offers a home to large numbers of breeding seabirds.

Birds: this is one of the most accessible gannetries in Britain, with over 20,000 breeding pairs of Gannets. To visit a large colony of this spectacular black and white seabird is a unique experience. The birds can be approached and photographed at close range, though the noise, smell and commotion are not to everyone's taste. Shag, Guillemot and Razorbill are also present.

Access: leave Edinburgh eastwards on the A1 and take the A198 to North Berwick. The boatman, Fred Marr, in North Berwick should be contacted in advance (Tel: 0620 2838). It is not always possible to land because of weather conditions and landing is not allowed in the earlier part of the season, when serious disturbance to the breeding birds could result.

Permits: contact the Scottish Ornithologists' Club, 21 Regent Terrace, Edinburgh EH7 5BT (Tel: 031 556 6042) for details of their own excursions and for permitted landing times.

BEACHY HEAD, EAST SUSSEX OS 199

Location: on the South Coast, between Eastbourne and Seaford.

Habitats: sheer chalk cliffs plunge vertically 150m to the sea with only one break, the Cuckmere Valley. The cliff-tops offer a mixture of grassland, scrub, arable fields and a few areas with trees.

Birds: Beachy is a migration point offering excellent seawatching together with the chance of grounded migrants, including exciting rarities. Between Eastbourne and Seaford there is only one 'major' wood (90 square metres) and only a few sheltered hollows where birds (and their insect food) can escape the wind – Whitebread Hollow, Belle Tout, Birling Gap and Cuckmere Haven. Each area should be thoroughly searched during spring and autumn passage periods. In spring Pomarine Skuas are something of a speciality, while small migrants are often abundant.

Access: from the promenade at Eastbourne, the South Downs Way continues to Beachy Head and beyond. A coast road also offers access. Birling Gap is good for spring seawatching. There is a car park at Exceat Bridge and a track down the valley to the sea, though this is much frequented by trippers.

Permits: not required.

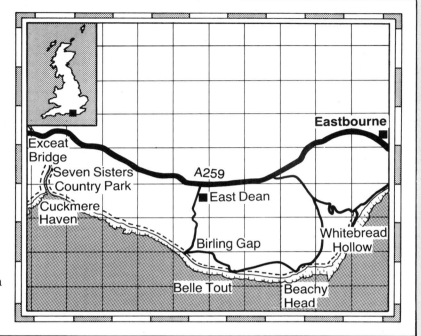

BEINN EIGHE, HIGHLAND OS 19 & 25

Location: 20 miles south-west of Ullapool.

Habitats: though Beinn Eighe National Nature Reserve, Britain's first, was created to protect one of the last remnants of the old Caledonian pine forests, it covers a huge area of mountain, moorland, loch and marsh.

Birds: this is a rugged landscape, boasting breeding Golden Eagle, Peregrine and Merlin, along with Red Grouse, Ptarmigan and Greenshank. Both Black-throated and Red-throated Divers breed, as do Dipper, Dunlin and Common Sandpiper. Both Crossbills and Scottish Crossbills may be found. Redwings breed among birches.

Access: start at Kinlochewe at the junction of the A896 and A832 at the head of Loch Maree. About 1 mile north on the A832 is the Reserve Visitor Centre, which offers advice and from which a pony trail runs westward into the highest part of the area. About 1 mile further north is a car park and the start of the Glas Leitire Nature Trail. The lower slopes here have Scots Pine with crossbills. Birders should take all the necessary precautions that wild mountainous country demands.

Permits: not required outside the deer-stalking season, currently between 1 September and 21 November (to check dates contact the British Field Sports Society, 59 Kennington Road, London SE1).

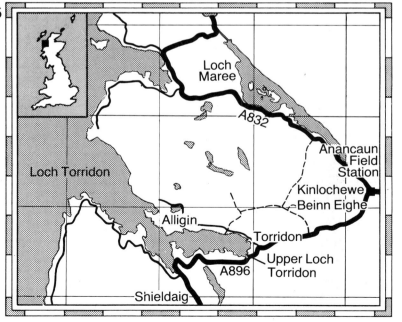

BEMPTON CLIFFS AND FLAMBOROUGH HEAD, HUMBERSIDE OS 101

Location: between Scarborough and Bridlington.

Habitats: vertical cliffs jutting out of what is otherwise a smooth and regular coast.

Birds: Bempton Cliffs supports tens of thousands of Kittiwakes, Guillemot, Razorbill, Puffin, Fulmar, Shag – and Britain's only mainland gannetry.

The cliffs at Flamborough are some 75m high, perhaps too high for perfect seawatching, but the Head's position makes it one of the top two or three seawatching spots in Britain. All four skuas occur every year, especially Arctic and Great Skuas. Manx Shearwaters are regular and even the Mediterranean race appears most years. Sooty Shearwaters are seen throughout the autumn and there are reports most years of both Cory's and Great Shearwaters. In winter there are divers offshore as well as gulls, seaducks and even the odd skua.

With small migrants, autumn is usually more spectacular than spring. All the usual warblers, chats, flycatchers and thrushes, including Pied Flycatcher, Whinchat, Redstart and Wryneck, are regular passage migrants. Semi-rarities such as Ortolan Bunting and Yellow-browed Warbler turn up annually. Most of these birds are found among the hedges that separate the small fields, or in the scrub along the coastal path.

Access: leave Bridlington northwards on the B1255 and turn left to Bempton after 2 miles. Continue through the village and follow RSPB signs. From the car park, walk to the cliff top footpath and explore. There are observation points, an information centre and daily boat trips along the foot of the cliffs from Bridlington.

Take the B1259 to Flamborough Head, from where a path leads down from the lighthouse to sheltered crannies. There are alternative routes to North Landing, South Landing and the southern end of Danes' Dyke.

Permits: none required.

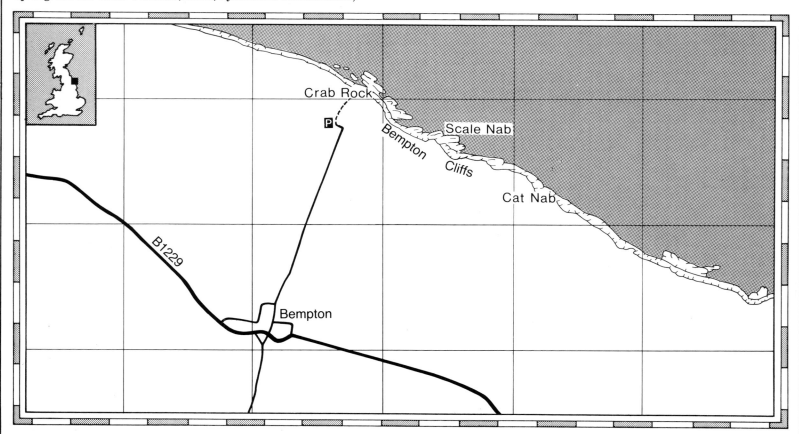

BENACRE, SUFFOLK OS 156

Location: on the coast a few miles south of Lowestoft.

Habitats: the large broad is separated from the sea by only a narrow shingle beach. The water is fresh and the inland part is densely overgrown with reeds. The broad's shoreline includes exposed mud. The whole area is surrounded by mature, mixed woodland. To the north is a series of disused gravel pits that are now flooded, providing more fresh water. An area of scrubby hedges frequently holds a good variety of small birds during spring and autumn passage. To the south is a line of crumbling cliffs.

Birds: the reed beds hold a good selection of East Anglian specialities, but there is no access. In winter the broad has a good collection of ducks and the odd harrier. During migration, there is often a good range of waders, and gulls regularly include Glaucous and Mediterranean. Terns regularly come to bathe and the occasional skua may do the same. The bushes hold chats, warblers and flycatchers, though rarities are surprisingly few. The East Anglian coast is poor for seawatching.

Access: leave the A12 at Wrentham, taking the minor road to Covehithe. Park beyond the church and walk north. There is a hide on the southern shore.

Permits: not required – but do not trespass on to the Reserve.

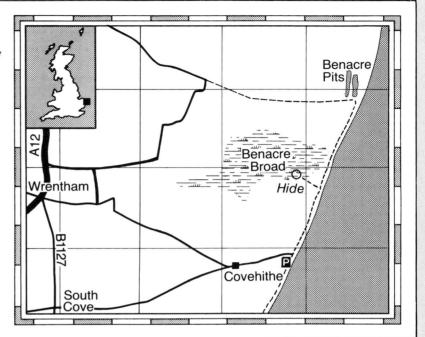

BIRSAY MOORS AND COTTASGARTH, ORKNEY OS 6

Location: one of the largest RSPB reserves, it lies in the extreme north of Mainland, to the east of Brough Head.

Habitat: rough, windswept heather moorland with large bogs as well as lochs and streams. Fortunately, much can be seen from the public roads.

Birds: with the dedicated help of the RSPB's local man, the late Eddie Balfour, the Hen Harrier survived here and has since spread back to the mainland. Many birds find conditions perfect here, including Short-eared Owls, Arctic and Great Skuas and Red-throated Diver.

Access: the B9057 crosses the moors between Dounby and the north coast, while a minor road runs from it north-westwards to Loch of Hundland and Twatt. The lochs are worth exploring. There is a hide at Lower Cottasgarth, reached by turning left just beyond the Norseman Garage, 3 miles north of Finstown. Another hide at Burgar Hill, near the wind generators, is approached from Evie. Further access is possible at Durkadale, reached by taking a rough track from the southern end of Loch of Hundland.

Permits: not required.

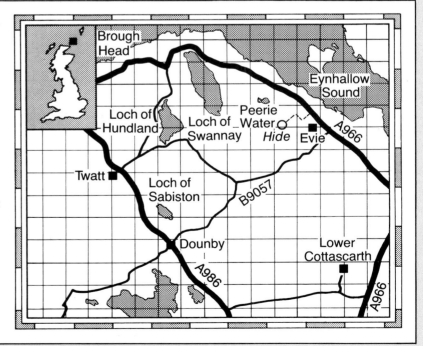

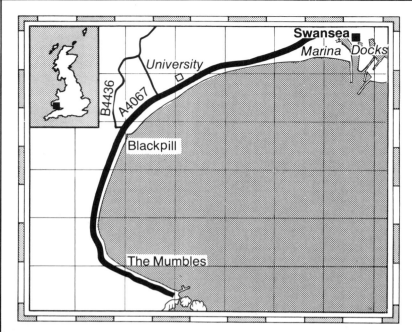

BLACKPILL, WEST GLAMORGAN OS 159

Location: this is no more than a seaside suburb of Swansea, lying to the south-west of the city and overlooking Swansea Bay.

Habitat: the intertidal area here is blessed by having a small stream entering the sea, providing freshwater in which birds can bathe. There are large areas of mud and sand, a promenade and a boating pool. All in all, it is not a place that would seem to have anything special to offer the birder – but it does.

Birds: the first ever Ring-billed Gull from America was discovered here in 1973 and Blackpill has been famous for rare gulls ever since. Ring-billed Gulls still occur here more regularly than at any other British site, with up to five present, mainly in March. The roost here attracts several thousand gulls, among which Mediterranean, Glaucous and Iceland may be found. There are also winter waders, including a good flock of Sanderling, plus the occasional seaduck and diver. Autumn passage produces a wider range of species, but Blackpill remains primarily a gull-watching spot, with other birds simply a sideshow.

Access: the A4067 southward from Swansea runs behind the beach to the Boating Pool, where most birders gather.

Permits: none required.

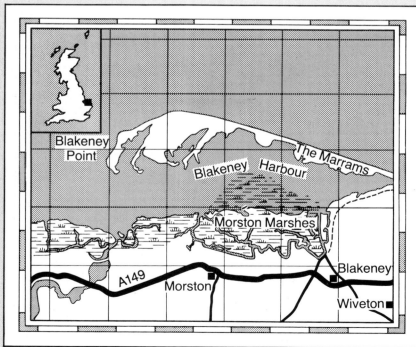

BLAKENEY POINT AND HARBOUR, NORFOLK OS 132

Location: the Norfolk coast offshore from Blakeney and Morston.

Habitats: the Point forms the climax to a lengthy shingle bar that extends westwards from Cley Beach. Areas of shingle and sand are overgrown, in parts, with dense patches of seablite (*Sueda*) and other low vegetation. There is a small plantation. The Harbour is a vast intertidal basin that exposes large areas of mud at low tide, with huge areas of saltmarsh.

Birds: Blakeney Point has a large colony of Common Terns, watched over by the National Trust warden. Among these birds are a few Little and Arctic Terns and, sometimes, a colony of Sandwich Terns. During the summer some areas are fenced off. In autumn the Point becomes one of the top migration spots in the country and many birders walk the whole way from Cley Beach to the Point and back, examining every bush along the way. Scarce migrants turn up every year, including Wryneck, Bluethroat and Barred Warbler.

Access: from Cley Beach car park walk west to the Point and back. Alternatively, in summer, take a boat from Morston Quay. In Blakeney itself there is a large quayside car park, from which a sea-wall leads out along the eastern shore of the Harbour.

Permits: not required.

BLACKTOFT SANDS, HUMBERSIDE OS 112

Location: this RSPB reserve lies where the Rivers Ouse and Trent meet to form the Humber, upstream from Hull to the north of Scunthorpe.

Habitat: a vast area of intertidal mud and extensive reed beds. Though a noted haunt of Pink-footed Geese and a good variety of duck for many years, it was always a difficult area to watch, with passage waders offering little more than fleeting glimpses in the distance. Then the RSPB arrived and created their Blacktoft Sands Reserve, with artificial lagoons and hides among the reeds, and the area was transformed. This is now a splendid place to watch a wide variety of different species.

Birds: in summer the reed beds are alive with Sedge and Reed Warblers, together with Water Rail and Bearded Tit. At this time the lagoons have several species of ducks and waders, including Little Ringed Plover. It is, however, during migration that Blacktoft really sparkles, with all the usual waders passing through in good numbers. These include Black-tailed Godwit, Ruff, Little Stint and Curlew Sandpiper, along with a scattering of rarities. Exotic wanderers such as Red-necked and Long-tailed Stints, and Semipalmated and Western Sandpipers may prove difficult to identify.

In winter there is usually a good collection of ducks together with the more regular waders, especially at high tide. Marsh Harriers are reasonably regular, as are Short-eared Owl, Marsh and Hen Harrier. Geese sometimes put in an appearance and, particularly early in the season, Bearded Tits are often very active.

Access: leave the M62 at Exit 36 to Goole and take the A161 southwards. After 2–2½ miles turn left to Reedness and on to Ousefleet. The reserve centre will be seen on the left, by a sharp right-hand turn in the road. Several hides overlook the lagoons.

Permits: open six days a week (not Tuesday at time of going to press) with a charge for non-RSPB members.

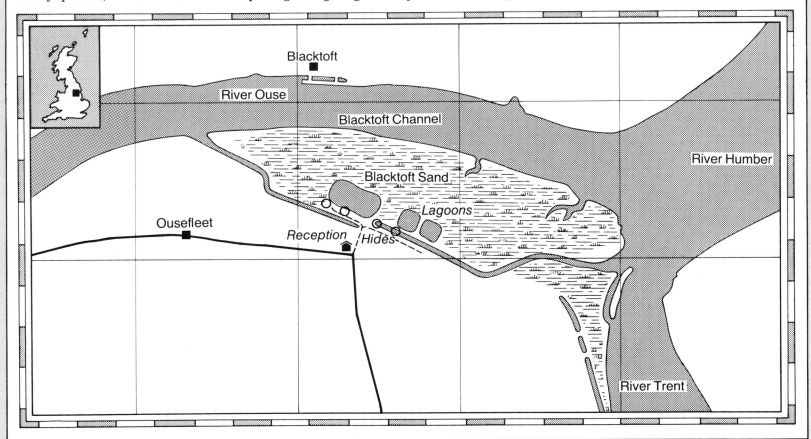

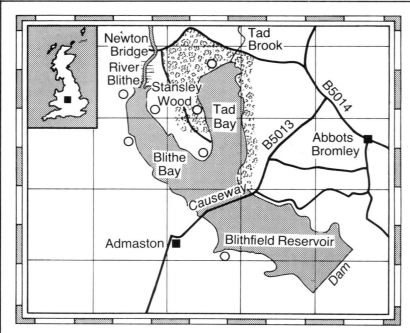

BLITHFIELD RESERVOIR, STAFFORDSHIRE OS 128

Location: 10 miles west of Burton-on-Trent.

Habitats: created in 1952, the natural banks offer varying amounts of muddy edge, depending on weather and season. By early autumn the mud attracts waders. In winter the shallows at the head of the reservoir are reflooded and are sometimes high enough to flood the surrounding grassland, offering fine feeding opportunities for wildfowl. The eastern shore has a conifer plantation and there is a mixed wood at the northern end of the reservoir.

Birds: one of the best reservoirs for birds in the country. The winter collection of ducks is always very impressive, with outstanding numbers of Mallard, Teal and Wigeon. There are also usually several of the scarcer duck species present, including Pintail, Goosander, Ruddy Duck and Goldeneye, together with a regular herd of Bewick's Swans. During passage periods waders and terns are regular and, in autumn, these include Green and Curlew Sandpipers, Little Stint and Black Tern, with Little Gulls regular.

Access: the B5013 northwards to Uttoxeter from Rugeley crosses the reservoir by a causeway that offers good views.

Permits: annual permits are issued by the West Midland Bird Club.

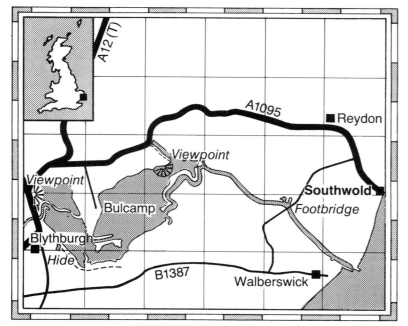

BLYTH ESTUARY, SUFFOLK

OS 156

Location: a partly reclaimed estuary on the Suffolk coast at Blythburgh, on the A12 south of Lowestoft.

Habitats: channelized for much of its lower course, the River Blyth has burst its banks to re-establish this estuary, which thus lies a little way inland rather than at the mouth of the river. It is an extensive area of intertidal mud banks with saltmarsh and reed beds on the southern shore. The surrounding farmland, heath and pine coverts are strictly out of bounds.

Birds: though terns and common waders breed here, spring and autumn passage periods are outstanding, with good numbers of Black-tailed Godwit and Spotted Redshank. Autumn brings Little Stint, Curlew Sandpiper and Greenshank, while in winter there are usually good numbers of Redshank, Bar-tailed Godwits, Marsh and Hen Harriers, and Short-eared Owls regularly quarter the surrounding rough fields.

Access: access is strictly limited. Just north of the village, there is a layby on the left hand side of the A12. Cross the road and view from the bank. Walk back toward The White Hart and take a track about 175m before the pub. A footpath leads to a hide among the reeds.

Permits: not required.

BRADWELL, ESSEX OS 168

Location: a surprisingly lonely area on the southern shore of the Blackwater estuary, 8½ miles north of Burnham-on-Crouch.

Habitats: a huge sea-wall separates a vast area of grazing marshes from the mud banks of the Dengie Flats. Here a group of enthusiasts have established and maintained the Bradwell Bird Observatory.

Birds: though a bird observatory with an inevitable bias toward migration periods, Bradwell is really better during the winter for general birdwatching. Then there are vast flocks of Brent Geese, wildfowl and waders. Grey Plover, Knot, Curlew, Turnstone and Dunlin are all very numerous. Hen Harriers and Short-eared Owls are often present and Merlins regularly winter. Just a short way along the shore to the south, a good variety of breeding waders – Redshank, Ringed Plover and Oystercatcher – can be observed in summer. Common Terns also breeds there.

Access: from Maldon or South Woodham Ferrers, follow signs to Southminster and then to Bradwell. In Bradwell-on-Sea take a road right to a car park by Eastlands Farm and then walk 1 mile to St Peter's-on-the-Wall and the Observatory.

Permits: not required.

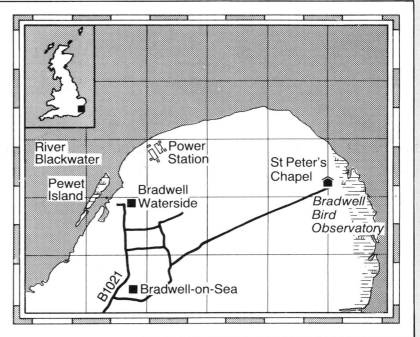

BROWNSEA ISLAND, DORSET

OS 195

Location: the largest of several islands in Poole Harbour, near Bournemouth.

Habitats: large areas of intertidal mud and sand, and heathland. Once a derelict and overgrown privately-owned 'sanctuary', Brownsea has been converted into a first-class bird reserve.

Birds: in summer the lagoon holds a colony of Sandwich Terns and there is a large heronry. Nightjar, Dartford Warbler and feral Golden Pheasant breed on the heaths. Waders seen in spring and autumn, include Little Stint, Curlew Sandpiper, Black-tailed Godwit, Greenshank and Spotted Redshank. Avocets frequently winter here.

In winter there is a good chance of a scarce grebe, a diver or Red-breasted Merganser, while the population of Black-tailed Godwits is one of the most important in the country. Ruff are also frequently present, but all of these birds must be sought from the mainland because Brownsea is closed from September to March.

Access: by regular boat from Sandbanks on Poole Quay.

Permits: on arrival.

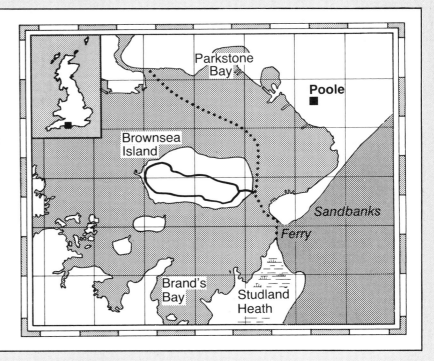

BREYDON WATER, NORFOLK OS 134

Location: this 'inland' estuary lies west of Great Yarmouth, the mouth of several rivers that drain the Norfolk Broads.

Habitats: huge area of intertidal mud flats, with low-lying grazing marshes intersected by dykes and with patches of mud.

Birds: there may be good numbers of waders in the northern part, with roosts easily viewable from the area west of the railway station. The most abundant species are Grey Plover, Knot, Redshank, Curlew and Dunlin. Spring and autumn passage can be productive, with Avocet, Whimbrel, both godwits, Ruff, Spotted Redshank all regular, and rarer visitors, such as Broad-billed Sandpiper, a possibility. Other reasonably regular migrants include Spoonbill and Black Tern, both in spring and autumn.

Many of the more exciting winter birds frequent the marshes south of the estuary where harriers, Rough-legged Buzzard (in some winters), Merlin, Peregrine, Short-eared Owl, both Bewick's and Whooper Swans, Twite, Snow Bunting and a regular, if elusive, flock of Lapland Buntings may be found. This huge area is well worth the effort of exploration and, though there are usually birders present at weekends, the weekday watcher may well walk for miles without seeing another soul.

At the end of the day a short trip to the mouth of the river at Gorleston-on-Sea may produce a rarer gull or two among the flocks of the more common species. Glaucous Gulls, in particular, are often present and there may well be a seaduck or two.

Access: from Great Yarmouth railway station walk along the wall westwards to two hides. Views are perfectly satisfactory without entering. A footpath along the southern shore starts at the Haven Bridge, but many birders prefer to start at Burgh Castle at the head of the estuary. It is this area that most regularly produces the more interesting species of winter visitors.

Permits: available for the hides, but casual observers usually do not bother to enter.

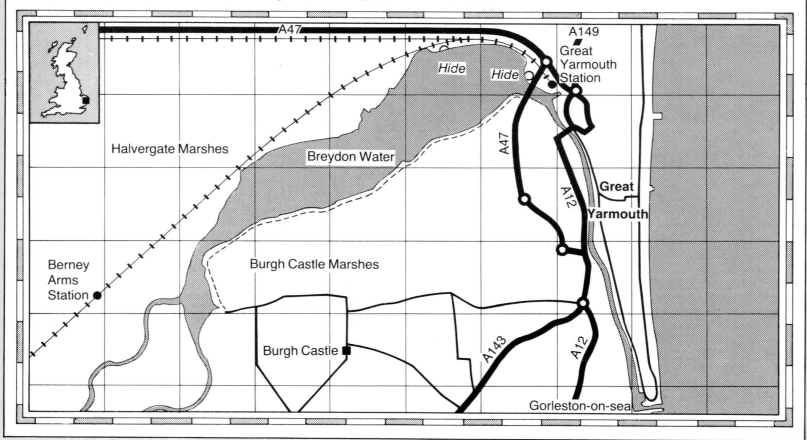

BULLERS OF BUCHAN, GRAMPIAN OS 30

Location: these cliffs lie on the east coast about 23 miles north of Aberdeen and 7 miles south of Peterhead.

Habitats: the area of sea cliffs here is one of the most accessible of seabird colonies, while the little wooded valley behind Cruden Bay is often worth searching for small migrants, especially in autumn.

Birds: though there is nothing rare or unusual here, Bullers of Buchan is a delightful seabird colony, with thousands of birds wheeling and calling at close range. All the usual species are present, including Guillemot, Razorbill and Puffin, Kittiwake, Shag and Fulmar. Many birders rank these cliffs as some of the best for seabirds in mainland Scotland.

Access: stop on the A975 north of Aberdeen just beyond Cruden Bay, where a track leads to Robie's Haven. Check that you have the correct track with the OS map. Another track leads via the wooded valley to Port Errol.

Permits: not required.

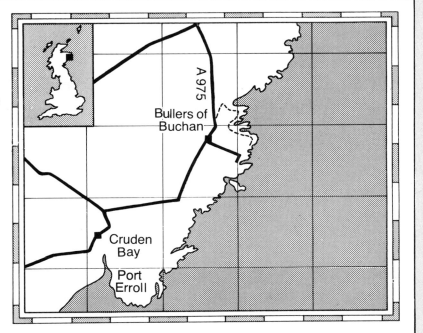

BURRY INLET, WEST GLAMORGAN OS 159

Location: about 7 miles west of Swansea, and partially enclosed by the Gower Peninsula to the south.

Habitats: the inlet is the huge intertidal estuary of the river Loughor. The sand and mud here attract a huge population of birds, but access is made awkward by the presence of large areas of saltmarsh. At the estuary mouth is Whiteford Burrows, a large dune system with marram grass and plantations of conifers.

Birds: primarily a winter birdwatching site, known internationally for huge numbers of Oystercatchers. Knot and Dunlin are plentiful, as are Curlew, Redshank and Turnstone. Other birds include Brent and Eider duck, a few scarcer grebes, both godwits and even the occasional overwintering Greenshank. Viewing is difficult in passage periods though.

Access: good views can be obtained along the B4295 west of Penclawdd, notably at Crofty. Access to Whiteford Burrows is restricted to a marked path that runs from Cwm Ivy (where there is a National Nature Reserve Information Centre) through the pine woods. Opposite Berges Island is a hide that is often good on a rising tide. Continue to Whiteford Point for the high-tide wader roost.

Permits: not necessary, except off the footpaths at the Point.

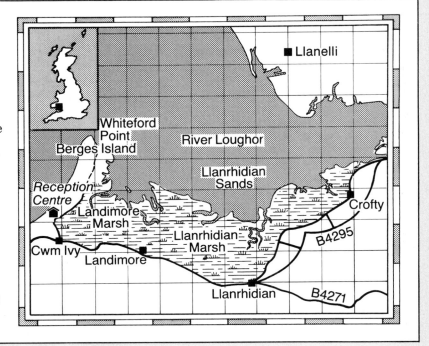

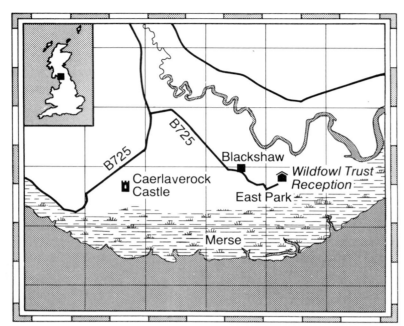

CAERLAVEROCK, DUMFRIES AND GALLOWAY OS 84 & 85

Location: this famous marsh lies on the northern shore of the Solway Firth about 9 miles to the south of Dumfries.

Habitats: the intertidal mud banks of this part of the Solway are backed by extensive areas of saltmarshes, known locally as 'merse'. Sea walls protect an area of farmland divided by well-kept hedges and fences. There are two artificial pools in the grounds of the Wildfowl Trust.

Birds: the merse is the winter home of the entire population of Barnacle Geese that breed on the Arctic island of Spitsbergen. Up to 10,000 can be seen throughout the winter, though in March they split into smaller groups. Also present are even larger numbers of Pink-footed Geese. Like the Greylags they prefer feeding on farmland. There are plenty of ducks and waders in winter here with attendant Peregrine, Merlin and Hen Harrier. Also good during passage periods.

Access: from Dumfries southward on the B725 and park by Caerlaverock Castle. Take a minor road right to the Wildfowl Trust Centre at East Park Farm.

Permits: admission fee at the Wildfowl Trust Centre.

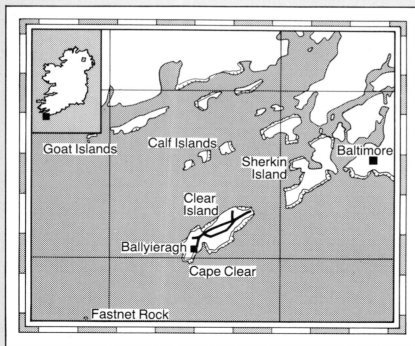

CAPE CLEAR, CO. CORK, IRISH REPUBLIC IOS½ 24

Location: the extreme south-west of Ireland, facing the open Atlantic, 50 miles west of Cork.

Habitats: an inhabited island with a crofting and fishing community. There are moors, cliffs and comparatively little cover. It is the geographical position rather than specific habitats that gives Clear its excellent reputation as a birdwatching site.

Birds: breeding birds include Black Guillemot and Chough, while migration brings a wide variety of scarce and rare species. One of the best seawatch stations around the shores of the British Isles, the current fashion for ocean-going small boat trips in autumn can trace its origins to the pioneering work of the Cape Clear Bird Observatory.

From the southern headlands of Pointanbullig, Blananarragaun and Pointabullaun autumn seawatchers may observe spectacular movements of shearwaters, including Great, Cory's and Sooty. There are vast numbers of Manx Shearwaters, together with petrels, Great Skuas, Gannets and the odd albatross. There are records of Little Shearwater and claims of Wilson's Petrel.

Access: by boat from Baltimore, about 7 miles south-west of Skibbereen.

CAIRNGORMS, HIGHLAND OS 35 & 36

Location: this vast area, covering 180 square miles, is centred on the growing holiday resort of Aviemore.

Habitats: as diverse as it is large, this area offers the visiting birder the chance of a lengthy holiday of exploration, with a host of excellent birds to find. There are grassy fields and even hedgerows along the banks of the River Spey, but these quickly give way to more rocky areas of heath, with deciduous and coniferous trees. There are remnants of the old Caledonian forest of Scots Pine (particularly at Rothiemurchus) as well as modern plantations. At higher altitudes open heather moorland becomes dominant and this gradually becomes more sparse until on the high tops of Cairn Gorm one finds a sort of Scottish tundra with rocks and dwarf vegetation.

Birds: essentially a summer haunt of breeding birds, many in need of protection, so exact directions cannot always be given. There are Golden Eagles and Peregrines here, though the only 'public' site for either is the cliffs above Craigellachie where the falcon is frequently seen. The elusive Honey Buzzard, Goshawk and Greenshank also breed here, along with the more common Black Grouse, Capercaillie, Scottish Crossbill and Crested Tit. Finally, on the high tops, there are Ptarmigan, Snow Bunting and Dotterel. The region has, in recent years, been the home of breeding Temminck's Stint, Wood and Green Sandpipers, as well as Brambling, Lapland Bunting and Shore Lark.

Access: a good map, compass and sensible waterproof clothing are essential. Start at Aviemore and take the road to Loch Morlich for the old Scots Pine forests. Continue up to the ski-lift station and, if the weather is good, take a lift to the top for high-level birds. Further south take the track starting at Feshiebridge along Glen Feshie; this penetrates remote country and for the energetic there is a climb up Carn Ban Mor. For those who prefer wild, unfrequented country an approach from the south via Deeside is charming.

Permits: none required.

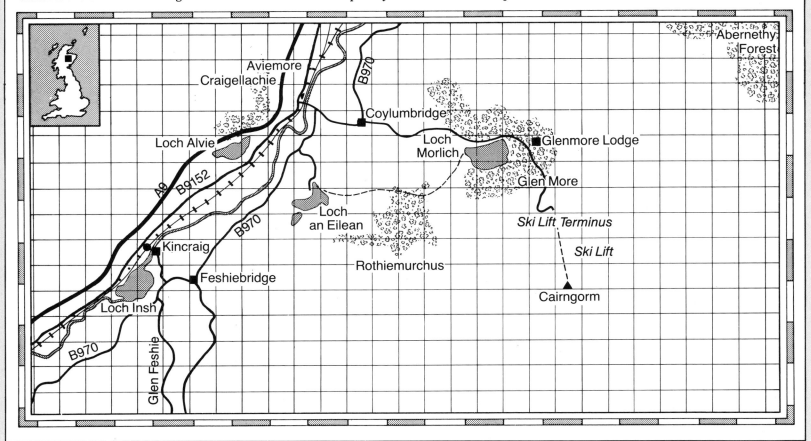

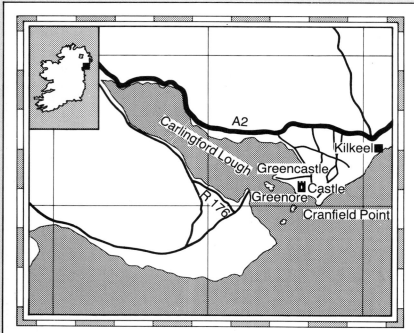

CARLINGFORD LOUGH, CO. DOWN, NORTHERN IRELAND

OSNI 29

Location: this inlet lies on the east coast of Ireland and stretches inland as far as Newry, forming the boundary between Northern Ireland and the Irish Republic.

Habitats: less an estuary than a sunken valley carved by a former glacier. Intertidal areas are thus confined to the narrow inner area toward Newry and a large bay west of Greencastle Point.

Birds: Curlew, Redshank, Dunlin and other waders are numerous, especially in winter. Several of the more widespread species of duck reach good numbers, though the flock of Scaup is fast declining. Brent Geese also winter here. In summer there are sizeable colonies of terns on Green Island, which is an RSPB reserve. These include Common, Arctic, Sandwich and the rare Roseate Tern. Black Guillemot breed at Cranfield Point.

Access: the inner estuary can be seen from the roads that line each side. The eastern one, the A2, leads to the largest area of mud viewable from Greencastle. This is also the best viewpoint for the birds of Green Island, which is out of bounds.

Permits: not required; not available for Green Island.

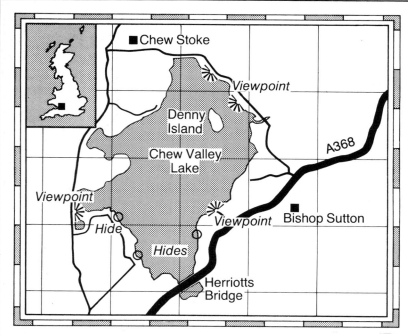

CHEW VALLEY LAKE, AVON

OS 172 & 182

Location: this large artificial lake lies about 5 miles south of Bristol, between the city and the Mendip Hills.

Habitats: the reservoir was flooded in 1953. It is shallow in many places with gently shelving banks. There are reed beds as well as areas of woodland and bushes.

Birds: winter brings an excellent collection of wildfowl that regularly includes Bewick's Swan, together with good flocks of Wigeon, Shoveler, Pochard and Tufted Duck. Ruddy Duck are present throughout the year and Garganey regularly spend the summer here. Less numerous in winter, but nevertheless regular, are Goldeneye, Goosander, Golden Plover and Dunlin. Other waders, including Ruff, Greenshank, Spotted Redshank, Black-tailed Godwit and Little Stint, are regular on passage, especially in autumn. Terns also pass through, Black Terns being regular both in spring and autumn.

Access: the A368 crosses the south-eastern arm of the reservoir near Herriot's Bridge. Public roads allow viewing at many spots. There is a nature reserve at Herriott's Bridge and there are several hides along the southern and western shores.

Permits: not required.

CHICHESTER HARBOUR, WEST SUSSEX   OS 197

Location: this huge area lies between Portsmouth and Chichester, alongside Langstone Harbour, which is in Hampshire (*see page* 287).

Habitats: an intertidal basin that, at low water, exposes a huge expanse of mud. The central channels remain full of water, even at low tide, and the surroundings are a mixture of urban, suburban and rural landscapes, but Chichester is far more popular with the yachting fraternity than Langstone where the birds are generally less disturbed.

Birds: wildfowl and waders in autumn and winter are the main attraction. Brent Geese, numbering up to 10,000, can be seen, along with good numbers of ducks, including Pintail and Wigeon. Red-breasted Merganser and Goldeneye are regular along with the occasional scarce grebe, though these species are more often found at Langstone. Waders include good numbers of Knot and Grey Plover, together with both godwits.

Access: leave Havant and the A27 southwards on the A3023 to Langstone Bridge, where good views can be obtained. Continue to Hayling Island, turn left to North Hayling and take the road to the sea-wall at Tye. Continue to South Hayling and to Black Point.

Permits: not required.

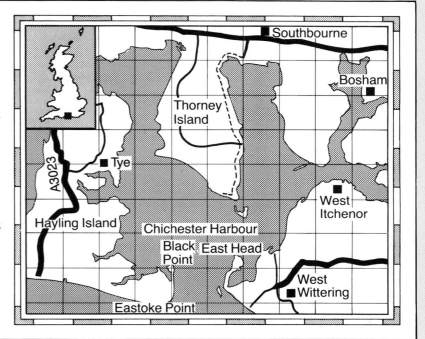

CLIFFE AND HALSTOW, KENT

OS 178

Location: on the southern shore of the Thames estuary to the north of the Medway towns of Chatham, Gillingham and Rochester.

Habitats: from Cliffe to Allhallows lies a huge area of low-lying grazing land, separated from intertidal mud banks by a large sea-wall. Inland, there are bushy hedgerows and woods. Both the clay pits at Cliffe and the mudflats at Yantlett Creek attract birds.

Birds: waders on passage are excellent, with good numbers at Cliffe Pools, including Little Stint, Curlew and Wood Sandpipers, Ruff, Black-tailed Godwit and often a rarity. Black Terns are regular, both in spring and autumn. In winter White-fronted Geese can be seen, along with Bewick's Swans and a good variety of duck on the Thames. The nearby RSPB heronry is worth a visit. Merlin, Hen Harrier and Short-eared Owl all visit during hard weather.

Access: from Cliffe village follow a track westwards to the pools and then turn right out to the coastguard cottages. Several pools can be seen from this footpath as well as from other tracks to the south. St Mary's and Egypt Bay are reached by turning northwards ½ mile east of High Halstow to Decoy Farm and Swigshole. Walk to the sea-wall. Northward Hill RSPB Reserve is famous for its heronry.

Permits: required only for the RSPB reserve.

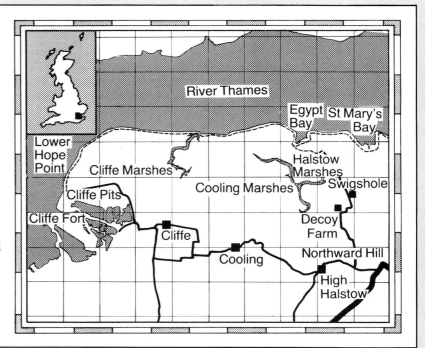

CLEY, NORFOLK OS 133

Location: the North Norfolk coast 1 mile to the east of Blakeney.
Habitats: an outstanding and varied wetland on an excellent coast.
Birds: Cley has long been regarded as the best birding spot in Britain. In summer, there are breeding Bittern, Bearded Tit, Avocet, and Sedge and Reed Warblers. But it is the passage periods that bring peak numbers of both birds and birders. In spring, waders include Kentish Plover and Temminck's Stint, Spoonbills are often present, and Black-tailed Godwit, Ruff and Garganey may or may not stay to breed. In autumn Greenshank, Wood Sandpiper, Little Stint, Curlew Sandpiper and Spotted Redshank are more or less continually present, along with minor rarities. All can be seen from the hides opposite the warden's house. Seawatching is also good. A northerly wind may produce Manx Shearwater, Arctic, Great and Pomarine Skuas, Gannet and divers, but several other scarcer seabirds are also seen every year. Small migrants turn up around the village. Barred Warbler is regular every autumn, along with many of the commoner warblers, chats and flycatchers.

In winter, Brent and Greylag Geese are plentiful and there are good flocks of waders and gulls, the latter including a regular Glaucous Gull. Shore Lark and Snow Bunting are also seen.
Access: Cley Marshes are a reserve of the Norfolk Naturalists' Trust and are open daily from April to October except Mondays. There are well-marked paths, hides and a visitor centre. Cley Coastguards is an excellent public spot. A small car park giving access to the East Bank – a great meeting place for birders. From here there are excellent views over the reed beds and, near the shore, over Arnold's Marsh, one of the best wader pools in Britain.
Permits: available at 10.00 a.m. from the Norfolk Naturalists' Trust centre on the A149 east of the village. Essential for autumn visits.

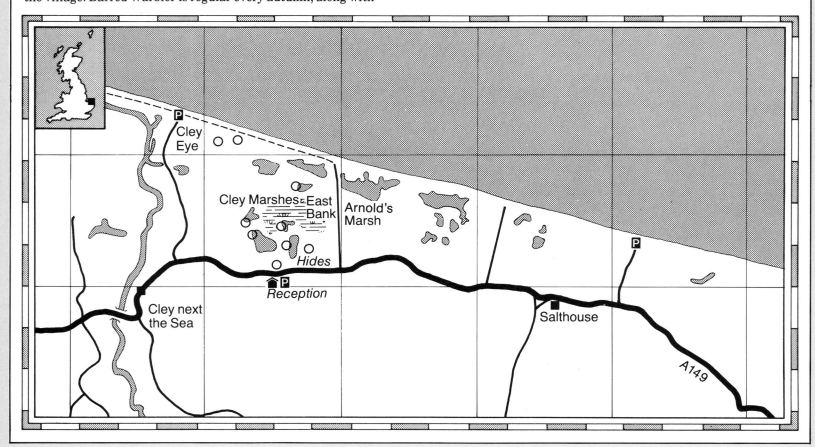

CLO MOR, HIGHLAND OS 9

Location: these fearsome cliffs are more or less the north-western tip of mainland Scotland near Cape Wrath.

Habitats: the cliffs are the highest on the British mainland and boast a major and spectacular seabird colony. Inland, the rolling moors are bleak and hostile, but hold exciting birds in summer.

Birds: the usual collection of cliff-nesting seabirds can be seen, but in fantastic numbers and against a spectacular backdrop. The colonies of Guillemot and Puffin are huge, but there are Razorbills, Black Guillemots and Kittiwakes along with Fulmars and a continuous offshore movement of Gannets that do not, however, breed here. Peregrines do breed, however, and there are Golden Eagle and Ptarmigan, Greenshank and Great Skua here as well.

Access: take the foot ferry across the Kyle of Durness and then the minibus towards Cape Wrath. Get off at a track that leads northwards to Kearvaig and walk to the right along the cliff tops to Clo Mor. It is possible to return to the road 'overland' via Loch Inshore, but this is tough country and should be treated with the respect it merits. Make sure you are equipped with proper weatherproof hiking gear, map, compass and other survival equipment.

Permits: not required.

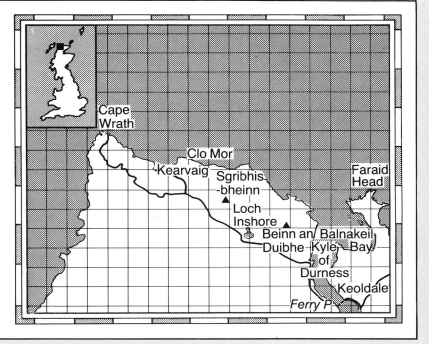

CLUMBER AND THE DUKERIES, NOTTINGHAM OS 120

Location: between M1 and A1 north of Nottingham is a series of large mansions and estates collectively known as the Dukeries.

Habitats: parkland, ornamental lakes, woodland and estate farms.

Birds: the Clumber-Welbeck area is a stronghold of the Honey Buzzard, a fact which remained unpublished until quite recently. Even now birders should restrict their activities to the roads and other areas of public access. May to August is the best time. Otherwise there is a good cross section of woodland birds that includes Sparrowhawk, all three woodpeckers, the commoner warblers, Hawfinch and Redstart. The Hawfinches, as elsewhere, are easiest to see in winter.

Access: from the B6034 south of Worksop turn west towards Norton. The lakes of Welbeck Park are on the right, and there is parking space for a few cars. Here there are good views across the water to the woods beyond for soaring Honey Buzzard. Return to the B6005 and cross it to Carburton and fork right to the chapel in Clumber Park where woodland can be explored.

Permits: parking fee at Clumber.

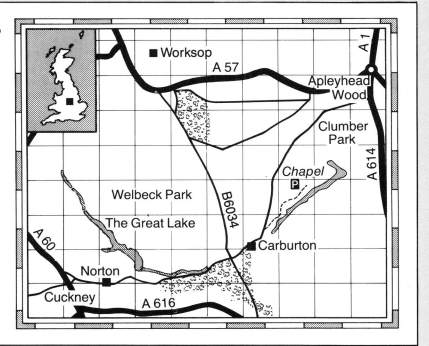

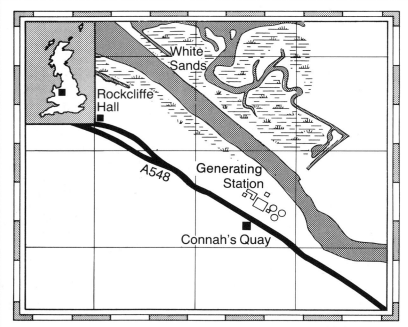

CONNAH'S QUAY, CLWYD OS 117

Location: this area lies at the head of the Dee Estuary about 7 miles to the west of Chester in a predominantly industrial landscape.

Habitats: the Central Electricity Generating Board has declared a large area surrounding its power station a nature reserve. It includes fields, saltmarshes and intertidal mud. A 'scrape' has been created – an area of shallow, brackish water and mud dotted with small islands to attract breeding birds – and there are hides and a reserve centre.

Birds: waders use the pools here as a high-tide roost and are best at the highest tides, but there are always good numbers of these birds on passage and in winter. Spotted Redshank are something of a local speciality, especially in winter, and in autumn Little Stint, Curlew Sandpiper, Ruff and Black-tailed Godwit are regular. Ducks include most of the species found on the estuary, including Pintail, Wigeon, Shoveler, Goldeneye and Red-breasted Merganser, and both Peregrine and Merlin are regular winter visitors.

Access: from the A548 at Connah's Quay Power Station.

Permits: are essential and may be obtained from The Station Manager, Connah's Quay Power Station, Connah's Quay, Deeside; or from the Deeside Naturalist's Society, Melrose, 38 Kelsterton Road, Connah's Quay, Clwyd. There is an open day once a month.

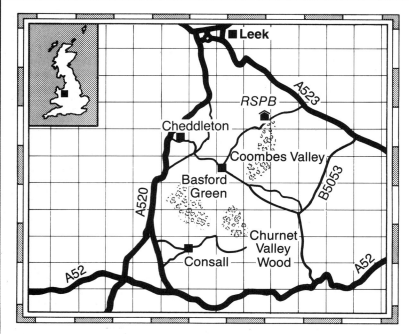

COOMBES VALLEY, STAFFORDSHIRE OS 118

Location: to the south of Leek the RSPB has established three reserves centred on its original Coombes Valley site. They can all be visited in a day: Coombes Valley, Rough Knipe, Booth's Wood. Stoke-on-Trent is about 13 miles to the south-west.

Habitats: this area is deeply dissected by steep-sided valleys with rough, tumbling streams. The valley sides are covered with mixed deciduous woodland, with a surrounding network of grassy fields broken by more extensive areas of woodlands and scrub.

Birds: a typical woodland fauna exists here and a visit to this site offers a chance to enjoy beautiful walks and a day of pleasant, relaxed birding. Birds include all three British species of woodpecker, Pied Flycatcher, Wood Warbler, Tawny and Long-eared Owls, Tree Pipit and Sparrowhawk, plus Dipper, Kingfisher and Grey Wagtail.

Access: leave Leek southwards on the A523. Turn left signposted Apesford and the reserve entrance is on the left after about 1 mile. The two other reserves lie off the A520, turning left to Consall and then following a footpath. Coombes Valley is open every day except Tuesday and there is a nature trail and hides.

Permits: free on arrival.

COPINSAY, ORKNEY OS 6

Location: this small island lies to the east of the Orkney Mainland about 2 miles south-east of Point of Ayre.

Habitats: this is a mainly cliff-bound island, with a green interior and a low-lying rocky shoreline that is neither isolated nor exposed to the prevailing westerly winds.

Birds: Copinsay is an RSPB reserve purchased in memory of James Fisher, the ornithologist and bird publicist/author who had a profound influence on 20th-century British ornithology. Its cliffs hold major seabird colonies, including 15,000 pairs of Guillemot, along with Razorbill, Black Guillemot and Puffin. There are countless Kittiwake and Fulmar, a large colony of Shag and a colony of Arctic Tern.

Access: by boat from Skaill, which lies north of Point of Ayre. Contact Mr S. Foubister (Tel: 085 674252) to make arrangements for a day trip at any time. Best in May and June. Visitors are requested to take great care when approaching the cliff tops.

Permits: not required.

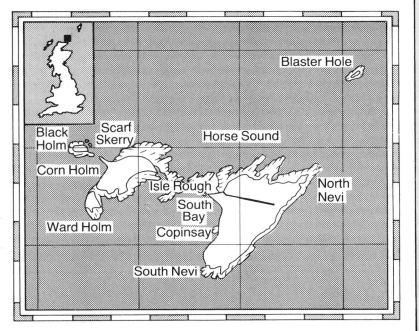

COQUET ISLAND, NORTHUMBERLAND OS 81

Location: this RSPB reserve lies just off the coast of Northumberland, opposite the village of Amble (just north of Hauxley: *see page* 274) and near the mouth of the River Coquet, about 24 miles to the north of Newcastle.

Habitat: this is a relatively low island with a grassy flat top that, while being quite unsuited to cliff-nesting seabirds, does provide a home for large colonies of terns and other birds, similar to those of the Farne Islands (*see page* 266) about 24 miles to the north.

Birds: among the terns that breed here are large colonies of both Common and Arctic, along with more densely packed Sandwich Terns. A few pairs of Roseate Terns still breed each year but it is difficult to pick them out from among the milling masses of the more abundant and widespread species. The top of the island offers ideal conditions for Puffins to excavate their burrows. Several hundred of these attractive little auks breed here, as do a number of Eider.

Access: from the A1068 to Amble. Arrange with the boatman Mr Easton (Tel: 0665 710384 or 712460) to take a trip around the island.

Permits: no landing is allowed, but the birds can be seen well from the boat.

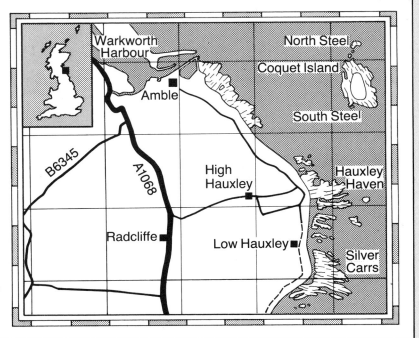

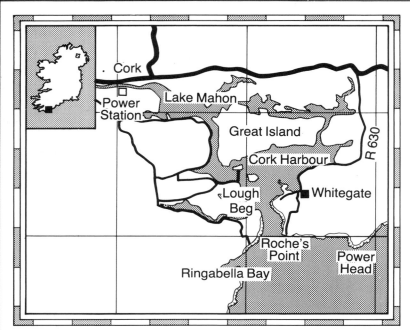

CORK HARBOUR, CO. CORK, IRISH REPUBLIC IOS½ 25

Location: immediately south of Cork on the southern coast.

Habitats: this is a deep inlet with a maze of channels and backwaters similar to those found along the coasts of south Devon and Cornwall. Large intertidal areas exist, but are separated from one another by narrow, steep-sided shorelines.

Birds: this is one of the finest wildfowl and wader sites in Ireland with several species reaching significant numbers. Ducks are often abundant, with the Shelduck flock being, at one time, the largest in the country. There are also Wigeon, Teal, and a regular flock of Pintail. Mostly these are concentrated in the North Channel that extends west to east at the top of the estuary. Here too are many waders, including an autumn roost of Oystercatcher as well as Dunlin, Redshank and an important flock of Black-tailed Godwit. Waders are generally more widespread and less concentrated than ducks. Cork also has the largest gull roost on the southern coastline and unusual species may occasionally be found alongside the commoner ones.

Access: the whole area can be explored via public roads from Cork, starting at Tivoli and Lough Beg in the west.

Permits: not required.

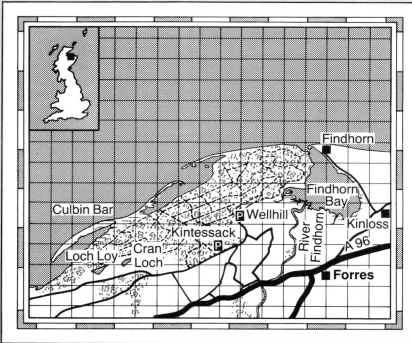

CULBIN BAR AND FINDHORN BAY, GRAMPIAN & HIGHLAND

OS 27

Location: on the Moray Firth, 4 miles north of Forres.

Habitats: an offshore sand bar protects a large dune system that has been planted with conifers. To the east, Findhorn Bay is an almost land-locked intertidal basin.

Birds: Crested Tit and Scottish Crossbill are present, along with Capercaillie, Long-eared Owl and Buzzard. The shoreline supports a few Eider, Ringed Plover and terns. On passage waders are often good, especially at Findhorn Bay, where Greenshank, Spotted Redshank and Whimbrel are regular. The sea in winter is excellent for divers and ducks, and on occasions huge numbers of Scoter, Velvet Scoter and Long-tailed Duck may be observed.

Access: explore a network of tracks through the forest by leaving Forres westward on the A96 and taking a minor road north to Kintessack. Continue to Welhill Gate; park and walk from there. Findhorn Bay is also reached from Forres by following the B9011 east and north to Findhorn and viewing from the road.

Permits: not required.

DORNOCH FIRTH, HIGHLAND

OS 21

Location: on the east coast of Scotland 28 miles north of Inverness.

Habitats: extensive intertidal areas along both shorelines, mainly in large bays, but fortunately the best birds are concentrated on the sea at the north, and on the small Skibo Inlet.

Birds: waders and wildfowl are the main attraction, with a significant population of seaducks occurring regularly at the mouth of the firth northwards to Embo. These include Long-tailed Duck, Eider and both British species of scoter, along with Merganser and Goldeneye, and reasonably regular King Eider and Surf Scoter. Winter waders include the more common species, along with regular Purple Sandpiper. Hen Harrier, Peregrine and Short-eared Owl are sometimes present at this season. Passage waders are not outstanding, but Osprey is regular in summer and autumn and Arctic Tern sometimes abundant; they breed at Loch Fleet (*see page* 292) a little way to the north.

Access: the surrounding roads offer good views, particularly at Tain and the Skibo Inlet, which is reached via the A9, turning southwards at Clashmore to Meikle Ferry. Embo lies north of Dornoch, east of the A9. Loch Eye should not be missed in winter.

Permits: none required.

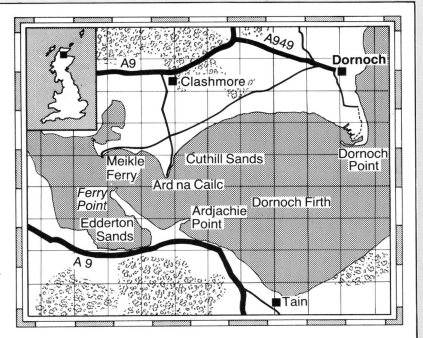

DRAYCOTE WATER, WARWICKSHIRE   OS 151

Location: this large reservoir lies about 4 miles south of Rugby off the M45.

Habitats: covering 700 acres Draycote offers waterbirds a refuge in what is otherwise a rather barren area. It has part natural and part concrete-lined banks, with a shallow area in the north. It is widely used for water sports, but still attracts birds.

Birds: this is essentially a winter site, with ducks the main attraction. There are decent numbers of Wigeon and Shoveler, and good-sized flocks of the more common diving ducks. It is, however, the possibility of seeing the less usual species, such as Scoter, Scaup, Smew and Goosander, that makes this reservoir attractive to local birders. Spring and autumn passage bring terns, including Black Terns, and there are a few waders in autumn.

Access: for the non-regular visitor there is access from the A45 or the A426 via a public footpath that runs along the northern shoreline between Thurlaston and Toft. This passes a hide. Regulars can obtain a permit that enables them to drive all the way round the reservoir.

Permits: available annually from Severn-Trent Water Authority, Avon House, Demountford Way, Cannon Park, Coventry CV4 7EJ.

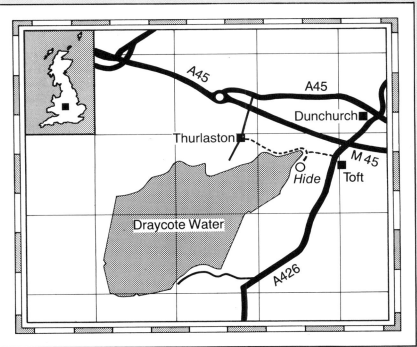

DUNGENESS, KENT OS 189

Location: the peninsula extends into the English Channel, 3 miles south-east of Lydd.

Habitats: low-lying shingle that has been excavated for gravel forming extensive freshwater lakes. The point attracts hosts of migrants. There is a well-run bird observatory and a large RSPB reserve.

Birds: in winter the gravel pits are a haunt of ducks, divers, waders and gulls. Smew, Goldeneye and Goosander are frequently present, as are divers (mostly Red-throated, but sometimes Black-throated and Great Northern) and Black-necked Grebes.

During passage periods waders and terns are usually good, with Little Gulls in autumn. Gulls and terns frequent 'The Patch', the warm-water outlets of the nuclear power station. Small birds include all the usual warblers, chats and flycatchers together with a few major rarities. Seabird passage regularly produces skuas, shearwaters, Gannet, terns and auks, with Pomarine Skua in the first half of May. In summer, there are good breeding colonies of Common and Sandwich Terns, with a few Mediterranean Gulls. Black Redstarts breed on the power station and a few pairs of Wheatear breed at specially created nest sites.

Access: several roads lead southwards from the A259 to Dungeness. The road between Lydd and Lydd-on-Sea passes the best gravel pits and the RSPB reserve lies to the west of this at Boulderwall Farm. It is open daily except Tuesday throughout the year and has four hides overlooking the main water. Dungeness proper is reached by following signs over a private road that starts near 'The Pilot' pub.

The bird observatory is situated at the end of a small terrace of houses and is reached by taking a left at the old lighthouse. It offers accommodation and information, and holds regular open days. The power station must be approached via the old lighthouse, *not* the access road near the pits. 'The Patch' can be reached on foot.

Permits: only required for the RSPB reserve.

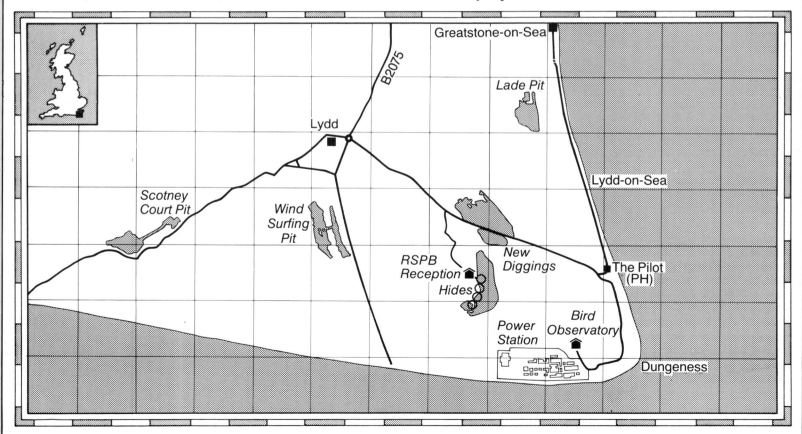

DUNNET HEAD, HIGHLAND OS 12

Location: the most northerly point of mainland Scotland.

Habitats: this is a rocky promontory extending northwards into the Pentland Firth, with extensive areas of cliffs in the north and east. The top is rolling rather than rugged, with areas of moorland broken by many lochs. To the south is the sandy Dunnet Bay, with St John's Loch to the west.

Birds: a fine collection of breeding seabirds, including Guillemot, Razorbill, Black Guillemot, Puffin and Kittiwake. There are usually Gannets and Great Skuas offshore and the doves are probably the genuine wild Rock Dove. The sandy bay to the south has Arctic Tern and Great Northern Diver in summer and is a regular haunt of divers and seaducks in winter. Other ducks, together with Whooper Swan, can be found at this time on St John's Loch.

Access: leave the A836 at Dunnet on the B855 to Dunnet Head, where there is a car park a short distance from the lighthouse. Walk north and east for the cliffs, but be careful. The lochs on the Head can be seen from the road or via paths. The A836 east of Dunnet passes St John's Loch, while to the west there is a parking area at the north-eastern corner of Dunnet Bay.

Permits: not required.

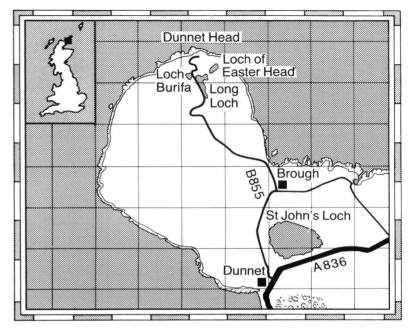

DYFI ESTUARY, DYFED & GWYNEDD OS 135

Location: below Machynlleth and Aberdyfi (formerly called Aberdovey).

Habitats: a large intertidal area with good areas of mud. The northern shoreline is steep, but to the south are large areas of saltmarsh backed by grazing marshes. Cors Fochno (Borth Bog), with extensive sand dunes all but closes the river mouth.

Birds: in winter a small flock of Greenland White-fronted Geese can often be seen from the northern shore along the A493 at the head of the estuary. There are also good flocks of Wigeon, Red-breasted Merganser and Goldeneye. Birds of prey include Hen Harrier and Merlin. Divers, mainly Red-throated, may sometimes be seen at the estuary mouth, but are always present offshore. There are some waders but gulls may be more interesting during passages.

Access: near the mouth at Ynyslas is a National Nature Reserve information centre with good views over estuary and sea. There is further access on the south shore by following the footpath along the bank of the Afon Leri where it crosses the B4353 just over ½ mile east of Ynyslas. The A493 along the northern shore will produce geese and ducks, but the views are too distant for much else.

Permits: not required.

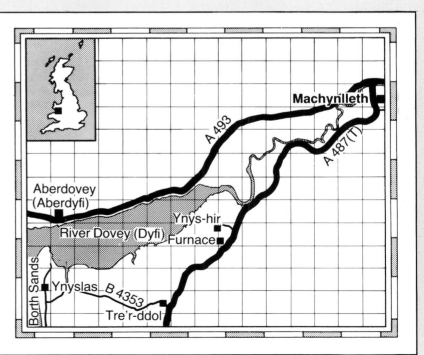

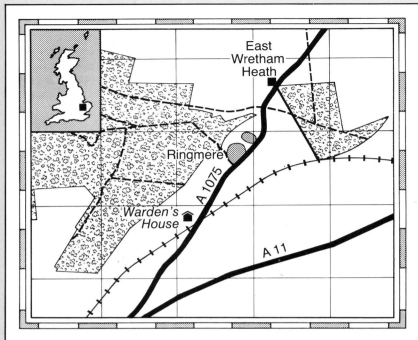

EAST WRETHAM HEATH, NORFOLK OS 144

Location: this area of Breckland lies north of Thetford along the A1075.

Habitat: originally a stony wasteland of infertile soils grazed by sheep, Breckland has been broken up by the planting of Scots pine windbrakes and more recently by extensive conifer plantations and conversion to arable farmland. Here and there, mainly in nature reserves, areas similar to the original landscape can be found.

Birds: this Norfolk Naturalists' Trust Reserve holds a cross section of the birds for which Breckland is best known. There is not, however, a single area left where all of the specialities can be seen, so dashing around is usually a necessary ingredient of a day in the Brecks. Here there is a good cross-section of heath and woodland specialities. Breckland is best known for Stone-curlew, Crossbill, Woodlark and the all-but-gone Red-backed Shrike.

Access: from Thetford northwards on the A11 and take the A1075. Stop at the first house on the left after the railway where the warden will issue permits from 10.00 a.m. (except Tuesdays). The reserve lies some 2 miles north on the left and is well signposted.

Permits: as above for a small charge.

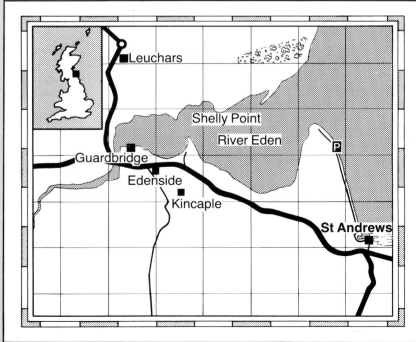

EDEN ESTUARY, FIFE OS 59

Location: this site lies on the east coast of Scotland immediately north of the famous Royal & Ancient golf course at St Andrews.

Habitats: this is, by Scottish standards, a small estuary that enables the visitor to see most of the birds that frequent the intertidal banks of mud. There are extensive areas of dunes at the mouth and a rocky shoreline at St Andrews.

Birds: the Eden is one of the very best of Scottish estuaries for waders and, in autumn in particular, there are really good numbers of several species, including Greenshank as well as Black-tailed and Bar-tailed Godwits. In winter, too, there are good numbers of waders, with Grey Plover and Black-tailed Godwit being notable for Scotland. At this season there are also good concentrations of seaducks, divers and grebes at the estuary mouth.

Access: there is a road from St Andrews northwards along the coast to the estuary mouth at Out Head, from where there are excellent views of the sea and estuary. At the head of the estuary there are good views from the bridge where the A91 crosses the river at Guardbridge.

Permits: though a large area of the estuary is a local nature reserve, permits are not required to view from the locations described above.

ELMLEY MARSHES, KENT OS 178

Location: on the southern shore of the Isle of Sheppey in north Kent, 4 miles north-east of Sittingbourne.

Habitats: the Sheppey shore of the Swale is a maze of rough grazing land, broken here and there by large 'fleets' – old backwaters that have been reclaimed from the estuary. The RSPB has established its Elmley Reserve here and created a large floodwater that now acts as a major high tide roost for wildfowl and waders, as well as a fine stop-over site for migrant waders.

Birds: Elmley is often regarded as predominantly a winter spot, with White-fronted Goose, thousands of ducks and even more waders, with regular Hen Harrier, Peregrine, Merlin and Rough-legged Buzzard. But the passage periods are also excellent for waders, including Little Stint, Curlew, Sandpiper, Ruff, Black-tailed Godwit and Spotted Redshank. In summer there are visiting Montagu's and Marsh Harriers, Avocet, and breeding Little Tern and Ringed Plover.

Access: cross Kingsferry Bridge on to the Isle of Sheppey and watch out for a track on the right after about one mile. Thereafter follow signs to the RSPB car park, the flood and hides.

Permits: available daily on arrival, except Tuesday.

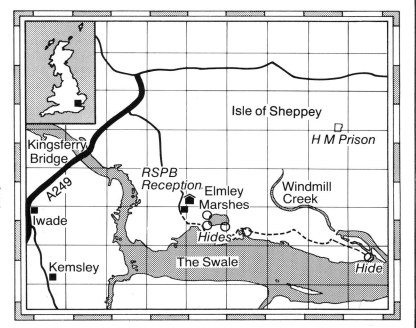

EXE ESTUARY, DEVON OS 192

Location: this fine estuary lies between Exeter and Exmouth on the south Devon coast. Birdwatching is better on the west side.

Habitats: intertidal mud and sand with a reed bed near Exminster. At the mouth is Dawlish Warren, a dune system with interesting slacks (damp hollows between the dunes).

Birds: 600 Black-tailed Godwit, 2000 Brent and 4500 Wigeon winter here, along with Ruff, Greenshank, Grey Plover and thousands of the more common waders. A few Avocets, a Peregrine and a collection of water birds that includes Slavonian Grebe and divers can also be found. During passage periods there is a wider variety of waders, with Whimbrel in spring and Greenshank in autumn. Dawlish Warren may hold interesting small birds and there are terns at the estuary mouth. Fields and hedgerows nearby may hold Cirl Bunting in summer.

Access: approach the head of the estuary from Exminster by parking at the Swans Nest pub and walking the footpath to the Topsham foot ferry. Walk southwards from here to Turf. Also on the west bank there is a tunnel under the railway at Powderham and a track leads northwards from the church. There is free access to the estuary mouth at Dawlish Warren (where there is a hide).

Permits: not required.

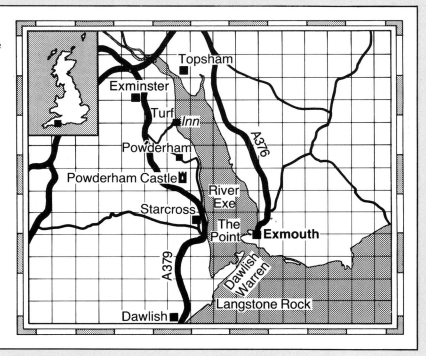

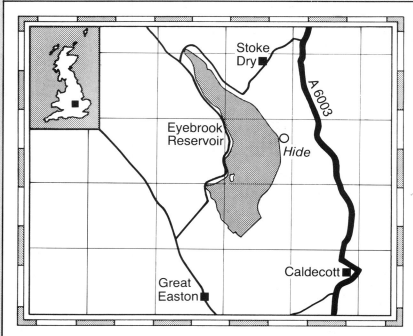

EYEBROOK RESERVOIR, LEICESTERSHIRE OS 141

Location: between Leicester and Peterborough, 4 miles north of Corby.

Habitats: some reservoirs are vast, daunting and give only poor chances of observation. Eyebrook is a complete contrast. An attractive place, it is large enough to hold birds but easily viewed over its entire area. It has mainly shallow, natural banks, with a fine marsh at the northern inlet end. The eastern shore has been planted with conifers.

Birds: in winter Eyebrook is an important wildfowl site, with regular herds of Bewick's Swan and flocks of Greylag Geese. Ducks include Wigeon, Pintail, Goosander and Goldeneye, and there are sometimes a few Smew. Grebes and divers are often present in the new year, though Black-necked Grebes are more frequent in autumn. At this time the western shore and marsh are excellent for waders, including Little Stint, Curlew Sandpiper and Greenshank. Autumn also brings Black and other terns. Ruddy Duck can be seen throughout the year.

Access: from the A6003 or B664. A road runs around the western and northern parts of the reservoir.

Permits: unnecessary for non-regular visitors.

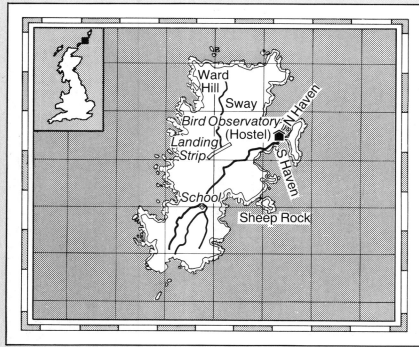

FAIR ISLE, SHETLAND OS 4

Location: roughly half way between Shetland and Orkney.

Habitats: Fair Isle attracts storm-driven waifs from a huge area. On arrival, they find shelter where they can; among the crofters' vegetable patches, along dry-stone walls and in the few areas of scrub. Otherwise Fair Isle is open moorland, with some towering, precipitous sea-cliffs.

Birds: there are thriving colonies of seabirds, including Guillemot, Razorbill, Black Guillemot and Puffin, Kittiwake and Fulmar, plus good numbers of Great and Arctic Skuas, Common and Arctic Terns, Storm Petrel and a gannetry. During spring and autumn Fair Isle becomes really outstanding, attracting many birds that have wandered north of their migration routes. It is also visited by extremely rare Siberian birds, particularly in autumn. Rarities include Lanceolated and Arctic Warblers, Pechora and Olive-backed Pipits, Yellow-breasted Bunting and even Siberian Rubythroat.

Access: there are regular flights by Loganair from Shetland that connect with mainland services. There is also a regular mail boat from Shetland, though the crossing can be rough. Full-board accommodation can be booked at the Bird Observatory, Fair Isle, Shetland, ZE2 9JU.

Permits: none required.

FAIRBURN INGS, NORTH YORKSHIRE OS 105

Location: Fairburn lies on the A1, just north-east of Castleford.
Habitats: the 'Ings' are a series of shallow lagoons, created by mining subsidence, that have matured to produce a number of reed-fringed waters, with some areas of mud and much shallow water. They now form an RSPB reserve with access paths and hides.
Birds: winter wildfowl are a primary attraction. There is a good herd of Whooper Swan, and ducks include Teal, Shoveler, Pochard and Tufted Duck in good numbers, plus regular Goldeneye and Goosander. A gull roost produces the occasional semi-rarity. During passage (particularly after easterly winds during spring) terns may be interesting, with Black Tern regular. In summer the breeding scene is dominated by a large colony of Black-headed Gulls.
Access: leave the A1 at Fairburn and turn westwards toward Allerton. The reserve centre is well marked after one mile and is open at weekends, with access to a board walk and hides. A footpath from the village (off Cut Lane) leads to public hides that are open at all times and good views can also be obtained along the roadsides.
Permits: only needed at weekends: available on arrival at the information centre at Newton, about 1½ miles west of Fairburn (opening hours 10.00 a.m.–5.00 p.m.). Otherwise unnecessary.

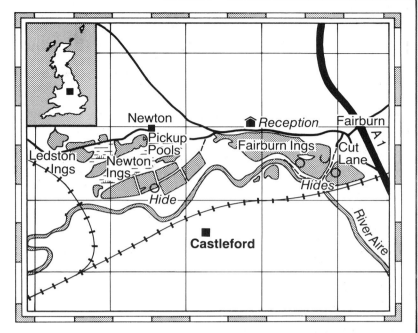

FARAID HEAD, HIGHLAND OS 9

Location: this headland is situated on the north coast of Scotland 3 miles north of Durness and about 9 miles east of Cape Wrath. It is a superb alternative to the better known Clo Mor (*see page* 255) to the west.
Habitats: magnificent cliffs that, though lower and holding fewer birds than those at Clo Mor, are of decidedly easier access and quite magnificent in their own right. The headland is otherwise a windswept moor broken only by a few tracks.
Birds: the usual cliff-dwelling species are present in good numbers, with Fulmar, Kittiwake, Guillemot, Razorbill, Black Guillemot and Puffin all on view. The latter have honeycombed the tops of the eastern cliffs. Gannets are regular offshore, sometimes accompanied by Great Skuas. The bay to the west, as well as the Kyle of Durness itself, is a regular haunt of divers, often including Great Northern, which remain well into summer.
Access: leave Durness on the road to Balnakeil, inspecting the lochs along the way. Continue on tracks to Faraid Head and explore the whole coastline.
Permits: none required.

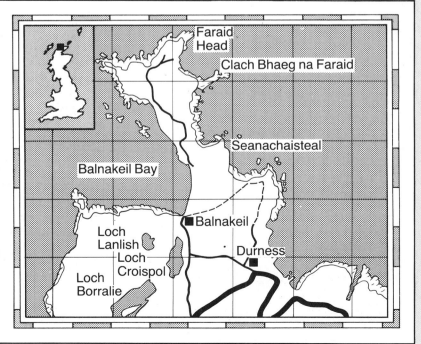

265

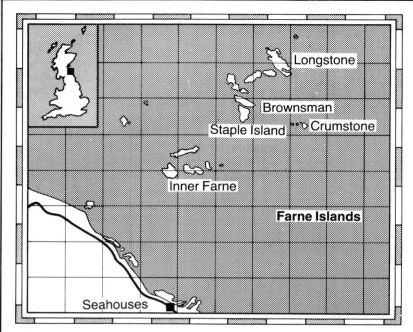

FARNE ISLANDS, NORTHUMBERLAND OS 75

Location: these scattered islands lie 1½ miles off the Northumberland coast near Bamburgh.

Habitats: though they are all rocky, the larger inner islands are lower and flatter, while the outer areas are cliff-girt with deep clefts and gullies. There are also some magnificent isolated stacks.

Birds: the Farnes have long been famous for their connections with the 7th-century Benedictine hermit St Cuthbert, who established Britain's oldest bird sanctuary. They are one of the most visited seabird colonies in the country with thousands of visitors every year. The birds seem quite unconcerned. All the usual auks breed, including vast numbers of Puffin, along with huge numbers of terns that are mainly Arctic and Sandwich, but also Common and a few Roseate. Eider too are numerous and, as elsewhere, remarkably tame, and there are also Shag, Fulmar and Kittiwake.

Access: there are daily boat trips from nearby Seahouses to Staple Island in the mornings and Inner Farne in the afternoons. The latter is best. It is a good idea to book in advance. Contact the National Trust Information Centre, 16 Main Street, Seahouses, Northumberland (Tel: 0665 720424).

Permits: a landing fee is payable on arrival.

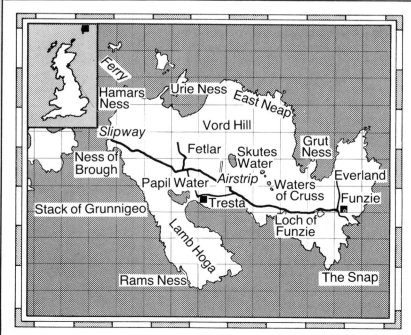

FETLAR, SHETLAND OS 1

Location: south of Unst (*see page 328*) and to the east of Yell.

Habitats: in contrast with the rest of Shetland, Fetlar is a 'green' island, with lushy grassy fields covering much of the southern half. The north has more typically Shetland landscape, with open moors and hills rising gradually to the top of quite extensive cliffs.

Birds: this island has for long been the jewel in the Shetland crown. Snowy Owls bred here in the mid-1960s, but do not breed today for lack of a male. Even so, other specialities, Whimbrel and Red-necked Phalarope, are still present and the cliffs hold vast numbers of auks, Shag, Fulmar and Kittiwake. A boat trip to view the screaming hordes of seabirds on the cliffs is an unforgettable experience, and should be arranged if at all possible – Mid-Yell is the place to try.

Access: the inter-island ferry service, developed as Shetland entered the 'oil-age', makes travel within the islands both simple and cheap. Fetlar can thus be reached via Yell and Unst. There are also regular air services by Loganair. Crofters take paying guests. Explore eastwards to the Loch of Funzie for Whimbrel and Red-necked Phalarope and on Vord Hill for the Snowy Owls.

Permits: available for the Snowy Owls from the RSPB warden at Bealance, Fetlar, Shetland ZE2 9DJ.

FIFE NESS, FIFE OS 59

Location: 10 miles south-east of St Andrews, the headland extends eastwards at the mouth of the Firth of Forth on its northern shore.

Habitats: a low-lying, rocky shore is broken by sandy bays and backed by a golf course and agricultural land. The lack of cover makes it easy to find small migrants.

Birds: this site is best in spring and autumn, when it is visited by a good range of passage migrants, including all the regular chats, flycatchers and warblers. Among them is a scattering of rarities and semi-rarities that regularly includes Wryneck and Bluethroat – both most likely to be visitors from Scandinavia. With a good easterly or north-easterly wind, seawatching can be excellent, with regular Manx and Sooty Shearwaters in autumn, as well as Little Gull, plus Arctic and Great Skuas (and the occasional Pomarine Skua). Common, Arctic and Sandwich Terns, and sometimes Little Terns, too, can be seen on passage in spring and autumn. Divers, auks and seaducks are regularly seen in winter.

Access: from the A917 at Crail. Take the road to the airfield and continue to Fife Ness. Park at the car park by the golf club. All of the small areas of cover can be explored on foot, but do not trespass on private property.

Permits: none required save for parking fees.

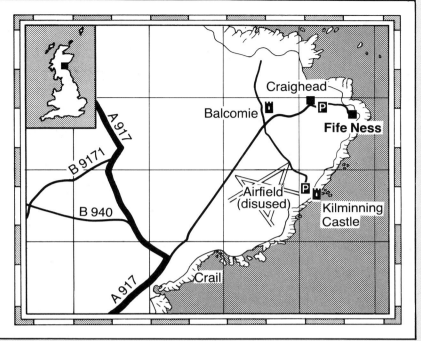

FINGRINGHOE WICK, ESSEX OS 168

Location: this reserve lies on the western shore of the Colne estuary about 5 miles south of Colchester.

Habitats: the open shoreline of the Colne estuary offers a considerable area of mud at low tide. The Essex Naturalists' Trust have created a reserve inside the sea-walls based on an area of disused gravel pits which, together with the surrounding reeds, fields and a small area of woodland, has become one of the finest sites for estuary birds along this coast.

Birds: in winter the area is widely used for feeding and roosting by wildfowl and waders, with many of the more common species present in quite respectable numbers. Red-throated Diver and Slavonian Grebe are also regular visitors. Fingringhoe also attracts Hen Harriers, Short-eared Owl, Merlin and sometimes even a Peregrine. During passage periods there is a greater variety of waders, with Little Stint and Curlew Sandpiper often present in autumn. In summer there are breeding Shelduck, Redshank and Ringed Plover.

Access: leave Colchester southwards on the B1025 toward Mersea and turn left after 2½ miles, following signs to South Green. The car park, nature trails, hides and nature centre lie off this road.

Permits: available on arrival. The reserve is closed on Mondays and reserved for members-only on Sundays.

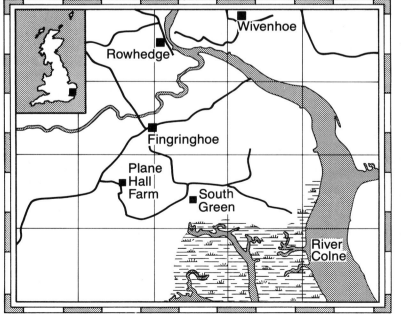

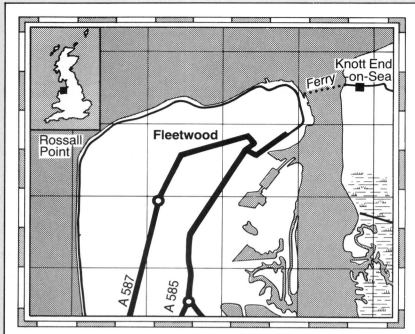

FLEETWOOD, LANCASHIRE OS 96

Location: the town of Fleetwood lies immediately north of Blackpool at the mouth of Morecambe Bay, but the area described here extends eastward for about 10 miles along the southern shore of this great intertidal area as far as Cockerham.

Habitats: Morecambe Bay is one of Europe's most important intertidal zones for both waders and wildfowl, with several species forming flocks of international significance. There are large mussel beds and saltmarshes and huge flats of sand and mud. This means that unless a visit is made at the correct state of the tide, the sea and the birds can be miles away.

Birds: huge flocks of Knot, Dunlin, Oystercatcher and Redshank are the dominant birds throughout the winter, but there are also good numbers of Bar-tailed Godwit, Curlew and Turnstone, together with smaller numbers of Purple Sandpiper. Although passage brings more waders, including outstanding numbers of Sanderling, these are generally more 'open-shore' birds than the commoner species.

Access: from Fleetwood head west to Rossall Point for rocky-shore waders and the chance of a Glaucous Gull. To the east Knott End is another good spot, as is Pilling (*see page* 310).

Permits: not required.

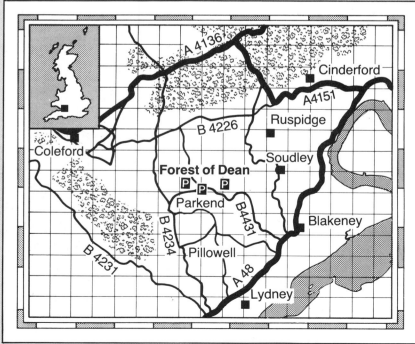

FOREST OF DEAN, GLOUCESTERSHIRE OS 162

Location: within 25 miles of Gloucester and Newport, this old-established forest lies between the east bank of the River Wye and the north bank of the Severn.

Habitats: the woodlands here are extensive and old. Though there are new plantations, there are also areas of mature mixed hardwoods that include oak, together with beech, rowan and birch. There are more open areas too, and several forest streams that tumble over rocky beds.

Birds: the bird community consists of relatively commonplace species that can be seen throughout lowland Britain, though there is a distinct westerly bias. There is, for example, a large population of Pied Flycatchers, mainly as a result of an intensive programme of erecting nest boxes. Here too are Wood Warblers, Buzzards and Dippers, as well as Tree Pipits and the three British woodpeckers. The RSPB's Nagshead Reserve is near the centre of the forest.

Access: leave the A48 northward on the B4431. Beyond Parkend watch for a track on the right to the RSPB car park. There are well marked trails and hides. Otherwise there are plentiful roads from which to explore the forest.

Permits: not required.

FOULA, SHETLAND OS 4

Location: among the most isolated of all inhabited islands in Britain, Foula lies to the west of the main island of Shetland, Mainland, near the meeting of the Atlantic Ocean and North Sea.

Habitats: the 4 square miles of this small island consist essentially of a mountain surrounded by an often fierce sea, which has cut huge cliffs from almost the whole of the coastline. At over 350m, some are among the highest to be found in Britain and are teeming with birds. Yet Foula remains largely unvisited by birdwatchers, though it has regular transport services and a welcoming local population.

Birds: all of the usual cliff-breeding seabirds can be found, including large numbers of Fulmar, Kittiwake, Guillemot and Puffin. There are Razorbill, Black Guillemot and Shag too, as well as a small colony of Gannet, a sizeable colony of Manx Shearwater and both Storm and Leach's Petrels. The Great Skua has a major breeding stronghold here. Despite its isolated position, there has been little investigation of migration here, even though rare birds have been found. What an opportunity awaits.

Access: there are flights from Shetland once a week during the summer and twice weekly sailings throughout the year. Be prepared for the ferry to be cancelled or delayed.

Permits: none required.

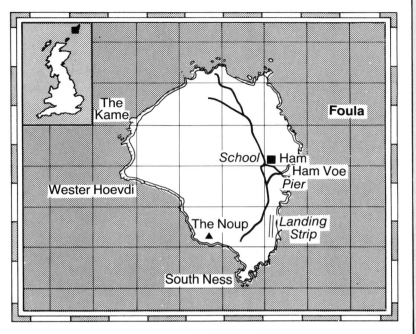

FOWLSHEUGH, GRAMPIAN OS 45

Location: the cliffs here lie on the east coast, next to the village of Crawton, about 16 miles south of Aberdeen and 4 miles south of Stonehaven.

Habitats: though nowhere near as formidable as some of the island seabird cliffs, these are among the best in mainland Britain. Only 60m high, they are readily accessible – though, as always at such sites, great care should be taken near the cliff-edge.

Birds: the most abundant species are Guillemot and Kittiwake, with about 30,000 pairs of each breeding regularly. With a good breeding colony of 5000 pairs of scarcer Razorbill, this a particularly important site nationally for all three species. As a bonus, there are smaller numbers of Puffin, Fulmar, Shag and Herring Gull. All these species combine to produce that hurly-burly, non-stop noise of a truly great seabird site. Eider are also regularly present on the sea itself.

Access: about 3 miles beyond Stonehaven turn left to Crawton and park at the small cliff-top car park. Walk northward along the cliff top path for views at many places. Though 1½ miles of the cliffs are an RSPB reserve, there is no warden.

Permits: not required.

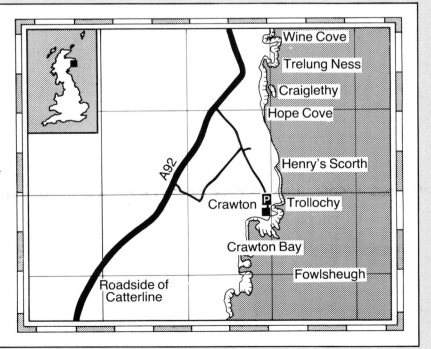

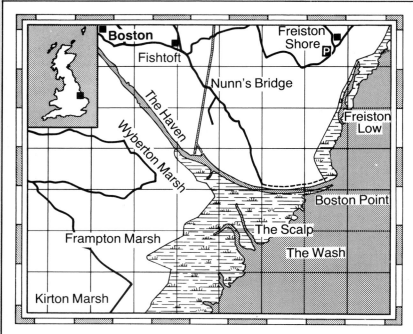

FRAMPTON MARSH, LINCOLNSHIRE OS 131

Location: 3 miles south of Boston at the western point of The Wash.

Habitats: three rivers have their estuaries at this corner of The Wash and all have been artificially embanked and straightened to ease the passage of flood waters. Where they meet there is a maze of saltmarshes and, behind the sea-wall, a system of dykes between the fields. This is a lonely place, usually ignored by birders, but it is what most of our coastal marshes were like before reclamation.

Birds: all the waders that frequent The Wash, one of Europe's top wetland sites, can be seen here – sometimes in spectacular numbers at passage seasons and in winter. Arrive an hour before one of the highest tides for the impressive spectacle of vast numbers of Knot, Dunlin, Curlew, Bar-tailed Godwit, Grey Plover and other waders. There are also wintering Hen Harrier, Merlin and Short-eared Owl, ducks and possibly geese too.

Access: leave Boston southwards on the A16 and turn left on to a maze of roads through Wyberton to Frampton Marsh. Continue to the sea-wall and the mouth of the River Witham. The area can also be approached from the north bank of the river via Fishtoft: walk to the sea-wall and walk 1¼ miles to the wader roost at Boston Point.

Permits: none required.

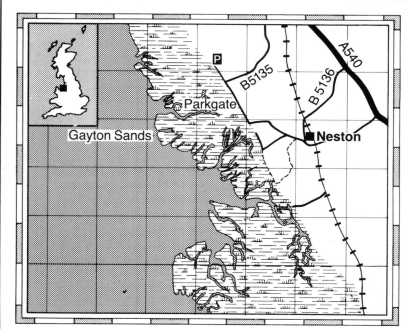

GAYTON SANDS, CHESHIRE OS 117

Location: this intertidal area lies on the north-east shore of the Dee Estuary at Parkgate, about 6 miles from Birkenhead.

Habitat: the huge sand flats here are backed by a large area of saltmarsh that was purchased by the RSPB and now constitutes its Gayton Sands reserve. There is also a reed bed.

Birds: this is predominantly a site for wintering wildfowl and waders. These include 30,000 each of Knot and Dunlin, plus lesser numbers of Bar-tailed Godwit, Grey Plover, and a nationally important flock of 1000 Black-tailed Godwit. Pintail are often the most common of the ducks, along with Wigeon and Shelduck, and there are regular Peregrine, Merlin and Hen Harrier. Often difficult to see are the flocks of small birds among the saltings, but careful watching may produce Water Pipit, Brambling and Twite. Just occasionally, a party of Pink-footed Geese or Bewick's Swans will put in an appearance.

Access: leave the main A540 between Hoylake and Chester on to the B5135 to Parkgate, where there is parking at the Old Baths car park, near the Boathouse Restaurant. Walk north along the public footpath or south to a reed bed at Neston that may hold Water Rail and Jack Snipe in winter, Grasshopper Warbler in summer.

Permits: not required.

GELTSDALE, CUMBRIA OS 86

Location: immediately south of the A69 from Carlisle to Newcastle-upon-Tyne. Its north-western boundary lies about 4 miles south of Brampton.

Habitat: open moorland, with large areas of heather and rough grass but also grassy fields and valley floors. Woodland along the valley sides, and tumbling rivers.

Birds: the heather moors hold breeding Red Grouse, Curlew and Golden Plover. Pied Flycatcher, Wood Warbler and Redstart breed in the woodlands, and Common Sandpiper, Dipper and Grey Wagtail on the streams. There are breeding Buzzard, Sparrowhawk, Hen Harrier, Merlin and Peregrine, as well as Goosander and Short-eared Owl. In winter, Whooper Swan may be seen on the tarn.

Access: the RSPB has established a reserve here consisting of 12,000 acres of moorland, with 300 acres of woods. Leave Brampton eastwards on the A69 and fork right on to the A689 to Tindale. A road southward leads to a disused railway, where there is parking for Tindale Tarn. Alternatively, take the A69 westwards from Brampton and turn left to Low Geltbridge. Park and walk south-eastwards through woods along the bank of the river. The third approach is to leave Brampton southward on the B6413 to Castle Carrock and turn left to Jockey Shield, where there is a track.

Permits: none required, but keep to rights of way on the moors.

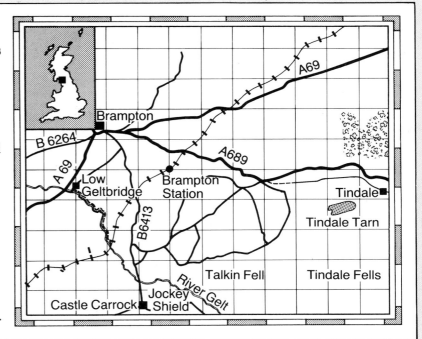

GIBRALTAR POINT, LINCOLNSHIRE OS 122

Location: 3 miles south of Skegness on The Wash.

Habitats: the coastline is backed by dunes, with 'slacks' (damp hollows) between. There is a good growth of scrub, broken by areas of fresh water and marsh – a perfect combination of habitats for small migrants. There is also a golf course, a 'scrape' (an artificial area of brackish water with small islands) and an area of saltmarsh.

Birds: the area is a National Nature Reserve and the site of Gibraltar Point Field Station, a bird observatory and a visitor centre. During passage periods there are all the regular chats and warblers with, in autumn, a fair chance of a 'fall' of large numbers of migrants, including rarities. Even in winter large numbers of waders can be seen at a nearby roost, also divers, Brent Geese and a variety of raptors that regularly includes Peregrine. Migration in spring and autumn can be very dramatic.

Access: follow the minor road south along the coast from Skegness to the Point, where parking is available at two sites. There is a hide at The Mere and the visitor centre is open daily in the summer and at weekends throughout the year.

Permits: none required. Contact Gibraltar Point Field Station, Skegness, Lincolnshire, PE24 4SU, for accommodation.

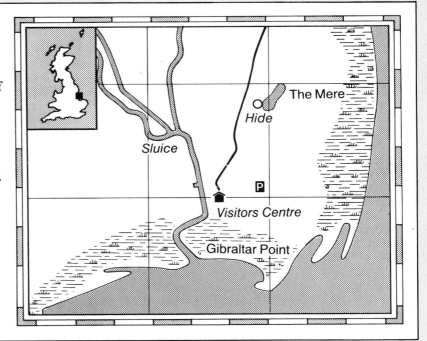

271

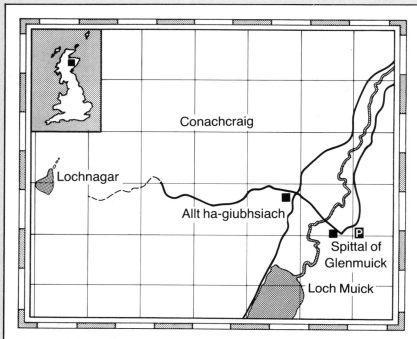

GLEN MUICK AND THE EAST GRAMPIANS, DEE OS 44

Location: the River Dee rises in the Grampian Mountains. The area described here includes the Dee Valley east and west of Ballater, as well as Glen Muick to the south and lies about 40 miles west of Aberdeen, where the Dee reaches the sea.

Habitats: mountains, valleys, old woods and new plantations, lakes, ponds, marshes and streams – all are to be found in this remarkable area, that has almost all the Scottish specialities usually associated with Speyside.

Birds: though there are geese here in winter, this is primarily a superb summer spot for the best of Scottish birds. Golden Eagle cruise over the higher hillsides and there are Ptarmigan and Dotterel on the tops, Hen Harriers on the lower slopes, and Goshawk and Sparrowhawk in the woods. These also hold Black Grouse and Capercaillie, along with Scottish Crossbill, Redstart and Wood Warbler. In fact, the only Scottish woodland speciality that is missing is the Crested Tit.

Access: take the A93 westward from Aberdeen and explore the minor roads to the north and south between Aboyne and Braemar. One of the best leaves Ballater southwards to Glen Muick.

Permits: not required, but keep to public rights of way.

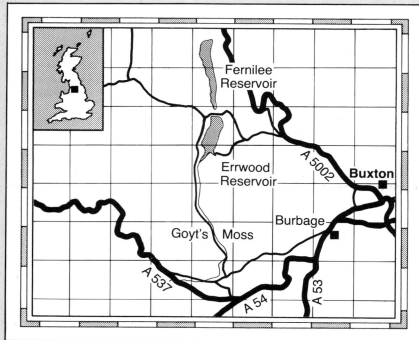

GOYT VALLEY, DERBYSHIRE

OS 118

Location: the north-western corner of Derbyshire, close to its borders with Greater Manchester, Cheshire and Staffordshire.

Habitats: this is one of those beauty spots that attracts people from all directions. At certain times, particularly summer weekends, it may be chock-a-block with visitors, making birding all but impossible. The valley is beautiful and the Goyt here is a stream tumbling over a rocky bed before entering a string of reservoirs, whose banks are clothed by magnificent woods. High above are open sheep moors.

Birds: a community of typical upland breeding birds of a variety of habitats makes this very much a spring and summer place. The high tops, easily accessible by road, hold Red Grouse, Curlew and Golden Plover. Along the stream live Dipper, Grey Wagtail and Common Sandpiper, while the woods contain Redstart, Tree Pipit and Wood Warbler. Also there are Great and Lesser Spotted Woodpeckers, Ring Ousel, Whinchat and, on the reservoirs, Great Crested and Little Grebes.

Access: by minor roads from the A537, A54 or A5002. There is a car park at Errwood Reservoir. This is a partially traffic-free zone.

Permits: none required.

GRAFHAM WATER, CAMBRIDGESHIRE OS 153

Location: this lowland reservoir lies just 1¼ miles west of the A1 about 5 miles south-west of Huntingdon.

Habitats: most of the banks of this huge reservoir are natural and gently shelving. For years it was England's largest reservoir (this title now rests with Rutland Water, *see page* 314) and is in great demand for various leisure pursuits, but there are protected areas.

Birds: in winter there are good numbers of the commoner ducks, including Wigeon, Teal and Shoveler, along with smaller numbers of Goosander and Goldeneye. Bewick's Swan is regular and there may be really impressive numbers of Great Crested and Little Grebes. During passage periods Black and Common Terns are regular and, chiefly in autumn, waders include a scattering of the usual 'freshwater' species, such as Common, Green and Wood Sandpiper.

Access: leave the A1 westwards on the B661 to the dam. There are roads to the north and the south which lead to car parks with views over the water. Just beyond West Perry, in the south, the car park gives access to a waterside footpath that leads to a hide.

Permits: the Bedfordshire and Huntingdonshire Wildlife Trust reserve at the western end has no access and even the hide is open only on winter Sundays, for a small charge.

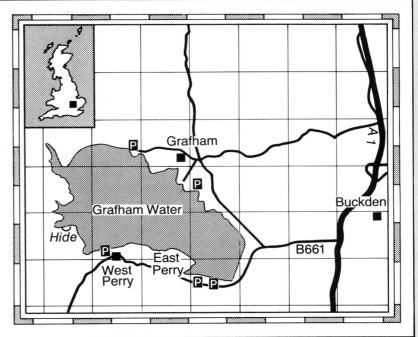

GWENFFRWD AND DINAS, DYFED OS 146 or 147

Location: these RSPB reserves lie to the north-west of the A483 about 8 miles north of Llandovery.

Habitats: though much of the reserves consists of open moorland and rough grass, the main centre of interest lies in the lovely old oakwoods and the rippling streams that cut through them.

Birds: the Red Kite, still persecuted and still endangered, finds a stronghold hereabouts and a good view of one of these lovely birds is one of the primary objects of a visit. They can be seen soaring gracefully over the woods, though most larger raptors seen here are Buzzards. The woods are alive with Pied Flycatcher, Wood Warbler, Redstart, woodpeckers, Woodcock and Tree Pipit. The streams have Dipper, Grey Wagtail and Common Sandpiper, and there are Merlin, Red Grouse and possible Peregrine, too.

Access: leave Llandovery on minor roads to Rhandirmwyn. The Dinas reserve is found off the road to Llyn Brianne dam. There is a summer information centre by the car park and the start of a nature trail here. For the Gwenffrwd reserve and its two nature trails report to the Dinas centre and check details with the warden. Access is restricted by the lack of parking space.

Permits: see access; no Friday access.

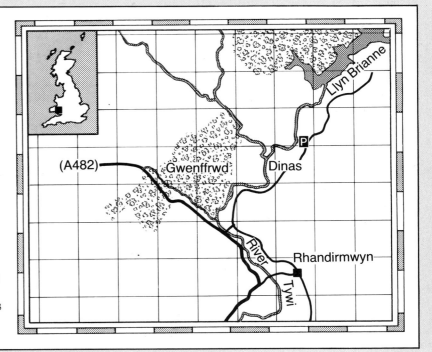

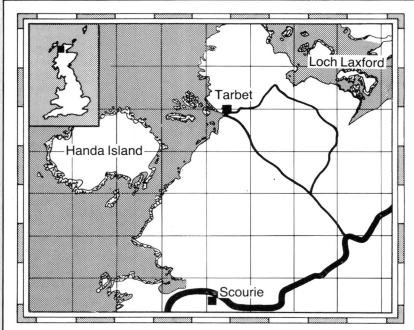

HANDA, HIGHLAND OS 9

Location: just a mile's ferry crossing from the north-west coast of Scotland – and about 17 miles south of Cape Wrath.

Habitats: Handa is a large island consisting mainly of rough, steep grazing land and heather, but with impressive cliffs in the north and sandy bays and beaches in the south and east. Its position and its cliffs make Handa one of the best seabird colonies in Britain.

Birds: altogether there are some 100,000 pairs of breeding seabirds here; Guillemot alone number nearly 30,000 pairs. They include Razorbill, Puffin, Kittiwake, Fulmar and Shag, plus strong populations of Great and Arctic Skuas. Peregrine and Buzzard are regular visitors. On the boat crossing watch for Red-throated and Black-throated Divers, plus Great Northern Diver in early summer.

Access: there are regular boats from Tarbet, which is reached from the A894 via a minor road north-west, about 3 miles north-east of Scourie. The boats depart from about 10.00 a.m. daily except Sunday throughout summer. Handa is open between 1 April and 10 September. There is a warden, and visitors are requested to keep to the marked paths. By arrangement with the RSPB's Scottish office members may stay at Handa, at a bothy.

Permits: see access above.

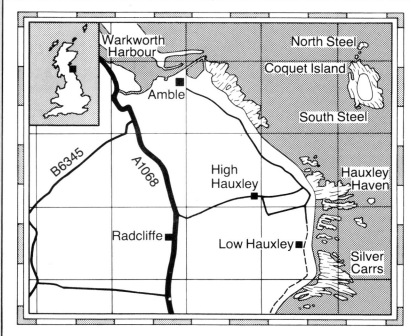

HAUXLEY, NORTHUMBERLAND OS 81

Location: Hauxley is situated on a bulge in the rugged stretch of coastline about 25 miles to the north of the Tyneside conurbation.

Habitats: a long sandy foreshore is broken by a rocky area that juts into the sea, forming a headland that regularly attracts birds.

Birds: the main attractions at Hauxley are the migrants, the foreshore waders and the seabirds. The latter include all the species that regularly breed on nearby Coquet Island (*see page* 257) and among which Common, Arctic and Sandwich Tern are often numerous. Careful watching may produce one or two of the rare Roseate Tern. It is, however, in late summer and autumn that the area really begins to shine. The terns then feed and rest along the shoreline and skuas regularly appear among them. These are mostly Arctic, but Great and Pomarine Skua are sometimes present as well. Manx Shearwater, too, are regular and Sooty, Cory's and Great Shearwaters are seen annually. Small migrants may be good in autumn too; an easterly element in the wind helps. Among the warblers, chats and flycatchers there are always some semi-rarities.

Access: south of Amble, off the A1068. Continue to Low Hauxley where the road south to Bondicare is a public footpath.

Permits: none required, but do not trespass on private land.

HAVERGATE ISLAND, SUFFOLK OS 169

Location: in the estuary of the River Alde about 2½ miles south of Orford; Ipswich lies 16 miles to the west.

Habitats: after widening out below Snape and forming a minor estuary, the River Alde is diverted southwards by the huge sweep of Orfordness, eventually reaching the sea at Shingle Street. Along this narrow part it divides in two, with Havergate forming the island between. Wartime flooding enabled Avocets to recolonize Britain in 1947 here and at nearby Minsmere (*see page* 303).

Birds: the Avocet still has a major colony here and Common and Sandwich Terns, too. Short-eared Owl also breed, as do a few waders. In autumn the exposed mud attracts many waders, including Spotted Redshank, Little Stint, Curlew Sandpiper and Greenshank, yet rarities are seldom found – presumably because access to birders is restricted outside the breeding season.

Access: by boat several days each week during the summer, less frequently from September through the winter.

Permits: there is a charge for the boat trip – RSPB members pay less than half price. Details of arrangements for the current season and reservations by post only from The Warden, 30 Mundays Lane, Orford, Woodbridge, IP12 2LX.

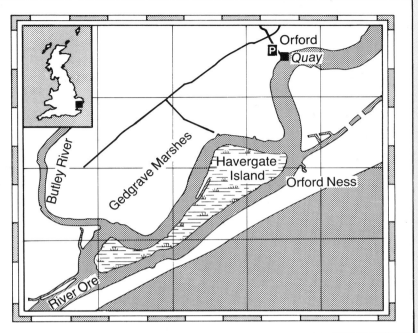

HAYLE ESTUARY, CORNWALL OS 203

Location: the Hayle is the nearest estuary to Land's End – and the nearest in England to North America. The town of Hayle all but embraces it and the resort of St Ives, with its outstanding seawatching site (*see page* 316), is about 3 miles to the north-west.

Habitats: this is a small estuary, with mud banks at low tide, a small saltmarsh and a detached tidal lagoon called Carnsew Pool.

Birds: the peak season is autumn, when waders include Greenshank, Spotted Redshank, Common Sandpiper, Little Stint, Curlew Sandpiper and the chance of an American rarity or two. Dowitchers are among the most likely of these, but a variety of rare waders, including Pectoral and White-rumped Sandpipers, have turned up here. Terns and gulls include a scattering of semi-rarities, though winter is usually better for the gulls. At this time divers and the scarcer grebes are regular and there are always a few ducks.

Access: the Hayle as well as Copperhouse Creek can be seen well from the B3301, from which there is also access to Carnsew Pool. The RSPB have a public hide on the south of the estuary near the Old Quay House Inn, which has a large car park that can be used by birders.

Permits: not required.

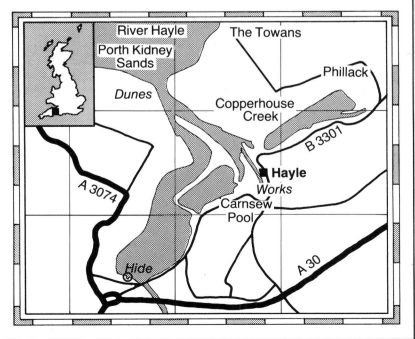

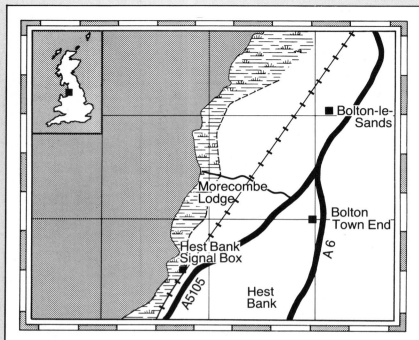

HEST BANK, LANCASHIRE OS 97

Location: this area lies on the shores of the huge Morecambe Bay, at the southern end of the RSPB reserve, just to the north of Morecambe itself (*see page 302*).

Habitats: Morecambe Bay is vast intertidal complex and one of the most important wetlands in Europe. Hest Bank is one of the best sites on the shores of this great area.

Birds: this is a spot that, if visited at the right time, can produce an unforgettable bird spectacle. If visited casually it can, on the contrary, produce no more than a few common waders. The secret is timing. Choose a winter spring tide during the daylight hours and arrive at Hest Bank an hour or so before high tide. Then watch for waders pouring in by the thousand. Numbers of wintering waders in Morecambe Bay can be staggering, with totals of 80,000 Knot, 50,000 Dunlin, 45,000 Oystercatcher, 8000 Bar-tailed Godwit and 7000 Redshank. Hest Bank is one of the prime wader roosts. Passage brings large numbers of Sanderling and Ringed Plover and there may be other species such as Greenshank present.

Access: leave Morecambe northwards on the A5105 to Hest Bank and cross the railway at the level crossing, to reach a large car park. Walk northwards toward the wader roost.

Permits: none required.

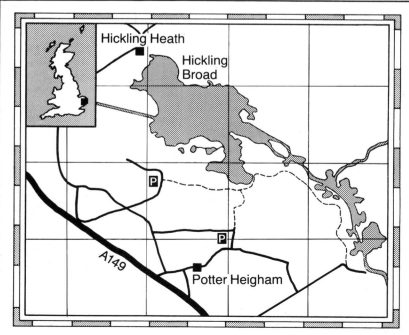

HICKLING BROAD, NORFOLK

OS 134

Location: to the north-east of the more famous 'boating' broads. Great Yarmouth lies some 11 miles to the south-east.

Habitats: this is a large open water surrounded by vast reed beds. It is a National Nature Reserve and partly a reserve of the Norfolk Naturalists' Trust, with a series of shallow lagoons that attract many passage waders.

Birds: all the Broadland specialities can be found here in summer, including Bittern and Bearded Tit, Sedge, Reed, Grasshopper and Savi's Warbler, and visiting Marsh Harrier. There are Common Terns nesting on specially sited rafts and Black Terns are regular in both spring and autumn. Waders include Green and Wood Sandpipers, Greenshank, Little Stint, Curlew Sandpiper and Spotted Redshank.

Access: by permit to a nature trail and series of hides in the north-east of the broad via the Norfolk Naturalists' Trust. Much of the southern part can be seen via a footpath along the shore starting from Decoy Lane, or via another from Potter Heigham church.

Permits: the Norfolk Naturalists' Trust Warden has an office along Stubb Lane, which is next to the Greyhound Inn. Permits are issued in half-day sessions, except on Tuesdays, and fees are modest.

HILBRE, MERSEYSIDE OS 108

Location: three separate islands off the Wirral peninsula at the mouth of the River Dee, about 8 miles west of Birkenhead.

Habitats: these are three low, flat rocky islands – Hilbre, Little Hilbre and Little Eye. Though there is a bird observatory on Hilbre Island, as well as good visible migration through the late autumn and rewarding seawatching after gales, these islands are famous chiefly as a major roost for waders on the Dee estuary.

Birds: though wader numbers are smaller than they were, due to disturbance, this is still a spectacular spot for these birds. Dunlin, Knot, Redshank, Bar-tailed Godwit and Grey Plover dominate, but there are also good numbers of Oystercatcher, Purple Sandpiper and Turnstone. At other times the islands hold little of interest, though autumn gales often drive Leach's Petrel close to the islands.

Access: the islands can be reached on foot at low tide, but it is essential to start at least three hours before high water from West Kirby on the mainland. The nearby Red Rocks are another wader roost, which can be reached with considerably less walking.

Permits: no access without a permit from Wirral Borough Council which manages the islands as a local nature reserve. Write to Wirral Borough Council Department of Leisure, Town Hall, Brighton Street, Wallasey, Merseyside L44 8ED.

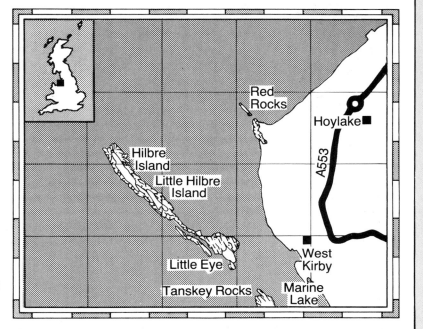

HOBBISTER, ORKNEY OS 6

Location: this large RSPB reserve (1875 acres) lies in the south of Orkney Mainland, about 3 miles to the south-west of Kirkwall. Its southern boundary lies on the shores of Scapa Flow.

Habitats: an area of open moorland dominated by heather, with bogs and marshes and a corner of the Loch of Kirbister. It also includes a substantial length of shoreline, part of which comprises low cliffs.

Birds: this is one of several Orkney breeding strongholds of the Hen Harrier, and there is a good chance of seeing one from the road. Short-eared Owl and Merlin also breed, as do Red-throated Diver, Curlew and Snipe. There is a good breeding population of Red Grouse on the moor. The cliffs hold Fulmar and Black Guillemot. In winter divers, grebes and seaducks are regular. Hobbister is a pleasant area of open countryside and shore with a good chance of seeing several exciting birds.

Access: there is a track that loops across the southern half of the reserve from the A964 near Waulkmill Bay, starting at a minor road or nearby track. This is the only access.

Permits: not required for access described above.

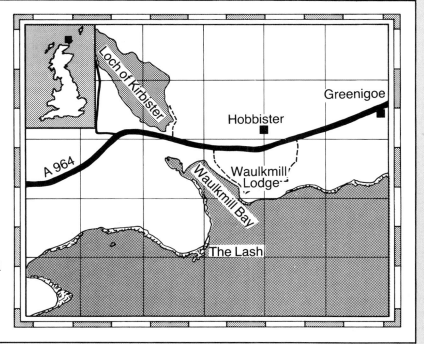

HOLKHAM AND WELLS, NORFOLK OS 132

Location: the north Norfolk coast about 10 miles to the west of Blakeney (*see page* 244).

Habitats: the foreshore here is mainly sandy. A muddy deep channel extends inland to Wells Quay. The dunes to the west have been stabilized with extensive pine plantations. Inland lies Holkham Hall, a large park with specimen trees and several lakes. Much of the seaward side of the A149 is a National Nature Reserve.

Birds: the grounds of Holkham Hall, particularly the birchy scrub on the landward side, are splendidly productive during both spring and autumn passage, with birds such as Pied Flycatcher, Wryneck and Barred Warbler turning up annually. In the autumn, this same area regularly produces an impressive number of rarities, including Yellow-browed and Pallas's Warblers, and sometimes extreme rarities such as Radde's and Dusky Warblers.

In winter, Brent Geese, Wigeon, seaducks, grebes, the common waders, Red-breasted Merganser, Common Scoter, Slavonian Grebe, Knot, Bar-tailed Godwit and Grey Plover can be seen at the shoreline and harbour mouth. Winter also sees geese flock to the fields between the pines and Holkham Hall. Egyptian Goose are invariably present here, as are feral Greylags. Search for Hawfinch on the hornbeam trees just inside the Park.

Access: explore the pines from the Wells end, taking the road northwards along the western side of the quay to a car park at the far end. Walk up the sea-wall to the right and view the channel mouth. From the western side of the car park walk westwards, along the northern side of the boating lake (check for terns in season) and explore the scrub on the landward side of the pines. Turn north opposite Holkham Hall along Lady Anne's Drive to the pines. Walk over the boardwalk to the sea and also east and west behind the pines. Holkham Park can be visited via a small gate to the right of the main gate. Further west, the A149 gives excellent views over the grazing meadows for the goose flocks.

Permits: not required for the access detailed above.

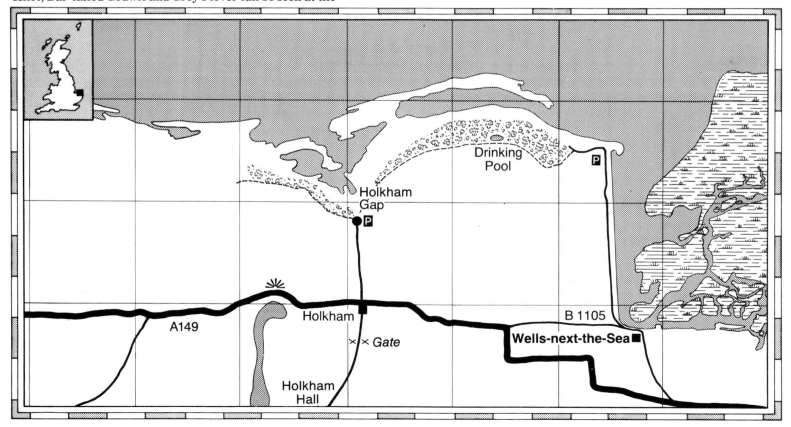

HOLBEACH, LINCOLNSHIRE

OS 122 & 131

Location: these marshes lie at the western corner of The Wash between the outlets of the River Welland and the River Nene.

Habitats: this is a huge area of reclaimed fen that lies below sea level, protected by a sea-wall and drained by dykes. Beyond the sea-wall a vast area of saltmarshes extends to the mud banks of The Wash.

Birds: Holbeach has long been famous as one of the major wader resorts of The Wash. Spring tides are virtually essential for success here – the higher the better. At such times a proportion of the huge wader flocks of this major wetland are forced off the saltmarshes and over the sea-wall at Flushing Creek Wall. Knot, Dunlin, Oystercatcher and Redshank are the most numerous species, but there are also good numbers of Bar-tailed Godwit and Curlew. The area also attracts a good selection of wintering raptors, including Merlin and Hen Harrier.

Access: leave the A17 at Chapelgate northwards on the B1359 and turn left on to a minor road, signposted Holbeach St Matthew. Continue through the village to the sea-wall. Walk out to Flushing Creek Wall at the mouth of the River Welland.

Permits: not required.

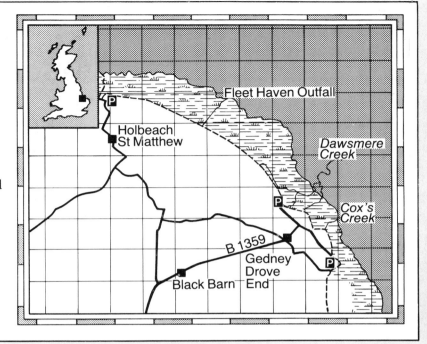

HOLME, NORFOLK OS 132

Location: where the north Norfolk coast turns into The Wash. The best area lies between Holme-next-the-Sea and Thornham Harbour.

Habitats: the shoreline here is wide and sandy, and is backed by extensive dunes. A large pool, called Broad Water, is surrounded by reeds, while to the west is an area of 'scrapes' (artificial areas of shallow, brackish water with low-lying islets for attracting birds). Thornham Harbour has large mud banks and saltmarshes.

Birds: the Norfolk Ornithologists' Association has a private bird observatory here, while the Norfolk Naturalists' Trust's reserve covers the larger part of the area. In summer the latter holds Avocet, Little Tern, Bearded Tit and both Reed and Sedge Warbler. In winter there are divers, ducks and grebes offshore, and Brent Goose on the fields. Hen Harrier, Snow Bunting and Shore Lark are regular. During spring and autumn passage periods the 'scrapes' hold waders, while the scrub and pines sometimes produce scarce migrant warblers, chats and flycatchers, including Barred and Yellow-browed Warblers and Red-breasted Flycatcher.

Access: leave the A149 northward to Holme along Beach Road and turn right along a track (a small toll is payable in summer).

Permits: are available every day except Tuesday for the NNT reserve and every day for the NOA area. These are available on site.

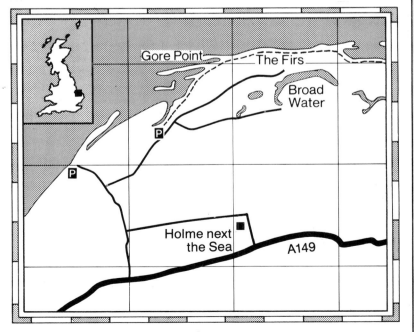

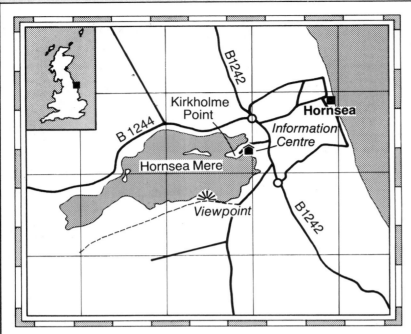

HORNSEA MERE, HUMBERSIDE OS 107

Location: just west of the B1242 and the small coastal town of Hornsea. Hull is about 12 miles to the south-west.

Habitats: this is a large freshwater lake surrounded by extensive reed beds just a short distance from the North Sea coast. There are areas of woodland and much surrounding farmland.

Birds: Hornsea is an RSPB reserve that is most interesting in winter and during spring and autumn passage periods. Ducks include hundreds of Teal, Wigeon, Gadwall, Pochard and Goldeneye, the latter forming a notable flock for a freshwater site. Divers and grebes are often present during hard weather. If the water level is low enough to expose the muddy shoreline, waders can be interesting in autumn, though they are never as regular as the Little Gull that is present all season. Black and other terns are regularly present during spring and autumn passage seasons.

Access: the RSPB have an information centre at Kirkholme Point open during summer weekends, and cars may be parked here. Simply follow signs to 'The Mere' from Hornsea town centre. There is also an excellent public footpath along the southern shore that starts in Hull Road.

Permits: not required.

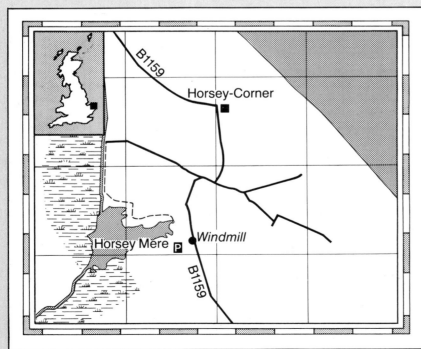

HORSEY MERE, NORFOLK OS 134

Location: less than a mile from the coast, and about 10 miles to the north of Great Yarmouth. As a birdwatching site, it is often overshadowed by the neighbouring Hickling Broad (*see page* 276).

Habitats: Horsey is a medium-sized broad surrounded by extensive reed beds and is a nature reserve belonging to the National Trust.

Birds: for many years, Horsey was a stronghold of the Broadland specialities, but several of these sadly no longer breed there, though Bearded Tit and Water Rail still hold on. The Marsh Harrier is now only a visitor and the status of the Bittern is precarious to say the least. Nevertheless, the reeds are full of warblers and there are often good numbers of waders and terns during spring and autumn passage periods. In winter Hen Harrier, Short-eared Owl and a good population of ducks visit the area and Bewick's Swan are sometimes present in small numbers.

Access: viewing the mere is difficult as access is restricted, and most birders give it no more than a quick once-over. A more active conservation policy, including strategically sited hides, might well produce more birds. At present, the mere can be viewed only from the track that leads from the windmill, where there is a car park.

Permits: not required for access detailed above; not available otherwise.

HOY, ORKNEY OS 7

Location: Hoy is one of the southern Orkney islands, separated from the mainland of Scotland by the Pentland Firth and from Mainland Orkney by the narrow Hoy Sound.

Habitats: this is the bleakest of the Orkneys with huge areas of moorland with heather, rough grass, bogs and lochs. In the west are some of the most spectacular of seabird cliffs. The RSPB reserve of North Hoy contains all of these habitats, culminating in the fearsome 335m St John's Head cliffs, and the 140m Old Man of Hoy, Britain's highest sea stack.

Birds: seabirds in summer include many Guillemot, Razorbill, Shag and Kittiwake. The cliffs also hold nesting Peregrine, and there is a Manx Shearwater colony. Off the north-west coast are colonies of Great and Arctic Skuas, while inland there are Golden Plover, Dunlin and Curlew. The lochs have the largest population of Red-throated Diver in Orkney and there are Hen Harrier and Merlin on the hills inland.

Access: Hoy can be reached by passenger ferry from Stromness to Moress and a car ferry from Houton to Lyness. Take the B9047 and turn westward to Rackwick. Here there are paths leading to the Old Man and inland between Ward Hill and the Cuilags. Take care on the cliff-tops, as these are crumbling in places.

Permits: none required.

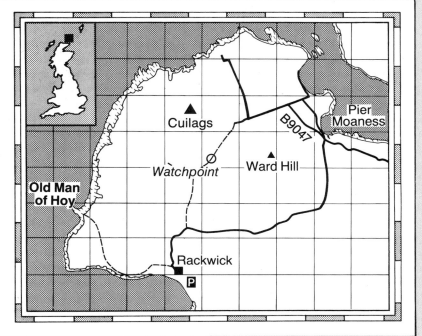

HUNSTANTON, NORFOLK OS 132

Location: the Victorian resort of Hunstanton lies at the north-east corner of The Wash, between the major bird sites of Holme (*see page* 279), and Snettisham (*see page* 321).

Habitats: the prime attractions are the sea and shoreline. As the tide rises, it pushes wildfowl and waders towards the promenade. Here they can be watched from a few strategically-sited shelters. To the north of the town, the sandy cliffs offer another viewpoint.

Birds: wildfowl and waders here are predominantly winter birds and, in summer, there are only a few Fulmars along the cliffs. Brent Geese are regular in small numbers and Bar-tailed Godwit, Curlew, Grey Plover, Redshank and Turnstone are invariably present. All of these birds are best watched on a rising tide, while at high water there may be quite impressive flocks flighting along the coast to roost. At this time, seaducks move inshore, including good numbers of Scoter, along with Velvet Scoter, Long-tailed Duck, Eider and Goldeneye. Red-throated Diver are also present.

Access: from the centre of town and turn north-east along a road with open grass on the left and the cliffs beyond. There are several shelters to choose from. Continue to the higher sandy cliffs with Fulmar, but less winter shelter.

Permits: none necessary.

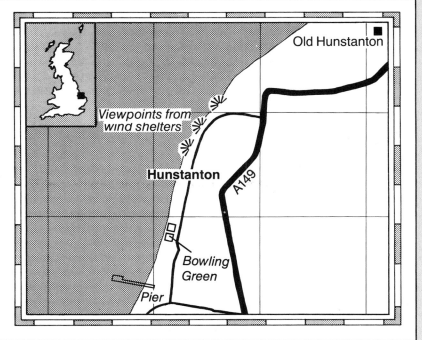

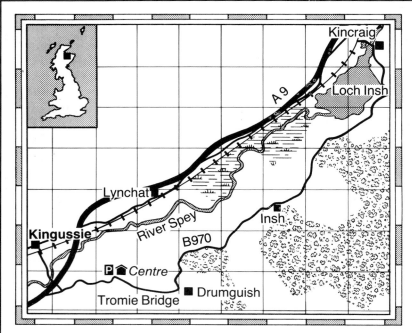

INSH MARSHES, HIGHLAND OS 35

Location: these marshes lie between Kingussie and the Cairngorm Mountains, immediately south of the main A9 road.

Habitats: this is an RSPB reserve covering the low-lying floodlands along the River Spey. Additionally there is the large Loch Insh to the north and Glen Tromie to the south. The valley itself is a mixture of rough grass with open pools in a setting of birch and willow scrub. In winter the whole area is frequently flooded.

Birds: most birdwatchers visit Insh Marshes in summer, when a variety of ducks breed, including Wigeon, Teal and Shoveler, as well as Goldeneye, which use nest-boxes. Greylag Geese also breed at this site. Tree Pipit, Redstart, Great Spotted Woodpecker breed in the woods, together with the occasional pair of Pied Flycatcher. The streams have nesting Dipper and Grey Wagtail, while Redshank, Curlew and Grasshopper Warbler breed on the marshes themselves. The Osprey is a regular visitor throughout the summer. In winter there is a regular herd of Whooper Swan, plus Greylag and Pink-footed Geese, and a variety of ducks.

Access: leave Kingussie on the B970 toward Insh and after 1¼ miles the RSPB reserve centre is on the left before Tromie Bridge.

Permits: the reserve is open every day except Tuesday.

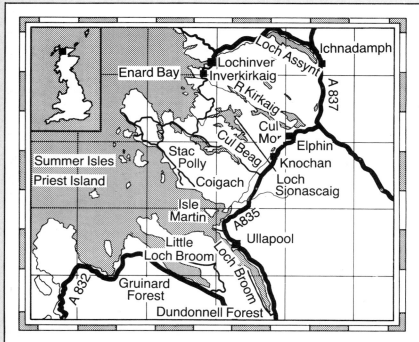

INVERPOLLY, HIGHLAND OS 15

Location: wild country in the north-west of Scotland, one of the remotest parts of Britain. Ullapool is the nearest town of any size.

Habitats: this is a dramatic landscape of rugged mountains, vast moors, innumerable lochs, wild sea coasts and delightful islands, much of it protected in a huge National Nature Reserve, covering 26,827 acres. Offshore are the Summer Isles, with breeding seabirds.

Birds: all of the open-country, non-woodland Scottish bird specialities occur here. Divers, Red-breasted Merganser, Goosander, Wigeon, Golden Eagle, Peregrine, Merlin, Ptarmigan, Red Grouse, Dunlin, Greenshank, Redwing and Twite all breed. The cliffs and islands have Black Guillemot, Eider, Greylag Goose, Arctic Tern and even Storm Petrels. There is a chance of finding breeding Scottish Crossbill in the woods and Snow Bunting on the higher slopes. A good deal of walking and serious preparation are essential: make sure you are equipped with a compass, map, torch, food, water and warm, weatherproof clothing.

Access: leave Ullapool northwards on the A835 and after about 14 miles, stop at the Knockan Information Centre, open from May to mid-September. Otherwise explore off the minor roads with the OS map. Boats from Ullapool regularly visit the Summer Isles.

Permits: only needed from 15 July to 21 October.

ISLAY, STRATHCLYDE OS 60

Location: this is one of the larger Inner Hebrides, lying some 14 miles west of the Kintyre and about 70 miles west of Glasgow.

Habitats: there are areas of farmland and grazing, of loch and moor; there are streams and bogs, and cliffs and dune beaches.

Birds: up to 20,000 Barnacle Geese winter here, mainly in the Loch Gruinart area where the RSPB has a reserve. These birds come from Greenland and they are often accompanied by several thousand Greenland Whitefronts. To the south Loch Indaal is a good place for wintering seabirds, with Great Northern Diver, Slavonian Grebe, Scaup, Goldeneye, Red-breasted Merganser, Common Scoter and Eider. Resident birds that may be seen include Chough, Golden Eagle and Peregrine, plus the chance of a wandering White-tailed Eagle from the island of Rhum, about 70 miles to the north, where this magnificent raptor was re-introduced between 1975 and 1985. In summer there are divers, terns and auks.

Access: the B8017 and the road northwards to Ardnave along the western side of Loch Gruinart are both excellent for geese. Loch Indaal is easily explored from the A847 which, in the east, leads to the cliffs of The Oa. There are daily ferries from Kennacraig in Kintyre and Loganair operates regular air services from Glasgow.

Permits: none required.

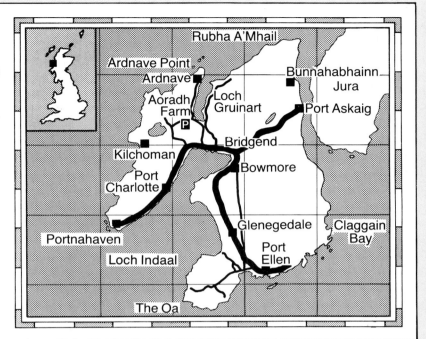

ISLE OF MAY, FIFE OS 59

Location: 'the May', as it is affectionately called, lies at the mouth of the Firth of Forth, with Anstruther, about five miles to the north-west, the nearest port on the mainland.

Habitats: this is a rather bleak island, so migrants tend to find their way to the observatory garden. There are also fine sea-cliffs.

Birds: breeding seabirds include Guillemot, Razorbill, Puffin, Kittiwake, Shag and Fulmar, together with Arctic and Common Tern. But the real objective of a visit is for migrants. The Isle of May has been known as a major migrant watch point since 1907 and a bird observatory was established in 1934. The regular chats, warblers and flycatchers are best in autumn with easterly winds and sometimes occur in dramatic 'falls' of large numbers. With them are Bluethroat and Wryneck and sometimes Barred and Icterine Warblers with a chance of extreme rarities. Almost any bird can turn up here. Seabirds are often visible offshore in autumn.

Access: the observatory operates on a self-catering basis and the 1 hour crossing from Anstruther can be arranged when booking. Contact Mrs R. Cowper, 9 Oxgangs Road, Edinburgh EH10 7BG. Day trips can be arranged in Anstruther.

Permits: none required. The island is a National Nature Reserve.

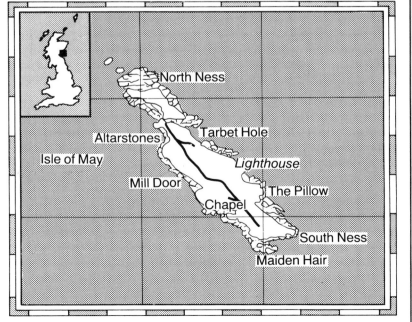

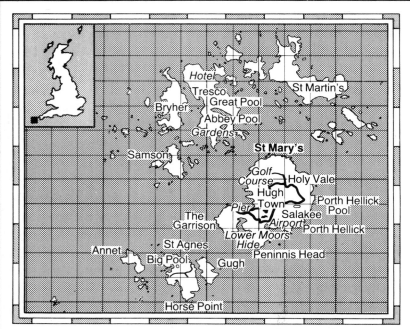

ISLES OF SCILLY OS 203

Location: over 150 islands off the coast of Land's End in Cornwall, with nothing between them and America but the Atlantic Ocean.

Habitats: only five of the islands are inhabited. The rest are mostly rocky with areas of rough grass. These are low-lying islands with few significant cliffs. Much of the landscape on the larger islands is agricultural, with early vegetables and flowers.

Birds: Scilly does have breeding seabirds, including Razorbill, Puffin, Manx Shearwater and Storm Petrel, but a boat trip around Annet is usually as close as anyone gets to them. Tresco has both Common and Roseate Tern, the latter as rare as ever. Spring passage can be good and regularly produces a rarity that has overshot its destination, including Hoopoe, Golden Oriole and Woodchat Shrike but it is October that is the prime time for Scilly birdwatching. Over 375 species have been recorded on the islands, including the rarest of rare birds and many 'firsts' for Britain.

Access: most visitors stay on St Mary's, the main centre. There are regular helicopter flights from Penzance, but early booking is essential. There are also flights by plane from Plymouth and Exeter and daily sailings by boat from Penzance. The boat is good for seabirds, but the 2½ hour crossing may be very rough.

Permits: none required, but do not trespass on private land.

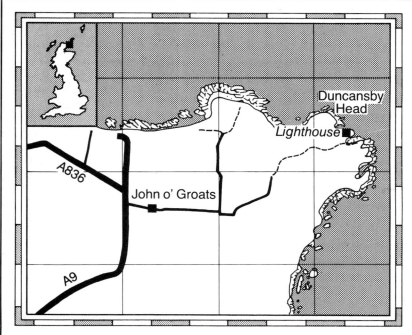

JOHN O'GROATS, HIGHLAND OS 12

Location: the north-eastern-most point of Scotland, more or less the furthest point on the mainland from Land's End. The nearest town is Wick, about 17 miles to the south.

Habitats: John O'Groats is a scattering of tourist shops just a short distance from Duncansby Head, which is the real centre of birding interest. Here the cliffs fall directly to the sea, offering a home to large colonies of seabirds. These cliffs extend southwards along the east coast to Brough Head.

Birds: the cliff-dwelling seabirds are abundant along this stretch of coastline, and include Guillemot, Razorbill, Puffin, Black Guillemot, Fulmar and Kittiwake. There are Shags here too, as well as Great and Arctic Skuas nesting a short distance inland. Though they do not breed, Gannets are abundant throughout the summer and reasonably pure Rock Doves can also be found.

Access: from John O'Groats take the minor road to the lighthouse at Duncansby Head, where you can enjoy good views of the highest cliffs. Return southwards on the A9 and stop where the cliffs are closest. Walk to the edge to view the low cliffs teeming with birds. Brough Head is a good place to stop.

Permits: none required.

KENFIG, MID-GLAMORGAN OS 170

Location: between Cardiff and Swansea, three miles north of Porthcawl and strategically situated near the South Wales coast.

Habitats: this 70-acre freshwater dune-slack lake lies among over 1000 acres of open dunes and is surrounded by extensive marshy areas with reed and scrub. The coastline itself is mainly sandy, with intertidal areas and a rocky outcrop at Sker Point.

Birds: in summer there are warblers among the lakeside vegetation, including Reed and Grasshopper Warbler, both of which breed. Spring and autumn passage periods bring terns, including regular Black Tern, and a good variety of ducks and waders, including substantial flocks of Whimbrel. In winter the shoreline holds Grey Plover, Purple Sandpiper and Turnstone and, at high tide, some of these birds move to Kenfig to roost, bathe or continue feeding. There are usually plenty of gulls here, but rarities are seldom found. Water Rail, Hen Harrier and Ruff are also reasonably regular at this time.

Access: leave the M4 at Exit 37 or 38 and join the B4283, from where a road leaves southward across the motorway to Kenfig. South of the village there is a reserve centre of the Mid-Glamorgan County Council with paths around the pools, where there is a hide.

Permits: not required, but check at the centre that the hide is open.

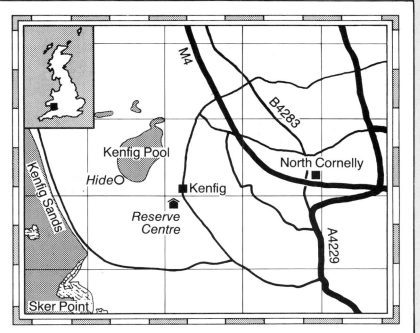

KYLE OF TONGUE, HIGHLAND

OS 10

Location: this sea inlet is situated on the north coast of Sutherland, between John O'Groats and Cape Wrath.

Habitats: the Kyle is a long tidal inlet that is remarkably shallow, with large areas of mud exposed at low tide. Offshore there are several substantial islands that hold seabirds, while inland lies one of the remotest moorland and mountain areas in Britain.

Birds: there are Britain's most northerly Rooks here and a good seabird population, especially on Roan Island with its Black Guillemot, Great Skua and Storm Petrel, along with Peregrine. The inland lochs attract breeding Red-throated and Black-throated Diver, Dunlin and Greenshank, with the occasional Wood Sandpiper and even Red-necked Phalarope. Golden Eagle, Merlin, Ptarmigan and Ring Ousel breed on the moors.

Access: the coastal A838 gives good views of the Kyle of Tongue and the A836 leads past Loch Loyal and Ben Loyal. Otherwise it is a matter of exploring all the roads and tracks and not being afraid of cross-country trekking. Roan can be reached by boat from Tongue.

Permits: this is grouse-shooting and deer-stalking country, with restrictions during late summer and autumn. Look out for notices giving details of deer-stalking.

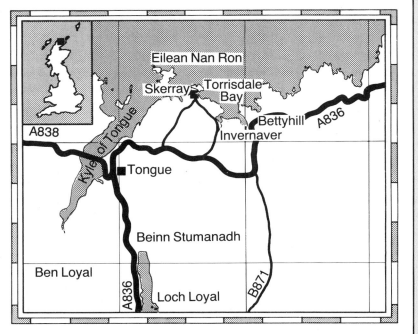

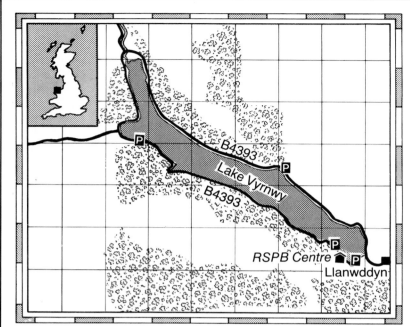

LAKE VYRNWY, POWYS OS 125

Location: this large reservoir lies in the Berwyn Hills of northern Powys, a remote area of mid-Wales. Welshpool lies about 18 miles to the south-east, Machynlleth about 25 miles to the south-west.

Habitats: the reservoir is surrounded by typical Welsh hill country, with extensive heather moors broken by conifer plantations, but also features delightful wooded valleys and rippling streams. The lake has shallow margins in several areas and there are considerable areas of scrub.

Birds: in this lovely range of hills it is possible to find a typical cross-section of Welsh woodland and mountain breeding birds. The oaks have Wood Warbler, Pied Flycatcher and Redstart; the streams hold Grey Wagtail, Dipper and Common Sandpiper; the lake boasts Goosander and Kingfisher. Overhead there are Buzzard and Sparrowhawk, while the conifers, when young, are home to Hen Harrier, and, when mature, to Crossbill. Providing the heather moors can be protected, the Vyrnwy area will remain the best place to go birding in this part of Wales.

Access: the B4393 from Llanfyllin goes right round the reservoir. There is an RSPB centre at the dam, a hide in the north-west and plenty of good woodland walks.

Permits: not required.

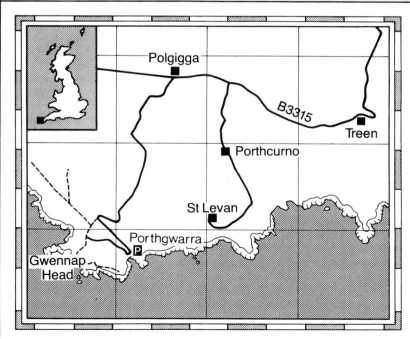

LAND'S END, CORNWALL OS 203

Location: famous as the extreme south-western tip of England, surrounded by the Atlantic Ocean.

Habitats: surrounded by dramatic granite sea cliffs, the Land's End peninsula is an area of moorland, heath and small fields, broken here and there by deep valleys.

Birds: the area is good for migrants in both spring and autumn, and October sees a scattering of rare birds. Every year there is an American species or two, along with eastern rarities such as Red-breasted Flycatcher and southern ones like Woodchat Shrike. Scarce waders, such as Dotterel, are regular on St Just Airfield and this is also a good spot for Buff-breasted Sandpiper.

Access: from Penzance take the B3315 to Treen and later a minor road at Polgigga to Porthgwarra. Walk up the Porthgwarra valley west to the coastguard cottages and on a choice of paths around Gwennap Head. Check the village gardens in Porthgwarra and the dense bushes in the valley for birds. Continue on the B3315 to Land's End, turn right on the A30, then left on the B3306 to St Just Airfield. Turn left to Nanquidno and scan the short grass for waders. To the west of the airfield the Nanquidno valley, with its dense cover, also produces migrants, including American rarities.

Permits: none required.

LANDGUARD POINT, SUFFOLK

OS 169

Location: the southernmost tip of the Suffolk coast, at the mouth of the joint estuary of the Rivers Stour and Orwell, it lies between Harwich and the docks of Felixstowe.

Habitats: this is a shingle spit extending southwards across the estuary mouth, with large areas of low cover surrounded by sprawling docks. There are disused pits, wartime defences, and a small pool. It was not until the 1980s that Landguard became a notable birdwatching site. In 1983 a bird observatory was established and scarce migrants have been recorded ever since. There is also a reserve here, managed by the Suffolk Trust for Nature Conservation. The main emphasis is on small migrants in spring and autumn, with birds arriving and departing during day and night, particularly in autumn. Pied Flycatcher, Bluethroat and Wryneck are all regular, along with the more widespread warblers and chats. The docks and old fort provide nesting sites for Black Redstart, while Ringed Plover and Little Tern breed on the shingle.

Access: leave Felixstowe southwards on a minor road to Landguard nature reserve.

Permits: these are not required for the nature reserve and not available for the observatory. There is no accommodation.

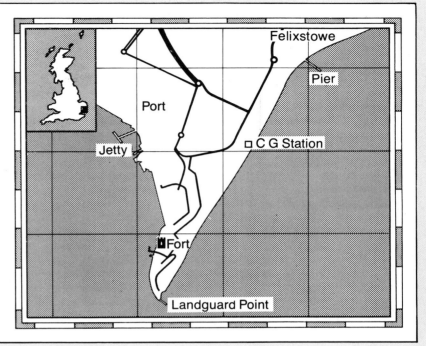

LANGSTONE HARBOUR AND FARLINGTON MARSHES, HAMPSHIRE   OS 196 & 197

Location: the large tidal inlet of Langstone Harbour is east of Portsmouth. Farlington Marshes extend into it.

Habitats: the areas of mud exposed at low tide offer shorebirds good feeding opportunities and there are low-lying islands that offer safe roosts to waders. Farlington is an area of rough grazing land intersected by dykes and a few low-lying freshwater marshes.

Birds: winter brings up to 10,000 Brent Geese. Wigeon, Teal and Pintail are also numerous and waders include good flocks of Knot, Black-tailed Godwit, Grey Plover and especially Dunlin, and a few wintering Greenshank, Spotted Redshank and Ruff. Goldeneye and Red-breasted Merganser feed in the deep channels and Black-necked Grebe frequent the Langstone Bridge area. On spring and autumn passage there is a wider variety of waders. Gulls have included the rarest species found in Britain.

Access: leave the A27 at its junction with the A2030 and take a track off the roundabout leading eastward to the marshes. A footpath leads around the peninsula.

Permits: though partly an RSPB reserve, no permits are required.

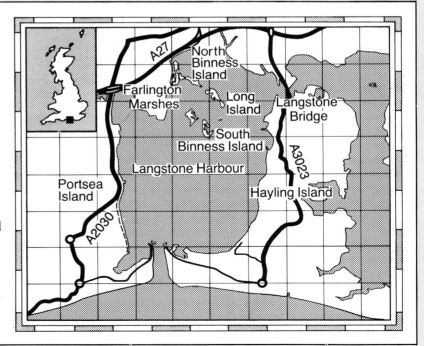

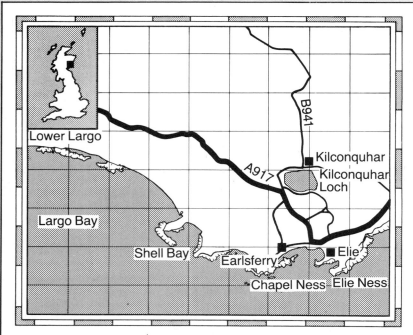

LARGO BAY AND KILCONQUHAR LOCH, FIFE

OS 59

Location: on the northern shore of the Firth of Forth, east of Leven.

Habitats: the sea itself is the major attraction here. Loch Kilconquhar has a roost of Greylag Geese – and much more besides.

Birds: though grebes and ducks breed on the loch, this is mainly a winter site, when seaducks are particularly good. Scoter, Goldeneye and Scaup are dominant, but Long-tailed Duck is regular in good numbers, often approaching quite close inshore. Both Red-throated and Black-throated Divers are regular, the former being by far the most numerous, and Slavonian Grebe can usually be seen. The rocky shorelines hold Purple Sandpiper, as well as the more widespread Turnstone, Dunlin, Grey Plover and Redshank. Spring and autumn passage periods bring in good numbers of terns, including a few Roseate Terns, while Little Gull is something of a local speciality, with several hundred sometimes appearing at Loch Kilconquhar.

Access: Leven is worth a look as is Lower Largo to the east. Elie Ness and Earlsferry are probably the best seawatching spots. For Kilconquhar Loch leave the A917 on to the B941 to the village and view from the north by the church.

Permits: none necessary.

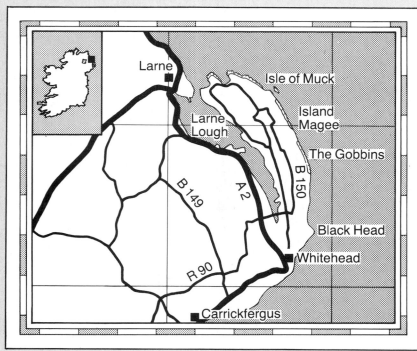

LARNE LOUGH, CO. ANTRIM, NORTHERN IRELAND   OSNI 9

Location: this is an inlet of the sea less than 30 miles to the north-east of Belfast that almost cuts off Island Magee from the mainland. Larne itself is a ferry terminal.

Habitats: there are extensive mud banks that offer good feeding opportunities to wildfowl and waders, but comparatively small areas of saltmarsh. Sadly, the estuary is being used as a dump by industry.

Birds: there is a small flock of Brent Geese here through the winter, along with up to 2000 Wigeon, and smaller numbers of Teal and Shelducks. Goldeneye (sometimes 50 or more) can be regularly seen on the channels. The tiny (¼-acre) RSPB reserve of Swan Island, on the inner part of the lough, is a major high-tide wader roost and shelters large numbers of ducks, and has small breeding colonies of Roseate and Sandwich Terns, as well as breeding Red-breasted Mergansers.

Access: the main A2 from Larne to Belfast passes along the western shoreline, though the railway line between it and the lough prevents complete exploration of the site. The B90 crosses the head of the estuary and offers access at several sites along the eastern shoreline.

Permits: there is no access to Swan Island; no permit is required for the rest of the area.

LAVAN SANDS, GWYNEDD OS 115

Location: on the North Wales coast, to the east of Anglesey.

Habitats: the massive intertidal sands are broken only by the Ogwen estuary. The Conwy estuary, about 10 miles to the north-east, is an excellent site, while 5 miles to the north of the Conwy are the dramatic limestone sea-cliffs of Great Ormes Head.

Birds: the Ogwen estuary has Wigeon, Shelduck, Goldeneye and Red-breasted Merganser. Waders are found here too, though the largest roost is usually just to the west of Llanfairfechan. This is also a good area for the scarcer winter grebes, and for wintering Firecrest, Chiffchaff and even Water Pipit. Winter also brings Red-throated Diver, a few Great Northern Divers, and small flocks of Twite on the saltmarshes, while at Great Orme there are Purple Sandpiper. There is a hide overlooking the estuary on one side and a small pool in a wood on the other; Kingfisher and Water Rail are often seen here in winter. Spring and autumn passage brings a greater variety of waders, especially to the 6000-acre Traeth Lavan Local Nature Reserve.

Access: from the A55 at Tal-y-bont a minor road leads north to the reserve and hide. The other sites are reachable from the A55.

Permits: none required at present, but check with the reserve on arrival for access to Traeth Lavan.

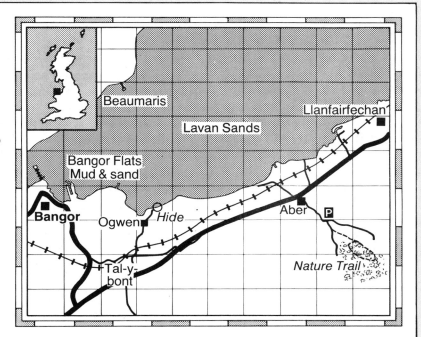

LEIGHTON MOSS, LANCASHIRE OS 97

Location: this RSPB reserve lies in a limestone valley in north-western Lancashire, near the head of Morecambe Bay.

Habitats: this is now one of the largest reed beds in the country. There is plenty of scrub and open water, surrounded by hilly woods.

Birds: this is now the main breeding stronghold of the Bittern in Britain. Bearded Tit, too, breed, along with Reed, Sedge and Grasshopper Warblers. Several duck species (including Shoveler and sometimes Gadwall and Garganey), also breed, as do Buzzard and Sparrowhawk. Spring and autumn passage brings regular Garganey, Marsh Harrier and Black Tern. Passage waders include Greenshank, Green Sandpiper and Spotted Redshank. In winter there are many ducks, Greylag Goose, Water Rail, as well as resident Bittern.

Access: from the A6 or M6 at junction 35 (via Carnforth) or 36 (via Milnthorpe). The reserve entrance is on the left near Silverdale railway station. There is public access across the middle of the reserve, and a public hide, as well as four RSPB-only hides. The reserve is open daily, except Tuesday; the car park and reserve centre lies to the south of the public track.

Permits: a fee is payable by non-RSPB members.

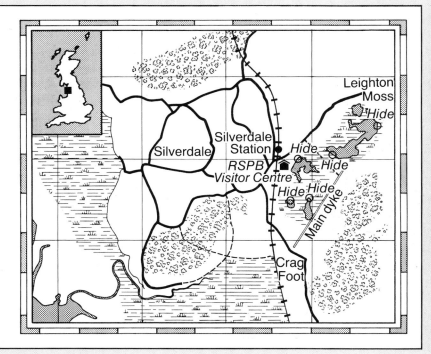

289

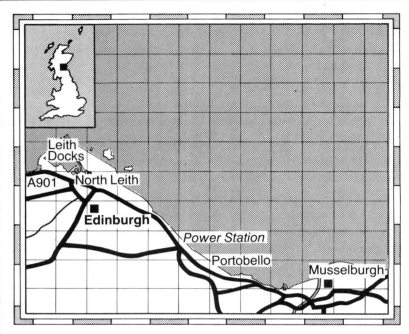

LEITH AND MUSSELBURGH, EAST LOTHIAN OS 66

Location: this bay extends from the dockland of Leith eastwards along the southern shore of the Firth of Forth.

Habitats: the rich feeding grounds of the Forth have attracted both wildfowl and waders to this area for many years. For a long time this attraction was enhanced by a sewage outfall, but sadly that has now gone. One result is that, instead of boasting one of the largest flocks of Scaup in the country (with a peak of 30,000 or more in 1968–9), the bay now rarely holds more than a handful of these seaducks.

Birds: Merganser, Long-tailed Duck, Common and Velvet Scoter, Goldeneye and Eider are all present here in good numbers. Red-throated Diver is regular too, along with Slavonian Grebe. Waders tend to be the regular Redshank, Turnstone and Dunlin, but during spring and autumn the Goose Green Ash Lagoon may hold a wider variety of species. There may also be Gulls.

Access: the A1 runs parallel with the shores of the Firth of Forth east of Edinburgh and there is a promenade giving excellent views to the west. It is worth exploring the whole of this shoreline, stopping to view the birds from the many vantage points. The Goose Green Ash Lagoon lies at Musselburgh, just off the A1.

Permits: none required.

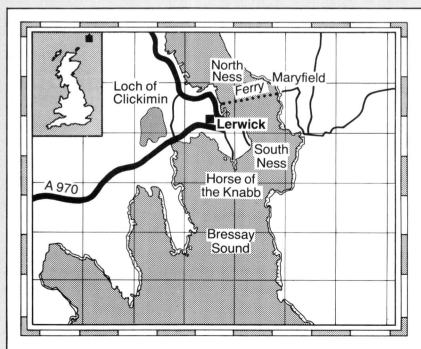

LERWICK, SHETLAND OS 4

Location: the capital of Shetland, Lerwick lies on the eastern side of Mainland, the biggest island, and is sheltered by the island of Bressay, to the east.

Habitats: the main attraction of Lerwick to birders is its busy harbour, where scavenging seabirds regularly gather in large numbers. There are also gardens offering cover to migrants, but no convenient spot from which these birds can be easily watched.

Birds: in summer, there are always gulls and Black Guillemot, but the real time for a visit is mid-winter, especially after gales. Then the local gulls are regularly joined by both Glaucous and Iceland Gulls and, just occasionally, by one of the really rare species, such as Ivory Gull. These same storms may force some of the birds that winter elsewhere in Shetland to seek shelter: these include Long-tailed Duck, Eider and Slavonian Grebe. Great Northern Diver occurs every winter and each one should be checked carefully in case it is a rare White-billed Diver.

Access: there are regular connections to Lerwick from Aberdeen by air and ferry. A good place to start exploring the area is the sewage outfall immediately south of Loch of Clickimin. Respect the islanders' privacy when looking into gardens.

Permits: not required.

LINDISFARNE, NORTHUMBERLAND OS 75

Location: this island, also known as Holy Island, is joined to the north Northumberland coast at low tide by a causeway. It lies about 9 miles south of Berwick-upon-Tweed and the Scottish border. The Lindisfarne National Nature Reserve is mainly intertidal and includes Budle Bay. The area described here includes the mainland from Goswick in the north to Bamburgh in the south. The A1 provides both a boundary and convenient access.

Habitats: predominantly an intertidal area of mud and sand, sheltered from the open sea by a coastline of large dunes. The largest area of dunes lies at the northern end of Holy Island. The causeway to the mainland is covered by the tide for several hours each day. This is no place to run out of petrol, though people do every year. The largest area of sand is Fenham Flats, but in Budle Bay to the south large areas of mud and sand are exposed at low tide. About 9 miles to the south the castle at Bamburgh stands atop cliffs that are frequented by seabirds.

Birds: the number of birds here in winter can be quite staggering, with Dunlin the dominant wader and Wigeon the commonest duck. The latter have reached 40,000 on occasion. Of the waders there are 14,000 Dunlin, 10,000 Knot, 4500 Bar-tailed Godwit, 1000 Redshank and lesser numbers of Sanderling, Turnstone and Grey Plover. As well as Wigeon, wildfowl include about 600 Scoter, 200 Long-tailed Duck, 600 Shelduck and virtually the whole British wintering population of the Pale-bellied sub-species of Brent Goose, which breeds on the island of Spitsbergen (Svalbard) in the Arctic Ocean and which is rapidly declining. There is also a 400-strong herd of Whooper Swan. Red-throated Diver are regular and Black-throated Diver are often present, too. Slavonian is the most common grebe, but Red-necked Grebe is also regular.

Spring and autumn passage periods bring a wider variety of waders, including Spotted Redshank, both Black-tailed and Bar-tailed Godwits and, in autumn, Little Stint. Terns, too, are regular (mainly Common, Arctic and Sandwich), and are often accompanied by Arctic Skua. Small migrants are often good, but rarities are few and even species such as Bluethroat and Wryneck that turn up regularly at other east-coast sites are scarce.

Access: there are several easy access points that make exploration straightforward. They are, from north to south, Goswick; Beal for the causeway to Holy Island, which is certainly worth exploring as far as Castle Point; Fenham; Ross to Ross Links and Ross Back Sands; via Budle to Budle Point; and from Bamburgh northwards. Take careful note of the tide times and instructions prominently displayed at the causeway before attempting to cross to Holy Island.

Permits: permits are not necessary, but keep strictly to the public rights of way as outlined above.

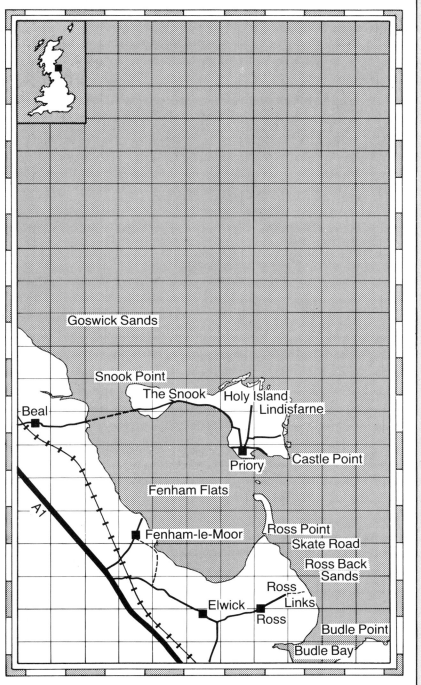

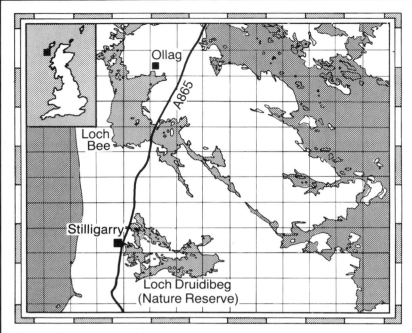

LOCH DRUIDIBEG, OUTER HEBRIDES OS 22

Location: this National Nature Reserve is situated in the northern part of the island of South Uist.

Habitats: Druidibeg is a shallow freshwater loch with grassy margins and fields; there are damp areas and some taller vegetation. To the west the land rolls gently toward the shellsand beaches, while to the east the coast is more rugged and hostile.

Birds: the flock of about 150 Greylag Geese is the largest native population in Britain. The birds breed here and spend the winter grazing the surrounding grasslands. Some are also found on Loch Bee to the north. Though mainly winter visitors, Whooper Swans sometimes stay for the summer, though there has been no proof of breeding for over 40 years. The area holds Corncrake in summer.

Access: the main A865 passes the western shore of Druidibeg and there are minor roads running eastward to facilitate exploration, especially the B890. South Uist can be reached by British Airways flights to Benbecula; alternatively, there are Caledonian MacBrayne ferries from Oban to Lochboisdale (voyage 6–9 hours), or from Uig, on Skye, to Lochmaddy, North Uist (voyage 2 hours).

Permits: none required outside the breeding season; keep to the public roads at other times.

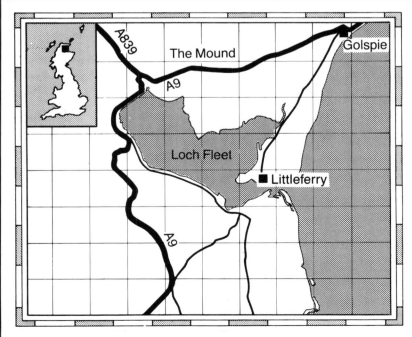

LOCH FLEET, HIGHLAND OS 21

Location: five miles north of the Dornoch Firth and 3 miles to the south-west of Golspie on the east coast of northern Scotland.

Habitats: the loch is almost totally enclosed by land and has only a narrow opening to the sea, at Littleferry. Its intertidal banks offer feeding opportunities to waders and wildfowl, while the attempted draining of the upper part of the estuary with 'The Mound' in 1815 simply created a freshwater marsh that has become a dense 'fen'. Near the coast the dunes extend northwards to Golspie.

Birds: winter is probably the best season here, with good numbers of the more common waders and plentiful wildfowl. The latter include Whooper Swan and Greylag Goose, along with good numbers of seaducks, including Long-tailed Duck and Eider. The area seems to have an attraction for long-stay rarities, including King Eider and Surf Scoter. Breeding birds include Scottish Crossbill, Arctic Tern and Eider. Ospreys visit in summer.

Access: the main A9 runs along The Mound and gives views over the fen and upper estuary. The best birds are often near the mouth, or just outside, and can be viewed by taking the road southward near Golspie to Littleferry then walking along the shore back toward the town. Embo, to the south, should not be ignored.

Permits: not required for access along rights of way.

LOCH GARTEN, HIGHLAND OS 36

Loch: this famous Scottish loch lies about 3½ miles east of the A9 at the point at which the road leaves the Spey valley, about 25 miles south-east of Inverness.

Habitats: the loch actually lies within Abernethy Forest which is treated separately (*see page* 235) because of its appeal to a different kind of birdwatcher. Loch Garten is surrounded by old Scots pine forest with open areas of heather and juniper.

Birds: this reserve celebrates the return of the Osprey to breed in Britain and is an important PR exercise for the RSPB. The number of visitors is extraordinary and the staff ensure that the observation post and the powerful fixed binoculars are used to maximum effect. Most visitors see the birds, buy a souvenir and are soon on their way to the next tourist site. Birders may walk the paths in their search for Scottish Crossbill, Crested Tit, Redstart and Siskin, but would be well advised to follow a different approach for the scarcer species.

Access: leave the B970 on a minor road 1 mile north east of Boat of Garten and follow signs marked 'To the Ospreys'. There is ample parking and information, an RSPB shop, the observation post and helpful staff.

Permits: none required and nothing to pay.

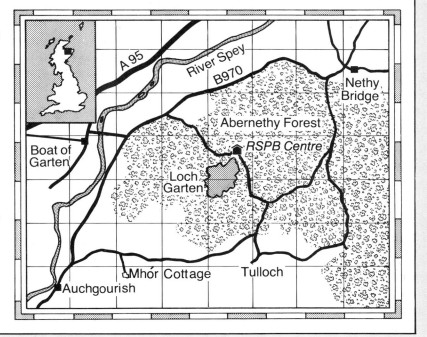

LOCH KEN, DUMFRIES AND GALLOWAY OS 77, 83 & 84

Location: inland of the north shore of the Solway, extending from just west of Castle Douglas to New Galloway.

Habitats: the damming of the River Dee has created a long and narrow loch with natural grassy banks and marshes. There is an RSPB reserve (the Ken–Dee Marshes Reserve).

Birds: for many years, this has been one of the finest sites for wintering geese in Britain. Greylag and Greenland Whitefront are the major species, but the decidedly scarce Bean Goose also occurs, mainly after Christmas, and there are also Pink-footed Goose as well as Whooper Swan. Ducks include Wigeon, Teal, Shoveler, Pintail, Goldeneye, Goosander and Merganser. Raptors are regular, including Buzzard, Merlin and Hen Harrier.

Access: starting at Castle Douglas, view Carlingwark Loch to the west before continuing on the A75 to Threave Wildfowl Refuge. Take the track to the right to Kelton Lodge where there are free hides. Explore Loch Ken from the A713 on the east and A762 on the west. The RSPB reserve may be visited only escorted and by previous appointment, but all the birds can be seen from the roads.

Permits: only necessary for escorted visits to RSPB reserve: contact The Warden, Midtown, Laurieston, near Castle Douglas, DG7 2PP.

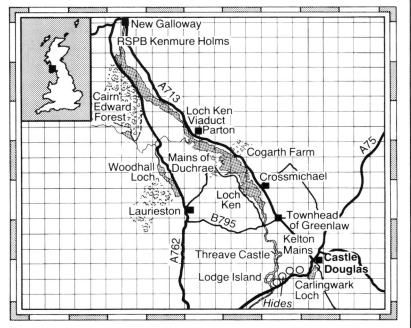

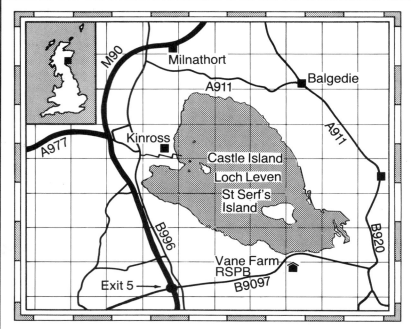

LOCH LEVEN, TAYSIDE   OS 58

Location: between the Firths of Forth and Tay.
Habitats: Loch Leven is one of the richest lowland lakes in the country and is surrounded by agricultural land. It has several islands, marshy banks, and a 'scrape' at the RSPB's Vane Farm Reserve.
Birds: Loch Leven has long been famous as the most important breeding site for ducks (with over 1000 pairs) in Britain and one of the major arrival points for wintering geese. In autumn over 12,000 Pink-footed Geese use the water as a roost, with large numbers remaining all winter, with many Greylag Geese. Wintering ducks include very good numbers of Goosander and Goldeneye, as well as huge numbers of the more common species. Peregrine is frequently to be seen. The geese are best seen at dusk and dawn.
Access: though there is access at Kirkgate Park, Burleigh Sands and from roads at other points, the RSPB reserve at Vane Farm is usually the best entry point at all seasons. Leave the M90 at Exit 5 and take the B9097 eastwards along the southern shore. There is an excellent visitor centre that is open daily except during January to March, when opening is restricted to weekends, and good hides.
Permits: available from the RSPB reserve centre. Non-members pay a small charge.

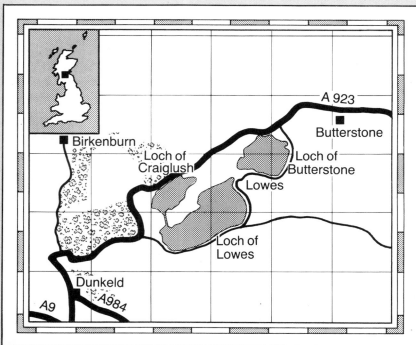

LOCH OF LOWES, TAYSIDE   OS 53

Location: this Scottish Wildlife Trust reserve lies immediately east of Dunkeld only a short distance from the A9 trunk road.
Habitats: this is a shallow loch with a good growth of emergent vegetation that offers food and shelter to a good range of birds. It is surrounded by mature woodlands that provide protection from casual disturbance.
Birds: Ospreys breed every year and this is only the second (after Loch Garten) eyrie of these birds to be widely publicized and open to visiting, despite the continued increase in numbers of these charismatic raptors. Other breeders include Great Crested Grebe and both Sedge and Grasshopper Warblers. Despite rumours, this is not a regular site for breeding Slavonian Grebe. The woodlands hold all the species one would expect in this region and there are Black Grouse and Capercaillie nearby. In winter the loch acts as a major roost for Greylag Geese.
Access: leave the A9 at Dunkeld on the A923 and turn right after 1½ miles. There is a visitor centre here that is open daily from April to September, and the hide is open throughout the year.
Permits: not required, but you will help ensure the birds will continue to bring enjoyment by joining the Scottish Wildlife Trust: donations are also gratefully received.

LOCH OF SPIGGIE, SHETLAND

OS 4

Location: this lowland loch lies in the southern part of Shetland's chief island, Mainland, to the west of the main Lerwick–Sumburgh road and only about ¼ mile from the Bay of Scousburgh.

Habitats: Spiggie is a shallow freshwater loch that is rich and fertile. It is surrounded by grassland, with dunes to the north and a marsh to the south that separates it from the neighbouring Loch of Brow. Part of the latter, as well as the whole of Loch of Spiggie, is included in an RSPB reserve.

Birds: breeding birds include Shelduck and Curlew, and it is regularly used by a variety of seabirds for bathing and resting. These include Great and Arctic Skuas and Arctic Terns. In spring there is a regular gathering of Long-tailed Duck that indulge in courtship displays prior to nesting elsewhere. In winter Whooper Swan are regular visitors and there are usually also Greylag Geese and a variety of duck present. During passage periods various waders, often including Red-necked Phalarope, appear.

Access: though there is a summer warden, there are no visiting arrangements. Much can be seen from the surrounding roads. Leave the A970 westwards on the B9122 and view to the south.

Permits: not available.

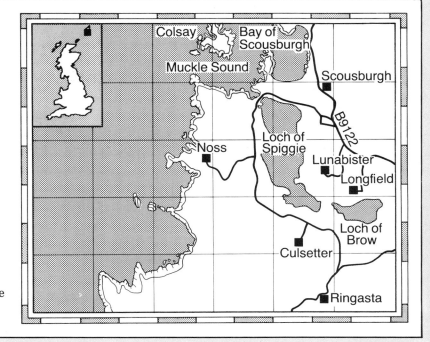

LOCH OF STRATHBEG, GRAMPIAN OS 30

Location: the largest dune lake in Britain. It lies between Peterhead and Fraserburgh in the north-east of Scotland.

Habitats: this is a shallow 'dune-slack' lake that varies greatly in size according to the water-level. It is surrounded by farmland and grassy marshes, with some reedy areas, and is separated from the sea by a large dune system. Much of the area is an RSPB reserve.

Birds: the main interest is in winter, when Strathbeg is a major gathering place for huge flocks of migrating geese. Nearly 40,000 geese, mainly Pinkfeet and Greylags, regularly use the area, and there are good numbers of Whooper Swan, Goldeneye and Goosander. The sea holds all three regular British species of diver, and Hen Harrier are also regular. More irregular visitors include Marsh Harrier and Merlin.

Access: leave Peterhead northwards on the A952 and turn right before Crimond to the reserve headquarters. Access is across MoD property. The south side of the loch can be seen from the minor road to the south which leads to Rattray Head.

Permits: no access without a permit: write in advance to The Warden, RSPB, The Lythe, Crimonmogate, Lonmay, Fraserburgh, AB4 4UB. There is a charge to non-RSPB members.

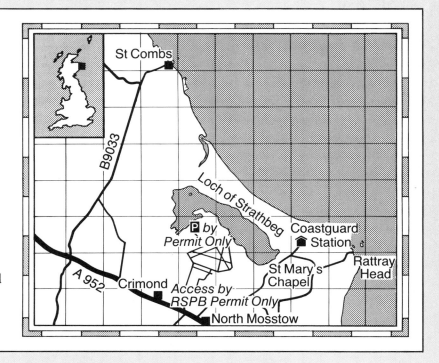

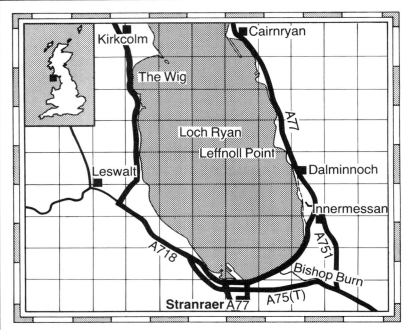

LOCH RYAN, DUMFRIES AND GALLOWAY OS 76 & 82

Location: at the western end of Galloway, enclosed by the northern arm of the hammerhead-shaped western tip of Galloway, with Luce Bay about 6 miles to the south.

Habitats: this is a large sea loch that is well sheltered by the surrounding hills. There are small intertidal areas of mud.

Birds: this is a favourite site for a good variety of wintering seabirds. Though Red-throated Diver is most common, both Black-throated and Great Northern also occur regularly. Grebes usually include both Slavonian and Black-necked, and seaducks include Wigeon, Scaup, Common Scoter, Red-breasted Merganser, Goldeneye and Eider. The occasional King Eider turns up among the Common Eider; indeed, Loch Ryan is one of the best spots in Britain for this handsome northern vagrant. Most of these birds concentrate on the southern shore off Stranraer, where there is a muddy foreshore that attracts waders. To the south-east lie the twin waters of Black Loch and White Loch, separated by Castle Kennedy. Here Greylag Geese are regular.

Access: the A77 and A718 provide many excellent vantage points, in particular, check east of Stranraer, Cairnryan and The Wig.

Permits: not required.

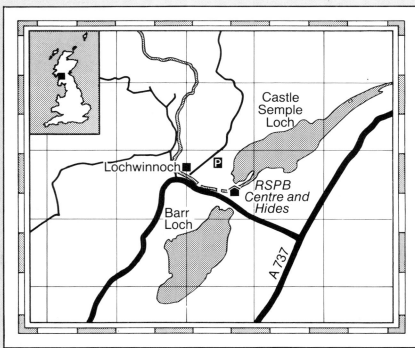

LOCHWINNOCH, STRATHCLYDE OS 70

Location: this is an RSPB reserve that consists of the south-western shore of Castle Semple Loch, Aird Meadow, a large area of sedge marsh that extends southward almost to the A760 and some way beyond it. Only about 18 miles south-west of Glasgow, it serves an important function as an educational centre encouraging inner-city children to become involved in conservation.

Habitats: as well as the Barr Loch, there is willow and alder scrub, deciduous woodland and the sedge marsh of Aird Meadow.

Birds: breeding birds include Great Crested Grebe, which here finds its Scottish stronghold, plus several duck species, including Shoveler and Teal. There is a Black-headed Gull colony and both Grasshopper and Sedge Warblers breed among the reeds. In winter both Whooper Swan and Greylag Goose use the area, along with many ducks, including up to 1000 or more each of Tufted Duck and Pochard.

Access: leave the A737 on the A760 to Lochwinnoch Station. The reserve centre is beyond this on the right. There is a shop, a fine visitor centre, with a tower hide, and a nature trail that leads to other hides. A small admission charge is made to non-members. The reserve is open throughout the year.

Permits: available on arrival.

THE LODGE, BEDFORDSHIRE OS 153

Location: the headquarters of the RSPB, The Lodge lies just 1 mile east of the town of Sandy, on the A1 between Stevenage and St Neots.

Habitats: chiefly parkland surrounding a Victorian country mansion which houses the RSPB staff: the whole area has been improved to offer a variety of different habitats. There are areas of sandy heath, bracken slopes, birch scrub, mature wood and with old Scots pine, an artificial lake, three ponds and formal gardens surrounding the lodge itself.

Birds: no less than 130 species have been recorded, which is not surprising in view of the presence of so many pairs of expert eyes. They include 50 breeding species, among which Redstart, Lesser Whitethroat, Tree Pipit and all three British woodpeckers are notable. There is a shop and exhibition centre, a nature trail and a hide. The Lodge itself is not open to visitors.

Access: leave the A1 at Sandy eastwards on the B1042. Pass through the town and watch out for The Lodge on the right after 1 mile. The reserve is open daily.

Permits: not required, though only RSPB members and their guests may visit on Sundays.

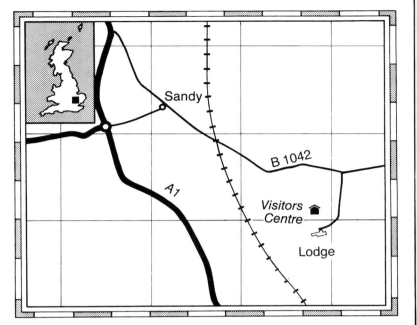

THE LOONS, ORKNEY OS 6

Location: this RSPB reserve lies in the north-western part of Mainland, the chief island of Orkney, directly west of Twatt, which is on the A986.

Habitats: The Loons is a substantial marsh lying in a basin of Old Red Sandstone and covered with an extensive growth of sedges and reeds. To the south it borders the western shore of the Loch of Isbister.

Birds: the marsh has a good breeding population of ducks that includes Shoveler, Wigeon, Pintail and Red-breasted Merganser, along with a mixed colony of gulls and terns that includes Arctic Tern and Common Gull. Though rare, Corncrake may still breed here. Winter brings many wildfowl, among which a small flock of Greenland Whitefronted Geese is notable. The marsh is, of course, a regular haunt of Hen Harrier.

Access: leave Twatt and the A986 just north of its junction with the A967, turning left on to a minor road. The reserve can be viewed from the south side of this minor road at several points. Just before reaching the B9056 there is a hide on the south side of the road giving good views.

Permits: not available; the only access is to the hide, which is open throughout the year.

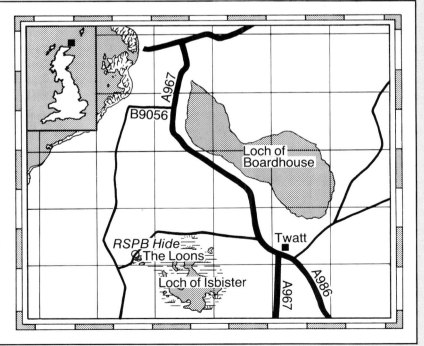

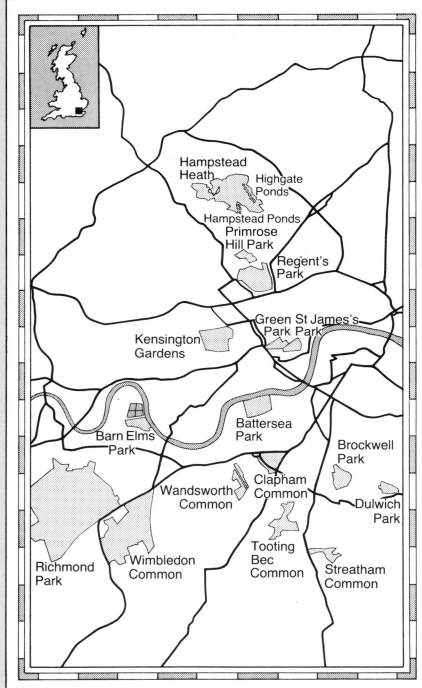

Hampstead Heath

Highgate Ponds

Hampstead Ponds

Primrose Hill Park

Regent's Park

Green Park   St James's Park

Kensington Gardens

Barn Elms Park

Battersea Park

Brockwell Park

Wandsworth Common

Clapham Common

Dulwich Park

Richmond Park

Wimbledon Common

Tooting Bec Common

Streatham Common

LONDON OS 176 & 177

Location: the capital, with an area of over 600 sq miles (Greater London), has grown up around the River Thames, some 40 miles from its estuary and the North Sea.

Habitats: though a gigantic urban sprawl, London is surprisingly green when viewed from the air. There are numerous open areas of grassland and parkland, many with ornamental lakes, and in the suburbs the combined area of gardens is larger than that of the buildings. The total area of parks, gardens, squares and playing fields exceeds 20,000 acres, including 6000 acres of Royal Parks.

There has been a tradition of watching birds in London for many years, with attention concentrated on the Royal Parks and the reservoirs. The reservoirs at Barn Elms are treated separately (*see pages* 240). More recently the parks and commons of the suburbs have been treated to more intensive study and shown to be mini-Fair Isles set in a sea of concrete. Because breeding birds are so few, it is much easier to count common migrants here than in open countryside.

Birds: ducks and feral geese breed on many ponds and there are Blackbird, Song Thrush and Blue Tit in most open areas, including back gardens. Black Redstart still breed on central redevelopment sites and the River Thames holds good populations of wintering ducks. The tiny reservoirs at Stoke Newington are always worth a winter watch. Since before the First War, diurnal migrants have been watched, particularly in October, from rooftops throughout the capital. In the north, Hampstead Heath has long been a favoured bird haunt, while in the south Wimbledon Common is one of the best sites. Watching for migrant warblers, chats and flycatchers can be rewarding at any substantial open space with trees or bushes and will produce daily Willow Warbler, Chiffchaff, Whitethroat, Lesser Whitethroat, Blackcap and other small migrants in season. Pied Flycatcher is regular and rarities have included Pallas's Warbler.

Access: the best area for migrants is the nearest open space that can be explored adequately in a morning. Over the years the following places have produced good birds: Hyde Park, Kensington Gardens, St James's Park, Regent's Park, Green Park and the string of southern commons that includes Clapham, Tooting, Wandsworth and Streatham. Breeding birds are better at Hampstead Heath and Wimbledon Common which retain more undergrowth, while any rooftop in October will produce birds soon after dawn. If your nearest open space is not listed, do not be put off. A few early morning walks during passage periods will soon show which areas are most productive, though try copses and bushy areas first. Be warned, however: the habit of watching daily can become almost an obsession, although it may produce the occasional real surprise.

Permits: none required.

LOUGH FOYLE, CO. LONDONDERRY, NORTHERN IRELAND OSNI 4 & 7

Location: this large open bay lies at the mouth of the River Foyle beginning about 5 miles downstream from Londonderry.

Habitats: Lough Foyle is a substantial sea lough with mud flats along the southern and eastern shores. The water is shallow and large areas of mud are exposed at low tide.

Birds: this is a major gathering place for migrating waders and wildfowl, with up to 29,000 Wigeon being particularly noteworthy in autumn. Winter numbers are generally much smaller. Brent Goose too is regular and both Whooper and Bewick's Swans form sizeable winter flocks. Several species of wader occur including Oystercatcher, Curlew, Redshank and Bar-tailed Godwit. Migrants include Little Stint, Curlew Sandpiper, Spotted Redshank and Greenshank.

Access: there is a National Nature Reserve (NNR) at the mouth of the River Roe, while the RSPB reserve extends from Longfield Point eastwards almost to the NNR. There is free access to viewpoints at Longfield, Faughanvale and Ballykelly, found by taking minor roads north off the A2. Magilligan Point also has waders.

Permits: none required.

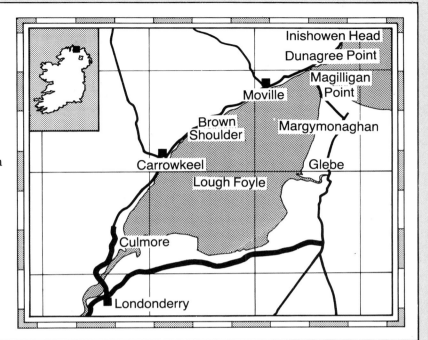

LOUGH NEAGH, CO. ANTRIM, NORTHERN IRELAND OSNI 14, 19 & 20

Location: the eastern shores of this huge lake lie some 15 miles west of Belfast.

Habitats: this is the largest area of freshwater in Britain and Ireland. Some of the newly created dry land has been turned over to agriculture, but much has been allowed to go wild, forming reed beds and swampy fens. To the north is Lough Beg, a similar but smaller water that is even richer in underwater life.

Birds: Lough Neagh is one of the major wildfowl sites in Europe, with massive winter populations of Tufted Duck and Pochard. Total numbers of both these species have, on occasion, exceeded 30,000 birds. More than 2000 each of Teal, Wigeon and Scaup have been recorded, while Goldeneye numbers have exceeded 5000 several times. All three British swans and Greylag Geese are regular. Diving ducks and geese are seen on Lough Neagh, while swans and surface-feeding ducks are more often found on Lough Beg. In summer there is a large breeding population of ducks.

Access: start at Shanes Castle, an RSPB reserve and estate open to the public. Find the Randalstown Road just west of Antrim.

Permits: contact The Warden, Shanes Castle, RSPB Reserve, 67 Greenview Avenue, Antrim.

299

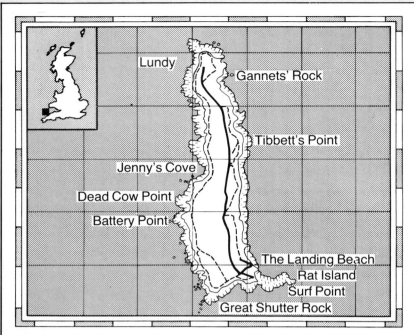

LUNDY, DEVON OS 180

Location: this island lies in the Bristol Channel 11 miles off the north coast of Devon and is reached via Ilfracombe.

Habitats: Lundy is about 3½ miles long, with 100-metre cliffs along its western shoreline. Most of the interior is windswept and virtually devoid of cover, though there are a few sheltered valleys in the east. It is position rather than habitat that makes the island so attractive to birds. Lundy was declared Britain's first Statutory Marine Nature Reserve in 1986.

Birds: though the island's name, given it by Viking raiders, is Old Norse for 'Isle of Puffins', these birds are now down to less than a hundred pairs. Two other species of auks, Guillemot and Razorbill, are more numerous, as are Kittiwake and Fulmar. Gannet are frequently seen offshore and Manx Shearwater and Storm Petrel both breed. During summer and autumn passage periods, all sorts of small birds turn up including a good selection of rarities.

Access: there is a regular boat service from Ilfracombe. Day trips from Ilfracombe allow too little time for exploration. Contact the Island Administrator (Tel: 0271 870870) for details. Accommodation may be booked through The Landmark Trust, Shottesbrooke, Maidenhead, Berks SL6 3SW (Tel: 062 882 5925).

Permits: none required.

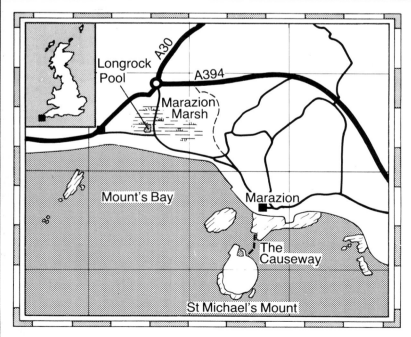

MARAZION MARSH, CORNWALL OS 203

Location: this coastal marsh lies about 3 miles east of Penzance between Longrock and Marazion overlooking Mount's Bay.

Habitats: Marazion Marsh is a largely overgrown swamp, broken here and there by pools of open water. By autumn these usually have muddy margins that attract waders. These also occur along the shoreline, along with gulls.

Birds: the position of Marazion, only 11 miles east of Land's End, makes it an inevitable port of call for various transatlantic vagrants. In particular, it regularly boasts an American wader or two in autumn. At this season it is also one of the best places in the country, along with Slapton Ley (*see page* 320), for Aquatic Warbler. Spring sees a regular influx of southern birds rarities that have 'overshot' their normal summer range in southern Europe, with Hoopoe and Little Egret the most likely. Many rarities have been found here, including now almost regular Ring-billed Gull from North America.

Access: leave Penzance eastward on the A30 and turn right in Longrock along the coast road, from which the marsh can be seen. At the eastern end is a car park from where a footpath leads northwards across the marsh to the railway and beyond.

Permits: none required.

MARTIN MERE, LANCASHIRE OS 108

Location: between the Mersey and Ribble estuaries, some 7½ miles east of the Lancashire coast and about 5 miles east of Southport.

Habitats: at one time a large lake, Martin Mere was drained and converted for agricultural use before being purchased by the Wildfowl Trust in 1969 and, partially at least, reconverted back to open water. There is now a series of pools housing the Trust's collection of captive wildfowl and flamingoes, plus some larger lagoons intended for wild birds.

Birds: Martin Mere is a major arrival point for Pink-footed Goose migrating to Britain. There are both Whooper and Bewick's Swans, tens of thousands of ducks, including one of the country's largest flocks of Pintail, and an impressive selection of raptors. The latter include Peregrine and Hen Harrier. Waders may be good on passage and Ruff and Black-tailed Godwit have bred here. Although it is often a busy place, with thousands of children paying educational visits each year, this is a stunningly good birding spot, and is generously provided with 9 hides.

Access: the Trust is signposted at Mere Brow from the A565, and Burscough Bridge from the A59. It is open daily.

Permits: entrance fee to non-members.

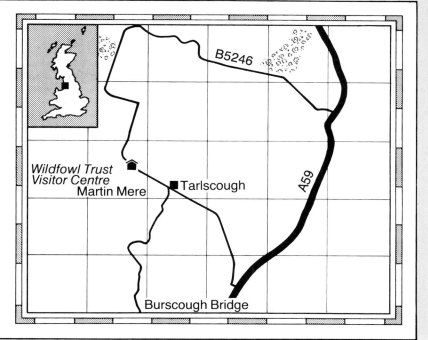

MARWICK HEAD, ORKNEY OS 6

Location: this headland lies on the north-western coast of Mainland, the chief island of Orkney, and is easily located by the memorial to Lord Kitchener who perished offshore in 1916, when the cruiser on which he was travelling was sunk by a German mine.

Habitats: the cliffs here rise to almost 90m and are decidedly crumbly, with some huge landslides. They are backed by grassy fields sloping away to a gentle valley.

Birds: despite their comparatively low height, these cliffs contain one of Britain's most spectacular seabird breeding colonies, and the RSPB recognized this by establishing a reserve here. There are birds everywhere, in the air, crammed together on cliff ledges, and swimming or diving in the sea. Huge numbers of Guillemots, estimated at 35,000, are everywhere, with over 10,000 pairs of Kittiwakes. There are also Razorbills and Puffins, Fulmars and Shags, and sometimes a Peregrine. Both Great and Arctic Skuas are regular visitors and Ravens utter their deep, resonant croaks.

Access: take the B9056 and turn westward on a minor road that leads to Marwick. Watch out for the Kitchener Memorial and walk the track to the cliff-tops. Take great care not to disturb the birds. Take care, also, not to approach the cliff-tops too closely.

Permits: not required.

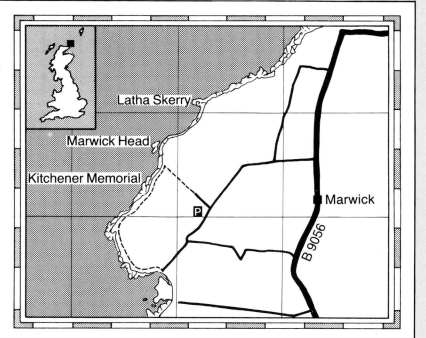

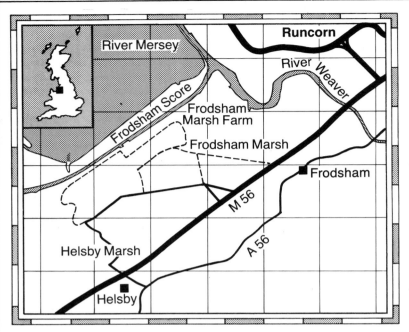

MERSEY ESTUARY, CHESHIRE OS 117

Location: the Mersey extends inland from Liverpool and is one of the most heavily industrialized estuaries in the whole country.

Habitats: access is decidedly awkward and the best places revel in names such as 'the sludge lagoon' and 'the ICI tank'.

Birds: despite its industrialization, the Mersey is of considerable importance for wintering waders and wildfowl, with a population of over 35,000 Dunlin and four-figure totals for Shelduck, Wigeon, Teal and Pintail. Numbers of the latter usually exceed those at any other site in Britain and are among the greatest in north-west Europe. Despite the pollution, the birds are protected from both shooting and disturbance. The best areas are near the head of the estuary, at Hale on the northern shore and at Frodsham on the south. In particular, the sludge lagoons at the latter (especially Number 5) and the ICI Tank are good for waders at all times of the year.

Access: leave the M56 at Exit 12 and follow the A56 to Frodsham. Take Ship Street back across the motorway and follow a gravel track northwards. Continue on foot northwards to Weaver Bend via the ICI Tank. Return via the sludge lagoon.

Permits: though much of the area is private, birders are usually tolerated.

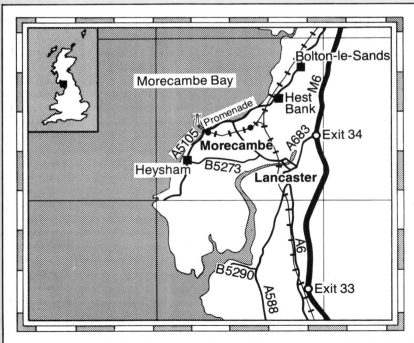

MORECAMBE, LANCASHIRE OS 96

Location: this seaside resort lies at the heart of Morecambe Bay about 20 miles to the north of Blackpool.

Habitats: the huge intertidal area of Morecambe Bay (with about 120 square miles of mud and sand at low tide) extends to north and south and is acknowledged as one of the major wetland areas of Europe. Morecambe promenade offers the easiest access to what can otherwise be a daunting area because of its vast size.

Birds: the birds of Morecambe Bay are abundant and of international importance. Up to 80,000 Knot – more than a quarter of the total population wintering in Britain – can be found here, and both Oystercatcher and Dunlin exceed 40,000 birds. Bar-tailed Godwit, Curlew, Redshank and Turnstone are all abundant and Ringed Plover and Sanderling are numerous on passage, when numbers of Knot may rise to 100,000. In winter there are many seaducks, including Goldeneye, Red-breasted Merganser, Scaup and Long-tailed Duck, and usually also a few divers present. The best time is on a rising tide.

Access: easily reached via the M6; leave the motorway at Exit 34 and follow the signs to Lancaster and Morecambe. When you reach the town, find the promenade.

Permits: not required.

MINSMERE, SUFFOLK OS 156

Location: this famous RSPB reserve is situated on the Suffolk coast between Southwold and Aldeburgh.

Habitats: Minsmere's fame results from the variety of habitats that can be found in its relatively small area of 1470 acres and the wealth of birds that these attract. Basically, it is a low-lying area separated from the sea by a high beach and a protective seawall. One of the most important habitats is the famous 'scrape' (an artificial area of shallow brackish water, mud and low islets), which has been imitated at many other sites. The major part of the reserve is dominated by reed beds. There are open waters here and there, belts of woodland, dry heathland, some farmland and meadow and even a couple of sand pits.

Birds: when the Avocet returned to breed in Britain after the Second World War, it chose Minsmere. The RSPB promptly created a reserve to protect them and the birds equally promptly moved away down the coast to Havergate. The birds returned to breed at Minsmere however, and today they are one of the prime attractions in summer. There are Common and Little Terns here, too, while the reed beds hold Bearded Tit, Bittern and Marsh Harrier. Both Savi's and Cetti's Warblers established breeding colonies at Minsmere, but their present status is precarious. A more recent arrival is Ruddy Duck. The woods hold a fine cross section of woodland birds, and the heaths still have breeding Nightjar, though Woodlark, Stone-curlew and Red-backed Shrike have all disappeared.

Passage can be excellent, with good numbers of waders passing through in both spring and and autumn. Species regularly include Kentish Plover and Temminck's Stint in spring and Little Stint, Curlew Sandpiper, Ruff, Greenshank and Spotted Redshank in autumn. Black Tern, Little Gull, Spoonbill and even Purple Heron are present every year. In winter there are swans and geese, also Hen Harrier and sometimes Rough-legged Buzzard. Snow Bunting and Twite frequent the shoreline and there are usually some seaducks and divers offshore.

Access: the public hide along the shore is open every day of the year. It is reached by taking the Dunwich road eastward from the B1125 at Westleton. Minsmere is signposted before reaching Dunwich. The track at the end is owned by the National Trust and a fee is payable in summer. Park at the cliff end and walk southwards. The reserve proper is reached via Westleton or Eastbridge on minor roads best found with the aid of an OS map. Both routes pass through Scott's Hall Farm to the RSPB reserve centre. Minsmere is closed on Tuesdays and is usually overcrowded during peak weekends and bank holidays.

Permits: not required to view 'The Scrape' from the shore hides; otherwise they are available from the reserve centre on arrival, but are limited, so arrive promptly at 9 a.m.

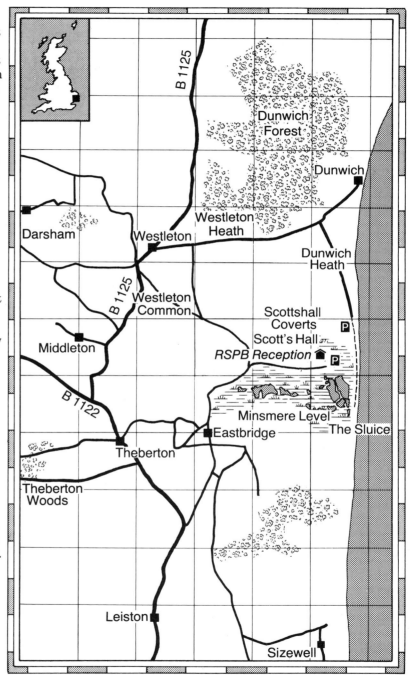

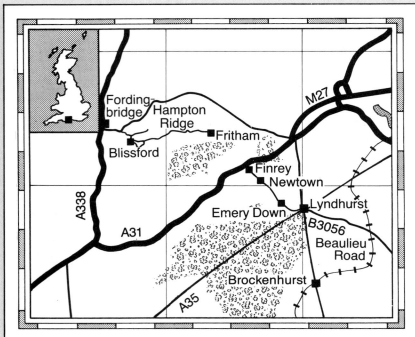

NEW FOREST, HAMPSHIRE

OS 195 & 196

Location: between Southampton and Bournemouth with its centre around the small town of Lyndhurst.

Habitats: much of the New Forest is open heathland and rough grazing, broken by extensive 'inclosures' of deciduous woodland and substantial belts of conifers. Despite its name, it includes one of the biggest areas of open land in southern Britain.

Birds: 'The Forest', as it is generally known, has long provided sites for rare breeding birds that were widely known, but never publicized. Even today it is impossible to give precise locations for birds such as Dartford Warbler, Woodlark, Hobby, Goshawk and Honey Buzzard, though all can be found by a combination of hard work and good fortune. There are breeding Nightjar, Buzzard, Firecrest, Siskin, Wood Warbler and a fine range of other species.

Access: most of The Forest is of open access and can be explored on minor roads, tracks and footpaths with the aid of the OS maps cited above, or OS Outdoor Leisure Map 22. The classic site is Beaulieu Road on the B3056, but Acres Down, Hampton Ridge and Rhinefield are also worth finding and exploring.

Permits: none required, but take care to respect private property and park only in public car parks.

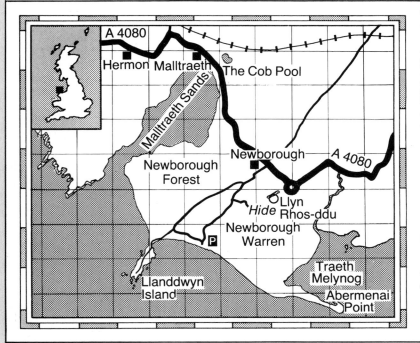

NEWBOROUGH WARREN, GWYNEDD OS 114

Location: in the south-western corner of the island of Anglesey.

Habitats: these include the extensive dune system of the Warren proper, the estuary of the River Cefni with the extensive Malltraeth Sands, and a low-lying marshy interior, partly reclaimed by a huge embankment called the Cob. Half of the Warren area is managed by the Nature Conservancy Council as a National Nature Reserve.

Birds: the breeding season brings a number of common birds to the area. In winter, there are many waders, together with Wigeon, the occasional Pink-footed and White-fronted Goose, and feral Canada and Greylag Geese. Raptors regularly include Hen Harrier, Merlin and Peregrine. Spring and autumn migration periods see regular Greenshank, Spotted Redshank and Little Stint.

Access: Malltraeth Sands, Malltraeth Pool and the damp fields beyond can all be viewed from The Cob or the A4080. The Warren can be explored from a track leading from Newborough Village south-westward. There are marked tracks that can be walked.

Permits: none required for public rights of way. Permits are necessary to visit areas away from designated routes in the National Nature Reserve. Contact the warden at 'Serai', Malltraeth, Bodorgan, Anglesey, Gwynedd LL62 5AS.

NORTH BULL, DUBLIN, IRISH REPUBLIC IOS½ 16

Location: this island lies in the northern part of Dublin Bay at the mouth of the River Liffey, surrounded by the suburbs of Dublin.

Habitats: though the best known of Irish wetlands, North Bull is really only a part of the much larger area that is the estuary of the Liffey. The island is a low ridge of dunes and saltmarsh surrounded by intertidal mud flats. Sadly, it is under continual threat from local authorities in search of dumps for rubbish as well as civic improvement works.

Birds: this is a major haunt of wildfowl and waders, with 1000 Brent and 2500 Wigeon along with lesser numbers of Teal and Pintail. Several species of wader top the 1000 mark, with Knot and Dunlin both exceeding 6000 in winter. Bar-tailed Godwit are also of international importance here, and only Dundalk Bay has larger numbers of waders on the Irish east coast. North Bull is the major wader resort for Dublin Bay, while most of the area's wildfowl can be found on the creek that separates the island from the mainland.

Access: the island is joined to the mainland by a causeway that offers excellent views over the creek and gives access to easy birding over the area.

Permits: not required.

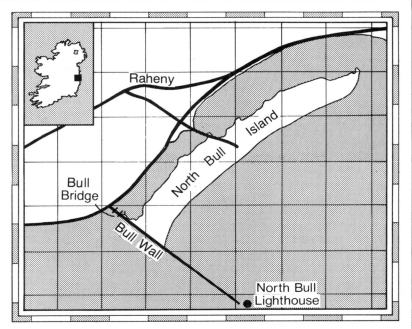

NOSS, SHETLAND OS 4

Location: this small uninhabited island lies about 12 miles east of Lerwick (*see page* 290) and just east of the isle of Bressay.

Habitats: Noss is managed by the Nature Conservancy Council as a National Nature Reserve with an area of almost 1000 acres. Its highest point, the Noup, rises to almost 180m, and it has some fearsome sea-cliffs, but is otherwise rather green and lush compared with most of Shetland.

Birds: Noss boasts one of Britain's most accessible gannetries, with nearly 7000 pairs of Gannets in summer. These numbers are, however, dwarfed by the 65,000 Guillemots, along with good numbers of Razorbill, Puffin, Kittiwake and Fulmar. Both Great and Arctic Skua breed here, too, among a grand total of twelve breeding seabirds.

Access: leave Lerwick on the regular car ferry to Bressay and continue by road across the island to Noss Sound. The nature reserve wardens will then ferry you across to Noss for a small fee. The island may be visited from mid-May to August except Monday and Thursday, but check with the Shetland Tourist Organisation, Market Cross, Lerwick (Tel: 0595 3434) in case these arrangements are changed.

Permits: none required, but keep to the clifftop paths while visiting the reserve.

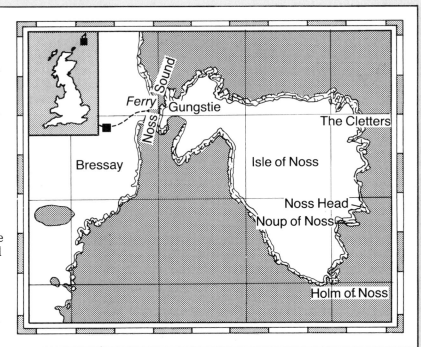

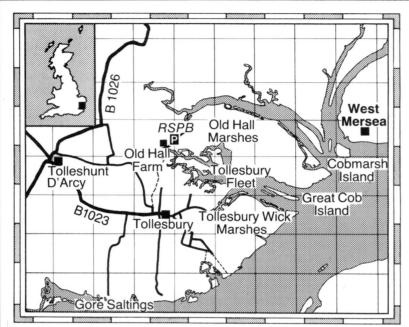

OLD HALL MARSHES, ESSEX OS 168

Location: this RSPB reserve lies on the Essex coast at the mouth of the Blackwater Estuary between Maldon and Colchester.

Habitats: this is a low-lying area of grazing marshes intersected by drainage dykes and broken here and there by a maze of old backwaters, 'fleets' (shallow creeks) and marshy reed beds.

Birds: during the summer, Common Terns breed on the islands and other breeding species include Shelduck, Pochard, Water Rail, Redshank, Yellow Wagtail and Bearded Tit. During spring and autumn passage periods waders include Black-tailed and Bar-tailed Godwits, Curlew Sandpiper, Little Stint and the occasional rarity. Avocet and Marsh Harrier are also regular. The peak season is winter, with up to 4000 Brent Geese, thousands of Wigeon, Teal and Shoveler on the marshes and Goldeneye, Red-breasted Merganser and Eider on the surrounding creeks. Slavonian Grebe find a winter stronghold here and there are usually a few Hen Harrier and Merlin to be seen.

Access: take the B1023 to Tolleshunt D'Arcy. Turn right on a minor road at the village and after 1¼ miles watch out for the track to Old Hall Farm on the left. Park and continue on foot around the sea-wall, but please do not walk or stand on it.

Permits: from The Warden, 1 Old Hall Lane, Tollesbury on arrival.

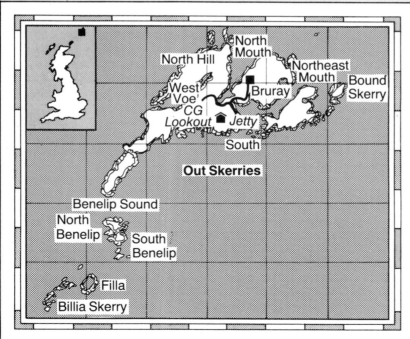

OUT SKERRIES, SHETLAND OS 2

Location: this group of small islands lies about 22 miles east of Mainland, the chief island of Shetland, and about 10 miles north-east of the island of Whalsay.

Habitats: the fact that there is a small crofting community that can offer accommodation, combined with their small size and geographical position at the easternmost point of Shetland makes the Skerries ideal for watching migrant birds.

Birds: migrants and rarities are the species that birders with a sense of independence come to Skerries to search for. In the number of rarities that are recorded each year, the islands are second only to Fair Isle (*see page 264*). Yet, even during the peak autumn period, there are seldom more than a handful of enthusiasts present, whereas Fair Isle can be booked up years ahead. Work on the assumption that anything that turns up at that more famous location can turn up here . . . but then have the satisfaction of finding it for yourself.

Access: there is a regular ferry from Lerwick to Out Skerries twice a week (journey time 3 hours) and flights once a week from Tingwall Airstrip near Lerwick in summer. Contact the Shetland Tourist Organisation, Market Cross, Lerwick.

Permits: none required.

OUSE WASHES, CAMBRIDGESHIRE & NORFOLK OS 143

Location: extending from Earith, Cambridgeshire, in the south to Denver, Norfolk, in the north.

Habitats: the Washes are a great strip of grassland, just over ½ mile wide and over 20 miles long, enclosed between high embankments, intentionally created to act as a reservoir for excess winter floodwater when the Fens were drained during the seventeenth century. Much of the area is now owned by conservation bodies which have improved the habitat with excavations, feeding programmes and suchlike schemes.

Birds: in winter, ducks, especially Wigeon, dominate the scene, with over 35,000 of this species alone. Teal, Shoveler, Pochard and Pintail are also present in good numbers, along with over 2000 Bewick's Swans and 200 Whooper Swans. The Washes have long been the major British haunt of Bewick's Swan, but the creation of a Wildfowl Trust refuge at Welney, plus an intensive feeding programme, has enabled the birds to become habituated to humans in close up. Winter also brings Hen Harrier, Merlin and Short-eared Owl.

By spring the wildfowl are on their way and their place is taken by a fine collection of breeding birds. Black-tailed Godwit and Ruff both returned here to breed after periods of absence from the country. Black Tern sometimes breeds and Little Gull has done so. During spring and autumn passage periods there are even more of these birds and they are joined by many waders that breed farther north.

Rarities regularly turn up here including ducks, herons and waders, and the Washes are worth visiting at any time of the year.

Access: there are two major access points, plus the excellent area at Welney that can be seen from the road. In the southern section the RSPB reserve is centred on Welches Dam, with a series of hides situated along the western embankment that are best visited in the afternoon when the light is better. As this side of the Washes floods first, it is better to visit it when the water level is low rather than high. Head southwards from Manea to the visitor centre. The Wildfowl Trust Refuge, too, is better at times of lower water levels, for here has been created a series of artificial pools that conveniently concentrates the birds immediately in front of a series of hides. Members of the Trust can enjoy the luxury of large glass windows in what is probably Britain's most comfortable hide. Feeding brings wild swans almost within touching distance, enabling individuals to be recognized year after year. The Refuge is reached by heading across the Washes from Welney and turning left on the far bank.

Permits: there is an admission charge to non-members of the Wildfowl Trust to the hide at Welney; in summer it is also possible to take a 2-mile walk across part of the Washes. The RSPB centre is open at weekends, but the hides are free throughout the year.

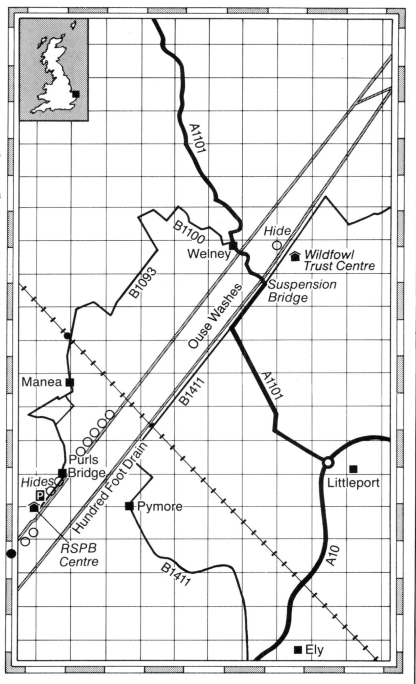

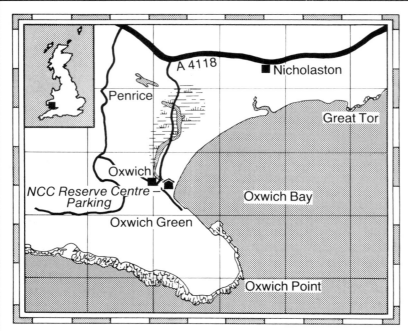

OXWICH BAY, WEST GLAMORGAN OS 159

Location: this delightful area lies on the south coast of the beautiful Gower Peninsula, about 10 miles west of Swansea.

Habitats: Oxwich is enclosed by limestone hills and consists of a low-lying valley floor contained by a broad sandy beach, backed by dunes, which partially dams the drainage stream. There are large reed beds broken by open pools, shallow marshes and dense thickets of willow. The whole area is a National Nature Reserve.

Birds: Oxwich is the major western stronghold of Reed Warbler in Britain and the reed beds also hold breeding Cetti's Warbler and Bearded Tit. Grasshopper Warblers, Sedge Warblers and Water Rail breed, too and Buzzards nest in the woods, along with Sparrowhawk and all three British woodpecker species. Regular migrants include harriers, Osprey and Hobby. In winter there are gulls, divers, seaducks and waders. A few Blackcap and Chiffchaff overwinter.

Access: leave Swansea on the A4118 and turn left on a minor road to Oxwich village. The National Nature Reserve centre, on the seaward side of the village is open on weekdays all year, and at weekends as well from spring to autumn; it has access maps.

Permits: obtain permission from the warden to use the hide (although this is not available in July and August).

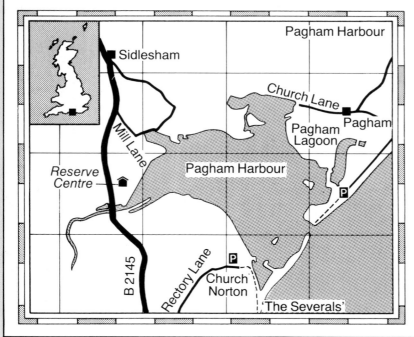

PAGHAM HARBOUR, WEST SUSSEX OS 197

Location: this tidal inlet lies on the western side of Selsey Bill immediately west of Bognor Regis.

Habitats: at low tide banks of mud, sand and shingle attract a wide variety of birds to feed. The mouth is narrow and has its own special birds. Sidlesham Ferry Pool is a tiny backwater that is superb during passage periods, while Pagham Lagoon is an abandoned gravel pit with a fen-like annexe at the northern end.

Birds: in summer Pagham is a major haunt of Little Tern, along with Ringed Plover and Shelduck. In winter there are regular Red-throated Diver, Slavonian Grebe, Brent Goose, Goldeney, Red-breasted Merganser and Eider. Waders winter as well, with Black-tailed Godwit and Ruff regular in small numbers. Spring and autumn passage waders include many Spotted Redshank, Greenshank, Little Stint and Curlew Sandpiper. Often, small numbers of these birds frequent the Ferry Pool.

Access: the West Sussex County Council has a reserve here with a centre at Sidlesham Ferry and a car park. From the Chichester by-pass follow signs to Selsey (not Pagham). Continue to Church Norton and walk to the Harbour mouth.

Permits: not required.

PAPA WESTRAY, ORKNEY OS 5

Location: situated in the extreme north of the Orkney Islands, this little island is less than a mile east of its neighbour, Westray.

Habitats: a crofting community occupies much of the central area; to north and east are maritime heath with low sandstone cliffs. The large Loch of St Tredwell is set in gently undulating country.

Birds: together with nearby Westray, these islands hold the greatest diversity of breeding seabirds in Britain. The northern part of the island is the RSPB reserve of North Hill, with over 6000 pairs of breeding Arctic Tern. Here, too, is a thriving colony of Arctic Skua, and breeding Guillemot, Razorbill, Black Guillemot, Kittiwake and Fulmar. Probably the best area is Fowl Craig on the east coast. Several pairs of Corncrake still breed here and there is a small breeding colony of Storm Petrel on the Holm of Papa. Migrants have included rarities. Sooty Shearwaters are regular in late summer.

Access: the island is easily reached by air from Westray. For details of accommodation, contact the Papa Community Co-op, Papa Westray, Orkney (Tel: 085 74 267).

Permits: none required, but contact the summer warden on arrival. Be careful not to disturb the breeding terns. By writing well before your visit, you can arrange an escorted tour of the nesting colonies.

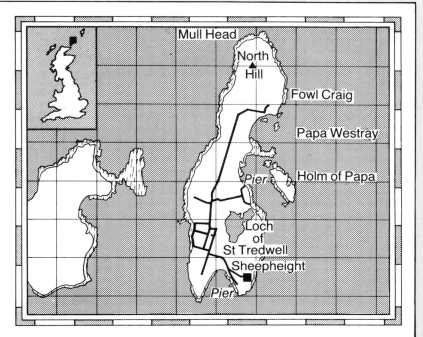

PENNINGTON MARSHES, HAMPSHIRE OS 196

Location: at the western end of the Solent, opposite the Isle of Wight, between Lymington and Keyhaven.

Habitats: an area of low-lying marshes and fields, broken up by freshwater 'borrow pits' that have gently shelving edges. On the seaward side there are also 'enclosed' areas that provide saline feeding grounds, and saltmarsh.

Birds: this is a fine area in winter, with good numbers of Brent Goose, along with Wigeon and the more widespread waders, including Grey Plover, Turnstone and Sanderling. Spotted Redshank and Ruff, on the marshes, also overwinter. During spring and autumn there is a wider variety of waders, though the two last-mentioned species, along with Greenshank, often dominate the freshwater pools. Little Stint and Curlew Sandpiper are regular in autumn and there is a good passage of Black Tern. In summer the colony of Black-headed Gulls may play host to a visiting Mediterranean Gull, and Little Tern breed.

Access: leave Lymington southwards on the A337 and turn left on Lower Pennington Lane. Continue through the village on a track past the grazing marshes, then walk to the sea-wall.

Permits: not required.

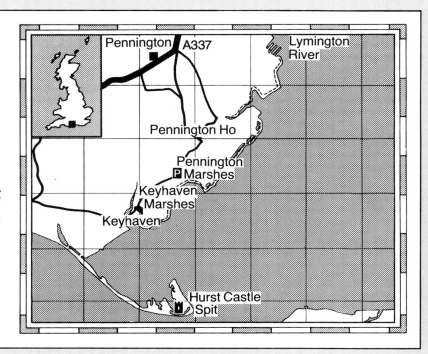

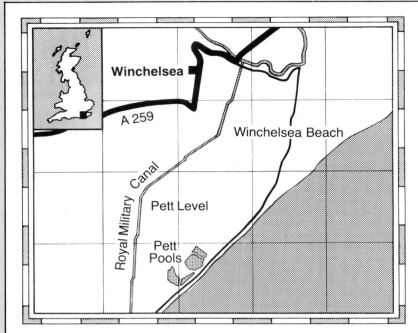

PETT LEVEL, EAST SUSSEX OS 189

Location: this wetland area lies at the eastern end of the county, about 4 miles south of Rye. It can be approached via Winchelsea Beach by taking the Fairlight road toward Hastings.

Habitats: this is an area of low-lying grazing marshes criss-crossed by a network of drainage ditches and broken by a few splashy areas that flood in winter. The sea-wall is backed by several large 'borrow pits', one of which is pumped out in mid-July each year by the Sussex Ornithological Society to expose an area of mud that attracts waders in autumn. The society maintains a small reserve here.

Birds: winter sees Brent Goose, as well as Wigeon and other ducks, along with a variety of waders that flight in at high tide. There are usually a few raptors around, too, mostly Hen Harrier and Short-eared Owl, and the sea holds Great Crested Grebe, Scoter and Eider. During the autumn passage, when the pool nearest the coast is pumped out, a fine variety of waders put in an appearance, including Little Stint, Curlew Sandpiper, Ruff, Greenshank, Knot and often a rarity. Black Tern, Little and Mediterranean Gulls and the odd Marsh Harrier usually occur each autumn.

Access: leave Rye westward on the A259. Turn left at Winchelsea on to a minor road to Winchelsea Beach. Follow this to the pools.

Permits: none required; view the site from the road.

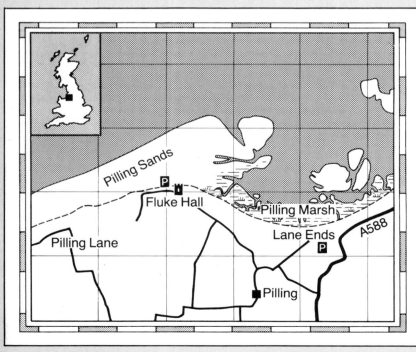

PILLING, LANCASHIRE OS 102

Location: this is another spot on the vast area of Morecambe Bay that is highly productive of both waders and wildfowl. It lies on the southern shore of the bay about 9 miles north of Blackpool.

Habitats: the vast intertidal sands are separated from the low-lying grazing and arable land by a sea-wall. Birds flight between the two different habitats.

Birds: the area between Pilling and Cockerham has long been the favourite haunt of Morecambe's flock of Pink-footed Geese, which feed on the fields here before flighting out to the sand banks to roost. They may number up to 4000 and are often accompanied by a few White-fronted Geese. Finding them is a matter of careful searching from the network of small lanes that run through the area. Pilling is also a major wader resort and in winter thousands of Knot, Dunlin, Redshank, Oystercatcher and Bar-tailed Godwit may be present.

Access: the network of lanes can be explored for geese between Pilling and Cockerham via the A588, which lies north-east of Blackpool. The geese may also be seen late in the day from the sea-wall. This is reached by driving northwards from the village to a car park, from where the waders can also be watched as they fly in to roost.

Permits: none required.

PITSFORD RESERVOIR, NORTHAMPTONSHIRE OS 141 & 152

Location: about 5 miles to the north of Northampton, between the villages of Brixworth and Holcot.

Habitats: many of the banks are gently shelving. The northern part, a nature reserve, has several sheltered bays and also some plantations and woodland. The southern part is more open.

Birds: winter brings a variety of ducks, including good numbers of Wigeon, along with Gadwall, Shoveler, Goldeneye and Pintail. There are also Bewick's Swan here, though usually they move on before the onset of hard weather. During spring and autumn passage periods waders can be interesting, particularly in autumn when Little Stint and Curlew Sandpiper are regular. Terns, including Black Terns, also pass through. In summer, there is a variety of warblers and an occasional Hobby. There are usually a few Ruddy Duck present throughout the year.

Access: Pitsford reservoir car park is found by turning left in the village. Return to Pitsford and turn left to Holcot and then left again across the causeway to view the more interesting northern half.

Permits: write (enclosing a s.a.e.) for a day permit to visit the reserve to: The Warden, c/o Northants Trust for Nature Conservation, Lings House, Billing Lings, Northampton NN3 4BE.

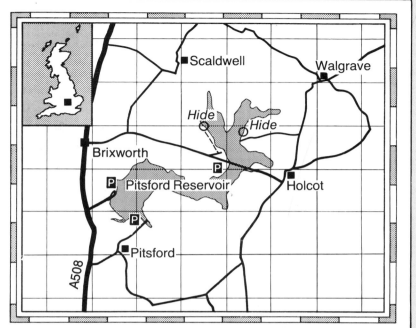

PORTLAND, DORSET OS 194

Location: the Isle of Portland extends southwards into the English Channel south of Weymouth. It is joined to the mainland by a causeway (Ferrybridge), with Portland Harbour to the east.

Habitats: Portland is a virtually treeless island of limestone rock. Birdwatching interest centres on the bird observatory at Portland Bill, as the southern tip of the island is known, the muddy foreshore at Ferrybridge and the sheltered waters of Portland Harbour.

Birds: the gardens and small fields around the Old Lower Light attract a wonderful range of small birds in spring and autumn, including many rarities. The Obelisk at the Bill is an excellent seawatch point, while to the north, Portland Harbour offers winter shelter to divers, grebes and seaducks (including Red-breasted Merganser and Eider).

Access: leave Weymouth on the A354 after checking for birds on Portland Harbour near Sandsfoot Castle. Stop on the south side of Ferrybridge at a car park on the right hand side and check the bay. Continue to Portland Bill.

Permits: none required. Accommodation is available at the Observatory: contact The Warden, Portland Bird Observatory, Old Lower Light, Portland Bill, Dorset DT5 2JT.

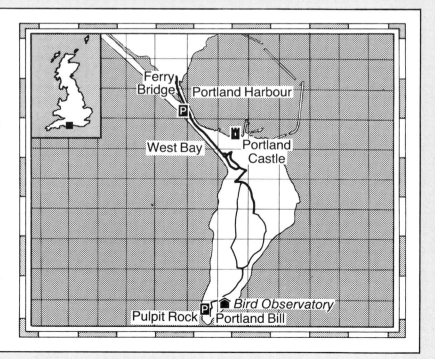

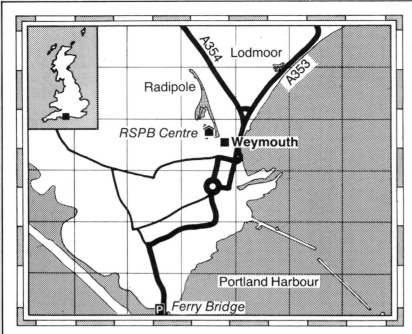

RADIPOLE AND LODMOOR, DORSET OS 194

Location: these two RSPB reserves are at Weymouth. Radipole is within the town itself, while Lodmoor lies just to the north-east.

Habitats: Radipole is the inland extension of Weymouth Harbour. Since 1924, when a bridge was built across the River Wey, this estuary has gradually become a freshwater site. It is now a reedy backwater with areas of open water, muddy banks and scrub. Lodmoor is damp grassland with marshy pools and some reed beds.

Birds: migrants have always been the main attraction, along with waders, terns, gulls: this is a prime spot for Little, Mediterranean and Ring-billed Gulls, and Black Terns are regular during both spring and autumn passage periods. Waders may include a rarity from time to time, while Garganey are present each spring. Warblers, including Cetti's, breed in the reed beds, and there are small numbers of breeding Water Rail, Kingfisher and Bearded Tit.

Access: the RSPB reserve centre is situated at the car park, near the bus station just north of Westham Bridge. For Lodmoor leave the town on the coastal A353 to the Sea Life Centre, where the entrance to the reserve and hides can be found.

Permits: car parking tickets purchased at Radipole can be used at Lodmoor. Otherwise, access is free.

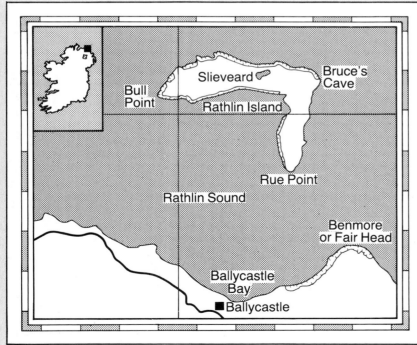

RATHLIN ISLAND, CO. ANTRIM, NORTHERN IRELAND OSNI 5

Location: Rathlin lies off the north-eastern coast of Northern Ireland and is, more or less, the nearest point of Ireland to Scotland. It is separated from the mainland by the five miles of Rathlin Sound.

Habitats: this is quite a large island extending some five miles from east to west and about four miles north to south. Extensive cliffs along the northern coast are now an RSPB reserve and, in the west, are a nature reserve of the Northern Ireland Department of the Environment. There are guest houses and caravans to be hired.

Birds: large colonies of cliff-breeding species including Guillemot, Razorbill, Black Guillemot, Fulmar and Kittiwake. There is a thriving puffinny and Manx Shearwaters breed in the same cliff-top burrows. Peregrine and Chough round off the collection. During passage periods Rathlin may attract many small migrants and has a number of rarities to its credit. It is, however, strategically sited to watch for migrant seabirds entering or leaving the Irish Sea and skuas and shearwaters are regularly seen in autumn.

Access: there is a regular boat service from Ballycastle on the adjacent mainland and the local minibus service runs somewhat erratically between Church Bay and Kebble.

Permits: none required.

RHUM, HIGHLAND OS 39

Location: Rhum is the largest of the group of islands that lies south of Skye in the Inner Hebrides. Skye is 8 miles away, and the nearest mainland port is Mallaig, 16 miles to the east.

Habitats: this is a moor-covered island rising to over 750m. There are cliff-girt shores, interrupted by sandy bays and coves, and some areas of rough pasture. A reafforestation programme is being carried out by the Nature Conservancy Council, who manage the whole of the island as a National Nature Reserve.

Birds: a few pairs of Golden Eagle, Merlin and Peregrine breed, and there are breeding Golden Plover, Short-eared Owl and Red Grouse on the moors. Other breeding birds include Dipper, Wheatear and Ring Ousel and the growing woodland is being colonized by an increasing variety of small birds. Between 1975 and 1985, 82 White-tailed Eagles were released here and, though they have spread throughout the Inner Hebrides, they may still be seen here.

Access: day visitors may land at Loch Scresort, but will have little time for exploration. Visitors can now stay at Kinloch Castle: contact Hebridean Holidays Ltd. (Tel: 0687 2026). Caledonian MacBrayne steamers leave Mallaig four times a week.

Permits: these are necessary to leave the Loch Scresort area. Write to the NCC Warden, White House, Kinloch, Isle of Rhum.

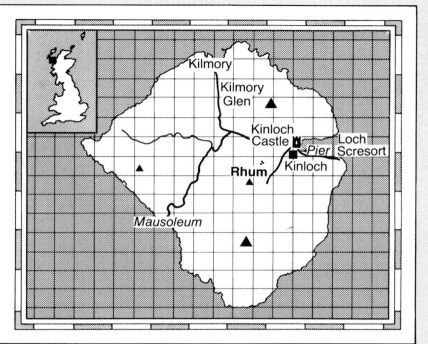

RIBBLE ESTUARY, LANCASHIRE OS 102 & 108

Location: this estuary lies some 10 miles downstream of Preston, on the coast between Blackpool and Southport.

Habitats: the Ribble is mainly sandy. The inner estuary has vast sand banks, but they are guarded by large areas of saltmarsh that make access difficult.

Birds: this is one of Britain's most important estuaries. In winter, over 70,000 Knot and 42,000 Dunlin have been counted, along with thousands of Oystercatchers, Sanderling, Redshank and both Bar-tailed and Black-tailed Godwits. Pink-footed Geese may number 14,000 in early winter – almost a quarter of the total world population. Additionally there are Bewick's Swan, many ducks, Hen Harrier, and a fine passage of autumn waders.

Access: Southport Marine Parade is a splendid birding spot. Further in, Crossens Marsh, Bank Marsh and Hesketh Marshes can all be viewed from the sea-wall, which is accessible via minor roads off the A565. In the north St Anne's, Fairhaven and Lytham offer good watching from the promenades. Squire's Gate, south Blackpool, has a narrow shoreline, allowing superb views of divers, grebes and seaducks at high tide in autumn and winter.

Permits: none required on public rights of way.

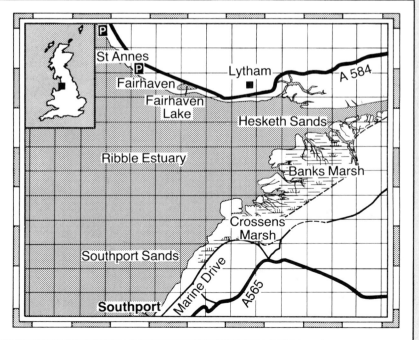

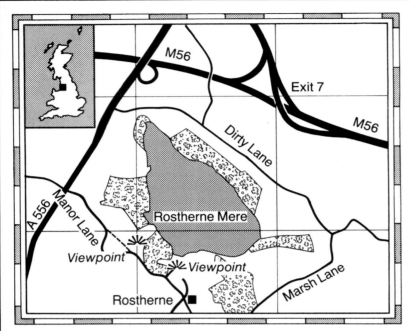

ROSTHERNE MERE, CHESHIRE OS 109

Location: this fine lake lies on the southern outskirts of Greater Manchester, about 2 miles south-west of Altrincham.

Habitats: with its surrounding reed beds and bushy scrub, Rostherne bears a remarkable resemblance to a Norfolk Broad rather than a suburban lake. It is a National Nature Reserve.

Birds: the shallow waters attract a fine variety of surface-feeding ducks, especially Mallard, Teal, Wigeon, Shoveler and Pintail. Diving ducks are also present, though generally in smaller numbers; these are mainly Tufted Duck and Pochard, though most winters see a scattering of Goldeneye and Goosander. Scarcer duck species turn up from time to time. Winter also brings Water Rail, and on passage Black Tern and other terns are regular. Breeding birds include Great Crested and Little Grebes.

Access: there is no formal access to this National Nature Reserve, but much can be seen from the surrounding lanes. Leave the M56 at Exit 7 and proceed along the A556. Turn along Manor Lane to Rostherne village where the churchyard offers a good viewpoint.

Permits: annual permits for the A. W. Boyd Memorial Observatory can be obtained from the Manchester Ornithological Society, 13 Kingston Drive, Sale, M33 2FS.

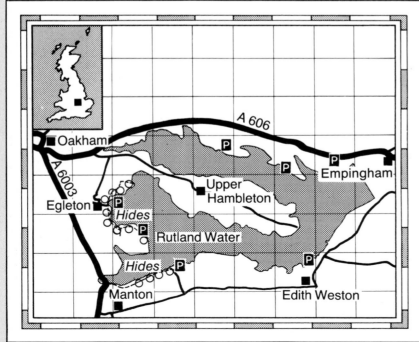

RUTLAND WATER, LEICESTERSHIRE OS 141

Location: between Leicester and Peterborough, 4 miles from the A1.

Habitats: this reservoir, England's largest, was created in 1975. Its 3000 acres and mile upon mile of gently shelving natural shoreline offer security and food for wintering ducks and passage waders and the western end of the southern area is a nature reserve of the local naturalists' trust and the Anglian Water Authority.

Birds: winter ducks include over 1000 Gadwall and reasonably regular Goosander, Smew, Ruddy Duck and Scaup. Grebes include all the regular British species, though most are more likely to be seen in autumn than in winter. The same is also true of waders. Spring and autumn passage periods regularly bring Little Stint, Curlew Sandpiper, Greenshank and Black-tailed Godwit, along with terns, including Black Tern.

Access: take the A606 towards Empingham. In the south-west the Lyndon Reserve is reached via the minor road east of Manton. The Egleton Reserve, in the west, is reached via the A6003.

Permits: are available to non-members of the Leicestershire and Rutland Trust for Nature Conservation at the centres on various days of the week: at present, on weekends throughout the year and, during the summer (May–October), also from Tuesday to Thursday.

RYE HARBOUR, EAST SUSSEX OS 189

Location: this local nature reserve lies 2 miles south of Rye. The huge promontory of Dungeness (*see page* 260) lies to the east.

Habitats: Rye Harbour is a shingle area built up by the sea at the mouth of the River Rother. A succession of old shorelines extends inland for 1–3 miles, and here the gravel-extraction industry has dug out a series of pits, now abandoned and flooded. Areas of offshore mud are exposed at low tide. There is also arable land and scrub.

Birds: breeding birds include Little Tern, plus Common and Sandwich Terns on specially constructed islands in the Ternery Pool nearest the coast. There is a thriving Black-headed Gull colony. In winter, ducks, grebes and Water Rail are regular and Hen Harrier and Merlin are often present. Spring and autumn passage brings the usual waders – high tide is best. In a good year Curlew Sandpiper, Little Stint, Spotted Redshank and Greenshank may all be abundant and in spring there is a large flock of Whimbrel. For most of the year the reserve is the major wader roost for Rye Bay.

Access: leave Rye westwards and turn left from the A259 on the outskirts of the town to Rye Harbour. Park near the nature centre and walk along the concrete track opposite to the sea and the hides.

Permits: not required, but there are collecting boxes.

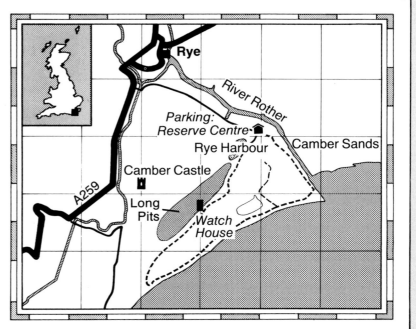

ST ABB'S HEAD, BORDERS OS 67

Location: on the east coast just north of the Scottish border and 12 miles north of Berwick-upon-Tweed; it is easily accessible to anyone travelling to and from Edinburgh on the A1.

Habitats: the cliffs here rise to 90m and are conveniently indented to offer excellent views of the breeding seabirds. The Head is also a good spot for watching seabird migration and there is a freshwater pool, Mire Loch, with plenty of bushy cover for small migrants.

Birds: the breeding seabirds here include thousands of Guillemot, Razorbill, Fulmar, Shag and Kittiwake, along with much less numerous Puffin. Though they do not breed, Gannets are regularly seen offshore and, during passage periods, they are often accompanied by marauding Great Skuas. Other skuas are regular in autumn and shearwaters, terns, seaducks and divers may also occur at this time. The latter are also present during the winter. Small migrants include the regular chats, warblers and flycatchers. A scattering of rarities is reported every year.

Access: from the A1107, turn right in Coldingham to St Abb's village on the B6438. A path leads northward to the Head, which may also be approached by the road to the lighthouse. Mire Loch lies east of this road.

Permits: none required.

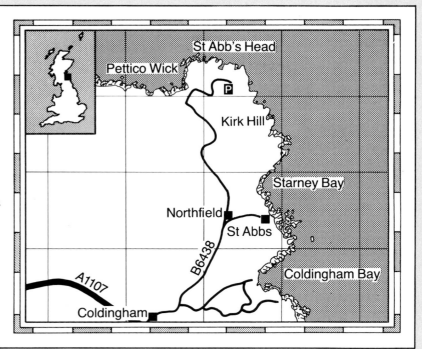

315

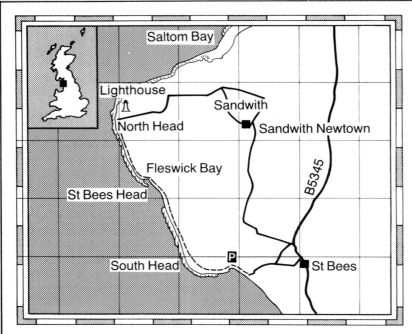

ST BEES HEAD, CUMBRIA OS 89

Location: the westernmost point of the Lake District, this headland lies just 2 miles north-west of the village of St Bees.

Habitats: the red sandstone cliffs rise to 90m and are eroded, forming perfect ledges for breeding seabirds. The tops are grassy, with clumps of gorse.

Birds: this is an RSPB reserve that contains large colonies of breeding seabirds, with Guillemot, Kittiwake and Fulmar the most numerous. Indeed, it is one of England's largest west coast seabird breeding colonies and the site of the country's only breeding Black Guillemots. Razorbill are comparatively scarce, as are Puffin, but Shag and Cormorant both breed, as do Peregrine. Seawatching can be productive, especially with south-westerly winds, when Gannet, skuas and shearwaters may all be seen.

Access: leave Whitehaven southwards on the B5345 and turn left in St Bees to the beach car park. Walk northwards along the cliff-top footpath, which has several excellent (and safe) vantage points. It is a 2½-mile walk from the car park to the lighthouse; disabled visitors only may approach the lighthouse by car on a private road from Sandwith.

Permits: a summer warden is present at the lighthouse, but no permits are required.

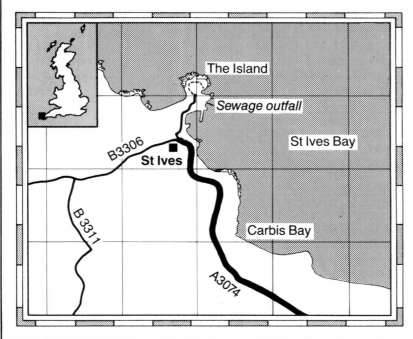

ST IVES, CORNWALL OS 203

Location: this is a flourishing seaside resort situated on the north Cornish coast near Penzance and Land's End.

Habitats: St Ives Island is actually a rocky headland, while to the south is the sewage outfall and the harbour.

Birds: this is an outstanding seabird spot at the right time and in the right conditions. Autumn, particularly September, is the right time, and north-west winds, especially following a south-westerly gale the right conditions. Both Storm and Leach's Petrels, Great and Arctic Skuas, Manx Shearwaters (including the Balearic race) and Sooty Shearwaters, thousands of Guillemots and Razorbills, Kittiwakes and Gannets and often Sabine's Gulls are to be seen; Grey Phalarope may occur in late autumn. In winter there are divers, Slavonian Grebe and often Glaucous or Iceland Gulls. The sheltered St Ives Bay has seabirds throughout the year, and nearby sites also have much to offer the birdwatcher: try the Hayle Estuary (*see page* 275), Marazion Marsh (*see page* 300), Lands End (*see page* 286), and the Isles of Scilly (*see page* 284).

Access: the Island is at the north end of the town: follow signs to the car park. The sewage outfall is just east of the car park. There is a footpath to the coastguard lookout station.

Permits: none required.

SANDWICH BAY, KENT OS 179

Location: on the east coast of Kent, immediately south of the estuary of the River Stour between the North and South Forelands.

Habitats: the offshore sand and mud banks here form part of the intertidal Pegwell Bay and the Stour estuary, immediately to the north, where there are Kent Trust for Nature Conservation and National Trust reserves. Much of the large area of dunes has been turned into a famous golf course. There are fields, hedges, marshy pools and reed beds.

Birds: this is a migration watch point, with the emphasis on seabirds and small migrant chats, flycatchers and warblers. There are, however, several areas for waders, and Kentish Plover in spring, and Little Stint and Curlew Sandpiper in autumn, are regular. It is a poor autumn that does not produce Pallas's Warbler and other eastern vagrants.

Access: the whole area is private and is accessible only via a toll road between Sandwich and Sandwich Bay. The observatory offers hostel accommodation to keen migrant watchers. There is a road northward along the coast from Sandwich Bay which gives access to the nature reserves at the mouth of the Stour.

Permits: contact The Honorary Warden, Bird Observatory, 2 Old Downs Farm, Guildford Road, Sandwich, Kent CT13 9PF.

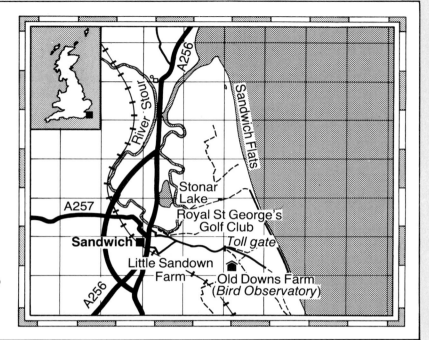

SHANNON ESTUARY, CO. LIMERICK, IRISH REPUBLIC

IOS½ 17

Location: on the west coast of Ireland, this is Ireland's largest estuary, extending for over 50 miles downstream from Limerick.

Habitats: vast mud banks are exposed at low tide, especially where the River Fergus joins the Shannon on its northern shore, at Poulnasherry Bay and the inlets east of Aughinish Island.

Birds: this is a major wetland, one of the most significant in Europe. In an average winter it holds over 10,000 wildfowl and twice as many waders, but may hold much larger numbers of both during peak spring and autumn passage periods. This is a major haunt of Black-tailed Godwit, with regular winter numbers over 8000 and a spring passage record of over 16,000 birds. Most of these concentrate at the Fergus inlet–Shannon Airport area. Here, too, are vast flocks of Dunlin (up to 30,000), Bar-tailed Godwit, Curlew, Knot and Redshank, along with up to 100 Greenshank. Wigeon are the most abundant duck, and other wildfowl include Scaup, Whooper Swan, Brent Goose and Greylag Goose.

Access: there is road access off the N18 to Shannon Airport and the R473 west of the Fergus inlet. Other access requires a detailed map.

Permits: none required.

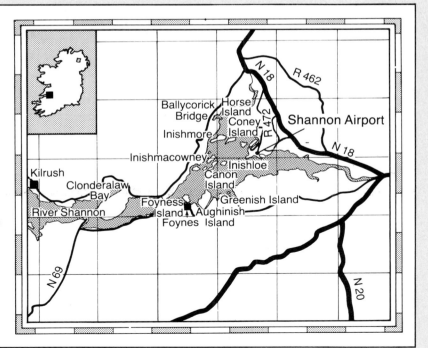

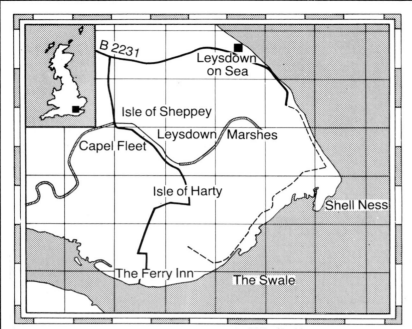

SHELL NESS, KENT OS 178

Location: on the north Kent coast at the mouth of the Swale estuary, forming the easternmost point of the Isle of Sheppey.

Habitats: Shell Ness is a headland constructed of shells by tidal action. Inland lie fields, while to the west are extensive saltmarshes.

Birds: the sea here is a regular haunt of seabirds, including winter divers and grebes, along with Brent Goose, Eider, scoters and Red-breasted Merganser. Waders are abundant, with Knot and Dunlin the most common, but with Turnstone and Sanderling also sometimes numerous. Twite and Snow Bunting are local specialities, and there are good numbers of Hen Harrier and Short-eared Owl, and the occasional Peregrine. Though passage periods bring a wider variety of species, there are other sites on the Isle of Sheppey, notably Elmley Marshes (*see page* 263), that are usually better at these times.

Access: follow the A249 on to the Isle of Sheppey, then take the B2231 to Leysdown-on-Sea. Leave Leysdown eastwards on a minor road along the coast until you reach a few houses, where it is possible to park. From here it is a short walk southwards to the Ness beyond which is a bay with roosting waders. The shoreline to the north is also productive, especially on a rising tide.

Permits: none required, but make sure you do not disturb the birds.

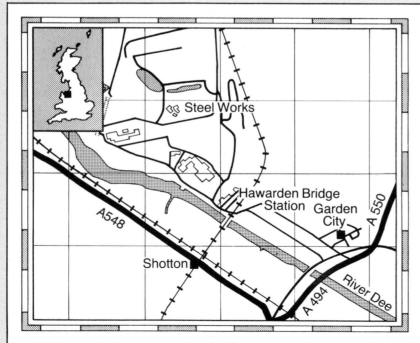

SHOTTON POOLS, CLWYD OS 117

Location: this site lies within the confines of Shotton Steelworks at the head of the Dee estuary. Chester is 10 miles to the south-east.

Habitats: the saltmarshes are surrounded by lagoons and marshes as well as several reservoirs. There are areas of reeds and several of the pools have rafts to encourage breeding and resting birds. There are also areas of farmland to add diversity to this highly successful little reserve.

Birds: the specially constructed rafts offer breeding sites to a substantial colony of Common Terns. Elsewhere, species as varied as Ringed Plover, Reed Warbler and Yellow Wagtail find a summer home. It is, however, during spring and autumn passage periods that Shotton shines. In autumn, in particular, the pools attract a wide variety of waders, with Little Stint, Curlew and Wood Sandpipers, Greenshank and Spotted Redshank among the more common and widespread species. Whimbrel are more abundant in spring. Autumn also brings a good passage of Black Terns and there is a rarity of some sort most years.

Access: The British Steel Corporation Works are signposted on the A550 and access is strictly by permit.

Permits: write to the PR Manager, BSC, Shotton Steelworks, Deeside, Clwyd. Permits are accompanied by a map showing access.

SKELLIGS, CO. KERRY, IRISH REPUBLIC IOS½ 20

Location: the Skelligs are the smallest and most isolated of the islands that lie off the rugged coast of south-west Ireland.

Habitats: these are uninhabited cliff-girt islands that rise spectacularly straight from the sea.

Birds: the Skelligs form the middle group of Kerry bird islands, between the 'Inish' group to the north and the 'Bull' group to the south. They are more isolated than either and hold some outstanding seabird colonies. All the Skellig islands are worth visiting, though none are of easy access. The best localities and their specialities are: Inishtooskert for Storm Petrel and Manx Shearwater; Inishtearaght for Puffin, Storm Petrel and Manx Shearwater; Inishabro for Storm Petrel and Manx Shearwater; Inishvickillane for Puffin, Razorbill, Storm Petrel and Manx Shearwater; and Puffin Island for its huge Manx Shearwater colony. Little Skellig itself has a huge gannetry, while Great Skellig has good colonies of Storm Petrel and Manx Shearwater.

Access: boats may be chartered from the nearby mainland fishing villages (try Ballinskelligs), but choose a calmish day, as landing is far from easy. Day trips are fun, but longer stays require a tent.

Permits: not required.

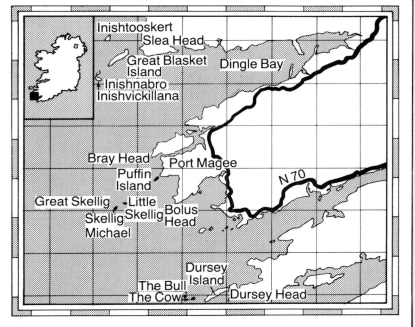

SKOMER, DYFED OS 157

Location: this is the best known and most easily accessible of the 'Pembrokeshire' islands. It lies a mile off the south-west coast of Wales about 10 miles west of Milford Haven.

Habitats: Skomer has some fine cliffs, broken by deeply cut gullies that make viewing both easy and safe. The interior is grassy and honeycombed by the burrows of rabbits and Puffins.

Birds: the three 'Pembrokeshire' islands each have their own specialities. Grassholm has a huge gannetry; Skokholm has breeding seabirds, but is primarily a migration watch point; while Skomer is a classic seabird island. Puffin, Guillemot, Razorbill, Fulmar and Kittiwake are all abundant breeders and there are breeding Shags, Buzzard, gulls and Chough as well. Inland there is a breeding colony of 100,000 pairs of Manx Shearwater.

Access: the island can be visited daily, except Monday, throughout the summer months via Martin's Haven, which is 2 miles west of Marloes towards Wooltack Point. There is an information centre and car park (fee charged) at Martin's Haven. A boat fee and landing fee are both payable and there is limited single accommodation for members of the West Wales Trust for Nature Conservation, 7 Market Street, Haverfordwest, Dyfed SA61 1NF.

Permits: Landing fee on arrival; as above to stay.

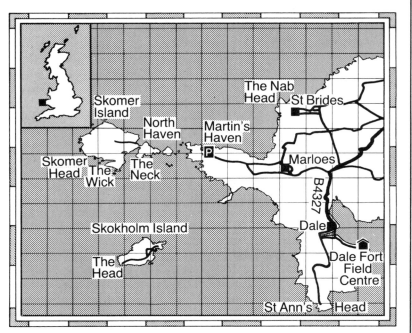

319

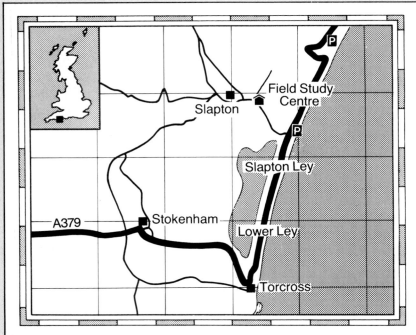

SLAPTON LEY, DEVON OS 202

Location: this large lagoon lies on the south coast of Devon between Dartmouth and Start Point.

Habitats: the shoreline of Start Bay consists of a huge shingle beach that has enclosed a series of freshwater lagoons. They are fringed by bushy scrub and there are field and woodland inland. Slapton Ley is a nature reserve of the Field Studies Council.

Birds: the reed beds here are full of Sedge and Reed Warblers in summer and Cetti's Warbler is resident. A variety of species breeds inland, including Buzzard, Sparrowhawk, Raven and Cirl Bunting (a South Devon speciality). In winter, Water Rails are often quite obvious, a variety of ducks, and perhaps the odd diver or grebe, too. Most years see a few Bittern and Bearded Tit during hard weather. On passage there are frequently terns and skuas and occasionally Sooty Shearwater; warblers, chats and flycatchers among the shoreside bushes; the occasional Marsh Harrier or Hoopoe; regular Garganey in spring; and a regular autumn arrival of Aquatic Warblers among the reeds.

Access: the coastal A379 from Dartmouth runs along the beach.

Permits: on arrival, contact Slapton Ley Field Centre for information. It also offers accommodation and study courses: write to Slapton Ley Field Centre, Slapton, Kingsbridge, Devon TQ7 2QP.

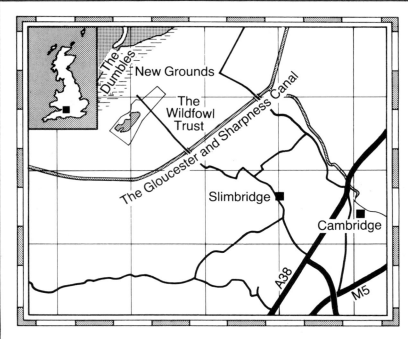

SLIMBRIDGE, GLOUCESTERSHIRE OS 162

Location: on the bank of the Severn, 10 miles from Gloucester.

Habitats: the Wildfowl Trust, founded in 1946 by Sir Peter Scott, have their headquarters here and the collection of ducks, geese, swans and flamingoes is the largest in the world. The birds are housed in enclosures with ponds or lakes. There are hedges and woodland within the collection area, while outside the sea-wall lie grassy saltmarsh and reclaimed meadows, with the tidal river beyond.

Birds: apart from the wildfowl collection, wild birds flight in. Outstanding is the wild flock of Bewick's Swan, one of the largest in the country, that swim around the Rushy Pen for most of the winter. Wild ducks are invariably present, including Wigeon, Pintail and Shoveler. White-fronted Geese regularly exceed 5000 after Christmas. Among them, the occasional Lesser Whitefront or Red-breasted Goose. Waders are less in evidence, but there are good winter numbers of the more common species as well as a wider variety on passage. A Peregrine usually winters.

Access: leave the M5 at Exit 13 or 14 and follow signs to the Wildfowl Trust on the A38. Open daily.

Permits: admission charge for non-members of the Wildfowl Trust.

SNETTISHAM, NORFOLK OS 132

Location: this RSPB reserve is situated on the eastern shore of the Wash between Kings Lynn and Hunstanton.

Habitats: shingle banks with extensive mud flats extending seawards and a hinterland of rough grazing fields. A series of old gravel pits forms a major high-tide roost for waders.

Birds: The Wash is one of Europe's major wetlands and Snettisham is one of its major high-tide wader roosts. Knot, Dunlin, Bar-tailed Godwit, Oystercatcher and Redshank are dominant, but there are always other species present, too. The pits are also used by many wildfowl, with Shoveler, Teal, Wigeon, Gadwall, Goldeneye and Red-breasted Merganser all regular. Occasional seaducks and divers also put in appearances. Both Brent and Pink-footed Geese use the area, mostly roosting on the sand and mud banks offshore. During spring and autumn passage periods, good numbers of waders use the pools as a resting and feeding ground.

Access: leave the A149 at Snettisham and take a minor road westward to the beach. Park in the public car park and walk southwards along the seaward side of the gravel pits until you reach the hides around the southernmost of the pits. Timing is crucial: arrive an hour before high tide – preferably a really high one.

Permits: none required.

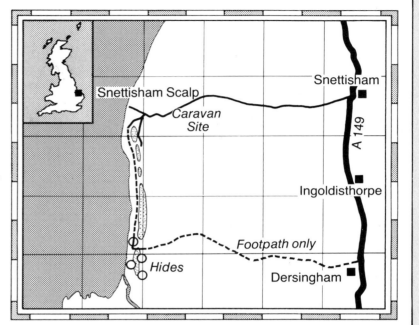

SOUTH STACK, GWYNEDD OS 114

Location: these cliffs lie at the north-western corner of Anglesey, less than 3 miles west of the port of Holyhead and the end of the A5.

Habitats: this is an RSPB reserve covering much of Holyhead Mountain and extending along a cliff-girt coast from North Stack to South Stack. There is also a separate section around Penrhyn Mawr. The area is basically heather and grass moorland, but the main birdwatching interest is centred on the seabird cliffs.

Birds: there are thousands of Guillemot, Razorbill and Kittiwake here, along with smaller numbers of Fulmar, Puffin and Shag. Outstandingly, there are several pairs of Peregrine and Chough, as well as a good population of Raven. Visitors in summer should not ignore the seawatching possibilities, for both Manx Shearwater and Gannet regularly pass by offshore.

Access: leave Holyhead and the A5 westward, signposted South Stack. There is a car park and an information centre at Ellin's Tower that is open daily throughout the summer. A network of good paths leads to North Stack, Holyhead Mountain and across the bridge to South Stack itself. A road also leads southward to another car park at Penrhosfeilw Common where there are more paths to explore.

Permits: none required, but do visit the information centre, where there is a summer warden.

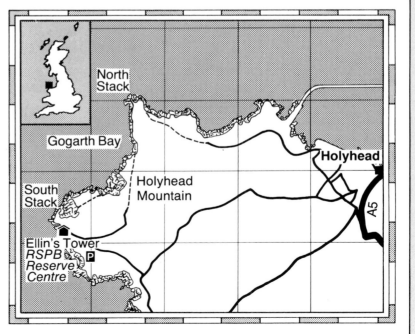

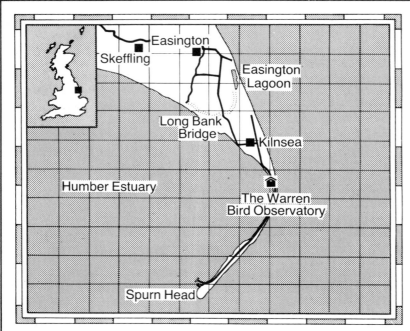

SPURN HEAD, HUMBERSIDE OS 113

Location: at the mouth of the Humber, 25 miles from Hull.

Habitats: this 3-mile long, shingle spit contains large areas of intertidal mud, including Spurn Bight, and small areas of saltmarsh lie to the west, and a sandy shore to the east. Marram grass, bushy thickets and elder scrub offer cover to migrant birds. There are lagoons and small areas of farmland and gardens.

Birds: in winter there are divers and Brent Geese, hosts of waders, winter raptors and Snow Buntings, but during spring and autumn passage periods 'Spurn' really comes into its own. Northerly winds produce skuas and shearwaters, often including Pomarine Skua and Sooty Shearwater. Terns are often numerous and waders include a sprinkling of the scarcer species. Small nocturnal migrants include chats, warblers and flycatchers, with Wryneck, Bluethroat and Barred Warbler in September, and Yellow-browed and Pallas's Warblers in October. Spurn Nature Reserve is owned by the Yorkshire Wildlife Trust, and includes the whole of Spurn Head.

Access: from the A1033 turn south at Patrington on to the B1445 to Kilnsea. A toll is payable beyond Kilnsea. Self-catering accommodation is available: write to The Warden, Spurn Bird Observatory, Kilnsea, Patrington, Hull, Humberside, HU12 0UG.

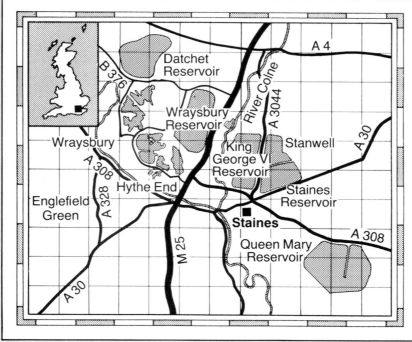

STAINES RESERVOIR, SURREY OS 176

Location: 17 miles west of the centre of London next to Staines, very near the M4 and M25 motorways, among a maze of roads, many of them heading for Heathrow Airport.

Habitats: these are two large concrete-banked reservoir pools, separated by a public causeway, offering open water to a variety of species. Other good sites are Queen Mary Reservoir, which can be visited; Datchet Reservoir, with only partial access; Wraysbury and King George VI Reservoirs, completely out of bounds.

Birds: winter wildfowl include many Tufted and Pochard, along with fewer Goldeneye and Goosander, and the occasional rarity. There are usually a few Black-necked Grebes, reaching their highest numbers in late summer, and a few Little Gulls regularly in spring and autumn. Passage also brings small numbers of waders and terns, the latter regularly including Black Terns. When a pool is drained it may then attract a fine selection of waders.

Access: the A3044 between Staines and Colnbrook runs between the Staines and King George VI Reservoirs. On the west side is a pumping station beside the road. Park here and walk up the path opposite between railings to the causeway.

Permits: none required.

STODMARSH, KENT OS 179

Location: in the valley of the River Stour about 5 miles north-east of Canterbury.

Habitats: mining subsidence along the valley has created a series of shallow lagoons and floods, most of which have been colonized by reeds to form the largest freshwater marsh in Kent. At Stodmarsh these have been incorporated into a National Nature Reserve.

Birds: in the 1960s colonizing Savi's Warblers chose this as their first British breeding stronghold. They were followed, in 1972, by Cetti's Warbler. Sadly, being susceptible to hard winters, both species have declined. Other attractions include Bearded Tit and Bittern, abundant Sedge and Reed Warblers, a sprinkling of Grasshopper Warblers, and often the earliest Garganey in the country. Passage brings Black Tern and many waders, especially Ruff and Black-tailed Godwit, and the odd Marsh Harrier, Osprey, Hobby and Short-eared Owl. Winter brings ducks and Hen Harrier.

Access: leave Canterbury eastwards on the A257 and turn left on an unmarked lane just past a British Telecom yard. Follow this to Stodmarsh. In the village take the turning next to the Red Lion to the Reserve car park. Walk to the Lampen Wall which runs across the marsh to the river. This path continues to Grove Ferry.

Permits: not required.

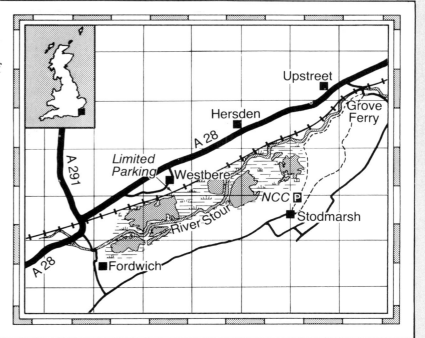

STRANGFORD LOUGH, CO. DOWN, NORTHERN IRELAND

OSNI 21

Location: this large sea lough lies on the east coast of Northern Ireland only a few miles to the south-east of Belfast.

Habitats: huge mud flats are exposed at low tide and there are many small islands. A barrage across the mouth of the River Quoile has created a freshwater which is a National Nature Reserve, and there are three reserves at the seaward end of the lough.

Birds: wintering species include Pale-bellied Brent and Wigeon. There are good numbers of Whooper Swan, Shelduck and Teal, along with smaller but significant numbers of Pintail, Goldeneye and Red-breasted Merganser. Seaducks are regular, as are grebes and Great Northern Diver. Waders, too, are abundant, with Knot, Dunlin, Oystercatcher, Curlew, Redshank and Bar-tailed Godwit all reaching four-figure populations in winter. Greenshank and Black-tailed Godwit winter regularly. Passage brings the same species, together with Grey Plover.

Access: view from the A20 south of Newtownards. The best areas, however, lie on the western shore. From Comber take the A22 southwards and turn left on to a maze of roads to the shore.

Permits: not required.

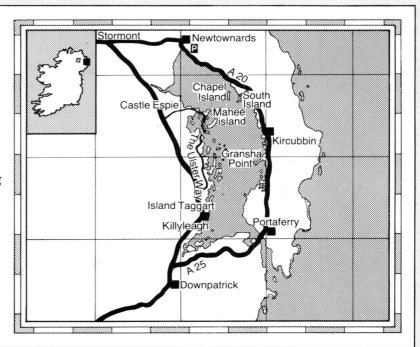

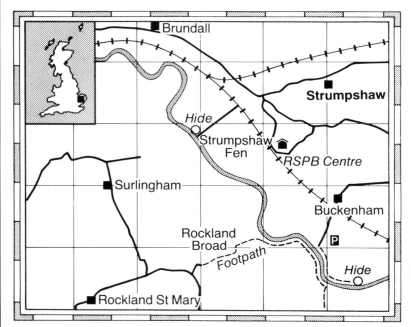

STRUMPSHAW FEN, NORFOLK

OS 134

Location: this RSPB reserve is just 5 miles east of the suburbs of Norwich, in the Yare valley, immediately north of Rockland Broad.
Habitats: this is an area of reed beds, broken by alder carr, willow scrub and areas of open water, surrounded by rough grazing fields. To the east, outside the reserve, lie Buckenham grazing marshes.
Birds: Buckenham has long been a haunt of a flock of Bean Geese. The reserve holds breeding Marsh Harrier and Bearded Tit, Water Rail, Woodcock, Kingfisher and Reed Warbler. Cetti's Warbler was common but has been affected by severe winters, but Grasshopper Warbler is still quite common. During the winter, Hen Harrier, Short-eared Owl and Great Grey Shrike occur regularly.
Access: leave Norwich on the A47 toward Great Yarmouth and turn right on to a minor road to Brundall. Beyond the village take a right towards Hassingham and then another right along Low Road. The RSPB car park is on the right, with the reception centre across a pedestrian level-crossing beyond. For Buckenham and the Bean Geese, continue eastwards from the RSPB car park, then turn right and continue to Buckenham Station. Turn right on a track to the river and car park. Walk eastwards to the mill and nearby hide.
Permits: open daily; no permits required.

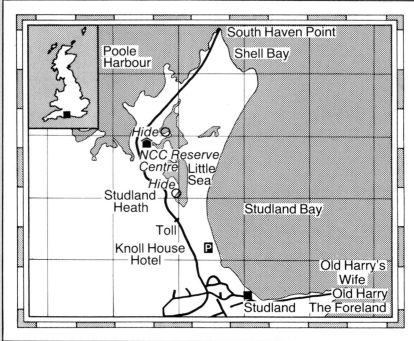

STUDLAND HEATH, DORSET

OS 195

Location: this National Nature Reserve lies on the coast between Poole Harbour and the Isle of Purbeck.
Habitats: sandy heathland with heather, gorse pines and birch scrub. In the east are extensive dunes, among which is Little Sea, a dune-slack lake. Beyond this lies the sea at Studland Bay.
Birds: like the nearby Arne Reserve of the RSPB (*see page* 237), this is a major stronghold of the scarce and highly localized Dartford Warbler. Nightjars also breed here. During passage periods there is a fine collection of waders at Little Sea. Winter brings ducks, including Red-breasted Merganser and Scoter, to the Bay and Sanderling to the beach. Avocet and Black-tailed Godwit usually winter. Bearded Tit usually occur among the reeds at Little Sea.
Access: from Wareham, in the north of the Isle of Purbeck, take the A351 southwards and turn left on to the B3351 at Corfe Castle. Follow the signs to Studland village. Alternatively, from Bournemouth, take the Sandbanks Ferry to South Haven Point. The Nature Reserve observation point lies along a minor road, Ferry Road, between Studland and South Haven Point. There are hides overlooking Little Sea and paths and tracks of free access.
Permits: none for marked paths; toll payable for Ferry Road.

TACUMSHIN LAKE, CO. WEXFORD, IRISH REPUBLIC

IOS½ 23

Location: this wetland lies at the south-eastern corner of Ireland. Wexford, about 10 miles north, is the nearest town, but the ferry terminal of Rosslare is much closer, only 6 miles to the north-west.

Habitats: until 1974 Tacumshin Lake was an area of intertidal mud, all but cut off from the sea by a narrow shingle bar. Then the exit was artificially closed and a drainage sluice dug through the beach. The result has been to reduce considerably the area of wetland and convert it from a tidal basin into a freshwater lake. In late summer the muddy edges provide food for waders.

Birds: in winter wildfowl include up to 400 Brent Geese and 100 Bewick's Swans, the latter doubtless flying in from the nearby Wexford Slobs (*see page* 331). There is also a great variety of ducks, with large numbers of Wigeon; diving ducks include Scaup. Waders are neither outstanding nor particularly numerous in winter, but usually include Ruff. During passage periods, especially autumn, American waders now almost annual.

Access: leave Wexford southward on the N25 and explore the lake from the R736 and roads to the south.

Permits: none required.

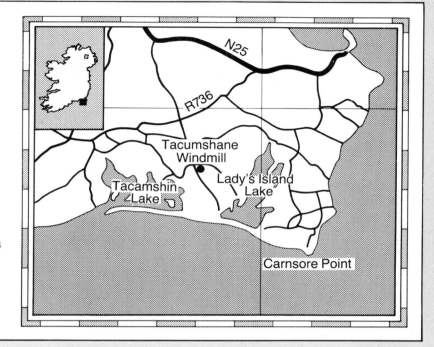

TEESSIDE AND COWPEN MARSH, CLEVELAND OS 93 & 94

Location: this area is the estuary of the River Tees, which reaches the North Sea beyond Middlesbrough.

Habitats: the estuary has been reclaimed for industry and much is covered by oil refineries. There are, however, major intertidal banks at Seal Sands and various pools, creeks and marshes remain.

Birds: winter brings Knot, Dunlin, Sanderling, Redshank, Bar-tailed Godwit, Ruff and Shelduck. Gulls usually include Glaucous, often Iceland, and occasionally a really rare species. The gulls congregate near the mouth where divers, grebes and seaducks can also be found. Autumn usually brings Manx and Sooty Shearwaters, Great and Arctic Skuas and masses of terns, plus a fine selection of waders, with major rarities every year.

Access: Cowpen Marsh lies on the A128. This reserve of the Cleveland Nature Conservation Trust (CTNC) is open to members (and RSPB members) from February to August. The pools to the east of the A178 have walking access and from Seaton Carew there are paths to North Gare. Contact the CNCT warden on arrival or write to Cleveland Nature Conservation Trust, Old Town Hall, Mandale Road, Thornaby, Stockton-on-Tees, TS17 6AW.

Permits: see above.

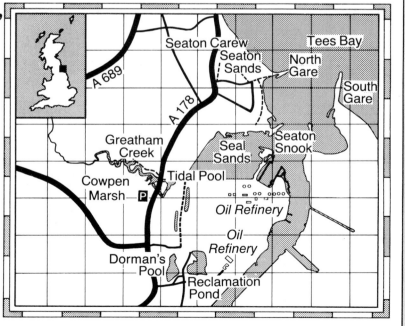

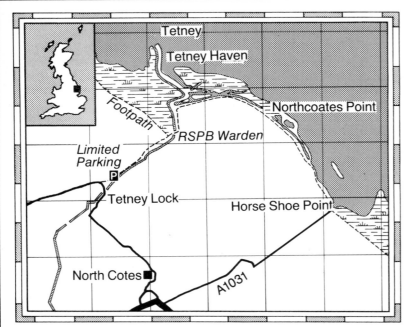

TETNEY, LINCOLNSHIRE OS 113

Location: these marshes lie at the mouth of the River Humber on its southern shore. Tetney is an RSPB reserve.

Habitats: there are large intertidal flats, areas of saltmarsh, an extensive dune system and several 'borrow pits', backed by fields.

Birds: in summer there is a major Little Tern colony here, while Oystercatcher, Redshank, Ringed Plover and Shelduck also breed. Access at this time is, however, highly restricted to protect the breeding birds. During the winter there is a major wader roost here, including Knot, Dunlin, Grey Plover, Oystercatcher and Bar-tailed Godwit. Wildfowl include Brent and Wigeon. Seaducks may include Scaup, Eider, Common and Velvet Scoters, Goldeneye and Red-breasted Merganser, and occasional Long-tailed Duck, while there are usually Red-throated Divers offshore. Merlin, Hen Harrier and Short-eared Owl are all regular winter visitors. Passage periods bring a selection of waders, especially in autumn, and many terns.

Access: leave Grimsby southwards on the A1031 to Tetney and turn left to Tetney Lock. Where the road turns left over the lock, continue on a road along the northern shore of the canal. Walk along the private road to the RSPB warden's caravan (warden present April–August). Continue to Tetney Haven and the sea-wall.

Permits: none required.

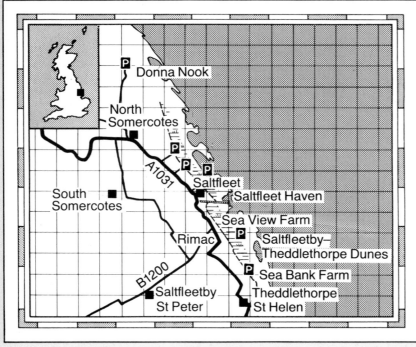

THEDDLETHORPE AND SALTFLEETBY, LINCOLNSHIRE OS 113

Location: this area lies on the coast between Grimsby and Skegness. Mablethorpe, 5 miles to the south is the nearest town.

Habitats: the whole area is a National Nature Reserve. The sand dunes have 'slacks' (damp hollows between the dunes), some having freshwater marshes with reeds and willow scrub.

Birds: Brent Geese are regular in winter and there are usually a few divers and seaducks offshore. Knot, Dunlin, Grey Plover and Oystercatcher are all present and both Marsh and Hen Harriers are regular. The beach holds Snow Bunting throughout winter. During spring and autumn passage periods there are waders and terns on the marshes and many migrant warblers, chats and flycatchers among the bushes. Shelduck, Water Rail, Ringed Plover, Snipe, Redshank and Short-eared Owl all breed.

Access: leave Mablethorpe northwards on the A1031, from which five tracks lead seawards, each with parking at the end. A footpath connects them. Look out for notices drawing attention to the danger area of the RAF bombing range.

Permits: not required.

THURSLEY COMMON, SURREY OS 186

Location: this National Nature Reserve lies roughly at the centre of a triangle with its corners at Farnham, Hindhead and Godalming, all of which give easy access.

Habitats: one of a string of heaths in this part of Surrey, Thursley is mainly dry heathland with heather and gorse, broken up by marshes and areas of birch scrub. Though offering similar habitats as Frensham and Hankley Commons to the west, it has always had a better birding reputation.

Birds: the heathland birds of southern England are fighting a losing battle, with species such as Stone-curlew, Red-backed Shrike and Woodlark all fast disappearing. Of these, only Woodlark can be found here, but there are also Dartford Warbler, Hobby, Tree Pipit, Lesser Spotted Woodpecker and Redstart. The Dartford Warbler is the main attraction, though numbers fluctuate year by year. The Hobby is usually much easier to see and late summer afternoons are generally productive.

Access: leave the A3 westwards to Thursley village; park here and walk northwards. Alternatively, continue to a T-junction and turn right to Moat Pond on the Elstead road. Keep to the paths.

Permits: not required.

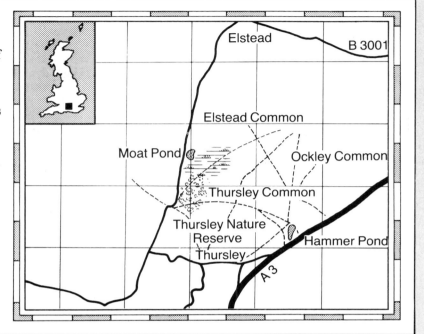

TITCHWELL, NORFOLK OS 132

Location: Titchwell lies at the eastern end of the North Norfolk coast, between Hunstanton and Burnham. The RSPB reserve is a short distance west of Titchwell village, next to the A149.

Habitats: a shallow fresh lagoon dotted with islands, a brackish lagoon, a small intertidal creek and a considerable area of reed beds with invading scrub.

Birds: the major East Anglian specialities all breed here, including Bittern, Marsh Harrier, Water Rail and Bearded Tit. Recently they have been joined by Avocet. In summer the reed beds are alive with warblers, and both Little and Common Terns breed near the beach. Spring brings many migrants, with Black Tern, Little Gull and Spoonbill all regularly present, and a good collection of waders. In autumn, waders are really excellent here. Though there are regular divers, grebes and seaducks offshore in winter, this is also an excellent season for waders on the pools. There are reasonable chances of seeing Short-eared Owl and Hen Harrier, and the beach holds Snow Buntings.

Access: leave Titchwell village westwards on the A149 and after 5 miles turn right on an inconspicuous track to the reserve centre and car park. A raised wall leads to the hides and the shore. At the end turn right to a further hide looking back into the reserve.

Permits: none required.

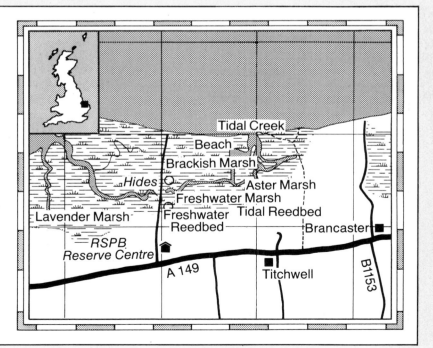

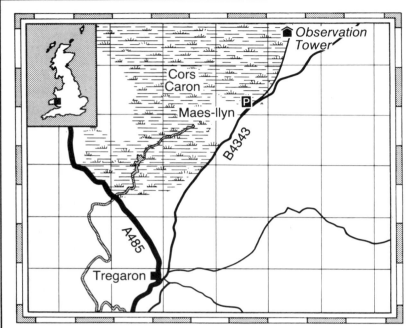

TREGARON, DYFED OS 146

Location: the small town of Tregaron lies among the hills of south-central Wales. A National Nature Reserve now known as Cors Caron (formerly Tregaron Bog) lies north of the town.

Habitats: Cors Caron is a superb raised bog, with a flat marshy landscape broken by clumps of scrub. There are several small ponds and an artificial pool bordered by reeds. The surrounding hills and stream-filled valleys are well wooded, with deciduous woodland and coniferous plantations, and open sheep pastures on the tops.

Birds: Tregaron has long been famous as Britain's most reliable place to see Red Kite. These splendid raptors are most regularly seen along the B4343 between town and reserve, and particularly from the car park, where a nature trail leads north across the bog. Another good spot is about 1 mile south of the town on the same road – look for the rubbish tip, which attracts the birds. A minor road to Llanwrtyd Wells gives further chances of seeing Red Kite. The area holds usual breeding species one would expect in upland western Britain, including Dipper, Grey Wagtail, Pied Flycatcher, Redstart, Buzzard, Sparrowhawk and, in winter, Peregrine and Hen Harrier.

Access: leave Tregaron northwards on the B4343 for 2½ miles. Park on the left and walk along the trail to a windy tower hide.

Permits: not needed, but no access other than detailed above.

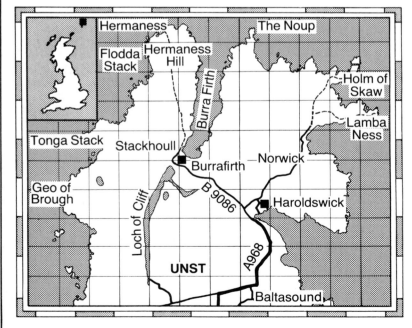

UNST, SHETLAND OS 1

Location: this is the northernmost island of the British Isles, with only a few rock stacks lying offshore further north.

Habitats: the main breeding centre for birds is the promontory of Hermaness in the north-west of Unst. This is a National Nature Reserve, with spectacular cliff scenery.

Birds: the cliffs hold all the usual breeding seabirds, including a fine gannetry, with over 10,000 pairs. The Gannets nest on the broken areas near the cliff foot as well as on the offshore stacks. Among them is a solitary Black-browed Albatross, which has summered here since 1972. There are also Guillemots, Razorbills, thousands of Puffins, Black Guillemots, Shags and Fulmars, and masses of Kittiwakes. Unfortunately, the cliffs here are broken on a dramatic scale, with many huge landslides, and are decidedly dangerous. Walk along the cliff-tops, but take great care on the steep grass slopes, which are especially slippery after rain. The moors hold both Great and Arctic Skuas in good numbers. To the south the Loch of Cliff is favoured by seabirds as a bathing site.

Access: there are regular inter-island car ferries from Yell and daily flights on weekdays from Tingwall Airstrip near Lerwick, or Mainland Shetland, by Loganair.

Permits: none required.

WALBERSWICK, SUFFOLK OS 156

Location: this is a small village on the Suffolk coast immediately south of the mouth of the River Blyth, a mile south of the small town of Southwold. There is a National Nature Reserve here.

Habitats: the shingle beach protects a low-lying area of marshy pools and extensive reed beds. There are open pools and deep dykes, and an overgrown fen, heath and coverts at the western end.

Birds: Bittern, Water Rail, Marsh Harrier and Bearded Tit are present in summer, along with masses of Sedge, Reed and Grasshopper Warblers. Both Savi's and Cetti's Warblers bred here, too. The heaths have nesting Nightjar and Woodcock, and there is still a pair or two of Stone-curlew on the stony fields. Passage waders in spring and autumn include a good collection on the shore pools, though they are much disturbed. Snow Buntings and Twite winter, though Shore Larks tend to occur only in autumn. Winter also brings Hen Harrier, Short-eared Owl and sometimes Rough-legged Buzzard.

Access: leave the A12 just south of Blythburgh, turning right on to the B1387 and following signs to Walberswick. Park at the beach car park and walk southwards along the path behind the sea-wall. Take the second embankment opposite the old windpump to reach the latter, and then head inland to Hoist Covert.

Permits: none required for rights of way.

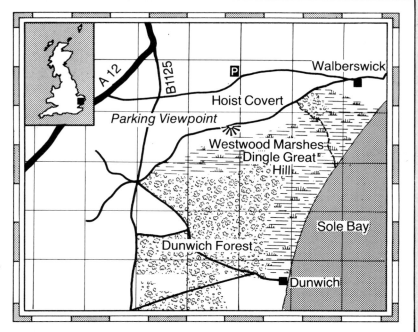

WALNEY ISLAND, CUMBRIA OS 96

Location: this large sand and shingle bar forms the north-western corner of Morecambe Bay (*see page* 302) and lies immediately offshore of Barrow-in-Furness. It is joined to the mainland by road.

Habitats: this is a low-lying island with sandy beaches and large areas of shingle broken by pools of freshwater. Cover is very limited.

Birds: Walney is one of the prime wader sites in Britain, with a massive roost of these birds that includes over 10,000 wintering Oystercatchers, yet it is renowned chiefly as a migration site for small migrants and a massive gull breeding colony. Among the latter are close to 10,000 pairs each of Lesser Black-backed and Herring Gulls, along with small numbers of Great Black-backed Gulls. Other summer breeding birds include Eider, Little Tern and Shelduck. Seawatching is also productive, especially after westerly gales. Shearwaters, skuas and petrels all occur annually and Little Auk most years. In winter Walney is good for Hen Harrier, Merlin, Peregrine (which also breed locally) and Short-eared Owl.

Access: take the bridge from Barrow and head south via Biggar to the nature reserve and observatory, where there is a nature trail and several hides. Contact the Warden, Coastguard Cottages, South Walney Nature Reserve, Barrow-in-Furness LA14 3YQ.

Permits: there is a small charge on arrival.

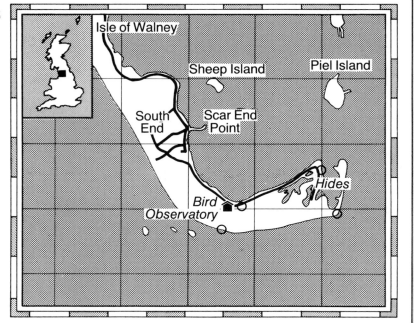

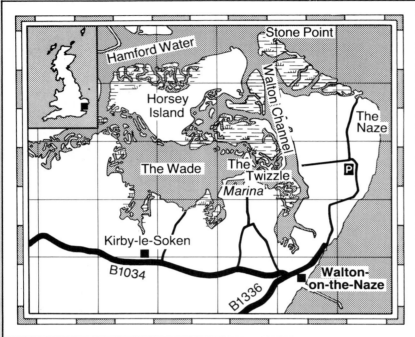

WALTON-ON-THE-NAZE, ESSEX OS 169

Location: on the Essex coast between Clacton and Harwich.

Habitats: this is a largely intertidal area with areas of saltings backed by rough grazing. The sea-wall defences have created deep dykes, but there are still several marshy pools and backwaters.

Birds: though Little Tern and Ringed Plover breed, this is mainly a winter and passage area with waders and wildfowl the main draw. Greenshank, Little Stint and Curlew Sandpiper are all regular in autumn, while in winter they are replaced by Dunlin, Curlew and Redshank. Golden Plover may be abundant but the scene is dominated by over 3000 Brent Geese. The major wader roosts are on Hamford's islands, but Stone Point regularly holds a flock of Sanderling at high tide. Bewick's Swan are regular and there are many ducks, including Wigeon. Red-breasted Merganser have a winter stronghold here and there are regular Hen Harrier, Short-eared Owl and Twite.

Access: Walton-on-the-Naze is easily reached via the A12 and Colchester. Park in the cliff-top car park. Walk northwards. Low water allows access as far as Stone Point, but wellies are essential as is good information about the timing of the tides.

Permits: none required.

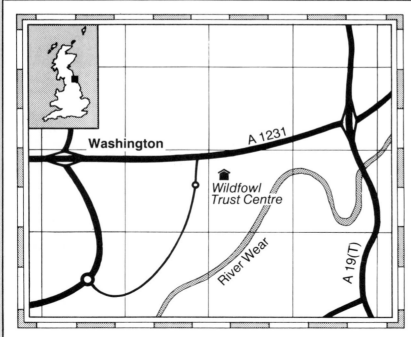

WASHINGTON WATERFOWL PARK, TYNE AND WEAR OS 88

Location: this Wildfowl Trust refuge is situated on the north bank of the River Wear, on the eastern outskirts of Washington New Town, itself a suburb of the great Tyneside conurbation.

Habitats: low-lying riverside marshes have been converted to extensive shallow pools, and imaginative landscaping has created a series of excavated ponds rising in a terraced arrangement.

Birds: this is a typical Wildfowl Trust collection, with a fine visitor centre and well laid out paths giving access and splendid views of an excellent collection of captive ducks and other wildfowl. Unlike some of the other Trust centres, there was no tradition of wildfowl use prior to the reserve's establishment, so that wild birds have had to be encouraged to use the area. The new marshy pools have certainly done so. Specially planted reeds now attract Reed Warbler in summer and Water Rail in winter. Passage periods, especially autumn, bring waders, including Wood Sandpiper, Greenshank, Black-tailed Godwit and the occasional Temminck's Stint. It can only be a matter of time before wild swans discover the area.

Access: take the A1231 to Washington New Town and follow the Wildfowl Trust signs to the refuge.

Permits: charge for non-members.

WEETING HEATH, NORFOLK

OS 144

Location: the village of Weeting lies on the Norfolk–Suffolk border within the huge area known as Breckland (or the Brecks), and about 6 miles north-west of the town of Thetford. The heath itself lies about a mile west of the village on the Hockwold road.

Habitats: dry, infertile soils have created a substantial area of poor grassland typical of what the Brecks once were. This poor sheep pasture is broken by belts of conifers, with other ungrazed areas covered by thicker ground vegetation.

Birds: typical Breckland birds here include Long-eared Owl, Nightjar, Woodcock, Grasshopper Warbler and Crossbill. Weeting Heath is also established as the top spot for Stone-curlew in Britain. Several pairs still breed here and these fine birds can be watched at leisure from the end of March well into the summer.

Access: leave the A1065 at Weeting village turning left on to a minor road westwards toward Hockwold. After 1½ miles, look out for a small car park on the left among a belt of pines. There is a warden at the caravan throughout the Stone-curlew breeding season. A marked path leads to two hides giving fine views of these exciting birds.

Permits: available for a small fee from the warden.

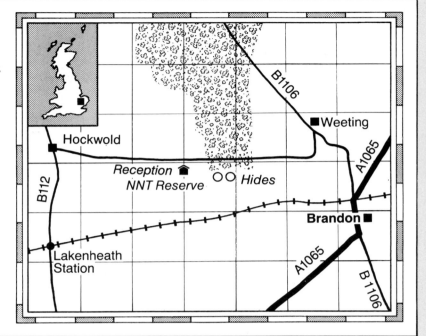

WEXFORD SLOBS, CO. WEXFORD, IRISH REPUBLIC

IOS½ 23

Location: at the south-eastern corner of Ireland, where the town of Wexford itself overlooks much of the best habitat.

Habitats: the North and South Slobs are extensive mud banks and large areas of saltmarsh that have been reclaimed and converted to low-lying grassland, intersected by a network of drainage ditches.

Birds: this is Ireland's major wetland, where the winter population of Greenland White-fronted Geese regularly exceeds 5000, representing about half the total world population. Brent Geese also winter, but in smaller numbers, with a scattering of Pink-footed and Barnacle Goose and the occasional Snow Goose, the latter are mostly regarded as genuine wild birds rather than escapees. Nearly a thousand Pintail also winter and there is a growing herd of Bewick's Swan. Bar-tailed and Black-tailed Godwits are more numerous on spring and autumn passage. Spotted Redshank are notable in autumn. Summer brings large colonies of terns on Tern Island, including Europe's major Roseate Tern colony.

Access: the best area is usually northwards from Rosslare to the Point, where there is a major wader roost.

Permits: none required.

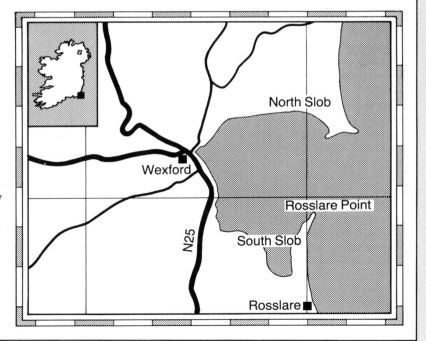

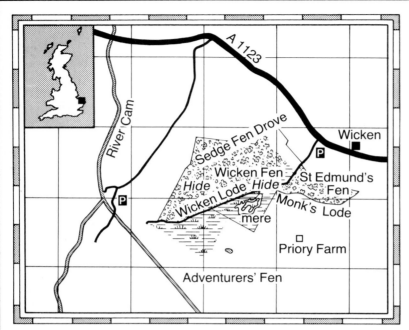

WICKEN FEN, CAMBRIDGESHIRE OS 154

Location: this area of old fenland lies about 7 miles north-west of Newmarket and is marked as 'Adventurers' Fen' on most maps.

Habitats: parts of this important reserve are the last remnants of the original Fens which, prior to drainage, covered so much of the hinterland of The Wash. Adventurers' Fen has been drained, but never with great success. It is now a mere with reed beds.

Birds: many birds breed here, but few are easily seen. They include Bearded Tit, Water Rail and the highly elusive Spotted Crake, as well as Snipe, Redshank and Woodcock, Long-eared Owl, Lesser Spotted Woodpecker and Willow Tit. Breeding warblers include Grasshopper, Cetti's and Savi's, though the latter two have declined. Winter brings many ducks, mainly Wigeon, along with Bittern, Hen Harrier, Water Rail and Short-eared Owl.

Access: leave the A45 Newmarket by-pass, turning right on to the A142 northbound towards Ely. Turn left about a mile after Fordham on to the A1123 to Wicken. On the far side of the village turn left, signposted 'Wicken Fen'. There is a car park, visitor centre and an automatic permit dispenser. Follow tracks and paths for easy exploration and hides. The tower hide is excellent in winter.

Permits: available on arrival. National Trust members enter free.

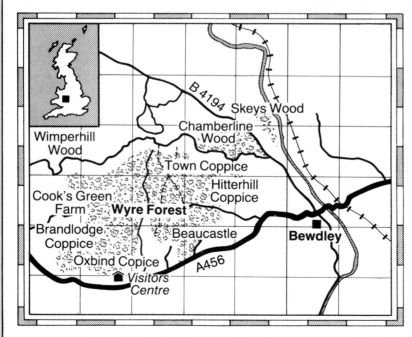

WYRE FOREST, SHROPSHIRE

OS 138 & 139

Location: this remarkably fine forest lies immediately west of the Midlands conurbation on the Shropshire–Worcestershire border and only a few miles west of Kidderminster, the nearest large town.

Habitats: this is a large forest by British standards extending over some six square miles. It is a mature, old forest dominated by deciduous trees, but with an interesting mix of conifers and open heathland. The attractive Dowles Brook bisects the area.

Birds: Wyre Forest offers a good cross-section of the woodland birds of this part of Britain with the western specialities of Pied Flycatcher, Redstart and Wood Warbler present in variable numbers. There are all three woodpeckers, Tree Pipit, Crossbill and Hawfinch to be found, with Dipper and Kingfisher along the streams. Walking the many footpaths in spring it is difficult to realise just how close one is to the great urban sprawl of Birmingham.

Access: leave Birmingham south-eastwards on the A456 to Kidderminster and continue to Bewdley. Turn right on to the B4194. After a couple of miles the forest will be signed. It is a NNR and LNR and the Forestry Commission have a centre here.

Permits: none required for the footpaths that facilitate exploration.

YNYS-HIR, DYFED OS 135

Location: this RSPB reserve lies on the southern shore of the Dyfi estuary (*see page* 261). Machynlleth lies 7 miles to the west.

Habitats: though covering a large area of the saltmarsh that flanks the estuary at this point and containing a typical selection of waders and wildfowl, Ynys-hir is also a fine site for the other birds of this part of Wales, thanks to its outcrops, grassy meadows and woods.

Birds: in summer the woods here are alive with birds and, despite its other attractions, this is probably the best time for visiting. There are breeding Lesser Spotted Woodpecker, Redstart, Pied Flycatcher and Wood Warbler, and all the other more common woodland birds. Both Buzzard and Sparrowhawk breed, too, and Whinchat, Stonechat and Tree Pipit all nest on the more open areas. Red-breasted Merganser and Common Sandpiper can be found along the streams, but Red Kite is only an irregular visitor. In winter there are White-fronted Goose, Wigeon and the more common waders, and the latter include a good selection of species during spring and autumn passage periods.

Access: leave the A487 between Machynlleth and Aberystwyth at Furnace. There is a road to the RSPB car park and information centre and a nature trail with hides. The reserve is open daily.

Permits: on arrival; there is a charge to non-members.

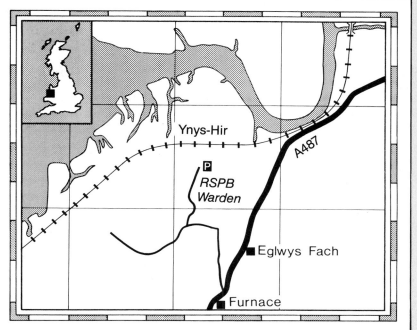

YTHAN ESTUARY, GRAMPIAN

OS 30 & 38

Location: on the Scottish east coast 12 miles north of Aberdeen, and is crossed by the A975. The village of Newburgh lies on the southern shore and the National Nature Reserve of the Sands of Forvie, on the northern shore, is included in this account.

Habitats: there are mud and sand banks at low tide. To the north lie the sandy wastes of Forvie while further north still are several lochs.

Birds: summer sees good numbers of Eider and terns at this site, all breeding at Forvie, but easily seen at the estuary mouth. The colonies of Little, Common, Arctic and Sandwich Terns attract a few skuas at all seasons, and there is usually a flock of Common Scoter offshore, often with some Velvet Scoter. During spring and autumn passage periods waders are often good, with species such as Greenshank, Ruff and sometimes Little Stint. In winter there are Greylag and Pink-footed Geese, which roost mainly on Meikle Loch, and up to 250 Whooper Swans.

Access: the A975 gives excellent views, from both village and bridge. The Sleek of Tarty, with its winter wader roost, can be examined from the bridge before crossing. From here a track leads south to the Point where a hide overlooks the ternery.

Permits: none required.

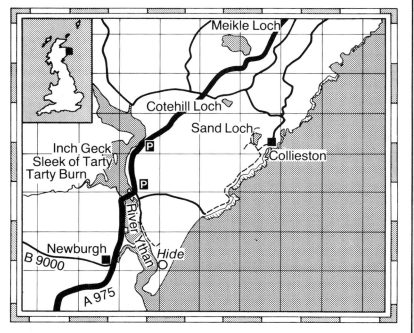

The Checklist

The official British and Irish List is determined by the Records Committee of the British Ornithologists Union (BOU) and amendments are published from time to time in the Union's journal *The Ibis*. Such records, as well as subsequent records, are also published in the annual report of the Rarities Committee of the monthly journal *British Birds*, though final acceptance of a new British bird rests with the BOU.

The BOU list is divided into four categories, A to D, and this letter code follows the name of each species in the most recent version of the list given below, which is complete to 31 December 1986. Category D species are listed separately at the end.

- A Species which have been recorded in an apparently wild state in Britain or Ireland at least once within the last 50 years.
- B Species which have been recorded in an apparently wild state in Britain or Ireland at least once, but not within the last 50 years.
- C Species which, although introduced by man, have now established a regular feral breeding stock which apparently maintains itself without necessary recourse to further introduction.
- D Species which have been recorded within the last 50 years and would otherwise appear in category A except that (1) there is a reasonable doubt that they have ever occurred in a wild state, or (2) they have certainly arrived with ship-assistance, or (3) they have only ever been found dead on the tideline; also species which would otherwise appear in category C except that their feral populations may or may not be self-supporting.

☐ **Red-throated Diver** A
Gavia stellata
Widespread breeder in north and west Scotland and in Northern Ireland though nowhere common. Regular winter visitor to most coastlines where it is usually the most common diver.

☐ **Black-throated Diver** A
Gavia Arctica
Breeds in north and west Scotland as far south as the southern uplands, but is decidedly local. Winter visitor to most coasts in small numbers, more numerous in the west.

☐ **Great Northern Diver** A
Gavia immer
Bred in 1970. Otherwise a regular winter visitor in small numbers to most coasts, though may be the dominant diver in parts of the north and west.

☐ **White-billed Diver** A
Gavia adamsii
A rare winter visitor from the Arctic that is recorded annually in Scotland and exceptionally further south.

☐ **Pied-billed Grebe** A
Podilymbus podiceps
A rare vagrant from North America that was recorded nine times up to 1986.

☐ **Little Grebe** A
Tachybaptus ruficollis
A widespread resident almost throughout Britain and Ireland with some immigration during the winter.

☐ **Great Crested Grebe** A
Podiceps cristatus
A widespread resident from the Scottish lowlands southwards. More widespread in winter with some immigration from the Continent.

☐ **Red-necked Grebe** A
Podiceps grisegena
Increasing evidence that a pair will eventually breed in southern Scotland. Otherwise a regular, if scarce, winter visitor to the east and south coasts.

☐ **Slavonian Grebe** A
Podiceps auritus
Highly localized breeder, mainly in northern Scotland, where some 60–80 pairs can be found. Elsewhere mainly a winter visitor in small numbers to coasts, and tend to return to favoured haunts.

☐ **Black-necked Grebe** A
Podiceps nigricollis
Scarcer breeder in England and especially southern Scotland, and in western Ireland. Otherwise scarce winter visitor and passage migrant to coasts and reservoirs.

☐ **Black-browed Albatross** A
Biomedea melanophris
Exceptional vagrant from the southern hemisphere. One individual has been resident every summer at Hermaness in Shetland since 1971.

☐ **Fulmar** A
Fulmarus glacialis
Common breeder along almost every stretch of cliffs in Britain and Ireland. Widespread at sea outside the breeding season.

☐ **Capped Petrel** (A) B
Pterodroma lasitata
Exceptional vagrant. One found long dead at Barmiston, Humberside in 1984. Only previous record was in 1850.

☐ **Bulwer's Petrel** A
Bulweria bulwerii
Exceptional vagrant with only four records.

☐ **Cory's Shearwater** A
Calonectris diomedia
Very scare, but regular, migrant mainly in autumn to the western approaches that may be seen from southern Irish seawatch stations and occasionally elsewhere.

☐ **Great Shearwater** A
Puffinus gravis
Scarce autumn visitor from South Atlantic to western approaches that may be seen from Irish seawatch stations and elsewhere. Often seen from "western" ferries and pelagic trips, sometimes in good numbers.

☐ **Sooty Shearwater** A
Puffinus griseus
Regular late summer and autumn visitor in small numbers to most seawatch stations.

☐ **Manx Shearwater** A
Puffinus puffinus
The most abundant shearwater around out coasts with large, but highly concentrated, breeding colonies, especially in the north and west. Scarce, mainly autumn, migrant elsewhere.

☐ **Little Shearwater** A
Puffinus assimilis
Rare autumn visitor to main seawatch stations that is difficult to identify and for which reports are often rejected.

☐ **Wilson's Petrel** A
Oceanites oceanicus
Exceptionally rare vagrant from southern hemisphere that is probably present offshore in the western approaches, but which is hardly ever seen from land.

☐ **White-faced Petrel** B
Pelagodroma marina
No records for over 50 years.

☐ **Storm Petrel** A
Hydrobates pelagicus
Breeds on isolated islands in north and west. Otherwise mainly storm-driven autumn visitor to the top seawatch stations, and may then occur inland.

☐ **Leach's Petrel** A
Oceanodroma leucorhoa
Breeds at a handful of isolated island sites in the extreme north-west and also probably in Ireland. Elsewhere only storm-driven in autumn.

☐ **Madeiran Petrel** A
Oceanodroma castro
Extremely rare vagrant from the Atlantic that has not been recorded in the past 50 years.

☐ **Gannet** A
Sula bassana
Fast increasing and spreading as a breeding bird, though still mainly confined to large colonies in the north and west. Elsewhere regularly seen offshore.

☐ **Cormorant** A
Phalacrocorax carbo
Widespread resident that breeds along most of the west coasts of Britain and Ireland and occasionally inland. More widespread on all coasts in winter.

☐ **Shag** A
Phalacrocorax aristotelis
Breeds at many places along the north and west coasts, often in large colonies. Mainly resident, but some birds wander to reach most coastlines in winter.

☐ **Magnificent Frigatebird** A
Frigata magnificens
Exceptional. One record, plus two other frigatebirds not specifically identified.

☐ **Bittern** A
Botaurus stellaris
Slowly declining resident that is confined to a few sites in East Anglia and one in Cumbria. Elsewhere only a very rare winter rarity.

☐ **American Bittern** A
Botaurus lentiginosus
Exceptional transatlantic vagrant that has occurred on 58 occasions, most recently in 1982.

☐ **Little Bittern** A
Ixobrychus minutus
First proved to breed at South Potteric Carr, Yorkshire in 1984 after years of rumour elsewhere. Otherwise only a summer vagrant, mainly in late spring, to Southern England.

☐ **Night Heron** A
Nycticorax nycticorax
Irregular vagrant mainly to southern England with about five records a year, though sometimes considerably more.

☐ **Green Heron** A
Butorides striatus
No records since 1889 until one was found at Stone Creek, Humberside on 27 November 1982.

☐ **Squacco Heron** A
Ardeola ralloides
Vagrant northwards from southern Europe mainly to southern England. Some 119 have been recorded, but it is by no means of annual occurrence.

☐ **Castle Egret** A
Bubulcus ibis
Spreading outwards as a breeding bird from its Iberian stronghold, this small heron is slowly becoming more regular in Britain. Though there are only 44 records, no less than 9 were in 1986.

☐ **Little Egret** A
Egretta garzetta
Rare, but annual, visitor, mainly in spring, to southern England, with 20 or more records a year.

☐ **Great White Egret** A
Egretta alba
Rare, but annual, visitor with one or two records each year.

☐ **Great Heron** A
Ardea cinerea
Widespread resident throughout Britain and Ireland. Some immigrants spend the winter here.

☐ **Purple Heron** A
Ardea purpurea
Regular visitor in small numbers that everyone expects to breed in the future. Most regular along the Suffolk coast and elsewhere in southern England.

☐ **Black Stork** A
Ciconia nigra
Vagrant northwards in tiny numbers most years. Maximum was eight in 1985.

☐ **White Stork** A
Ciconia circonia
Irregular summer visitor that occurs almost every year in small numbers, mainly in the spring.

☐ **Glossy Ibis** A
Plegadis falcinellus
Irregular vagrant from south-eastern Europe that occurs most years, but with a major influx in 1986. One or two birds have been apparently resident along the east coast southward to Kent in recent years.

☐ **Spoonbill** A
Platalea leucorodia
Regular, if scarce, passage migrant and exceptional winter visitor, mainly to south and east England presumably *en route* to and from Dutch breeding colonies.

☐ **Mute Swan** A
Cygnus olor
Resident throughout Britain and Ireland save for the major upland regions in the north and west. Slow decline apparently due to lead poisoning.

☐ **Bewick's Swan** A
Cygnus columbianus
Regular, but localized, winter visitor. Most large herds tend to occur in southern and eastern England.

☐ **Whooper Swan** A
Cygnus cygnus
Widespread winter visitor to Scotland and Ireland that is more localized in England and Wales. Most birds are apparently of Icelandic origin. Feral pairs have bred in Scotland in recent years:

☐ **Bean Goose** A
Anser fabalis
Regular, but highly localized, winter visitor from northern Europe with only a handful of traditional haunts. Recent increases in East Anglia, which is now the stronghold in Britain.

☐ **Pink-footed Goose** A
Anser brachyrhynchus
The most abundant of our winter geese with the entire Icelandic population, plus birds from Greenland, wintering in Scotland and at a few major sites in England.

☐ **White-fronted Goose** A
Anser albifrons
Widespread winter visitor to many parts of the country. Birds in Ireland and western Scotland come from Greenland. Those in England are from Russia. Welsh birds originate from both directions, but keep quite separate.

Lesser White-fronted Goose A
Anser erythropus
Rare, but almost annual, vagrant from eastern Europe, most often found among large flocks of winter Whitefronts.

Greylag Goose A
Anser anser
Widespread resident as a result of reintroductions. Original native stock confined to Outer Hebrides and other parts of north-west Scotland. Common winter visitor mainly to Scotland.

Snow Goose A
Anser caerulescens
A regular straggler from North America that also escapes from wildfowl collections. Birds in Ireland tend to be regarded as genuine migrants, those in southern England are often suspect.

Canada Goose A
Branta canadensis
Widespread resident in England and locally elsewhere. Originally introduced, the species is prospering and has developed a pattern of moult migration. Genuine vagrants occur in Ireland and western Scotland annually.

Barnacle Goose A
Branta leucopsis
Locally abundant winter visitor. Greenland birds winter in Ireland and north-west Scotland; Spitzbergen birds on the Scottish Solway. Siberian birds now occur in small numbers annually in south-east England.

Brent Goose A
Branta bernicla
Increasing winter visitor to many coasts and estuaries. The dark-bellied form which comes from the Soviet Union frequents east and south coasts: the pale-bellied from Greenland occurs in Ireland. Pale-bellied Spitzbergen birds are found in north-east England.

Red-breasted Goose A
Branta ruficollis
Vagrant from eastern Europe that is now of annual occurrence, most often with flocks of Brent Geese, one of two per year, but probably increasing.

Egyptian Goose C
Alopochen aegyptiacus
Introduced in the eighteenth century and now well established in Norfolk where the population is self-supporting.

Ruddy Shelduck A
Tadorna ferruginea
Widely kept in wildfowl collections, these ducks are mostly regarded as escapees, though a few are probably truly wild birds from north-west Africa and southern Eurasia.

Shelduck A
Tadorna tadorna
Resident breeding bird along many stretches of coastline and inland in some areas. More widespread, but still mainly coastal, in winter.

Mandarin C
Aix galericulata
Introduced from China where it is now decidedly rare and may be endangered. Highly localized with most populations resident in south and east England.

Wigeon A
Anas penelope
Widespread, often abundant, winter visitor to coastal and lowland areas throughout Britain and Ireland. Breeds in the north and at several places southward to Kent.

American Wigeon A
Anas americana
Regular transatlantic vagrant in small numbers to Ireland, but also to Britain. Several birds have been shot bearing American rings.

Gadwell A
Anas strepera
Originally introduced to Britain, but with genuine wild birds occurring additionally as winter visitors. Now breeds at scattered localities throughout these islands with dispersal in winter elsewhere. Rather local in Ireland.

Baikal Teal A
Anas formosa
Extremely rare vagrant from Siberia with a total of ten records, two of which at least are regarded as genuine wild birds. The last was in southern Scotland in 1973.

Teal A
Anas crecca
Widespread breeding bird mainly in the north and west, but also elsewhere in suitable habitats. Abundant winter visitor to all parts of Britain and Ireland.

Mallard A
Anas platyrhynchos
Abundant and widespread breeding bird and winter visitor.

Black Duck A
Anas rubripes
Rare transatlantic vagrant. Females show a remarkable tendency to pair with male Mallard and produce confusing hybrid young.

Pintail A
Anas acuta
Widespread winter visitor, mainly to coastal areas, with large flocks confined to traditional sites. Scattered breeding in several parts of Britain and Ireland in small numbers.

Garganey A
Anas querquedula
Summer visitor, mainly to southern England, from Africa, south of the Sahara. Regular spring and autumn passage migrant in Ireland and southern Scotland.

Blue-winged Teal A
Anas discors
Rare transatlantic vagrant that is now recorded every year in small numbers.

Shoveler A
Anas clypeata
Widespread breeding bird in England and eastern Scotland. More localized in Ireland and largely absent from Wales and the south-west. Large number of immigrants from Iceland and northern Europe in winter.

Red-crested Pochard A
Netta rufina
Scarce autumn and winter visitor mainly to south-eastern England, though status confused by frequent escapes from wildfowl collections.

Pochard A
Aythya ferina
Widespread breeding bird to most of Britain and Ireland except for the hill regions of the north and west. Abundant winter visitor, particularly to lowland reservoirs.

Ring-necked Duck A
Aythya collaris
Scarce, though regular transatlantic vagrant that is now of annual occurrence and often long-staying. Numbers vary from six to 35 per year.

Ferruginous Duck A
Aythya nyroca
Rare annual visitor to south and east England from south-eastern Europe mainly between autumn

and spring. Beware relatively common escapes.

☐ **Tufted Duck** A
Aythya fuligula
Common breeding bird throughout most of Britain and Ireland and abundant winter visitor that forms large flocks on suitable inland waters.

☐ **Scaup** A
Aythya morila
Locally common winter visitor to suitable coasts and sheltered bays. May form really large flocks at favoured localities.

☐ **Eider** A
Somateria mollissima
Common breeding bird along the coasts of Scotland and Northern Ireland. Disperses along most coasts in winter, though most birds are resident. Some immigration across the southern North Sea.

☐ **King Eider** A
Somateria spectabilis
Rare, but annual, vagrant from the Arctic, mainly to northern Britain. Most are males and many are long-staying.

☐ **Steller's Eider** A
Polysticta stelleri
Extremely rare vagrant that has occurred 13 times mostly in northern Britain. The last was a long-stay individual in the Outer Hebrides from 1972 to 1984.

☐ **Harlequin Duck** A
Histrionicus histrionicus
An extremely rare vagrant that breeds as near as Iceland, but which has wandered southwards to northern Britain in winter on nine occasions.

☐ **Long-tailed Duck** A
Clangula hyemalis
A widespread winter visitor to most coastlines with major

populations concentrated in the north and north-east. Occasionally found inland and has bred on occasion.

☐ **Common Scoter** A
Melanitta nigra
Widespread and common winter visitor to most coastlines, with flocks of subadults present in many areas throughout the year. Breeds in small numbers in north-western Scotland and Ireland.

☐ **Surf Scoter** A
Melanitta perspicillata
Scarce, but annual, visitor in small numbers to the north and west, several of which have proved long stayers. Breeds in Arctic North America.

☐ **Velvet Scoter** A
Melanitta fusca
Winter visitor from northern Europe to most coastlines, though absent from western Ireland. Generally outnumbered by Common Scoter, with which it associates.

☐ **Buffhead** A
Bucephala albeola
Extremely rare vagrant from North America that has occurred only six times, most recently in the Outer Hebrides in 1980.

☐ **Goldeneye** A
Bucephala clangula
Scarce, but increasing, breeder in specially erected nest boxes in the Scottish Highlands, about seventy pairs in 1985. Widespread and common winter visitor to most of Britain and Ireland, both inland and along the coasts.

☐ **Hooded Merganser** A
Mergus cucullatus
Extremely rare transatlantic vagrant that has occurred only five times, mostly in Ireland in winter.

☐ **Smew** A
Mergus albellus
Scarce, but regular, winter visitor mainly to south-eastern England, mostly seen on gravel pits and reservoirs, particularly early in the year. May occasionally summer in far north, but not breeding as yet.

☐ **Red-breasted Merganser** A
Mergus serrator
Breeds in northern Britain as far south as North Wales and in north and west of Ireland. Widespread along most coasts in winter when there is some immigration.

☐ **Goosander** A
Mergus merganser
Breeds in northern Britain, but absent from Ireland. Mainly resident, but immigrants from the Continent are found at many inland waters in England in winter.

☐ **Ruddy Duck** A
Oxyura jamaicensis
Introduced from North America; escapees have bred in the wild since 1960. Nowe well established in Midlands and spreading. Wanders as far as Kent in winter.

☐ **Honey Buzzard** A
Pernis apivorus
Very rare summer visitor that breeds in small numbers every year. Total pairs less than a dozen.

☐ **Black Kite** A
Milvus migrans
Rare vagrant, mainly in late spring, with most records from southern England. Apparently increasing with 13 records in 1986.

☐ **Red Kite** A
Milvus milvus
Slow, steady increase from the verge of extinction as resident breeding bird in central Wales. Maximum 50 pairs in 1985, but

still robbed every year. Rare, but annual, vagrant elsewhere.

☐ **White-tailed Eagle** A
Haliaeetus albicilla
Has bred once more following a ten-year reintroduction scheme centred on Rhum in the Inner Hebrides. Four pairs laid eggs in 1985. Elsewhere, extremely rare vagrant, mainly in winter.

☐ **Egyptian Vulture** B
Neophron percnopterus
Rare vagrant from southern Europe that has not occurred for over 50 years.

☐ **Griffon Vulture** B
Gyps fulvus
Rare vagrant from southern Europe that has not occurred for over 50 years.

☐ **Marsh Harrier** A
Circus aeruginosus
Scarce breeding bird that is steadily building up its numbers after a period of near extinction. Some 31 nests in 1985 was a new peak in this century. More widespread on passage and in winter.

☐ **Hen Harrier** A
Circus cyaneus
Increasing and spreading as a breeding species, from an all time low between the wars, when it was more or less confined to the Orkneys. Now breeds as far south as Wales. Widespread winter visitor to coasts and heaths.

☐ **Pallid Harrier** A
Circus macrourus
Exceptional vagrant from eastern Europe that has occurred only three times.

☐ **Montagu's Harrier** A
Circus pygargus
Very rare summer visitor mainly to eastern England that has not exceeded ten pairs in the past

decade. Otherwise a scarce passage migrant.

☐ **Goshawk** A
Accipiter gentilis
Slowly increasing as a breeding bird, mainly as a result of escapees from falconry. Widespread, with 35–65 breeding pairs, but still robbed annually.

☐ **Sparrowhawk** A
Accipiter nisus
Widespread breeder throughout Britain and Ireland and mainly resident. Considerable increase since the pesticide fiasco of the 1960s.

☐ **Buzzard** A
Buteo buteo
Widespread and common resident in north and west Britain, but highly local in Ireland and in south and eastern England. Regular winter visitor and passage migrant in small numbers elsewhere.

☐ **Rough-legged Buzzard** A
Buteo lagopus
Scarce winter visitor, mainly to the east coast, in variable numbers each year. Tendency to reach peak every five or six years.

☐ **Spotted Eagle** A
Aquila clanga
Extremely rare vagrant from eastern Europe that has not occurred within the past 50 years.

☐ **Golden Eagle** A
Aquila chrysaetos
Healthy population resident in Scottish Highlands and Islands with several pairs in the Southern Uplands and, more recently, a pair in the Lake District.

☐ **Osprey** A
Pandion haliaetus
Gradual increase as breeder since recolonization. In 1985 there were 34 pairs, of which 28 bred, rearing 53 young. Elsewhere an increasing passage migrant throughout Britain and Ireland.

☐ **Lesser Kestrel** A
Falco naumanni
Extrmeley rare vagrant from southern Europe where it is declining. There have been 20 records, the last in 1983 in Humberside.

☐ **Kestrel** A
Falco tinnunculus
The most widespread and abundant British and Irish bird of prey.

☐ **American Kestrel** A
Falco sparverius
Exceptional transatlantic vagrant with only two records, both in 1976, from Cornwall in June and Fair Isle in May.

☐ **Red-footed Falcon** A
Falco vespertinus
Rare passage migrant, that occurs in small numbers annually, mostly in late spring, sometimes in small flocks.

☐ **Merlin** A
Falco columbarius
Widespread, but uncommon, resident in mostly hilly districts of the north and west. Winter visitor in small numbers to most coastlines.

☐ **Hobby** A
Falco subbuteo
Summer visitor to southern England, that is steadily increasing in numbers after years of persecution by egg-collectors. Passage migrant elsewhere

☐ **Eleonora's Falcon** A
Falco eleonorae
Exceptionally rare vagrant northwards from the Mediterranean that has appeared on only two occasions; in 1977 on Merseyside, and in 1981 on Humberside – the latter dead in a cabbage patch!

☐ **Gyrfalcon** A
Falco rusticolus
Rare, but annual, vagrant averaging about three a year, mainly in winter and mainly in the north of Britain.

☐ **Peregrine** A
Falco peregrinus
Breeds in most mountain and cliff-girt coastal districts of the north and west and has made a significant recovery since its numbers were decimated by pesticides. Elsewhere mainly a coastal passage migrant and winter visitor.

☐ **Red Grouse** A
Lagopus lagopus
Resident in all hill districts of the north and west. Unknown elsewhere.

☐ **Ptarmigan** A
Lagopus mutus
Resident among the highest ranges of the Scottish Highlands. Unknown elsewhere.

☐ **Black Grouse** A
Tetrao tetrix
Resident in hilly districts of north and west. Unknown Ireland and elsewhere.

☐ **Capercaillie** A
Tetrao urogallus
Exterminated in eighteenth century, reintroduced from Sweden in the mid-nineteenth century. Resident in Scottish Highlands and unknown elsewhere.

☐ **Red-legged Partridge** C
Alectoris rufa
Introduced in eighteenth century, now well established resident in eastern and central England, and in eastern Scotland.

☐ **Grey Partridge** A
Perdix perdix
Resident almost throughout Britain and Ireland, though steady decline in numbers continues, despite artificial rearing.

☐ **Quail** A
Coturnix coturnix
Summer visitor that has a patchy distribution throughout Britain and Ireland, but which has become decidedly rare in many areas.

☐ **Pheasant** C
Phasianus colchicus
Introduced from Asia possibly by the Romans, but certainly since Norman times. Now widespread and common resident throughout Britain and Ireland, including huge numbers artificially reared – and shot – every year.

☐ **Golden Pheasant** A
Chrysolophus pictus
Introduced in late nineteenth century, mainly in the Brecks and western Norfolk, but also in Galloway. Continued introductions today, but highly confined distribution.

☐ **Lady Amherst's Pheasant** C
Chrysolophus amherstiae
Introduced at the turn of the century with a self-supporting feral population now established in Bedfordshire.

☐ **Water Rail** A
Rallus aquaticus
Widespread resident, except in the hilly districts, and winter visitor from the Continent. Nowhere common.

☐ **Spotted Crake** A
Porzana porzana
Rare summer visitor that probably breeds every year in very small numbers. Equally scare passage migrant.

☐ **Sora Rail** A
Porzana carolina
Exceptionally rare transatlantic vagrant, mainly in autumn. The total of 11 includes the latest in West Sussex in 1985.

☐ **Little Crake** A
Porzana parva
Rare vagrant from southern Europe, mainly in early spring. The latest was in East Sussex in 1985.

☐ **Baillon's Crake** A
Porzana pusilla
Rare vagrant from southern Europe, mostly in late winter or early spring. There have been no records since 1976 until when it has been more or less of annual occurrence.

☐ **Corncrake** A
Crex crex
Once widespread, this bird has declined rapidly this century due to changing agricultural techniques. It is now a summer visitor only to north-west Scotland and Ireland in any numbers. Elsewhere a scarce passage migrant.

☐ **Moorhen** A
Gallinula chloropus
Widespread and abundant resident throughout Britain and Ireland.

☐ **Allen's Gallinule** B
Porphyrula alleni
Exceptionally rare vagrant that has not occurred within the past 50 years.

☐ **American Purple Gallinule** A
Porphyrula martinica
Exceptional transatlantic vagrant that has occurred once in the Isles of Scilly.

☐ **Coot** A
Fulica atra
Widespread and numerous resident and abundant winter visitor.

☐ **American Coot** A
Fulica americana
Exceptional transatlantic vagrant. One found at Ballycotton in Ireland in 1981.

☐ **Crane** A
Grus grus
Rare passage migrant, mainly in small numbers, but with the occasional large autumn influx. Breeds in Scandinavia, winters from France through to Spain. A small group is at present resident in east Norfolk.

☐ **Sandhill Crane** A
Grus canadensis
Exceptional transatlantic vagrant with only two records: Co. Cork in 1905 and Fair Isle in 1981.

☐ **Little Bustard** A
Tetrax tetrax
Rare vagrant from south or east, mainly in winter. Formerly reasonably regular, it is now quite exceptional. (One in Hampshire on New Year's Eve 1987 broke the duck for hundreds of observers.)

☐ **Husbara Bustard** A
Chlamydotis undulata
Exceptionally rare vagrant from Middle East or North Africa. There are five records, the last in Suffolk in 1962.

☐ **Great Bustard** A
Otis tarda
Rare vagrant from southern and eastern Europe that averages about one record a year at the present time. Mostly winter.

☐ **Oystercatcher** A
Haematopus ostralegus
Widespread and common shoreline breeder, found inland in summer in northern England and Scotland. Abundant on estuaries in winter.

☐ **Black-winged Stilt** A
Himantopus himantopus
Regular, if scarce, passage migrant mainly to the south in spring, usually at the beginning of May. Bred in Nottinghamshire in 1945 (and again in Norfolk in 1987).

☐ **Avocet** A
Recurvirostra avosetta
Steadily increasing and spreading as a breeding bird since its war time recolonization. In 1985 there was a record 269 pairs at 14 sites, including some that were not bird reserves. Elsewhere, a scarce passage migrant and a winter visitor to the south-east.

☐ **Stone-curlew** A
Burhinus oedicnemus
A scarce summer visitor to south and east England that is steadily declining in numbers due to agricultural destruction, egg collecting and disturbance.

☐ **Cream-coloured Courser** A
Cursorius cursor
Very rare vagrant from North Africa, that has occurred on 33 occasions, most recently in Essex in 1984.

☐ **Collared Pratincole** A
Glareola pratincola
Vagrant northwards from southern Europe that occurs most years in late spring, usually in the south.

☐ **Black-winged Pratincole** A
Glareola nordmanni
Rare vagrant northwards from south-eastern Europe that is of less than annual occurrence, mainly in autumn.

☐ **Little Ringed Plover** A
Charadrius dubius
First bred in 1938 and now established as a regular summer visitor to England, though with a decidedly eastern bias. Elsewhere a passage migrant, mostly inland.

☐ **Ringed Plover** A
Charadrius hiaticula
Breeds along most coasts and in many hilly districts in good numbers. Abundant along many shorelines on passage, but numbers are smaller in winter.

☐ **Semipalmated Plover** A
Charadrius semipalmatus
Exceptional transatlantic vagrant. One on Scilly in 1978.

☐ **Killdeer** A
Charadrius vociferus
Rare transatlantic vagrant that is recorded in very small numbers most winters. Last was in Herefordshire in 1985.

☐ **Kentish Plover** A
Charadrius alexandrinus
Formerly bred in small numbers in western Kent and adjacent Sussex. Now mainly a scarce passage migrant, mainly in spring, but bred again in 1979.

☐ **Greater Sand Plover** A
Charadrius leschenaultii
Exceptional vagrant from the Middle East that was first recorded in 1978 and has appeared six times since, the last being in Norfolk in 1985.

☐ **Caspian Plover** B
Charadrius asiaticus
Exceptionally rare vagrant that has not been recorded within the past 50 years.

☐ **Dotterel** A
Charadrius marinellus
Regular summer visitor to the highest of the Scottish hills where some 15–30 pairs regularly breed.

Otherwise a scarce passage migrant that has the habit of stopping off at the same spots at the same time each year.

☐ **American Golden Plover** A
Pluvialis dominica
A rare transatlantic vagrant that occurs most years mainly in late summer and autumn.

☐ **Pacific Golden Plover** A
Pluvialis fulva
A rare vagrant from north-east Asia that has recently been 'split' from the American Golden Plover and which had been identified on only four occasions until 1986. Non-specific records of American/Pacific Golden Plovers, previously lumped as Lesser Golden Plover, may include this species.

☐ **Golden Plover** A
Pluvialis apricaria
Widespread breeder among hills of north and west. Abundant winter visitor over much of lowland Britain and Ireland.

☐ **Grey Plover** A
Pluvialis squatarola
Numerous passage migrant and winter visitor to most coasts and estuaries.

☐ **Sociable Plover** A
Chettusia gregaria
Rare vagrant from south-east Russia and Central Asia, mainly in October to southern England that is now almost of annual occurrence. There were 29 records up to 1986.

☐ **White-tailed Plover** A
Chettusia leucura
An exceptionally rare vagrant westwards from Russia and the Middle East that has occurred on four occasions, most recently in 1984.

☐ **Lapwing** A
Vanelus vanellus
Widespread and abundant breeding bird, passage migrant and winter visitor.

☐ **Knot** A
Calidris canutus
Abundant winter visitor, particularly to favoured estuaries, though in smaller numbers along most coastlines.

☐ **Sanderling** A
Calidris alba
Common winter visitor to most shorelines, with largest numbers usually present in the west in spring.

☐ **Semipalmated Sandpiper** A
Calidris pusilla
Rare transatlantic vagrant that was recorded 49 times up to 1986, mainly in autumn.

☐ **Western Sandpiper** A
Calidris mauri
Exceptionally rare transatlantic vagrant that was recorded on only seven occasions up to 1986. The last was in 1975.

☐ **Little Stint** A
Calidris minuta
Widespread passage migrant, mainly in autumn, that occasionally overwinters in small numbers.

☐ **Temminck's Stint** A
Calidris temminckii
Scarce double passage migrant that is more regular in spring than autumn. Tiny numbers have bred in northern Scotland during the past decade, but permanent colonization seems far away.

☐ **Long-toed Stint** A
Calidris subminuta
Extremely rare vagrant from Asia that occurred on only one occasion up to 1986, in Cleveland in 1982.

☐ **Least Sandpiper** A
Calidris minutilla
A very rare transatlantic vagrant that was recorded 27 times prior to 1986, when one was reported from Cornwall. Most have been in autumn, though the 1986 bird was present from February to April.

☐ **White-rumped Sandpiper** A
Calidris fuscicollis
Regular transatlantic vagrant, mainly in autumn, usually with up to 20 records a year.

☐ **Baird's Sandpiper** A
Calidris bairdii
More or less annual transatlantic vagrant in small numbers, mainly in autumn.

☐ **Pectoral Sandpiper** A
Calidris melanotus
Scarce but regular transatlantic passage migrant every autumn. Regular sightings in spring suggest that this species may become established this side of the Atlantic.

☐ **Sharp-tailed Sandpiper** A
Calidris acuminata
Exceptionally rare vagrant from north-eastern Siberia, mainly in autumn. There were 18 records up to 1986.

☐ **Curlew Sandpiper** A
Calidris ferruginea
Widespread passage migrant, especially in autumn, to coastal and inland marshes. Occasional in winter.

☐ **Purple Sandpiper** A
Calidris maritima
Regular winter visitor to rocky shorelines, mostly in small numbers. Since 1978 has bred in Scotland, with a maximum of three pairs in 1985.

☐ **Dunlin** A
Calidris alpina
Abundant along shores, estuaries and inland marshes in winter and on passage. Widespread breeder among northern and western moors.

☐ **Broad-billed Sandpiper** A
Limicola falcinellus
Rare passage migrant in small numbers in May and June most years. The best ever year was 1984 with 12 records.

☐ **Stilt Sandpiper** A
Micropalama himantopus
A very rare transatlantic vagrant that occurred on only 17 occasions until 1986, the last in Kent in 1985. Most are in autumn, in the south.

☐ **Buff-breasted Sandpiper** A
Tryngites subruficollis
A regular transatlantic migrant in small numbers, mostly in autumn, often to golf courses, airfields and similar grasslands.

☐ **Ruff** A
Philomachus pugnax
A common and widespread passage migrant throughout Britain and Ireland, that now winters regularly in smallish numbers at several sites and which has returned to breed irregularly over the past 20 years.

☐ **Jack Snipe** A
Lymnocryptes minimus
A scarce winter visitor and passage migrant throughout Britain and Ireland.

☐ **Snipe** A
Gallinago gallinago
Widespread resident and abundant winter visitor to all parts of Britain and Ireland.

☐ **Great Snipe** A
Gallinago media
Rare autumn vagrant mainly to Fair Isle and the east coast with

no more than one or two records in most recent years.

Short-billed Dowitcher A
Limnodromus griseus
Exceptionally rare vagrant from America that was positively identified on only five occasions up to 1986. Many dowitchers are not identified as to species.

Long-billed Dowitcher A
Limnodromus scolopaceus
Rare transatlantic vagrant, mainly in autumn, that also stays on to winter on occasion. Averages some half dozen records a year at present.

Woodcock A
Scolopax rusticola
Widespread resident in damp woodlands that is also a passage migrant and winter visitor from the Continent.

Black-tailed Godwit A
Limosa limosa
Scarce and localized breeding bird with some 36–90 pairs grouped in 5–13 localities, mostly in England. Regular and widespread passage migrant and winter visitor.

Hudsonian Godwit A
Limosa haemastica
Exceptional vagrant from America. One on Humberside in 1981 was also seen (presumed the same bird) in 1983.

Bar-tailed Godwit A
Limosa lapponica
Widespread and common passage migrant and winter visitor to many estuaries and shorelines.

Little Whimbrel A
Numenius minutus
Extremely rare vagrant from Asia that was first recorded in Glamorgan in 1982 and subsequently in Norfolk in 1985. These were the only records up to 1986.

Eskimo Curlew B
Numerius borealis
Transatlantic vagrant last century that is all but extinct and highly unlikely to occur again.

Whimbrel A
Numenius phaeopus
Regular double passage migrant, especially in spring, that breeds in small numbers in the Scottish islands.

Curlew A
Numenius arquata
Common and widespread summer visitor to much of Britain and Ireland, and is also common around most coasts and estuaries on passage and in winter.

Upland Sandpiper A
Bartramia longicauda
Rare transatlantic vagrant that occurred 39 times up to 1986. Now regarded as more or less annual in October on the Isles of Scilly.

Spotted Redshank A
Tringa erythropus
Regular double passage migrant mainly in the south and east that has definite favoured areas. Small numbers also winter.

Redshank A
Tringa totanus
Widespread breeding bird that is an abundant winter visitor and passage migrant.

Marsh Sandpiper A
Tringa stagnatilis
Rare vagrant from eastern Europe that is now recorded annually in small numbers, mostly in summer. Total of 59 records up to 1986.

Greenshank A
Tringa nebularia
Regular and widespread double passage migrant that breeds in small numbers in Scotland and Ireland. Small numbers in winter, mainly in the south-west.

Greater Yellowlegs A
Tringa melanoleuca
Very rare transatlantic vagrant, mostly in autumn, that occurred only 28 times up to 1986, most recently in 1985.

Lesser Yellowlegs A
Tringa flavipes
Rare transatlantic visitor that occurs in tiny numbers every year, mostly in autumn.

Solitary Sandpiper A
Tringa solitaria
Very rare transatlantic vagrant that occurred only 24 times up to 1986, mostly in autumn. Most recent was on Scilly in 1985, where about half the records now derive.

Green Sandpiper A
Tringa ochropus
Widespread passage migrant and scarce winter visitor that has bred on occasion.

Wood Sandpiper A
Tringa glareola
Widespread passage migrant, particularly in autumn, that has bred in northern Scotland in small numbers in recent years.

Terek Sandpiper A
Xenus cinereus
Rare vagrant from eastern Europe that is mainly a late spring and early summer visitor to the south and east coasts. Only 28 were recorded until 1986, when no less than four were found.

Common Sandpiper A
Actitis hypoleucos
Widespread summer visitor to the hilly districts of the north and west, and elsewhere a common passge migrant to fresh waters and marshes. A few winter in the south-west.

Spotted Sandpiper A
Actitis macularia
Rare transatlantic vagrant, mostly in autumn, but also in winter. Now recorded in small numbers every year and has bred once in Scotland in 1975.

Grey-tailed Tattler A
Heteroscelus brevipes
Exceptional vagrant from Siberia that was first recorded on the Dyfed-Gwynedd borders in 1981. This remains the only record.

Turnstone A
Arenaria interpres
Widespread winter visitor and passage migrant to all coastlines.

Wilson's Phalarope A
Phalaropus tricolor
Rare transatlantic vagrant that has occurred with increasing frequency in recent years, even in summer.

Red-necked Phalarope A
Phalaropus lobatus
Scarce breeding bird in extreme north and west. Double passage migrant, mainly in autumn and particularly after gales when it may be widespread inland.

Grey Phalarope A
Phalaropus fulicarius
Regular autumn migrant, especially after autumn storms. Rare at other times.

Pomarine Skua A
Stercorarius pomarinus
Regular double passage migrant in small numbers, mainly to north-west and south coasts in spring and to the east coast in autumn.

Arctic Skua A
Stercorarius parasiticus
Breeds in the far north in good numbers. Elsewhere, a regular double passage migrant and the most common of the skuas along all coastlines.

☐ **Long-tailed Skua** A
Stercorarius longicaudus
Scarcest of the four skuas and
only a rare passage migrant in
spring and autumn to our coasts.

☐ **Great Skua** A
Stercorarius skua
Scarce breeding bird in far north.
Elsehwere a scarce passage
migrant.

☐ **Great Black-headed Gull** A
Larus ichthyaetus
Extremely rare vagrant from
southern Russia that has not
occurred since 1932, though a few
have been claimed.

☐ **Mediterranean Gull** A
Larus melanocephalus
Regular, but scarce, visitor
throughout the year that has bred
erratically on the south coast over
the past two decades.

☐ **Laughing Gull** A
Larus atricilla
Rare transatlantic vagrant that is
now recorded in small numbers
every year.

☐ **Franklin's Gull** A
Larus pipixcan
Very rare transatlantic vagrant
that was recorded 11 times up to
1986, but which is now recognised
most years.

☐ **Little Gull** A
Larus minutus
Regular double passage migrant
throughout England, Wales,
southern Scotland and south-
eastern Ireland, that may form
quite large flocks in favoured
areas. Scarce in winter, and
attempted to breed in 1975 and
1978.

☐ **Sabine's Gull** A
Larus sabini
Passage migrant through south-
western approaches that may be
blown onshore by autumn storms.

Probably more abundant at sea
than status indicates.

☐ **Bonaparte's Gull** A
Larus philadelphia
Rare transatlantic vagrant,
mainly to the south-west, that is
becoming of annual occurrence.

☐ **Black-headed Gull** A
Larus ridibundus
The most abundant and
widespread of the gulls in most
parts of the country. Breeds in
many areas, including inland, and
is an abundant winter visitor.

☐ **Slender-billed Gull** A
Larus genei
Extremely rare vagrant from
southern Europe, with only a
handful of records. (Two appeared
in Norfolk in 1987.)

☐ **Ring-billed Gull** A
Larus delawarensis
First recorded only in 1973 as a
transatlantic vagrant. Now
regarded as a scarce but regular
visitor, mainly in early spring,
with up to 50 records each year.
Many reports are still rejected.

☐ **Common Gull** A
Larus canus
Widespread breeding bird in the
north and west and abundant
winter visitor and passage
migrant throughout Britain and
Ireland.

☐ **Lesser Black-backed
Gull** A
Larus fuscus
Breeds in large numbers at many
places, particularly around the
coasts. Common passage migrant
and numerous winter visitor.

☐ **Herring Gull** A
Larus argentatus
Breeds commonly along most cliff-
bound coastlines, particularly in
the north and west. Abundant
winter visitor to all areas.

☐ **Iceland Gull** A
Larus glaucoides
Scarce winter visitor that may
occur along any coastline, but
which is primarily a bird of the far
north.

☐ **Glaucous Gull** A
Larus hyperboreus
Widespread, but scarce, winter
visitor to all coastlines.
Outnumbers Iceland Gull in all
areas. Some individuals return to
regular wintering area year after
year.

☐ **Great Black-backed Gull** A
Larus marinus
Widespread breeding bird in north
and west, and is a regular winter
visitor elsewhere, though largely
confined to the coast.

☐ **Ross's Gull** A
Rhodostethia rosea
Rare winter visitor from the far
north, mainly to northern Britain
that occurred 46 times up to 1986,
but which is becoming annual.

☐ **Kittiwake** A
Rissa tridactyla
Breeds along most cliff-girt
coastlines, thus mainly in the
north and west. Pelagic outside
the breeding season, but occurs off
all shorelines in winter.

☐ **Ivory Gull** A
Pagophila eburnea
Very rare vagrant from the Arctic
that occasionally appears, usually
in the far northern islands.
Becoming even more irregular
despite increasing gull-watching.

☐ **Gull-billed Tern** A
Gelochelidon nilotica
Rare passage migrant, mainly to
the south-east, in spring and
autumn with 1–13 records each
year. Breeds as near as the Baltic.

☐ **Caspian Tern** A
Sterna caspia
Rare passage migrant that occurs
in tiny numbers each year, mainly
on the south and east coasts.
Breeds in the Baltic.

☐ **Royal Tern** A
Sterna maxima
Extremely rare vagrant from the
tropics that has occurred only
four times, most recently in south
Wales in 1979. Easily confused
with Lesser Crested Tern.

☐ **Lesser Crested Tern** A
Sterna bengalensis
Extremely rare vagrant that has
been seen annually since first
recorded in 1982. It is possible that
all records refer to the single
individual that was seen on
television on the Farne Islands.

☐ **Sandwich Tern** A
Sterna sandvicensis
Widespread, but local, summer
visitor to many coastal areas and
regular passage migrant along all
shorelines.

☐ **Roseate Tern** A
Sterna dougallii
Very localized summer visitor,
mainly to Ireland, with small
colonies in eastern Scotland and
north-eastern England. Elsewhere
a scarce passage migrant to
coasts. Slowly declining.

☐ **Common Tern** A
Sterna hirundo
Widespread and numerous
summer visitor to coasts and
inland wetlands. Common passage
migrant elsewhere.

☐ **Arctic Tern** A
Sterna paradisaea
Abundant summer visitor to
coasts of north and west with
smaller numbers south to East
Anglia. Widespread passage
migrant to other coasts.

☐ **Aleutian Tern** A
Sterna aleutica
Exceptionally rare vagrant. One record of one in Northumberland in 1979.

☐ **Forster's Tern** A
Sterna forsteri
Exceptionally rare vagrant, first recorded as recently as 1980, that is now seen annually in late autumn and winter. There were 13 records until 1986.

☐ **Bridled Tern** A
Sterna anaethetus
Exceptional vagrant from tropical waters that was seen only ten times up to 1986, most recently with two in 1984.

☐ **Sooty Tern** A
Sterna fuscata
Extremely rare vagrant from the tropics that occurred 26 times up to 1986, most recently in Kent and East Sussex in 1984.

☐ **Little Tern** A
Sterna albifrons
Scarce, but widespread, summer visitor to many coastlines, that is declining in many areas. Passage migrant elsewhere.

☐ **Whiskered Tern** A
Chlidonius hybridus
Rare vagrant that occurs in tiny numbers most years, mainly along the south coast in spring.

☐ **Black Tern** A
Chlidonias niger
Regular double passage migrant, mainly to south and east England, that occasionally breeds.

☐ **White-winged Black Tern** A
Chlidonias leucopterus
Rare double passage migrant in small numbers each year, mainly to south and east England.

☐ **Guillemot** A
Uria aalge
Confined to cliffs of north and west where large numbers form dense breeding colonies. Found in small numbers along all coasts in winter.

☐ **Brünnich's Guillemot** A
Uria lomvia
Exceptionally rare vagrant from the Arctic that occurred 21 times until 1986, mainly in the far northern islands in winter. Most were dead when found.

☐ **Razorbill** A
Alca torda
Breeds among the cliffs of the north and west, but is nowhere as abundant as the Guillemot. Found in small numbers along many coasts in winter.

☐ **Great Auk** A
Pinguinus impennis
Extinct. Last British birds were killed on St Kilda about 1840. Final World Extinction on Eldey, Iceland on 4 June 1844.

☐ **Black Guillemot** A
Cepphus grylle
Widespread breeder in north-west, though nowhere very numerous. Mainly resident and decidedly rare in south and east.

☐ **Little Auk** A
Alle alle
Regular autumn passage migrant that is blown onshore by gales in late October and November and which may then occur inland. Scarce at other times.

☐ **Puffin** A
Fratercula arctica
Localized breeding bird on north and west coasts. Forms dense colonies on many offshore islands. Seen in winter in small numbers elsewhere.

☐ **Pallas's Sandgrouse** A
Syrrhaptes paradoxus
Irregular visitor, sometimes in significant numbers, at the beginning of this century, that exceptionally stayed on to breed in subsequent years. Last irruption was 1909 and only six have been recorded since.

☐ **Rock Dove** A
Columba livia
Widespread and numerous as 'Feral Pigeon'. Genuine Rock Doves probably now confined to the extreme north and west.

☐ **Stock Dove** A
Columba oenas
Widespread resident throughout Britain, except the north-western Highlands

☐ **Woodpigeon** A
Columba palumbus
Common and widespread resident throughout Britain and Ireland and abundant winter visitor.

☐ **Collared Dove** A
Streptopelia decaocto
Widespread resident throughout Britain and Ireland after first colonization in 1955.

☐ **Turtle Dove** A
Streptopelia turtur
Summer visitor to south, central and eastern England and eastern Wales. Passage migrant elsewhere.

☐ **Rufous Turtle Dove** A
Streptopelia orientalis
Exceptional vagrant from the east that occurred on only eight occasions up to 1968, most recently in Cornwall in 1978.

☐ **Rose-ringed Parakeet** C
Psittacula krameri
Thinly spread and rather localized resident over much of England as far north as eastern Scotland after introduction in the 1960s.

☐ **Great Spotted Cuckoo** A
Clamator glandarius
Very rare vagrant, mainly to southern England in spring. There were 28 records up to 1986, the latest being on the Ise of Wight in that year.

☐ **Cuckoo** A
Cuculus canorus
Widespread summer visitor to Britain and Ireland

☐ **Black-billed Cuckoo** A
Coccyzus erythrophthalmus
Exceptional transatlantic vagrant that occurred only 12 times up to 1986. The latest was typically in autumn 1985 in Scilly.

☐ **Yellow-billed Cuckoo** A
Coccyzus americanus
Rare transatlantic vagrant mainly in autumn. The latest was in 1986 in Co. Cork.

☐ **Barn Owl** A
Tyto alba
Widespread, but declining, resident throughout Britain and Ireland, save for the extreme north and west.

☐ **Scops Owl** A
Otus scops
Rare vagrant from southern Europe, mostly in early summer. There were 78 records by 1986, the most recent being one in Wiltshire in 1982.

☐ **Eagle Owl** B
Bubo bubo
Exceptional vagrant that has not been recorded in the past 50 years.

☐ **Snowy Owl** A
Nyctea scandiaca
Irregular autumn and winter visitor that bred in Shetland from 1967 until 1975. Several females have been resident there since. Vagrant elsewhere.

☐ **Hawk Owl** A
Surnia ulula
Exceptional vagrant from the north-east that was recorded 11 times up to 1986, most recently in Shetland in 1983.

☐ **Little Owl** A
Athene noctua
Widespread resident in England and in north and south Wales. Winter visitor to central Wales, vagrant elsewhere. Originally introduced in late nineteenth century.

☐ **Tawny Owl** A
Strix aluco
Common and widespread resident, but absent from Ireland.

☐ **Long-eared Owl** A
Asio otus
Widespread resident, though absent from many parts of southern England. Winter visitor elsewhere.

☐ **Short-eared Owl** A
Asio flammeus
Resident in hilly regions of north and west and along coasts of East Anglia. Elsewhere, widespread winter visitor.

☐ **Tengmalm's Owl** A
Aegolius funereus
Rare vagrant from the Continent that has occurred 57 times, most recently in Orkney in 1986.

☐ **Nightjar** A
Caprimulgus eruopaeus
Widespread summer visitor, mainly to southern Britain, and passage migrant elsewhere.

☐ **Red-necked Nightjar** B
Caprimulgus ruficollis
Exceptional vagrant from southern Europe that has not been recorded within the last 50 years.

☐ **Egyptian Nightjar** B
Caprimulgus aegyptius
Exceptional vagrant from Africa and Asia that has not been recorded within the past 50 years.

☐ **Common Nighthawk** A
Chordeiles minor
Exceptional transatlantic vagrant that occurred on 13 occasions up to 1986. The most recent was on Merseyside in 1985. Most are seen in the south-west in October.

☐ **Chimney Swift** A
Chaetura pelagica
Exceptional transatlantic vagrant that was recorded only three times up to 1986. Two were seen in Cornwall in 1982, and one in Scilly in 1986.

☐ **Needle-tailed Swift** A
Hirundapus caudacutus
Exceptionally rare vagrant from Siberia that was recorded six times up to 1986, most recently in Yorkshire in 1985.

☐ **Swift** A
Apus apus
Common and widespread summer visitor to almost all parts of Britain and Ireland.

☐ **Pallid Swift** A
Apus pallidus
Exceptional vagrant from southern Europe that occurred only on six occasions up to 1986, no less than four of which were in November 1984.

☐ **Pacific Swift** A
Apus pacificus
Exceptional vagrant from eastern Asia that occurred only once, on a North Sea gas platform in 1981.

☐ **Alpine Swift** A
Apus melba
Rare vagrant from southern Europe in spring and summer, mainly to southern England. Now regarded as annual in small numbers.

☐ **Little Swift** A
Apus affinis
Exceptional vagrant from North Africa that occurred only seven times up to 1986. The first was in Co. Cork in 1981.

☐ **Kingfisher** A
Alcedo atthis
Widespread resident as far north as central Scotland. Recent decline due to hard winters and river pollution.

☐ **Belted Kingfisher** A
Ceryle alcyon
Exceptional transatlantic vagrant that was recorded only five times up to 1986. Most recent was in Co. Tipperary in 1985.

☐ **Blue-cheeked Bee-eater** A
Merops superciliosus
Exceptionally rare vagrant that was seen on only three occasions up to 1986. The most recent was in a lorry park in Cambridgeshire in September 1982.

☐ **Bee-eater** A
Merops apiaster
Vagrant northwards from the Mediterranean, mostly to southern England in the early summer, often in small flocks.

☐ **Roller** A
Coracias garrulus
Rare vagrant northwards from southern Europe that is almost of annual occurrence in very small numbers.

☐ **Hoopoe** A
Upupa epops
Rare spring and autumn visitor that exceptionally nests in southern England.

☐ **Wryneck** A
Jynx torquilla
Formerly a scarce breeder in southern England that has now colonized Scotland where a few pairs probably breed each year.

☐ **Great Spotted Woodpecker** A
Dendrocopos major
Widespread and common resident except in northernmost Scotland and in Ireland.

☐ **Lesser Spotted**
Otherwise a scarce passage migrant mainly to the south and east coasts.

☐ **Green Woodpecker** A
Picus viridis
Widespread and common resident in England, Wales and the southern half of Scotland. Unknown in Ireland.

☐ **Yellow-bellied Sapsucker** A
Sphyrapicus varius
Exceptional transatlantic vagrant that has found its way to the Isles of Scilly once.

Woodpecker A
Dendrocopos minor
Widespread resident over most of England and Wales that is easily overlooked.

☐ **Calandra Lark** A
Melanocorypha calandra
Exceptional vagrant northward from southern Europe that occurred only three times in Britain up to 1986.

☐ **Bimaculated Lark** A
Melanocorypha bimaculata
Exceptional vagrant from south-eastern Europe that occurred only three times up to 1986.

☐ **White-winged lark** A
Melanocorypha leucoptera
Exceptional vagrant from Russia that occurred only five times up to 1986, most recently in Norfolk in 1981.

☐ **Short-toed Lark** A
Calandrella brachydactyla
Scarce annual visitor from Africa and southern Eurasia in small numbers, mainly in autumn.

☐ **Lesser Short-toed Lark** A
Calandrella rufescens
Exceptionally rare visitor to western Ireland in the early part of the year. Only four records, though 42 birds were involved.

☐ **Crested Lark** A
Galerida cristata
Exceptional vagrant from across the Channel. There were 19 records up to 1986, the latest in Gwynedd in 1982.

☐ **Woodlark** A
Lullula arborea
Scarce and declining resident in southern England and East Anglia; rare elsewhere

☐ **Skylark** A
Alauda arvensis
Common and widespread resident, passage migrant and winter visitor throughout Britain and Ireland.

☐ **Shore Lark** A
Eremophila alpestris
Scarce winter visitor to the east coast that is apparently declining. Bred on at least two occasions in the 1970s.

☐ **Sand Martin** A
Riparia riparia
Widespread summer visitor to all parts of Britain and Ireland except the northern and western isles. Serious decline in 1980s due to drought in wintering zone.

☐ **Swallow** A
Hirundo rustica
Common and widespread summer visitor.

☐ **Red-rumped Swallow** A
Hirundo daurica
Rare vagrant northwards from southern Europe that is spreading northwards and has become of annual occurrence in recent years.

☐ **Cliff Swallow** A
Hirundo pyrrhonota
Exceptional transatlantic vagrant. One on the Isles of Scilly in October 1983.

☐ **House Martin** A
Delichon urbica
Common and widespread summer visitor to all parts of Britain and Ireland, except north and western Scotland.

☐ **Richard's Pipit** A
Anthus novaeseelandiae
Scarce passage migrant, mainly in autumn, to most coasts in small numbers.

☐ **Blythe's Pipit** B
Anthus godlewskii
Exceptional vagrant that has not been recorded in the past 50 years.

☐ **Tawny Pipit** A
Anthus campestris
Scarce passage migrant, mostly in autumn, to south and east coasts of England.

☐ **Olive-backed Pipit** A
Anthus hodgsoni
Rare vagrant from Russia that has been increasingly identified over the past 20 years. Now averages about three records a year.

☐ **Tree Pipit** A
Anthus trivalis
Widespread summer visitor to most of England, Wales and Scotland. Only a passage migrant to southern and eastern Ireland.

☐ **Pechora Pipit** A
Anthus gustavi
Very rare vagrant from Russia, mainly in September and October, mostly to Fair Isle. Total up to 1986 was 29.

☐ **Meadow Pipit** A
Anthus pratensis
Widespread and common resident throughout. Also common passage migrant and winter visitor.

☐ **Red-throated Pipit** A
Anthus cervinus
Rare vagrant from eastern Europe that occurs in variable numbers each year, mainly in autumn.

☐ **Rock Pipit** A
Anthus petrosus
Resident along most rocky shorelines. Also passage migrant and winter visitor.

☐ **Water Pipit** A
Anthus spinoletta
Scarce winter visitor from the Continent, most often found inland on watercress beds.

☐ **American Pipit** A
Anthus rubescens
Rare transatlantic vagrant that has only recently been accorded the status of a separate species.

☐ **Yellow Wagtail** A
Motacilla flava
Common and widespread summer visitor to England, the Welsh lowlands and lowland Scotland. Elsewhere, including Ireland, double passage migrant.

☐ **Citrine Wagtail** A
Motacilla citreola
Rare vagrant from Russia that occurs in small numbers most years, mostly on the east and south coasts. Expanding range westwards and males have summered.

☐ **Grey Wagtail** A
Montacilla cinerea
Resident over most of southern Britain and Ireland, and summer visitor to northern Scotland.

☐ **Pied Wagtail** A
Montacilla alba
Common and widespread resident. White Wagtail *M. a. alba* is a regular double passage migrant.

☐ **Waxwing** A
Bombycilla garrulus
Irregular autumn and winter visitor in variable numbers, mainly to eastern Britain. Irrupts from Scandiavia.

☐ **Dipper** A
Cinclus cinclus
Resident along suitable streams in all hilly districts of the north and west. Few winter vagrants from the Continent each year.

☐ **Wren** A
Troglodytes troglodytes
Common and widespread resident.

☐ **Brown Thrasher** A
Toxostoma rufum
Exceptional transatlantic vagrant. One in Dorset in 1966–67.

☐ **Grey Catbird** A
Dunetella carolinensis
Exceptional transatlantic vagrant. One on Co. Cork in November 1986.

☐ **Dunnock** A
Prunella modularis
Common and widespread throughout Britain and Ireland.

☐ **Alpine Accentor** A
Prunella collaris
Very rare vagrant from mountains of south and central Europe that has occurred on 35 occasions, but which remains as irregular as ever. Last records were in Dorset and Norfolk in 1978.

☐ **Rufous Bush Robin** A
Cercotrichas galactotes
Exceptionally rare vagrant northwards from the Mediterranean that has occurred on 11 occasions, most recently in Devon in 1980.

☐ **Robin** A
Erithacus rubecula
Common and widespread resident and winter visitor.

☐ **Thrush Nightingale** A
Luscinia luscinia
Rare vagrant from eastern
Europe, with most birds trapped
for ringing in spring and autumn.

☐ **Nightingale** A
Luscinia megarhynchos
Widespread summer visitor to
southern, central and eastern
England.

☐ **Siberian Rubythroat** A
Luscinia calliope
Exceptionally rare vagrant from
north-eastern Europe that
occurred on eight occasions up to
1986, most recently in
Lincolnshire in 1978.

☐ **Bluethroat** A
Luscinia svecica
Scarce double passage migrant,
but mainly in autumn on the east
coast. A nest and eggs were found
in 1968, and a pair bred
successfully in 1985. Both were in
northern Scotland.

☐ **Red-flanked Bluetail** A
Tarsiger cyanurus
Exceptionally rare vagrant from
Asia that occurred on ten
occasions up to 1986, most
recently on Fair Isle in 1984.

☐ **White-throated Robin** A
Irania gutturalis
Exceptional vagrant from Asia
Minor. One on the Isle of Man in
1983.

☐ **Black Redstart** A
Phoenicurus ochruros
Localized summer visitor to south,
central and eastern England, but a
more widespread double passage
migrant.

☐ **Redstart** A
Phoenicurus phoenicurus
Widespread summer visitor,
though highly localized in Ireland,
and double passage migrant.

☐ **Whinchat** A
Saxicola rubetra
Widespread summer visitor and
double passage migrant in good
numbers.

☐ **Stonechat** A
Saxicola torquata
Widespread resident, particularly
in the west, passage migrant and
scarce winter visitor.

☐ **Isabelline Wheatear** A
Oenanthe isabellina
Exceptionally rare vagrant from
south-eastern Europe that
occurred only four times up to
1986, the most recent was in
Northumberland in 1980.

☐ **Wheatear** A
Oenanthe oenanthe
Common and widespread summer
visitor to hilly and coastal
districts. Elsewhere, regular
double passage migrant.

☐ **Pied Wheatear** A
Oenanthe pleschanka
Exceptionally rare vagrant from
south-east Europe that occurred
ten times up to 1986, almost all in
autumn.

☐ **Black-eared Wheatear** A
Oenanthe hispanica
Rare vagrant from southern
Europe that occurred 39 times up
to 1986, mostly in spring.

☐ **Desert Wheatear** A
Oenanthe deserti
Very rare vagrant that occurred
only 24 times up to 1986, mostly in
autumn.

☐ **White-crowned Black
Wheatear** A
Oenanthe leucopyga
Exceptionally rare vagrant from
North Africa. One record in
Suffolk in June 1982.

☐ **Black Wheatear** A
Oenanthe leucura
Exceptionally rare vagrant from

southern Europe that occurred
only six times up to 1986.

☐ **Rock Thrush** A
Monticola saxatilis
Rare vagrant northwards from the
Mediterranean that occurred only
21 times up to 1986, most recently
in Gwynedd in that year.

☐ **White's Thrush** A
Zoothera dauma
Rare vagrant from Siberia that
has occurred on 41 occasions
mainly in autumn, most recently
in Shetland in 1985.

☐ **Siberian Thrush** A
Zoothera sibirica
Exceptional vagrant, mainly in
autumn, from Siberia. Only five
have been recorded, the most
recent in Co. Cork in 1985.

☐ **Hermit Thrush** A
Catharus guttatus
Exceptionally rare transatlantic
vagrant that occurred only twice
up to 1986. The first was on Fair
Isle in 1975, the second on Scilly in
1984.

☐ **Swainson's Thrush** A
Catharus ustulatus
Exceptional transatlantic vagrant
that occurred only ten times up to
1986; all in autumn, four in Scilly.

☐ **Grey-cheeked Thrush** A
Catharus minimus
Exceptionally rare transatlantic
vagrant that also breeds in
eastern Siberia. It was recorded on
30 occasions up to 1986, ten of
which were in that year, the vast
majority in October in Scilly.

☐ **Veery** A
Catharus fuscescens
Exceptional transatlantic vagrant
that occurred once up to 1986.

☐ **Ring Ousel** A
Turdus torquatus
Summer visitor to all hilly
districts of the north and west,

though nowhere common.
Otherwise scarce passage migrant.

☐ **Blackbird** A
Turdus merula
Abundant widespread resident
and winter visitor.

☐ **Eye-browed Thrush** A
Turdus obscurus
Exceptional vagrant westwards
from Siberia that occurred only
eight times up to 1986, most
recently in Orkney and Scilly in
the autumn of 1984.

☐ **Dusky Thrush** A
Turdus naumanni
Exceptionally rare vagrant from
Siberia that occurred on only
seven occasions up to 1986, most
recently in Cornwall in 1983.

☐ **Black-throated (Red-
throated) Thrush** A
Turdus ruficollis
Exceptional Asian vagrant that
occurred only 14 times up to 1986,
most recently in 1983 in Greater
Manchester.

☐ **Fieldfare** A
Turdus pilaris
Common and widespread winter
visitor that has bred most years
since 1967, though numbers were
fewer in 1985 than in the mid
1970s.

☐ **Song Thrush** A
Turdus philomelos
Common and widespread resident
and winter visitor.

☐ **Redwing** A
Turdus iliacus
Common and widespread winter
visitor that has bred in northern
Scotland since the mid 1950s and
which gradually increased in
numbers until 1984.

☐ **Mistle Thrush** A
Turdus viscivorus
Widespread and common resident
throughout Britain and Ireland.

☐ **American Robin** A
Turdus migratorius
Rare transatlantic vagrant that occurred 29 times up to 1986, mostly in autumn and winter. The most recent record was of one in Surrey that was probably killed by a Magpie.

☐ **Cetti's Warbler** A
Cettia cetti
A recent colonizing and resident warbler that suffered during the bitter winters of the mid 1980s, but which maintains a good population in south and south-west England.

☐ **Fan-tailed Warbler** A
Cisticola juncidis
Exceptionally rare vagrant from continental Europe that occurred only four times between 1962 and 1986.

☐ **Pallas's Grasshopper Warbler** A
Locustella certhiola
Exceptionally rare vagrant from Siberia in autumn, mainly to Fair Isle, that occurred nine times up to 1986. The last was at that island in 1986.

☐ **Lanceolated Warbler** A
Locustella lanceolata
Exceptionally rare autumn vagrant from Russia mainly to Fair Isle that occured 37 times up to 1986.

☐ **Grasshopper Warbler** A
Locustella naevia
Widespread summer visitor throughout Britain and Ireland, except to the higher hills.

☐ **River Warbler** A
Locustella fluviatilis
Exceptional vagrant from eastern Europe that occurred only ten times up to 1986. The most recent were on Fair Isle in 1984, the same year that a male was seen singing in East Anglia. The species is spreading westwards through the Continent.

☐ **Savi's Warbler** A
Locustella luscinioides
Summer visitor in decreasing numbers to south and east England after successful colonization in the 1960s.

☐ **Moustached Warbler** A
Acrocephalus melanopogon
Exceptional vagrant from southern Europe that occurred only ten times up to 1986, including breeding in Cambridgeshire in 1946.

☐ **Aquatic Warbler** A
Acrocephalus paludicola
Regular, but scarce, autumn passage migrant along the south coast of England. Most trapped in south Devon.

☐ **Sedge Warbler** A
Acrocephalus schoenobaenus
Widespread and common summer visitor, except to the hilly districts.

☐ **Paddyfield Warbler** A
Acrocephalus agricola
Exceptional vagrant from Russia westwards that occurred on 13 occasions up to 1986, mostly in September on Fair Isle.

☐ **Blyth's Reed Warbler** A
Acrocephalus dumetorum
Exceptional vagrant from eastern Europe that had occurred 13 times until 1986, most recently on Humberside in 1984.

☐ **Marsh Warbler** A
Acrocephalus palustris
Highly localized summer visitor mainly to the west Midlands that is apparently declining at its main Worcestershire stronghold. Scarce passage migrant in south and eastern England.

☐ **Reed Warbler** A
Acrocephalus scirpaceus
Widespread and common summer visitor, mainly to southern half of England.

☐ **Great Reed Warbler** A
Acrocephalus arundinaceus
Scarce vagrant northwards from the Continent that appears most years in southern England, usually in spring, in small numbers.

☐ **Thick-billed Warbler** A
Acrocephalus aedon
Exceptional vagrant from Asia that was recorded twice up to 1986.

☐ **Olivaceous Warbler** A
Hippolais pallida
Exceptionally rare vagrant from the south and east that occurred only 14 times up to 1986, most recently in Scilly in 1985.

☐ **Booted Warbler** A
Hippolais caligata
Rare vagrant from Russia that is now of almost annual occurrence, but which was recorded only 22 times up to 1986.

☐ **Icterine Warbler** A
Hippolais icterina
Scarce passage migrant, mainly to the south and east coasts in autumn.

☐ **Melodious Warbler** A
Hippolais polyglotta
Scarce passage migrant, mainly to the south and west coasts in autumn.

☐ **Marmora's Warbler** A
Sylvia sarda
Exceptional vagrant from Mediterranean. A male was in song through the summer of 1982 on Midhope Moor, Yorkshire. This is the only record.

☐ **Dartford Warbler** A
Sylvia undata
Rare resident in southern England that suffers severe population crashes during hard winters. Some 300–400 pairs probably breed in good years.

☐ **Spectacled Warbler** A
Sylvia conspicillata
Exceptionally rare vagrant northwards from the Mediterranean that occurred only three times up to 1986, the last being on Fair Isle in 1979.

☐ **Subalpine Warbler** A
Sylvia cantillans
Rare vagrant northwards from the Mediterranean that occurs annually in small numbers, usually in spring.

☐ **Sardinian Warbler** A
Sylvia melanocephala
Extremely rare vagrant from southern Europe that occurred on 14 occasion up to 1986, the last in Lincolnshire in that year.

☐ **Ruppell's Warbler** A
Sylvia rueppelli
Exceptionally rare vagrant from the eastern Mediterranean that occurred twice up to 1986. The first was in Shetland in 1977, the second on Lundy in 1979.

☐ **Desert Warbler** A
Sylvia nana
Exceptionally rare vagrant from Asia that occurred only on four occasions up to 1986. The last was on Merseyside in 1979.

☐ **Orphean Warbler** A
Sylvia hortensis
Exceptionally rare vagrant from southern Europe that occurred five times up to 1986. The most recent was in Aberdeen in 1982.

☐ **Barred Warbler** A
Sylvia nisoria
Scarce passage migrant, mainly to the east coast in autumn.

☐ **Lesser Whitethroat** A
Sylvia curruca
Widespread summer visitor to most of England. Regular passage migrant elsewhere.

☐ **Whitethroat** A
Sylvia communis
Widespread summer visitor to whole of Britain and Ireland, except the highest hills of the north. Double passage migrant. Decline in numbers due to drought in wintering zone.

☐ **Garden Warbler** A
Sylvia borin
Widespread summer visitor except to Scottish Highlands and much of Ireland.

☐ **Blackcap** A
Sylvia atricapilla
Widespread and common summer visitor to Britain and Ireland and absent only from western Ireland and Scottish hills and extreme north. Common passage migrant that winters in small numbers in southern England and Ireland.

☐ **Green Warbler** A
Phylloscopus nitidus
Exceptional vagrant from the Middle East that was first recorded on Scilly in 1983. This remains the only record.

☐ **Greenish Warbler** A
Phylloscopus trochiloides
Rare, but regular, vagrant mostly in late August and mainly to the east coast. Usually four or five records each year.

☐ **Arctic Warbler** A
Phylloscopus borealis
Rare vagrant, mostly in September, that averages about six records each year.

☐ **Pallas's Warbler** A
Phylloscopus proregulus
Rare vagrant from Asia that is of annual occurrence in late October

– early November. Numbers vary from a handful up to 20 each year, but there was a record 116 in 1982.

☐ **Yellow-browed Warbler** A
Phylloscopus inornatus
Scarce autumn visitor from Asia, mainly to the east coast, but also to the south and south-west.

☐ **Radde's Warbler** A
Phylloscopus schwarzi
Rare autumn vagrant from Asia, mainly to south and east England. Occurred 51 times up to 1986, averaging two or three a season in recent years.

☐ **Dusky Warbler** A
Phylloscopus fuscatus
Rare autumn vagrant from Asia, mainly to south and east coasts. Occurred 51 times up to 1986, with about three new records a year.

☐ **Bonelli's Warbler** A
Phylloscopus bonelli
Rare vagrant from southern Europe, mainly in autumn, that occurred on almost a hundred occasions up to 1986.

☐ **Wood Warbler** A
Phylloscopus sibilatrix
Widespread summer visitor that is common in the west of Britain, but all but absent from Ireland. Scarce passage migrant where it does not breed.

☐ **Chiffchaff** A
Phylloscopus collybita
Common and widespread summer visitor that is absent from the northern hills. Passage migrant that winters in small numbers in the south-west.

☐ **Willow Warbler** A
Phylloscopus trochilus
Abundant summer visitor throughout Britain and Ireland. Common double passage migrant.

☐ **Goldcrest** A
Regulus regulus
Widespread resident throughout and regular winter visitor from the Continent.

☐ **Firecrest** A
Regulus ignicapillus
Regular passage migrant, particularly in autumn, that winters in the south-west and breeds in small (but variable) numbers each year in southern England.

☐ **Spotted Flycatcher** A
Muscicapa striata
Widespread and common summer visitor and regular double passage migrant.

☐ **Red-breasted Flycatcher** A
Ficedula parva
Scarce passage migrant from eastern Europe, mainly in autumn.

☐ **Collared Flycatcher** A
Ficedula albicollis
Extremely rare vagrant from the Continent that occurred on 15 occasions up to 1986, most recently in Suffolk and Yorkshire in 1985. Most records are of males in spring.

☐ **Pied Flycatcher** A
Ficedula hypoleuca
Summer visitor to western hilly districts, but not Ireland. Passage migrant elsewhere, often quite common along the east coast in autumn.

☐ **Bearded Tit** A
Panurus biarmicus
Highly localized resident in reed beds of the south and east of England. Usually irrupts across southern England in autumn.

☐ **Long-tailed Tit** A
Aegithalos caudatus
Widespread and common resident throughout Britain and Ireland.

☐ **Marsh Tit** A
Parus palustris
Common resident throughout England, Wales and south-eastern Scotland.

☐ **Willow Tit** A
Parus montanus
Resident in England, Wales and southern Scotland, but somewhat local in distribution.

☐ **Crested Tit** A
Parus cristatus
Resident in the pine forests of the central Scottish Highlands. Unknown elsewhere.

☐ **Coal Tit** A
Parus ater
Common resident throughout Britain and Ireland.

☐ **Blue Tit** A
Parus caeruleus
Common resident throughout Britain and Ireland.

☐ **Great Tit** A
Parus major
Common resident throughout Britain and Ireland.

☐ **Nuthatch** A
Sitta europaea
Widespread resident in England and Wales, becoming scarcer to the north.

☐ **Wallcreeper** A
Tichodroma muraria
Extremely rare vagrant from high continental mountains that is mostly seen on south coast cliffs and which has overwintered. The total up to 1986 was ten, the most recent on the Isle of Wight in 1985.

☐ **Treecreeper** A
Certhia familiaris
Widespread resident throughout Britain and Ireland.

☐ **Short-toed Treecreeper** A
Certhia brachydactyla
Extremely rare vagrant from the Continent that occurred on seven

occasions up to 1986. The most recent were two in Kent in 1978.

☐ **Penduline Tit** A

Remiz pendulinus

Extremely rare vagrant that is expanding its range northwards on the Continent and which occurred 11 times up to 1986. The most recent was in Kent in 1984.

☐ **Golden Oriole** A

Oriolus oriolus

Rare summer visitor, mainly to East Anglia, with up to 15 pairs breeding. Otherwise scarce passage migrant.

☐ **Isabelline Shrike** A

Lanius isabellinus

Extremely rare vagrant from Asia that occurred 20 times up to 1986, mostly in autumn. The most recent were in Dorset and Gwynedd in 1985.

☐ **Red-backed Shrike** A

Lanius collurio

A fast declining summer visitor to south and east England, with a 1985 population of 6–11 pairs. Otherwise only a scarce passage migrant.

☐ **Cretzschmar's Bunting** A

Emberiza coesia

Exceptional vagrant from south-western Europe that was recorded only twice up to 1986. Both were in June on Fair Isle, in 1967 and 1979.

☐ **Yellow-browed Bunting** A

Emberiza chrysophris

Exceptionally rare vagrant from Asia that was recorded only once, on Fair Isle in 1980.

☐ **Rustic Bunting** A

Emberiza rustica

Extremely rare migrant from Scandinavia, mainly in autumn, that is recorded in single figures each year.

☐ **Little Bunting** A

Emberiza pusilla

Regular, but scarce, passage migrant mainly in October with about twenty records each year. Breeds as near as Scandinavia.

☐ **Yellow-breasted Bunting** A

Emberiza aureola

Scarce passage migrant, mainly in autumn, to the northern isles and predominantly to Fair Isle where a handful occur each year.

☐ **Reed Bunting** A

Emberiza schoeniclus

Widespread and common resident throughout Britain and Ireland.

☐ **Pallas's Reed Bunting** A

Emberiza pallasi

Exceptional vagrant from Siberia that occurred twice up to 1986. Both were on Fair Isle in autumn, in 1976 and 1981.

☐ **Black-headed Bunting** A

Emberiza melanocephala

Rare vagrant from south-western Europe that occurred 69 times up to 1986. Most have been males and may have been escapees from avaries.

☐ **Corn Bunting** A

Milaria calandra

Widespread, but localized, resident that is absent from many parts of the north and west.

☐ **Rose-breasted Grosbeak** A

Pheucticus ludovicianus

Extremely rare transatlantic vagrant, almost always in October, that occurred 18 times up to 1986. The latest was on Scilly in 1986.

☐ **Bobolink** A

Dolichonyx oryzivorus

Rare vagrant from North America that was recorded a total of 13 times up to 1986, when the latest occurred on Fair Isle in September.

☐ **Northern Oriole** A

Icterus galbula

Extremely rare transatlantic vagrant that was recorded 14 times up to 1986, most recently on Scilly in 1983.

☐ **Lesser Grey Shrike** A

Lanius minor

Decidedly rare, mainly autumn vagrant from southern Europe with three or four records a year.

☐ **Great Grey Shrike** A

Lanius excubitor

Scarce winter visitor from the Continent, mainly to the eastern side of Britain. Some individuals turn up at the same location year after year.

☐ **Woodchat Shrike** A

Lanius senator

Regular, but rare, migrant mainly in May in variable numbers.

☐ **Jay** A

Garrulus glandarius

Widespread resident that is absent only from northern Scotland, the hills and western Ireland.

☐ **Magpie** A

Pica pica

Resident throughout Britain and Ireland, though sporadically distributed in Scotland.

☐ **Nutcracker** A

Nucifraga caryocatactes

Rare winter vagrant that occasionally irrupts from its continental forest home. A total of 401 has been recorded of which 315 were in 1968. The most recent were three in 1985.

☐ **Chough** A

Pyrrhocorax pyrrhocorax

Highly localized resident along the coasts of Wales and inland in slate quarries, at Islay and along the west coast of Ireland.

☐ **Jackdaw** A

Corvus monedula

Common resident throughout Britain and Ireland.

☐ **Rook** A

Corvus frugilegus

Common resident throughout Britain and Ireland, except the Scottish mountains.

☐ **Carrion Crow** A

Corvus corone

Common resident throughout the British Isles except in Isle of Man, north-west Scotland and Ireland, where the subspecies, the Hooded Crow *C. c. cornix* replaces it. The two races interbreed readily and there is a narrow overlap zone where hybrids are common.

☐ **Raven** A

Corvus corax

Resident in the hilly districts of the north and west and along adjacent coasts.

☐ **Starling** A

Sturnus vulgaris

Common and widespread resident throughout Britain and Ireland and an abundant winter visitor.

☐ **Rose-coloured Starling** A

Sturnus roseus

Rare vagrant from eastern Europe that occurs about seven or eight times a year on average, mostly in summer and autumn.

☐ **House Sparrow** A

Passer domesticus

Common and widespread resident in all areas except the Scottish Mountains.

☐ **Spanish Sparrow** A

Passer hispaniolensis

Extremely rare vagrant from the Mediterranean that occurred on only three occasions until 1986. The most recent was in Scilly in 1977.

☐ **Tree Sparrow** A

Passer montanus

Widespread resident in all lowland districts of England, Scotland and Wales. Rather localized around the coasts in Ireland.

☐ **Rock Sparrow** A

Petronia petronia

Exceptional vagrant from southern Europe. One was seen in Norfolk in 1981.

☐ **Philadelphia Vireo** A

Vireo philadelphia

Exceptional transatlantic vagrant that was first recorded in 1985 in Co. Cork. This is the only record.

☐ **Red-eyed Vireo** A

Vireo olivaceus

Rare transatlantic vagrant that is now more or less annually recorded in Scilly which boasted 15 of the 36 recorded by 1986.

☐ **Chaffinch** A

Fringilla coelebs

Common resident throughout Britain and Ireland and abundant winter visitor.

☐ **Brambling** A

Fringilla montifringilla

Widespread winter visitor from northern Europe that has started to breed in Scotland in small numbers during the past decade.

☐ **Serin** A

Serinus serinus

Scarce migrant and summer visitor to southern England that has bred in tiny numbers for several years, mostly in Devon.

☐ **Citril Finch** B

Serinus citrinella

Exceptional vagrant that has not been recorded in the past 50 years.

☐ **Greenfinch** A

Carduelis chloris

Common and widespread resident, except in the Scottish mountains.

☐ **Goldfinch** A

Carduelis carduelis

Common and widespread resident as far north as the Scottish lowlands. Further north it is a summer visitor or migrant.

☐ **Siskin** A

Carduelis spinus

Resident in the hilly districts of the north and west and at a few places in lowland England. Elsewhere, a widespread winter visitor.

☐ **Linnet** A

Carduelis cannabina

Common resident everywhere, except for northernmost Scotland, also a winter visitor.

☐ **Twite** A

Carduelis flavirostris

Resident in north-western Scotland, in the Pennines and along the coasts of north-western Ireland. Winter visitor, mainly to the east coast.

☐ **Redpoll** A

Carduelis flammea

Widespread resident except in south-central England, but a common winter visitor throughout Britain and Ireland.

☐ **Arctic Redpoll** A

Carduelis hornemanni

Rare vagrant from northern Europe in variable numbers that occurs annually, mainly in autumn in the north and east. Exceptionally, there were 25 on Fair Isle in 1984.

☐ **Two-barred Crossbill** A

Loxia leucoptera

Rare vagrant from northern Europe that occurs erratically during Common Crossbill irruptions, mainy in the north and east in autumn. There were 66 records up to 1986.

☐ **Common Crossbill** A

Loxia curvirostra

Patchily distributed in England and southern Scotland as a breeding resident. More widespread following periodic irruptions from the Continent.

☐ **Scottish Crossbill** A

Loxia scotica

Resident in north-central Scottish Highlands.

☐ **Parrot Crossbill** A

Loxia pytyopsittacus

Rare vagrant from northern Europe, that occurs in small numbers along with irrupting Common Crossbills. A pair or two bred in East Anglia in 1983–1986.

☐ **Trumpeter Finch** A

Bucanetes githagineus

Exceptionally rare vagrant from North Africa that was recorded only five times up to 1986. Most recent was in Essex in 1985.

☐ **Scarlet Rosefinch** A

Carpodacus erythrinus

Scarce autumn migrant, mainly to the north, that regularly summers in Scotland in small numbers, but which has been proved to breed only in 1982.

☐ **Pine Grosbeak** A

Pinicola enucleator

Extremely rare vagrant from nothern Europe that occurred only nine times up to 1986.

☐ **Bullfinch** A

Pyrrhula pyrrhula

Widespread resident throughout Britain and Ireland, except for the bleakest of moors and hills.

☐ **Hawfinch** A

Coccothraustes coccothrautes

Patchily distributed resident in England, Wales and southern Scotland. Nowhere common.

☐ **Evening Grosbeak** A

Hesperiphona vespertina

Exceptional transatlantic vagrant that has been recorded twice: first on St Kilda in 1969; second in Highland in 1980. The possibility of escapees cannot be excluded.

☐ **Black-and-white Warbler** A

Mniotilta varia

Exceptional transatlantic vagrant that occurred only ten times until 1986, most recently in Norfolk in 1985.

☐ **Tennessee Warbler** A

Vermivora peregrina

Exceptional transatlantic vagrant that occurred only three times up to 1986, all in the northern isles. The most recent was in Orkney in 1982.

☐ **Northern Parula** A

Parula americana

Exceptional transatlantic vagrant that occurred only ten times up to 1986. The most recent were three in October 1985 in Scilly, Cornwall and Dorset.

☐ **Yellow Warbler** A

Dendroica petechia

Exceptional transatlantic vagrant that has occurred only once, in Gwynedd in 1984.

☐ **Cape May Warbler** A

Dendroica tigrina

Exceptional transatlantic vagrant that has been found only once in Strathclyde in 1978.

☐ **Magnolia Warbler** A

Dendroica magnolia

Exceptional transatlantic vagrant that was found on the Scillys in 1981.

☐ **Yellow-rumped Warbler** A

Dendroica coronata

Exceptional transatlantic vagrant that was recorded 15 times up to 1986, most recently in 1985 when four were recorded. These included two on Scilly, one on the Calf of Man and one in Co. Cork.

☐ **Blackpoll Warbler** A
Dendroica striata
Extremely rare transatlantic vagrant that occurred 24 times up to 1986, mostly to the south-west. Most recent were on Shetland and Co. Wexford in 1985.

☐ **American Redstart** A
Setophaga ruticilla
Exceptional transatlantic vagrant that occurred on only six occasions up to 1986, most recently in Co. Cork in 1985.

☐ **Ovenbird** A
Seiurus aurocapillus
Exceptionally rare transatlantic vagrant that occurred only three times up to 1986. The most recent was found dead in south Devon in 1985.

☐ **Northern Waterthrush** A
Seiurus noveboracensis
Exceptional transatlantic vagrant to the south-west in late September that occurred four times until 1986, most recently in Co. Cork in 1983.

☐ **Common Yellowthroat** A
Geothlypis trichas
Exceptionally rare transatlantic vagrant that was recorded only three times up to 1986, most recently in spring in Shetland and Scilly in autumn, both in 1984.

☐ **Hooded Warbler** A
Wilsonia citrina
Exceptional transatlantic vagrant that has reached here only once, in Scilly in September.

☐ **Summer Tanager** A
Piranga rubra
Exceptional transatlantic vagrant that was recorded once, in Gwynedd in September, up to 1986.

☐ **Scarlet Tanager** A
Piranga olivcea
Exceptional transatlantic vagrant that occurred seven times up to 1986, most recently in Co. Cork in 1985.

☐ **Rufous-sided Towhee** A
Pipilo erythrophthalmus
Exceptional transatlantic vagrant that occurred only once, in Devon in June, up to 1986.

☐ **Savannah Sparrow** A
Ammodramus sandwichensis
Exceptional transatlantic vagrant that was added to the List in 1982 when one appeared in Dorset. It has not been recorded since.

☐ **Fox Sparrow** A
Zonotrichia iliaca
Exceptional transatlantic vagrant that was recorded only once up to 1986, in Co. Down in June.

☐ **Song Sparrow** A
Zonotrichia melodia
Exceptional transatlantic vagrant that was recorded just five times up to 1986, all in spring. The most recent was in Shetland in 1979.

☐ **White-crowned Sparrow** A
Zonotrichia leucophrys
Exceptional transatlantic vagrant that occurred only twice until 1986. Both were in spring 1977 at Humberside and Fair Isle.

☐ **White-throated Sparrow** A
Zonotrichia albicollis
Extremely rare transatlantic vagrant that occurred on 14 occasions up to 1986, most recently one that overwintered in Belfast in 1984–1985.

☐ **Slate-coloured Junco** A
Junco hyemalis
Exceptional transatlantic vagrant that was recorded just 12 times up to 1986. Most recent were three records in May 1983 in Cornwall, Dorset and Somerset.

☐ **Lapland Bunting** A
Calcarius lapponicus
Scarce winter visitor to the east coast that may form small flocks at favoured locations. Has bred erratically since 1977 in the Scottish Highlands.

☐ **Snow Bunting** A
Plectrophenax nivalis
Winter visitor to the east coasts of Britain and Ireland and passage migrant in small numbers to other coasts. Sometimes forms large flocks in favoured areas. Breeds in small numbers every year on highest Scottish mountains.

☐ **Pine Bunting** A
Emberiza leucocephalos
Extremely rare vagrant from Siberia that occurred only nine times up to 1986, most recently in Scilly and North Yorkshire in 1985, both in spring.

☐ **Yellowhammer** A
Emberiza citrinella
Widespread and common resident throughout Britain and Ireland, except to the higher hills of Scotland.

☐ **Cirl Bunting** A
Emberiza cirlus
Scarce and declining resident in southern England that has its stronghold in south Devon and a total population of no more than 60 pairs.

☐ **Rock Bunting** A
Emberiza cia
Exceptional vagrant from southern Europe that occurred only five times up to 1986.

☐ **Ortolan Bunting** A
Emberiza hortulana
Scarce passage migrant, mainly in autumn to the east coast and elsewhere in small numbers.

Category D
White Pelican
Pelicanus onocrotalus
Greater Flamingo
Phoenicopterus ruber
Wood Duck
Aix sponsa
Borrow's Goldeneye
Bucephala islandica
Bald Eagle
Haliaeetus leucocephalus
Saker
Falco cherrug
Bobwhite
Colinus virginianus
Northern Flicker
Colaptes auratus
Blue Rock Thrush
Monticola solitarius
Snow Finch
Montifringilla nivalis
Palm Warbler
Dendroica palmorum
Lark Sparrow
Chondestes grammacus
Chestnut Bunting
Emberiza rutila
Red-headed Bunting
Emberiza bruniceps
Blue Grosbeak
Guiraca caerulea
Indigo Bunting
Passerina cyanea
Painted Bunting
Passerina ciris

Useful Addresses and Societies

NATIONAL ORGANISATIONS

BIRD OBSERVATORIES COUNCIL Secretary: Sean McMinn, Dungeness Bird Observatory, Dungeness, Romney Marsh, Kent TN29 9NA

BIRDS OF PREY CONSERVATION & FALCONRY CENTRE (1966) Mr & Mrs J. Parry-Jones, Newent, Glos GL18 1JJ (0531) 820286

BRITISH BIRDS Fountains, Park Lane, Blunham, Bedford, MK44 3NJ

BRITISH BIRDS RARITIES COMMITTEE Bag End, Churchtown, Towednack, Cornwall TR26 3AZ

BRITISH LIBRARY OF WILDLIFE SOUNDS Curator: Ron Kettle, National Sound Archive, 29 Exhibition Road, London SW7 2AS

BRITISH ORNITHOLOGISTS' UNION c/o British Museum (Natural History), Sub-department of Ornithology, Tring, Herts HP23 6AP

BRITISH TRUST FOR ORNITHOLOGY Beech Grove, Station Roads, Tring, Herts HP23 5NR (044 282) 3461

COUNTRYSIDE COMMISSION John Dower House, Crescent Place, Cheltenham, Glos GL50 3RA (0242) 521381

COUNTRYSIDE COMMISSION FOR SCOTLAND Battleby, Redgorton, Perth PH1 3EW (0738) 27921

EDWARD GREY INSTITUTE OF FIELD ORNITHOLOGY Department of Zoology, South Parks Road, Oxford OX1 3PS (0865) 271275

FAUNA AND FLORA PRESERVATION SOCIETY 8/12 Camden High Street, London NW1 0JH (01) 387 9656

FIELD STUDIES COUNCIL Preston Montford, Montford Bridge, Shrewsbury SY4 1HW (0743) 850674

FORESTRY COMMISSION 231 Corstorphine Road, Edinburgh EH12 7AT (031) 334 0303

GAME CONSERVANCY TRUST Burgate Manor, Fordingbridge, Hampshire SP6 1EF (0425) 52381

HAWK SOCIETY c/o Bird of Prey Section, Zoological Society of London, Regent's Park, London NW1 4RY

INSTITUTE OF TERRESTRIAL ECOLOGY (South): Monks Wood Experimental Station, Abbots Ripton, Huntingdon PE17 2LS (048 73) 381/8 (North): Edinburgh Research Station, Penicuick, Midlothian EH26 0QB (031) 445 4343/6

INTERNATIONAL COUNCIL FOR BIRD PRESERVATION: BRITISH SECTION c/o Fauna & Flora Preservation Society, 8–12 Camden High Street, London NW1 0JH (01) 387 9656

IRISH RARE BIRDS COMMITTEE Ballykenneally, Ballymacoda, Co. Cork

IRISH WILDBIRD CONSERVANCY Southview, Church Road, Greystones, Co. Wicklow. Dublin (01) 875759

NATIONAL TRUST 36 Queen Anne's Gate, London SW1H 9AS (01) 222 9251

NATIONAL TRUST FOR SCOTLAND Charlotte Square, Edinburgh EH2 4DU (031) 226 5922

NATURE CONSERVANCY COUNCIL Northminster House, Peterborough PE1 1UA (0733) 40345
Regional Offices: England
East Anglia Region: 60 Bracondale, Norwich, Norfolk NR1 2BE (0603) 620558
East Midlands Region: Northminster House, Peterborough, PE1 1UA (0733) 40345
North East Region: Archbold House, Archbold Terrace, Newcastle-upon-Tyne NE2 1EG (091) 281 6316
North West Region: Blackwell, Bowness-on-Windermere, Cumbria LA23 3JR (096 62) 5286
South Region: Foxhold House, Thornfold Road, Crookham Common, Newbury, Berkshire RG15 8EL. Headley (063 523) 429/439/533
South East Region: Zealds, Church Street, Wye, Ashford, Kent TN25 5BW (0233) 812525
South West Region: Roughmoor, Bishop's Hull, Taunton, Somerset TA1 5AA (0823) 83211
West Midlands Region: Attingham Park, Shrewsbury, Shropshire SY4 4TW. Upton Magna (074 377) 611

Regional Offices: Scotland
Headquarters for Scotland: 12 Hope Terrace, Edinburgh EH9 2AS (031) 447 4784
North East Region: Wynne-Edwards House, 17 Rubislaw Terrace, Aberdeen AB1 1XE (0224) 642863
North West Region: Fraser Darling House, 9 Culduthel Road, Inverness IV2 4AG (0463) 239431
South East Region: 12 Hope Terrace, Edinburgh EH9 2AS (031) 447 4784
South West Region: The Castle, Balloch Castle Country Park, Dumbartonshire G83 8LX. Alexandria (0389) 58511
Regional Offices: Wales
Headquarters for Wales: Plas Penrhos, Penrhos Road, Bangor, Gwynedd LL57 2LQ (0248) 370444
Dyfed-Powys Region: Plas Gogerddan, Aberystwyth, Dyfed SY23 3EB (0970) 828551
North Region: Plas Penrhos, Penrhos Road, Bangor, Gwynedd LL57 2LQ (0248) 370444
South Region: 44 The Parade, Roath, Cardiff CF2 3UH (0222) 485111

NORTHERN IRELAND BIRD RECORDS COMMITTEE 22 Marlborough Drive, Carrickfergus, Co. Antrim, Northern Ireland

ROYAL SOCIETY FOR NATURE CONSERVATION The Green, Nettleham, Lincoln LN2 2NR (0522) 752326

ROYAL SOCIETY FOR THE PROTECTION OF BIRDS The Lodge, Sandy, Beds SG19 2DL (0767) 80551

RSPB Scotland, 17 Regent Terrace, Edinburgh EH7 5BN (031) 556 5624/9042
RSPB Northern Ireland, Belvoir Park Forest, Belfast BT8 4QT (0232) 692547
RSPB Wales, Bryn Aderyn, Newtown, Powys SY16 2AB (0686) 26678
RSPB North England, E Floor, Milburn House, Dean St, Newcastle-upon-Tyne NE1 1LE (091) 232 4148
RSPB North West, Imperial House, Imperial Arcade, Huddersfield, West Yorkshire HD1 2BR (0484) 536331/517558
RSPB Midlands, 44 Friar Street, Droitwich, Worcs WR9 8ED (0905) 770581
RSPB East Anglia, Aldwych House, Bethel Street, Norwich NR2 1NR (0603) 615920
RSPB East Midlands, 12 Guildhall Street, Lincoln LN1 1TT (0522) 35596
RSPB South East, 8 Church Street, Shoreham, West Sussex BN4 5DQ (0273) 463642
RSPB South West, 10 Richmond Road, Exeter EX4 4JA (0392) 32691

SCOTTISH BIRDS RECORDS COMMITTEE Tyrol, Leswalt High Road, Stranraer, Wigtownshire DG9 0ED

SCOTTISH ORNITHOLOGISTS' CLUB 21 Regent Terrace, Edinburgh EH7 5BT (031) 556 6042

SCOTTISH WILDLIFE TRUST 25 Johnston Terrace, Edinburgh EH1 2NH (031) 226 4602

SEABIRD GROUP c/o NCC, Archway House, 7 Eastcheap, Letchworth, Herts SG6 3DG (0462) 675830

SOCIETY OF WILDLIFE ARTISTS c/o Federation of British Artists, 17 Carlton House Terrace, London SW1Y 5BD (01) 930 6844

WILDFOWL TRUST Slimbridge, Gloucester GL2 7BT. Cambridge (045 389) 333

WWF-UK 11–13 Ockford Road, Godalming GU7 1QU (048 68) 20551

YOUNG ORNITHOLOGISTS' CLUB The Lodge, Sandy, Beds SG19 2DL (0767) 80551

LOCAL ORGANISATIONS
England
Avon
BRISTOL NATURALISTS' SOCIETY 6 Bridle Way, Alveston, Avon (0272) 414180
BRISTOL ORNITHOLOGICAL CLUB 37 Spring Hill, Milton, Weston-super-Mare BS22 9AX (0934) 23148
AVON WILDLIFE TRUST The Old Police Station, 32 Jacobs Wells Road, Bristol BS8 1DR (0272) 268018/265490
Bedfordshire
BEDFORDSHIRE NATURAL HISTORY SOCIETY 7 Little Headlands, Putnoe, Bedford MK41 8JT (0234) 49307
BEDFORDSHIRE AND HUNTINGDONSHIRE WILDLIFE TRUST LTD (1961) Priory Country Park, Barkers Lane, Bedford MK41 9SH (0234) 64213

Berkshire
NEWBURY DISTRICT ORNITHOLOGICAL CLUB Brimstone Cottage, Little Lane, Upper Bucklebury, Nr. Reading RG7 6QX. Thatcham (0635) 60254
READING ORNITHOLOGICAL CLUB A.J. Hannan, Robin Cottage, Turners Green, Upper Bucklebury, Nr. Reading RG7 6RE (0635) 65682
BERKSHIRE, BUCKINGHAMSHIRE AND OXFORDSHIRE NATURALISTS' TRUST 3 Church Cowley Road, Rose Hill, Oxford OX4 3JR (0865) 775476
Buckinghamshire
AMERSHAM & DISTRICT ORNITHOLOGICAL SOCIETY 6 Howards Thicket, Gerrards Cross, Bucks SL9 7NX (0753) 885779
BUCKINGHAMSHIRE BIRD CLUB 319 Bath Road, Cippenham, Slough SL1 5PR. Burnham (062 86) 64386
MIDDLE THAMES NATURAL HISTORY SOCIETY 113 Holtspur Top Lane, Beaconsfield HP9 1DT (049 46) 71030
NORTH BUCKS BIRDERS 15 Jubilee Terrace, Stony Stratford MK11 1DU (0908) 565896
BERKSHIRE, BUCKINGHAMSHIRE AND OXFORDSHIRE NATURALISTS' TRUST 3 Church Cowley Road, Rose Hill, Oxford OX4 3JR (0865) 775476
Cambridgeshire
CAMBRIDGE BIRD CLUB 55 Arbury Road, Cambridge CB4 2JB (0223) 327477
CAMBRIDGESHIRE WILDLIFE TRUST 5 Fulbourn Manor, Fulbourn, Cambridge CB1 5ND (0223) 880788
Cheshire
CHESTER & DISTRICT ORNITHOLOGICAL SOCIETY 46 The Willows, Frodsham, Warrington WA6 7QS. Frodsham (0928) 31391
MID-CHESHIRE ORNITHOLOGICAL SOCIETY Wynscot, Gazebank, Norley, via Warrington WA6 8LJ. Kingsley (0928) 88475
SOUTH EAST CHESHIRE ORNITHOLOGICAL SOCIETY 40 Carlisle Street, Crewe CW2 7NX (0270) 60288
CHESHIRE CONSERVATION TRUST Marbury Country Park, Northwich CW9 6AT (0606) 781868
Cleveland
TEESMOUTH BIRD CLUB 43 Hemlington Road, Stainton, Middlesborough TS8 9AG. Stockton (0642) 595845
CLEVELAND NATURE CONSERVATION TRUST Old Town Hall, Mandale Road, Thornaby, Stockton on Tees TS17 6AW (0642) 608405
Cornwall
CORNWALL BIRDWATCHING & PRESERVATION SOCIETY 13 Tregallas Road, Mullion, Cornwall TR12 7DX (0326) 240919
CORNWALL TRUST FOR NATURE CONSERVATION Dairy Cottage, Trelissick, Feock, Truro TR3 6QL (0872) 862202
Cumbria
ARNSIDE & DISTRICT NATURAL HISTORY SOCIETY Beachwood House, Redhills Road, Arnside, Carnforth LA5 0AX (0524) 761853
GRANGE & DISTRICT NATURAL HISTORY SOCIETY 31 Proiry Lane, Grange-over-Sands LA11 7BH (044 84) 3139
KENDAL NATURAL HISTORY SOCIETY Flat A, Gandy Nook, Low Fellside, Kendal LA9 4NZ (0539) 23686
CUMBRIA TRUST FOR NATURE CONSERVATION Church Street, Ambleside LA22 0BU (0966) 32476

Derbyshire
DERBYSHIRE ORNITHOLOGICAL SOCIETY 84 Moorland View Road, Walton, Chesterfield (0246) 36090
OGSTON BIRD CLUB 28 Welbeck Drive, Chesterfield (0246) 205939
DERBYSHIRE WILDLIFE TRUST Elvaston Castle Country Park, New Derby DE7 3EP (0332) 756610

Devon
DEVON BIRDWATCHING & PRESERVATION SOCIETY 14 Parkers Way, Totnes TQ9 5UF (0803) 862991
DEVON TRUST FOR NATURE CONSERVATION 35 New Bridge Street, Exeter EX4 3AH (0392) 79244

Dorset
DORSET NATURAL HISTORY & ARCHAEOLOGICAL SOCIETY Dorset County Museum, High West Street, Dorchester DT1 1XA (0305) 62735
NEW DORSET BIRD CLUB 20 Page Close, Colehill, Wilborne BH21 2SW (0202) 886885
DORSET TRUST FOR NATURE CONSERVATION 39 Christchurch Road, Bournemouth BH1 3NS (0202) 24241

Durham
DURHAM BIRD CLUB 6 Whitesmocks Avenue, Durham DH1 4HP (091) 384 3084
DURHAM COUNTY CONSERVATION TRUST 52 Old Elvet, Durham DH1 3HN (091) 386 9797

Essex
ESSEX BIRD WATCHING AND PRESERVATION SOCIETY 41 Repton Avenue, Gidea Park, Romford RM2 5LT (0708) 43859
ESSEX NATURALISTS' TRUST Fingringhoe Wick Nature Reserve, South Green Road, Fringringhoe, Colchester CO5 7DN. Rowhedge (020 628) 678

Gloucestershire
GLOUCESTERSHIRE NATURALISTS' SOCIETY Rowan Cottage, Dog Lane, Crickley Hill, Glos GL3 4UG (0452) 862248
GLOUCESTERSHIRE TRUST FOR NATURE CONSERVATION Church House, Standish, Stonehouse, Glos GL10 3EU (045 382) 2761

Hampshire
HAMPSHIRE ORNITHOLOGICAL SOCIETY Greenbanks, Broad Road, Monxton, Andover SP11 8AT (0264) 710518
HAMPSHIRE AND ISLE OF WIGHT NATURALISTS' TRUST 8 Market Place, Romsey, Hants SO51 8NB (0794) 513786

Herefordshire
HEREFORDSHIRE ORNITHOLOGICAL CLUB The Garth, Kington HR5 3BA (0544) 230502
HEREFORDSHIRE NATURE TRUST LTD Community House, 25 Castle Street, Hereford HR1 2NW (0432) 56872

Hertfordshire
HERTFORDSHIRE NATURAL HISTORY SOCIETY 16 Oliver Court, Crouchfield, Chapmore End, Weare SH12 0EX
HERTFORDSHIRE AND MIDDLESEX TRUST FOR NATURE CONSERVATION Grebe House, St Michael's Street, St Albans AL3 4SN (0727) 58901

Isle of Wight
ISLE OF WIGHT NATURAL HISTORY & ARCHAEOLOGICAL SOCIETY Ivy Cottage, New Barn Lane, Shorwell, Isle of Wight PO30 3JQ (0983) 740711
ISLE OF WIGHT ORNITHOLOGICAL GROUP 14 Churchill Close, Cowes, Isle of Wight PO31 8HQ (0983) 293244

HAMPSHIRE AND ISLE OF WIGHT NATURALISTS' TRUST 8 Market Place, Romsey, Hants SO51 8NB (0794) 513786

Kent
KENT ORNITHOLOGICAL SOCIETY 9 Greenfinches, New Barn, Longfield, Kent DA3 7ND (047 47) 4298
KENT TRUST FOR NATURE CONSERVATION The Annexe, 1A Bower Mount Road, Maidstone, Kent ME16 8AX (0622) 53017

Lancashire
FYLDE BIRD CLUB 11 Ulverston Crescent, Lytham St Annes FY8 3RZ (0253) 728025
ROSSENDALE ORNITHOLOGISTS' CLUB 17 Robert Street, Piercy, Rossendale BB4 9JF (0706) 227672
LANCASHIRE TRUST FOR NATURE CONSERVATION Cuerdon Park Wildlife Centre, Shady Lane, Bamber Bridge, Preston PR5 6AU (0772) 324129

Leicestershire
LEICESTERSHIRE & RUTLAND ORNITHOLOGICAL SOCIETY 28 Oakfield Avenue, Birdstall, Leicester LE4 3DQ (0533) 676476
LOUGHBOROUGH NATURALISTS 25 Craddock Drive, Quorn, Loughborough LE12 8ER (0509) 412531
LEICESTERSHIRE AND RUTLAND TRUST FOR NATURE CONSERVATION 1 West Street, Leicester LE1 6UU (0533) 553904

Lincolnshire
LINCOLNSHIRE BIRD CLUB 42 Wolsey Way, Glebe Park, Lincoln LN2 4QH (0522) 22474
LINCOLNSHIRE AND SOUTH HUMBERSIDE TRUST FOR NATURE CONSERVATION The Manor House, Alford LN13 9DL (052 12) 3468

London
LONDON NATURAL HISTORY SOCIETY 63 Ivinghoe Road, Bushey, Watford WD2 3SW (01) 950 5906
LONDON WILDLIFE TRUST 80 York Way, London N1 9AG (01) 278 6612

Manchester
MANCHESTER ORNITHOLOGICAL SOCIETY 5 Church Cottages, Holmes Chapel Road, Chelford, Macclesfield SK11 9AQ (0625) 861567

Merseyside
MERSEYSIDE NATURALISTS' ASSOCIATION 47 Woodsorrel Road, Liverpool L15 6UB (051) 722 2819
WIRRAL BIRD CLUB 8 Park Road, Meols, Wirral L47 7BG (051) 632 2705

Norfolk
NORFOLK & NORWICH NATURALISTS' SOCIETY Hillcrest, East Tuddenham, East Dereham NR20 3JJ. Norwich (0603) 880278
NORFOLK ORNITHOLOGISTS' ASSOCIATION Aslack Way, Holme-next-Sea, Hunstanton PE36 6LP. Holme (048 525) 266
NORFOLK NATURALISTS' TRUST 72 Cathedral Close, Norwich NR1 4DF (0603) 625540

Northamptonshire
NORTHAMPTONSHIRE NATURAL HISTORY SOCIETY & FIELD CLUB 41 Spinney Hill Road, Northampton NN3 1DH (0604) 42550
NORTHAMPTONSHIRE TRUST FOR NATURE CONSERVATION Lings House, Billing Lings, Northampton NN3 4BE (0604) 405285

Northumberland
NATURAL HISTORY SOCIETY OF NORTHUMBRIA Hancock Museum, Barras Bridge, Newcastle-upon-Tyne NE2 4PT (091) 232 6386
NORTHUMBERLAND AND TYNESIDE BIRD CLUB 27 Eddrington Grove, Chapel House, Newcastle-upon-Tyne NE5 1JG (091) 267 6974

Nottinghamshire
NOTTINGHAMSHIRE BIRDWATCHERS 330 Westdale Lane, Mapperley, Nottingham NG3 6ET (0602) 606979
NOTTINGHAMSHIRE TRUST FOR NATURE CONSERVATION 310 Sneinton Dale, Nottingham NG3 7DN (0602) 588242
Oxfordshire
OXFORD ORNITHOLOGICAL SOCIETY c/o Edward Grey Institute of Field Ornithology, Department of Zoology, South Parks Road, Oxford OX1 3PS (0865) 56789
BERKS, BUCKS & OXON NATURALISTS' TRUST 3 Church Cowley Road, Rose Hill, Oxford OX4 3JR (0865) 775476
Shropshire
SHROPSHIRE ORNITHOLOGICAL SOCIETY Arnsheen, Betley Lane, Bayston Hill, Shrewsbury SY3 0AS (074 372) 3118
SHROPSHIRE TRUST FOR NATURE CONSERVATION St George's Primary School, New Street, Frankwell, Shrewsbury (0743) 241691
Somerset
SOMERSET ORNITHOLOGICAL SOCIETY 109 Highbridge Road, Burnham-on-Sea, Somerset TA8 1LN (0278) 784161
SOMERSET TRUST FOR NATURE CONSERVATION Fyne Court, Broomfield, Bridgewater TA5 2EQ. Kingston St Mary (082 345) 587
Staffordshire
WEST MIDLAND BIRD CLUB 6 Franklyn Close, Perton, Wolverhampton WV6 7SB
STAFFORDSHIRE NATURE CONSERVATION TRUST Coutts House, Sandon ST18 0DN (088 97) 534
Suffolk
SUFFOLK ORNITHOLOGISTS' GROUP 1 Holly Road, Ipswich IP1 3QN (0473) 53816
SUFFOLK TRUST FOR NATURE CONSERVATION Park Cottage, South Entrance, Saxmundham IP17 1DQ (0728) 3765/3872
Surrey
SURREY BIRD CLUB Applegarth House, The Hildens, Westcott, Surrey RH4 3JX. Dorking (0306) 889095
SURREY WILDLIFE TRUST Hatchlands, East Clandon, Guildford GU4 7RT (0483) 223526
Sussex
SUSSEX ORNITHOLOGICAL SOCIETY 69 Farhalls Crescent, Horsham RH12 4BT (0403) 61509
SUSSEX TRUST FOR NATURE CONSERVATION Woods Mill, Henfield, West Sussex BN5 9SD (0273) 492630
Tyne and Wear
NATURAL HISTORY SOCIETY OF NORTHUMBRIA Hancock Museum, Barras Bridge, Newcastle-upon-Tyne NE2 4PT (091) 232 6386
NORTHUMBERLAND & TYNESIDE BIRD CLUB 27 Eddrington Grove, Chapel House, Newcastle-upon-Tyne NE5 1JG (091) 267 6974
Warwickshire
WEST MIDLAND BIRD CLUB 64 Cambridge Avenue, Solihull B91 1QF
WARWICKSHIRE NATURE CONSERVATION TRUST Montague Road, Warwick CV34 5LW (0926) 496848
West Midlands
WEST MIDLAND BIRD CLUB 74 Ivyfields Road, Erdington, Birmingham B23 7HH (021) 373 5489

Wiltshire
WILTSHIRE ORNITHOLOGICAL SOCIETY Westdene, The Ley, Box, Corsham SN14 9JZ. Box (0225) 742877
WILTSHIRE TRUST FOR NATURE CONSERVATION 19 High Street, Devizes SN10 1AT (0380) 5670
Worcestershire
WORCESTERSHIRE NATURE CONSERVATION TRUST Hanbury Road, Droitwich WR9 7DU (0905) 773031
Yorkshire
YORKSHIRE NATURALISTS' UNION 60 Saffron Crescent, Tickhill, Doncaster DN11 9RU (0302) 742672
YORKSHIRE WILDLIFE TRUST 10 Toft Green, York YO1 1JT (0904) 59570

Scotland
SCOTTISH ORNITHOLOGISTS' CLUB BORDERS BRANCH 79 Kingland Terrace, Rosetta Road, Peebles EH45 8HH (0721) 22926
SCOTTISH ORNITHOLOGISTS' CLUB CENTRAL BRANCH 4 Archers Avenue, Stirling FK7 7RJ (0786) 815797
SCOTTISH ORNITHOLOGISTS' CLUB DUMFRIES BRANCH 146 Golf Avenue, Dumfries DG2 9ER (0387) 64195
SCOTTISH ORNITHOLOGISTS' CLUB GALLOWAY BRANCH 60 Main Street, St Johns Town of Dalry, by Castle Douglas DG7 3UW. Dalry (064 43) 226
SCOTTISH ORNITHOLOGISTS' CLUB WIGTOWN BRANCH The Roddens, Leswalt, Stranraer, Wigtownshire DG9 0QR (077 687) 685
SCOTTISH ORNITHOLOGISTS' CLUB FIFE BRANCH St. Anthony's Rest, Star of Markinch, Fife KY7 6LE. Glenrothes (0592) 758447
SCOTTISH ORNITHOLOGISTS' CLUB GRAMPIAN BRANCH 24 Seafield Gardens, Aberdeen AB1 7YB (0224) 324334
SCOTTISH ORNITHOLOGISTS' CLUB CAITHNESS BRANCH Mill Cottage, Olrig, Castletown, Caithness KW14 8SN (084 782) 473
SCOTTISH ORNITHOLOGISTS' CLUB HIGHLAND BRANCH 7 Croft Road, Inverness IV3 6RS (0463) 220493
SCOTTISH ORNITHOLOGISTS' CLUB LOTHIAN BRANCH 13 Henderson Row Edinburgh EH3 5DH (031) 557 1369
SCOTTISH ORNITHOLOGISTS' CLUB AYRSHIRE BRANCH Knockshinnoch Bungalow, Rankinston, Ayr KA6 7HL (0292) 590274
SCOTTISH ORNITHOLOGISTS' CLUB CLYDE BRANCH 18 Roland Crescent, Newton Mearns, Glasgow G77 5JT (041) 639 6370
SCOTTISH ORNITHOLOGISTS' CLUB TAYSIDE BRANCH 6 Park Road, Invergowrie, Dundee DD2 5AM (082 67) 413

Wales
Clwyd
CLWYD ORNITHOLOGICAL SOCIETY 21 Plas Uchaf Avenue, Prestatyn, Clwyd LL19 9NR (074 56) 2844
DEESIDE NATURALISTS' SOCIETY 38 Kelsterton Road, Connah's Quay, Clwyd CH5 4BJ. Deeside (0244) 818339
NORTH WALES NATURALISTS' TRUST LTD. 376 High Street, Bangor, Gwynedd LL57 1YE (0248) 351541
Dyfed
WREXHAM BIRDWATCHERS' SOCIETY 10 Lake View, Gresford, Wrexham, Dyfed LL12 8PU (097 883) 4633

WEST WALES TRUST FOR NATURE CONSERVATION 7 Market Street, Haverfordwest SA61 1NF (0437) 5462

Glamorgan
CARDIFF NATURALISTS' SOCIETY Department of Geology, National Museum of Wales, Cardiff CF1 3NP (0222) 397951
GOWER ORNITHOLOGICAL SOCIETY 203 Penybanc Road, Ammanford, Dyfed SA18 3QP (0269) 4324
GLAMORGAN WILDLIFE TRUST Glamorgan Nature Centre, Fountain Road, Tondu, Bridgend CF32 0EH. Aberkenfig (0656) 724100

Gwent
GWENT ORNITHOLOGICAL SOCIETY The Sycamore, Tabernacle Lane, Llanvaches, Gwent NP6 3BL (0633) 400953
GWENT TRUST FOR NATURE CONSERVATION 16 White Swan Court, Monmouth NP5 3NY (0600) 5501

Gwynedd
CAMBRIAN ORNITHOLOGICAL SOCIETY 21 Benarth Court, Glan Conwy, Colwyn Bay LL28 5ED (049 268) 782
NORTH WALES NATURALISTS' TRUST LTD 376 High Street, Bangor, Gwynedd LL57 1YE (0248) 351541

Powys
RADNOR BIRD GROUP Garnfawr Bungalow, Bettws, Hundred House, Llandrindod Wells LD1 5RP (098 24) 334
BRECKNOCK WILDLIFE TRUST Lion House, 7 Lion Street, Brecon, Powys LD3 7AY (0874) 5708
MONTGOMERYSHIRE TRUST FOR NATURE CONSERVATION Severn Square, Newtown, Powys SY16 2AG (0686) 24751

Isle of Man
MANX ORNITHOLOGICAL SOCIETY Ivie Cottage, Kirk Michael (062 487) 266
MANX NATURE CONSERVATION TRUST 14 Bowling Green Road, Castletown, Isle of Man (062 487) 266

Northern Ireland
NORTHERN IRELAND ORNITHOLOGISTS' CLUB 1 Upper Cavehill Road, Belfast BT15 4EZ (0232) 714801
ULSTER TRUST FOR NATURE CONSERVATION Conservation Centre, Barnett's Cottage, Barnett's Demesne, Malone Road, Belfast BT9 5PB (0232) 612235
RADNORSHIRE WILDLIFE TRUST 1 Gwalia Annexe, Ithon Road, Llandrindod Wells, Powys LD1 6SD (0597) 3298

Republic of Ireland
IRISH WILDBIRD CONSERVANCY:
Athlone 5 Retreat Road, Athlone
Carlow Leamy, Ardaltun, Carlow
Cork Ashdale, Beaumont Drive, Ballintemple, Co. Cork
Donegal Knockbrack, Letterkenny, Co. Donegal
Dublin Central 123 O'Rourke Park, Sallynoggin, Dun Laoghaire, Co. Dublin
Dublin North 209 Clonlife Road, Drumcondra, Dublin 3
Dublin South 18 Maretimo Gardens East, Blackrock, Co. Dublin
Fingal 9 Shenick Grove, Skerries, Co. Dublin
Galway 69 Pairc nag Caor, Moycullen, Co. Galway
Kerry 1 Lisbeg, Tralee, Co. Kerry
Kilkenny 5 Riverview, Kilkenny
Liffey Valley 2 Hanbury Lane, Lucan, Co. Dublin
Mayo 29 Cormack Estate, Castlebar, Co. Mayo
North Munster 10 Ardykeohane, Bruff, Kilmallock, Co. Limerick
Sligo 26 Oakfield Park, Sligo
Tipperary An Grianan, Stokaun, Co. Tipperary
Waterford 8 Upper Johnstown, Waterford
West Waterford Ballinamult, Clonmel, Co. Tipperrary
Wexford Newtown, Fethard-on-Sea, Wexford
Wicklow 30 Wolfe Tone Square North, Bray, Co. Wicklow

Index

INDEX OF LATIN NAMES

GENERAL INDEX